GENDER AND SCIENTIFIC AUTHORITY

GENDER AND SCIENTIFIC AUTHORITY

EDITED BY

BARBARA LASLETT,

SALLY GREGORY KOHLSTEDT,

HELEN LONGINO, AND

EVELYNN HAMMONDS

The University of Chicago Press

Chicago and London

The essays in this volume originally appeared in various issues of
SIGNS: JOURNAL OF WOMEN IN CULTURE AND SOCIETY.
Acknowledgment of the original publication data can be found in the
first page of each essay.

The University of Chicago Press, Chicago 60637
The University of Chicago Press, Ltd., London
© 1996 by the University of Chicago
All rights reserved. Published 1996
Printed in the United States of America
00 99 98 97 96   5 4 3 2 1

Library of Congress Cataloging-in-Publication Data

Gender and scientific authority / edited by Barbara Laslett . . . [et al.].
    p.   cm.
    "The essays in this volume originally appeared in various issues of
Signs: journal of women in culture and society"—T.p. verso.
    Includes bibliographical references and index.
    ISBN 0-226-46917-4 (cloth).—ISBN 0-226-46918-2 (pbk.)
    1. Women in science.   I. Laslett, Barbara.
Q130.G44   1996
306.4'2—dc20   96-5442
                                                            CIP

The paper used in this publication meets the minimum requirements of
American National Standard for Information Sciences—Permanence of
Paper for Printed Library Materials, ANSI Z39.48-1984.

CONTENTS

SCIENCE AND THE CONSTRUCTION OF GENDERED BODIES

Acknowledgments

We are particularly grateful to Kerry Brooks, the *Signs* intern who very ably assisted us in the initial research for this volume and the correspondence with the contributors, and to Louisa Castner, the former assistant editor of *Signs*, who has coordinated the editing and production of this volume.

The Editors

Introduction

The Editors

FROM THE VERY outset, one major focus of feminist scholarship has been on the conceptions, practices, and exclusions in
Western science. As feminist studies of science have proceeded
in many disciplines, *Signs: Journal of Women in Culture and
Society* has disseminated this scholarship to a broad audience. *Sex and
Scientific Inquiry* (1987), edited by Sandra Harding and Jean F. O'Barr,
was the first collection of articles on the subject that had originally appeared in *Signs*. This present volume, *Gender and Scientific Authority*,
is both a continuation and a revision of the perspectives that organized
the earlier book. This volume begins with gender as its theoretical focus,
and consistent with work done in the field over the past ten years, the
substantive focus raises questions about scientific authority. We have
also expanded the meaning of the term *science* to include articles about
medicine and the social sciences, as well as considering the uses of scientific rhetoric in constructing public discourses of science. These choices
reflect the discursive theoretical focus of recent work in feminist science
studies as well as a continuation of an earlier emphasis on the social
construction of scientific knowledge.

A central theme in the feminist critique of science reflects the cognitive
authority granted to scientific knowledge and practices. This theme has
been forced on feminist analysis by the role of scientists in perpetuating
sexism and their claims, as preeminent practitioners, for objectivity and
rational belief. The nineteenth-century life sciences became sites for the
legitimation of women's subordination through the intersection of
women's increasing demand for social equality and the emergence of life
science as a source of understanding of human behaviors. Attempts to
identify socially meaningful behavioral and cognitive differences between
the sexes and to attribute them to inner, "natural" predispositions have
continued into our own time. Conceptions of gender-specific biological
structures and functions have been recruited as explanations of differential abilities and temperaments and are invoked as explanations of the
absence of women and the prevalence of men in positions of political,
artistic, commercial, and intellectual leadership. Because these abilities
and temperaments are seen as natural, no steps are needed to be taken

1

to change the social asymmetries, and, furthermore, any such steps would be futile, as nature would dictate their failure.

If the sciences were not granted authority to speak for the natural, that is, if they were not deemed the most authoritative sources of knowledge, such talk could be more easily dismissed as ideological rant. But such dismissal is not possible in the case of scientific legitimations of gender dominance and subordination without challenging very basic assumptions about the constitution of knowledge. If research offering biological legitimations of social inequality can be treated as "bad science," that is, as science that fails to meet certain common methodological standards, then the dilemma can be avoided and the cognitive authority of science is not threatened. Indeed, such authority is enhanced because the standards that ground that authority are the ones by reference to which bad science is identified as bad. The investigation of science by feminist scholars, however, has shown that while some suspect science *is* bad science, much of it satisfies the methodological requirements in place in the disciplines and subdisciplines at least as well as nonideologically problematic research does. Furthermore, in addition to their investigations of sciences directly concerned with sex and gender, feminist scholars have exposed the role of gender metaphors in modeling nongendered aspects of the natural world and the role of gender relations in constructing scientific thought and practices (Merchant 1980; Keller 1985, 1992; Laslett 1990; Schiebinger 1993).

The problems with traditional science of the natural and social worlds, then, and the critiques that feminists have leveled against it, go deeper than the exposure of methodologically inept science would suggest. Feminists are caught in a dilemma: either reject the cognitive authority of the sciences altogether or accept it and acquiesce in its masculinist order. In the face of such a choice, the first of these alternatives may seem appealing. Its cost, however, is the loss of a basis on which to argue for the soundness of feminist alternatives to the panoply of particular views we have rejected. Many feminist scholars, therefore, have sought a third way, a way that would recognize the role that ideologies and social locations play in the construction of scientific knowledge, while nevertheless retaining some conception of objectivity (Keller 1985; Haraway 1991; Harding 1991).

One early candidate for such a third way was feminist standpoint theory. This approach to knowledge transforms Marxist standpoint theory from a class-based to a gender-based view. Although first developed in a sociological context by Dorothy Smith (1987, 1990), it was taken up as a more general theory of knowledge by theorists such as Nancy Hartsock (1983) and Sandra Harding (1991). According to this theory, there are no neutral positions from which to ground knowledge claims.

Instead, everyone occupies some social position that provides a standpoint from which they observe and account for their world(s). Various social asymmetries generate different standpoints. Early feminist standpoint theorists argued that the sexual division of labor generated gender-specific standpoints. From this perspective, the standpoint of masculinity was the source of accounts of the world that mystified social relations by being blind both to the mechanisms perpetuating male supremacy and to the activities of women that enabled men to engage competently in the activities of the public world. Women, by contrast, were aware of their own activities, as well as knowing representations of the world generated from the privileged masculine position. Their knowledge was, therefore, more comprehensive, hence more objective.

The articles in this volume were selected by two historians, a philosopher, and a sociologist, all of whom have done primary work on the conceptions, practices, exclusions, and rhetorics of science. We had hoped, when we began work on this collection, to be able to offer a theoretical framework with which to bring together the many excellent studies that feminist scholars of science have undertaken over the recent past. Yet now as we introduce these materials to you, it is clear that our aspirations outstripped our capacities and the state of knowledge. What we can offer, we hope, is the identification of both new questions and continuing themes in feminist studies of scientific practices and discourses. The practices are too complex and the discourses too diverse for a single theoretical approach.

There are, however, recurrent themes that continue to intrigue and to puzzle. Three seem particularly clear. First are conceptions of nature and the natural and, related to them, the possibilities of change. As suggested above, ideas about nature's gifts and gratuities have been called on to justify and explain women's tasks, status, and physical and mental characteristics. Yet how do we both take account of the materiality of the natural world while, at the same time, recognizing that its study has been primarily the province of men, who have constructed scientific knowledge from positioned observations of privilege, where the desire for the continuation of that privilege cannot be ignored, even when cloaked in the guise of disinterested objectivity?

It is here that we can see a second recurrent theme in feminist studies of science. While recognizing that observations are shaped by social position and experiences, we, the editors of this volume, also believe that disciplined and systematic thought is not the exclusive domain of privilege. Importantly, feminists have raised questions about how scientific knowledge gets constructed, about who counts as an observer, about how discourses both reflect and shape observations. Yet this is done without requiring a relativism that would anchor observations and observer nowhere in the material world. We need to think through the complexities of how to evaluate what we see, and here the historically variable and multiple meanings of objectivity as such a standard for scientific behavior both challenge and puzzle us. Without some standard, we forgo tools with which to challenge women's subordination as well as the subordination of racial/ethnic minorities and nonelite class groups. Without some recognition of the variable meanings of objectivity as well as the multiple practices, such as quantification, that have been used to undergird its authority, we cannot move beyond those methods and epistemologies that have been part of women's subordination.

Connected to questions both of nature and of objectivity is a third theme—the theme of who counts as legitimate and authoritative observers of the natural and social worlds. How can we incorporate insights about the political and institutional dimensions of scientific practices so as to change them?

Expanding the conceptions of science that have informed this volume to include clinical practices, such as medicine, and the social sciences, such as psychology, is to mark explicitly the permeability of the disciplinary, institutional, and political boundaries that claim privileged status for one kind of knowledge over another. It is to recognize that the construction of all knowledge is a social and political process as well as an intellectual one. All occur within particular times and spaces. Much work remains for feminist scholars of science to bring together the complex of philosophical, historical, and sociological perspectives through which to advance our understandings of the relationship of gender to these complexities. Feminist scholars have gladly undertaken the challenge, and their accomplishments have been substantial. In bringing together the groups of articles discussed below, we coordinate and amplify that discussion.

Rethinking knowledge

Feminist standpoint theory encountered a number of criticisms, some concerning the centering of unmodified gender relations without acknowledging race or class differentiations in the sexual division of labor, others concerning the problematic retention of unexamined notions of truth and objectivity (Longino 1993). The articles included in this section develop issues raised in the critique of standpoint theory, either by moving away from the false universalism of subject positions constructed by gender alone or from the illusion of context-free validity or absolute truth or by exploring the ways in which some feminist work anticipated the postmodern turn in certain disciplines without thereby losing sight of important goals in the search for knowledge. What has grounded the feminist debate about scientific knowledge has been the need for a conception of knowledge that could avoid the false absolutes of modernism while at the same time not subverting our own efforts to analyze history, society, and culture.

Patricia Hill Collins deflects critiques of feminist standpoint theory by articulating what she takes to be the features of a specifically Black feminist standpoint. African American women's experiences can be assimilated neither to those of African American men nor to those of white women. They are instead the basis of a distinctive standpoint. Collins explores African American women's autobiographical writings to find certain common elements that characterize the ways they understand their worlds. She finds the primacy of concrete experience, validation through dialogue, attitudes of caring, and accountability recurring in these writings as well as in the work of African American feminist scholars; Collins argues that these traits constitute a distinctive Black feminist standpoint. Rather than aspire to universally valid knowledge claims or to an integration of Black women's knowledge into the extant body of academic knowledge, she argues for the necessity of "rearticulating a preexisting Black women's standpoint and recentering the language of existing academic discourse to accommodate these knowledge claims" (46).

While Collins finds it useful to think in terms of the "outsider within," Frances E. Mascia-Lees, Patricia Sharpe, and Colleen Ballerino Cohen think in terms of being neither inside nor outside. This double—and unstable—position of the outsider (in their case, women) seeking to generate knowledge in the context of a traditional discipline (in their case, anthropology) already models the situation postmodern ethnography strives to realize. The new ethnography does so, however, without acknowledging the work feminists have already done, and according to Mascia-Lees, Sharpe, and Cohen, in many cases reobscures the marginalized subject rather than making it visible and acknowledging its agency. The new ethnography, while seeking to give a voice to "the other," is still performed by members of a dominant culture (even when "studying up"). Without sufficient self-reflexivity, such work will continue to privilege the voice of the culture of those who do the studying, who have the power to interpret the other. What protects feminist scholarship from such self-subversion is its avowedly political engagement: knowledge is pursued in order to change "the power relationships that underlie women's oppression" (68). Such a goal has encouraged the development by feminist social scientists of specific techniques to preserve and make audible the subjectivity of their subjects within the very framing of the research project. The new ethnography would be well served, Mascia-Lees, Sharpe, and Cohen argue, if it learned from the feminists who have already blazed the trail of politically sensitive and relevant anthropological and sociological research.

Mary E. Hawkesworth's article reviews problems in the three main candidates for feminist epistemology: feminist empiricism, feminist standpoint theory, and feminist postmodernism. All share certain problematic features that disable feminist attempts to support political action with informed analysis. The focus on the subject of knowledge in all three of these epistemologies has trapped feminists between an untenable homogeneity incapable of doing justice to the fallibility and diversity of human knowers and an unstable heterogeneity that transmutes into "authoritarian assertion or uncritical relativism" (88). Hawkesworth recommends abandoning the foundationalism characteristic of empiricism and standpoint theories for a view of cognition as a complex set of human practices activated in particular contexts and in relation to particular problems. Postmodernism, in contrast, while evincing a salutary rejection of univocality, has not developed analytic resources to prevent a slide into relativism. Pluralism must not mean that any account is as good or has as much claim on our beliefs as any other. Like Mascia-Lees, Sharpe, and Cohen, Hawkesworth emphasizes the concrete political dimensions of feminist cognitive activity: our need to speak clearly about rape, domestic violence, workplace harassment, and discrimination. She calls for a critical feminist epistemology that recognizes the limits of reason without jettisoning the resources of knowledge and rational argumentation.

Although none of the articles in this section purports to offer a wholly revamped epistemological theory, all three point to the constraints any new theory must satisfy: respect for the variety of subject positions from which inquiry can be carried out; tolerance of fallibilism and pluralism; and recognition of the positive role of ordinary, situated rationality in the construction of knowledge. A new understanding satisfying such constraints is most likely to emerge from attending to the concrete practices of feminists as they challenge old myths and create new knowledge.

Gendering scientific and technological knowledge

Situating gender issues—masculinity as the dominant mode—in science and technology requires close attention to the context of time and place. Historians initially researched the effect of this controlling culture on individual women or on women's prescribed roles by examining biographies of individual women who somehow defied the norm or by studying the records of the gatekeeping institutions that enabled or prevented women's participation (Jordanova 1993; Kohlstedt 1995). While such research revealed the social, political, and economic strains of influence exercised primarily by men, the circumstances were often complex because women themselves participated in defining activities and were thus unwilling to risk losing traditional responsibilities and opportunities (Rossiter 1982, 1995; Abir-Am and Outram 1987). Feminist scholars probed more deeply into the historical record, with particular emphasis on the origins of modern science. At the same time, social studies of science challenged the claims for scientific objectivity and shifted the attention of philosophers and sociologists to investigation of the practices and codification of values in science. Such research, including several reprinted in this volume, revealed the relative invisibility and silence of women in the emergence of scientific disciplines and the relative absence of effective feminist challenges until the past two decades. Organized chronologically, the four case studies in the section "Gendering Scientific and Technological Knowledge" suggest the authority of experts as well as the often subtle and subversive challenges that are part of the continuing redefinition of scientific practice and policy.

The power of expert, or scientific, knowledge applied to social circumstances became particularly significant in the nineteenth century as European-influenced governments around the world centralized and codified economic behavior. For the most part, women were pushed to the periphery of the colleges, learned societies, and state agencies where such knowledge built political power. Desley Deacon uses the example of demography in nineteenth-century Australia as new methods of quantification and analysis shaped definitions of women's work during the decade-by-decade census. During the early years of the official census, farm women were counted as productive and contributing to Australian wealth. By the end of the century, however, farm women were classified as dependents and described by their presumed consumer status. The official pronouncements of demographers somewhat ironically denigrated household work despite its necessity; the pressure to view women as consumers at the end of the century coincided, Deacon argues, with a conservative outlook that viewed married women who worked as antithetical to family life and social progress. In Australia and elsewhere, white women were challenging that narrow definition by working, by necessity, in ever-increasing numbers and often outside their homes. Some of them inevitably would challenge the social assumptions that tried to limit them and their colleagues.

Precisely how the dynamic of participation and challenge worked has been the object of studies, particularly in the social sciences and medicine. Nancy M. Theriot's article on women medical doctors in the United States at the end of the nineteenth century looks at a rather significant population of women, often educated in women's medical colleges, who were pushed into occupational settings that offered less prestige and pay

than private practice. Like other women working for wages in professions dominated by men, many female physicians accepted assignments
to work with women, doing so in ways that extended, clarified, and
challenged the theories and practices of some colleagues. Theriot examines the role of women doctors assigned to work in the ubiquitous mental
asylums of the period. Using patient and other records, she uncovers the
ambiguous role of female patients and documents the challenges to the
initial diagnoses of hysteria and other so-called female diseases. In fact,
while cautious about conflating gender and sex, she argues that the
women physicians, and indeed their women patients, were important,
often as a counterweight, in the widespread practice of medicalizing
women's bodies, emotions, and intellects during the period of fierce professionalization (Walsh 1977).

While nineteenth-century case studies of growing scientific authority
indicate that some were challenged and reshaped by women's activity,
the powerful presence of modern technologies raises new issues about
the exercise of expert authority where outcomes are unresolved (McGaw
1989; Wajcman 1991). Since World War II, perhaps the most important
technology to touch everyday lives has been the personal computer. The
masculinization of the instrumentation, its languages, and the workplace
are evident. Ruth Perry and Lisa Greber's comprehensive introduction
to a special issue on women and computing revisits the early history of
computing to discover the important role played by women and yet the
surprising limits of their influence on theory and implementation. This
outcome, they argue, is not technologically determined but, rather, directly connected to social and political decisions that have had a negative
impact on women's wages, health, and opportunities.

A firsthand view of how a pervasively gendered culture operates and
its impact on an outsider is revealed in Carol Cohn's compelling account
in "Sex and Death in the Rational World of Defense Intellectuals." In-
vited to join a workshop within the defense establishment, she learned
the language of "clean bombs" and "collateral damage" (or human
death). She ultimately concludes that the technostrategic language intrin-
sically limits outsiders from conversing about social and ethical concerns
and thus fundamentally limits access to policy decision making within
the establishment (Gurak and Bayer 1994).

Science and the construction of gendered subjectivities

The third section includes four articles that analyze the uses of science
as rhetoric and as practice in relation to women's subjectivities, identities, and sexualities and how the changing specificities of historical contexts shaped these processes. In "The Trials of Alice Mitchell: Sensation-

alism, Sexology, and the Lesbian Subject in Turn-of-the-Century America," Lisa Duggan argues that the scientific (sexological) and sensationalist (journalistic) representations of a "love murder" of one teenaged girl by another was part of how a new, erotic sense of self was constructed among women who desired women. But, Duggan argues, the stories told and the social conversations through which erotic lesbian identities were constructed were not solely the result of discourses of violence or deviance imposed by a sensationalist press or by turn-of-the-century sexologists. It was from women's own stories, as reported by the press, that sexologists based their theories. Out of this intersection of journalists' images, sexologists' formulations, and women's own stories, the identity of the mannish lesbian was constructed—an identity that both reproduced and challenged conventional gender hierarchies.

Daphne de Marneffe, in "Looking and Listening: The Construction of Clinical Knowledge in Charcot and Freud," provides another case study of the intersection of the social and the scientific. Tracing one part of the history of hysteria, de Marneffe discusses the uses of photography by the French neuropathologist, Jean-Martin Charcot, in late nineteenth-century France. Meticulous observations of patients were central to Charcot's views that associated hysteria and degeneracy through heredity. For Charcot and the clinicians who worked with him, photography was the perfect method for recording symptoms and the progression of behaviors. But reliance on observation was pursued at the price of direct interaction with patients. Despite having collected detailed case histories from patients, Charcot did not attend to their words or their accounts of life experiences. Instead, he based his diagnoses and theories of hysteria on photographic records and observations. "Looking," for him, was the key scientific method. Sigmund Freud, who studied with Charcot the "reigning expert on the neurological aspects of hysteria" (261), greatly admired various aspects of Charcot's studies of neurosis. But between 1886, when he returned from Paris, and 1895, when his *Studies on Hysteria* was published, Freud's views sharply diverged from those of his teacher. Freud's developing theories of hysteria—locating its etiology in trauma rather than heredity and questioning the association with degeneracy—was a sharp deviation from Charcot's theories and practices. Freud focused on verbal communication and the relation between the therapist and patient to diagnose and treat hysteria. But why did Charcot only look while Freud listened? De Marneffe suggests that social reasons explain why Charcot did not listen to his patients, who were mostly poor, sick women. Freud's patients suffering from hysteria, in contrast, were often respectable and intelligent bourgeois women. As de Marneffe puts it, "Had Charcot consciously and explicitly admitted these women's words as evidence . . . he would also have had to admit that they could be tellers of truth and possessors of knowledge. . . . The fact that Freud did listen to his patients' accounts may rest in part on the fact that he saw a different group of patients, patients who were not warehoused en masse in an asylum but were able to visit his consulting room and to pay his fees" (275).

Looking at more recent developments in psychology, Janice Haaken and Janet Shibley Hyde examine the construction of scientific knowledge about psychological gender differences, although in different ways. In "Field Dependence Research: A Historical Analysis of a Psychological Construct" and "Meta-Analysis and the Psychology of Gender Differences" Haaken and Hyde, respectively, examine how science has been used to establish and question the nature and extent of gender differences in psychological characteristics. Haaken analyzes a series of psychological experiments, begun in the 1940s and extending over thirty years, that were used to assess the dependence or independence of perception on context. Sex differences emerged as a specific theme in this research, building on and fostering new beliefs about "natural sex differences" in personality and perception. Haaken links these developments to the postwar context, which emphasized enduring and essential sex differences in support of a "domestic mystique," as men returned home to reclaim jobs held during the war by women. This mystique, in turn, led to a gendered division of labor that belied women's labor force participation during the war. Furthermore, Haaken argues, "in a society that valued independence and individual autonomy, field dependence had negative connotations" (289)—connotations that had gendered as well as cultural implications. By placing this work in its historical as well as its epistemological context, that is, by viewing the experimental method on which so much of psychology's claim for scientific status rested, Haaken shows the ways in which political, cultural, and ideological forces in the United States in the 1940s and 1950s constructed the "scientific" study of psychological sex differences.

Hyde reviews the history of psychological research of gender differences in abilities, beginning with the mental testing movement as developed in the intellectual worlds of Alfred Binet, Lewis Terman, and L. L. Thurstone. Their work constructed a basis for viewing intelligence not as a general characteristic of individuals but as a composite of separable components (spatial, mathematical, verbal, and so on) that could be identified using a statistical technique—factor analysis. Using meta-analysis, a statistical method developed in the 1980s to combine findings from different studies, Hyde concludes that the cumulated evidence about gender differences in cognitive abilities are, for the most part, either not large or nonexistent. In terms of social behaviors, such as aggressive or helping behaviors, the observation of gender differences was dependent on which behaviors were measured and the settings in which the studies were done. Furthermore, Hyde argues, "meta-analyses demonstrate a trend over approximately two decades toward a decline in the magnitude of gender differences" (319).

Each of these articles shows how subjectivities are shaped by scientific practices, scientific claims, and existing scientific knowledges. But they also demonstrate the importance of the historical and social contexts in which knowledge is constructed. The use of newspaper accounts by sexologists at the turn of the century about women's erotic interests, the "looking"and "listening" that shaped and contested medical discourses about hysteria as well as the class characteristics of the mostly female subjects of its treatment, created space for women's voices to be heard and yet confined those voices to preconceived notions about class and gender. The continuing impact of social forces in the formation of beliefs about gender differences in perceptions and mental abilities, however, is not merely an artifact of "early" science or "bad" science but, as the experimental methods used in studies of perception demonstrate, was also part of a particular historical period and the beliefs about gender that were shaped by it. Yet feminists do not have to eschew the scientific and objectivist methods that have often been criticized as "male science." Such techniques are also available to feminist scholars seeking, in Janet Hyde's words, to smash the "many myths about gender differences" (320).

Science and the construction of gendered bodies

The four articles in this section describe the ways in which feminists have exposed the infusion of gender stereotypes in scientific discourses. These case studies demonstrate the construction and exposure of gender dimorphism in biological and social sciences at multiple sites and levels of analysis. The first site is medicine, at the level of the cell and in the language used to describe the activities of egg and sperm in Emily Martin's "The Egg and the Sperm: How Science Has Constructed a Romance Based on Stereotypical Male-Female Roles." Second, we view another area of medicine, at the level of the body in practices of physicians who assign the gender of infants, in Suzanne J. Kessler's "The Medical Construction of Gender: Case Management of Intersexed Infants." Third, at the level of human development through the ways in which evolutionary and behavioral studies of primates are used to establish the "naturalness" of gendered behaviors in human societies, we find Susan Sperling's "Baboons with Briefcases: Feminism, Functionalism, and Sociobiology in the Evolution of Primate Gender." And last, at the level of populations in the interpretation of demographic data of reproductive outcomes in large populations is Susan Greenhalgh and Jiali Li's, "Engendering Reproductive Policy and Practice in Peasant China: For a Feminist Demography of Reproduction." Their article shows how a feminist analysis can expose presumptions that reproductive processes are gendered by nature and culture, that is, by state practices, which are political and public and which, in turn, shape the "natural" and private choices of individuals.

Although the methodologies used in these case studies differ markedly, they connect in several ways. In each, the authors take for granted that scientific theories and hypotheses are shaped by the cultural, political, and economic interests of scientists and social scientists in terms of material technologies and discursive practices. In particular with respect to gender dimorphism, they assert the impossibility of drawing a line between gender identity as a social construct and biological differentiation (Jacobus, Keller, and Shuttlesworth 1990).

Martin is intrigued by the language that biological and medical scientists use to describe the egg and the sperm in medical textbooks and journal articles. She finds that the picture of the egg and sperm drawn in both popular and scientific accounts relies on stereotypes central to our cultural definitions of male and female. The persistence of language that describes female biological processes as less worthy than those of their male counterparts implies that women are less worthy than men. For Martin, the gendered metaphors that scientists use to describe the egg and sperm both reflect and impose meanings on social relations and in turn reify existing gender stereotypes. Martin argues that because "these stereotypes are now being written in at the level of the *cell*" they constitute "a powerful move to make them seem so natural as to be beyond alteration" (338). But what are feminists to do about these metaphors beyond pointing them out? Martin suggests that feminists must wake up these sleeping metaphors in scientific texts in order to rob them of their cultural and scientific power, and they must also try substituting more egalitarian ones in their places.

Susan Sperling begins by arguing that fully alternative feminist accounts of science must do more than simply tell a better story than other male-biased accounts. Instead of merely changing the narrative element so that "the category 'female,' like 'male,' is constructed as active, dominant, and looking out for genetic advantages," she argues instead for "a deconstruction of all functionalist models, including sociobiological ones, of sex-linked primate behaviors" (367). For Sperling, neither the old sexist accounts of primate behavior nor the new feminist accounts engage the developmental factors that bring about gendered behaviors in primates. While feminist postmodernists like Donna Haraway (1991) have contextualized primatology both historically and culturally as a "mythic science of 'good stories' and 'bad stories' " about the iconic role that primates play for us humans, Sperling argues that primatology in both its androcentric and feminist versions has suffered from a functionalist framework that has predominated in the field (386). This framework has facilitated empirically unsupported generalizations about behaviors across species as well as inventing adaptationist stories about putative sex-differentiated behaviors. Sperling calls instead for detailed life history studies in primate ethology that would make it possible to account for sexual and reproductive behavior in ways that represent genuine integrations of genetic and extragenetic factors. Such detailed studies would, she suggests, reveal cross-species differences and undermine the tendency to extend adaptationist stories from nonhuman primates to human ones. Sperling locates her assessment of the feminist primatology in relation to the empiricist, standpoint, and postmodernist epistemological stances advocated by feminists, thus making concrete the issues that are discussed more abstractly in the first section of this volume, "Rethinking Knowledge."

Metaphors about the diversity of gendered behaviors and gender itself are largely absent from medicine and primatology. Thus the idea that gender dimorphism is given by nature is also enhanced by the lack of alternative metaphors. The effectiveness of scientific metaphors, as Evelyn Fox Keller has argued, "depends not only on social resources but also on the technical and natural resources that are available" (Keller 1985, xiii). The gendering of intersexed infants represents a "border case" between the cellular and evolutionary levels described by Martin and Sperling. The bodies of these infants serve as sites where biological and cultural notions of gender clash. Physicians now have the techniques to manipulate and alter the bodies of infants so that they conform to their belief that gender dimorphism is compelled by nature. Yet, as Suzanne Kessler argues, these same physicians paradoxically also believe that gender identity is determined primarily by social factors. The physician sees his or her job then as merely to provide the "right genitals to go along with the socialization" (354). Language and imagery, argues Keller—and we would add, the technical apparatus to manipulate the body—support Kessler's belief that "gender consists of two exclusive types . . . maintained and perpetuated by the medical community in the face of incontrovertible physical evidence that it is not mandated by biology" (362).

The case of intersexed infants moves us from a focus on the social construction of science and medicine to the social construction of gender. The management of intersexed infants is a manifestation of what Martin warns against: the possibly disturbing social consequences of endowing egg and sperm with personhood. As Kessler notes, if intersexuality is to be "managed differently . . . physicians would have to take seriously [the] assertion that it is a misrepresentation of epistemology to consider any cell in the body authentically male or female" (362).

If cases of intersexuality illustrate how society's accountability is masked by the assumption that gender is a given, the case of China's missing girls makes the point even clearer. Susan Greenhalgh and Jiali Li describe the shocking fact that little girls are being eliminated from Chinese society on a massive scale. In this case, as with primatology, the question becomes, what can feminists do? Greenhalgh and Li argue that demography, because it presents "a bird's-eye view of the whole population under study, can provide stark clues to the changing relations between the genders in the society as a whole" (392). Traditionally, demographers have not paid enough attention to sex-based disparities in populations, nor have they adequately developed theories to explain reproduction. In the case of the missing girls, however, demographers were able to expose the growing discrimination against baby girls in China, yet they could shed little light on the complex processes that led up to it. As Greenhalgh and Li note, demographic interpretations have had little to say about politics, the role of the state, and the historical transformations in gender values. The fact that the state has been an everpresent force in reproductive decision making means that "gender ideologies . . . ha[ve] been made and remade many times" in Chinese society (394).

A feminist demography would trace the ways in which male bias in reproductive behavior evolved over time, according to Greenhalgh and Li, drawing from both aggregate data sets and local case studies that can show the impact of state policies on individual lives. The one-child policy has had a devastating impact on Chinese society. In this case, nature exposed what the state would have kept hidden, that is, the increasing deviations from the normal range of sex ratios in the Chinese population as a result of the one-child policy.

Feminists are not alone in probing the fundamental assumptions and practices of science in the 1980s and 1990s, but their perspectives insist that gender be taken into account. This volume highlights the multiple facets of feminist commentary, the range of insights emerging within and among the scholarly disciplines, and the impact of the humanities, especially the analysis of discourses and language, on recent feminist studies of science. All the authors included agree that issues of gender, so long ignored or disdained by those exercising authority over formal knowledge, production, and dissemination, must be reintroduced into areas of study ranging from primatology and anthropology to physics and computer science.

Signs has been a leader in advancing the discussion of gender and scientific authority over the past two decades. There is little doubt that these works, widely cited, have had an impact on the disciplines from which they sprang and on some of the women and men in the scientific and technological communities under investigation. We hope that this volume, situated near the beginning of such discussions, may also prove to be a useful tool in extending the discourse.

References

Abir-Am, Pnina G., and Dorinda Outram, eds. 1987. *Uneasy Careers and Intimate Lives: Women in Science, 1789–1979*. New Brunswick, N.J.: Rutgers University Press.

Gurak, Laura J., and Nancy L. Bayer. 1994. "Making Gender Visible: Extending Feminist Critiques of Technology to Technical Communication." *Technical Communication Quarterly* 3:257–70.

Haraway, Donna. 1991. *Simians, Cyborgs, and Women: The Reinvention of Nature*. New York: Routledge.

Harding, Sandra. 1991. *Whose Science? Whose Knowledge? Thinking from Women's Lives*. Ithaca, N.Y.: Cornell University Press.

Harding, Sandra, and Jean F. O'Barr. 1987. *Sex and Scientific Inquiry*. Chicago: University of Chicago Press.

Hartsock, Nancy. 1983. "The Feminist Standpoint: Developing the Ground for a Specifically Feminist Historical Materialism." In *Discovering Reality*, ed. Sandra Harding and Merrill B. Hintikka, 283–310. Dordrecht: Reidel.

Jacobus, Mary, Evelyn Fox Keller, and Sally Shuttlesworth, eds. 1990. *Body/Politics: Women and the Discourses of Science*. New York: Routledge.

Jordanova, Ludmilla. 1993. "Gender and the Historiography of Science." *British Journal for the History of Science* 16:469–83.

Keller, Evelyn Fox. 1985. *Reflections on Gender and Science*. New Haven, Conn.: Yale University Press.

———. 1992. *Secrets of Life, Secrets of Death: Essays in Language, Gender, and Science*. London: Routledge.

Kohlstedt, Sally Gregory. 1995. "Women in the History of Science: An Ambiguous Place." *Osiris* 10:27–38.

Laslett, Barbara. 1990. "Unfeeling Knowledge: Emotion and Objectivity in the History of Sociology." *Sociological Forum* 5 (September): 413–33.

Longino, Helen E. 1993. "Feminist Standpoint Theory and the Problems of Knowledge: Review Essay." *Signs: Journal of Women in Culture and Society* 19 (Autumn): 201–12.

McGaw, Judith. 1989. "No Passive Victims, No Separate Spheres: A Feminist Perspective on Technology's History." In *In Context: History and the History of Technology*, ed. Stephen H. Cutcliffe and Robert Post. Bethlehem, Pa.: Lehigh University Press.

Merchant, Carolyn. 1980. *The Death of Nature: Women, Ecology, and the Scientific Revolution*. San Francisco: Harper & Row.

Rossiter, Margaret W. 1982. *Women Scientists in America: Struggles and Strategies to 1940*. Baltimore: Johns Hopkins University Press.

————. 1995. *Women Scientists in America: Before Affirmative Action, 1940–1972*. Baltimore: Johns Hopkins University Press.

Schiebinger, Londa. 1993. *Nature's Body: Gender in the Making of Modern Science*. Boston: Beacon.

Smith, Dorothy. 1987. *The Everyday World as Problematic*. Boston: Northeastern University Press.

————. 1990. *The Conceptual Practices of Power: A Feminist Sociology of Knowledge*. Boston: Northeastern University Press.

Wajcman, Judith. 1991. *Feminism Confronts Technology*. University Park: Pennsylvania State University Press.

Walsh, Mary Roth. 1977. *"Doctors Wanted: No Women Need Apply": Sexual Barriers in the Medical Profession, 1835–1975*. New Haven, Conn.: Yale University Press.

RETHINKING
KNOWLEDGE

The Social Construction of Black Feminist Thought

Patricia Hill Collins

Sojourner Truth, Anna Julia Cooper, Ida Wells Barnett, and Fannie Lou Hamer are but a few names from a growing list of distinguished African-American women activists. Although their sustained resistance to Black women's victimization within interlocking systems of race, gender, and class oppression is well known, these women did not act alone.[1] Their actions were nurtured by the support of countless, ordinary African-American women who, through strategies of everyday resistance, created a powerful foundation for

Special thanks go out to the following people for reading various drafts of this manuscript: Evelyn Nakano Glenn, Lynn Weber Cannon, and participants in the 1986 Research Institute, Center for Research on Women, Memphis State University; Elsa Barkley Brown, Deborah K. King, Elizabeth V. Spelman, and Angelene Jamison-Hall; and four anonymous reviewers at *Signs*.

[1] For analyses of how interlocking systems of oppression affect Black women, see Frances Beale, "Double Jeopardy: To Be Black and Female," in *The Black Woman*, ed. Toni Cade (New York: Signet, 1970); Angela Y. Davis, *Women, Race and Class* (New York: Random House, 1981); Bonnie Thornton Dill, "Race, Class, and Gender: Prospects for an All-Inclusive Sisterhood," *Feminist Studies* 9, no. 1 (1983): 131–50; bell hooks, *Ain't I a Woman? Black Women and Feminism* (Boston: South End Press, 1981); Diane Lewis, "A Response to Inequality: Black Women, Racism, and Sexism," *Signs: Journal of Women in Culture and Society* 3, no. 2 (Winter 1977): 339–61; Pauli Murray, "The Liberation of Black Women," in *Voices of the New Feminism*, ed. Mary Lou Thompson (Boston: Beacon, 1970), 87–102; and the introduction in Filomina Chioma Steady, *The Black Woman Cross-Culturally* (Cambridge, Mass.: Schenkman, 1981), 7–41.

[*Signs: Journal of Women in Culture and Society* 1989, vol. 14, no. 4]

this more visible Black feminist activist tradition.[2] Such support has been essential to the shape and goals of Black feminist thought.

The long-term and widely shared resistance among African-American women can only have been sustained by an enduring and shared standpoint among Black women about the meaning of oppression and the actions that Black women can and should take to resist it. Efforts to identify the central concepts of this Black women's standpoint figure prominently in the works of contemporary Black feminist intellectuals.[3] Moreover, political and epistemological issues influence the social construction of Black feminist thought. Like other subordinate groups, African-American women not only have developed distinctive interpretations of Black women's oppression but have done so by using alternative ways of producing and validating knowledge itself.

A Black women's standpoint
The foundation of Black feminist thought

Black women's everyday acts of resistance challenge two prevailing approaches to studying the consciousness of oppressed groups.[4] One approach claims that subordinate groups identify with the powerful and have no valid independent interpretation of their own oppression.[5] The second approach assumes that the oppressed are

[2] See the introduction in Steady for an overview of Black women's strengths. This strength-resiliency perspective has greatly influenced empirical work on African-American women. See, e.g., Joyce Ladner's study of low-income Black adolescent girls, *Tomorrow's Tomorrow* (New York: Doubleday, 1971); and Lena Wright Myers's work on Black women's self-concept, *Black Women: Do They Cope Better?* (Englewood Cliffs, N.J.: Prentice-Hall, 1980). For discussions of Black women's resistance, see Elizabeth Fox-Genovese, "Strategies and Forms of Resistance: Focus on Slave Women in the United States," in *In Resistance: Studies in African, Caribbean and Afro-American History*, ed. Gary Y. Okihiro (Amherst, Mass.: University of Massachusetts Press, 1986), 143–65; and Rosalyn Terborg-Penn, "Black Women in Resistance: A Cross-Cultural Perspective," in Okihiro, ed., 188–209. For a comprehensive discussion of everyday resistance, see James C. Scott, *Weapons of the Weak: Everyday Forms of Peasant Resistance* (New Haven, Conn.: Yale University Press, 1985).

[3] See Patricia Hill Collins's analysis of the substantive content of Black feminist thought in "Learning from the Outsider Within: The Sociological Significance of Black Feminist Thought," *Social Problems* 33, no. 6 (1986): 14–32.

[4] Scott describes consciousness as the meaning that people give to their acts through the symbols, norms, and ideological forms they create.

[5] This thesis is found in scholarship of varying theoretical perspectives. For example, Marxist analyses of working-class consciousness claim that "false consciousness" makes the working class unable to penetrate the hegemony of ruling-class ideologies. See Scott's critique of this literature.

less human than their rulers and, therefore, are less capable of articulating their own standpoint.[6] Both approaches see any independent consciousness expressed by an oppressed group as being not of the group's own making and/or inferior to the perspective of the dominant group.[7] More important, both interpretations suggest that oppressed groups lack the motivation for political activism because of their flawed consciousness of their own subordination.

Yet African-American women have been neither passive victims of nor willing accomplices to their own domination. As a result, emerging work in Black women's studies contends that Black women have a self-defined standpoint on their own oppression.[8] Two interlocking components characterize this standpoint. First, Black women's political and economic status provides them with a distinctive set of experiences that offers a different view of material reality than that available to other groups. The unpaid and paid work that Black women perform, the types of communities in which they live, and the kinds of relationships they have with others suggest that African-American women, as a group, experience a different world than those who are not Black and female.[9] Second,

[6] For example, in Western societies, African-Americans have been judged as being less capable of intellectual excellence, more suited to manual labor, and therefore as less human than whites. Similarly, white women have been assigned roles as emotional, irrational creatures ruled by passions and biological urges. They too have been stigmatized as being less than fully human, as being objects. For a discussion of the importance that objectification and dehumanization play in maintaining systems of domination, see Arthur Brittan and Mary Maynard, *Sexism, Racism and Oppression* (New York: Basil Blackwell, 1984).

[7] The tendency for Western scholarship to assess Black culture as pathological and deviant illustrates this process. See Rhett S. Jones, "Proving Blacks Inferior: The Sociology of Knowledge," in *The Death of White Sociology,* ed. Joyce Ladner (New York: Vintage, 1973), 114–35.

[8] The presence of an independent standpoint does not mean that it is uniformly shared by all Black women or even that Black women fully recognize its contours. By using the concept of standpoint, I do not mean to minimize the rich diversity existing among African-American women. I use the phrase "Black women's standpoint" to emphasize the plurality of experiences within the overarching term "standpoint." For discussions of the concept of standpoint, see Nancy M. Hartsock, "The Feminist Standpoint: Developing the Ground for a Specifically Feminist Historical Materialism," in *Discovering Reality,* ed. Sandra Harding and Merrill Hintikka (Boston: D. Reidel, 1983), 283–310, and *Money, Sex, and Power* (Boston: Northeastern University Press, 1983); and Alison M. Jaggar, *Feminist Politics and Human Nature* (Totowa, N.J.: Rowman & Allanheld, 1983), 377–89. My use of the standpoint epistemologies as an organizing concept in this essay does not mean that the concept is problem-free. For a helpful critique of standpoint epistemologies, see Sandra Harding, *The Science Question in Feminism* (Ithaca, N.Y.: Cornell University Press, 1986).

[9] One contribution of contemporary Black women's studies is its documentation of how race, class, and gender have structured these differences. For representative

these experiences stimulate a distinctive Black feminist consciousness concerning that material reality.[10] In brief, a subordinate group
not only experiences a different reality than a group that rules, but
a subordinate group may interpret that reality differently than a
dominant group.

Many ordinary African-American women have grasped this
connection between what one does and how one thinks. Hannah
Nelson, an elderly Black domestic worker, discusses how work
shapes the standpoints of African-American and white women:
"Since I have to work, I don't really have to worry about most of the
things that most of the white women I have worked for are worrying
about. And if these women did their own work, they would think
just like I do—about this, anyway."[11] Ruth Shays, a Black inner city
resident, points out how variations in men's and women's experiences lead to differences in perspective: "The mind of the man and
the mind of the woman is the same. But this business of living
makes women use their minds in ways that men don't even have to
think about."[12] Finally, elderly domestic worker Rosa Wakefield
assesses how the standpoints of the powerful and those who serve
them diverge: "If you eats these dinners and don't cook 'em, if you
wears these clothes and don't buy or iron them, then you might start
thinking that the good fairy or some spirit did all that. . . . Blackfolks
don't have no time to be thinking like that. . . . But when you don't

---

works surveying African-American women's experiences, see Paula Giddings, *When
and Where I Enter: The Impact of Black Women on Race and Sex in America* (New
York: William Morrow, 1984); and Jacqueline Jones, *Labor of Love, Labor of
Sorrow: Black Women, Work, and the Family from Slavery to the Present* (New
York: Basic, 1985).

[10] For example, Judith Rollins, *Between Women: Domestics and Their Employers*
(Philadelphia: Temple University Press, 1985); and Bonnie Thornton Dill, " 'The
Means to Put My Children Through': Child-Rearing Goals and Strategies among
Black Female Domestic Servants," in *The Black Woman*, ed. LaFrances Rodgers-
Rose (Beverly Hills, Calif.: Sage Publications, 1980), 107–23, report that Black
domestic workers do not see themselves as being the devalued workers that their
employers perceive and construct their own interpretations of the meaning of their
work. For additional discussions of how Black women's consciousness is shaped by
the material conditions they encounter, see Ladner (n. 2 above); Myers (n. 2 above);
and Cheryl Townsend Gilkes, " 'Together and in Harness': Women's Traditions in
the Sanctified Church," *Signs* 10, no. 4 (Summer 1985): 678–99. See also Marcia
Westkott's discussion of consciousness as a sphere of freedom for women in
"Feminist Criticism of the Social Sciences," *Harvard Educational Review* 49, no. 4
(1979): 422–30.

[11] John Langston Gwaltney, *Drylongso: A Self-Portrait of Black America* (New
York: Vintage, 1980), 4.

[12] Ibid., 33.

have anything else to do, you can think like that. It's bad for your mind, though."[13]

While African-American women may occupy material positions that stimulate a unique standpoint, expressing an independent Black feminist consciousness is problematic precisely because more powerful groups have a vested interest in suppressing such thought. As Hannah Nelson notes, "I have grown to womanhood in a world where the saner you are, the madder you are made to appear."[14] Nelson realizes that those who control the schools, the media, and other cultural institutions are generally skilled in establishing their view of reality as superior to alternative interpretations. While an oppressed group's experiences may put them in a position to see things differently, their lack of control over the apparatuses of society that sustain ideological hegemony makes the articulation of their self-defined standpoint difficult. Groups unequal in power are correspondingly unequal in their access to the resources necessary to implement their perspectives outside their particular group.

One key reason that standpoints of oppressed groups are discredited and suppressed by the more powerful is that self-defined standpoints can stimulate oppressed groups to resist their domination. For instance, Annie Adams, a southern Black woman, describes how she became involved in civil rights activities.

> When I first went into the mill we had segregated water fountains. . . . Same thing about the toilets. I had to clean the toilets for the inspection room and then, when I got ready to go to the bathroom, I had to go all the way to the bottom of the stairs to the cellar. So I asked my boss man, "What's the difference? If I can go in there and clean them toilets, why can't I use them?" Finally, I started to use that toilet. I decided I wasn't going to walk a mile to go to the bathroom.[15]

In this case, Adams found the standpoint of the "boss man" inadequate, developed one of her own, and acted upon it. In doing so, her actions exemplify the connections between experiencing oppression, developing a self-defined standpoint on that experience, and resistance.

[13] Ibid., 88.

[14] Ibid., 7.

[15] Victoria Byerly, *Hard Times Cotton Mill Girls: Personal Histories of Womanhood and Poverty in the South* (New York: ILR Press, 1986), 134.

The significance of Black feminist thought

The existence of a distinctive Black women's standpoint does not mean that it has been adequately articulated in Black feminist thought. Peter Berger and Thomas Luckmann provide a useful approach to clarifying the relationship between a Black women's standpoint and Black feminist thought with the contention that knowledge exists on two levels.[16] The first level includes the everyday, taken-for-granted knowledge shared by members of a given group, such as the ideas expressed by Ruth Shays and Annie Adams. Black feminist thought, by extension, represents a second level of knowledge, the more specialized knowledge furnished by experts who are part of a group and who express the group's standpoint. The two levels of knowledge are interdependent; while Black feminist thought articulates the taken-for-granted knowledge of African-American women, it also encourages all Black women to create new self-definitions that validate a Black women's standpoint.

Black feminist thought's potential significance goes far beyond demonstrating that Black women can produce independent, specialized knowledge. Such thought can encourage collective identity by offering Black women a different view of themselves and their world than that offered by the established social order. This different view encourages African-American women to value their own subjective knowledge base.[17] By taking elements and themes of Black women's culture and traditions and infusing them with new meaning, Black feminist thought rearticulates a consciousness that already exists.[18] More important, this rearticulated consciousness gives African-American women another tool of resistance to all forms of their subordination.[19]

Black feminist thought, then, specializes in formulating and rearticulating the distinctive, self-defined standpoint of African-American women. One approach to learning more about a Black women's standpoint is to consult standard scholarly sources for the

[16] See Peter L. Berger and Thomas Luckmann, *The Social Construction of Reality* (New York: Doubleday, 1966), for a discussion of everyday thought and the role of experts in articulating specialized thought.

[17] See Michael Omi and Howard Winant, *Racial Formation in the United States* (New York: Routledge & Kegan Paul, 1986), esp. 93.

[18] In discussing standpoint epistemologies, Hartsock, in *Money, Sex, and Power*, notes that a standpoint is "achieved rather than obvious, a mediated rather than immediate understanding" (132).

[19] See Scott (n. 2 above); and Hartsock, *Money, Sex, and Power* (n. 8 above).

ideas of specialists on Black women's experiences.[20] But investigating a Black women's standpoint and Black feminist thought requires more ingenuity than that required in examining the standpoints and thought of white males. Rearticulating the standpoint of African-American women through Black feminist thought is much more difficult since one cannot use the same techniques to study the knowledge of the dominated as one uses to study the knowledge of the powerful. This is precisely because subordinate groups have long had to use alternative ways to create an independent consciousness and to rearticulate it through specialists validated by the oppressed themselves.

The Eurocentric masculinist knowledge-validation process[21]

All social thought, including white masculinist and Black feminist, reflects the interests and standpoint of its creators. As Karl Mannheim notes, "If one were to trace in detail . . . the origin and . . . diffusion of a certain thought-model, one would discover the . . . affinity it has to the social position of given groups and their manner of interpreting the world."[22] Scholars, publishers, and other experts represent specific interests and credentialing processes, and their knowledge claims must satisfy the epistemological and political criteria of the contexts in which they reside.[23]

[20] Some readers may question how one determines whether the ideas of any given African-American woman are "feminist" and "Afrocentric." I offer the following working definitions. I agree with the general definition of feminist consciousness provided by Black feminist sociologist Deborah K. King: "Any purposes, goals, and activities which seek to enhance the potential of women, to ensure their liberty, afford them equal opportunity, and to permit and encourage their self-determination represent a feminist consciousness, even if they occur within a racial community" (in "Race, Class and Gender Salience in Black Women's Womanist Consciousness" [Dartmouth College, Department of Sociology, Hanover, N.H., 1987, typescript], 22). To be Black or Afrocentric, such thought must not only reflect a similar concern for the self-determination of African-American people, but must in some way draw upon key elements of an Afrocentric tradition as well.

[21] The Eurocentric masculinist process is defined here as the institutions, paradigms, and any elements of the knowledge-validation procedure controlled by white males and whose purpose is to represent a white male standpoint. While this process represents the interests of powerful white males, various dimensions of the process are not necessarily managed by white males themselves.

[22] Karl Mannheim, *Ideology and Utopia: An Introduction to the Sociology of Knowledge* (New York: Harcourt, Brace, 1936, 1954), 276.

[23] The knowledge-validation model used in this essay is taken from Michael Mulkay, *Science and the Sociology of Knowledge* (Boston: Allen & Unwin, 1979). For a general discussion of the structure of knowledge, see Thomas Kuhn, *The Structure of Scientific Revolutions* (Chicago: University of Chicago Press, 1962).

Two political criteria influence the knowledge-validation process. First, knowledge claims must be evaluated by a community of experts whose members represent the standpoints of the groups from which they originate. Second, each community of experts must maintain its credibility as defined by the larger group in which it is situated and from which it draws its basic, taken-for-granted knowledge.

When white males control the knowledge-validation process, both political criteria can work to suppress Black feminist thought. Since the general culture shaping the taken-for-granted knowledge of the community of experts is one permeated by widespread notions of Black and female inferiority,[24] new knowledge claims that seem to violate these fundamental assumptions are likely to be viewed as anomalies.[25] Moreover, specialized thought challenging notions of Black and female inferiority is unlikely to be generated from within a white-male-controlled academic community because both the kinds of questions that could be asked and the explanations that would be found satisfying would necessarily reflect a basic lack of familiarity with Black women's reality.[26]

The experiences of African-American women scholars illustrate how individuals who wish to rearticulate a Black women's standpoint through Black feminist thought can be suppressed by a white-male-controlled knowledge-validation process. Exclusion from basic literacy, quality educational experiences, and faculty and administrative positions has limited Black women's access to influential academic positions.[27] Thus, while Black women can produce knowledge claims that contest those advanced by the white male community, this community does not grant that Black women scholars have competing knowledge claims based in another knowledge-validation process. As a consequence, any

[24] For analyses of the content and functions of images of Black female inferiority, see Mae King, "The Politics of Sexual Stereotypes," *Black Scholar* 4, nos. 6–7 (1973): 12–23; Cheryl Townsend Gilkes, "From Slavery to Social Welfare: Racism and the Control of Black Women," in *Class, Race, and Sex: The Dynamics of Control*, ed. Amy Smerdlow and Helen Lessinger (Boston: G. K. Hall, 1981), 288–300; and Elizabeth Higginbotham, "Two Representative Issues in Contemporary Sociological Work on Black Women," in *But Some of Us Are Brave*, ed. Gloria T. Hull, Patricia Bell Scott, and Barbara Smith (Old Westbury, N.Y.: Feminist Press, 1982).

[25] Kuhn.

[26] Evelyn Fox Keller, *Reflections on Gender and Science* (New Haven, Conn.: Yale University Press, 1985), 167.

[27] Maxine Baca Zinn, Lynn Weber Cannon, Elizabeth Higginbotham, and Bonnie Thornton Dill, "The Cost of Exclusionary Practices in Women's Studies," *Signs* 11, no. 2 (Winter 1986): 290–303.

credentials controlled by white male academicians can be denied to Black women producing Black feminist thought on the grounds that it is not credible research.

Those Black women with academic credentials who seek to exert the authority that their status grants them to propose new knowledge claims about African-American women face pressures to use their authority to help legitimate a system that devalues and excludes the majority of Black women.[28] One way of excluding the majority of Black women from the knowledge-validation process is to permit a few Black women to acquire positions of authority in institutions that legitimate knowledge and to encourage them to work within the taken-for-granted assumptions of Black female inferiority shared by the scholarly community and the culture at large. Those Black women who accept these assumptions are likely to be rewarded by their institutions, often at significant personal cost. Those challenging the assumptions run the risk of being ostracized.

African-American women academicians who persist in trying to rearticulate a Black women's standpoint also face potential rejection of their knowledge claims on epistemological grounds. Just as the material realities of the powerful and the dominated produce separate standpoints, each group may also have distinctive epistemologies or theories of knowledge. It is my contention that Black female scholars may know that something is true but be unwilling or unable to legitimate their claims using Eurocentric masculinist criteria for consistency with substantiated knowledge and Eurocentric masculinist criteria for methodological adequacy.

For any particular interpretive context, new knowledge claims must be consistent with an existing body of knowledge that the group controlling the interpretive context accepts as true. The methods used to validate knowledge claims must also be acceptable to the group controlling the knowledge-validation process.

The criteria for the methodological adequacy of positivism illustrate the epistemological standards that Black women scholars

[28] Berger and Luckmann (n. 16 above) note that if an outsider group, in this case African-American women, recognizes that the insider group, namely, white men, requires special privileges from the larger society, a special problem arises of keeping the outsiders out and at the same time having them acknowledge the legitimacy of this procedure. Accepting a few "safe" outsiders is one way of addressing this legitimation problem. Collins's discussion (n. 3 above) of Black women as "outsiders within" addresses this issue. Other relevant works include Franz Fanon's analysis of the role of the national middle class in maintaining colonial systems, *The Wretched of the Earth* (New York: Grove, 1963); and William Tabb's discussion of the use of "bright natives" in controlling African-American communities, *The Political Economy of the Black Ghetto* (New York: Norton, 1970).

would have to satisfy in legitimating alternative knowledge claims.[29] Positivist approaches aim to create scientific descriptions of reality by producing objective generalizations. Since researchers have widely differing values, experiences, and emotions, genuine science is thought to be unattainable unless all human characteristics except rationality are eliminated from the research process. By following strict methodological rules, scientists aim to distance themselves from the values, vested interests, and emotions generated by their class, race, sex, or unique situation and in so doing become detached observers and manipulators of nature.[30]

Several requirements typify positivist methodological approaches. First, research methods generally require a distancing of the researcher from her/his "object" of study by defining the researcher as a "subject" with full human subjectivity and objectifying the "object" of study.[31] A second requirement is the absence of emotions from the research process.[32] Third, ethics and values are deemed inappropriate in the research process, either as the reason for scientific inquiry or as part of the research process itself.[33] Finally, adversarial debates, whether written or oral, become the preferred method of ascertaining truth—the arguments that can withstand the greatest assault and survive intact become the strongest truths.[34]

Such criteria ask African-American women to objectify themselves, devalue their emotional life, displace their motivations for furthering knowledge about Black women, and confront, in an adversarial relationship, those who have more social, economic,

[29] While I have been describing Eurocentric masculinist approaches as a single process, there are many schools of thought or paradigms subsumed under this one process. Positivism represents one such paradigm. See Harding (n. 8 above) for an overview and critique of this literature. The following discussion depends heavily on Jaggar (n. 8 above), 355–58.

[30] Jaggar, 356.

[31] See Keller, especially her analysis of static autonomy and its relation to objectivity (67–126).

[32] Ironically, researchers must "objectify" themselves to achieve this lack of bias. See Arlie Russell Hochschild, "The Sociology of Feeling and Emotion: Selected Possibilities," in *Another Voice: Feminist Perspectives on Social Life and Social Science*, ed. Marcia Millman and Rosabeth Kanter (Garden City, N.Y.: Anchor, 1975), 280–307. Also, see Jaggar.

[33] See Norma Haan, Robert Bellah, Paul Rabinow, and William Sullivan, eds., *Social Science as Moral Inquiry* (New York: Columbia University Press, 1983), esp. Michelle Z. Rosaldo's "Moral/Analytic Dilemmas Posed by the Intersection of Feminism and Social Science," 76–96; and Robert Bellah's "The Ethical Aims of Social Inquiry," 360–81.

[34] Janice Moulton, "A Paradigm of Philosophy: The Adversary Method," in Harding and Hintikka, eds. (n. 8 above), 149–64.

and professional power than they. It seems unlikely, therefore, that Black women would use a positivist epistemological stance in rearticulating a Black women's standpoint. Black women are more likely to choose an alternative epistemology for assessing knowledge claims, one using standards that are consistent with Black women's criteria for substantiated knowledge and with Black women's criteria for methodological adequacy. If such an epistemology exists, what are its contours? Moreover, what is its role in the production of Black feminist thought?

The contours of an Afrocentric feminist epistemology

Africanist analyses of the Black experience generally agree on the fundamental elements of an Afrocentric standpoint. In spite of varying histories, Black societies reflect elements of a core African value system that existed prior to and independently of racial oppression.[35] Moreover, as a result of colonialism, imperialism, slavery, apartheid, and other systems of racial domination, Blacks share a common experience of oppression. These similarities in material conditions have fostered shared Afrocentric values that permeate the family structure, religious institutions, culture, and community life of Blacks in varying parts of Africa, the Caribbean, South America, and North America.[36] This Afrocentric consciousness permeates the shared history of people of African descent through the framework of a distinctive Afrocentric epistemology.[37]

[35] For detailed discussions of the Afrocentric worldview, see John S. Mbiti, *African Religions and Philosophy* (London: Heinemann, 1969); Dominique Zahan, *The Religion, Spirituality, and Thought of Traditional Africa* (Chicago: University of Chicago Press, 1979); and Mechal Sobel, *Trabelin' On: The Slave Journey to an Afro-Baptist Faith* (Westport, Conn.: Greenwood Press, 1979), 1–76.

[36] For representative works applying these concepts to African-American culture, see Niara Sudarkasa, "Interpreting the African Heritage in Afro-American Family Organization," in *Black Families*, ed. Harriette Pipes McAdoo (Beverly Hills, Calif.: Sage, 1981); Henry H. Mitchell and Nicholas Cooper Lewter, *Soul Theology: The Heart of American Black Culture* (San Francisco: Harper & Row, 1986); Robert Farris Thompson, *Flash of the Spirit: African and Afro-American Art and Philosophy* (New York: Vintage, 1983); and Ortiz M. Walton, "Comparative Analysis of the African and the Western Aesthetics," in *The Black Aesthetic*, ed. Addison Gayle (Garden City, N.Y.: Doubleday, 1971), 154–64.

[37] One of the best discussions of an Afrocentric epistemology is offered by James E. Turner, "Foreword: Africana Studies and Epistemology; a Discourse in the Sociology of Knowledge," in *The Next Decade: Theoretical and Research Issues in Africana Studies*, ed. James E. Turner (Ithaca, N.Y.: Cornell University Africana Studies and Research Center, 1984), v–xxv. See also Vernon Dixon, "World Views and Research Methodology," summarized in Harding (n. 8 above), 170.

Feminist scholars advance a similar argument. They assert that women share a history of patriarchal oppression through the political economy of the material conditions of sexuality and reproduction.[38] These shared material conditions are thought to transcend divisions among women created by race, social class, religion, sexual orientation, and ethnicity and to form the basis of a women's standpoint with its corresponding feminist consciousness and epistemology.[39]

Since Black women have access to both the Afrocentric and the feminist standpoints, an alternative epistemology used to rearticulate a Black women's standpoint reflects elements of both traditions.[40] The search for the distinguishing features of an alternative epistemology used by African-American women reveals that values and ideas that Africanist scholars identify as being characteristically "Black" often bear remarkable resemblance to similar ideas claimed by feminist scholars as being characteristically "female."[41] This similarity suggests that the material conditions of oppression can vary dramatically and yet generate some uniformity

[38] See Hester Eisenstein, *Contemporary Feminist Thought* (Boston: G. K. Hall, 1983). Nancy Hartsock's *Money, Sex, and Power* (n. 8 above), 145–209, offers a particularly insightful analysis of women's oppression.

[39] For discussions of feminist consciousness, see Dorothy Smith, "A Sociology for Women," in *The Prism of Sex: Essays in the Sociology of Knowledge,* ed. Julia A. Sherman and Evelyn T. Beck (Madison: University of Wisconsin Press, 1979); and Michelle Z. Rosaldo, "Women, Culture, and Society: A Theoretical Overview," in *Woman, Culture, and Society,* ed. Michelle Z. Rosaldo and Louise Lamphere (Stanford, Calif.: Stanford University Press, 1974), 17–42. Feminist epistemologies are surveyed by Jaggar (n. 8 above).

[40] One significant difference between Afrocentric and feminist standpoints is that much of what is termed women's culture is, unlike African-American culture, created in the context of and produced by oppression. Those who argue for a women's culture are electing to value, rather than denigrate, those traits associated with females in white patriarchal societies. While this choice is important, it is not the same as identifying an independent, historic culture associated with a society. I am indebted to Deborah K. King for this point.

[41] Critiques of the Eurocentric masculinist knowledge-validation process by both Africanist and feminist scholars illustrate this point. What one group labels "white" and "Eurocentric," the other describes as "male-dominated" and "masculinist." Although he does not emphasize its patriarchal and racist features, Morris Berman's *The Reenchantment of the World* (New York: Bantam, 1981) provides a historical discussion of Western thought. Afrocentric analyses of this same process can be found in Molefi Kete Asante, "International/Intercultural Relations," in *Contemporary Black Thought,* ed. Molefi Kete Asante and Abdulai S. Vandi (Beverly Hills, Calif.: Sage, 1980), 43–58; and Dona Richards, "European Mythology: The Ideology of 'Progress,' " in Asante and Vandi, eds., 59–79. For feminist analyses, see Hartsock, *Money, Sex, and Power.* Harding also discusses this similarity (see chap. 7, "Other 'Others' and Fractured Identities: Issues for Epistemologists," 163–96).

in the epistemologies of subordinate groups. Thus, the significance of an Afrocentric feminist epistemology may lie in its enrichment of our understanding of how subordinate groups create knowledge that enables them to resist oppression.

The parallels between the two conceptual schemes raise a question: Is the worldview of women of African descent more intensely infused with the overlapping feminine/Afrocentric standpoints than is the case for either African-American men or white women?[42] While an Afrocentric feminist epistemology reflects elements of epistemologies used by Blacks as a group and women as a group, it also paradoxically demonstrates features that may be unique to Black women. On certain dimensions, Black women may more closely resemble Black men, on others, white women, and on still others, Black women may stand apart from both groups. Black feminist sociologist Deborah K. King describes this phenomenon as a "both/or" orientation, the act of being simultaneously a member of a group and yet standing apart from it. She suggests that multiple realities among Black women yield a "multiple consciousness in Black women's politics" and that this state of belonging yet not belonging forms an integral part of Black women's oppositional consciousness.[43] Bonnie Thornton Dill's analysis of how Black women live with contradictions, a situation she labels the "dialectics of Black womanhood," parallels King's assertions that this "both/or" orientation is central to an Afrocentric feminist consciousness.[44] Rather than emphasizing how a Black women's standpoint and its accompanying epistemology are different than those in Afrocentric and feminist analyses, I use Black women's experiences as a point of contact between the two.

Viewing an Afrocentric feminist epistemology in this way challenges analyses claiming that Black women have a more accurate view of oppression than do other groups. Such approaches suggest that oppression can be quantified and compared and that adding layers of oppression produces a potentially clearer standpoint. While it is tempting to claim that Black women are more oppressed than everyone else and therefore have the best standpoint from which to understand the mechanisms, processes, and effects of oppression, this simply may not be the case.[45]

[42] Harding, 166.

[43] D. King (n. 20 above).

[44] Bonnie Thornton Dill, "The Dialectics of Black Womanhood," Signs 4, no. 3 (Spring 1979): 543–55.

[45] One implication of standpoint approaches is that the more subordinate the group, the purer the vision of the oppressed group. This is an outcome of the origins of standpoint approaches in Marxist social theory, itself a dualistic analysis of social

African-American women do not uniformly share an Afrocentric feminist epistemology since social class introduces variations among Black women in seeing, valuing, and using Afrocentric feminist perspectives. While a Black women's standpoint and its accompanying epistemology stem from Black women's consciousness of race and gender oppression, they are not simply the result of combining Afrocentric and female values—standpoints are rooted in real material conditions structured by social class.[46]

Concrete experience as a criterion of meaning

Carolyn Chase, a thirty-one-year-old inner city Black woman, notes, "My aunt used to say, 'A heap see, but a few know.' "[47] This saying depicts two types of knowing, knowledge and wisdom, and taps the first dimension of an Afrocentric feminist epistemology. Living life as Black women requires wisdom since knowledge about the dynamics of race, gender, and class subordination has been essential to Black women's survival. African-American women give such wisdom high credence in assessing knowledge.

Allusions to these two types of knowing pervade the words of a range of African-American women. In explaining the tenacity of racism, Zilpha Elaw, a preacher of the mid-1800s, noted: "The pride of a white skin is a bauble of great value with many in some parts of the United States, who readily sacrifice their intelligence to their prejudices, and possess more knowledge than wisdom."[48] In describing differences separating African-American and white women, Nancy White invokes a similar rule: "When you come right down to it, white women just *think* they are free. Black women

---

structure. Because such approaches rely on quantifying and ranking human oppressions—familiar tenets of positivist approaches—they are rejected by Blacks and feminists alike. See Harding (n. 8 above) for a discussion of this point. See also Elizabeth V. Spelman's discussion of the fallacy of additive oppression in "Theories of Race and Gender: The Erasure of Black Women," *Quest* 5, no. 4 (1982): 36–62.

[46] Class differences among Black women may be marked. For example, see Paula Giddings's analysis (n. 9 above) of the role of social class in shaping Black women's political activism; or Elizabeth Higginbotham's study of the effects of social class in Black women's college attendance in "Race and Class Barriers to Black Women's College Attendance," *Journal of Ethnic Studies* 13, no. 1 (1985): 89–107. Those African-American women who have experienced the greatest degree of convergence of race, class, and gender oppression may be in a better position to recognize and use an alternative epistemology.

[47] Gwaltney (n. 11 above), 83.

[48] William L. Andrews, *Sisters of the Spirit: Three Black Women's Autobiographies of the Nineteenth Century* (Bloomington: Indiana University Press, 1986), 85.

know they ain't free."[49] Geneva Smitherman, a college professor specializing in African-American linguistics, suggests that "from a black perspective, written documents are limited in what they can teach about life and survival in the world. Blacks are quick to ridicule 'educated fools,' . . . they have 'book learning' but no 'mother wit,' knowledge, but not wisdom."[50] Mabel Lincoln eloquently summarizes the distinction between knowledge and wisdom: "To black people like me, a fool is funny—you know, people who love to break bad, people you can't tell anything to, folks that would take a shotgun to a roach."[51]

Black women need wisdom to know how to deal with the "educated fools" who would "take a shotgun to a roach." As members of a subordinate group, Black women cannot afford to be fools of any type, for their devalued status denies them the protections that white skin, maleness, and wealth confer. This distinction between knowledge and wisdom, and the use of experience as the cutting edge dividing them, has been key to Black women's survival. In the context of race, gender, and class oppression, the distinction is essential since knowledge without wisdom is adequate for the powerful, but wisdom is essential to the survival of the subordinate.

For ordinary African-American women, those individuals who have lived through the experiences about which they claim to be experts are more believable and credible than those who have merely read or thought about such experiences. Thus, concrete experience as a criterion for credibility frequently is invoked by Black women when making knowledge claims. For instance, Hannah Nelson describes the importance that personal experience has for her: "Our speech is most directly personal, and every black person assumes that every other black person has a right to a personal opinion. In speaking of grave matters, your personal experience is considered very good evidence. With us, distant statistics are certainly not as important as the actual experience of a sober person."[52] Similarly, Ruth Shays uses her concrete experiences to challenge the idea that formal education is the only route to knowledge: "I am the kind of person who doesn't have a lot of education, but both my mother and my father had good common sense. Now, I think that's all you need. I might not know how to use thirty-four words where three would do, but that does not mean that

[49] Gwaltney, 147.

[50] Geneva Smitherman, *Talkin and Testifyin: The Language of Black America* (Detroit: Wayne State University Press, 1986), 76.

[51] Gwaltney, 68.

[52] Ibid., 7.

I don't know what I'm talking about . . . I know what I'm talking about because I'm talking about myself. I'm talking about what I have lived."[53] Implicit in Shays's self-assessment is a critique of the type of knowledge that obscures the truth, the "thirty-four words" that cover up a truth that can be expressed in three.

Even after substantial mastery of white masculinist epistemologies, many Black women scholars invoke their own concrete experiences and those of other Black women in selecting topics for investigation and methodologies used. For example, Elsa Barkley Brown subtitles her essay on Black women's history, "how my mother taught me to be an historian in spite of my academic training."[54] Similarly, Joyce Ladner maintains that growing up as a Black woman in the South gave her special insights in conducting her study of Black adolescent women.[55]

Henry Mitchell and Nicholas Lewter claim that experience as a criterion of meaning with practical images as its symbolic vehicles is a fundamental epistemological tenet in African-American thought-systems.[56] Stories, narratives, and Bible principles are selected for their applicability to the lived experiences of African-Americans and become symbolic representations of a whole wealth of experience. For example, Bible tales are told for their value to common life, so their interpretation involves no need for scientific historical verification. The narrative method requires that the story be "told, not torn apart in analysis, and trusted as core belief, not admired as science."[57] Any biblical story contains more than characters and a plot—it presents key ethical issues salient in African-American life.

June Jordan's essay about her mother's suicide exemplifies the multiple levels of meaning that can occur when concrete experiences are used as a criterion of meaning. Jordan describes her mother, a woman who literally died trying to stand up, and the effect that her mother's death had on her own work:

> I think all of this is really about women and work. Certainly this is all about me as a woman and my life work. I mean I am

[53] Ibid., 27, 33.

[54] Elsa Barkley Brown, "Hearing Our Mothers' Lives" (paper presented at the Fifteenth Anniversary Faculty Lecture Series, African-American and African Studies, Emory University, Atlanta, 1986).

[55] Ladner (n. 2 above).

[56] Mitchell and Lewter (n. 36 above). The use of the narrative approach in African-American theology exemplifies an inductive system of logic alternately called "folk wisdom" or a survival-based, need-oriented method of assessing knowledge claims.

[57] Ibid., 8.

not sure my mother's suicide was something extraordinary. Perhaps most women must deal with a similar inheritance, the legacy of a woman whose death you cannot possibly pinpoint because she died so many, many times and because, even before she became your mother, the life of that woman was taken. . . . I came too late to help my mother to her feet. By way of everlasting thanks to all of the women who have helped me to stay alive I am working never to be late again.[58]

While Jordan has knowledge about the concrete act of her mother's death, she also strives for wisdom concerning the meaning of that death.

Some feminist scholars offer a similar claim that women, as a group, are more likely than men to use concrete knowledge in assessing knowledge claims. For example, a substantial number of the 135 women in a study of women's cognitive development were "connected knowers" and were drawn to the sort of knowledge that emerges from first-hand observation. Such women felt that since knowledge comes from experience, the best way of understanding another person's ideas was to try to share the experiences that led the person to form those ideas. At the heart of the procedures used by connected knowers is the capacity for empathy.[59]

In valuing the concrete, African-American women may be invoking not only an Afrocentric tradition, but a women's tradition as well. Some feminist theorists suggest that women are socialized in complex relational nexuses where contextual rules take priority over abstract principles in governing behavior. This socialization process is thought to stimulate characteristic ways of knowing.[60] For example, Canadian sociologist Dorothy Smith maintains that two modes of knowing exist, one located in the body and the space it occupies and the other passing beyond it. She asserts that women, through their child-rearing and nurturing activities, mediate these two modes and use the concrete experiences of their daily lives to assess more abstract knowledge claims.[61]

Amanda King, a young Black mother, describes how she used the concrete to assess the abstract and points out how difficult mediating these two modes of knowing can be:

[58] June Jordan, On Call: Political Essays (Boston: South End Press, 1985), 26.
[59] Mary Belenky, Blythe Clinchy, Nancy Goldberger, and Jill Tarule, Women's Ways of Knowing (New York: Basic, 1986), 113.
[60] Hartsock, Money, Sex and Power (n. 8 above), 237; and Nancy Chodorow, The Reproduction of Mothering (Berkeley and Los Angeles: University of California Press, 1978).
[61] Dorothy Smith, The Everyday World as Problematic (Boston: Northeastern University Press, 1987).

The leaders of the ROC [a labor union] lost their jobs too, but it just seemed like they were used to losing their jobs. . . . This was like a lifelong thing for them, to get out there and protest. They were like, what do you call them—intellectuals. . . . You got the ones that go to the university that are supposed to make all the speeches, they're the ones that are supposed to lead, you know, put this little revolution together, and then you got the little ones . . . that go to the factory everyday, they be the ones that have to fight. I had a child and I thought I don't have the time to be running around with these people. . . . I mean I understand some of that stuff they were talking about, like the bourgeoisie, the rich and the poor and all that, but I had surviving on my mind for me and my kid.[62]

For King, abstract ideals of class solidarity were mediated by the concrete experience of motherhood and the connectedness it involved.

In traditional African-American communities, Black women find considerable institutional support for valuing concrete experience. Black extended families and Black churches are two key institutions where Black women experts with concrete knowledge of what it takes to be self-defined Black women share their knowledge with their younger, less experienced sisters. This relationship of sisterhood among Black women can be seen as a model for a whole series of relationships that African-American women have with each other, whether it is networks among women in extended families, among women in the Black church, or among women in the African-American community at large.[63]

Since the Black church and the Black family are both woman-centered and Afrocentric institutions, African-American women traditionally have found considerable institutional support for this dimension of an Afrocentric feminist epistemology in ways that are unique to them. While white women may value the concrete, it is

[62] Byerly (n. 15 above), 198.
[63] For Black women's centrality in the family, see Steady (n. 1 above); Ladner (n. 2 above); Brown (n. 54 above); and McAdoo, ed. (n. 36 above). See Gilkes, " 'Together and in Harness' " (n. 10 above), for Black women in the church; and chap. 4 of Deborah Gray White, *Ar'n't I a Woman? Female Slaves in the Plantation South* (New York: Norton, 1985). See also Gloria Joseph, "Black Mothers and Daughters: Their Roles and Functions in American Society," in *Common Differences: Conflicts in Black and White Feminist Perspectives,* ed. Gloria Joseph and Jill Lewis (Garden City, N.Y.: Anchor, 1981), 75–126. Even though Black women play essential roles in Black families and Black churches, these institutions are not free from sexism.

questionable whether white families, particularly middle-class nuclear ones, and white community institutions provide comparable types of support. Similarly, while Black men are supported by Afrocentric institutions, they cannot participate in Black women's sisterhood. In terms of Black women's relationships with one another then, African-American women may indeed find it easier than others to recognize connectedness as a primary way of knowing, simply because they are encouraged to do so by Black women's tradition of sisterhood.

The use of dialogue in assessing knowledge claims

For Black women, new knowledge claims are rarely worked out in isolation from other individuals and are usually developed through dialogues with other members of a community. A primary epistemological assumption underlying the use of dialogue in assessing knowledge claims is that connectedness rather than separation is an essential component of the knowledge-validation process.[64]

The use of dialogue has deep roots in an African-based oral tradition and in African-American culture.[65] Ruth Shays describes the importance of dialogue in the knowledge-validation process of enslaved African-Americans: "They would find a lie if it took them a year . . . the foreparents found the truth because they listened and they made people tell their part many times. Most often you can hear a lie. . . . Those old people was everywhere and knew the truth of many disputes. They believed that a liar should suffer the pain of his lies, and they had all kinds of ways of bringing liars to judgement."[66]

The widespread use of the call and response discourse mode among African-Americans exemplifies the importance placed on dialogue. Composed of spontaneous verbal and nonverbal interaction between speaker and listener in which all of the speaker's statements or "calls" are punctuated by expressions or "responses" from the listener, this Black discourse mode pervades African-American culture. The fundamental requirement of this interactive network is active participation of all individuals.[67] For ideas to be tested and validated, everyone in the group must participate. To

[64] As Belenky et al. note, "Unlike the eye, the ear requires closeness between subject and object. Unlike seeing, speaking and listening suggest dialogue and interaction" (18).

[65] Thomas Kochman, *Black and White: Styles in Conflict* (Chicago: University of Chicago Press, 1981); and Smitherman (n. 50 above).

[66] Gwaltney (n. 11 above), 32.

[67] Smitherman, 108.

refuse to join in, especially if one really disagrees with what has been said is seen as "cheating."[68]

June Jordan's analysis of Black English points to the significance of this dimension of an alternative epistemology.

> Our language is a system constructed by people constantly needing to insist that we exist. . . . Our language devolves from a culture that abhors all abstraction, or anything tending to obscure or delete the fact of the human being who is here and now/the truth of the person who is speaking or listening. Consequently, *there is no passive voice construction possible in Black English.* For example, you cannot say, "Black English is being eliminated." You must say, instead, "White people eliminating Black English." The assumption of the presence of life governs all of Black English . . . every sentence assumes the living and active participation of at least two human beings, the speaker and the listener.[69]

Many Black women intellectuals invoke the relationships and connectedness provided by use of dialogue. When asked why she chose the themes she did, novelist Gayle Jones replied: "I was . . . interested . . . in oral traditions of storytelling—Afro-American and others, in which there is always the consciousness and importance of the hearer."[70] In describing the difference in the way male and female writers select significant events and relationships, Jones points out that "with many women writers, relationships within family, community, between men and women, and among women— from slave narratives by black women writers on—are treated as complex and significant relationships, whereas with many men the significant relationships are those that involve confrontations— relationships outside the family and community."[71] Alice Walker's reaction to Zora Neale Hurston's book, *Mules and Men,* is another example of the use of dialogue in assessing knowlege claims. In *Mules and Men,* Hurston chose not to become a detached observer of the stories and folktales she collected but instead, through extensive dialogues with the people in the communities she studied, placed herself at the center of her analysis. Using a similar process, Walker tests the truth of Hurston's knowledge claims: "When I read *Mules and Men* I was delighted. Here was this perfect book! The 'perfection' of which I immediately tested on my

---

[68] Kochman, 28.
[69] Jordan (n. 58 above), 129.
[70] Claudia Tate, *Black Women Writers at Work* (New York: Continuum, 1983), 91.
[71] Ibid., 92.

relatives, who are such typical Black Americans they are useful for every sort of political, cultural, or economic survey. Very regular people from the South, rapidly forgetting their Southern cultural inheritance in the suburbs and ghettos of Boston and New York, they sat around reading the book themselves, listening to me read the book, listening to each other read the book, and a kind of paradise was regained."[72]

Their centrality in Black churches and Black extended families provides Black women with a high degree of support from Black institutions for invoking dialogue as a dimension of an Afrocentric feminist epistemology. However, when African-American women use dialogues in assessing knowledge claims, they might be invoking a particularly female way of knowing as well. Feminist scholars contend that males and females are socialized within their families to seek different types of autonomy, the former based on separation, the latter seeking connectedness, and that this variation in types of autonomy parallels the characteristic differences between male and female ways of knowing.[73] For instance, in contrast to the visual metaphors (such as equating knowledge with illumination, knowing with seeing, and truth with light) that scientists and philosophers typically use, women tend to ground their epistemological premises in metaphors suggesting speaking and listening.[74]

While there are significant differences between the roles Black women play in their families and those played by middle-class white women, Black women clearly are affected by general cultural norms prescribing certain familial roles for women. Thus, in terms of the role of dialogue in an Afrocentric feminist epistemology, Black women may again experience a convergence of the values of the African-American community and woman-centered values.

The ethic of caring

"Ole white preachers used to talk wid dey tongues widdout sayin' nothin', but Jesus told us slaves to talk wid our hearts."[75] These words of an ex-slave suggest that ideas cannot be divorced from the individuals who create and share them. This theme of "talking with the heart" taps another dimension of an alternative epistemology used by African-American women, the ethic of caring. Just as the ex-slave used the wisdom in his heart to reject the ideas of the

[72] Alice Walker, *In Search of Our Mothers' Gardens* (New York: Harcourt Brace Jovanovich, 1974), 84.

[73] Keller (n. 26 above); Chodorow (n. 60 above).

[74] Belenky et al. (n. 59 above), 16.

[75] Thomas Webber, *Deep Like the Rivers* (New York: Norton, 1978), 127.

preachers who talked "wid dey tongues widdout sayin' nothin'," the ethic of caring suggests that personal expressiveness, emotions, and empathy are central to the knowledge-validation process.

One of three interrelated components making up the ethic of caring is the emphasis placed on individual uniqueness. Rooted in a tradition of African humanism, each individual is thought to be a unique expression of a common spirit, power, or energy expressed by all life.[76] This belief in individual uniqueness is illustrated by the value placed on personal expressiveness in African-American communities.[77] Johnetta Ray, an inner city resident, describes this Afrocentric emphasis on individual uniqueness: "No matter how hard we try, I don't think black people will ever develop much of a herd instinct. We are profound individualists with a passion for self-expression."[78]

A second component of the ethic of caring concerns the appropriateness of emotions in dialogues. Emotion indicates that a speaker believes in the validity of an argument.[79] Consider Ntozake Shange's description of one of the goals of her work: "Our [Western] society allows people to be absolutely neurotic and totally out of touch with their feelings and everyone else's feelings, and yet be very respectable. This, to me, is a travesty. . . . I'm trying to change the idea of seeing emotions and intellect as distinct faculties."[80] Shange's words echo those of the ex-slave. Both see the denigration of emotion as problematic, and both suggest that expressiveness should be reclaimed and valued.

A third component of the ethic of caring involves developing the capacity for empathy. Harriet Jones, a sixteen-year-old Black woman, explains why she chose to open up to her interviewer: "Some things in my life are so hard for me to bear, and it makes me

[76] In her discussion of the West African Sacred Cosmos, Mechal Sobel (n. 35 above) notes that Nyam, a root word in many West African languages, connotes an enduring spirit, power, or energy possessed by all life. In spite of the pervasiveness of this key concept in African humanism, its definition remains elusive. She points out, "Every individual analyzing the various Sacred Cosmos of West Africa has recognized the reality of this force, but no one has yet adequately translated this concept into Western terms" (13).

[77] For discussions of personal expressiveness in African-American culture, see Smitherman (n. 50 above); Kochman (n. 65 above), esp. chap. 9; and Mitchell and Lewter (n. 36 above).

[78] Gwaltney (n. 11 above), 228.

[79] For feminist analyses of the subordination of emotion in Western culture, see Hochschild (n. 32 above); and Chodorow.

[80] Tate (n. 70 above), 156.

feel better to know that you feel sorry about those things and would change them if you could."[81]

These three components of the ethic of caring—the value placed on individual expressiveness, the appropriateness of emotions, and the capacity for empathy—pervade African-American culture. One of the best examples of the interactive nature of the importance of dialogue and the ethic of caring in assessing knowledge claims occurs in the use of the call and response discourse mode in traditional Black church services. In such services, both the minister and the congregation routinely use voice rhythm and vocal inflection to convey meaning. The sound of what is being said is just as important as the words themselves in what is, in a sense, a dialogue between reason and emotions. As a result, it is nearly impossible to filter out the strictly linguistic-cognitive abstract meaning from the sociocultural psycho-emotive meaning.[82] While the ideas presented by a speaker must have validity, that is, agree with the general body of knowledge shared by the Black congregation, the group also appraises the way knowledge claims are presented.

There is growing evidence that the ethic of caring may be part of women's experience as well. Certain dimensions of women's ways of knowing bear striking resemblance to Afrocentric expressions of the ethic of caring. Belenky, Clinchy, Goldberger, and Tarule point out that two contrasting epistemological orientations characterize knowing—one, an epistemology of separation based on impersonal procedures for establishing truth, and the other, an epistemology of connection in which truth emerges through care. While these ways of knowing are not gender specific, disproportionate numbers of women rely on connected knowing.[83]

The parallels between Afrocentric expressions of the ethic of caring and those advanced by feminist scholars are noteworthy. The emphasis placed on expressiveness and emotion in African-American communities bears marked resemblance to feminist perspectives on the importance of personality in connected knowing. Separate knowers try to subtract the personality of an individual from his or her ideas because they see personality as biasing those ideas. In contrast, connected knowers see personality as adding to an individual's ideas, and they feel that the personality of each group member enriches a group's understanding.[84] Similarly, the significance of individual uniqueness, personal expressiveness,

[81] Gwaltney, 11.
[82] Smitherman, 135 and 137.
[83] Belenky et al. (n. 59 above), 100–130.
[84] Ibid., 119.

and empathy in African-American communities resembles the importance that some feminist analyses place on women's "inner voice."[85]

The convergence of Afrocentric and feminist values in the ethic-of-care dimension of an alternative epistemology seems particularly acute. While white women may have access to a women's tradition valuing emotion and expressiveness, few white social institutions except the family validate this way of knowing. In contrast, Black women have long had the support of the Black church, an institution with deep roots in the African past and a philosophy that accepts and encourages expressiveness and an ethic of caring. While Black men share in this Afrocentric tradition, they must resolve the contradictions that distinguish abstract, unemotional Western masculinity from an Afrocentric ethic of caring. The differences among race/gender groups thus hinge on differences in their access to institutional supports valuing one type of knowing over another. Although Black women may be denigrated within white-male-controlled academic institutions, other institutions, such as Black families and churches, which encourage the expression of Black female power, seem to do so by way of their support for an Afrocentric feminist epistemology.

The ethic of personal accountability

An ethic of personal accountability is the final dimension of an alternative epistemology. Not only must individuals develop their knowledge claims through dialogue and present those knowledge claims in a style proving their concern for their ideas, people are expected to be accountable for their knowledge claims. Zilpha Elaw's description of slavery reflects this notion that every idea has an owner and that the owner's identity matters: "Oh, the abominations of slavery! . . . every case of slavery, however lenient its inflictions and mitigated its atrocities, indicates an oppressor, the oppressed, and oppression."[86] For Elaw, abstract definitions of slavery mesh with the concrete identities of its perpetrators and its victims. Blacks "consider it essential for individuals to have personal positions on issues and assume full responsibility for arguing their validity."[87]

---

[85] See ibid., 52–75, for a discussion of inner voice and its role in women's cognitive styles. Regarding empathy, Belenky et al. note: "Connected knowers begin with an interest in the facts of other people's lives, but they gradually shift the focus to other people's ways of thinking. . . . It is the form rather than the content of knowing that is central. . . . Connected learners learn through empathy" (115).

[86] Andrews (n. 48 above), 98.

[87] Kochman (n. 65 above), 20 and 25.

Assessments of an individual's knowledge claims simultaneously evaluate an individual's character, values, and ethics. African-Americans reject Eurocentric masculinist beliefs that probing into an individual's personal viewpoint is outside the boundaries of discussion. Rather, all views expressed and actions taken are thought to derive from a central set of core beliefs that cannot be other than personal.[88] From this perspective, knowledge claims made by individuals respected for their moral and ethical values will carry more weight than those offered by less respected figures.[89]

An example drawn from an undergraduate course composed entirely of Black women, which I taught, might help clarify the uniqueness of this portion of the knowledge-validation process. During one class discussion, I assigned the students the task of critiquing an analysis of Black feminism advanced by a prominent Black male scholar. Instead of dissecting the rationality of the author's thesis, my students demanded facts about the author's personal biography. They were especially interested in concrete details of his life such as his relationships with Black women, his marital status, and his social class background. By requesting data on dimensions of his personal life routinely excluded in positivist approaches to knowledge validation, they were invoking concrete experience as a criterion of meaning. They used this information to assess whether he really cared about his topic and invoked this ethic of caring in advancing their knowledge claims about his work. Furthermore, they refused to evaluate the rationality of his written ideas without some indication of his personal credibility as an ethical human being. The entire exchange could only have occurred as a dialogue among members of a class that had established a solid enough community to invoke an alternative epistemology in assessing knowledge claims.[90]

The ethic of personal accountability is clearly an Afrocentric value, but is it feminist as well? While limited by its attention to middle-class, white women, Carol Gilligan's work suggests that there is a female model for moral development where women are more inclined to link morality to responsibility, relationships, and the ability to maintain social ties.[91] If this is the case, then African-

[88] Ibid, 23.

[89] The sizable proportion of ministers among Black political leaders illustrates the importance of ethics in African-American communities.

[90] Belenky et al. discuss a similar situation. They note, "People could critique each other's work in this class and accept each other's criticisms because members of the group shared a similar experience. . . . Authority in connected knowing rests not on power or status or certification but on commonality of experience" (118).

[91] Carol Gilligan, *In a Different Voice* (Cambridge, Mass.: Harvard University Press, 1982). Carol Stack critiques Gilligan's model by arguing that African-Americans invoke a similar model of moral development to that used by women (see

American women again experience a convergence of values from Afrocentric and female institutions.

The use of an Afrocentric feminist epistemology in traditional Black church services illustrates the interactive nature of all four dimensions and also serves as a metaphor for the distinguishing features of an Afrocentric feminist way of knowing. The services represent more than dialogues between the rationality used in examining biblical texts/stories and the emotion inherent in the use of reason for this purpose. The rationale for such dialogues addresses the task of examining concrete experiences for the presence of an ethic of caring. Neither emotion nor ethics is subordinated to reason. Instead, emotion, ethics, and reason are used as interconnected, essential components in assessing knowledge claims. In an Afrocentric feminist epistemology, values lie at the heart of the knowledge-validation process such that inquiry always has an ethical aim.

Epistemology and Black feminist thought

Living life as an African-American woman is a necessary prerequisite for producing Black feminist thought because within Black women's communities thought is validated and produced with reference to a particular set of historical, material, and epistemological conditions.[92] African-American women who adhere to the idea that claims about Black women must be substantiated by Black women's sense of their own experiences and who anchor their knowledge claims in an Afrocentric feminist epistemology have produced a rich tradition of Black feminist thought.

Traditionally, such women were blues singers, poets, autobiographers, storytellers, and orators validated by the larger community of Black women as experts on a Black women's standpoint. Only a few unusual African-American feminist scholars have been able to defy Eurocentric masculinist epistemologies and explicitly embrace an Afrocentric feminist epistemology. Consider Alice Walker's description of Zora Neale Hurston: "In my mind, Zora Neale Hurston, Billie Holiday, and Bessie Smith form a sort of unholy trinity. Zora *belongs* in the tradition of Black women singers, rather than among 'the literati.' . . . Like Billie and Bessie she followed

---

"The Culture of Gender: Women and Men of Color," *Signs* 11, no. 2 [Winter 1986]: 321–24). Another difficulty with Gilligan's work concerns the homogeneity of the subjects whom she studied.

[92] Black men, white women, and members of other race, class, and gender groups should be encouraged to interpret, teach, and critique the Black feminist thought produced by African-American women.

her own road, believed in her own gods, pursued her own dreams, and refused to separate herself from 'common' people."[93]

Zora Neale Hurston is an exception for, prior to 1950, few Black women earned advanced degrees, and most of those who did complied with Eurocentric masculinist epistemologies. While these women worked on behalf of Black women, they did so within the confines of pervasive race and gender oppression. Black women scholars were in a position to see the exclusion of Black women from scholarly discourse, and the thematic content of their work often reflected their interest in examining a Black women's standpoint. However, their tenuous status in academic institutions led them to adhere to Eurocentric masculinist epistemologies so that their work would be accepted as scholarly. As a result, while they produced Black feminist thought, those Black women most likely to gain academic credentials were often least likely to produce Black feminist thought that used an Afrocentric feminist epistemology.

As more Black women earn advanced degrees, the range of Black feminist scholarship is expanding. Increasing numbers of African-American women scholars are explicitly choosing to ground their work in Black women's experiences, and, by doing so, many implicitly adhere to an Afrocentric feminist epistemology. Rather than being restrained by their "both/and" status of marginality, these women make creative use of their outsider-within status and produce innovative Black feminist thought. The difficulties these women face lie less in demonstrating the technical components of white male epistemologies than in resisting the hegemonic nature of these patterns of thought in order to see, value, and use existing alternative Afrocentric feminist ways of knowing.

In establishing the legitimacy of their knowledge claims, Black women scholars who want to develop Black feminist thought may encounter the often conflicting standards of three key groups. First, Black feminist thought must be validated by ordinary African-American women who grow to womanhood "in a world where the saner you are, the madder you are made to appear."[94] To be credible in the eyes of this group, scholars must be personal advocates for their material, be accountable for the consequences of their work, have lived or experienced their material in some fashion, and be willing to engage in dialogues about their findings with ordinary, everyday people. Second, if it is to establish its legitimacy, Black feminist thought also must be accepted by the community of Black women scholars. These scholars place varying amounts of importance on rearticulating a Black women's standpoint using an Afro-

[93] Walker (n. 72 above), 91.
[94] Gwaltney (n. 11 above), 7.

centric feminist epistemology. Third, Black feminist thought within academia must be prepared to confront Eurocentric masculinist political and epistemological requirements.

The dilemma facing Black women scholars engaged in creating Black feminist thought is that a knowledge claim that meets the criteria of adequacy for one group and thus is judged to be an acceptable knowledge claim may not be translatable into the terms of a different group. Using the example of Black English, June Jordan illustrates the difficulty of moving among epistemologies: "You cannot 'translate' instances of Standard English preoccupied with abstraction or with nothing/nobody evidently alive into Black English. That would warp the language into uses antithetical to the guiding perspective of its community of users. Rather you must first change those Standard English sentences, themselves, into ideas consistent with the person-centered assumptions of Black English."[95] While both worldviews share a common vocabulary, the ideas themselves defy direct translation.

Once Black feminist scholars face the notion that, on certain dimensions of a Black women's standpoint, it may be fruitless to try to translate ideas from an Afrocentric feminist epistemology into a Eurocentric masculinist epistemology, then the choices become clearer. Rather than trying to uncover universal knowledge claims that can withstand the translation from one epistemology to another, time might be better spent rearticulating a Black women's standpoint in order to give African-American women the tools to resist their own subordination. The goal here is not one of integrating Black female "folk culture" into the substantiated body of academic knowledge, for that substantiated knowledge is, in many ways, antithetical to the best interests of Black women. Rather, the process is one of rearticulating a preexisting Black women's standpoint and recentering the language of existing academic discourse to accommodate these knowledge claims. For those Black women scholars engaged in this rearticulation process, the social construction of Black feminist thought requires the skill and sophistication to decide which knowledge claims can be validated using the epistemological assumptions of one but not both frameworks, which claims can be generated in one framework and only partially accommodated by the other, and which claims can be made in both frameworks without violating the basic political and epistemological assumptions of either.

Black feminist scholars offering knowledge claims that cannot be accommodated by both frameworks face the choice between accepting the taken-for-granted assumptions that permeate white-male-controlled academic institutions or leaving academia. Those

---

[95] Jordan (n. 58 above), 130.

Black women who choose to remain in academia must accept the possibility that their knowledge claims will be limited to those claims about Black women that are consistent with a white male worldview. And yet those African-American women who leave academia may find their work is inaccessible to scholarly communities.

Black feminist scholars offering knowledge claims that can be partially accommodated by both epistemologies can create a body of thought that stands outside of either. Rather than trying to synthesize competing worldviews that, at this point in time, may defy reconciliation, their task is to point out common themes and concerns. By making creative use of their status as mediators, their thought becomes an entity unto itself that is rooted in two distinct political and epistemological contexts.[96]

Those Black feminists who develop knowledge claims that both epistemologies can accommodate may have found a route to the elusive goal of generating so-called objective generalizations that can stand as universal truths. Those ideas that are validated as true by African-American women, African-American men, white men, white women, and other groups with distinctive standpoints, with each group using the epistemological approaches growing from its unique standpoint, thus become the most objective truths.[97]

Alternative knowledge claims, in and of themselves, are rarely threatening to conventional knowledge. Such claims are routinely ignored, discredited, or simply absorbed and marginalized in existing paradigms. Much more threatening is the challenge that alternative epistemologies offer to the basic process used by the powerful to legitimate their knowledge claims. If the epistemology used to validate knowledge comes into question, then all prior knowledge claims validated under the dominant model become suspect. An alternative epistemology challenges all certified knowledge and opens up the question of whether what has been taken to be true can stand the test of alternative ways of validating truth. The existence of an independent Black women's standpoint using an Afrocentric feminist epistemology calls into question the content of what currently passes as truth and simultaneously challenges the process of arriving at that truth.

Department of Afro-American Studies
University of Cincinnati

---

[96] Collins (n. 3 above).

[97] This point addresses the question of relativity in the sociology of knowledge and offers a way of regulating competing knowledge claims.

The Postmodernist Turn in Anthropology: Cautions from a Feminist Perspective

Frances E. Mascia-Lees, Patricia Sharpe, and Colleen Ballerino Cohen

At this profoundly self-reflexive moment in anthropology—a moment of questioning traditional modes of representation in the discipline—practitioners seeking to write a genuinely new ethnography would do better to use feminist theory as a model than to draw on postmodern trends in epistemology and literary criticism with which they have thus far claimed allegiance.[1] Unlike postmod-

We wish to thank Mary Margaret Kellogg for her generous support of the Women's Studies Program at Simon's Rock of Bard College and its Faculty Development Fund. Support from that fund and from Vassar College made it possible for us to present an earlier version of this paper at the 86th annual meetings of the American Anthropological Association in Chicago, Illinois. We also wish to thank Francis C. Lees for keeping us warm and well fed while we worked, Nancy Hartsock for her inspiration and helpful suggestions, and Alissa Rupp and William Maurer for their assistance.

[1] The term "new ethnography" is commonly used to refer to cultural accounts that are reflexive in a sense seldom seen in traditional ethnographic writing. This reflexivity can take the form of identification of the fieldworker as an actor in the ethnographic situation, as in Paul Rabinow's *Reflections on Fieldwork in Morocco* (Berkeley and Los Angeles: University of California Press, 1977); Barbara Myerhoff's *Number Our Days* (New York: Simon & Schuster, 1978); Paul Friedrich's *The Princes of Naranja: An Essay in Anthrohistorical Method* (Austin: University of Texas Press, 1986); Marianne Alverson's *Under African Sun* (Chicago and London: University of Chicago Press, 1987); J. Favret-Saada's *Deadly Words: Witchcraft in the Bocage* (Cambridge: Cambridge University Press, 1980); and Manda Cesara's *Reflections of a Woman Anthropologist: No Hiding Places* (New York: Academic

[*Signs: Journal of Women in Culture and Society* 1989, vol. 15, no. 1]

ernism, feminist theory is an intellectual system that knows its politics, a politics directed toward securing recognition that the feminine is as crucial an element of the human as the masculine, and thus a politics skeptical and critical of traditional "universal truths" concerning human behavior. Similarly, anthropology is grounded in a politics: it aims to secure a recognition that the non-Western is as crucial an element of the human as the Western and thus is skeptical and critical of Western claims to knowledge and understanding.

Anthropologists influenced by postmodernism have recognized the need to claim a politics in order to appeal to an anthropological audience. This is evident even in the titles of the two most influential explications of this reflexive moment: *Anthropology as Cultural Critique: An Experimental Moment in the Human Sciences* and *Writing Culture: The Poetics and Politics of Ethnography.*[2] Indeed, the pop-

---

Press, 1982). It can present a commentary on cultural difference through the highlighting of intersubjective interactions, as in Marjorie Shostak's *Nisa: The Life and Words of a !Kung Woman* (Cambridge, Mass.: Harvard University Press, 1981); Kevin Dwyer's *Moroccan Dialogues* (Baltimore: Johns Hopkins University Press, 1982); and Vincent Crapanzano's *Tuhami: Portrait of a Moroccan* (Chicago: University of Chicago Press, 1980). It can experiment with traditional ethnographic rhetorical forms, as in Edward Schieffelin's *The Sorrow of the Lonely and the Burning of the Dancers* (New York: St. Martin's Press, 1976); and Michelle Rosaldo's *Knowledge and Passion: Ilongot Notions of Self and Social Life* (New York: Cambridge University Press, 1980); or it can offer a close scrutiny of global systems of domination through the examination of symbolic manifestations in the lives of individuals, as in Michael Taussig's *The Devil and Commodity Fetishism in South America* (Chapel Hill: University of North Carolina Press, 1980); June Nash's *We Eat the Mines and the Mines Eat Us: Dependency and Exploitation in Bolivian Tin Mines* (New York: Columbia University Press, 1979); and Gananath Obeyesekere's *Medusa's Hair: An Essay on Personal Symbols and Religious Experience* (Berkeley and Los Angeles: University of California Press, 1981). In addition, there is a recent movement to read traditional ethnographic texts, such as Bronislaw Malinowski's *Argonauts of the Western Pacific* (New York: Dutton, 1961); and E. E. Evans-Pritchard's *The Nuer* (Oxford: Oxford University Press, 1940), for their narrative structure or rhetorical style, as well as to claim early texts once presented as "mere fiction," such as Elenore Bowen's (pseudonym for Laura Bohannan) *Return to Laughter: An Anthropological Novel* (New York: Harper & Row, 1954); and Gregory Bateson's *Naven: A Survey of the Problems Suggested by a Composite Picture of a Culture of a New Guinea Tribe Drawn from Three Points of View* (Stanford, Calif.: Stanford University Press, 1936), as precursors to the "new ethnography." This list is not exhaustive or particularly selective; many of these ethnographies employ several reflexive strategies. Among people talking about the new ethnography there is only limited consensus on which works are exemplars of the trend.

[2] George E. Marcus and Michael M. J. Fischer, *Anthropology as Cultural Critique: An Experimental Moment in the Human Sciences* (Chicago and London: University of Chicago Press, 1986); James Clifford and George E. Marcus, eds., *Writing Culture: The Poetics and Politics of Ethnography* (Berkeley and Los Angeles: University of California Press, 1986).

ularity of these books may be due as much to their appeal to anthropologists' traditional moral imperative—that we must question and expand Western definitions of the human—as to the current concern with modes of expression. Postmodern in their attention to texture and form as well as in their emphasis on language, text, and the nature of representation, these two works seek to connect this focus with the politics inherent in the anthropological enterprise. George Marcus and Michael Fischer's *Anthropology as Cultural Critique*, for example, starts off with a restatement of anthropology's traditional goals: to salvage "distinct cultural forms of life from the processes of global Westernization" and to serve "as a form of cultural critique of ourselves."[3] In keeping with postmodernism's emphasis on style, the authors claim that it is through new types of experimental ethnographic writing that anthropology can best expose the global systems of power relations that are embedded in traditional representations of other societies.

Underlying the new ethnography are questions concerning anthropology's role in the maintenance of Western hegemony: how have anthropological writings constructed or perpetuated myths about the non-Western "other"? How have these constructed images served the interest of the West? Even when critiquing colonialism and questioning Western representations of other societies, anthropology cannot avoid proposing alternative constructions. This has led to the recognition that ethnography is "always caught up with the invention, not the representation, of cultures."[4] And, as James Clifford suggests, the resultant undermining of the truth claims of Western representations of the "other" has been reinforced by important theorizing about the limits of representation itself in diverse fields.[5]

Postmodernist anthropologists, with their focus on classic ethnographies as texts, wish to call attention to the constructed nature of cultural accounts. They also wish to explore new forms of writing that will reflect the newly problematized relationships among writer, reader, and subject matter in anthropology in an age when the native informant may read and contest the ethnographer's characterizations—indeed, may well have heard of Jacques Derrida and have a copy of the latest Banana Republic catalog.[6] Postmod-

[3] Marcus and Fischer, esp. 1.

[4] James Clifford, "Introduction," in Clifford and Marcus, eds., 1–26, esp. 2. See Roy Wagner, *The Invention of Culture* (Chicago: University of Chicago Press, 1975) for an elaboration of this idea.

[5] Clifford, "Introduction," 10.

[6] Marilyn Strathern, "Out of Context: The Persuasive Fictions of Anthropology," *Current Anthropology* 28, no. 3 (June 1987): 251–70, esp. 269; James Clifford, "On

ernist anthropologists claim that the aim of experimentation with such forms as intertextuality, dialogue, and self-referentiality is to demystify the anthropologist's unitary authority and thus to include, and structure the relationships among, the "many voices clamoring for expression"[7] in the ethnographic situation. However, these new ways of structuring are more subtle and enigmatic than traditional modes of anthropological writing: they may serve to make the new ethnographies more obscure and, thus, difficult for anyone but highly trained specialists to dispute.

The essays in James Clifford and George Marcus's *Writing Culture: The Poetics and Politics of Ethnography* are concerned with the explication of the relation between the ethnographic field situation and the style of the ethnographic text. In his introduction to the book, for example, Clifford explains the effects of the new ethnographers' use of dialogue: "It locates cultural interpretations in many sorts of reciprocal contexts, and it obliges writers to find diverse ways of rendering negotiated realities as multisubjective, power-laden, and incongruent. In this view, 'culture' is always relational, an inscription of communicative processes that exist, historically, *between* subjects in relation to power."[8]

Thus, Clifford argues that new ethnographers, those anthropologists who do not just theorize about textual production but who write cultural accounts, employ experimental writing techniques in an attempt to expose the power relations embedded in any ethnographic work and to produce a text that is less encumbered with Western assumptions and categories than traditional ethnographies have been. Michelle Rosaldo, for example, has attempted to make the initial cultural unintelligibility of the voice of an Ilongot headhunter persuasive not so much through argumentation or explication as through repetition.[9] In *Nisa: The Life and Words of a !Kung Woman*, Marjorie Shostak juxtaposes the voice of the "other" with the voice of the ethnographer to offer the reader the possibility of confronting the difference between two distinct modes of understanding.[10] In *Moroccan Dialogues*, Kevin Dwyer experiments with a dialogic mode of representation to emphasize that the ethnographic text is a collaborative endeavor between himself and

---

Ethnographic Allegory," in Clifford and Marcus, eds., 98–121, esp. 117; and Paul Stoller, "A Dialogue on Anthropology between a Songhay and an Inquirer" (paper presented at the eighty-seventh annual meeting of the American Anthropological Association, Phoenix, Ariz., November 16–20, 1988).

[7] Clifford, "Introduction," 15.
[8] Ibid. (emphasis Clifford's).
[9] Rosaldo (n. 1 above).
[10] Shostak (n. 1 above).

a Moroccan farmer.[11] Other experimental works have concentrated on exposing how the observation, as well as the interpretation, of another culture are affected by a researcher's cultural identity and mode of expression. In *The Princes of Naranja: An Essay in Anthrohistorical Method*, for example, Paul Friedrich gives an extensive discussion of his own personal history, showing how his childhood farm experiences predisposed him to a study of agrarian life and how an almost unbelievable series of physical mishaps led him to reorganize his entire book. He also shows how this reordering and his choice of stylistic devices such as texturing and "historical holography" help convey a sense of Naranjan life as complex.[12]

However, what appear to be new and exciting insights to these new postmodernist anthropologists—that culture is composed of seriously contested codes of meaning, that language and politics are inseparable, and that constructing the "other" entails relations of domination[13]—are insights that have received repeated and rich exploration in feminist theory for the past forty years. Discussion of the female as "other" was the starting point of contemporary feminist theory. As early as 1949, Simone de Beauvoir's *The Second Sex* argued that it was by constructing the woman as "other" that men in Western culture have constituted themselves as subjects.[14] An early goal of this second wave of feminism was to recover women's experience and thereby to find ways that we as women could constitute ourselves—claim ourselves—as subjects. This early feminist theory does have similarities with traditional anthropology. Both were concerned with the relationship of the dominant and the "other," and with the need to expand and question definitions of the human. However, even in this early stage, a crucial difference existed between anthropological and feminist inquiries. While anthropology questioned the status of the participant-observer, it spoke from the position of the dominant and thus for the "other." Feminists speak from the position of the "other."

This is not to oversimplify. It was not possible for feminists to speak directly *as* "other." Women in consciousness-raising groups were not simply giving voice to already formulated but not yet articulated women's perspectives; they were creatively constructing them. In telling stories about their experiences, they were

---

[11] Dwyer (n. 1 above).

[12] Friedrich (n. 1 above).

[13] Clifford, "Introduction," 2.

[14] Simone de Beauvoir, *The Second Sex* (1949 in French; reprint, New York: Alfred Knopf, 1953).

giving them new meanings, meanings other than those granted by patriarchy, which sees women only as seductresses or wives, as good or bad mothers. Similarly, feminist scholars sought to construct new theoretical interpretations of women. Yet, even when attempting to speak for women, and as women, feminist scholars wrote within a patriarchal discourse that does not accord subject status to the feminine. In this way feminists exposed the contradictions in a supposedly neutral and objective discourse that always proceeds from a gendered being and thereby questioned the adequacy of academic discourse. Thus, feminist theory, even in the 1970s, was concerned not simply with understanding women's experience of otherness but also with the inscription of women as "other" in language and discourse. This was particularly evident in feminist literary criticism, which moved from the cataloging of stereotypes[15] to the study of female authorship as resistance and reinscription.[16] French feminists, notably Hélène Cixous and Luce Irigaray, playfully exploited language's metaphoric and polysemic capacities to give voice to feminist reinterpretations of dominant myths about women.[17]

A fundamental goal of the new ethnography is similar: to apprehend and inscribe "others" in such a way as not to deny or diffuse their claims to subjecthood. As Marcus and Fischer put it, the new ethnography seeks to allow "the adequate representation of other voices or points of view across cultural boundaries."[18] Informed by the notion of culture as a collective and historically contingent construct, the new ethnography claims to be acutely sensitive to cultural differences and, within cultures, to the multiplicity of individual experience.

However, despite these similarities, when anthropologists look for a theory on which to ground the new ethnography, they turn to postmodernism, dismissing feminist theory as having little to teach

---

[15] See esp. Mary Ellmann, *Thinking about Women* (New York: Harcourt, Brace, Jovanovich, 1968); and Annis Pratt, *Archetypal Patterns in Women's Fiction* (Bloomington: Indiana University Press, 1982).

[16] See esp. Sandra Gilbert and Susan Gubar, *The Madwoman in the Attic: The Woman Writer and the Nineteenth-Century Literary Imagination* (New Haven, Conn.: Yale University Press, 1980); Elaine Showalter, *A Literature of Their Own: British Women Novelists from Brontë to Lessing* (Princeton, N.J.: Princeton University Press, 1977); and Ellen Moers, *Literary Women* (New York: Doubleday, 1976).

[17] Hélène Cixous, "The Laugh of the Medusa," trans. Keith Cohen and Paula Cohen, in *The Signs Reader: Women, Gender and Scholarship*, ed. Elizabeth Abel and Emily K. Abel (Chicago and London: University of Chicago Press, 1983), 279–97; and Luce Irigaray, "This Sex Which Is Not One," in *New French Feminisms*, ed. Elaine Marks and Isabelle de Courtivron (New York: Schocken, 1981), 99–106.

[18] Marcus and Fischer (n. 2 above), 2.

that anthropology does not already know. For example, Marcus and Fischer claim, "The debate over gender differences stimulated by feminism . . . often [falls] into the same rhetorical strategies that once were used for playing off the dissatisfactions of civilized society against the virtues of the primitive."[19] By focusing exclusively on those feminists who valorize "essential" female characteristics like motherhood and peaceableness, Marcus and Fischer construe feminism as little more than the expression of women's dissatisfactions with a sinister patriarchy. Thus, their ignorance of the full spectrum of feminist theory may partly explain their dismissal of it.

Similarly, Clifford justifies the exclusion of feminist anthropologists from *Writing Culture: The Poetics and Politics of Ethnography* with a questionable characterization of the feminist enterprise in anthropology: "Feminist ethnography has focused either on setting the record straight about women or revising anthropological categories. . . . It has not produced either unconventional forms of writing or a developed reflection on ethnographic textuality as such."[20] Clifford nonetheless uses Margorie Shostak's *Nisa: The Life and Words of a !Kung Woman* as a primary example in his essay "On Ethnographic Allegory" in the same volume. In this essay, he calls Shostak's work at once "feminist" and "original in its polyvocality, . . . manifestly the product of a collaboration with the other," reflexive of "a troubled, inventive moment in the history of cross-cultural representation."[21] He therefore reveals not only that he clearly knows of at least one feminist ethnography that has employed "unconventional forms of writing," but also that he prefers to write about feminists rather than inviting them to write for themselves.

This contradiction makes sense in the context of Clifford's essay on ethnographic allegory. In it he seeks to demonstrate that the new ethnography is like traditional anthropological writings about the "other" in that both use allegory. He argues that all ethnography is inevitably allegorical since it at once presents us with a representation of a different reality and continuously refers to another pattern of ideas to make that difference comprehensible. It is odd that Clifford uses a feminist ethnography as his only example of how new ethnography is allegorical since, in view of his statement about feminist ethnography's lack of experimentation in his introduction, he himself should suspect that Shostak's work is not representative of the new ethnography. Such a contradiction seems

---

[19] Ibid., 135.
[20] Clifford, "Introduction," 20–21.
[21] Clifford, "On Ethnographic Allegory" (n. 6 above), 104–9.

to betray Clifford's tendency to equate women with forces of cultural conservatism. In dismissing the novelty of feminist work in anthropology, Clifford seeks to validate *Writing Culture* as truly innovative: "The essays in this volume occupy a new space opened up by the disintegration of 'Man' as *telos* for a whole discipline."[22] Like European explorers discovering the New World, Clifford and his colleagues perceive a new and uninhabited space where, in fact, feminists have long been at work.

How can we understand this dismissal of feminism in favor of postmodernism, the dismissal of political engagement in favor of a view that "beholds the world blankly, with a knowingness that dissolves feeling and commitment into irony"?[23] Anthropologists should be uncomfortable with an aesthetic view of the world as a global shopping center and suspicious of an ideology that sustains the global economic system.[24] Of course, there are many postmodernisms, just as there are many feminisms, and within both movements definitions are contested.[25] While there is also considerable overlap, postmodernism is unlike feminism in its relationship to the ferment of the 1960s.[26] While contemporary feminism is an ongoing political movement with roots in the 1960s, "post-modernism is above all post-1960s; its keynote is cultural helplessness. It is post-Viet Nam, post-New Left, post-hippie, post-Watergate. History was ruptured, passions have been expended, belief has become difficult. . . . The 1960s exploded our belief in progress. . . . Old verities crumbled, but new ones have not settled in. Self-regarding irony and blankness are a way of staving off anxieties, rages, terrors, and hungers that have been kicked up but cannot find resolution."[27] The sense of helplessness that postmodernism expresses is broader, however, than the disillusionment of the 1960s' leftists; it is an experience of tremendous loss of mastery in traditionally dominant groups. In the postmodern period, theorists "stave off" their anxi-

---

[22] Clifford, "Introduction," 4.

[23] Todd Gitlin, "Hip-Deep in Post-Modernism," *New York Times Book Review* (November 6, 1988), 1, 35–36, esp. 35.

[24] See Fredric Jameson, "Postmodernism and Consumer Society," in *The Anti-Aesthetic: Essays on Postmodern Culture*, ed. H. Foster (Port Townsend, Wash.: Bay Press, 1983), 111–25.

[25] This point recently has been made by Daryl McGowan Tress, "Comment on Flax's 'Postmodernism and Gender Relations in Feminist Theory,' " *Signs: Journal of Women in Culture and Society* 14, no. 1 (Autumn 1988): 196–200.

[26] See Jane Flax, "Postmodernism and Gender Relations in Feminist Theory," *Signs* 12, no. 4 (Summer 1987): 621–43; Craig Owens, "The Discourse of Others: Feminists and Postmodernism," in Foster, ed., 57–82. Nancy Fraser and Linda Nicholson, "Social Criticism without Philosophy: An Encounter between Feminism and Postmodernism," *Theory, Culture, and Society* 5 (June 1988): 373–94, was very helpful to us on this point.

[27] Gitlin, 36.

ety by questioning the basis of the truths that they are losing the privilege to define.

Political scientist Nancy Hartsock has made a similar observation; she finds it curious that the postmodern claim that verbal constructs do not correspond in a direct way to reality has arisen precisely when women and non-Western peoples have begun to speak for themselves and, indeed, to speak about global systems of power differentials.[28] In fact, Hartsock suggests that the postmodern view that truth and knowledge are contingent and multiple may be seen to act as a truth claim itself, a claim that undermines the ontological status of the subject at the very time when women and non-Western peoples have begun to claim themselves as subject. In a similar vein, Sarah Lennox has asserted that the postmodern despair associated with the recognition that truth is never entirely knowable is merely an inversion of Western arrogance.[29] When Western white males—who traditionally have controlled the production of knowledge—can no longer define the truth, she argues, their response is to conclude that there is not a truth to be discovered. Similarly, Sandra Harding claims that "historically, relativism appears as an intellectual possibility, and as a 'problem,' only for dominating groups at the point where the hegemony (the universality) of their views is being challenged. [Relativism] is fundamentally a sexist response that attempts to preserve the legitimacy of androcentric claims in the face of contrary evidence."[30] Perhaps most compelling for the new ethnography is the question Andreas Huyssen asks in "Mapping the Postmodern": "Isn't the death of the subject/author position tied by mere reversal to the very ideology that invariably glorifies the artist as genius? . . . Doesn't post-structuralism where it simply denies the subject altogether jettison the chance of challenging the ideology of the subject (as male, white, and middle-class) by developing alternative notions of subjectivity?"[31]

These analyses clearly raise questions about the experience of Western white males and how that experience is reflected in postmodern thought. To the extent that this dominant group has in

[28] Nancy Hartsock, "Rethinking Modernism," *Cultural Critique* 7 (Fall 1987): 187–206.

[29] Sarah Lennox, "Anthropology and the Politics of Deconstruction" (paper presented at the ninth annual conference of the National Women's Studies Association, Atlanta, Ga., June 1987).

[30] Sandra Harding, "Introduction: Is There a Feminist Method?" in *Feminism and Methodology*, ed. Sandra Harding (Bloomington and Indianapolis: Indiana University Press, 1987), 1–14, esp. 10.

[31] Andreas Huyssen's "Mapping the Postmodern," quoted in Nancy K. Miller, "Changing the Subject: Authorship, Writing, and the Reader," in *Feminist Studies: Critical Studies*, ed. Teresa de Lauretis (Bloomington: Indiana University Press, 1986), 102–20, esp. 106–7.

recent years experienced a decentering as world politics and economic realities shift global power relations, postmodern theorizing can be understood as socially constructed itself, as a metaphor for the sense of the dominant that the ground has begun to shift under their feet. And this social construction, according to Hartsock, Lennox, Harding, and Huyssen, is one that potentially may work to preserve the privileged position of Western white males. If so, then the new ethnography, in its reliance on postmodernism, may run the risk of participating in an ideology blind to its own politics. More than that, it may help to preserve the dominant colonial and neocolonial relations from which anthropology, and especially the new ethnography, has been trying to extricate itself.

But to phrase this argument exclusively in these terms is to obscure the fact that the significant power relations for many of these new postmodernist anthropologists are not global but parochial, those that are played out in the halls of anthropology departments, those that are embedded in the patriarchal social order of the academy in which male and female scholars maneuver for status, tenure, and power. In a recent article in *Current Anthropology*, P. Steven Sangren argues that although postmodernist anthropologists call for a questioning of *textually* constituted authority, their efforts are actually a play for *socially* constituted authority and power.[32] He thus suggests that it is first and foremost academic politics that condition the production and reproduction of ethnographic texts. Moreover, according to him, "whatever 'authority' is created in a text has its most direct social effect not in the world of political and economic domination of the Third World by colonial and neocolonial powers, but rather in the academic institutions in which such authors participate."[33] While postmodernist anthropologists such as Clifford, Marcus, and Fischer may choose to think that they are transforming global power relations as well as the discipline of anthropology itself, they may also be establishing first claim in the new academic territory on which this decade's battles for intellectual supremacy and jobs will be waged.[34] The exclusion of feminist voices in Clifford and Marcus's influential volume and Clifford's defensive, convoluted, and contradictory

[32] P. Steven Sangren, "Rhetoric and the Authority of Ethnography," *Current Anthropology* 29, no. 3 (June 1988): 405–24, esp. 411.

[33] Ibid., 412.

[34] In their reply to Sangren, Michael Fischer and George Marcus (written with Stephen Tyler) call Sangren's concern an "*obsession* with academic power and status" (emphasis ours). See Michael M. J. Fischer, George E. Marcus, and Stephen A. Tyler, "Comments," *Current Anthropology* 29, no. 3 (1988): 426–27, esp. 426.

explanation for it are strategies that preserve male supremacy in the academy. Clifford seems well aware of this when we read in the same introductory pages in which he presents his defense of excluding feminist writers his statement that "all constructed truths are made possible by powerful 'lies' of exclusion and rhetoric."[35]

The lie of excluding feminism has characterized most postmodernist writing by males, not simply that in anthropology. One notable exception, Craig Owens's "The Discourse of Others: Feminists and Postmodernism," demonstrates the richness of insight into cultural phenomena that the conjunction of feminist and postmodern perspectives offers. For anthropologists, his analysis of the message we humans transmit to possible extraterrestrials, the space-age "other," is particularly telling. Of the schematic image of a nude man and woman, the former's right arm raised in greeting, which was emblazoned on the Pioneer spacecraft, Owens observes, "Like all representations of sexual difference that our culture produces, this is an image not simply of anatomical difference but of the values assigned to it."[36] A small difference in morphology is marked or underscored by the erect right arm, a signal that speech is the privilege of the male. Owens notes that deconstructions of this privilege by male postmodernists is rare: "If one of the most salient aspects of our postmodern culture is the presence of an insistent feminist voice . . . theories of postmodernism have tended either to neglect or to repress that voice. The absence of discussions of sexual difference in writings about postmodernism, as well as the fact that few women have engaged in the modernism/postmodernism debate, suggest that postmodernism may be another masculine invention engineered to exclude women."[37]

While "engineered," with its suggestions of conscious agency, may grant academic males too much sinister awareness, Owens's observation of the evidence is accurate: "Men appear unwilling to address the issues placed on the critical agenda by women unless those issues have been first neut(e)ralized."[38] This suggests their fear of entering into a discourse where the "other" has privilege. Intellectual cross-dressing, like its physical counterpart, is less disruptive of traditional orders of privilege when performed by women than by men.[39] Fearing loss of authority and masculinity,

[35] Clifford, "Introduction" (n. 4 above), 7.
[36] Owens (n. 26 above), 61.
[37] Ibid.
[38] Ibid., 62.
[39] Owens notes that writing for women requires intellectual cross-dressing: "In order to speak, to represent herself, a woman assumes a masculine position; perhaps that is why femininity is frequently associated with masquerade, with false repre-

male critics have preferred to look on feminism as a limited and peripheral enterprise, not as one that challenges them to rethink their own positions in terms of gender.[40] "Although sympathetic male critics respect feminism (an old theme: respect for women)," Owens acknowledges that "they have in general declined to enter into the dialogue in which their female colleagues have been trying to engage them."[41]

The case of Paul Rabinow is illustrative. His is the one article in *Writing Culture* that appears to deal seriously with feminism. However, he concludes that feminism is not an intellectual position he personally can hold. Seeing himself as "excluded from direct participation in the feminist dialogue," he constructs an alternative "ethical" position for anthropologists: critical cosmopolitanism. "This is an oppositional position," he argues, "one suspicious of sovereign powers, universal truths . . . but also wary of the tendency to essentialize difference." Ironically, however, Rabinow not only universalizes, stating "we are all cosmopolitans," but also essentializes difference when he excludes himself from the feminist dialogue solely because he is male. Seeing himself as unable to participate in feminist and Third World discourses, he identifies with the Greek Sophists, "cosmopolitan insider's outsiders of a

---

sentation, with simulation and seduction" (ibid., esp. 59). See also Mary Russo's "Female Grotesques: Carnival and Theory," in de Lauretis, ed. (n. 31 above), esp. 213–29. For a broad discussion of the advantages of cross-dressing for women, see Susan Gubar's "Blessings in Disguise: Cross-Dressing as Re-Dressing for Female Modernists," *Massachusetts Review* 22, no. 3 (Autumn 1981): 477–508. A suspicious look at some male responses to feminist literary criticism in terms of current interest in male cross-dressing, as evidenced by the film *Tootsie*, is Elaine Showalter's "Critical Cross-Dressing: Male Feminists and the Woman of the Year," *Raritan* 3, no. 2 (Fall 1983): 130–49. Male anxiety about the implications of doing feminist criticism was voiced by Dominick LaCapra in a discussion of his "Death in Venice: An Allegory of Reading" (paper delivered at the Woodrow Wilson Institute's "Interpreting the Humanities," June 1986). When asked about gender issues in Mann's story, he replied: "I can't do transvestite criticism like Jonathan Culler," a reference to the chapter "Reading as a Woman" in Jonathan Culler, *On Deconstruction: Theory and Criticism After Structuralism* (Ithaca, N.Y.: Cornell University Press, 1982), esp. 43–64. Freud's similar fear of identification with the feminine is discussed in C. Bernheimer and Claire Kahane, eds., *Dora's Case: Freud-Hysteria-Feminism* (New York: Columbia University Press, 1985).

[40] Evelyn Fox Keller has described the recurrent mistranslation of gender and science as women and science, showing how gender questions are considered to be of concern only to women in "Feminist Perspectives on Science Studies," *Barnard Occasional Papers on Women's Issues* 3 (Spring 1988): 10–36.

[41] Owens, esp. 62. This observation, of course, is well known to feminists who have been consistently frustrated by the marginalization of feminist insights. See, e.g., Miller (n. 31 above).

particular historical and cultural world."[42] In thus constructing himself as just one more "other" among the rest, Rabinow risks the danger he ascribes to critics like James Clifford: "obliterating meaningful difference," obliterating and obscuring some of the privileges and power granted to him by race, nationality, and gender.[43] He describes his decision to study elite French male colonial officials as proceeding from this oppositional ethical stance: "By 'studying up' I find myself in a more comfortable position than I would be were I 'giving voice' on behalf of dominated or marginal groups." An exclusive focus on the elite, eschewing the dominated or marginal, is a dangerous, if comfortable, correction. Feminists have taught us the danger of analyses that focus exclusively on men: they have traditionally rendered gender differences irrelevant and reinforced the Western male as the norm. Rabinow's earlier *Reflections on Fieldwork in Morocco* relied exclusively on male informants, presenting women only marginally and as objects of his sexual desire, communicating through "the unambiguity of gesture."[44] Ironically, he claims his new work will broaden "considerations of power and representation" which were "too localized in my earlier work on Morocco," yet he focuses even more explicitly on men. This can be defended only if Rabinow struggles with his earlier insensitivity to gender issues and, in this study of elite powerful males, undertakes that part of the feminist project particularly suited to male practitioners: deconstructing the patriarchy.[45]

Feminists' call for self-reflexivity in men is related to postmodernist anthropology's goal of self-critique; when anthropologists include themselves as characters in ethnographic texts instead of posing as objective controlling narrators, they expose their biases. This coincides with the goals of postmodernism as characterized by Jane Flax: "Postmodern discourses are all 'deconstructive' in that they seek to distance us from and make us skeptical about beliefs

[42] Paul Rabinow, "Representations Are Social Facts: Modernity and Post-Modernity in Anthropology," in Clifford and Marcus, eds. (n. 2 above), 234–61, esp. 257–59.

[43] Deborah Gordon has noted recently that not only is the critical cosmopolitan "not clearly marked by any 'local' concerns such as gender, race, nationality, etc.," but also "the Greek sophists who are Rabinow's fictive figure for this position were European men," in "Writing Culture, Writing Feminism: The Poetics and Politics of Experimental Ethnography," *Inscriptions*, nos. 3/4 (1988), 7–24.

[44] Rabinow (n. 1 above), esp. 67.

[45] Lois Banner argued that this is the appropriate task for males who are sympathetic to feminism in her response to Peter Gabriel Filene's plenary address, "History and Men's History and What's the Difference," at the Conference on the New Gender Scholarship: Women's and Men's Studies, University of Southern California, Los Angeles, February 1987.

concerning truth, knowledge, power, the self, and language that are often taken for granted within and serve as legitimation for contemporary Western culture."[46] Yet interest in these questions in postmodernism is abstract and philosophical, paradoxically grounded in a search for a more accurate vision of truth. Feminist theory shares similar concerns to these postmodern ideas, as Flax notes, but feminist theory differs from postmodernism in that it acknowledges its grounding in politics.

The one theorist who has grappled with the problems that arise when feminism and anthropology are merged is Marilyn Strathern, who notes that "anthropology has interests parallel to those of feminist scholarship," which would lead us to "expect 'radical' anthropology to draw on its feminist counterpart."[47] She notes, however, that feminism has affected only the choice of subjects of study in social anthropology, not its scholarly practices: where social anthropological categories of analysis have changed, "it has been in response to internal criticism that has little to do with feminist theory." Strathern seeks to explain why anthropology has failed to respond to feminism as a profound challenge by showing how the two endeavors are parallel, yet mock each other. Feminism mocks experimental anthropology's search for an ethnography that is a "collaborative production . . . a metaphor for an ideal ethical situation in which neither voice is submerged by the Other," while anthropology mocks feminists' pretensions to separate themselves from Western "cultural suppositions about the nature of personhood and of relationships . . . shared equally by the [male] Other."[48]

Strathern thus suggests that there can be no true merging of feminism and the new ethnography, but this contention is based on a problematic formulation. Even the brief quotations above indicate Strathern's disturbing use of the term "other" to refer to " 'patriarchy,' the institutions and persons who represent male domination, often simply concretized as 'men.' " This, she believes, is the "other" of feminism, the "other" that feminists must remain in opposition to for "the construction of the feminist self."[49] This feminist need to remain distinct from a wrongheaded male "other" is at odds, she argues, with the new ethnography's desire to get close to and know the "other." But in this latter usage of the word "other," she refers to the traditional anthropological subject of study, non-Western peoples. In her awkward parallel usage, Strath-

---

[46] Flax (n. 26 above), 624.

[47] Marilyn Strathern, "An Awkward Relationship: The Case of Feminism and Anthropology," *Signs* 12, no. 2 (Winter 1987): 276–92, esp. 277–80.

[48] Ibid., 281, 290–91.

[49] Ibid., 288.

ern seems to ignore differential power relations, failing to acknowledge that one term in each pair is historically marked by privilege.
She does not see that women are to men as natives are to
anthropologists. And, thus, even if as feminists we remain in
opposition to men to construct ourselves, it does not mean that we
must fear getting to know the non-Western "other." We may,
however, be cautious in our desire to do so. Feminists can teach
new ethnographers that their ideal of collaboration "is a delusion,
overlooking the crucial dimension of different social interests,"
Strathern suggests, wrongly attributing this insight to the oppositional position feminists strike in relation to the patriarchal
"other."[50] Our suspicion of the new ethnographers' desire for
collaboration with the "other" stems not from any such refusal to
enter into dialogue with that "other," but from our history and
understanding of being appropriated and literally spoken for by the
dominant, and from our consequent sympathetic identification with
the subjects of anthropological study in this regard.

This leads to the questioning, voiced recently by Judith Stacey,
of whether any ethnography of the "other" can be compatible with
feminist politics. Stacey argues that despite the appearance of
compatibility between feminist researchers seeking an "egalitarian
research process characterized by authenticity, reciprocity, and
intersubjectivity between the researcher and her 'subjects,' " and
the face-to-face and personalized encounter of the ethnographic
field experience, major contradictions exist. First, the highly personalized relationship between ethnographer and research subject,
which masks actual differences in power, knowledge, and structural
mobility, "places research subjects at grave risk of manipulation
and betrayal by the ethnographer." Additionally, Stacey points to
the contradiction between the desire for collaboration on the final
research product and the fact that "the research product is ultimately that of the researcher, however modified or influenced by
informants."[51] Stacey's response to these contradictions is to despair
of a fully feminist ethnography. "There can be ethnographies that
are partially feminist, accounts of culture enhanced by the application of feminist perspectives," she argues, and there can be "feminist research that is rigorously self-aware and therefore humble
about the partiality of its ethnographic vision and its capacity to
represent self and other."[52] But how are these goals to be realized?
Has feminism nothing more to teach the new ethnography?

    [50] Ibid., 290.
    [51] Judith Stacey, "Can There Be a Feminist Ethnography?" *Women's Studies
International Forum* 11, no. 1 (1988): 21–27, esp. 22–23.
    [52] Ibid., 26.

We have suggested that an important aspect of feminist scholarship is its relationship to a politics. Strathern notes that within feminist writing, "play with context [similar to that used by the new ethnographers] is creative because of the expressed continuity of purpose between feminists as scholars and feminists as activists."[53] Feminism teaches us to take up a particularly moral and sensitive attitude toward relationships by emphasizing the importance of community building to the feminist project, and it also demands scrutiny of our motivations for research. In their current experimentation, anthropologists need a renewed sensitivity to "the question of relationships involved in communication."[54] They need to learn the lessons of feminism and consider for whom they write.

Throughout her discussion of postmodernist anthropology, Strathern displays suspicions, like those that feminists have, of its claims to use free play and jumble, to present many voices in flattened, nonhierarchical, plural texts, to employ "heteroglossia (a utopia of plural endeavour that gives all collaborators the status of authors)." Irony, she argues, rather than jumble is the postmodern mode, and "irony involves not a scrambling but a deliberate juxtaposition of contexts, pastiche perhaps but not jumble."[55]

Strathern contrasts this illusion of free play in postmodernist anthropology with feminist writing: "Much feminist discourse is constructed in a plural way. Arguments are juxtaposed, many voices solicited. . . . There are no central texts, no definitive techniques." Unlike postmodern writing, however, which masks its structuring oppositions under a myth of jumble, feminist scholarship has "a special set of social interests. Feminists argue with one another in their many voices because they also know themselves as an interest group."[56] Thus, although feminism originally may have discovered itself by becoming conscious of oppression, more recently feminists have focused on relations among women and the project of conceiving difference without binary opposition. Feminist politics provide an explicit structure that frames our research questions and moderates the interactions in which we engage with other women. Where there is no such explicit political structure, the danger of veiled agendas is great.

Anthropologists could benefit from an understanding of this feminist dialogue. Just as early feminist theory of the "other" is grounded in women's actual subordination to men, so more recent

[53] Strathern, "Out of Context: The Persuasive Fictions of Anthropology" (n. 6 above), 268.

[54] Ibid., 269.

[55] Ibid., 266–67.

[56] Ibid., 268.

trends in feminist theorizing about difference are grounded in actual differences among women. For example, the recent focus in mainstream feminist theory upon the diversity of women's experiences bears relation to the postmodern deconstruction of the subject, but it stems from a very different source: the political confrontation between white feminists and women of color.[57] In response to accusations by women of color that the women's movement has been in actuality a white middle-class women's movement, Western white feminists, together with women of color, have had to reconsider theories of *the* woman and replace them with theories of multiplicity. In a similar vein, the need for building self-criticism into feminist theory has been expressed with the recognition that what once appeared to be theoretically appropriate mandates for change may have very different results for different populations of women. For example, some scholars claim that antirape activism has served to reinforce racial stereotypes (the rapist as black male), that pro-choice legislation has provided a rationale for forced sterilization and abortions among the poor and women of color, and that feminist-backed no-fault-divorce legislation has contributed to the feminization of poverty. The new ethnography draws on postmodernist epistemology to accomplish its political ends, but much feminism derives its theory from a practice based in the material conditions of women's lives.

Both postmodernist anthropology and feminism assume a self-consciously reflexive stance toward their subjects, but there are significant differences between them. For, as Sandra Harding has suggested, at the moment that feminist scholars begin to address themselves to women's experiences, their inquiry necessarily becomes concerned with questions of power and political struggle, and their research goals become defined by that struggle. This is because "the questions an oppressed group wants answered are rarely requests for so-called pure truth. Instead, they are questions about how to change its conditions; how its world is shaped by forces beyond it; how to win over, defeat or neutralize those forces arrayed against its emancipation, growth or development; and so forth."[58] The feminist researcher is led to design projects that, according to Harding, women want and need.

Indeed, in this sense, feminist research is more closely aligned with applied anthropology, whose practitioners also often derive

---

[57] See Maria C. Lugones and Elizabeth Spelman, "Have We Got a Theory for You! Feminist Theory, Cultural Imperialism and the Demand for 'The Woman's Voice,' " *Women's Studies International Forum* 6, no. 6 (1983): 573–81, for a compelling representation of this dialogue.

[58] Harding, "Introduction: Is There a Feminist Method?" (n. 30 above), 8.

their questions from and apply their methods to the solution of problems defined by the people being studied, than with new ethnographers.[59] Applied anthropologists frequently function as "power brokers," translating between the subordinate, disenfranchised group and the dominant class or power. To understand the difference in approach between the new ethnographer and the applied anthropologist, it is useful to look at Clifford's recent article on "Identity in Mashpee."[60]

The Mashpee are a group of Native Americans who in 1976 sued in federal court for possession of a large tract of land in Mashpee, Massachusetts. The case revolved around claims of cultural identity: if the individuals bringing suit could prove an uninterrupted historical identity as a tribe, then their claim for compensation would be upheld. In his article, Clifford makes use of trial transcripts, transcripts of interviews with witnesses for the defense, and snippets of information from the documents used in the case to reconstruct Mashpee history. As a new ethnographer, Clifford analyzes these as commentaries on "the ways in which historical stories are told" and on "the alternative cultural models that have been applied to human groups."[61] Such readings as this can and do elucidate who speaks for cultural authenticity and how collective identity and difference are represented. Indeed, for the new ethnographer, the Mashpee trial emerges as a sort of natural laboratory in which multiple voices contributing to a collectively constituted cultural reality can be heard. It illustrates how the postmodernist emphasis on dialogue helps anthropologists to study native populations as they change and interact in response to the dominant culture rather than simply as representatives of a pure and dying past. However, Mascia-Lees, as someone who has worked with and for the Mashpee in their federal recognition appeal, would argue that it is highly doubtful whether Clifford's

---

[59] Applied anthropologists, like feminist scholars, also frequently participate in collaborative research projects, helping to undermine the traditional, and largely unjustified and false, notion of research and scholarship as the heroic quest by the lone scholar for "truth." Sandra Harding recently has made the point that this notion often obscures the contributions made by women to the scientific enterprise, since what they do, especially in the laboratory, can be dismissed as domestic work in the service of the male scientist. Sandra Harding, *The Science Question in Feminism* (Ithaca, N.Y.: Cornell University Press, 1986).

[60] James Clifford, "Identity in Mashpee," in his *The Predicament of Culture: Twentieth-Century Ethnography, Literature, and Art* (Cambridge, Mass.: Harvard University Press, 1988), 277–346.

[61] Ibid., 289.

insights provide the Mashpee with explanations of social phenomena that they either want or need.

We must question whether the appearance of multiple voices in Clifford's text can act to counter the hegemonic forces that continue to deny the Mashpee access to their tribal lands. Who is the intended audience for this analysis: the Mashpee or other scholars in institutions under Western control? And whose interests does it serve? Following Harding's claim that feminist research seeks to use women's experiences "as the test of adequacy of the problems, concepts, hypotheses, research design, collection, and interpretation of data,"[62] we might even go so far as to ask whether Clifford's representation uses the Mashpee's experience as a test of the adequacy of his research. Clifford sees himself as rejecting the Western privileging of visualism in favor of a paradigm of the interplay of voices. Yet, perhaps dialogue, even the proliferating Bakhtinian dialogic processes Clifford favors, is saturated with Western assumptions. We need to ask whose experience of the world this focus on dialogue reflects: that of the ethnographer who yearns to speak with and know the "other," or that of Native Americans, many of whom have frequently refused dialogue with the anthropologist whom they see as yet one more representative of the oppressive culture and for some of whom dialogue may be an alien mode?

This yearning to know the "other" can be traced to the romanticism so frequently associated with anthropologists' scholarly pursuits. Traditionally, this romantic component has been linked to the heroic quests, by the single anthropologist, for "his soul"[63] through confrontation with the exotic "other."[64] This particular avenue for self-exploration has been closed recently by the resistance of Third World peoples to serving in therapeutic roles for Westerners as well as by the sense on the part of anthropologists

[62] Harding, "Introduction: Is There a Feminist Method?" 11.

[63] We have chosen to retain the masculine pronoun here and in subsequent parts of the text when referring to individuals steeped in traditional anthropological ideas and practices. As feminist anthropologists have shown, even though anthropology has traditionally included women as researchers, the field has been plagued with androcentric assumptions. See Sally Slocum's "Woman the Gatherer: Male Bias in Anthropology," in *Toward an Anthropology of Women*, ed. R. Rapp (New York and London: Monthly Review Press, 1975), esp. 36–50, for one of the earliest works to expose this bias.

[64] Susan Sontag, "The Anthropologist as Hero," in her *Against Interpretation* (New York: Farrar, Straus, Giroux, 1966), esp. 69–81; Clifford Geertz, *Works and Lives: The Anthropologist as Author* (Stanford, Calif.: Stanford University Press, 1988), esp. 73–101.

that twentieth-century "natives" may themselves be in need of therapy, "neutered, like the rest of us, by the dark forces of the world system."[65]

Yet the romantic tradition in anthropology is being sustained by the postmodernist mandate for self-reflection. For in turning inward, making himself, his motives, and his experience the thing to be confronted, the postmodernist anthropologist locates the "other" in himself. It is as if, finding the "exotic" closed off to him, the anthropologist constructs himself as the exotic.[66] This is clearly the case, for example, in *The Princes of Naranja*.[67] Here, Paul Friedrich's characterization of the salient features of his own life history connects in the reader's mind with images of the Tarascan princes who have appeared on earlier pages: home-bred fatalism, peer rivalry, and personal experiences with death and danger. Since Friedrich's self-reflection was written some thirty years after his initial fieldwork experience in Naranja, it seems likely, although Friedrich does not suggest it, that this inscription of his own childhood history may have been as much affected by his Naranja experience as vice versa. Ironically, Friedrich's book, which opens up the possibility of demystifying the "other," reveals that this process may lead to a mystification of the self. In this light, it is hardly surprising that Clifford's work is so popular. Clifford the historian has turned ethnographers into the natives to be understood and ethnography into virgin territory to be explored.

This current focus on self-reflexivity in postmodernist anthropology is expressed not only in works that make the ethnographer into a character in the ethnographic text but also in analyses of earlier ethnographic writing.[68] Of this process Marilyn Strathern comments, "Retrospectively to ask about the persuasive fictions of earlier epochs is to ask about how others (Frazer, Malinowski, and the rest) handled our moral problems of literary construction. In answering the question, we create historic shifts between past writers in terms persuasive to our own ears, thereby participating in a postmodern history, reading back into books the strategies of

[65] Stephen A. Tyler, "Post-Modern Ethnography: From Document of the Occult to Occult Document," in Clifford and Marcus, eds. (n. 2 above), 122–140, esp. 128.

[66] On the use of the generic he, see n. 63 above. Here we wish to highlight that postmodern ethnographers, like their traditional forebears, speak from the male/ dominant position and have seen self-reflection, collaboration, and textual experimentation as "new" only when it has been practiced by men.

[67] Friedrich (n. 1 above), 246–61.

[68] Geertz; Clifford, *The Predicament of Culture* (n. 60 above), esp. 92–113, 117–151; and Strathern, "Out of Context: The Persuasive Fictions of Anthropology" (n. 6 above).

fictionalisation. To construct past works as quasi-intentional literary games is the new ethnocentrism. There is no evidence, after all, that 'we' have stopped attributing our problems to 'others.' "[69]

Furthermore, much of this historical analysis deals with colonialism, affording the contemporary anthropologist a field of study in which it is possible to hold a critical and ethical view. Paradoxically, however, it simultaneously replays a time in which Western white males were of supreme importance in the lives of the "other" just at this moment when the anthropologist fears his irrelevance.

Such paradoxes, which emerge from the wedding of postmodernism with anthropology, pose the most difficult questions for practitioners of the new ethnography at present: once one articulates an epistemology of free play in which there is no inevitable relationship between signifier and signified, how is it possible to write an ethnography that has descriptive force? Once one has no metanarratives into which the experience of difference can be translated, how is it possible to write any ethnography? Here, too, lessons from feminism may be helpful; since current feminist theory lives constantly with the paradoxical nature of its own endeavor, it offers postmodernism models for dealing with contradiction. As Nancy Cott suggests, feminism is paradoxical in that it "aims for individual freedoms by mobilizing sex solidarity. It acknowledges diversity among women while positing that women recognize their unity. It requires gender consciousness for its basis, yet calls for the elimination of prescribed gender roles." Postmodern thought has helped feminists to argue that women's inferior status is a product of cultural and historical constructions and to resist essentialist truth claims, but the danger for feminists is that "in deconstructing categories of meaning, we deconstruct not only patriarchal definitions of 'womanhood' and 'truth' but also the very categories of our own analysis—'women' and 'feminism' and 'oppression.' "[70]

That feminist theory, with its recent emphasis on the diversity of women's experience, has not succumbed entirely to the seduction of postmodernism and the dangers inherent in a complete decentering of the historical and material is due in part to feminist theory's concern with women as the central category of analysis and with feminism's political goal of changing the power relationships that underlie women's oppression. Feminists will not relinquish

[69] Strathern, "Out of Context: The Persuasive Fictions of Anthropology," 269.

[70] Nancy Cott, quoted in Joanne Frye, "The Politics of Reading: Feminism, the Novel and the Coercions of 'Truth' " (paper presented at the annual meeting of the Midwest Modern Language Association, Columbus, Ohio, November 1987), esp. 2.

the claim to understanding women's gendered experience in the hierarchical world in which we continue to live.[71]

This situatedness affords feminists a ground for reclaiming objectivity for our enterprise while at the same time recognizing the partiality of truth claims. Recent works by feminist critics of science have challenged traditional definitions of objectivity as disinterestedness and have reappropriated the term for the situated truth that feminism seeks. This argument is well stated by Mary Hawkesworth: "In the absence of claims of universal validity, feminist accounts derive their justificatory force from their capacity to illuminate existing social relations, to demonstrate the deficiencies of alternative interpretations, to debunk opposing views. Precisely because feminists move beyond texts to confront the world, they can provide concrete reasons in specific contexts for the superiority of their accounts. . . . At their best, feminist analyses engage both the critical intellect and the world; they surpass androcentric accounts because in their systematicity more is examined and less is assumed."[72] Truth can only emerge in particular circumstances; we must be wary of generalizations. Such a politics demands and enables feminists to examine for whom we write. Strathern is one anthropologist who has found this lesson of value: "In describing Melanesian marriage ceremonies, I must bear my Melanesian readers in mind. That in turn makes problematic the previously established distinction between writer and subject: I must know on whose behalf and to what end I write."[73]

Hidden power relations constitute problems not only for women and for feminist scholarship but also for men and for the dominant discourse whose claims to objectivity are marred by distortions and mystification. The very fictional forms that in postmodern epistemology are the ideal vehicles for uncovering these power relations actually may tempt the new ethnographer to write without deciding who the audience is. The new ethnography must embed its theory in a grounded politics rather than turning to a currently popular aesthetic without interrogating the way in which that thinking is potentially subversive of anthropology's own political agenda.

It is true that postmodernism, with its emphasis on the decentering of the Cartesian subject, can be invigorating to those traditionally excluded from discourse. Jane Flax has stressed this liberating potential, arguing that postmodern experimentation encourages us "to tolerate and interpret ambivalence, ambiguity, and

---

[71] Ibid.

[72] Mary E. Hawkesworth, "Knowers, Knowing, Known: Feminist Theory and Claims of Truth," *Signs* 14, no. 3 (Spring 1989): 533–57, esp. 557.

[73] Strathern, "Out of Context: The Persuasive Fictions of Anthropology," esp. 269.

multiplicity."[74] Similarly, historian Joan Scott has recently argued that the postmodern rejection of the notion that humanity can be embodied in any universal figure or norm to which the "other" is compared acts to decenter the Western white male.[75] In Craig Owens's words: "The postmodern work attempts to upset the reassuring stability of [the] mastering position [of the] subject of representation as absolutely centered, unitary, masculine."[76] Indeed, this seems to be the political motivation underlying the new ethnography, but actual postmodern writing may not serve these political ends. Rather, it may erase difference, implying that all stories are really about one experience: the decentering and fragmentation that is the current experience of Western white males.

Moreover, even if we grant that postmodernism's potential lies in its capacity to decenter experience, a number of questions still arise. Can we think of difference without putting it against a norm? Can we recognize difference, but not in terms of hierarchy?[77] Perhaps more to the point in terms of the new ethnography, what are the implications of polyvocality? If the postmodernist emphasis on multivocality leads to a denial of the continued existence of a hierarchy of discourse, the material and historical links between cultures can be ignored, with all voices becoming equal, each telling only an individualized story. Then the history of the colonial, for example, can be read as independent of that of the colonizer. Such readings ignore or obscure exploitation and power differentials and, therefore, offer no ground to fight oppression and effect change. Moreover, in light of the diversity of the experience that the new ethnography wishes to foreground, anthropologists need to consider what provisions will have to be made for interdiscursive unintelligibility or misinterpretation. The traditional ethnographer's translation of other cultures into the discourse of Western social science long has been recognized to be problematic. A text that subtly orchestrates the translation of that experience in the mind of each reader, an interpreter who may be able to draw only on commonsense categories saturated with the assumptions of the Western tradition, is certainly no less so. However brilliant the deconstruction of the text of culture, however eloquent the oral history of the informant, the "other" may still be reconstituted in the language of the dominant discourse if there is not an analysis that "regards every discourse as a result of a practice of production

[74] Flax (n. 26 above), 643.

[75] Joan Scott, "History and the Problem of Sexual Difference" (lecture presented at Simon's Rock of Bard College, Great Barrington, Mass., November 1987).

[76] Owens (n. 26 above), 58.

[77] Scott.

which is at once material, discursive, and complex."[78] Without a politically reflexive grounding, the "other" too easily can be reconstituted as an exotic in danger of being disempowered by that exoticism.

Furthermore, the new ethnography's shift from a scientific to a more literary discourse may constitute a masking and empowering of Western bias rather than a diffusing of it. When the new ethnography borrows from literary narrative in an effort to rid itself of a unitary, totalizing narrative voice, it turns understandably, if ironically, to modern fiction for its models. The disappearance of the omniscient, controlling narrative voice that comments on the lives of all characters and knows their inner secrets is crucial to the modernist transformation of fiction evident in the works of writers like Joseph Conrad, Henry James, Virginia Woolf, James Joyce, Gertrude Stein, and William Faulkner, a transformation that coincided with the breakdown of colonialism. As critics have pointed out, authors who experiment with point of view, presenting a seeming jumble of perspectives and subjectivities in a variety of voices, may well be writing no more open texts than classic works in which all action is mediated by a unitary narrative voice.[79] The literary techniques of fragmentation, metaphor, thematic and verbal echo, repetition, and juxtaposition, which the new ethnography borrows, are all devices through which an author manipulates understanding and response. They function to structure the reader's experience of the apparently discontinuous, illogical, and fragmentary text. Through them, and by refusing to speak his or her views and intentions directly, the author achieves a more complete mastery.[80] Anthropologists seeking to write new ethnography and borrowing this range of devices from literature may unknowingly in the process pick up literary emphasis on form and the aesthetic of wholeness, both of which constitute traps for the ethnographer. These aesthetic criteria invite the manipulation of narrative devices in polyvocal works, whose apparent cacophony mirrors the diversity and multiplicity of individual and cultural perspectives, subtly to resolve all elements into a coherent and pleasing whole. These narrative devices potentially structure and control as surely as does

---

[78] J. Henriques, W. Holloway, C. Urwin, C. Venn, and V. Walkerdine, *Changing the Subject* (London and New York: Methuen, 1984), esp. 106.

[79] See Roland Barthes, *S/Z*, trans. Richard Miller (New York: Hill & Wang, 1974); and Wayne Booth, *The Rhetoric of Fiction* (Chicago: University of Chicago Press, 1961).

[80] Shoshana Felman, "Turning the Screw of Interpretation," *Yale French Studies* 55/56 (1977): 94–208, esp. 203–7.

the narrator of classic works, whether literary, historical, or ethnographic.[81]

These cautions can, of course, be viewed as excessively formalist, as failing to see the new ethnography as more than stylistic innovation. Stephen Tyler, in his incantatory, wildly enthusiastic—though, perhaps, self-contradictory—celebration of new ethnography, labels such a view a "modernist perversion."[82] To him, the new ethnographic writing is evocative rather than representational; like ritual or poetry "it makes available through absence what can be conceived but not represented."[83] Indeed, readers wishing to experience the self-congratulatory ideology underlying the new ethnography, unqualified by subtlety or academic caution, should read Tyler's unproblematized claims: that postmodernist ethnography emphasizes "the cooperative and collaborative nature of the fieldwork situation" and "the mutual dialogical production of discourse";[84] that in privileging discourse over text it is concerned "not ... to make a better representation, but ... to avoid representation";[85] that it is "the meditative vehicle for a transcendence of time and place."[86] Tyler says that "ethnographic discourse is not part of a project whose aim is to create universal knowledge,"[87] but rather the "consumed fragment" of an understanding that is only experienced in the text, the text which is evocative and participatory, bringing the joint work of ethnographer and his native partners together with the hermeneutic process of the reader.[88]

However, Jonathan Friedman, coming at this from a Marxist perspective, and Judith Stacey, from a feminist one, are highly skeptical of the claim that postmodernist revision of ethnographic practice is significantly more than a matter of style. Friedman calls

---

[81] This has been acknowledged by Clifford in *The Predicament of Culture* (n. 60 above) as well as by Geertz (n. 64 above), and has been well described by Bruce Kapferer in his review of both books in "The Anthropologist as Hero: Three Exponents of Post-Modernist Anthropology," *Critique of Anthropology* 8, no. 2 (1988): 77–104, esp. 98. According to Kapferer, "Present attempts to give voice— edited texts of tape recorded interviews, for example—can be made into the vehicle for the ethnographer's own views. The ethnographer hides behind the mask of the other. This could be more insidious than in the less self-conscious ethnography of yore. It can be another mode by which the other is appropriated and controlled."

[82] Tyler (n. 65 above), 129.

[83] Ibid., 123.

[84] Ibid., 126.

[85] Ibid., 128.

[86] Ibid., 129.

[87] Ibid., 131.

[88] Ibid., 129–30.

for a dialogue that is intertextual, not merely intratextual, since "it is clearly the case that the single dialogic text may express the attempt to recapture and thus neutralize, once more, the relation between us and them by assuming that the anthropologist can represent the other's voice."[89] Stacey argues that "acknowledging partiality and taking responsibility for authorial construction" are not enough: "The postmodern strategy is an inadequate response to the ethical issues endemic to ethnographic process and product."[90] The new ethnography threatens to subsume the "other" either in a manipulative, totalizing form whose politics is masked, or in the historically contingent discourse of each reader's response. In their borrowing of techniques from fiction, new ethnographers do not claim to write purely imaginative works. They continue to make some truth claims: their use of dialogue is presented as reflecting their experience in the field, and the fragmentation of their texts is presented as mirroring their postmodern condition. As Tyler puts it, "We confirm in our ethnographies our consciousness of the fragmentary nature of the post-modern world, for nothing so well defines *our world* as the absence of a synthesizing allegory."[91]

This is not true for non-Western males or for all women. The supposed absence of all metanarratives—the experience of helplessness and fragmentation—is the new synthesizing allegory that is being projected onto white women and Third World peoples who only recently have been partially empowered. To the extent that the new ethnography's political strength lies in a social criticism based on the "sophisticated reflection by the anthropologist about herself and her own society that describing an alien culture engenders," as Marcus and Fischer have suggested, it is disheartening as anthropology.[92] It has lost its claim to describe the "other" and yet seems devoid of the capacity to empower anyone but the writer and the reader for whom it serves as academic collateral or therapy. Anthropology is potentially reduced to an identity ritual for the anthropologist. If the new ethnography is that, then it must be seen as a facet of postmodernism's ultimate defense of the privilege of the traditional subject, even as, paradoxically, it deconstructs subject status.

While postmodern thinking has indeed invigorated many academic disciplines, anthropology must reconsider the costs of embracing it. Those anthropologists sensitive to the power relations in

[89] Jonathan Friedman, "Comment," *Current Anthropology* 29, no. 3 (June 1988): 426–27, esp. 427.

[90] Stacey (n. 51 above), 26.

[91] Tyler, 132 (emphasis ours).

[92] Marcus and Fischer (n. 2 above), 4.

the ethnographic enterprise who wish to discover ways of confronting them ethically would do better to turn to feminist theory and practice than to postmodernism. Ultimately, the postmodern focus on style and form, regardless of its sophistication, directs our attention away from the fact that ethnography is more than "writing it up." From women's position as "other" in a patriarchal culture and from feminists' dialogue and confrontation with diverse groups of women, we have learned to be suspicious of all attempts by members of a dominant group to speak for the oppressed, no matter how eloquently or experimentally. Politically sensitive anthropologists should not be satisfied with exposing power relations in the ethnographic text, if that is indeed what the new ethnography accomplishes, but rather should work to overcome these relations. By turning to postmodernism, they may instead be (unwittingly or not) reinforcing such power relations and preserving their status as anthropologists, as authoritative speakers. Anthropologists may be better able to overcome these power relations by framing research questions according to the desires of the oppressed group, by choosing to do work that "others" want and need, by being clear for whom they are writing, and by adopting a feminist political framework that is suspicious of relationships with "others" that do not include a close and honest scrutiny of the motivations for research.

Within Western culture, women's position has been paradoxical. Like a Third World person who has been educated at Oxbridge, we feminist scholars speak at once as the socially constituted "other" and as speakers within the dominant discourse, never able to place ourselves wholly or uncritically in either position. Similarly, although ethnographers are speakers of the dominant discourse, they know the experience of otherness, albeit a self-inflicted and temporally limited one, from their time in the field. They may be able to draw on their experiences as outsiders in that situation to help them clarify their political and personal goals and to set their research agendas. While it is complex and uncomfortable to speak from a position that is neither inside nor outside, it is this position that necessitates that we merge our scholarship with a clear politics to work against the forces of oppression.

Women's Studies and Anthropology
Simon's Rock of Bard College (Mascia-Lees)

Women's Studies and Literature
Simon's Rock of Bard College (Sharpe)

Department of Anthropology
Vassar College (Cohen)

Knowers, Knowing, Known: Feminist Theory and Claims of Truth

Mary E. Hawkesworth

Despite a growing philosophical movement away from preoccupations with epistemology in general, and foundationalism in particular, feminist theorists continue to explore theories of knowledge.[1] Recurrent tendencies within the dominant disciplines to marginalize feminist scholarship as a subject of interest to "women only"

I would like to thank Philip Alperson, Frank Cunningham, Judith Grant, and three anonymous reviewers for their helpful comments on an earlier version of this paper.

[1] For general arguments against an excessive philosophical preoccupation with epistemology, see Jacques Derrida, *Dissemination* (Chicago: University of Chicago Press, 1981); John Gunnell, *Between Philosophy and Politics* (Amherst: University of Massachusetts Press, 1986); Mark Krupnick, ed., *Displacement* (Bloomington: University of Indiana Press, 1983); Paul Kress, "Against Epistemology," *Journal of Politics* 41, no. 2 (May 1979): 526–42. For specific arguments against foundationalism, see Richard Rorty, *Philosophy and the Mirror of Nature* (Princeton, N.J.: Princeton University Press, 1979); Richard Bernstein, *Beyond Objectivism and Relativism* (Philadelphia: University of Pennsylvania Press, 1983); Don Herzog, *Without Foundations: Justification in Political Theory* (Ithaca, N.Y.: Cornell University Press, 1985). It is worth noting the irony that even those most intent on repudiating epistemology on the grounds that traditional epistemological concerns involve claims altogether beyond the possibilities for human knowledge are themselves advancing epistemological claims.

[*Signs: Journal of Women in Culture and Society* 1989, vol. 14, no. 3]

inspire a quest for an epistemological foundation that can rescue feminist claims from trivialization by demonstrating their truth and importance.[2] The discovery of a pervasive androcentrism in the definition of intellectual problems as well as in specific theories, concepts, methods, and interpretations of research fuels efforts to distinguish between knowledge and prejudice.[3] The recognition that epistemological assumptions have political implications stimulates efforts to attain theoretical self-consciousness concerning the intellectual presuppositions of feminist analysis.[4] Dissatisfaction with paternalistic politics premised on malestream conceptions of "women's nature" sustains feminist epistemological challenges to men's claims to "know" women's nature or what constitutes "women's best interests."[5] Objections raised by Third World women and women of color to the political priorities of white, Western feminists generate profound skepticism about the ability of any particular group of women to "know" what is in the interest of all women.[6]

[2] Sandra Harding and Merrill Hintikka, eds., *Discovering Reality: Feminist Perspectives on Epistemology, Metaphysics, Methodology and Philosophy of Science* (Dordrecht: D. Reidel, 1983); Dale Spender, ed., *Men's Studies Modified: The Impact of Feminism on the Academic Disciplines* (Oxford: Pergamon, 1981).

[3] In addition to the works of Harding and Hintikka, eds., and Spender, ed. (*Men's Studies Modified*) mentioned above, see also Sandra Harding, *The Science Question in Feminism* (Ithaca, N.Y.: Cornell University Press, 1986); Carol Pateman and Elizabeth Gross, eds., *Feminist Challenges* (Boston: Northeastern University Press, 1986); Marion Lowe and Ruth Hubbard, eds., *Women's Nature: Rationalizations of Inequality* (New York: Pergamon, 1983); Evelyn Fox Keller, *Reflections on Gender and Science* (New Haven, Conn.: Yale University Press, 1984); and Jean Grimshaw, *Philosophy and Feminist Thinking* (Minneapolis: University of Minnesota Press, 1986).

[4] Nancy Hartsock, "The Feminist Standpoint: Developing a Ground for a Specifically Feminist Historical Materialism," in Harding and Hintikka, eds., 283–310, and *Money, Sex and Power: Towards a Feminist Historical Materialism* (Boston: Northeastern University Press, 1985); Alison Jaggar, *Feminist Politics and Human Nature* (Totowa, N.J.: Rowman & Allanheld, 1983); and Rita Mae Kelly, Bernard Ronan, and Margaret Cawley, "Liberal Positivistic Epistemology and Research on Women and Politics," *Women and Politics* 7, no. 3 (Fall 1987): 11–27.

[5] Such challenges of men's claims to "know" women's nature have been a staple of feminist criticism since its inception. For examples of early critiques, see Christine de Pisan's fifteenth-century treatise, *The Book of the City of the Ladies*, trans. Earl Jeffrey Richards (New York: Persea, 1982); Mary Wollstonecraft, *Vindication of the Rights of Women*, ed. Charles Hagelman (New York: Norton, 1967); and John Stuart Mill, *The Subjection of Women* (Cambridge, Mass.: MIT Press, 1970). For more recent criticisms, see Mary Daly, *Gyn/Ecology: The Metaethics of Radical Feminism* (Boston: Beacon, 1978); Dale Spender, ed., *Women of Ideas and What Men Have Done to Them* (London: Ark Paperbacks, 1983).

[6] Angela Davis, *Women, Race and Class* (New York: Random House, 1981); Gloria Joseph and Jill Lewis, *Common Differences: Conflicts in Black and White Feminist Perspectives* (New York: Anchor Press/Doubleday, 1981); Paula Giddens, *When and Where I Enter: The Impact of Black Women on Race and Sex in America* (New York: Bantam, 1984).

The identification of conflicts experienced by many women between the contradictory demands of "rationality" and "femininity"
stimulate a search for theoretical connections between gender and
specific ways of knowing.[7]

The various issues that have inspired feminist interest in theories of knowledge have also produced divergent arguments concerning the premises of a "feminist epistemology." Three models
for a feminist theory of knowledge surface with great regularity:
feminist empiricism, feminist standpoint theories, and feminist
postmodernism.[8]

Feminist empiricism accepts the tenets of philosophical realism
(which posit the existence of the world independent of the human
knower) and empiricist assumptions about the primacy of the senses
as the source of all knowledge about the world. Feminist empiricists
maintain that sexism and androcentrism are identifiable biases of
individual knowers that can be eliminated by stricter application
of existing methodological norms of scientific and philosophical
inquiry. From this view, the appropriate method for apprehending
the truth about the world involves a process of systematic observation in which the subjectivity of the observer is controlled by
rigid adherence to neutral procedures designed to produce identical
measurements of the real properties of objects. The eradication of
misogynist bias is compatible with, indeed, is a necessary precondition for, the achievement of objective knowledge, for it promotes
the acquisition of an unmediated truth about the world; it frees
substantive knowledge about reality from the distorting lenses of
particular observers.[9]

[7] Genevieve Lloyd, The Man of Reason: Male and Female in Western Philosophy
(London: Methuen, 1984); Carol McMillan, Women, Reason and Nature (Oxford:
Basil Blackwell, 1982); Helen Weinrich-Haste, "Redefining Rationality: Feminism
and Science" (guest lecture presented at the Ontario Institute for Studies in Education, Toronto, Ontario, October 9, 1986).

[8] This characterization of the alternatives is developed most clearly by Sandra
Harding in The Science Question in Feminism (n. 3 above). For alternative characterizations of the options available to feminism, see Jaggar; Eloise Buker, "Hermeneutics: Problems and Promises for Doing Feminist Theory" (paper presented
at the Annual Meeting of the American Political Science Association, New Orleans,
August 30, 1985); and Susan Hekman, "The Feminization of Epistemology: Gender
and the Social Sciences," Women and Politics 7, no. 3 (Fall 1987): 65–83.

[9] For examples of feminist empiricist arguments, see Janet Richards, The Skeptical Feminist (London: Penguin, 1982); S. C. Bourque and J. Grossholtz, "Politics
an Unnatural Practice: Political Science Looks at Female Participation," Politics and
Society 4, no. 2 (Winter 1974): 225–66; M. Goot and E. Reid, "Women and Voting
Studies: Mindless Matrons or Sexist Scientism," Sage Professional Papers in Comparative Political Sociology (Newbury Park, Calif.: Sage, 1975); Jill McCalla Vickers,
"Memoirs of an Ontological Exile: The Methodological Rebellions of Feminist Research," in Feminism in Canada, ed. Geraldine Finn and Angela Miles (Montreal:
Black Rose, 1982).

Drawing on historical materialism's insight that social being determines consciousness, feminist standpoint theories reject the notion of an "unmediated truth," arguing that knowledge is always mediated by a host of factors related to an individual's particular position in a determinate sociopolitical formation at a specific point in history. Class, race, and gender necessarily structure the individual's understanding of reality and hence inform all knowledge claims. Although they repudiate the possibility of an unmediated truth, feminist standpoint epistemologies do not reject the notion of truth altogether. On the contrary, they argue that while certain social positions (the oppressor's) produce distorted ideological views of reality, other social positions (the oppressed's) can pierce ideological obfuscations and attain a correct and comprehensive understanding of the world. Thus, feminist analysis grounded on the privileged perspective that emerges from women's oppression constitutes the core of a "successor science" that can replace the truncated projects of masculinist science with a more systematic and sophisticated conception of social and political life.[10]

Taking the perspectivism intimated by standpoint epistemologies to its logical conclusion, "feminist postmodernism" rejects the very possibility of *a* truth about reality. Feminist postmodernists use the "situatedness" of each finite observer in a particular sociopolitical, historical context to challenge the plausibility of claims that any perspective on the world could escape partiality. Extrapolating from the disparate conditions that shape individual identities, they raise grave suspicions about the very notion of a putative unitary consciousness of the species. In addition, the argument that knowledge is the result of invention, the imposition of form on the world rather than the result of discovery, undermines any belief that the Order of Being could be known even if it exists. As an alternative to the futile quest for an authoritative truth to ground feminist theory, feminist postmodernists advocate a profound skepticism regarding universal (or universalizing) claims about the existence, nature, and powers of reason.[11] Rather than succumb to the authoritarian impulses of the will to truth, they urge instead the

[10] For examples of feminist standpoint arguments, see Hartsock, "The Feminist Standpoint," and *Money, Sex and Power;* Jaggar; Mary O'Brien, *The Politics of Reproduction* (London: Routledge & Kegan Paul, 1981); Hilary Rose, "Hand, Brain and Heart: A Feminist Epistemology for the Natural Sciences," *Signs: Journal of Women in Culture and Society* 9, no. 1 (Autumn 1983): 73–90; Dorothy Smith, "Women's Perspective as a Radical Critique of Sociology," *Sociological Inquiry* 44, no. 1 (1974): 7–13.

[11] Jane Flax, "Gender as a Social Problem: In and For Feminist Theory," *American Studies/Amerika Studien* 31, no. 2 (1986): 193–213.

development of a commitment to plurality and the play of difference.[12]

Even so brief a summary of the alternative epistemologies currently vying for feminist allegiance indicates that no single contender can address all of the concerns that have fueled feminists' turn to epistemology. The elements of feminist empiricism and feminist standpoint epistemologies that sustain feminist claims concerning a privileged perspective on the world are at odds with the insight generated by the long struggle of women of color within the feminist movement, that there is no uniform "women's reality" to be known, no coherent perspective to be privileged. Yet the feminist postmodernists' plea for tolerance of multiple perspectives is altogether at odds with feminists' desire to develop a successor science that can refute once and for all the distortions of androcentrism. So intractable is the pull of these competing demands that it has led one of the most astute feminist scholars to recommend that feminists simply recognize and embrace the tensions created by these alternative insights. As Sandra Harding puts it: "Feminist analytical categories *should* be unstable at this moment in history. We need to learn how to see our goal for the present moment as a kind of illuminating 'riffing' between and over the beats of the various patriarchal theories and our own transformations of them, rather than as a revision of the rhythms of any particular one (Marxism, psychoanalysis, empiricism, hermeneutics, postmodernism . . .) to fit what we think at the moment we want to say. The problem is that we do not know and we should not know just what we want to say about a number of conceptual choices with which we are presented—except that the choices themselves create no-win dilemmas for our feminisms."[13]

---

[12] For additional examples of feminist postmodernism, see Jane Flax, "Postmodernism and Gender Relations in Feminist Theory," *Signs* 12, no. 4 (Summer 1987): 621–43; Donna Haraway, "A Manifesto for Cyborgs: Science, Technology and Socialist Feminism in the 1980s," *Socialist Review* 80 (March/April 1985): 65–107; Claudine Hermann, "The Virile System," in *New French Feminisms*, ed. Elaine Marks and Isabelle de Courtivron (New York: Schocken, 1981); Hekman, "The Feminization of Epistemology," and Susan Hekman, "Derrida, Feminism and Epistemology" (paper presented at the Annual Meeting of the American Political Science Association, Washington, D.C., September 2, 1988); Luce Irigaray, *Speculum of the Other Woman*, trans. Gillian Gill (Ithaca, N.Y.: Cornell University Press, 1985), and *This Sex Which Is Not One*, trans. Catherine Porter (Ithaca, N.Y.: Cornell University Press, 1985).

[13] Harding (n. 3 above), 244; see also 194–96. This ambivalence is also apparent in Jane Flax's article, "Postmodernism and Gender Relations in Feminist Theory," which categorizes feminist theory as a "a type of postmodern philosophy" (624) while simultaneously illuminating some of the deficiencies of postmodernism for

Has feminism arrived at such an impasse that its best hope with respect to epistemological issues is to embrace incompatible positions and embed a contradiction at the heart of its theory of knowledge? There is an alternative approach to epistemological questions that can avoid this unhappy resolution. The purpose of this paper is to explore certain troublesome shifts in feminist arguments about knowledge that lead to the no-win dilemmas outlined by Harding. By changing the focus of feminist epistemological investigations from questions about knowers to claims about the known, feminism can both preserve important insights of postmodernism and serve as a corrective to a variety of inadequate conceptions of the world. By adopting a conception of cognition as a human practice, a critical feminist epistemology can identify, explain, and refute persistent androcentric bias within the dominant discourses without privileging a putative "woman's" perspective and without appealing to problematic conceptions of "the given."

Knowers

Both in academic institutions and in interpersonal interactions, feminists often become acquainted with the claims of established knowledge from the underside. The classic texts of Western history, philosophy, literature, religion, and science, riddled with misinformation about women, are handed down as sacred truths. When individual women attempt to challenge the adequacy of such misogynist accounts, they are frequently informed that their innate inabilities preclude their comprehension of these classic insights. Hence it is not surprising that brilliant feminists have agreed that reason has served as a weapon for the oppression of women, that it has functioned as "a kind of gang rape of women's minds,"[14] that "in masculine hands, logic is often a form of violence, a sly kind of tyranny."[15]

In response to such widespread abusive intellectual practices, feminist analysis often shifts very subtly from a recognition of misinformation about women to a suspicion concerning the dissemi-

---

feminists committed to human emancipation. Thus Flax concludes that "the relation of feminist theorizing to the postmodern project of deconstruction is necessarily ambivalent" (625).

[14] Mary Daly, *Beyond God the Father* (Boston: Beacon, 1973), 9.

[15] Simone de Beauvoir, *The Second Sex*, trans. and ed. H. M. Parshley (New York: Bantam, 1960), 201.

nation of disinformation about women. The fact that the Western intellectual tradition has been conceived and produced by men is taken as evidence that this tradition exists to serve the misogynist interests of men. The existence of the misinformation is taken as evidence of "sexual ideology, a set of false beliefs deployed against women by a conscious, well-organized male conspiracy."[16] The slide from misinformation to disinformation has a number of dire consequences for feminist approaches to epistemology. In focusing attention on the source of knowledge, that is, on men, rather than on the validity of specific claims advanced by men, the terms of debate are shifted toward psychological and functionalist analyses and away from issues of justification. This in turn allows a number of contested epistemological assumptions about the nature of knowledge, the process of knowing, standards of evidence, and criteria of assessment to be incorporated unreflectively into feminist arguments.

In feminist treatments of knowledge one frequently encounters the curious claim that reason is gendered.[17] The claim takes a variety of different forms. It is said that rationality, a tough, rigorous, impersonal, competitive, unemotional, objectifying stance, "is inextricably intertwined with issues of men's gender identities" such as obsession with separation and individuation.[18] It is said that "distinctively (Western) masculine desires are satisfied by the preoccupation with method, rule and law-governed behavior and activity."[19] It is said that the connections between masculinization, reification, and objectification are such that should women attempt to enter the male realm of objectivity, they have only one option: to deny their female nature and adopt the male mode of being.[20] It is said that all dichotomies—objective/subjective, rational/irrational, reason/emotion, culture/nature—are a product of the basic male/

[16] Toril Moi traces this subtle shift in the work of a number of contemporary French feminists and offers an insightful critique of this slide (see *Sexual/Textual Politics: Feminist Literary Theory* [New York: Methuen, 1985], 28).

[17] For a detailed and illuminating discussion of the arguments that sustain this claim, see Judith Grant, "I Feel Therefore I Am: A Critique of Female Experience as a Basis for Feminist Epistemology," *Women and Politics* 7, no. 3 (Fall 1987): 99–114.

[18] Harding, 63. For similar claims, see Susan Bordo, "The Cartesian Masculinization of Thought," *Signs* 11, no. 3 (Spring 1986): 439–56; Kathy Ferguson, "Male Ordered Politics: Feminism and Political Science" (paper presented at the Annual Meeting of the American Political Science Association, New Orleans, August 30, 1985).

[19] Harding (n. 3 above), 229. See also Isaac Balbus, *Marxism and Domination* (Princeton, N.J.: Princeton University Press, 1982); Keller (n. 3 above).

[20] For a sustained consideration of the possibility that the "ideals of reason have incorporated an exclusion of the feminine," see Genevieve Lloyd, *The Man of Reason* (London: Methuen, 1982), 8.

female hierarchy that is central to patriarchal thought and society.[21] It is said that reason is morphologically and functionally analogous to the male sex organ, linear, hard, penetrating but impenetrable.[22] And it is said that representational conceptions of knowledge that privilege evidence based on sight/observation/"the gaze" are derived from men's need to valorize their own visible genitals against the threat of castration posed by women's genitalia, which exist as "nothing to be seen."[23]

Underlying all these claims are speculative psychological notions about a fragile, defensive male ego that impels men constantly to "prove" their masculinity by mastering women, to affirm their own value by denigrating that which is "other."[24] Whether one wishes to defend these psychological claims or to attack them, it is important to note that at issue are certain psychological theories, particular conceptions of psychosexual development, specific notions about the role of the body and of sexuality in the formation of individual identity, and speculations about the relationship between personal identity and sociability. While all of these questions are important and worthy of systematic investigation, they are not epistemological questions per se. The slide from consideration of claims about knowledge and about the truth of certain propositions about women contained in classical texts to concerns about the "will to power" embodied in the claims of "male reason" moves feminist inquiry to a set of highly complex psychological issues that in principle could be completely irrelevant to the resolution of the initial epistemological questions.

---

[21] Elizabeth Fee, "Whither Feminist Epistemology?" (paper presented at Beyond the Second Sex Conference, Philadelphia, University of Pennsylvania, 1984). Hekman discusses a number of feminist works that link dichotomous thinking to gender hierarchy in "The Feminization of Epistemology" (n. 8 above).

[22] Irigaray, *Speculum of the Other Woman* (n. 12 above), and *This Sex Which Is Not One* (n. 12 above); Hélène Cixous, "Le rire de la Méduse," *L'Arc* 61 (1975): 39–54, trans. Keith Cohen and Paula Cohen, "The Laugh of the Medusa," *Signs* 1, no. 4 (Summer 1976): 875–93, and "Le sexe ou la tête," *Les Cahiers du GRIF* 13 (1976): 5–15, trans. Annette Kuhn, "Castration or Decapitation?" *Signs* 7, no. 1 (Autumn 1981): 41–55; and Ferguson.

[23] Irigaray, *Speculum of the Other Woman*, 48.

[24] Whether these contentious claims are drawn directly from the theories of Freud or indirectly from Freud by means of Klein, Winnicott, and Chodorow, or by means of Lacan and Irigaray, the ultimate blame for the fragility of male identity is attributed to women qua mothers. Despite their theoretical complexities, the various interpretations of the "oedipal conflict" manage to insinuate that it is women-only childcare practices that are the cause of psychic needs to oppress women. That a good deal of feminist theorizing should be premised on such "blame the victim" assumptions is itself very puzzling.

Feminist discussions of epistemology often devolve into modes of functionalist argument. Unlike psychological arguments that attempt to explain phallocentric claims in terms of the psychic needs of male knowers, functionalist arguments focus attention on the putative "interests" served by particular beliefs, whether they be the interests of discrete individuals, groups, classes, institutions, structures, or systems.[25] Thus it is said that "male reason" promotes the interests of men as a sex-class by securing women's collusion in their own oppression, transforming each woman from a forced slave into a willing one.[26] It is said that sexist beliefs serve the interests of individual men, for each man reaps psychological, economic, and political advantages in a society organized according to patriarchal imperatives.[27] It is said that sexist ideology serves the interests of capitalism, for it reproduces the relations of dominance and subordination required by capitalist production; it facilitates the reproduction of labor power on a daily as well as a generational basis; it creates a marginal female labor force willing to work for less than subsistence wages; and it creates divisions within the working class on the basis of gender that thwart the development of unified class consciousness and revolutionary action.[28] And it is said that "male rationality," functioning in accordance with the "logic of identity," operates as a mechanism of social control. In the interests of unrelenting domination, "thought seeks to have everything under control, to eliminate all uncertainty, unpredictability, to eliminate otherness."[29] Authoritarian reason imposes conformity

[25] For the purposes of developing a logical taxonomy, it might be preferable to identify psychological arguments as one form of functionalism, a form that emphasizes the psychological needs and interests served by particular ideas. Because of the frequency with which psychological claims surface in feminist epistemology, in the foregoing analysis I have treated psychological claims independently, but they are also vulnerable to the kinds of problems associated with functionalism.

[26] Mill (n. 5 above); Germaine Greer, *The Female Eunuch* (London: St. Albans, 1971).

[27] Sara Ann Ketchum and Christine Pierce, "Separatism and Sexual Relationships" in *Philosophy and Women,* ed. Sharon Bishop and Marjorie Weinsweig (Belmont, Calif.: Wadsworth Press, 1979), 163–71.

[28] Wally Seccombe, "The Housewife and Her Labour under Capitalism," *New Left Review* 83 (January–February 1973): 3–24; John Berger and Jean Mohr, *A Seventh Man* (London: Harmondsworth, 1975); Victoria Beechey, "Some Notes on Female Wage Labour in the Capitalist Mode of Production," *Capital and Class* 3 (Fall 1977): 45–64, and "Women and Production," in *Feminism and Materialism,* ed. Annette Kuhn and Ann Marie Wolpe (London: Routledge & Kegan Paul, 1978).

[29] Iris Young, "Impartiality and the Civic Public: Some Implications for Feminist Critiques of Moral and Political Theory," *Praxis International* 5, no. 4 (1986): 381–401, esp. 384.

by policing thoughts, purging from the realm of the thinkable all that differs from its own narrow presuppositions.

Functionalist arguments are frequently offered as causal explanations for the existence of particular ideas on the assumption that the function served constitutes the raison d'être for the belief; for example, misogynist notions were/are invented precisely to serve as mechanisms of social control. Yet this teleological assumption, which equates function with first and final cause, overlooks the possibility that the origin of an idea may be totally unrelated to specific uses made of the idea.[30] Functionalist explanations also tend to gloss over complex sociological, political, and historical issues that arise when one attempts to demonstrate that a particular idea or belief actually serves the latent or manifest functions attributed to it in a contemporary setting and that it served this function in a variety of different historical epochs. As feminists pursue the intractable problems associated with functionalist explanations, they are once again carried away from questions concerning the validity of particular claims about women. In the search for the putative purposes served by androcentric notions, arguments concerning the merits of these claims are abandoned.

Feminist analyses that focus on men as the source of knowledge and on the psychological needs and social purposes served by androcentric rationality as *the* central epistemological issues are premised on a number of highly problematic assumptions about the nature of reason and the process of knowing. Rather than acknowledging that reason, rationality, and knowledge are themselves essentially contested concepts that have been the subject of centuries of philosophical debate, there is a tendency to conflate all reasoning with one particular conception of rationality, with instrumental reason.[31] Associated with Enlightenment optimism about the possibility of using reason to gain technical mastery over nature, with rigorous methodological strictures for controlled observation and experimentation, with impartial application of rules to ensure replicability, with the rigidity of the fact/value dichotomy and means-ends analysis that leave crucial normative questions unconsidered, with

[30] For critiques of functionalist arguments within feminism, see Richards (n. 9 above); and Michèle Barrett, *Women's Oppression Today: Problems in Marxist Feminist Analysis* (London: Verso, 1980).

[31] Feminist approaches to epistemology are not alone in reducing a variety of theoretical conceptions of reason to a monolithic notion of instrumental rationality. Richard Bernstein has argued that this is a problem in a number of postmodern theories (see "The Rage against Reason," *Philosophy and Literature* 10, no. 2 [October 1986]: 186–210). For an insightful critique of this tendency within feminism, see Grimshaw (n. 3 above).

processes of rationalization that threaten to imprison human life in increasingly dehumanized systems, and with the deployment of technology that threatens the annihilation of all life on the planet, instrumental reason makes a ready villain.[32] When this villain is in turn associated with uniquely male psychological propensities, it is all too easy to assume that one comprehends not only that men have gotten the world wrong but also why they have gotten it wrong. The supposition that error is the result of willful deception dovetails patly with uncritical notions about unrelenting male drives for dominance and mastery.

The notion that instrumental reason is essentially male also sustains the appealing suggestion that the deployment of a uniquely female knowledge—a knowledge that is intuitive, emotional, engaged, and caring—could save humanity from the dangers of unconstrained masculinism.[33] To develop an account of this alternative knowledge, some feminists have turned to the body, to sexed embodiedness, to thinking in analogy with women's sexuality, to eros, and to women's psychosexual development.[34] Some have focused on the rich resources of women's intuition.[35] Others draw on insights from historical materialism, from theories of marginalization, and from the sociology of knowledge in an effort to generate an account of experiences common to all women that could provide a foun-

[32] For critiques of instrumental reason, see Max Weber, *The Protestant Ethic and the Spirit of Capitalism,* trans. Talcott Parsons (New York: Charles Scribner's Sons, 1958); Hans-Georg Gadamer, "Historical Transformations of Reason," in *Rationality Today,* ed. Theodore Geraets (Ottawa: University of Ottawa Press, 1979); Max Horkheimer and Theodore Adorno, *The Dialectic of Enlightenment* (New York: Herder & Herder, 1972); and Jurgen Habermas, "Dialectics of Rationalization," *Telos* 49 (Fall 1981): 5–31.

[33] See, e.g., Daly, *Gyn/Ecology* (n. 5 above); Marilyn French, *Beyond Power: On Women, Men and Morals* (New York: Summit, 1985); Sara Ruddick, "Maternal Thinking," *Feminist Studies* 6, no. 2 (1980): 342–67, and "Pacifying the Forces: Drafting Women in the Interests of Peace," *Signs* 8, no. 3 (Spring 1983): 471–89. Several feminist scholars have recently noted the irony that this oppositional conception of male and female reason reproduces the caricatures of masculine and feminine that have marked patriarchal social relations (see Grant [n. 17 above]; and Hekman, "The Feminization of Epistemology" [n. 8 above]).

[34] Consider Lorraine Code, "Is the Sex of the Knower Epistemologically Significant?" *Metaphilosophy* 12, nos. 3/4 (July/October 1981): 267–76; Cixous, "Le rire de la Méduse" (n. 22 above), and "Le sexe ou la tête" (n. 22 above); Irigaray, *Speculum of the Other Woman* (n. 12 above); H. K. Trask, *Eros and Power: The Promise of Feminist Theory* (Philadelphia: University of Pennsylvania Press, 1986); and Jane Flax, "Political Philosophy and the Patriarchal Unconscious: A Psychoanalytic Perspective on Epistemology and Metaphysics," in Harding and Hintikka, eds. (n. 2 above).

[35] Compare Daly's *Gyn/Ecology,* French's *Beyond Power,* and Susan Griffin's *Woman and Nature: The Roaring Inside Her* (New York: Harper Colophon, 1980).

dation for a women's standpoint or perspective.[36] The unification of manual, mental, and emotional capacities in women's traditional activities, the sensuous, concrete, and relational character of women's labor in the production of use-values and in reproduction, and the multiple oppressions experienced by women that generate collective struggles against the prevailing social order have all been advanced as the grounds for women's privileged epistemological perspective.[37] In appealing to certain physical, emotional, psychological, and social experiences of women, all of these approaches attempt to solve the problem of the source of knowledge and the validity of knowledge claims simultaneously by conflating the disparate issues of knower and known. They suggest that women's unique experience of reality enables them to pierce ideological distortions and grasp the truth about the world. Where men have gotten it wrong, women will get things right.

When stated so baldly, the claim that women will produce an accurate depiction of reality, either because they are women or because they are oppressed, appears to be highly implausible. Given the diversity and fallibility of all human knowers, there is no good reason to believe that women are any less prone to error, deception, or distortion than men. Appeals to the authority of the female "body" to substantiate such claims suffer from the same defects as the appeals to the authority of the senses so central to the instrumental conception of reason that these feminists set out to repudiate. Both fail to grasp the manifold ways in which all human experiences, whether of the external world or of the internal world, are mediated by theoretical presuppositions embedded in language and culture.[38]

[36] It is important to note that in contrast to claims concerning the immediate apprehension of reality characteristic of discussions of women's embodiedness and intuition, standpoint theories emphasize that a "privileged" standpoint is "achieved rather than obvious, a mediated rather than an immediate understanding . . . an achievement both of science (analysis) and of political struggle" (Hartsock, "The Feminist Standpoint" [n. 4 above], 288). Thus standpoint theories are far more sophisticated in their analysis of knowledge than feminist intuitionists and feminist empiricists. But standpoint theories still suffer from overly simplistic conceptions of the self and of science, which sustain problematic claims concerning the "universal" experiences of women that afford a foundation for a "privileged" standpoint.

[37] On the unification of capacities, see Rose (n. 10 above); the character of women's labor is examined in Hartsock "The Feminist Standpoint," and *Money, Sex and Power* (n. 4 above); and the multiple oppressions of women come under scrutiny in Jaggar (n. 4 above).

[38] In an effort to illuminate the extent to which conceptions of the "body" are socially mediated, Monique Wittig has noted that "in our [women's] case ideology goes far since our bodies as well as our minds are the product of this manipulation. We have been compelled in our bodies and our minds to correspond, feature by feature, with the idea of nature that has been established for us. Distorted to such

Both adhere to notions of transparency and a "natural" self who speaks a truth free of all ambiguity. Both adhere to the great illusion that there is one position in the world or one orientation toward the world that can eradicate all confusion, conflict, and contradiction.

These problems are not eliminated by moving from embodiedness to intuition. The distrust of the conceptual aspects of thought, which sustains claims that genuine knowledge requires immediate apprehension, presumes not only that an unmediated grasp of reality is possible but also that it is authoritative. Moreover, appeals to intuition raise the specter of an authoritarian trump that precludes the possibility of rational debate. Claims based on intuition manifest an unquestioning acceptance of their own veracity. When one assertion informed by the immediate apprehension of reality confronts another diametrically opposed claim also informed by the immediate apprehension of reality, there is no rational way to adjudicate such a dispute. Of course, one might appeal to a notion of adjudication on "intuitive" grounds, but this is the beginning of a vicious regress. Thus, intuition provides a foundation for claims about the world that is at once authoritarian, admitting of no further discussion, and relativist, since no individual can refute another's "immediate" apprehension of reality. Operating at a level of assertion that admits of no further elaboration or explication, those who abandon themselves to intuition conceive and give birth to dreams, not to truth.[39]

The theoretical monism that informs claims of truth rooted in the "body" and in intuition also haunts the arguments of feminist standpoint epistemologies. Although proponents of feminist standpoint theories are careful to note that conceptions of knowledge are historically variable and contestable, certain aspects of their arguments tend to undercut the force of that acknowledgment. For to claim that there is a distinctive women's "perspective" that is "privileged" precisely because it possesses heightened insights into the nature of reality, a superior access to truth, is to suggest that there is some uniform experience common to all women that generates this univocal vision. Yet if social, cultural, and historical differences

---

an extent that our deformed body is what they call 'natural,' is what is supposed to exist as such before oppression. Distorted to such an extent that at the end oppression seems to be a consequence of this 'nature' in ourselves (a nature which is only an idea)" (*Feminist Frameworks*, ed. Alison Jaggar and Paula Rothenberg [New York: McGraw Hill, 1984], 148–52, esp. 148).

[39] G. W. F. Hegel advances a detailed critique of intuitionism in his preface to the *Phenomenology of Spirit* (trans. J. B. Baillie [New York: Harper Colophon, 1967], 73–75).

are taken seriously, the notion of such a common experience becomes suspect. In the absence of such a homogeneous women's
experience, standpoint epistemologies must either develop complicated explanations of why some women see the truth while others
do not, a strategy that threatens to undermine the very notion of a
"women's standpoint," or collapse into a trivial and potentially contradictory pluralism that conceives of truth as simply the sum of all
women's partial and incompatible views.[40] It might be suggested
that this problem could be avoided by substituting the notion of a
"feminist perspective" for that of a "women's perspective." Such a
move could then account for the fact that some women grasp the
truth while others do not by appealing to the specific experiences
that make one a feminist. This move would also create the possibility that some men—those who are feminists—could also grasp
the truth, thereby freeing this claim from the specter of biologism.
But this strategy encounters other problems by assuming that there
is some unique set of experiences that create a feminist. The rich
and diverse histories of feminism in different nations and the rivalry
among competing feminist visions within contemporary American
society (e.g., liberal feminism vs. radical feminism vs. marxist feminism vs. socialist feminism vs. psychoanalytic feminism) raise serious challenges to the plausibility of claims concerning a uniform
mode of feminism or an invariant path to feminist consciousness.

Starting from a subjectivist approach to epistemology that focuses on issues pertaining to the faculties and sentiments of knowers as the source of knowledge, feminist inquiry arrives at an impasse.
Presuppositions concerning a "natural" subject/self capable of
grasping intuitively the totality of being, and a homogeneous wom-
en's experience that generates a privileged view of reality, fail to
do justice to the fallibility of human knowers, to the multiplicity
and diversity of women's experiences, and to the powerful ways in
which race, class, ethnicity, culture, and language structure individuals' understandings of the world. Claims concerning diverse
and incompatible intuitions about the essential nature of social reality premised on immediate apprehensions of that reality overlook
the theoretical underpinnings of all perception and experience and
consequently devolve into either authoritarian assertion or uncritical relativism. Moreover, the pervasive tolerance for and indul-
gence in "gender symbolism" within feminist discussions of
epistemology reproduce patriarchal stereotypes of men and women—

---

[40] This problem has been noted by Alan Soble, "Feminist Epistemology and
Women Scientists," *Metaphilosophy* 14, nos. 3/4 (July/October 1983): 291–307; Grant
(n. 17 above); and Harding (n. 3 above).

flirting with essentialism, distorting the diverse dimensions of human knowing, and falsifying the historical record of women's manifold uses of reason in daily life.[41]

Knowing

If the complex epistemological problems that confront feminist theory cannot be resolved by appeals to the authority of the body, intuition, or a universal Woman's experience, neither can they be solved by reference to a neutral scientific or philosophical method. Feminist empiricism, in its reliance on scientific techniques designed to control for subjectivity in the process of observation, and feminist standpoint theories that rely on historical/dialectical materialism as a method for achieving an objective grasp of reality depend on problematic conceptions of perception, experience, knowledge, and the self. An alternative account of human cognition can illuminate the defects of these conceptions. Critiques of foundationalism have emphasized that the belief in a permanent, ahistorical, Archimedean point that can provide a certain ground for knowledge claims is incompatible with an understanding of cognition as a human practice.[42] They have suggested that the belief that particular techniques of rational analysis can escape finitude and fallibility and grasp the totality of being misconstrues both the nature of subjective intellection and the nature of the objective world. Attacks on foundationalism therefore raise questions concerning specific forms of knowing, particular conceptions of subjectivity, and various theories of the external world. Insights drawn from these works can delineate the contours of a critical feminist epistemology, which avoids the limitations of feminist empiricism and feminist standpoint theories.

Standard critiques of foundationalism impugn deductive and inductive logic as the ground of objective knowledge. To challenge rationalists' confidence in the power of logical deduction as a method for securing the truth about the empirical world, critics typically point out that the truth of syllogistic reasoning is altogether dependent on the established truth of the syllogism's major and minor

---

[41] In *The Science Question in Feminism*, Harding defines gender symbolism in terms of the attribution of dualistic gender metaphors to distinctions that rarely have anything to do with sex differences, e.g., "male" reason vs. "female" intuition (17).

[42] See, e.g., Hans Albert, *Treatise on Critical Reason*, trans. Mary Varney Rorty (Princeton, N.J.: Princeton University Press, 1985); Bernstein, *Beyond Objectivism and Relativism* (n. 1 above); Stanley Cavell, *The Claim of Reason* (New York: Oxford University Press, 1979); Rorty (n. 1 above).

premises. Yet when one moves from relations of ideas governed by logical necessity to a world of contingency, the "established truth" of major and minor premises is precisely what is at issue. Thus, rather than providing an impeccable foundation for truth claims, deduction confronts the intractable problems of infinite regress, the vicious circle, or the arbitrary suspension of the principle of sufficient reason through appeals to intuition or self-evidence.[43]

Attacks on empiricist exuberance have been equally shattering. It has been repeatedly pointed out that inductive generalizations, however scrupulous and systematic, founder on a host of problems: observation generates correlations that cannot prove causation; conclusions derived from incomplete evidence sustain probability claims but do not produce incontestable truth.[44] Moreover, where rationalism tends to overestimate the power of theoretical speculation, empiricism errs in the opposite extreme by underestimating the role of theory in shaping perception and structuring comprehension.[45] Thus, the "objectivity" of the empiricist project turns on the deployment of an untenable dichotomy between "facts" and "values"—a dichotomy that misconstrues the nature of perception, fails to comprehend the theoretical constitution of facticity, and uncritically disseminates the "myth of the given."[46]

As an alternative to a conception of knowledge that is dependent on the existence of an unmediated reality that can be grasped directly by observation or intellection, antifoundationalists suggest a conception of cognition as a human practice.[47] In this view, "knowing" presupposes involvement in a social process replete with rules of compliance, norms of assessment, and standards of excellence that are humanly created. Although humans aspire to unmediated knowledge of the world, the nature of perception precludes such direct access. The only possible access is through theory-laden con-

---

[43] These arguments were developed forcefully by David Hume in his *Enquiry concerning Human Understanding* (Oxford: Clarendon, 1975). For more recent treatment of the issues, see Albert.

[44] For a review of these arguments, see Albert; and Karl Popper, *Conjectures and Refutations* (New York: Basic, 1962).

[45] Albert.

[46] The "myth of the given" is discussed in Wilfred Sellars, *Science, Perception and Reality* (New York: Humanities Press, 1963), 64. For helpful introductions to Sellars's work, see Gibson Winter, *Elements for a Social Ethic: Scientific and Ethical Perspectives on Social Process* (New York: Macmillan, 1966), 61–166; Richard Bernstein, *The Restructuring of Social and Political Theory* (Philadelphia: University of Pennsylvania Press, 1976), 121–35; and Gunnell (n. 1 above), 68–90.

[47] For a detailed discussion of the conception of practice invoked here, see Alasdair MacIntyre, *After Virtue* (Notre Dame, Ind.: University of Notre Dame Press, 1981), 174–89.

ventions that organize and structure observation by according meanings to observed events, bestowing relevance and significance on phenomena, indicating strategies for problem solving, and identifying methods by which to test the validity of proposed solutions. Knowledge, then, is a convention rooted in the practical judgments of a community of fallible inquirers who struggle to resolve theory-dependent problems under specific historical conditions.

Acquisition of knowledge occurs in the context of socialization and enculturation to determinate traditions that provide the conceptual frameworks through which the world is viewed. As sedimentations of conventional attempts to comprehend the world correctly, cognitive practices afford the individual not only a set of accredited techniques for grasping the truth of existence but also a "natural attitude," an attitude of "suspended doubt" with respect to a wide range of issues based on the conviction that one understands how the world works. In establishing what will be taken as normal, natural, real, reasonable, expected, and sane, theoretical presuppositions camouflage their contributions to cognition and their operation on the understanding. Because the theoretical presuppositions that structure cognition operate at the tacit level, it is difficult to isolate and illuminate the full range of presuppositions informing cognitive practices. Moreover, any attempt to elucidate presuppositions must operate within a "hermeneutic circle." Any attempt to examine or to challenge certain assumptions or expectations must occur within the frame of reference established by mutually reinforcing presuppositions. That certain presuppositions must remain fixed if others are to be subjected to systematic critique does not imply that individuals are "prisoners" trapped within the cognitive framework acquired through socialization.[48] Critical reflection on and abandonment of certain theoretical presuppositions is possible within the hermeneutic circle; but the goal of transparency, of the unmediated grasp of things as they are, is not, for no investigation, no matter how critical, can escape the fundamental conditions of human cognition.

Thus, the conception of cognition as a human practice challenges the possibility of unmediated knowledge of the world, as well as notions such as "brute facts," the "immediately given," "theory-free research," "neutral observation language," and "self-evident truths," which suggest that possibility. Because cognition is always theoretically mediated, the world captured in human knowledge and designated "empirical" is itself theoretically constituted. Divergent

---

[48] In *Beyond Objectivism and Relativism*, Bernstein characterizes this erroneous conclusion as the "myth of the framework" (84).

cognitive practices rooted in conventions such as common sense, religion, science, philosophy, and the arts construe the empirical realm differently, identifying and emphasizing various dimensions, accrediting different forms of evidence, different criteria of meaning, different standards of explanation, different tokens of truthfulness. Such an understanding of the theoretical constitution of the empirical realm in the context of specific cognitive practices requires a reformulation of the notion of "facts." A fact is a theoretically constituted proposition, supported by theoretically mediated evidence and put forward as part of a theoretical formulation of reality. A fact is a contestable component of a theoretically constituted order of things.[49]

The recognition that all cognition is theory-laden has also generated a critique of many traditional assumptions about the subject/self that undergird rationalist, empiricist, and materialist conceptions of knowing. Conceptions of the "innocent eye," of the "passive observer," of the mind as a "tabula rasa" have been severely challenged.[50] The notion of transparency, the belief that the individual knower can identify all his/her prejudices and purge them in order to greet an unobstructed reality has been rendered suspect.[51] Conceptions of an atomistic self who experiences the world independent of all social influences, of the unalienated self who exists as potentiality awaiting expression, and of a unified self who can grasp the totality of being have been thoroughly contested.[52] The very idea of the "subject" has been castigated for incorporating assumptions about the "logic of identity" that posit knowers as undifferentiated, anonymous, and general, possessing a vision independent of all identifiable perspectives.[53] Indeed, the conception of the knowing "subject" has been faulted for failure to grasp that rather than being the source of truth, the subject is the product of particular

[49] For an intriguing discussion of some of the most fundamental presuppositions that have shaped Western cognitive practices since the seventeenth century, see Michel Foucault, *The Order of Things: An Archaeology of the Human Sciences* (New York: Vintage, 1973).

[50] See Popper; Harold Brown, *Perception, Theory and Commitment: The New Philosophy of Science* (Chicago: Precedent, 1977); and Norman Stockman, *Anti-Positivist Theories of Science: Critical Rationalism, Critical Theory and Scientific Realism* (Dordrecht: D. Reidel, 1983).

[51] Albert (n. 42 above); Popper (n. 44 above); Brown; and Stockman.

[52] Seyla Benhabib, *Critique, Norm and Utopia* (New York: Columbia University Press, 1986); Charles Taylor, "Foucault on Freedom and Truth," *Political Theory* 12, no. 2 (1984): 152–83; William E. Connolly, "Taylor, Foucault and Otherness," *Political Theory* 13, no. 3 (1985): 365–76.

[53] See, e.g., Alan Megill, *Prophets of Extremity: Nietzsche, Heidegger, Foucault, Derrida* (Berkeley and Los Angeles: University of California Press, 1985); Young (n. 29 above), 381–401.

regimes of truth.[54] In postmodernist discourses, the notion of a sovereign subject who possesses unparalleled powers of clairvoyance affording direct apprehension of internal and external reality has been supplanted by a conception of the self as an unstable constellation of unconscious desires, fears, phobias, and conflicting linguistic, social, and political forces.

In addition to challenging notions of an unmediated reality and a transparent subject/self, the conception of cognition as a human practice also takes issue with accounts of reason that privilege one particular mode of rationality while denigrating all others. Attempts to reduce the practice of knowing to monadic conceptions of reason fail to grasp the complexity of the interaction between traditional assumptions, social norms, theoretical conceptions, disciplinary strictures, linguistic possibilities, emotional dispositions, and creative impositions in every act of cognition. Approaches to cognition as a human practice emphasize the expansiveness of rationality and the irreducible plurality of its manifestations within diverse traditions. Perception, intuition, conceptualization, inference, representation, reflection, imagination, remembrance, conjecture, rationalization, argumentation, justification, contemplation, ratiocination, speculation, meditation, validation, deliberation—even a partial listing of the many dimensions of knowing suggests that it is a grave error to attempt to reduce this multiplicity to a unitary model. The resources of intellection are more profitably considered in their complexity, for what is involved in knowing is heavily dependent on what questions are asked, what kind of knowledge is sought, and the context in which cognition is undertaken.[55]

The conception of cognition as a human practice has a great deal to offer feminist analysis, for it provides an explanation of androcentric bias within dominant discourses that is free of the defects of psychological and functionalist arguments. Rather than imputing contentious psychological drives to all males or positing speculative structural interests for all social formations, feminists can examine the specific processes by which knowledge has been constituted within determinate traditions and explore the effects of the exclusion of women from participation in those traditions. Feminists can investigate the adequacy of the standards of evidence, criteria of relevance, modes of analysis, and strategies of argumentation privileged by the dominant traditions. By focusing on the theoretical constitution of the empirical realm, feminists can illuminate the presuppositions that circumscribe what is believed to exist and

---

[54] Michel Foucault, *Discipline and Punish* (New York: Vintage, 1977), and *The History of Sexuality* (New York: Vintage, 1980), vol. 1.

[55] Cavell (n. 42 above).

identify the mechanisms by which facticity is accredited and rendered unproblematic. In raising different questions, challenging received views, refocusing research agendas, and searching for methods of investigation adequate to the problems of feminist scholarship, feminists can contribute to the development of a more sophisticated understanding of human cognition.

The conception of cognition as a human practice suggests that feminist critique is situated within established traditions of cognition even as it calls those traditions into question. Thus feminists must deal deftly with the traditions that serve both as targets of criticism and as sources of norms and techniques essential to the critical project. Moreover, the conception of cognition as a human practice suggests that feminist analysis itself can be understood as a rich and varied tradition. To build feminist epistemology on an understanding of cognition as a human practice, then, requires careful consideration of the diverse cognitive practices that already structure feminist inquiry. Rather than privileging one model of rational inquiry, feminists must first consider the level of analysis, the degree of abstraction, the type of explanation, the standards of evidence, the criteria of evaluation, the tropes of discourse, and the strategies of argumentation that would be appropriate to feminist investigations of concrete problems. Awareness of the structuring power of tacit theoretical presuppositions requires detailed investigation of the political implications of determinate modes of inquiry. The politics of knowledge must remain a principle concern of feminist analysis, not only in the course of examining malestream thought but also in determining the most fruitful avenues for feminist research. For the analytic techniques developed in particular cognitive traditions may have unfortunate political implications when applied in different contexts. Cognitive practices appropriate for psychological analysis may not be appropriate for political and sociological analysis; hermeneutic techniques essential for an adequate interpretation of human action may be wholly inadequate to the task of structural analysis; statistical techniques crucial for the illumination of discrimination may be powerless to address problems relating to ideological oppression; semiotic analyses central to the development of feminist literary criticism may be insufficient to the task of feminist historical investigations; hormonal and endocrinological studies necessary for the creation of feminist health care may be altogether inapplicable as accounts of motivation or explanations of action. Causal, dialectical, genealogical, hermeneutic, psychological, semiotic, statistical, structural, and teleological explanations may all be important to specific aspects of feminist inquiry. But knowing which mode of analysis is appropriate in specific problem situations is an issue that feminist epistemology has not yet adequately addressed.

Feminist epistemology must be sufficiently sophisticated to account for the complexity and for the political dimensions of diverse cognitive practices. To equate feminist epistemology with any particular technique of rationality is to impose unwarranted constraints on feminist inquiry, impairing its ability to develop and deploy an arsenal of analytic techniques to combat the distortions that permeate the dominant malestream discourses. Neither feminist empiricism nor feminist standpoint theories afford an adequate framework for addressing these difficult issues. Feminist empiricism is committed to untenable beliefs about the nature of knowledge and process of knowing that render it unable to explain the persistence of sexist bias within established disciplines and unable to grasp the politics of knowledge. Feminist standpoint theories are far more attuned to the ideological dimensions of knowledge, yet they remain committed to an overly simplistic model of knowledge that tends to assume a "collective singular subject," to posit a false universality, to neglect the multiplicity of structuring processes that shape cognitive practices, and to underestimate the disjuncture between problems of oppression and questions of truth.[56] The conception of cognition as a human practice provides a context for the development of a critical feminist epistemology that can transcend these limitations.[57]

Known

Understanding cognition as a human practice does not, in itself, resolve the question of what, if anything, can be known. Skeptics, relativists, deconstructivists, structuralists, hermeneuticists, and

[56] For a detailed discussion of the problem of assuming a collective singular subject, see Benhabib.

[57] In suggesting that an understanding of cognition as a human practice can help feminist analysis avoid the problems of feminist empiricism and feminist standpoint theories while simultaneously illuminating fruitful strategies of inquiry, I do not mean to suggest that the notion of cognition as a human practice itself could or should supplant feminist investigations of knowledge claims. Feminist inquiry remains as important in the field of epistemology as in any other traditional academic area of investigation, precisely because most contemporary practitioners in these fields, like their predecessors in the Western tradition, suffer from a peculiar form of gender blindness. Even those most sensitive to the politics of knowledge in contexts involving race and class remain remarkably unaware of the unique issues raised by the problem of gender. Feminist analysis serves as a crucial corrective for this acute and pervasive form of masculinist myopia.

critical theorists might all concur about the social construction of cognition, yet come to different conclusions about the nature of truth claims. Within the context of feminist approaches to epistemology, many of the critiques of traditional conceptions of reason have been voiced by feminist postmodernists. Thus it is important to consider whether feminist postmodernism constitutes an adequate epistemology for feminist theory. Such an assessment requires an examination of the theoretical and political implications of postmodernism, as well as a discussion of the light that postmodernism sheds on the question of what can be known.

Discussions of the "situatedness" of knowers suggest that the claims of every knower reflect a particular perspective shaped by social, cultural, political, and personal factors and that the perspective of each knower contains blind spots, tacit presuppositions, and prejudgments of which the individual is unaware.[58] The partiality of individual perspectives in turn suggests that every claim about the world, every account, "can be shown to have left something out of the description of its object and to have put something in which others regard as nonessential."[59] Recognition of the selectivity of cognitive accounts, in terms of conscious and unconscious omission and supplementation, has led some postmodern thinkers to characterize the world in literary terms, to emphasize the fictive elements of "fact," the narrative elements of all discourse—literary, scientific, historical, social, political—and the nebulousness of the distinction between text and reality. The move to intertextuality suggests that the world be treated as text, as a play of signifiers with no determinate meaning, as a system of signs whose meaning is hidden and diffuse, as a discourse that resists decoding because of the infinite power of language to conceal and obfuscate.[60] Postmodernist discourses celebrate the human capacity to misunderstand, to universalize the particular and the idiosyncratic, to privilege the ethnocentric, and to conflate truth with those prejudices that advantage the knower. Postmodernist insights counsel that Truth be abandoned because it is a hegemonic and, hence, destructive illusion.

Postmodernism has much to commend it. Its sensitivity to the hubris of scientific reason has illuminated the manifold ways in which scientism sustains authoritarian tendencies. Its merger of the horizons of philosophical and literary discourses has loosened the

[58] See, e.g., Buker (n. 8 above); and Moi (n. 16 above).

[59] Hayden White, *Tropics of Discourse* (Baltimore: Johns Hopkins University Press, 1978), 3.

[60] For a helpful introduction to and critique of the postmodern shift from world to text, see Megill (n. 53 above).

disciplinary strictures of both traditions and produced creative deconstructions of the tacit assumptions that sustain a variety of unreflective beliefs. Its attentiveness to discourse has heightened our understanding of the integral relations between power and knowledge, and of the means by which particular power/knowledge constellations constitute us as subjects in a determinate order of things. Its refusal to validate univocal interpretations has generated a new appreciation of plurality and has stimulated creative thinking about ways to value difference.

But postmodernism also has a number of defects that militate against the uncritical adoption of all of its tenets into feminist epistemology. Indeed, crucial social and political insights of a critical feminist theory should serve as a corrective to some of the excesses of postmodernism.

The undesirable consequences of the slide into relativism that results from too facile a conflation of world and text is particularly evident when feminist concerns are taken as the starting point. Rape, domestic violence, and sexual harassment (to mention just a few of the realities that circumscribe women's lives) are not fictions or figurations that admit of the free play of signification. The victim's account of these experiences is not simply an arbitrary imposition of a purely fictive meaning on an otherwise meaningless reality. A victim's knowledge of the event may not be exhaustive; indeed, the victim may be oblivious to the fact of premeditation, may not comprehend the motive for the assault, may not know the identity of the assailant. But it would be premature to conclude from the incompleteness of the victim's account that all other accounts (the assailant's, defense attorney's, character witnesses' for the defendant) are equally valid or that there are no objective grounds on which to distinguish between truth and falsity in divergent interpretations. The important point here is not that it is easy to make these determinations or that they can always be made in particular cases but that standards related to the range of human cognitive practices allow us to distinguish between partial views (the inescapable condition of human cognition) and false beliefs, superstitions, irrebuttable presumptions, willful distortions. Although it is often extraordinarily difficult to explicate the standards of evidence, the criteria of relevance, paradigms of explanation, and norms of truth that inform such distinctions, the fact that informed judgments can be made provides sufficient ground to avoid premature plunges into relativism, to insist instead that there are some things that can be known.

The world is more than a text. Theoretical interpretations of the world must operate within different parameters than those of literary criticism. Although both theories of life and theories of literature are necessarily dependent on conceptual schemes that are themselves structured by language and, hence, contestable and contingent, theories of life must deal with more than the free play of signifiers. There is a modicum of permanence within the fluidity of the life-world: traditions, practices, relationships, institutions, and structures persist and can have profound consequences for individual life prospects, constraining opportunities for growth and development, resisting reconstitution, frustrating efforts toward direction and control. It is a serious mistake to neglect the more enduring features of existing institutional structures and practices while indulging the fantasies of freedom afforded by intertextuality. Contentment with relativist perspectivism does not do justice to the need for systematicity in analyses of the structural dimensions of social and political life. Although much can be gained from the recognition that there are many sides to every story and many voices to provide alternative accounts, the escape from the monotony of monologue should not be at the expense of the very notion of truth. The need to debunk scientistic assumptions about the unproblematic nature of the objective world does not require the total repudiation of either external reality or the capacity for critical reflection and rational judgment.[61]

A critical feminist epistemology must avoid both the foundationalist tendency to reduce the multiplicity of reasons to a monolithic "Reason" and the postmodernist tendency to reject all reasons *tout court*. Keenly aware of the complexity of all knowledge claims, it must defend the adoption of a minimalist standard of rationality that requires that belief be apportioned to evidence and that no assertion be immune from critical assessment. Deploying this minimalist standard, feminist analysis can demonstrate the inadequacies of accounts of human nature derived from an evidentiary base of only half the species; it can refute unfounded claims about women's "nature" that are premised on an atheoretical naturalism; it can identify androcentric bias in theories, methods, and concepts and show how this bias undermines explanatory force; it can demonstrate that the numerous obstacles to women's full participation in social, political, and economic life are humanly created and hence

[61] The conception of cognition as a human practice requires a coherence theory of truth. Due to the limitations of space, it is not possible to explore the dimensions of this conception in detail here; nor is it possible to provide a systematic defense of this conception of truth against the charge of relativism. For works that do undertake both those tasks, see Bernstein, *Beyond Objectivism and Relativism* (n. 1 above); Cavell (n. 42 above); Herzog (n. 1 above); and William E. Connolly, *Appearance and Reality in Politics* (Cambridge: Cambridge University Press, 1981).

susceptible to alteration. In providing sophisticated and detailed analyses of concrete situations, feminists can dispel distortions and mystifications that abound in malestream thought.

Based on a consistent belief in and acceptance of fallibility as inescapable and consonant with life in a world of contingencies, feminists need not claim universal, ahistorical validity for their analyses. They need not assert that theirs is the only or the final word on complex questions. In the absence of claims of universal validity, feminist accounts derive their justificatory force from their capacity to illuminate existing social relations, to demonstrate the deficiencies of alternative interpretations, to debunk opposing views. Precisely because feminists move beyond texts to confront the world, they can provide concrete reasons in specific contexts for the superiority of their accounts. Such claims to superiority are derived not from some privileged standpoint of the feminist knower nor from the putative merits of particular intuitions but from the strength of rational argument, from the ability to demonstrate point by point the deficiencies of alternative explanations. At their best, feminist analyses engage both the critical intellect and the world; they surpass androcentric accounts because in their systematicity more is examined and less is assumed.

Postmodernism's retreat to the text has a political dimension not altogether consonant with its self-proclaimed radicalism. There is an unmistakable escapist tendency in the shift to intertextuality, in the move from fact to fiction. The abandonment of reason(s) is accompanied by a profound sense of resignation, a nihilist recognition that there is nothing to do because nothing can be done. At a moment when the preponderance of rational and moral argument sustains prescriptions for women's equality, it is a bit too cruel a conclusion and too reactionary a political agenda to accept that reason is impotent, that equality is impossible. Should postmodernism's seductive text gain ascendancy, it will not be an accident that power remains in the hands of the white males who currently possess it. In a world of radical inequality, relativist resignation reinforces the status quo. For those affronted by the arrogance of power, there are political as well as intellectual reasons to prefer a critical feminist epistemology to a postmodernist one. In confrontations with power, knowledge and rational argumentation alone will not secure victory, but feminists can use them strategically to subvert male dominance and to transform oppressive institutions and practices.

Department of Political Science
University of Louisville

GENDERING SCIENTIFIC AND TECHNOLOGICAL KNOWLEDGE

Political Arithmetic: The Nineteenth-Century Australian Census and the Construction of the Dependent Woman

Desley Deacon

Official statistics, because they are widely disseminated and present a seemingly disinterested outline of socioeconomic conditions, are particularly effective in labeling groups and solidifying boundaries between them. They are, therefore, an ideal political tool in any struggle involving the manipulation of group images. The institutionalization of ascription in the labor market is one such conflict. This article examines the occupational statistics in the censuses of two Australian colonies during the second half of the nineteenth century as social constructs and social agents that developed out of struggles over labor market control. It traces the development in Britain and Australia of two rival methods of classifying women's work, one deriving from the laissez-faire doctrines of classical British liberalism and the other from the newer collectivist social philosophy. I argue that the latter's triumph in Australia at the end of the nineteenth century reflected the interests of male workers in effecting labor market closure and that its adoption was facilitated by the readier acceptance in Australia of collective resistance to market forces. I suggest that the method that eventually prevailed in Australia in effect heightened the boundary between men and women and labeled women as

Earlier versions of this article were presented at the conference of the Sociological Association of Australia and New Zealand in August 1982 and the meeting of the American Sociological Association in August 1983. It was co-recipient of an award from the Australian Political Studies Association for the best research article on women and politics in 1983. I am grateful to Jack Barbalet, Teresa Brennan, Richard Curtin, Robert G. Cushing, Lincoln Day, Catherine Hakim, Terence C. Halliday, John Higley, Bill Rubinstein, and two anonymous reviewers for helpful comments on earlier drafts of this article.

[*Signs: Journal of Women in Culture and Society* 1985, vol. 11, no. 1]

nonworkers during the crucial period of consolidation of modern Australian labor markets, which helped to institutionalize the idea that women were not legitimate competitors for jobs. In this way, the classification system of the census adversely affected women's access to the important distributive mechanism of the labor market and thus contributed to the social construction of the dependent woman.

The Power of Classification

In Australia and most other countries today, the labor force concept is generally accepted as the proper model for identifying those members of the population who "work." This concept, which was adopted for the Australian census in 1966, defines who is in the labor force on the basis of current economic activity. The labor force comprises the employed and the unemployed. The employed are those persons fifteen years old and over who did any work at all for wages, salary, payment, or profit in the week preceding the census, and those who had a job, business, profession, or farm, full-time or part-time, during that period, even if they were temporarily absent from it. The unemployed are those who did not work during the preceding week and who either looked for work or were temporarily laid off without pay for the entire week ("looking for work" is indicated by certain specified activities).

Although the labor force concept provides relatively objective criteria by which to classify a population, it involves definitions of economic activity that are to some extent arbitrary. A wife's work keeping house is not considered economic activity although it could be argued that she receives payment in kind for her services. Investors and landlords are earning money, but they are not considered to be working. Family members who help in a family business without pay for fifteen hours or more a week are defined as workers, but those who help for fourteen hours are not. A person may be ready and willing to work but is not considered unemployed if she has not carried out any of the activities that have been defined as looking for work. When examining the marginal cases in any classificatory system, officials make decisions that allow the importation of values. To this extent, definitions of work indicate the ideologies of their creators.

Interpretation of these definitions by the householder—who, in Australia, is responsible for completing the census form—again allows values to enter the classification system. The "person in charge" must decide, for instance, whether unpaid work carried out by a family member is work for profit or housework, and such decisions are likely to be made according to current ideologies about women's work.

Before the behavioral labor force concept was introduced, classifying occupations was even more open to the interpretations of householders and census officials. Householders were merely asked the "Profession or Occupation" or the "Industry, Trade or Service" of members of their households and were given vague instructions about the line between domestic duties and other occupations. As a result, people were enumerated according to the social perception of their usual occupation. For instance, under this older system a student who did casual work would probably be recorded as a student, whereas under the labor force concept she would be recorded as in the labor force even though she had done only one hour of work during the census week. A housewife who did seasonal agricultural work would be recorded as occupied with domestic duties, whereas a man, having no alternative social definition, would be recorded as an agricultural laborer. Women doing remunerative work in the home interspersed with household tasks would be recorded either as housewives or as workers according to prevailing ideas about what women should be doing. This nonbehavioral approach posed problems for householders, with the result that the task of classifying their womenfolk was often left to census officials.

The collection of occupational statistics provides, therefore, numerous opportunities for imposing definitions on groups of people and their activities, either by the groups themselves, by persons (such as householders) authorized to act on their behalf, or by census officials. This political usefulness of occupational statistics is enhanced by their apparent neutrality, which makes them an effective stalking-horse for ideology. Because of the degree of discretion allowed by the nonbehavioral concept of occupation, a study of census data compiled under this system can tell us as much about what householders and enumerators thought about work as it can about the actual occupations of people.

From "Husband-and-Wife" to Breadwinner and Dependent

The censuses of the Australian colonies of Victoria and New South Wales during the second half of the nineteenth century provided a battleground for two rival conceptions of women as workers. The first, derived from the 1851 British census and the 1861 and 1871 censuses of England and Wales, and ultimately from classical liberal doctrines, saw women as productive workers in the home, whether as housewives or as helpers in a family occupation, and presented an image of marriage as an economic partnership. The other, derived from collectivist doctrines, was accepted in the colonies more decisively than it was in Britain. It saw women's work in the home as unproductive, with the result that women were regarded as naturally dependent on their husbands, who were the sole legitimate breadwinners.

The Australian colonies had as their models during the late nineteenth century the 1851 British census and the censuses of England and Wales and of Scotland from 1861 to 1881.[1] The censuses of Britain and of England and Wales from 1851 to 1871 were under the direction of the great medical statistician, William Farr, who consolidated aims, concepts, and methods that had evolved since the census was introduced in Great Britain in 1801 and stamped them with his own distinctive ideas.[2] In his census work, Farr focused primarily on the size of the population, which was considered a measure of the nation's strength; he assumed that the unit of productive activity was the individual rather than the family; and he assumed a division of labor between men and women in the family that was complementary and equal. The British census had been introduced primarily because of an interest in population size. There was little interest in the activities of the population until 1831, and even then there was no clear differentiation of these activities on the grounds of productivity. Farr's occupational classification of 1851, refined in 1861, was the first official attempt to categorize such activities scientifically, and it was based on a generous conception of productive work that derived from his view of population as "living capital."[3] For Farr, the only unproductive classes were children, the infirm and sick, Gypsies and vagrants, "certain ladies" who "like the lilies of the field, neither toil nor spin," and "as many gentlemen" who "would perhaps find equal difficulty in pointing out anything of value which their head or their hand produce."[4]

1. New South Wales and Victoria held decennial censuses from 1861 to 1901. After federation, the Commonwealth of Australia held censuses in 1911, 1921, 1933, 1947, 1954, and at five-year intervals starting in 1961. Great Britain also held decennial censuses from 1801 to 1851, as did England and Wales together and Scotland separately after 1861 throughout the rest of the nineteenth century.

2. See *Dictionary of National Biography*, s.v. "Farr, William"; Michael J. Cullen, *The Statistical Movement in Early Victorian Britain: The Foundations of Empirical Social Research* (New York: Harvester Press, 1975), pp. 29–43; John M. Eyler, *Victorian Social Medicine: The Ideas and Methods of William Farr* (Baltimore: Johns Hopkins University Press, 1979); William Farr, *A Memorial Volume of Selections from the Reports and Writings of William Farr . . .* , ed. Noel Humphreys (London: Council of the Sanitary Institute, 1885).

3. See *Census of Great Britain, 1851, Population Tables II*, vol. 1 (Parliamentary Papers [hereafter PP] 1852–53, vol. 88, pt. 1), pp. lxxxii–c for Farr's 1851 classification, and pp. lxix–lxxv for history of occupational statistics; for 1861 classification and his ideas on productivity, see "The New Classification of the People according to Their Employments," in *Census of England and Wales, 1861* (PP 1863, vol. 53, pt. 1), pp. 225–48; for his economic ideas, see Eyler, pp. 90–96; and B. F. Kiker, *Human Capital: In Retrospect* (Columbia: University of South Carolina, Bureau of Business and Economic Research, College of Business Administration, 1968), pp. 5–11; quotation from William Farr, "Reports of the Official Delegates, 1863," *Journal of the Statistical Society of London* 26 (December 1863): 412–16, esp. 413, quoted in Eyler, p. 95.

4. *Census of England and Wales, 1861*, p. 225.

Farr's occupational statistics reversed the earlier presumption that productive activity took place in family units. Except for an abortive attempt to report individual occupations in 1801, census takers recorded family occupation up to 1831. Individual occupations of adult males and female domestics were recorded alongside family occupation in 1831, and individual occupations alone for the entire population beginning in 1841.[5] By 1851, the census differentiated the work of family members except in farming and some small businesses, where wives and adult children were assumed to be assisting their husbands and fathers and were automatically recorded in their menfolk's occupational category.[6] Even though the women in these family enterprises were placed in the "Domestic Class" in 1871, they were still distinguished from other wives and daughters.[7]

Although Farr distinguished in most cases between the work of family members, he did not value one sort of work over another; he considered the production of human capital through unpaid domestic labor just as important to the nation as other occupations, and he placed such labor in one of the productive classes along with paid work of a similar kind. In fact, in 1851 Farr stated that domestic work should be the extent of women's activities because "the most important production of a country is its population," and "where the women are much employed from home, the children and parents perish in great numbers."[8] By 1871, however, Farr's appreciation of women's contribution to national prosperity extended to those working outside the home. He observed with apparent approval that women's work was becoming "infinitely diversified" and that "noiselessly, there has been a rapid increase in the numbers and proportions of women engaged specifically in productive work." Propounding a laissez-faire attitude toward women's access to the labor market, Farr remarked that "a married woman of industry and talent aids her husband in his special occupation, or she follows different lines of her own . . . for it is only in a few cases that the whole of a wife's lifetime is filled up with childbearing, nursing and housekeeping"; that "many of the world's finest children are produced by hard-working women"; and that one of the principal questions of the day was whether women should be excluded from the professions or be allowed, "on the principle of free trade," to compete with men. As Farr pointed out, he found "no evidence of idle women."[9]

In painting this picture of Britain as a bustling community of workers, all contributing to the size and strength of the nation, Farr presented

---

5. *Census of Great Britain, 1851, Population Tables I*, vol. 1 (PP 1852–53, vol. 85), pp. ix–xi.

6. *Census of Great Britain, 1851* (n. 3 above), pp. lxxxviii–lxxxix, xci, xciv.

7. *Census of England and Wales, 1871* , vol. 3 (PP 1873, vol. 71, pt. 1), p. xxxv; *Census of England and Wales, 1871*, vol. 4 (PP 1873, vol. 71, pt. 2), p. 81.

8. *Census of Great Britain, 1851* (n. 3 above), p. lxxxviii.

9. *Census of England and Wales, 1871* , vol. 4 (n. 7 above), pp. xli–xlii.

an image of women as legitimate and productive workers inside and outside the home, and of marriage as an economic partnership; indeed, in one section of his 1851 report the head of a family is defined as the "husband-and-wife." This definition, however, was contradicted only a few pages away, where the census report defined the head as "the house-holder, master, husband, or father," apparently for the purpose of administering the census schedule. This administrative definition supplanted the other by 1871.[10] Farr's view of housework as an occupation was innovative in 1851, and it did not survive his resignation in 1880. Nor did his automatic classification of female relatives of farmers and small businessmen in a separate occupational category. In the census of 1881, women occupied with domestic duties and small businessmen's female relatives who were not reported as assisting were included among the "Persons without Specified Occupations" in the "Unoccupied Class."

This was a clear move toward defining women who did not have paid jobs as dependents, although the census reports of 1881 and 1891 were ambivalent about the new classification. The 1881 report stressed that categorizing women in the home as unoccupied was only a technicality—that if these women were taken into account, the proportion of occupied women would be similar to that of men.[11] The census of 1891 encouraged the reporting of women engaged in family enterprises as occupied;[12] it was not until 1911 that any uncertainty about the treatment of women working in the home disappeared.[13] The Scottish census officials, who presented independent reports beginning in 1861, were highly critical of Farr's scheme, and in 1871 eliminated the "Domestic Class" and redistributed its members to show how many were dependent on each occupation.[14] A similar scheme was proposed by Charles Booth, the great social investigator,[15] and a group of economists and social scientists, including Booth, who presented a memorandum to the 1890 Committee on the Census.[16] The Scots, more Malthusian in their fear of population

10. *Census of Great Britain, 1851* (n. 5 above), pp. xli, xxxiv.

11. *Census of England and Wales, 1881*, vol. 4 (PP 1883, vol. 80), pp. 29, 49.

12. *Census of England and Wales, 1891*, vol. 4 (PP 1893–94, vol. 106), pp. 57–58, 138.

13. Catherine Hakim, "Census Reports as Documentary Evidence: The Census Commentaries, 1801–1951," *Sociological Review* 28, no. 3 (1980): 551–80, esp. 557–58.

14. *Census of Scotland, 1861*, vol. 2 (PP 1864, vol. 51), pp. xlii–xlvii; *Census of Scotland, 1871*, vol. 2 (PP 1873, vol. 73), pp. xxxvi–xlviii. In 1881 the Scots returned to the system of England and Wales. I am grateful to F. L. Jones for drawing my attention to the Scottish censuses in his criticism of an earlier draft of this article in "Is It True What They Say about Women? The Census 1801–1911 and Women in the Economy" (Australian National University, Department of Sociology, Research School of Social Sciences, 1983, mimeographed).

15. Charles Booth, "Occupations of the People of the United Kingdom 1801–81," *Royal Statistical Society Journal* 49 (June 1886): 314–435.

16. Committee . . . to inquire into . . . the Census, *Report* (PP 1890, vol. 58), p. 119.

growth,[17] used the breadwinner/dependent distinction, as did Booth, to gain a more accurate picture of areas of deprivation.

In Australia, census officials in both New South Wales and Victoria adopted Farr's classification scheme for their censuses from 1861 to 1881, but neither followed the British model completely. The Australians never dwelt with the same enthusiasm on the importance of domestic work and were more reluctant to assign female relatives to the occupations of their menfolk. They attempted to elicit accurate reporting of women's work by giving the householder more explicit instructions about recording the work of relatives in family enterprises and by requiring him to state specifically if wives and daughters were employed with domestic duties (in the British system such women did not have to state their occupation).[18] Yet many Australian householders still failed to record an occupation for their female relatives, leaving census officials considerable discretion in determining classifications. This discretion could be used, if necessary, for political purposes, and we find that the classification of the work of farmers' and small businessmen's female relatives differed from year to year and from colony to colony even though the form of inquiry and instructions for recording such work were more or less uniform.

In New South Wales in 1861 and in Victoria in 1861 and 1871, apparently only the adult daughters of farmers were automatically recorded as farmers.[19] New South Wales began in 1871 to be concerned with the possible overenumeration of women workers, and from that time no female relatives were assumed to be assisting in family enterprises. This change seems to have been motivated more by the difficulties of getting comparable figures from census to census than by any consistent view of the productivity of women's work.[20] In contrast, Victoria took a clear and opposing position in 1881, when Henry Heylyn Hayter, the newly appointed government statist, or statistician, was completely in charge of the census for the first time.[21] Hayter was influenced by Farr's concern for showing how every member of the population was contributing to its

17. *Census of Scotland, 1861* (n. 14 above), p. xl.

18. *Census of Victoria, 1861, Population Tables, Pt. I, Report* (Melbourne, 1862), p. xxi; *Census of Great Britain, 1851* (n. 5 above), p. cxlvii.

19. *Census of Victoria, 1861, Population Tables, Pt. II, Report* (Melbourne, 1862–63), p. ix, states that the "Agricultural and Pastoral Class" included "farmers' wives, etc., if assisting on farm" and "male and female relatives of farmers living on farms if above 15 years of age and not otherwise described." *New South Wales Census of 1871, Report* (Sydney, 1873), p. xxvii, claims that most female relatives of food and drink sellers and of farmers were included in 1861 in their menfolks' classification, but a note to table 46 (p. lxix) indicates that this is merely an assumption. A comparison of figures for 1861 and 1871 suggests that their 1861 practice was the same as Victoria's.

20. *New South Wales Census of 1871*, p. xxvii.

21. *Australian Dictionary of Biography, 1851–1890*, s.v. "Hayter, Henry Heylyn"; *Dictionary of Australasian Biography*, s.v. "Hayter, Henry Heylyn."

prosperity, and apparently he was not satisfied that the method of self-classification gave an accurate picture of the colony's economic strength. Accordingly, he adopted the practice, which had by then been abandoned in Britain, of automatically counting farmers' wives and daughters and the wives of small businessmen in their menfolk's occupational category. To bring the 1871 statistics in line with those of 1881, he revised the 1871 figures rather arbitrarily, transferring 1,000 hotelkeepers' wives, 20,000 farmers' wives, 500 graziers' wives, 400 graziers' daughters, 400 shoemakers' wives, and 400 butchers' wives from the domestic to the nondomestic category. Hayter tried unsuccessfully to persuade the New South Wales statisticians to do likewise, and their refusal drew acerbic comments on their "peculiar" and outmoded methods.[22]

The conflict between the two colonies was resolved decisively in 1890 when, at an Australia-wide conference of statists, Hayter's method was rejected and all the colonies agreed to follow a new system of classification devised by the statist of New South Wales, T. A. Coghlan, and the Tasmanian statist, R. M. Johnston.[23] This new classification went further than the British censuses of 1881 and 1891 in dividing the population unequivocally into two categories, breadwinners and dependents. In addition, it followed the New South Wales practice of erring on the side of underenumerating as breadwinners the female relatives of farmers and small businessmen. The new system classified women's work as domestic in the absence of a clear statement to the contrary, and classified women

22. Henry Heylyn Hayter, *Census of Victoria, 1881, General Report* (Melbourne, 1883), pp. 105–20, 140–41.

23. Johnston's report on the conference is found in Tasmanian PP 1890, vol. 21, no. 146, pp. 1–19; Coghlan's in T. A. Coghlan, *General Report on the Eleventh Census of New South Wales* (Sydney, 1894), pp. 270–75; Hayter's in Henry Heylyn Hayter, *Census of Victoria, 1891, General Report* (Melbourne, 1893), pp. 190–92. For Coghlan, see *Australian Dictionary of Biography, 1851–1890*, s.v. "Coghlan, T. A."; Arndt, "A Pioneer of National Income Estimates," *Economic Journal* 59 (December 1949): 236–45; Joan M. Cordell, "T. A. Coghlan: Government Statist of New South Wales, 1886–1905" (unpublished manuscript, 1960); Desley Deacon, "The Naturalisation of Dependence: The New Middle Class, the State, and Women Workers, 1830–1930" (Ph.D. diss., Australian National University, 1985); E. C. Fry, "T. A. Coghlan as an Historian" (paper presented at the Australian and New Zealand Association for the Advancement of Science [ANZAAS] Congress, Hobart, Tasmania, 1965), and "Review Article: Labour and Industry in Australia," *Historical Studies* 14, no. 55 (1970): 430–39; Neville Hicks, *"This Sin and Scandal": Australia's Population Debate, 1891–1911* (Canberra: Australian National University Press, 1978); Paul Studenski, *The Income of Nations: Theory, Measurement, and Analysis: Past and Present* (New York: New York University Press, 1958), pp. 136–37. For Johnston, see *Dictionary of Australian Biography*, s.v. "Johnston, R. M."; Robert Mackenzie Johnston, *The R. M. Johnston Memorial Volume: Being a Selection of the Principal Writings in Connection with Geology and with Economic and Social Problems of the Day* (Hobart, Tasmania: Government Printer, 1921). For both, see Craufurd D. W. Goodwin, *Economic Enquiry in Australia* (Durham, N.C.: Duke University Press, 1966), hereafter *Economic Enquiry*, and *The Image of Australia: British Perception of the Australian Economy from the Eighteenth to the Twentieth Century* (Durham, N.C.: Duke University Press, 1974).

doing domestic work as dependents, a category that embraced "all persons dependent upon relatives or *natural guardians*, including wives, children, and others not otherwise engaged in pursuits for which remuneration is paid; and all persons depending upon private charity, or whose support is a burthen on the public revenue" (italics mine).[24]

These alternative methods of enumeration conveyed very different images of women. Hayter's addition of approximately 23,000 women to their male relatives' occupational categories in 1871 represented a major reclassification of women from domestic to nondomestic work in an adult female population of 177,000. In 1891, the number of women recorded in the farming sector in Victoria dropped by 32,000 from its 1881 level, in an adult female population of 350,000. In contrast, the total number of women recorded as doing nondomestic work fell by only 4,000, which indicates that the 1891 method covered up a sizable movement of women into paid work (table 1). The New South Wales method yielded participation rates of between 24 and 29 percent for the years 1871 to 1901, whereas Hayter's more generous method gave participation rates of 41 and 43 percent in 1871 and 1881 (table 2). By one method women were seen as minor economic actors, by the other as important contributors to the nation's prosperity.

Statistical Manipulation and Colonial Rivalry

The choices that these colonial statisticians made concerning the categorization of women's work appear to have been political ones. There was no apparent connection between changes in the organization of work and changes in the type of classification system used. The two colonies were almost identical in size, culture, politics, and degree of industrialization, yet each espoused a different method. Britain, at a similar stage of industrialization, used the method the Australians rejected in 1891 and was more tentative in taking up the new system, even though the British economy was much more developed. The Australians were not merely following British practice; until 1891 New South Wales hardly changed the classification scheme it had adopted from the 1851 British census, except to alter the way in which women working in family enterprises were enumerated in 1871, ten years before this change was made in England and Wales. The Victorian statist, Hayter, classified the work of such women in 1881 by a method England and Wales had abandoned in 1871; in advocating its continuation in 1891, he lagged far behind British practice. The New South Wales and Tasmanian innovators, Coghlan and Johnston, were prepared to take up the distinction between dependents

24. Coghlan, pp. 270–75, esp. p. 272.

Table 1

Women Reported as Engaged in Nondomestic Work in Victoria and New South Wales,
1861–1901

	Female Population over 15	Engaged in Nondomestic Work[a]			
		Total, Male and Female	Female	Total Farming, Male and Female	Female Farming
1861:					
Victoria[b]	124,833	251,627	38,702	50,301	7,118
New South Wales[b]..	86,200	161,214	28,776	53,902	6,986
1871:					
Victoria 1[b]	177,200	294,882	49,455	61,427	3,618
Victoria 2[c]	177,200	317,582	72,155	82,327	24,518
New South Wales 1[b]	124,862	204,226	30,411	64,929	2,027
New South Wales 2[b]	124,862	210,226	36,411	70,929	8,027
New South Wales 3[d]	124,862	207,693	36,373	70,929	8,027
1881:					
Victoria[b]	245,520	376,965	104,789	119,527	42,332
New South Wales 1[b]	192,816	312,254	49,559[e]	76,792	1,905
New South Wales 2[b]	192,816	318,140	55,559[e]	86,603[f]	8,905
New South Wales 3[d]	192,816	317,654	54,963[e]	86,603[f]	8,905
1891:					
Victoria 1[b]	346,586	484,073	100,984	97,778	10,842
Victoria 2[d]	346,586	493,977	114,229	97,778	10,842
New South Wales 1[b]	302,793	459,054	83,239	110,837	12,114
New South Wales 2[d]	302,793	471,887	89,502	110,862	12,114
1901:					
Victoria 1[b]	394,770	527,048	142,553	126,840	24,950
Victoria 2[d]	394,770	538,986	146,083	126,840	24,950
New South Wales 1[b]	404,245	549,027	103,929	127,456	4,614
New South Wales 2[d]	404,245	564,799	113,396	127,661	4,615

SOURCE.—Decennial censuses of Victoria and New South Wales, 1861–1901.

[a]Figures for work force for all ages because pre-1891 censuses did not give consistent breakdowns of occupational statistics by age. "Farming" includes grazing, agriculture, and dairying.

[b]My calculations based on published figures made as consistent as possible with post-1966 census figures and post-1911 figures given by Leonard Broom and F. Lancaster Jones on pp. 121–32 of *Opportunity and Attainment in Australia* (Canberra: Australian National University, 1967) by removal of retired persons, pensioners, and persons living on capital and inclusion of the unemployed and all but contemplative religious orders. Retired persons, etc., can be identified in New South Wales from 1891 by the category "Grade Not Applicable." Victoria did not use this category, so its numbers are probably inflated by comparison. I usually add the large "Not Stated" category to the work force as references in the census texts indicate this usually comprised adults and often contained numbers of unemployed; New South Wales in 1861 was an important exception. New South Wales 2 for 1871 and 1881 are based on Coghlan's revised figures of 1891; see text pp. 39–40.

[c]My calculations based on Hayter's revised figures of 1881; see text p. 34.

[d]Published figures based on Coghlan's 1891 system. New South Wales figures for 1871 and 1881 were revised in 1891; see text pp. 39–40. Coghlan regularly omitted the "Not Stated" category from the work force and included retired persons, etc. His 1861 figures are the same as mine because we treat the "Not Stated" category similarly that year; see n. b above. The Victorians in 1891 and 1901 gave a "Not Stated" figure but stated that it comprised mainly breadwinners, so it has been included in the work force figure in my table.

[e]There was an increase of only 6,000 in the total female work force, although 7,000 were added to the female farming figures because 1,000 women were removed from the commercial category. For differences between my figures and Coghlan's see nn. b and d above. The discrepancy between the increase in the female work force and the total male and female work force in New South Wales 1 and 3 is caused by minor differences between different sources of published figures.

[f]Coghlan also moved 2,811 males from other work force categories to the farming work force.

Table 2

Reported Participation Rates of Women Engaged in Nondomestic Work in Victoria and New South Wales, 1861–1901

	Participation Rates[a] (%)
1861:	
Victoria[a]	31
New South Wales[a]	33
1871:	
Victoria 1	28
Victoria 2	41
New South Wales 1	24
New South Wales 2	29
New South Wales 3	29
1881:	
Victoria	43
New South Wales 1	26
New South Wales 2	29
New South Wales 3	29
1891:	
Victoria 1	29
Victoria 2	33
New South Wales 1	27
New South Wales 2	30
1901:	
Victoria 1	36
Victoria 2	37
New South Wales 1	26
New South Wales 2	28

SOURCE.—Decennial censuses of Victoria and New South Wales, 1861–1901.

[a]See table 1, nn. a–d. Compare these female labor force participation rates to those for Australia as a whole in later years: 1911, 25 percent; 1921, 23 percent; 1933, 25 percent; 1947, 25 percent; 1954, 26 percent; 1961, 29 percent; 1966, 35 percent; 1971, 37 percent; 1976, 44 percent. These rates are based on those over fifteen years of age in the work force. The 1911–76 rates are calculated from Leonard Broom and F. Lancaster Jones, *Opportunity and Attainment in Australia* (Canberra: Australian National University Press, 1976), pp. 121–32; and the censuses of Australia for 1954, 1971, and 1976.

and workers that was suggested by British economists and social scientists and by earlier Scottish census officials—a distinction the census office of England and Wales rejected in 1890.[25] But the Australians adopted only the form and not the substance of the distinction; they did not use it to provide detailed information on the condition of different classes, which had been its original purpose. It seems, therefore, that the colonial statisticians were selecting from the alternatives available those classification systems that served their own interests and fitted with their own social philosophies.

25. Committee . . . to inquire into . . . the Census (n. 16 above), p. 121.

This statistical manipulation has to be understood in the context of colonial rivalry and the interrelations of the British and Australian economies. A major preoccupation of colonial governments during this period was the promotion of their colony to prospective British investors, and an important part of the work of the official statisticians was to convince Britain of their own colony's economic strength. Special offices of government statist were set up in Victoria in 1874 and New South Wales in 1886 with this object in view. Hayter in Victoria and Coghlan in New South Wales each used his office to disseminate information and propaganda about his colony in a rivalry that was exacerbated by their very different social philosophies.[26] In this competition for British investment, each used the classification of women's work that projected the most flattering image of his colony.

The rivalry between Hayter and Coghlan can be seen as a crystallization of the great late nineteenth-century debate between the proponents of laissez-faire economics and individualism on the one hand and state intervention and collectivism on the other. This debate was itself a source of tension between the colonies and British investors. Many British journals expressed concern about the increasingly divergent social and economic philosophies of the Australian colonies and their mother country. Through protectionist policies, increasing government intervention, immigration restrictions, and a general "excess" of democracy, the colonies were contravening laissez-faire doctrines. In the late 1880s, Britain's distrust of these trends and its fears of an approaching economic collapse intensified, in part because of growing unease about worker productivity under "State Socialism."[27]

Hayter and Coghlan responded to these British fears in different ways. A generation older than Coghlan, born into a well-connected British family and educated at a leading English public school, Hayter shared the assumptions of the British. He presented his statistics in conformity with the methods introduced by Farr, making his case for Victoria's progress within the framework of orthodox liberal economics. Accordingly, he used what discretion he had in the classification of women's work to depict a large and expanding work force. In contrast, Coghlan, who fitted the *Westminster Review*'s description of the colonist who demanded "our own science of wealth, our own theory of progress,"[28] was passionate in his attack on many laissez-faire assumptions, especially those concerning the labor market. Australian-born, of Irish-Catholic background, and

26. See Goodwin, *Economic Enquiry* and *Image of Australia* (n. 23 above). This and the following paragraph draw heavily on Goodwin's work. The interpretation concerning Coghlan and Hayter is mine.

27. Goodwin, *Image of Australia* (n. 23 above), pp. 122–35, 160–84.

28. "Democratic Government in Victoria," *Westminster Review* 33, no. 2 (April 1868): 481–523, quoted in Goodwin, *Image of Australia* (n. 23 above), p. 130.

the son of a builder of fluctuating fortunes, he had to make his own way in the world, and he trained as an engineer in the public service. His less privileged, native-born background gave him a political understanding of the Australian economy and labor market. He was sympathetic to state intervention and to the collectivist strategies of trade unions and professionals, identifying these strategies with his country's well-being and its superiority over the countries of Europe. He abandoned Hayter's and Farr's idea that a nation's prosperity was measured by the size and activity of its population and based his case for the progress of New South Wales on the quality of the working population and the standard of living it enjoyed. The uncertain occupational status of farmers' and small businessmen's female relatives was useful to his purposes as it was to Hayter's.

"A Political Economy Better Suited for the Working-man"

Coghlan's *General Report* on the 1891 census of New South Wales, which introduced the breadwinner/dependent distinction, articulated his new measure of the colony's prosperity and demonstrated its relationship to the image of women conveyed in the occupational statistics. In an essay on the employment of women in the report, Coghlan argued that both women's contributions to family economies and their competition for jobs lowered the wages of men and the community's standard of living. A high standard of living and good-quality workmen were found, he argued, where men had to support families, where competition was kept in check, and where workers were motivated to strike and organize to maintain or increase their wages. Therefore, he concluded, "The large employment of women in gainful pursuits is not a matter of gratulation." Instead, "it may . . . with some degree of certitude, be asserted that the condition of a country can in some measure be gauged by the number of such women as are compelled to seek occupations other than in their domestic sphere."[29]

Coghlan's conclusions about working women's impact on national prosperity led him to repudiate Hayter's assumption that "the sum of the male and female workers compared with the whole population is a measure of the relative advance made by the community in regard to productive or wealth-giving pursuits" and to characterize the movement of women into work outside the home as a matter for alarm. He was concerned, therefore, to depict an economy in which few women worked and the numbers of working women were not increasing. To this end, he revised figures from previous censuses to show that women had not replaced men as breadwinners and that their participation rate had not grown; he managed at one point to make female breadwinners disappear

29. Coghlan (n. 23 above), pp. 276–79, esp. p. 278.

altogether through what can only be described as statistical sleight of hand; and, most significantly, he advocated the widespread adoption of the minimal method of categorizing as breadwinners female relatives working in family enterprises.[30]

Classifying the work of farmers' female relatives was crucial in Coghlan's argument. Since one-quarter of the working men were farmers, classifying their wives or daughters as breadwinners could present an image of New South Wales contrary to the one he wished to convey. With his method of enumeration, Coghlan could report that only a small number of women assisted on farms and account for this by "the fact that domestic duties take up the whole of their time."[31] That this was not necessarily the case was suggested, however, by the Victorian statist's *Census Report* for the same year. There Hayter revealed that the new method for classifying farmers' female relatives was as much a deliberate act in the service of a particular image of Australia as were his own changes in 1881:

> Although no doubt the female relatives of farmers, if living on the farm, attend as a rule, to the lighter duties of the poultryyard and dairy, it was felt by the Conference [of statists] that the statement that so many females were engaged in agricultural pursuits would create an impression elsewhere that women were in the habit of working in the fields as they were in some of the older countries of the world, but certainly are not in Australia. It was therefore decided not to class any woman as engaged in agricultural pursuits except those respecting whom words were entered expressing that they were so occupied, the others to be classed in the same way as other women respecting whom no employment was entered—under the head of "Domestic Duties."[32]

Coghlan's new approach to the prosperity of the nation was informed by his sympathy for collective action in the labor market and the quality of workingmen such action produced. In rejecting the measures of Hayter and Farr, he was abandoning a laissez-faire faith in the "invisible hand" and attempting to develop what the *Westminster Review* called "a political economy better fitted for the working-man."[33] In asserting the benefits to all of a political stance by workingmen, he was advocating for the worker the injunction of the Australian nationalist magazine the *Bulletin* that "instead of figuring at the cannibal repast, trussed and

30. Ibid., pp. 276, 279, 281.

31. Ibid., pp. 280–81.

32. Hayter, *Census of Victoria, 1891* (n. 23 above), p. 192.

33. "Democratic Government" (n. 28 above), quoted in Goodwin, *Image of Australia* (n. 23 above), p. 131.

roasted on a dish," Australia should "sit down among the guests—but at the place of honour, with an appetite sharpened by the struggle for existence."[34]

The Victims of the "Cannibals' Repast"

Among the victims of the cannibals' feast, however, were working women. Coghlan's view of the nation's prosperity contained a number of implicit assumptions about woman's place and women's economic contributions. His classification of housewives as dependents and his under-enumeration of women working in family enterprises as breadwinners placed much of women's work outside the definition of economic activity. At this time, when Australia was beginning to industrialize but most work was still carried out in family enterprises,[35] the potential impact of such a conception of women's work was great. There was a large number of women whose work could be classified as either domestic or nondomestic, and the decision to classify doubtful cases as domestic and to consider domestic workers dependent meant that most Australian women were labeled nonworkers during the crucial period when the modern labor market was being established.[36]

These census definitions undoubtedly made an important contribution to the way the larger public viewed women as workers. The enormous interest in statistics in the late nineteenth century, their extensive publication in popular form, and the powerful position of statisticians as advisers to governments and expert commentators in public forums meant that men such as Coghlan had considerable influence on elite and popular opinion.[37] Women's contribution to the maintenance and reproduction of other workers became invisible, and, as economic activity moved more and more out of the family, their work was discounted as consumption rather than production.[38] Informal activities carried out in

34. "Protection—a National Necessity," *Bulletin* 9, no. 433 (1888): 4, quoted in Goodwin, *Economic Enquiry* (n. 23 above), p. 344.

35. Coghlan (n. 23 above), p. 280, remarks on the number of small employers and people working on their own account.

36. For the problems of recording women's work in developing countries, see Ruth B. Dixon, "Women in Agriculture: Counting the Labor Force in Developing Countries," *Population and Development Review* 8, no. 3 (September 1982): 539–66.

37. See Cordell (n. 23 above) for Coghlan's influence.

38. The nature of productivity and the productivity of housework are continuing subjects of debate. See Studenski (n. 23 above), pp. 11–12, 177; Simon Kuznets, *National Income and Its Composition, 1919–1938* (New York: National Bureau of Economic Research, 1941), pp. 6–21; John Kenneth Galbraith, *Economics and the Public Purpose* (Boston: Houghton Mifflin Publishing Co., 1973), pp. 29–37; Heidi Hartmann, "The Unhappy Marriage of Marxism and Feminism: Towards a More Progressive Union," in *Women and Revolution: A*

the home that might have fitted the definition of "breadwinning" also disappeared from public consciousness; Australian studies suggest that such activities were common but that they were seldom seen as work.[39] As the earlier heroic vision of the "colonial helpmeet" faded, farmers' wives lost public visibility, even though many worked just as hard.[40] As A. J. Jaffe and Charles Stewart conclude, "If the culture pretends that women do not work, then the women [or the men on their behalf] tend to reply that they have no occupation . . . regardless of what work they may actually do."[41] The snowballing effect of this public definition can be seen in the rapid decline in the percentage of women recorded in the farming work force after 1891 and the rapid rise after the introduction of the labor force concept in 1966 and the impact of the women's movement of the early 1970s (table 3, esp. n. a).

When one considers this power of definition, it seems likely that the labeling of women as nonworkers in this period had a strong prescriptive impact on their participation in paid work. Australian women had made important gains with regard to divorce law and access to higher education in the 1880s, and in the 1890s and the early 1900s they won the vote. They had begun to move into industry and the professions and had increased their participation in the public bureaucracy and teaching. Active unions emerged in some of women's main avenues of work, and public servants in New South Wales and the newly formed Commonwealth gained equal

---

Discussion of the Unhappy Marriage of Marxism and Feminism, ed. Lydia Sargent (Boston: South End Press, 1981), pp. 1–41. Renewed interest in the valuation of household work is found in Milton Moss, ed., *The Measurement of Economic and Social Performance* (New York: National Bureau of Economic Research, 1973); Martin Murphy, "Comparative Estimates of the Value of Household Work in the United States for 1976," *Review of Income and Wealth* 28, no. 2 (March 1982): 29–43.

39. Jill Julius Matthew, "Deconstructing the Masculine Universe: The Case of Women's Work," in *Third Women and Labour Conference Papers* (Salisbury East: South Australian College of Advanced Education, 1982), pp. 474–82; Patrick Mullins, "Theoretical Perspectives on Australian Urbanisation. 1. Material Components in the Reproduction of Australian Labour Power," *Australian and New Zealand Journal of Sociology* 17, no. 1 (March 1981): 65–76; Ann Aungles, "Family Economics in Transition: Adelaide Women in the Depression" (paper delivered at ANZAAS Congress, Perth, Western Australia, 1983).

40. See, e.g., Lino, "Women Who Work," *Argus* (Melbourne) (January 13, 1902). Research in other countries shows the underreporting of such work in censuses; see Lenore Davidoff, "The Separation of Home and Work? Landladies and Lodgers in Nineteenth and Twentieth Century England," in *Fit Work for Women*, ed. Sandra Burman (London: Croom Helm, 1979), pp. 64–97; Martha Norby Fraundorf, "The Labor Force Participation of Turn-of-the-Century Married Women," *Journal of Economic History* 39 (June 1979): 401–17, esp. 402–3; D. Ian Pool, "Changes in Canadian Female Labour Force Participation, and Some Possible Implications for Conjugal Power," *Journal of Comparative Family Studies* 9 (Spring 1978): 41–52, esp. 43–45, 50–51.

41. A. J. Jaffe and Charles D. Stewart, *Manpower Resources and Utilization: Principles of Working Force Analysis* (New York: John Wiley & Sons, 1951), pp. 452–53.

Table 3

Women as Percentage of Farming Work Force in Victoria and New South Wales, 1861–1901

	Women in Farming Work Force[a] (%)
1861:	
Victoria	14
New South Wales	13
1871:	
Victoria 1	6
Victoria 2	30
New South Wales 1	3
New South Wales 2	11
New South Wales 3	11
1881:	
Victoria	35
New South Wales 1	2
New South Wales 2	...
New South Wales 3	10
1891:	
Victoria 1	11
Victoria 2	11
New South Wales 1	11
New South Wales 2	11
1901:	
Victoria 1	20
Victoria 2	20
New South Wales 1	4
New South Wales 2	4

Source.—Decennial censuses of Victoria and New South Wales, 1861–1901.

[a]See table 1, nn. a–d. Compare these percentages to those for Australia as a whole in later years: 1911, 4 percent; 1921, 2 percent; 1933, 4 percent; 1947, 5 percent; 1954, 6 percent; 1961, 8 percent; 1966, 16 percent; 1971, 17 percent; 1976, 32 percent. These rates calculated from Leonard Broom and F. Lancaster Jones, *Opportunity and Attainment in Australia* (Canberra: Australian National University Press, 1976), pp. 121–32; and the censuses of Australia for 1954, 1971, and 1976.

pay in 1895 and 1902 respectively.[42] In these campaigns women received the support of liberal men, but a new climate of opinion, of which the 1891 census was a harbinger, slowed down this movement toward social and economic equality for women.

42. J. S. Baker, "The Women Telegraphists of Melbourne and Their Union, 1895–1920," *Recorder* (February 1978): 6–13; Judith Biddington, "The Role of Women in the Victorian Education Department, 1872–1925" (M.Ed. diss., Melbourne University, 1977); Desley Deacon, "State Formation, the New Middle Class and the Dual Labor Market. Women Clerks in an Australian Bureaucracy 1880–1930," in *Women and Politics: Activism, Attitudes and Office-holding*, vol. 2 of *Research in Politics and Society*, ed. Gwen Moore and Glenna Spitze (Greenwich, Conn.: JAI Press, 1985, forthcoming); M. Hutton Neve, *"This Mad Folly": The History of Australia's Pioneer Women Doctors* (Sydney: Library of Australian History, 1980); Margaret James, "Political Liberalism and the Oppression of Women,"

The ideas conveyed in the census were both a symptom of and a contribution to a new "conservative progressivism" that opposed women's equal participation in the labor market at the same time that its reformism in other areas earned Australia a reputation as the social laboratory of the world between 1890 and 1920. The practice of barring married women from occupations increased after 1887. Gains made by single women in areas such as the New South Wales and Commonwealth public services were eroded immediately by the establishment or intensification of dual labor markets.[43] Low pay for women (about 50 percent of the male wage) was institutionalized by the state industrial relations machinery.[44] These developments encouraged women to regard domesticity as a preferable alternative to the labor market. As one woman announced to her boss when she left work in 1909, "I'm going to better myself, I'm going to get married."[45]

There is little evidence, however, that women ceased to see themselves as legitimate workers. Women's groups continued to press for equal pay and opportunity, arguing that women's expenses and responsibilities were similar to men's.[46] Many women gave up work reluctantly on marrying in response to pressure from husbands, the threat of societal disapproval, or legal compulsion. Their considerable efforts to remain in the home even when they had to support their families seemed to be similarly motivated.[47] Women on the land were under no illusions about themselves; farmers' wives interviewed in 1902 by Melbourne's newspaper, the *Argus*, described how they cleared land, planted, plowed, harvested, and milked in an endless round of labor. As one remarked, "When we marry we've no time for nonsense, no time for anything else but work."[48] Their husbands gratefully acknowledged their necessary con-

---

Australia 1888 Bulletin 4 (May 1980): 28–36; Farley Kelly, "The 'Woman Question' in Melbourne, 1880–1914" (Ph.D diss., Melbourne University, 1982); Edna Ryan and Anne Conlon, *The Gentle Invaders: Australian Women at Work, 1788–1974* (Melbourne: Nelson, 1975); Dianne Scott, "Woman Suffrage: The Movement in Australia," *Journal of the Royal Australian Historical Society* 53, pt. 4 (December 1967): 299–322; Noeline Williamson, "The Feminization of Teaching in New South Wales: A Historical Perspective," *Australian Journal of Education* 27, no. 1 (April 1983): 33–44; Ailsa Zainu'ddin, "The Admission of Women to the University of Melbourne, 1869–1903," in *Melbourne Studies in Education*, ed. S. Murray-Smith (Melbourne: Melbourne University Press, 1973), pp. 50–106.

43. Desley Deacon, "The Employment of Women in the Commonwealth Public Service: The Creation and Reproduction of a Dual Labour Market," *Australian Journal of Public Administration* 41, no. 3 (September 1982): 232–50, and "State Formation," and "The Naturalisation of Dependence" (n. 23 above).

44. Ryan and Conlon.

45. Aungles, p. 7.

46. Deacon, "State Formation" (n. 42 above).

47. Aungles (n. 39 above); Ros Byrne, "Occupation—Secretary: An Historical Perspective" (paper delivered at Chisholm Institute of Technology, Melbourne, 1982), pp. 18–23.

48. Lino (n. 40 above).

tribution to the family economy, but even family members often did not recognize it when women supported their families by informal activities in the home. In one study, for example, a son was shocked when his mother took a factory job: "He said, 'Fancy my mother going out to work.' 'Yes I said, I've worked all my life'—*he didn't realise what I'd been doing you know.*"[49]

The new invisibility of women's household work and the lack of legitimacy accorded the paid work of married women helped clear the way for a prescriptive emphasis on housework and mothering as the exclusive duties of women. Middle-class experts castigated women for not carrying out these duties adequately and exhorted them to better efforts.[50] Despite such discussions of women's work in the home, the actual labor performed was ignored, even though most women were probably doing more of it in their increasingly servantless homes.[51] The experts' prescriptions were buttressed by the turn-of-the-century concern for a larger and better-nourished population, a concern that was heralded by Coghlan's 1900 and 1903 articles on the decline of the birth rate in New South Wales.[52] Adoption of the breadwinner/dependent distinction in the 1891 census helped, therefore, to circumscribe the socially approved activities of women. In doing so, it helped to consolidate a dual labor market in which women's marginal position was reproduced in a downward spiral of disadvantage.[53]

Conclusions

This study has examined the role of nineteenth-century Australian occupational statistics in the social construction of the dependent female

49. Aungles (n. 39 above), p. 19.

50. Bob Bessant, "Domestic Science Schools and Woman's Place," *Australian Journal of Education* 20, no. 1 (March 1976): 1–9; Desley Deacon, "Taylorism in the Home: The Medical Profession, the Infant Welfare Movement and the Deskilling of Women," *Australian and New Zealand Journal of Sociology* 21, no. 2 (July 1985), in press; Paige H. Porter, "The State, the Family, and Education: Ideology, Reproduction, and Resistance in Western Australia, 1900–1929," *Australian Journal of Education* 27, no. 2 (August 1983): 121–36; Kerreen M. Reiger, *The Disenchantment of the Home: Modernizing the Australian Family, 1880–1940* (Melbourne: Oxford University Press, 1985).

51. Beverley Kingston, *My Wife, My Daughter, and Poor Mary Ann: Women and Work in Australia* (West Melbourne: Nelson, 1977), pp. 29–55.

52. T. A. Coghlan, *Childbirth in New South Wales: A Study in Statistics* (Sydney: New South Wales Government Printer, 1900), and *The Decline of the Birth-Rate of New South Wales and other Phenomena of Childbirth: An Essay in Statistics* (Sydney: New South Wales Government Printer, 1903); Hicks (n. 23 above). For a similar concern in Britain and its connection with imperialism, see Anna Davin, "Imperialism and Motherhood," *History Workshop* 5 (Spring 1978): 9–65; Jane Lewis, *The Politics of Motherhood: Child and Maternal Welfare in England, 1900–1939* (London: Croom Helm, 1980).

53. For public employment, see Deacon, "Employment of Women" (n. 43 above).

and has suggested that the classification of women as dependents at the end of the century was in part a political act carried out in the interests of working-class men for the purpose of labor market closure. In the hands of the British statistician William Farr and his Australian follower Henry Hayter the classification system presented women as productive workers inside and outside of the home and as legitimate competitors in the labor market. In the hands of T. A. Coghlan, the system presented women as dependents whose rightful place was in the home; Coghlan's scheme was linked quite explicitly with a defense of collective action for labor market control.

This article has examined a particular instance of the ways in which class and gender have interacted to construct current sex roles. It suggests that the classification system adopted in the Australian colonies in 1891 was both a symptom of and a contribution to a heightening of differences between the sexes, which had previously been deemphasized. The earlier trend had been influenced by the laissez-faire doctrines of classical liberalism, which sought to remove traditional privilege and to open opportunity for all on the market principle. The subsequent movement was part of the resurgence of collectivism and its concomitant, market closure. The activities of Farr and Coghlan illustrate these two movements nicely. Both men were of working-class background and were trained as professionals, Farr in medicine and Coghlan in engineering. Both found power and influence through the expansion of the state bureaucracy. But each fought for very different labor market principles. Farr was one of that group of medical reformers who campaigned for the abolition of corporate privileges for the elite of the profession, and he continued throughout his life to defend the ideals associated with free markets.[54] Coghlan was of another generation, one disillusioned with or disbelieving in the "invisible hand," and he endorsed the principle of market restriction advocated by craft unions and increasingly by professional groups. In Frank Parkin's terms, the response of Farr's generation to privilege was usurpation, while the response of Coghlan's was closure.[55] Further research is needed on the changing material conditions and political resources of labor market participants in the second half of the nineteenth century in order to determine why usurpation was the appropriate strategy in one period and closure in another.[56] This will bring us closer to understanding the circumstances under which ascription becomes an important determinant of labor market participation.

54. Eyler (n. 2 above), pp. 3–4, 23–27.

55. Frank Parkin, *Marxism and Class Theory: A Bourgeois Critique* (London: Tavistock, 1979).

56. See Desley Deacon, "Women, Bureaucracy and the Dual Labour Market: An Historical Analysis," in *Public Sector Administration: New Perspectives*, ed. Alexander Kouzmin (Melbourne: Longman Cheshire, 1983), pp. 165–82 for an initial attempt.

Finally, this study reminds us of the pitfalls of comparing women's work force participation rates over time and between countries, since female occupational statistics are so sensitive to political and social influences. It is clear that the low numbers of women reported in the Australian work force between 1891 and 1961, and their increasing numbers since the introduction of the labor force concept in 1966, must be evaluated in this light. Interestingly, participation rates of women in nondomestic work derived from Farr's British censuses and Hayter's Victorian census, which were conducted under the influence of laissez-faire philosophies, are very close to those reported in recent years in Australia. In both cases, high reported participation rates are associated with increased legitimation of women as workers (table 2).[57] The symmetry, even when interpreted cautiously, does suggest that our view of women as economic actors may have been distorted in the intervening years. This does not mean, however, that reported figures need to be discarded altogether. This study has shown that a careful examination of census materials and of their social construction allows us to compile more accurate and comparable data.[58] As Robert Smuts wrote in 1960 concerning the female labor force in the United States, "When the numbers have been evaluated by the normal rules of historical evidence, they can be used as clues, hints, and sometimes even as facts."[59]

Department of Sociology
Australian National University

57. See Hakim (n. 13 above), p. 559 for rates for England and Wales.
58. See also ibid.
59. Robert W. Smuts, "The Female Labor Force: A Case Study in the Interpretation of Historical Statistics," *Journal of the American Statistical Association* 55, no. 289 (March 1960): 71–79, esp. 79.

Women's Voices in Nineteenth-Century Medical Discourse: A Step toward Deconstructing Science

Nancy M. Theriot

OR THE LAST DECADE, feminist scholars from various disciplinary perspectives have been reconceptualizing the ways in which medical science affects gender categories and is itself a gendered practice. Women's historians have moved away from the victimization model that dominated early studies of women patients and the male medical establishment and have begun to view medicine as more complicated and less villainous than previous studies had assumed. Similarly, the notion that nineteenth-century medicine was tainted by its maleness and that women patients could expect a different kind of care from women physicians has been challenged, particularly by the work of Regina Morantz-Sanchez. Feminists working in literary criticism also have pointed out how historically medical discourse has been a gendered discourse and, along with theorists working from the perspective of philosophy, have suggested ways to view the interaction between a dominant male discourse and women's minority-positioned subjectivities.

In spite of this work on the relationship between gender and science, however, each of us has a disciplinary blind spot that renders unseeable the best insights of our colleagues in other fields. Among many literary critics and philosophers, for example, the victimization model and the perception of medicine as a male system of knowledge/power still persist (see Showalter 1981, 1987; and Digby 1989). And, because history is perhaps the most antitheoretical of the disciplines, few women's historians make use of the theoretical models developed by critics, philosophers, and anthropologists that would allow us a way to problematize language and bodies.[1]

I want to thank my colleagues Ann Allen, John Cumbler, and Julia Dietrich for reading earlier drafts of this essay and the University of Louisville College of Arts and Sciences for providing grant support for this research.

[1] Women's historians who consciously make use of theoretical models include Jordanova 1980, 1989; Smith-Rosenberg 1985; Riley 1988; and Scott 1988.

[*Signs: Journal of Women in Culture and Society* 1993, vol. 19, no. 1]

For the past few years I have been reading nineteenth-century medical texts on women's nervousness and mental illness within an eclectic and evolving theoretical framework. I began with the assumption that medical writing would both reflect the ideas of the extramedical culture and prescribe a narrow field for sane or "normal" female behavior: in other words, that gender shapes science, which then reinforces gender. I also assumed that women patients were not "victims" of medical science but instead were able to use it to their advantage in their domestic power struggles. Both of these assumptions were conclusions of Carroll Smith-Rosenberg's early study of hysteria (1972), and I wanted to elaborate upon them by looking at a larger sample of medical writing. I read systematically through articles and monographs on women's insanity and nervousness as well as the editorials and book reviews in the major psychiatric, gynecological, and neurological journals of nineteenth-century American medicine. And the more I read, the more I doubted the simplicity of my original assumptions. The medical establishment did not present the unity I expected, women physicians differed more from their male colleagues than I anticipated, and, most surprising of all, women patients took on a presence of their own through physicians' recordings of their voices in case studies. My reading of nonhistorians such as Mary Poovey, Susan Bordo, Michel Foucault (whom many historians do not consider a "real" historian), Donna Haraway, Brian Turner, and Arthur Kleinman—to name a few—gradually led me to create another framework for a more complex and satisfying reading of the nineteenth-century material.[2]

Looking, then, at the late nineteenth-century medical discourse on women's insanity and nervousness from an interdisciplinary as opposed to a narrowly historical perspective, my purpose is to suggest that nineteenth-century medical science was a site of competing definitions of both gender and science and that women participated in the gender/science interaction as physicians and, more significantly, as patients. Specifically, I will argue that there was lively debate among nineteenth-century physicians over both gender and science; that women physicians, for professional, gender-specific reasons, articulated a self-interested view of women's insanity and nervousness; and that women patients were active participants in the process of medicalizing *woman*.

This reading of nineteenth-century medical discourse as a set of complex, multiauthored texts depends on an understanding of illness and disease as separate, mutually influential categories. Although Smith-Rosenberg and other feminist writers have treated illness and disease as

---

[2] See Foucault 1967, 1972, 1973, 1980; Kleinman 1980, 1986; Turner 1984; Poovey 1988; Bordo 1989; Haraway 1989a, 1989b.

distinct categories, Arthur Kleinman's work on neurasthenia as a diagnostic category in modern China has been more influential in my thinking about nineteenth-century insanity and nervousness (1980, 1986). Kleinman's interactive theory of illness and disease allows each to be considered separately but also provides a way to see their dynamic interconnection. Following Kleinman, I view illness as a self-defined state of less-than-optimum health, and disease as a form of knowledge that seeks to explain illness-affected behavior or physiological changes in the human organism. While illness is a matter of personal (and sometimes group) physiology and psychology, disease is a matter of representation. Disease is a scientific representation of illness that involves both a sorting of symptoms into discrete entities and a theorizing about causation and cure. As such, disease is not discovered but created. And any particular disease is never fixed but always open to constant redefinition, always dependent on changing representational practices. The representation of a particular illness pattern as a specific disease takes place in medical discourse, a discourse that not only is embedded in the larger, "extramedical" culture but also is shaped by time- and place-specific medical practices such as the constraints of doctor-patient interactions, the existence of medical institutions and technology, and the politics of medical specialization.[3] The nineteenth-century representation of women's nervousness and mental illness involved three specialties' border disputes, women physicians' special interest in the question, and women patients' illness narratives. Gender was both cause and effect in this representational process.

An article written in 1887 by Alice May Farnham, assistant physician at the Willard Asylum for the Insane in New York, provides an introduction to my three major points. Farnham's article appeared in *Alienist and Neurologist* and was titled "Uterine Disease as a Factor in the Production of Insanity." (*Alienist* was an earlier name for *psychiatrist*.) She began the article by reminding her readers of an "edict" popular "not so many years ago" among physicians and among the general public "that nearly all of those ills to which feminine flesh is heir are due either to disorders of the female reproductive organs, or so influenced by these organs as to constitute a peculiar class of diseases" (532). According to Farnham, the result of this widespread belief was that "the alienist and neurologist beheld his hysterical, melancholic and maniacal patients torn from his grasp and, by the wave of public opinion, cast into the hands of his brother practitioner, the gynaecologist" (532). Farnham went on to

---

[3] I am using the term *discourse* to mean a dialogue limited by discursive and nondiscursive practices that provide a context for meaning making. See Foucault 1967, 1972, 1973, and 1980. Scholars whose work on Foucault have been important in my thinking are Dreyfus and Rabinow 1982; Weedon 1987; Gutting 1989; and Sawicki 1991.

present case studies from the Willard Asylum to illustrate her conclusion that "uterine disease alone is seldom or never the cause of mental alienation [insanity]" (536).

Farnham's article indicates that the medical discourse on women's insanity and nervousness was multivocal, that women physicians (although a small minority in the profession) had a distinct professional voice, and that nonmedical voices were part of the discourse as well. First, and most obvious, Farnham's article was part of an ongoing struggle between gynecologists on the one hand and neurologists and alienists on the other for the right to define the nature of women's mental illness and nervousness. Second, Farnham was a woman physician attacking a narrow definition of womanhood, not as a scientific outsider but in the name of science. Finally—and this is most complex and interesting—Farnham alluded to "public opinion" and in her cases described patients and patients' family and friends as having significant input into the formation of medical ideas. Farnham's article was part of a medical dialogue in which women physicians and women patients influenced both the gendered construction of nervous disease and mental illness and the particular way *woman* was medicalized in the nineteenth century.

Professional turf battles

In the mid- to late nineteenth century, general practitioners, gynecologists, alienists, and neurologists saw women patients with mental or nervous complaints. Medical specialization was just beginning and required no formal examination, certification, or society membership until the twentieth century. Instead, a specialist was one who confined his or her cases to a certain group of people or to parts of the body or types of illnesses. Gynecologists specialized in the diseases of women, alienists specialized in mental illness and ran state or private insane asylums, and neurologists specialized in diseases of the nervous system. While these three categories might seem fairly straightforward and unproblematic, the boundaries of these specialties were sites of professional conflict in the nineteenth century. These three groups formed themselves into societies, held meetings, and published journals in order to define their subdisciplines.[4] A scientific understanding of gender was part of the knowledge each specialty created as its own.

In her 1887 article, Farnham challenged the gynecological definition of women's insanity and nervous disease, a definition she aptly characterized as obsessed with the notion that all of woman's illnesses were trace-

---

[4] For more information about these specialties in the nineteenth century see Blustine 1979, 1981; Sicherman 1980; Bynum 1985; Grob 1988; and Moscucci 1990.

able to her reproductive organs.[5] Although medicine from the late eighteenth century through the nineteenth century espoused an organicist notion of the individual/environment relationship—a notion stressing the entire life setting as an essential component of the patient's illness—gynecologists expressed a more mechanical, body-centered idea of women's illness than their contemporaries in other specialties (Jordanova 1989; Moscucci 1990). Horatio Storer, a mid-century Boston gynecologist, was representative of his fellow specialists when he asserted that "be the cases of insanity in females more or less in number [than in males], they are in great measure of reflex character, their exciting cause capable of being localized, and therefore, in a large proportion of cases, of being removed by treatment" (1864, 197). For Storer, the local causes of women's insanity were injured or dysfunctional reproductive organs that could be treated by the gynecologist with pessaries, applications of leeches or caustic chemicals, or, later in the century, surgery. Storer, like most other gynecologists, saw the uterus and ovaries as responsible for women's nervousness and mental illness. In an 1891 article titled "Can the Gynecologist Aid the Alienist in Institutions for the Insane," I. S. Stone outlined the position of gynecologists and then focused on the controversy between the gynecologists and the neurologists and alienists over the cause of women's insanity. Stone sent letters to alienists asking about the connection between gynecological problems and insanity in their patient populations. His extensive quotations from the letters, many very hostile, indicate that alienists found no causal relationship between women's reproductive organs and their mental alienation, yet Stone found it "logical" that "disease of the organs peculiar to women, which so much more than the corresponding organs in men, have to do with her physical and mental conditions, may cause psychical derangement" (1891, 873). Stone simply concluded that most of the alienists were incorrect in their evaluation of their patients. A professor of gynecology in Omaha, W. O. Henry, put it more succinctly: "A large majority of all insane women have some pelvic disturbance as an important, if not a chief causative factor" (1900–1901, 312).[6]

On the simplest level, gynecologists' physiological explanation for women's nervous complaints and insane behavior can be seen as stemming from economic self-interest. Just as they attempted to medicalize childbirth to drive out competition from midwives, gynecologists argued for a

---

[5] Moscucci 1990 found this assumption to be true of British gynecologists, but in the United States women gynecologists and some of their male colleagues differed from this dominant view.

[6] These physicians were representative of others in their specialty. Here, and throughout this article, I am citing only a small sample of the medical literature I found supporting my point.

theory of women's mental illness that held the gynecologist to be the specialist of choice to deal with women's nervousness and insanity. Although economics is always a factor in professional boundary disputes, the gynecological definition of women's insanity was prompted by much more than professional self-interest. Gynecologists saw women patients (and women) differently than nongynecologists did. Moscucci, in her 1990 study of British gynecology, has noted how the speculum influenced gynecological perception of women's illnesses. This new tool encouraged an anatomical representation of women's complaints partially because previously invisible problems, some serious and some benign, suddenly became viewable (Moscucci 1990, chap. 4). But even before the speculum, nineteenth-century gynecologists shaped a specialty around the otherness of woman; it was woman's difference, the "essential" femaleness of woman, that was the object of gynecological knowledge. It is no wonder that men who were in the process of creating a scientific specialty devoted to unveiling women's otherness would see all of their complaints as rooted in their ovaries and uterus. Horatio Storer, in the concluding part of his article, explained the logic of the gynecological view of woman's otherness. He marveled at woman's "possession of an inner mechanism, a central force, around which all her other systems and functions turn, and to which they are in reality, to a certain extent, but subsidiary," and reasoned that this mechanism is "so subtle and so easily disarranged by even slight external causes, that the real wonder is not that so many women are invalid, but that any are well" (1864, 199–200). George H. Rohe, a Maryland gynecologist, applied this logic more specifically to women's mental and nervous complaints and reasoned that women's reproductive organs rendered them unstable for their entire adult lives. He wrote, "Women are especially subject to mental disturbances dependent upon their sexual nature at three different epochs of life: the period of puberty when the menstrual function is established, the childbearing period, and the menopause" (1896, 802). The practice of gynecology in the nineteenth century encouraged male practitioners to define their specialty to include all of women's problems and therefore to define woman as inherently pathological.

In claiming women's physical and mental illness as gynecological territory, gynecological medical science collapsed the distinction between gender and sex: all of woman's complaints were reduced to her reproductive organs, her sex. When applied to women's mental illness and nervous complaints, gynecological medicine suggested that women were mentally ill or nervous simply because they were female and that their symptoms could be handled with physiological cures that, to late twentieth-century readers, appear to range from mildly punitive to unmistakably sadistic. As the early work of Smith-Rosenberg (1972) and Ann Douglas Wood (1973) has demonstrated, the gynecological view of women's sex-determined physical and mental debility—the woman-as-womb idea—was very influential in the early and mid-nineteenth century. According to physicians inside and outside of the specialty, this way of seeing women's nervousness and mental illness was widely shared by general practitioners as well as gynecologists.[7] But this point of view was neither universal nor uncontested within the medical community. Even while the gynecological view held sway, a spirited discourse among alienists and neurologists articulated a very different set of assumptions about the nature of women's mental illness and nervousness and a very different framework for understanding gender.

An 1882 editorial in *Alienist and Neurologist* judged "untenable" the "gynaecological reasoning which discerns through the speculum special and exclusive channels of communication with the brain, not revealed by physiological or anatomical research, and never dreamed of in regard to the other sex" (1882b, 133). The editor was writing specifically about removal of healthy ovaries for nervous complaints or insane behavior, but alienists and neurologists also argued against all "local" gynecological treatments for women's mental symptoms.[8] While they conceded that gynecological problems should be treated, the alienists and neurologists maintained that such problems were not the cause of women's mental complaints and symptoms. Instead, their theory of causation stressed the role of what today we would call sociological or environmental factors in the etiology of mental illness and nervousness.

In general, alienists and neurologists believed that a hereditary predisposition to insanity/nervousness was the root cause of mental problems in both women and men and that insanity was produced by a brain lesion not yet observable by medical science. Similar to the gynecologists' focus on their organs of specialty, the female reproductive organs, alienists and neurologists argued that the central nervous system was the body's control center for physical and emotional health. Like gynecologists' accolades to women's mysterious and powerful generative apparatus, neurologists and alienists described the central nervous system as the center that "intimately blended with all the other organs, controlling their actions and thus uniting

[7] I found a dozen examples of physicians from different specialties asserting that this view of the gynecological cause of women's mental and nervous complaints was widespread among gynecologists and general practitioners.

[8] This view was axiomatic among neurologists and alienists and was expressed in every review of gynecological texts appearing in *Alienist and Neurologist* and the *Journal of Nervous and Mental Disease*. It seems to be one of the few things about which alienists and neurologists agreed. For an excellent review of the nongynecological view, see Dwyer 1984.

them all in one harmonious whole" (Teed 1874, 139). According to these specialists, the "exciting cause"[9] of insanity or nervousness in either sex could be physical problems or situational ones, both of which could trigger insanity or nervousness through the nervous system. Most neurologists and alienists vigorously denied that women's reproductive organs were overinvolved in female insanity, and they heaped ridicule on the gynecological perspective. Representative of this neurological complaint was a review in *Alienist and Neurologist* that argued "modern gynecology . . . maintains that the uterus is the woman. As well say the testes, etc., is the man, for the nervous connections are about as intimate with the whole of his organism and testes as with the female uterus and ovaries" (1884, 735).[10] Most alienists and neurologists argued that female physiology contributed to women's mental problems only in that women had "finer tuned" nervous systems than men, so that physical or situational problems of any type were more likely to result in nervous breakdown in women than in men. These specialists conceded that gynecological problems, as well as other kinds of physical problems, could trigger a nervous response in women, but they maintained that once the reaction set in, the problem was one of nerves and not of reproductive organs. While they granted that the organic problem, reproductive or otherwise, should be treated, they argued that a cure was possible only by treating the nervous condition itself, usually with some combination of rest, massage, diet, exercise, and electricity.[11]

Some neurologists and alienists offered an even greater contrast to gynecological thinking, stressing women's gender role as the "exciting cause" of insanity or nervous symptoms. The demands of child rearing or nursing a sick family member, disappointment in love, boredom, an abusive husband, a lack of exercise or activity because of the restrictions of dress—all these were seen as causes of lowered physical and psychological resistance. In a person with "hereditary predisposition" to insanity or

[9] Physicians thought of the "exciting cause" as a necessary but not sufficient cause of the insanity or nervousness. The "exciting cause," although temporally related to the outbreak of the illness, could not produce the illness alone.

[10] Although this criticism was nearly universal among alienists and neurologists, there were some who argued for a special connection between woman's reproductive organs and her nervous system. For example, see Hersman 1899.

[11] Two of the most famous neurologists of the late nineteenth century, Beard and Mitchell, recommended complicated treatments including electricity, diet, rest, and exercise. Both believed physical problems, including problems of the reproductive organs, brought on nervous collapse, but neither singled out women's reproductive organs as particularly problematic. Most of Beard's work focusing on reproductive organs was with male patients (1879, 1898). Mitchell's infamous "rest cure" was first developed for male neurotics, not to "punish" women patients; his discussion of female neurotics clearly indicates his belief in sociological causes of women's nervous breakdowns (Mitchell 1871, 1879, 1900). Although both men, along with most of their generation of Americans, believed women and men to be more different than alike, neither argued for a gynecological theory of women's nervous disease.

nervous disease, such life situations were capable of producing a chain reaction that could end in slight nervousness or severe mental illness. Perhaps the most poignant explanation of this connection between women's life situations and nervous disease was given by E. H. Van Deusen, a Michigan physician who first used the word *neurasthenia* to name this condition. "The early married life of the wives of some of our smaller farmers seems especially calculated to predispose to this condition," he wrote. He went on to describe what he thought of as a typical situation:

> Transferred to an isolated farmhouse, very frequently from a home in which she had enjoyed a requisite measure of social and intellectual recreation, she is subjected to a daily routine of very monotonous household labor. Her new *home,* if it deserve the name, is . . . deprived of everything which can suggest a pleasant thought: not a flower blooms in the garden; books she has, perhaps, but no time to read them. Remote from neighbors . . . she sees only her husband and the generally uneducated man who shares his toil. . . . Her daily life, and especially if she have also the unaided care of one or two ailing little children, is exhausting and depressing to a degree of which but few are likely to form any correct conception. [1868–69, 447]

Similarly, physicians Joseph Collins and Carlin Phillips attributed the neurasthenia in their urban women patients to gender-related problems: "The entailments of marriage—anxiety concerning the material welfare of mate and offspring, incompatibility of partners, dread and depression attending sickness and death, the assumption of marital and maternal obligations, etc.—are contributing to the occurrence of this neurosis" (1899, 413). C. F. Folsom, the visiting physician for nervous disease at Boston City Hospital, went so far as to suggest that more education as well as "more physical exercise, more knowledge how to take care of themselves, more opportunities in every direction" would result in less nervous disease in women (1886, 185).

While the contrast between the gynecological view and the neurological and psychiatric view of women's nervousness and mental illness is important to note, I want to stress that nineteenth-century physicians, no matter what their specialty, assumed that women and men were more different than alike and that the physiological differences between the sexes translated "naturally" to different social roles.[12] In spite of all of

---

[12] For more about physicians' construction of women's otherness, see Jordanova 1986, esp. "Introduction" and "Naturalizing the Family: Literature and the Bio-Medical Sciences in the Late Eighteenth Century."

their complaints about gynecologists, most alienists and neurologists agreed with their gynecologist colleagues that women's reproductive organs dictated that women should restrict their activities and aspirations. In a review of Edward H. Clarke's *The Building of a Brain,* the *Psychological and Medico-Legal Journal* reviewer praised Clarke for writing "so forcibly, so overpoweringly, so thoroughly logically against the claims of some women to corporeal and mental identity with man" (1874, 401).

Although the gynecological view may appear more crude and more easily refutable with "scientific" evidence, the neurological/psychiatric view also rested on the assumption of difference at a more invisible level. As mentioned earlier, neurologists and alienists assumed that women had finer-tuned nervous systems than men. In fact, they imaged the nervous system as female. Illustrations of the nervous system in the nineteenth century were of female bodies, whereas illustrations of the muscular system were of male bodies. Nerves were inherently feminine, and women were inherently prone to nervousness and to manic, depressive, or hysterical responses to life's difficulties (see Jordanova 1989). While the gynecological view of women's problems was based on the reproductive organs—and therefore open to clinical refutation—the neurological/psychiatric view was based on the invisible femininity of the nervous system—and therefore closed to clinical refutation. Ironically, the neurological and psychiatric point of view was supported by women physicians in the name of clinical science.

Women physicians' professional position

The contribution of women physicians to the professional discourse on women's insanity and nervousness formed part of the neurological and psychiatric case against gynecological thinking, although most women physicians who participated in the discourse were technically gynecologists (i.e., most treated the diseases of women). While accepting as a truism the idea that mind and body interact and that all organs affect each other, women physicians drew broader and narrower conclusions about the nature of the interaction than did gynecologists. Amelia Gilmore, resident physician at the Philadelphia Hospital for the Insane, asserted that "all conditions of the body—all diseases, organic or specific,—may lead to insanity" (1893, 558). Likewise, Alice Bennett, working in the Norristown, Pennsylvania, asylum, noted that "it is understood, of course, that no organ or system of organs acts independently; that there can be no absolute separation of the study of one from the study of another" (1890, 569). Both women did studies of the relationship of kidney disease and insanity in their asylum populations, challenging the gynecological notion that women's reproductive organs were the only ones implicated in women's insanity.

Other women physicians focused on the relationship between women's reproductive organs and insanity but disputed gynecological views of cause and effect. Anne Hazen McFarland, medical superintendent of the Oak Lawn Retreat for the Insane (Illinois), ridiculed the gynecological hypothesis as "dull" and as serving the economic interest of physicians "who otherwise should have to take to a change of occupation to earn a livelihood" (1895, 115). Several women physicians employed in asylums as gynecologists conducted studies of the female patients specifically to test the gynecological hypothesis. Like Alice May Farnham, these women concluded that there was no cause-and-effect relationship between women's mental illness and diseases of the reproductive organs, although they conceded that physical problems should always be treated to make the patients more comfortable. One study of 450 asylum patients, coauthored by Mary E. Bassett, concluded that although many of the patients had some kind of pelvic disease, there was "no apparent relation between the pelvic disease and the mental disturbance" (Tomlinson and Bassett 1899, 831).[13] Designing empirical studies to refute the gynecological argument, women physicians "out-scienced" their male gynecologist colleagues; that is, women physicians argued their points from what they assumed to be a superior, more empirical, and therefore more scientific perspective. In arguing this way, women physicians also contributed to the scientific ammunition of neurologists and alienists.

The subject of gynecological surgery was very much a part of the debate over the origins and proper treatment of women's insanity and nervousness. Neurologists and alienists argued that when surgery of any kind "cured" insanity or nervousness, it was due to the power of suggestion and not to the physiological effect of the surgery.[14] Women physicians overwhelmingly supported the neurological and psychiatric point of view on the removal of women's reproductive organs in cases of insanity and nervousness. E. M. Roys Gavitt, a woman physician from Toledo and editor-in-chief of the *Woman's Medical Journal,* complained that "a desire to experiment has led ambitious surgeons to perform ovariotomy to cure insanity, nervous disorders and functional disturbances too numerous to mention." She went on to say that such surgery will be of no benefit "unless the woman has been under the influence of some

[13] Other women physicians who did empirical investigations or cited specific cases to demonstrate the invalidity of the gynecological hypothesis include Jacobi 1886, 399; Farnham 1887; Dr. Grace Peckham, cited by an unnamed author in *Alienist and Neurologist* 1888, 274; Davenport 1895, 368–70; and Gardner 1900.

[14] See, e.g., *Alienist and Neurologist* 1882a, 296; 1883, 499–500; and 1901, 737.

ambitious medical counselor, who has a mania that every pain and ache suffered by a woman is caused by some disturbance of the genital organs, *and the removal of the ovaries from the pelvis removes them from the head"* (1893, 123–24; emphasis in original). McFarland echoed Gavitt's opinion of physicians who perform ovariotomies as "ambitious and pretentious" and asserted that the "chief medical error of the present day is the mistaking of brain disease for pelvic disease" (1893, 146; 1894, 41). Mary Dixon Jones, a gynecologist who argued in favor of gynecological operations on diseased organs and in favor of the possible cure of insanity and nervousness by the removal of women's reproductive organs, insisted that the surgery should be done only when the physician suspected that the organs were physically diseased (1894a).[15] However, another woman physician, Flora Aldrich, complained that medical men misjudged women's nervous and mental illness as always related to the uterus and ovaries. She boasted of successfully treating "countless women" whose symptoms would have "doomed them to the knife" had they trusted their care to male physicians, many of them "young and thoughtless operators, aided if not by greed of gold, with errors in diagnosis" (1894, 107). Medical women consistently supported the neurological and psychiatric position against the gynecological essentialism that tied women's nervous and mental illness to their reproductive organs.

The women physicians who participated in this debate articulated a situational theory to explain women's mental illness and nervousness. Grace Peckham, a New York City physician, asserted that "many women are physically cripples from lack of use of their muscles, and the same is true of mental forces" (1887, 47). The assistant physician at the Iowa State Hospital for the Insane, Jennie McCowen, voiced a similar position that women's lives contributed to their mental problems. She wrote that one cause of insanity was "monotony of work and thought," "the treadmill of ceaseless care and toil to which so many conscientious souls are self-condemned" (1882–83, 17). She went on to say that "the largest numbers of victims to this cause is found among the mothers of the land" and gave a case study of a woman who was a "most domestic woman" much praised by her husband for her devotion to home and family (17). McCowen confidently asserted that the woman would not have gone insane had she been less domestic. A well-known New York neurologist, Mary Putnam Jacobi, similarly linked hysteria to women's life condi-

---

[15] Although Jones warned against too-aggressive surgery on women, she herself performed countless ovariotomies. I am grateful to Regina Morantz-Sanchez for sharing with me her unpublished paper (1992) in which Jones is a major character. Morantz-Sanchez found Jones to be a very active gynecological surgeon who was accused of not listening closely enough to her female patients, and she argues that this lack of feminine empathy was partially responsible for Jones's professional demise.

tions. Jacobi judged hysteria to be due ultimately to a brain lesion, but she argued that the narrow life of most women was the most frequent cause of the brain problem. "When hysteria develops," Jacobi wrote, "it implies that the mechanisms associated with the inmost individuality have succumbed to the accidents and calamities of life" (1886, 401). She went on to quote a male author who attributed hysteria to the "social conditions to which [women] are subject" that confine them to "a narrow and trivial existence" (401).[16]

In a similar vein, other women physicians argued that more education and greater freedom of life choices would prevent most cases of female insanity and nervousness. Women physicians took issue with their male colleagues who blamed women's nervousness on education. Jones, in a review of a gynecological textbook, praised the text in general but spent two pages of the five-page review chiding the author for his mistaken ideas about the detrimental effects of study on women's physical development. "As a woman, I must, especially, take exceptions to the above remarks," she wrote (1895b, 19). She went on to explain, "Developing or improving one part of the body certainly does not dwarf another, weaken it, deprive it of nerve power, or cause it to be diseased. . . . Certainly mental labor or assiduity in study does not produce disease" (21). Jones cited empirical, experiential evidence to prove her point, arguing that the best-educated women were generally "strong and vigorous" (23). Similarly, a series of editorials in the *Woman's Medical Journal* poked fun at medical authors opposing coeducation or higher education of women (1904a, 1904b, 1904c). Instead of education, women physicians blamed women's narrow life choices and self-sacrificial domesticity for women's nervousness and insanity and argued that opportunities and self-care would work wonders for women's mental health. Mary A. Spink argued that the most common cause of women's neurasthenia was the "lack of definite object in life. Eternal waiting and longing for something, they know not what, . . . disappointment and unhappiness from whatever cause" (1896, 36). She noted that women's colleges, women's clubs, the new permission for women to fence, cycle, play golf and tennis, and the new emphasis on proper clothing for exercise were all contributing to women's mental health (37). McFarland similarly linked women's nerves to domestic burdens. She recommended rest, the friendship of women, and having "something to do" as a cure (1895, 114). She particularly recommended against "misplaced self-denial" and urged women "to secure independence of thought and conduct, to pursue personal studies and interests" (116–17).

---

[16] Morantz-Sanchez (1985, 220–25) also notes that women physicians argued for an environmental view of women's insanity and nervousness.

Women physicians who stressed women's life situation, like those who did empirical studies of the relationship between uterine disease and insanity, were not unique in the profession. The point is not that they expressed views contrary to those of male physicians but that medical opinion about female insanity and nervousness was divided and women physicians contributed to the discourse almost entirely as opponents of the gynecological perspective. As women physicians, they had a professional as well as a personal stake in defeating the gynecological definition of gender. After all, many gynecologists argued throughout the nineteenth century that women's menstrual cycles rendered them biologically unfit to practice medicine.

In addition to being a part of the debate between the gynecologists and the alienists and neurologists, women physicians were participants in the discourse between alienists and neurologists over asylum politics. Alienists, who were asylum managers as well as physicians and who admitted only asylum superintendents into their small, male group, were opposed to other physicians' having access to asylum patients. Neurologists criticized alienists for sloppy asylum management, for keeping asylums closed to studies by other physicians, and basically for having wrong ideas about the nature of insanity. Women physicians entered this debate by siding with neurologists on points of contention, and, more important, by insisting that women asylum patients needed the care of women physicians. Louise Robinovitch, a New York City neurologist, expressed an almost territorial view of women asylum patients: "Insane women are the legitimate wards of the woman physician, and it is time that the woman physician entered into the practice of her art as applied to insane women" (1903, 74).[17] From a more patient-centered perspective, Calista Luther wrote that "it has long been recognized by a few professional men and women that the welfare of insane women demands that they should not only be treated by their own sex, but that none but women should be admitted to their presence" (1900, 39). Luther cited another woman physician, Margaret Cleaves, who supported her position, arguing that women patients who had gynecological problems would not be likely to tell male doctors of their distress. Cleaves also asserted that women asylum patients often misinterpreted gynecological treatment by male doctors and that the misinterpretation added to their mental illness. The *Woman's Medical Journal* suggested that the controversy over the relationship of pelvic disease and insanity was nearer a solution thanks to

[17] Further indication that women physicians saw the care of insane women as their special domain was the *Woman's Medical Journal's* publishing the names and positions of women physicians in asylums in each issue as the news was gathered, as well as two articles about such women (1894; and Coveny 1901). For more information about women physicians employed in asylums, see McGovern 1981 and MacKenzie 1983.

"more careful methods of research" established by "the introduction of medical women into the hospitals for the insane." The journal urged that "more medical women are needed in this work" (1900, 428). Amelia Gilmore, the resident physician to the Insane Department of the Philadelphia Hospital, went so far as to assert that a major symptom of puerperal insanity (insanity of childbirth) was prompted by male caretaking; she confidently wrote that "the tendency to eroticism [in behavior and language], is not provoked when the patients are under the medical care of women" (1892, 411).[18]

These women physicians were supported by many male neurologists who were interested in greater access to asylum patients, and as a result of their efforts several states passed laws by the end of the century that required that women physicians be appointed to state asylums to care for women patients. These laws were victories for neurologists and for all physicians who were not among the small group of asylum superintendents. In this controversy between neurologists and alienists, as in the controversy with gynecologists, women physicians were vocal, "inside" participants in a medical discourse about the nature of sex and gender. Sandra Harding has argued that the central "science question" in feminism is not one of "good" versus "bad" science but that it concerns instead the epistemology stemming from the scientist's position (1986). This is very much my point about nineteenth-century physicians: their specialties and genders determined the epistemological position upon which their different sciences depended. Like their male colleagues, nineteenth-century women physicians' ideas about women's insanity and nervousness expressed their gender and class situation. The knowledge that women physicians created about the female body and female consciousness was not "good science" as opposed to men physicians' "bad science"; instead, both women and men physicians formulated concepts of women's mental illness from their different positions in the medical and gender power structures, positions that limited their vision even as their vision helped define their positions.

While women physicians' gender set them apart from their male colleagues and contributed to their unique perception of women's insanity and nervousness, women physicians' middle-class professional position separated them from their women patients and prompted them to interpret women's illness in a particular way. Women who were physicians saw their lives as living testimony against the "woman-as-womb" idea. They likewise saw the domestic lives of the majority of women as oppressed with physical labor and psychological worry that was happily

[18] Three other women physicians who disagreed with male colleagues about the erotic nature of puerperal insanity were Burnet 1899; Hutchins 1900; and Cadwalader 1905.

absent from most of their lives. Women physicians' privileged class position encouraged them to see the lives of less privileged women as physically grueling and lacking in intellectual stimulation. Similarly, women
physicians saw the lives of upper-class women as frivolous and empty.
Because of their unique gender/professional situation, women physicians
"saw" their women patients' complaints as environmental and not essentially female—as related to gender role and not to biology. Their
working-class patients worked too hard, their upper-class patients had no
purpose in life, and neither group exercised their mental powers.

This vision, however, did not prompt a structural critique of gender;
women physicians treated women's mental alienation as a personal
problem that women could develop the "will" to overcome. In the turn-
of-the-century period, women physicians welcomed psychological and
psychoanalytical approaches to hysteria and neurasthenia that involved
isolating women patients from "sympathetic" friends, allowing patients
to talk to only the doctor, forcing them to "rest," showing no sympathy
for their symptoms, and encouraging the restoration of "mental control."[19] One New York City physician, Evelyn Garrigue, wrote in favor of
a psychotherapy aimed at "re-education." "The self-centered neurasthenics with their hyperfatigability and the self-deceiving hysterics with their
hypersuggestibility are specimens of abnormal development," she wrote;
"they need instruction how to make themselves normal" (1909a, 28).
The reeducation consisted of teaching these patients "to face the truth
about themselves," to understand that their symptoms or phobias are
"nothingness," and to develop habits of "industry and intelligently directed energy" (30). While Garrigue believed that reeducation "regarding
the complex relationship of the sexes" was needed, she cured her women
patients by giving them the "pluck and courage" to go back into their
domestic troubles with a "self-respecting power to cope with life's difficulties" (32). Women physicians' professional and gender position encouraged them to see women's nervousness and mental illness as situational, not biological, but also as indicative of a failure of will or energy.
Women patients, however, interpreted their illnesses differently.

Women patients' voices in medical discourse

Let me return to my earlier point about the difference between illness
and disease. If we think of women patients, their family and friends, and
their chosen physicians as participants in a dialogue about symptoms, a
dialogue in which symptoms of illness were transformed into disease
entities, we can begin to hear the voices of women patients in the medical

[19] For example, see Brown 1895; Coone 1904a, 1904b; *Woman's Medical Journal*
1908, 1909; Garrigue 1909a, 1909b, 1910; and Mackie 1909.

discourse on sex and gender. Like women physicians, women patients participated in the medical discourse on insanity and nervousness but in a more substantial, if less overt, manner. Although women physicians accounted for a tiny minority of medical writing about female insanity and nervous disease, women patients were present in almost every case study. In order to hear their voices in the discourse, however, we need to listen with an interactive theory of disease formation.

There were two subjects dominating the dialogue between medical practitioners and patients with nervous and mental complaints: the symptoms themselves and the perceived cause or causes of the symptoms. Many historians and critics of contemporary psychiatry have pointed out that symptoms of insanity vary depending on time and place and that attaching names to peculiar behavior can be seen as the medical community's medicalization and labeling of inappropriate behavior as disease.[20] According to this line of criticism, people displaying peculiar behavior are victimized by this medicalization. At first glance, this interpretation seems particularly fitting of nineteenth-century women's insane behavior, as the behavior was so gender-specific. The symptoms of nineteenth-century women's nervous and mental illnesses were numerous and varied, but the common characteristic of the symptoms was the unfeminine nature of the behavior or feeling. Insane and nervous women were described as antimaternal, selfish, willful, violent, erotic—all of these inappropriate in terms of nineteenth-century definitions of womanhood. Leaving aside for a moment the question of what the behavior labeled as insane meant in women patients' lives, we are concerned here with the question of how certain behavior and emotions were attached to the notion of insanity and nervousness within medical discourse. Case studies indicate that women patients and their families and friends were as responsible as physicians for linking unfeminine behavior with insanity and nervousness.[21] In many cases women came to physicians asking to be committed or to be given medication for behavior the patients themselves described as insane or nervous, including lack of interest in husband and family, violent feelings toward their children, and continual sadness or suicidal urges in spite of being well taken care of by husband or family.[22]

---

[20] See, e.g., Zola 1972; Waxler 1974; and Engelhardt 1975.

[21] A very small minority of the cases I read were cases named by physicians as *sexual inversion*, which, in the early twentieth century, was translated as *homosexual*. There are not enough of these cases in my sample for me to set them apart; however, these cases conform to my general point. The behavior seen as deviant by physicians and patients was not sexual behavior but was cross-dressing and performing "male" work (i.e., unfeminine behavior). This is the same conclusion drawn by Chauncey 1989.

[22] For example, Whitomore 1879 quotes a woman who related her second hysterical attack to her anger with her mother (522). Another woman's list of nervous symptoms included brooding, being unhappy, and having thoughts of suicide although married to a good man. See *Post-Graduate* 1896.

Most patients did not name their own behavior and feelings as nervous or insane; more frequently the connection was made by a family member or close friends. Husbands brought in wives for a variety of unwomanly offenses. Women who disagreed too vocally, lost interest in personal appearance, or neglected their children were brought to physicians by husbands who saw this behavior as insane or nervous. One woman was brought to the Boston Insane Hospital by her husband because she had begun going out, refused to say where she had been, came home smelling of whiskey, and neglected her children and household affairs (Boston Insane Hospital 1890–91a). Another husband brought his wife to a physician because "at uncertain, unexpected intervals of a few weeks, sometimes months . . . she would go into a paroxysm of scolding, fault-finding and vituperation, lasting a few hours" (Russell 1884, 467). A previously "refined wife and mother" was brought to a physician by her husband because she had developed a noticeable "coarseness not present before, and a tendency to malicious mischief toward her husband, whose sense of propriety she took an especial delight in outraging" (*Alienist and Neurologist* 1886, 505). The husbands of these women thought of them as insane or nervous because the women acted in ways a "normal" woman would not.

Even more numerous than cases of husbands bringing wives to physicians were cases of mothers bringing daughters. Girls and young women who were insubordinate, sexually promiscuous, or not interested enough in socializing were brought to physicians by anxious mothers. One fifteen-year-old was presented to Dr. J. Workman by her mother, "who gave . . . a terrorizing history of the daughter's misdeeds." Although Workman thought the deeds "savoured more of moral delinquency than of mental infirmity," he told the girl's mother he would admit her to the Toronto Asylum for the Insane if the mother could find three physicians to agree that the girl was insane; the mother obtained the necessary signatures (1883, 301). A New York City physician reported a case of "Insanity of Pubescence" involving a sixteen-year-old girl who had displayed "strange and willful" behavior since the age of twelve. "She would strike back if punished for any misdemeanor, and speak of those 'damn people,' although she had been carefully and religiously brought up"; she would not stay in school, and she displayed "very erotic" tendencies (Mann 1884, 503). In another case, an adolescent whose mother reported that "she had given her family much trouble" was brought to a physician by her mother (Arnold 1879, 118).

Behavior problems that threatened feminine propriety were often seen by mothers as evidence of mental or nervous illness. In a study titled "Insanity in Young Women," physician Clara Barrus listed "contradictoriness" as a major symptom (1896, 366), and physician G. R. Trowbridge also found erotic and willful behavior to be a symptom of insanity in young women (1891, 349). C. H. Hughes, a St. Louis physician, reported a case that included many of the symptoms listed thus far. The case appeared in *Alienist and Neurologist* as an extended quotation from a letter sent to Hughes by the mother of a twenty-seven-year-old woman. The mother cited her daughter's use of vile language as "a most striking sign of insanity" given that "all her life she has been surrounded by the most pure and lovely influences" (Hughes 1882, 519). Her daughter also made up "scandalous stories" about her younger sister, threw buckets of ash on the carpet, destroyed pictures, made scenes in public, and refused to help her mother take care of the home and family (520–21). All of this behavior was seen as insane by the mother, who wrote, "It is absurd to think a lady brought up as she has been . . . would act in that manner were she not insane. . . . Were she not mentally afflicted, knowing our circumstances and that I am trying to keep a home for my children, she would try to help me keep that home instead of destroying its peace and happiness and disgracing her family. . . . She has almost broken our hearts" (522–23).

Although a mother or husband was the most common person to accompany a woman to a physician's office or an asylum, sometimes other family members or the woman's friends were involved. A brother brought his "peculiar" thirty-six-year-old sister to the Boston Insane Hospital. He reported that her "irritable and unreasonable disposition" made her impossible to live with (Boston Insane Hospital 1884). Another young woman was brought in after she attacked her friend and pulled her hair, and a clergyman brought his daughter to a physician seeking to have her declared insane because of sexual misconduct (Fisher 1865a; *American Journal of Insanity* 1882–83). Many times a woman's friends accompanied her to a physician's office, explaining that the woman was troubled with crying spells, neglected her household when previously she had been an excellent housekeeper, or suddenly distrusted her husband. Isabel M. Davenport, assistant physician and gynecologist to the Eastern Illinois Hospital for the Insane, cited a case in which a woman's friends brought her to the asylum after the woman spent "three weeks of fearful debauchery in one of the large cities" (1895, 369). In all of these cases, certain unwomanly traits were linked by women patients, their families, or friends to the concept of insanity or nervousness.

Physicians recorded women's self-reported and other-reported symptoms, sometimes word for word and other times paraphrasing, and then translated those symptoms into various diseases: mania, melancholia, puerperal insanity, hysteria, neurasthenia, moral insanity. Even more significant, physicians' theories about the cause or causes of these insane and nervous symptoms echoed the patients' and patients' families' or friends' claims about causation. Women who went to general practitioners, gynecologists, and neurologists with nervous and insane symptoms linked their symptoms most frequently to physical problems with their reproductive organs. Doctors' theories about nervous and insane women, whether gynecological and related directly to the body or neurological and based on women's nervous sensibility, were formed from the testimony of their women patients and their patients' families and friends.

With and without prompting about the cause of their symptoms, women most often related their illness to their female bodies. A woman patient would report that she first noticed the nervous symptoms after the birth of her last child, or that they occurred at a particular time in her menstrual cycle, or that they were due to foolish behavior during her period, or that they were causally related to a physical problem with her reproductive organs.[23] The editor of *Alienist and Neurologist* complained in 1882 that the typical woman patient has "the imaginary notion that her womb is diseased" (1882a, 296). One of George Beard's patients attributed her neurasthenia to taking cold while on a mountain climb at the time of her menses (1877, 659), and another woman neurasthenic explained her submission to gynecological treatment thus: "I had a feeling, which many women I know also have, that the womb is the weak point and is the cause of most of their nervous ills" (*Post-Graduate* 1896, 364). In remembering her years as a woman physician to young college women in the 1890s, Lilian Welsh reported that "there was scarcely a student . . . with a neurotic history or a neurotic tendency whose mind was not fixed upon her reproductive organs as the source of all her troubles" (1925, 119).

Not only did women themselves relate their nervous and mental problems to their female bodies, but the friends and families of women patients also voiced similar theories about the cause of women's nervous and insane symptoms. Often a friend or family member of a patient related the patient's insane or nervous behavior to the onset of puberty or menopause or to dysfunctional menstruation.[24] One physician reported that for most of the women patients in the asylum where she worked, "the cause most frequently assigned by the friends and attending physician is 'pelvic disease'" (Davenport 1895, 368), and another physician similarly complained, "I am continually being asked by the friends of the insane, 'Is there not some uterine trouble?'" She went on to say, "People

[23] I found ten articles with case study examples of women who dated their nervous or mental symptoms from childbirth or who related them to menstrual irregularities, to their menstrual periods themselves, or to foolish activities during menstruation. These do not include cases defined as "puerperal insanity."

[24] Cases in which the friends or family of a woman attributed the woman's symptoms to menstruation or to menopause can be found in Boston Insane Hospital 1881a, 1882–83, and 1890–91b; Reed 1888–89; and Vinton 1899.

think that all mental disorder springs from uterine trouble. They forget that there are more insane men than insane women, so the uterus cannot be held responsible for all insanity" (Robinovitch 1903, 78).

However much women physicians resisted this physical explanation, women patients and their families and friends undoubtedly believed that the uterus was responsible for most nervous and mental symptoms. Even families more oriented toward the patient's life situation as the root of her problems reported "over-study" and "disappointment in love" as causes of women's symptoms, causes that were seen as inherently feminine.[25] Some families and friends of women patients gave "domestic trouble" as the cause of the woman's nervous or mental illness, but the domestic trouble was always accompanied by some physical cause as well.[26]

At a time when the medical wisdom held heredity responsible for mental illness and nervous disease, it is understandable both that families would resist the idea of hereditary "taint" and that physicians of all specialties would settle on something more tangible as a "secondary" or "exciting" cause of mental and nervous illness. In terms of treatment, heredity was untouchable, yet physicians definitely were expected to treat their nervous and insane patients. As I have pointed out earlier, both neurologists and gynecologists believed heredity was the root cause of insanity, although both treated nervous and insane women as if their female bodies were defective. The most dramatic examples of this treatment philosophy were "local" treatments and sexual surgery. If the symptoms of nervous and mental illness were unwomanly behavior and feelings, and if the causes were rooted in the female body, then the cures must produce some change in the woman patient's reproductive organs to change the woman's behavior. Women patients and their families and friends were vocal advocates of this line of reasoning.

The most popular form of surgery performed on nervous and insane women was removal of one or both ovaries. The vast majority of women with nervous and insane symptoms were not operated on, but many of those who underwent operations did so at the request or insistence of family or friends or, more frequently, at their own request. Mary Dixon Jones reported a case in which "the patient, as well as the relatives, were very anxious for an operation" to cure hystero-epilepsy (1895a, 5), and Isabel Davenport reported a case in which a patient's friends wanted an

[25] Cases in which patients' families/friends attributed the nervous symptoms to overstudy can be found in Boston Insane Hospital 1881b, 1890–91c; Hurd 1882–83. Cases in which friends and families of women patients related their insanity and nervous symptoms to life disappointments associated with the feminine role can be found in Barrus 1896. About the influence of families in women patients' admission to asylums, see Fox 1978 and MacKenzie 1983.

[26] Cases in which domestic trouble was seen by family or friends as a cause of symptoms can be found in Fisher 1865b; Boston Insane Hospital 1881c; Lane 1901.

ovario-hysterectomy performed to cure the woman's puerperal mania (1895, 369); the first operation was a success, but the second one was not.[27]

More common than family and friends influencing treatment, countless women patients also demanded or requested surgery to relieve their nervous symptoms. Jones had another patient who suffered from extreme pain and occasional seizures during her periods. When an operation was mentioned as a possibility, "eagerly she seized the idea at once and repeatedly urged that it should be done, and even grew angry that I delayed" (1895b, 23). Other physicians reported similar cases of women demanding surgery, hoping an operation would cure a physical or nervous problem.[28] Many times, physicians described themselves as reluctant operators, such as Edward Reynolds, whose neurasthenic patient "had become absolutely convinced that her only prospect of health lay in a cure of her local ailments." Although Reynolds was opposed to surgery, he reported that "after the complete failure of general treatment, and with her mento-nervous condition growing rapidly worse, I opened her abdomen" (1910, 114). Reynolds found nothing wrong, but the surgery had an immediate positive effect on his patient's nervous symptoms, and after a relapse she eventually recovered completely.

C. B. Burr, a physician from Pontiac, Michigan, even suggested that many women requested surgery for contraceptive reasons. Addressing the Michigan Medical Society in 1894, Burr said, "I do not believe that there is a man in this room . . . who has not been approached by patients to be operated upon for the purpose of bringing on an early change of life and preventing the bearing of children" (481). It is possible that other women were not as straightforward as the ones Burr referred to and instead came to their physicians with nervous and mental symptoms in order to request surgical treatment they knew would render them sterile. Whether to relieve emotional or behavioral symptoms or to end their childbearing potential, many women sought operations. Physicians reported that these operations cured many cases of nervous and mental illness, even among women in asylums.[29]

It is possible to argue that women patients and their families and friends were totally under the influence of selfish, ambitious physicians who persuaded these helpless victims that nervous and mental problems were caused by women's reproductive organs and could therefore be cured by surgery. In fact, some physicians (neurologists) accused other

[27] See also Clarke 1859 for a case in which the patient's friends were influential in the physician's use of medication.

[28] Additional cases of women patients demanding or requesting surgery can be found in Sims 1878; *Alienist and Neurologist* 1890, 1904; Jones 1894b; Davenport 1895.

[29] For examples of surgical cures and cures from other "local" treatments, see Scott 1871; Cross 1877; Sims 1878; Reed 1888–89; Burr 1894; Davenport 1895; Hall 1900; Hanley 1900–1901; Henry 1900–1901.

physicians (gynecologists and general practitioners) of being the cause of women patients' womb-centeredness.[30] However, this interpretation does not take seriously the interaction between doctor, patient, and family. General practitioners and specialists had to account for women's reproductive organs within their theories of insanity and nervous disease because women themselves, as well as their families and friends, related their emotional problems to reproductive dysfunction. In the nineteenth century, before sophisticated diagnostic techniques, women patients' self-reported symptoms and perceptions of causes formed the primary data of medical theorizing. Whether reproductive organs or life situation was stressed, the medical discourse elaborating the theory contained a chorus of professional, patient, and patient-advocate voices, with the professionals taking the other two perspectives as the raw material, the empirical basis of diagnosis. As we have seen, the specialty area as well as the sex of the doctor determined which set of patient-reported symptoms and causes the practitioner would take seriously, but neither the translation of symptoms into disease categories nor the theorizing about cause was the work of doctors alone.

A phenomenon illustrating this mixture of voices in the creation of a disease category was puerperal insanity, a disease defined in the nineteenth century by the medical community in general—alienists, neurologists, gynecologists, women physicians, and men physicians—from the illness behavior of women who believed childbirth itself could/would produce maniacal symptoms.[31] Women diagnosed by general practitioners and specialists as having puerperal insanity developed symptoms within hours or days of childbirth, and these symptoms included such behavior as suicidal tendencies, homicidal tendencies toward the baby or husband, talking incessantly and mostly incoherently, the inability to sleep, the refusal of food, and (according to male physicians) indecent language and sometimes indecent exposure. These symptoms were side effects of both normal and difficult labors and corresponded to no common set of physical or environmental factors. It is beyond the scope of this essay to speculate about the meaning of such behavior for women, but clearly the set of symptoms, unique and ubiquitous in the nineteenth century, translated by physicians into the disease category "puerperal insanity," illustrates the dependence of physicians on patient- or other-reported symptoms in the creation of disease categories. Physicians listened to their patients' stories and took seriously their patients' and their

---

[30] This point of view was expressed by *American Journal of Insanity* 1881, 1884; Robinovitch 1903; Reynolds 1910.

[31] One form of puerperal insanity was called "lactation insanity" and corresponds to what in the late twentieth century we call "postpartum depression." For a more complete discussion of puerperal insanity, see Theriot 1990.

patients' families' linking of symptoms to cause. The physician was not responsible for designating certain behavior as "symptoms" of nervous disease and insanity nor for linking "mad" or nervous behavior to women's reproductive organs. Instead, the interaction of physician, patient, and family and friends created symptoms, causes, and cures.

* * *

A reproductive theory of women's insanity and nervous disease dominated the nineteenth century partially because women experienced their reproductive lives as troublesome. Toward the end of the century, women physicians joined male neurologists and alienists to offer rebuttal to the gynecological theory. Ironically, the later environmental theory that we applaud today as a step toward an enlightened view of women's insanity and nervousness was based less on women patients' perceptions and more on empirical, "objective" studies that condemned patient perceptions as hopelessly subjective. As the gynecological theory, burdened by clinical refutation, lost professional support, it was replaced by a neurological/psychiatric theory of invisible femininity, insulated from the voices of women patients and immune to clinical evidence. Seen in this light, the neurological/psychiatric theory supported by women physicians led easily to the growing acceptance in the early twentieth century of a psychiatric point of view that totally discounted the perceptions of women patients in favor of a male-developed theory of repression. Freud's denial of the reality of Dora's sexual abuse was in keeping with the pattern established in the nineteenth century by women and men neurologists who combated the gynecological theory of women's insanity and nervous disease by increasingly disregarding women patients' self-reported symptoms and perceptions of causes.

The nervous symptoms and deviant behavior of nineteenth-century women patients were shaped by the constraints of gender and then were medicalized and therefore legitimized by medical representation as disease. The voices of women patients in case studies reported in medical periodicals and monographs indicate that women patients, as well as their family and friends, played a significant role in representing unfeminine behavior as nervous or insane and also in linking female insanity to women's reproductive organs. Although physicians' representations of women's illness varied by specialty, women's biological difference from men played some part in each specialty's explanatory scheme. Women physicians, unlike women patients, attempted to undermine the gynecological, organ-based explanation of female insanity and nervousness by empirical investigation and logical argument. Throughout the nineteenth century, medical science was shaped by women's "subjugated knowledge" just as it created a medicalized female subjectivity. Noticing women's voices in medical discourse, as patients and as physicians, forces us to reevaluate the unitary, male image of medical science and allows us to see gender and science as mutually constituting.

Department of History
University of Louisville

References

Aldrich, Flora L. 1894. "Another Consideration of Some Criticisms." *Woman's Medical Journal* 2:106–8.
Alienist and Neurologist. 1882a. "Attributing Undue Importance to Comparatively Trivial Uterine Affections." *Alienist and Neurologist* 3:296.
——— . 1882b. "Battey's Operation at the International Congress." *Alienist and Neurologist* 3:133.
——— . 1883. "Insanity in Hysterical Women." *Alienist and Neurologist* 4: 499–500.
——— . 1884. "Reviews of *On Visceral Neuroses.*" *Alienist and Neurologist* 5:735.
——— . 1886. "Moral Insanity." *Alienist and Neurologist* 7:505.
——— . 1888. "The Womb and Nerves." *Alienist and Neurologist* 9:274.
——— . 1890. "The Abuse of Uterine Treatment through Mistaken Diagnosis." *Alienist and Neurologist* 11:80.
——— . 1901. "Surgical Operations on the Insane." *Alienist and Neurologist* 22: 737.
——— . 1904. "Relation of Neurotic Cases to Abdominal Surgery." *Alienist and Neurologist* 25:556.
American Journal of Insanity. 1881. "Insanity and Uterine Diseases." *American Journal of Insanity* 37:443.
——— . 1882–83. "Proceedings of the Association of Medical Superintendents." *American Journal of Insanity* 39:133.
——— . 1884. "Proceedings of the Association of Medical Superintendents." *American Journal of Insanity* 40:247–325.
Arnold, A. B. 1879. "Hysteria." *Medical and Surgical Reporter* 41:118–21.
Barrus, Clara. 1896. "Insanity in Young Women." *Journal of Nervous and Mental Disease* 23:365–78.
Beard, Charles. 1877. "The Nature and Treatment of Neurasthenia (Nervous Exhaustion), Hysteria, Spinal Irritation, and Allied Neuroses." *Medical Record* 12:659.
——— . 1879. "Nervous Diseases Connected with the Male Genital Function." *Medical Record* 15:73–77, 555–59.
——— . 1898. *Sexual Neurasthenia (Nervous Exhaustion): Its Hygiene, Causes, Symptoms and Treatment.* New York: E. B. Treat.
Bennett, Alice. 1890. "Insanity as a Symptom of 'Bright's Disease.' " *Alienist and Neurologist* 11:566–605.
Blustine, Bonnie E. 1979. "New York Neurologists and the Specialization of American Medicine." *Bulletin of the History of Medicine* 53:170–83.

———. 1981. " 'A Hollow Square of Psychological Science': American Neurologists and Psychiatrists in Conflict." In *Madhouses, Mad-Doctors, and Madmen: The Social History of Psychiatry in the Victorian Era,* ed. Andrew Scull, 241–70. Philadelphia: University of Pennsylvania Press.

Bordo, Susan R. 1989. "The Body and the Reproduction of Femininity: A Feminist Appropriation of Foucault." In *Gender/Body/Knowledge: Feminist Reconstructions of Being and Knowing,* ed. Alison M. Jaggar and Susan R. Bordo, 13–33. New Brunswick, N.J.: Rutgers University Press.

Boston Insane Hospital (also known as Boston Lunatic Asylum). 1881a. Medical record. Case nos. 63, 67, 73, 292. Countway Library of Medicine, Boston.

———. 1881b. Medical record. Case no. 336. Countway Library of Medicine, Boston.

———. 1881c. Medical record. Case nos. 307, 335. Countway Library of Medicine, Boston.

———. 1882–83. Medical record. Case nos. 101, 253, 283, 318. Countway Library of Medicine, Boston.

———. 1884. Case records. Case no. 56. Countway Library of Medicine, Boston.

———. 1890–91a. Case records. Case no. 46. Countway Library of Medicine, Boston.

———. 1890–91b. Medical record. Case nos. 272, 290, 368. Countway Library of Medicine, Boston.

———. 1890–91c. Medical record. Case no. 82. Countway Library of Medicine, Boston.

Brown, Charlotte B. 1895. "Rest Therapy in Gynecology." *Woman's Medical Journal* 4:213–15.

Burnet, Anna. 1899. "Puerperal Insanity: Causes, Symptoms and Treatment." *Woman's Medical Journal* 9:267–73.

Burr, C. B. 1894. "The Relation of Gynaecology to Psychiatry." *Transactions of the Michigan Medical Society* 18:458–64, 478–87.

Bynum, W. F. 1985. "The Nervous Patient in Eighteenth- and Nineteenth-Century Britain: The Psychiatric Origins of British Neurology." In *The Anatomy of Madness: Essays in the History of Psychiatry,* ed. W. F. Bynum, Roy Porter, and Michael Shepherd, 89–102. London and New York: Tavistock Publications.

Cadwalader, Mary E. 1905. "The Insanity of Pregnancy and the Puerperium with Reports of Two Cases." *Woman's Medical Journal* 15:7–9.

Chauncey, George. 1989. "From Sexual Inversion to Homosexuality: Sexual Meanings and Homosexual Identities." In *Passion and Power: Sexuality in History,* ed. Kathy Peiss and Christina Simmons, 87–117. Philadelphia: Temple University Press.

Clarke, A. Bryant. 1859. "On the Treatment of Puerperal Mania by Veratrum Viride." *Boston Medical and Surgical Journal* 59:237–39.

Collins, Joseph, and Carlin Phillips. 1899. "The Etiology and Treatment of Neurasthenia: An Analysis of Three Hundred and Thirty-Three Cases." *Medical Record* 55:413.

Coone, Bethena. 1904a. "Hysteria and Neurasthenia." *Woman's Medical Journal* 14:236.

————. 1904b. "The Mental Diseases of Neurasthenia." *Woman's Medical Journal* 14:259–60.

Coveny, Mary A. 1901. "Women Physicians in Care of the State Insane." *Woman's Medical Journal* 11:262–63.

Cross, E. 1877. "Reflex Insanity." *St. Louis Clinical Record* 4:90–92.

Davenport, Isabel. 1895. "The Relation of Pelvic Disorders to Mental Disorders." *Medical News* 67:368–70, 560.

Digby, Anne. 1989. "Women's Biological Straitjacket." In *Sexuality and Subordination: Interdisciplinary Studies of Gender in the Nineteenth Century*, ed. Susan Mendus and Jane Rendall, 192–220. New York: Routledge.

Dreyfus, Hubert L., and Paul Rabinow. 1982. *Michel Foucault: Beyond Structuralism and Hermeneutics*. Chicago: University of Chicago Press.

Dwyer, Ellen. 1984. "A Historical Perspective." In *Sex Roles and Psychopathology*, ed. Cathy Spatz Widom, 19–48. New York: Plenum.

Engelhardt, H. Tristram, Jr. 1975. "The Concepts of Health and Disease." In *Evaluation and Explanation in the Biomedical Sciences*, ed. H. Tristram Engelhardt, Jr., and S. F. Spicker, 125–41. Dordrecht: D. Reidel.

Farnham, Alice May. 1887. "Uterine Disease as a Factor in the Production of Insanity." *Alienist and Neurologist* 8:532–47.

Fisher, Theodore. 1865a. Casebook, 1861–69. Case no. 56. Countway Library of Medicine, Boston.

————. 1865b. Casebook. Case nos. 58, 68. Countway Library of Medicine, Boston.

Folsom, Charles F. 1886. *The Relation of Our Public Schools to the Disorders of the Nervous System*. Boston: Grinn.

Foucault, Michel. 1967. *Madness and Civilization: A History of Insanity in the Age of Reason,* trans. Richard Howard. London: Tavistock.

————. 1972. *The Archaeology of Knowledge,* trans. A. M. Sheridan Smith. London: Tavistock.

————. 1973. *The Birth of the Clinic: An Archaeology of Medical Perception,* trans. A. M. Sheridan Smith. London: Tavistock.

————. 1980. *Power/Knowledge: Selected Interviews and Other Writings, 1972–1977,* trans. Colin Gordon. Brighton: Harvester.

Fox, Richard W. 1978. *So Far Disordered in Mind: Insanity in California, 1870–1930*. Berkeley: University of California Press.

Gardner, Miriam. 1900. "Retroversion of Uterus and Functional Neuroses." *Woman's Medical Journal* 10:36–37.

Garrigue, Evelyn. 1909a. "Psychotherapy and Re-education: Some Observations after Visiting Clinics in Paris and Nancy." *Woman's Medical Journal* 19:28–33.

————. 1909b. "Re-education in Medical Practice." *Woman's Medical Journal* 19:91–93.

————. 1910. "Some of the Causes and Prevention of Nervous Diseases." *Woman's Medical Journal* 20:78–80.

Gavitt, E. M. Roys. 1893. "Extraction of the Ovaries for the Cure of Insanity." *Woman's Medical Journal* 1:123–24.

Gilmore, Amelia. 1892. "Insanity of the Puerperium." *Journal of Nervous and Mental Disease* 19:408–18.

————. 1893. "A Contribution to the Study of Insanity and Nephritis." *Journal of Nervous and Mental Disease* 20:554–66.

Grob, Gerald N. 1988. "American Psychiatry: An Ambivalent Specialty." *Prospects* 12:149–74.

Gutting, Gary. 1989. *Michel Foucault's Archaeology of Scientific Reason.* Cambridge: Cambridge University Press.

Hall, Ernest. 1900. "The Gynecological Treatment of the Insane in Private Practice." *Pacific Medical Journal* 43:241–56.

Hanley, L. G. 1900–1901. "Mental Aberrations, Consequent Upon Pelvic Disease." *Buffalo Medical Journal* 40:672.

Haraway, Donna. 1989a. "The Biopolitics of Postmodern Bodies: Determinations of Self in Immune System Discourse." *differences: A Journal of Feminist Cultural Studies* 1:3–44.

————. 1989b. *Primate Visions: Gender, Race, and Nature in the World of Modern Science.* New York: Routledge.

Harding, Sandra. 1986. *The Science Question in Feminism.* Ithaca, N.Y.: Cornell University Press.

Henry, W. O. 1900–1901. "Insanity in Women Associated with Pelvic Diseases." *Annals of Gynecology and Pediatry* 14:312–20.

Hersman, C. C. 1899. "The Relationship between Uterine Disturbances and Some of the Insanities." *Journal of the American Medical Association* 33:709–11.

Hughes, C. H. 1882. "A Case of Moral Insanity: Described by a Mother and Reported by C. H. Hughes, M.D., St. Louis, Missouri." *Alienist and Neurologist* 3:519–23.

Hurd, Henry M. 1882–83. "The Treatment of Periodic Insanity." *American Journal of Insanity* 39:174–80.

Hutchins, Fannie C. 1900. "Puerperal Insanity." *Woman's Medical Journal* 10:253–57.

Jacobi, Mary Putnam. 1886. "Some Considerations on Hysteria." *Medical Record* 30:365–74, 396–401, 429–33.

Jones, Mary Dixon. 1894a. "A Consideration of Some Criticisms." *Woman's Medical Journal* 2:80–82.

————. 1894b. "Early Operations." *Woman's Medical Journal* 2:110–11.

————. 1895a. "Oophorectomy in Diseases of the Nervous System." *Woman's Medical Journal* 4:1–5.

————. 1895b. "Review of Henry J. Garrigues' *A Text-Book of the Diseases of Women.*" *Woman's Medical Journal* 4:19–23.

Jordanova, Ludmilla. 1980. "Natural Facts: A Historical Perspective on Science and Sexuality." In *Nature, Culture and Gender,* ed. Carol P. MacCormack and M. Strathern, 42–69. Cambridge: Cambridge University Press.

————. 1986. "Naturalizing the Family: Literature and the Bio-Medical Sciences in the Late Eighteenth Century." In *Languages of Nature: Critical Essays on Science and Literature,* ed. Ludmilla Jordanova, 86–116. New Brunswick, N.J.: Rutgers University Press.

————. 1989. *Sexual Visions: Images of Gender in Science and Medicine between the Eighteenth and Twentieth Centuries.* Madison: University of Wisconsin Press.

Kleinman, Arthur. 1980. *Patients and Healers in the Context of Culture*. Berkeley and Los Angeles: University of California Press.

———. 1986. *Social Origins of Distress and Disease: Depression, Neurasthenia, and Pain in Modern China*. New Haven, Conn.: Yale University Press.

Lane, Edward B. 1901. "Puerperal Insanity." *Boston Medical and S rgical Journal* 144:606–9.

Luther, Calista. 1900. "Woman's Work in the Care of the Insane." In *Transactions of the Twenty-fifth Meeting of the Alumnae Association of the Woman's Medical College of Pennsylvania*, 39–40. Alumnae Association of the Woman's Medical College of Pennsylvania, Philadelphia.

McCowen, Jennie. 1882–83. "The Prevention of Insanity." *Northwest Lancet* 2:14–19.

McFarland, Anne H. 1893. "Treatment of the Insane." *Woman's Medical Journal* 1:145–48.

———. 1894. "The Relation of Operative Gynecology to Insanity." *Woman's Medical Journal* 2:40–42.

———. 1895. "Nervous Men and Nervous Women." *Woman's Medical Journal* 4:113–17.

McGovern, Constance. 1981. "Doctors or Ladies? Women Physicians in Psychiatric Institutions, 1872–1900." *Bulletin of the History of Medicine* 55:88–107.

MacKenzie, Charlotte. 1983. "Women and Psychiatric Professionalization, 1790–1914." In *The Sexual Dynamics of History: Men's Power, Women's Resistance*, ed. the London Feminist History Group, 107–19. London: Pluto.

Mackie, Laura G. 1909. "Psychotherapy, Its Use and Abuse." *Woman's Medical Journal* 19:23–25.

Mann, Edward C. 1884. "A Case of Insanity of Pubescence (Hebephrenia), Associated with Epilepsy, Occurring in a Young Lady Sixteen Years of Age." *Alienist and Neurologist* 5:502–4.

Mitchell, S. Weir. 1871. *Wear and Tear, or Hints for the Overworked*. Philadelphia: J. B. Lippincott.

———. 1879. *Fat and Blood: And How to Make Them*. Philadelphia: J. B. Lippincott.

———. 1900. *Doctor and Patient*. Philadelphia: J. B. Lippincott.

Morantz-Sanchez, Regina. 1985. *Sympathy and Science: Women Physicians in American Medicine*. New York: Oxford University Press.

———. 1992. "The Gendering of Empathetic Expertise: How Women Doctors Became More Empathetic than Men." Unpublished manuscript, University of California, Los Angeles, Department of History.

Moscucci, Ornella. 1990. *The Science of Woman: Gynaecology and Gender in England, 1800–1921*. Cambridge: Cambridge University Press.

Peckham, Grace. 1887. "The Nervousness of Americans." *Journal of Social Science* 22:37–49.

Poovey, Mary. 1988. *Uneven Developments: The Ideological Work of Gender in Mid-Victorian England*. Chicago: University of Chicago Press.

Post-Graduate. 1896. "Confessions of a Nervous Woman." *Post-Graduate: The Journal of the New York Post-Graduate Medical School and Hospital* 11: 364–68.

Psychological and Medico-Legal Journal. 1874. "Review of Edward H. Clarke's *The Building of a Brain.*" *Psychological and Medico-Legal Journal* 1:401.

Reed, Charles A. L. 1888–89. "The Gynesic Element in Psychiatry—with Suggestions for Asylum Reform." *Buffalo Medical and Surgical Journal* 28: 569–81.

Reynolds, Edward. 1910. "Gynecological Operations on Neurasthenics: Advantages, Disadvantages, Selection of Cases." *Boston Medical and Surgical Journal* 163:113–18.

Riley, Denise. 1988. *"Am I That Name?" Feminism and the Category of "Women" in History.* Minneapolis: University of Minnesota Press.

Robinovitch, Louise G. 1903. "The Woman Physician and a Vast Field of Usefulness Unrecognized by Her." In *Transactions of the 28th Annual Meeting of the Alumnae Association of the Woman's Medical College of Pennsylvania,* 72–81. Alumnae Association of the Woman's Medical College of Pennsylvania.

Rohe, George H. 1896. "Some Causes of Insanity In Women." *American Journal of Obstetrics* 34:801–6.

Russell, Ira. 1884. "The Borderland of Insanity." *Alienist and Neurologist* 5: 457–71.

Sawicki, Jana. 1991. *Disciplining Foucault: Feminism, Power, and the Body.* New York: Routledge.

Scott, Joan Wallach. 1988. *Gender and the Politics of History.* New York: Columbia University Press.

Scott, John. 1871. "Reflex Puerperal Mania and Its Rational Treatment." *Proceedings of the Gynaecological Society of Boston* 5:222–24.

Showalter, Elaine. 1981. "Victorian Women and Insanity." In *Madhouses, Mad-Doctors, and Madmen: The Social History of Psychiatry in the Victorian Era,* ed. Andrew Scull, 313–31. Philadelphia: University of Pennsylvania Press.

———. 1987. *The Female Malady: Women, Madness, and English Culture, 1830–1980.* New York: Penguin.

Sicherman, Barbara. 1980. *The Quest for Mental Health in America, 1880–1917.* New York: Arno.

Sims, J. Marion. 1878. *Battey's Operation.* London: T. Richardo.

Smith-Rosenberg, Carroll. 1972. "The Hysterical Woman: Sex Roles and Role Conflict in Nineteenth-Century America." *Social Research* 39:562–84.

———. 1985. *Disorderly Conduct: Visions of Gender in Victorian America.* New York: Knopf.

Spink, Mary A. 1896. "Causes of Neurasthenia among the Women of To-Day." *Woman's Medical Journal* 5:33–37.

Stone, I. S. 1891. "Can the Gynecologist Aid the Alienist in Institutions for the Insane?" *Journal of the American Medical Association* 16:870–73.

Storer, Horatio R. 1864. "Cases Illustrative of Obstetric Disease—Deductions Concerning Insanity in Women." *Boston Medical and Surgical Journal* 70: 189–200.

Teed, J. L. 1874. "General Observations Preliminary to the Study of Nervous Disease." *Psychological and Medico-Legal Journal* 1:137–44.

Theriot, Nancy M. 1990. "Diagnosing Unnatural Motherhood: Nineteenth-Century Physicians and 'Puerperal Insanity.' " *American Studies* 26:69–88.

Tomlinson, H. A., and Mary E. Bassett. 1899. "Association of Pelvic Diseases and Insanity in Women, and the Influence of Treatment of the Local Disease Upon the Mental Condition." *Journal of the American Medical Association* 33: 827–31.

Trowbridge, G. R. 1891. "The Insanity of Pubescence." *Alienist and Neurologist* 12:341–49.

Turner, Bryan S. 1984. *The Body and Society: Explorations in Social Theory.* New York: Basil Blackwell.

Van Deusen, E. H. 1868–69. "Observations on a Form of Nervous Prostration (Neurasthenia), Culminating in Insanity." *American Journal of Insanity* 25:447.

Vinton, Maria Mitchell. 1899. "Studies of Melancholia." *Woman's Medical Journal* 9:103–10, 145–56.

Waxler, Nancy E. 1974. "Culture and Mental Illness: A Social Labeling Perspective." *Journal of Nervous and Mental Disease* 159:379–95.

Weedon, Chris. 1987. *Feminist Practice and Postructuralist Theory.* New York: Basil Blackwell.

Welsh, Lilian. 1925. *Reminiscences of Thirty Years in Baltimore.* Baltimore: Norman, Remington.

Whitomore, B. T. 1879. "Hystero-Epilepsy." *St. Louis Courier of Medicine and Collateral Sciences* 1:520–23.

Woman's Medical Journal. 1894. "Women Physicians in Insane Hospitals." *Woman's Medical Journal* 2:113.

———. 1900. "The Relation of Pelvic and Intra-Abdominal Diseases to Mental Diseases in Women." *Woman's Medical Journal* 10:428.

———. 1904a. "Sex Differentiation and Education." *Woman's Medical Journal* 14:83.

———. 1904b. "Sex Competition." *Woman's Medical Journal* 14:84.

———. 1904c. "The Overeducated Woman and the Race Question." *Woman's Medical Journal* 14:180–81.

———. 1908. "The Mental Origin of Neurasthenia and Its Bearing on Treatment." *Woman's Medical Journal* 18:30.

———. 1909. "Psychoanalysis in Psychotherapy." *Woman's Medical Journal* 19:210–11.

Wood, Ann Douglas. 1973. " 'The Fashionable Diseases': Women's Complaints and Their Treatment in Nineteenth-Century America." *Journal of Interdisciplinary History* 4:25–52.

Workman J. 1883. "Moral Insanity—What Is It?" *Alienist and Neurologist* 4:298–304.

Zola, Irving Kenneth. 1972. "Medicine as an Institution of Social Control." *Sociological Review* 20:487–504.

Women and Computers:
An Introduction

Ruth Perry and Lisa Greber

Sometimes technological change seems the only constant in our lives; in our darker moments, the Frankenstein specter of technology, embodied by the atomic bomb, haunts our collective dreams. The rapidity of technological innovation, and our urgent need to describe and adapt to its effects, may overwhelm the examination of more fundamental questions concerning its nature and its relation to human need. Popular consciousness as well as formal scholarship too often share an overriding concern with the effects of technological change while neglecting to look for the forces driving these changes. The exceptions, welcome and provocative, have been all too rare.[1] The relation of gender to technology—the effects of technology on women's and men's lives, the ways in which women and men construct and use technology, the theoretical implications of gender socialization for future needs and developments in technology—these connections have yet to be made, this story has yet to be written. Yet it is imperative that as feminists we try to sort out these forces and habits of thought if we want best to influence the directions and uses of rapidly changing technologies.

[1] See, e.g., Donald MacKensie and Judy Wajcman, eds., *The Social Shaping of Technology* (Philadelphia: Open University Press, 1985), an excellent collection of essays about the ways in which technologies—domestic, military, and productive technologies—are shaped by social forces. Particular attention is given to the interactions and contradictions between capitalism and patriarchy.

[*Signs: Journal of Women in Culture and Society* 1990, vol. 16, no. 1]

Most studies of the effects of technology assume the operation of an autonomous "technological determinism." In this view, tools themselves are considered to be neutral, and change is assumed to be inevitable, independent of other political or economic forces. Some versions of technological determinism claim that science shapes technology and that technology is merely a logical and pragmatic implementation of scientific ideas. Others posit that technology shapes technology—new technologies inexorably evolving from modifications of existing ones. Either way we humans are seen as ships before the storm of technology, lifted or buffeted by forces beyond our control; in the wake of the storm we adapt, choosing the least unpleasant from a limited set of options.[2]

Closer inspection of these images of technological change reveals complexities not sufficiently addressed by either formulation. Social, political, and economic factors, in conjunction with currents within the scientific and technical fields themselves, all combine to create the technologies of a particular era. To think that scientific knowledge alone determines technology implies that developments in science are themselves neutral. Yet recent theoretical work demonstrating the connections between the social order and scientific thought belie this belief in the objectivity of scientific pursuit, as objectivity traditionally has been understood. What is being called into question is not the validity of verifiable empirical data but, rather, the choice and construction of the questions asked, the methodology followed, and the relationship between the observer and the observed.[3] The socially determined

[2] For a more detailed discussion of technological determinism, see the introductory essay in MacKensie and Wajcman, eds., 2–25.

[3] There has been a tremendous outpouring of such critiques of science within the past twenty years. Perhaps one of the most far-reaching discussions, and one of particular interest to feminists, is Evelyn Fox Keller's collection of essays *Reflections on Gender and Science* (New Haven, Conn.: Yale University Press, 1985). Keller discusses the nature of scientific knowledge from its Baconian inception to its current practice and untangles the twisted strands of masculine and scientific ideology using examples of concrete practice in biology and physics. Ruth Bleier, in *Science and Gender: A Critique of Biology and Its Theories on Women* (New York: Pergamon, 1984), directs her attention primarily to biology and convincingly illustrates inherent masculine biases within the field. See also Sally Hacker, *Pleasure, Power, and Technology: Some Tales of Gender, Engineering and the Cooperative Workplace* (Boston: Unwin & Hyman, 1989); Cheris Kramarae, *Technology and Women's Voices: Keeping in Touch* (London and New York: Routledge & Kegan Paul, 1988); Joan Rothschild, *Teaching Technology from a Feminist Perspective: A Practical Guide* (New York: Pergamon, 1988); Ruth Bleier, *Feminist Approaches to Science* (New York: Pergamon, 1986); Pnina G. Abir-Am, *Uneasy Careers and Intimate Lives: Women in Science, 1789–1979* (New Brunswick, N.J.: Rutgers University Press, 1987).

constraints on science range from the obvious implications of funding priorities to much deeper criticisms of the practice of science: the factors involved in the selection of what is considered "compelling" evidence, the choice of paradigms and metaphorical explanations, and the criteria for good science. If science reflects at least some of a society's values, then technology developed from it must also embody these values. It is also shortsighted to theorize a simplistic one-way connection between technology and science because, for example, certain developments in science are made possible only by prior technical advances.

We do know that particular technological progressions are driven by complex economic and political imperatives. Thomas Hughes compared advances in the chemical industry in wartime Germany with those in the peacetime United States to demonstrate that a particular sequence of research and development is not inevitable. In the late 1930s, the German chemical firm I. G. Farben began to manufacture ammonia by the Haber-Bosch process—a technique for synthesizing new chemicals by combining precursor chemicals with hydrogen. Under the pressure of the wartime need for independent production of raw materials, the firm developed a parallel process for the synthesis of wood alcohol and, finally, petroleum. In the United States, Du Pont used similar processes for the production of ammonia and wood alcohol but, lacking the economic and political motivation to synthesize petroleum, found no need to continue the "natural" progression.[4]

Patriarchy, computers, and women's lives

If technological change is not simply inevitable, but in part determined by social, political, and economic forces, as feminists we must decipher how and to what extent technologies reflect or reinforce the patriarchal order. A few pioneering works on the subject have begun to explore the complex issues raised by this question.[5] Until recently, however, feminist thinkers have paid little

[4] See Thomas Hughes, "Edison and the Electric Light," in MacKensie and Wajcman, eds., 39–52.

[5] The pioneering work providing a feminist critique of technology has been invaluable. In a comprehensive set of essays, Jan Zimmerman, ed., *The Technological Woman: Interfacing with Tomorrow* (New York: Praeger, 1983), covers a wide range of issues from household technologies to abortion and reproductive technologies, in addition to dealing with office automation, jobs in high technology organizations, and computer education for girls. Another useful collection is Joan

attention to the linchpin of the new industrial revolution: the computer.[6] This omission is all the more striking given the veritable flood of material in recent years on the coming "information society" by proponents and critics alike. The reasons for this are complex. Feminist thinkers from the humanities and social sciences often feel insufficiently informed to address the subject. Even from within the fields of computer science and electrical engineering, women have been reluctant to challenge the socially constructed elements of computer science. In the past few years, however, as it has become more and more apparent that the computer will play a crucial role in all of our futures, feminist theorists have begun to address some of the issues raised by the use of computers.[7]

From the outset feminists have expressed concerns about differential access to computer education across racial and gender lines, about the construction of software for male and middle-class users, and about the effects on women's lives of the computer in the home and in the workplace. Feminists have been studying the

---

Rothschild, ed., *Machina ex Dea: Feminist Perspectives on Technology* (New York: Pergamon, 1983).

[6] Cynthia Cockburn's *Brothers: Male Dominance and Technological Change* (London: Pluto, 1983), focuses on the changes occurring in London's newspaper industry with the introduction of computer technology, and uses this example to explore the ways men use technology to maintain their patriarchal power. See also Diane Werneke, *Microelectronics and Office Jobs: One Impact of the Chip on Women's Employment* (London: International Labour Office, 1984); National Research Council, *Computer Chips and Paper Clips: Technology and Women's Development*, Report of the Panel on Technology and Women's Employment, vol. 1, ed. Heidi Hartmann, Robert E. Kraut, and Louise A. Tilly (Washington, D.C.: National Academy Press, 1986); and for the classroom, Rothschild, *Teaching Technology*.

[7] Much of the early thinking on this subject has been done by Scandinavian theorists, although not much of it has been distributed in this country. See, e.g., A. Olerup, L. Schneider, and E. Monod, eds., *Women, Work, and Computerization: Opportunities and Disadvantages* (North Holland: Elsevier Science Publishers, 1985). Other Scandinavian work on this subject includes *Women Challenge Technology: Papers from a European Conference on Women, Natural Sciences and Technology*, vols. 1–4, ed. Mona Dahms, Lone Dirckinck-Holmfeld, Kirsten Gronbaek Hansen, Anette Kolmos, and Janni Nielsen (Elsinore: Centertrykkeriet University Aalborg, 1986); Bente Rasmussen and Leslie Schneider, "Office Automation and Women's Work," *Tidsskrift for Samfunnsforskning* 23 (1982): 519–34; Tamar Bermann, "Data Technology and Women's Employment," *Psykolognytt, Organ för Sveriges Psykologförbund* (Oslo) 13 (1982): 24–26, 31–34; and Janni Neilsen, "Occupational Health Hazards: The Psychological Aspects with Special Reference to Office Workers" (paper presented at Internationales Fortbildungs-und Arbeitssem-nar fur Frauen, Salzburg, July 1982). New ways of formulating the work of systems development can be found in Gro Bjerkness, Pelle Ehn, and Morton Kyng, *Computers and Democracy—a Scandinavian Challenge* (London: Gower, 1987).

effects of computers on women's work as the dramatic changes brought about by the wide-scale use of computers in offices has begun to alter significantly both the quality and the scale of women's employment.

Taken as a whole, this research tends to show that computers are already affecting women's lives in very specific and predominantly negative ways. The pattern that emerges has historical resonances: women's work becomes more fragmented and isolated, output is tightly monitored and the pace and stress of the work is increased. The second industrial revolution begins to look very much like the first one.[8] Skilled craft knowledge is broken into smaller bits, requiring less training and commanding lower wages for workers; control is transferred from workers to management. Viewed this way, the computer's effects on women's lives appear not so much determined by the technology per se, as perpetuated and reinforced by particular social, economic, and political structures.

The U.S. economy is undergoing a shift from a primary emphasis on manufacturing to one based in the clerical and service sectors, in jobs traditionally considered women's work. Between 1973 and 1980, 70 percent of the new private sector jobs were in this area.[9] As the number of these jobs has increased, they have been increasingly automated. Complex skills have been broken into simple tasks which require less competence or discretion on the part of the individual worker. Automation within the Massachusetts welfare department, for example, has meant that the less easily defined, caring parts of the social workers' task can be lost as welfare workers are redefined as "financial assistance workers."[10] Now their main task is to process personal data and query the computer about the appropriate benefit level for a client.

Automation also enables managers to monitor more easily each individual's work—how much, how quickly, how many breaks he or she takes. Word-processing programs, for example, can monitor an operator's keystrokes or the amount of time he or she logs in on a machine. As more offices use computer networks instead of personal computers, the possibilities for monitoring increase. Network file access tends to be organized hierarchically; supervisors can read their employees' documents and memos before the

[8] Barbara Garson, *The Electronic Sweatshop: How Computers Are Transforming the Office of the Future into the Factory of the Past* (New York: Simon & Schuster, 1988).

[9] Barbara Ehrenreich and Frances Fox Piven, "The Feminization of Poverty," *Dissent* 31 (Spring 1984): 162–70, esp. 164.

[10] Garson, 75, 73–114. For a more general overview, see Roslyn L. Feldberg and Evelyn Nakano Glenn, "Technology and Work Degradation: Effects of Office Automation on Women Clerical Workers," in Rothschild, ed., 59–78.

employees have finished them—but not vice versa. Nor is monitoring restricted to computer terminals or even to any job-specific tasks. Barbara Garson describes an incident in the life of an airline reservation agent: "A woman sat down at the beginning of her shift, plugged in [her headset] and said to her friend, 'The doctor says it's cancer.' . . . Within an hour she was called into a supervisor's office, who asked sympathetically, 'Is there any way we can help about your cancer?' . . . The women thought they had to be talking to a customer to be overheard. They didn't know until then that the system picked up their voices as soon as they plugged in."[11] While managers can claim remarkable results by monitoring everything from a trucker's highway speed to a factory worker's pace, workers themselves may feel that such surveillance is dehumanizing and degrading, reducing their already limited control over their work environment and increasing their stress.

Video display terminal (VDT) use appears in some cases to be hazardous to workers' health as well as their privacy. Those who work with VDTs report suffering from eye strain and deteriorated vision as well as headaches, back problems, insomnia, and increased anxiety and depression.[12] There is some evidence that VDTs may be harmful, particularly to pregnant women. A recent study at the Northern California Kaiser Permanent Medical Care Program in Oakland found that office workers using VDTs more than twenty hours per week during the first three months of pregnancy doubled their risk for miscarriages. It is not clear whether these health effects are caused by the technology itself or by the stresses of the faster workplace and electronic monitoring.[13]

Increasingly automated and monitored, clerical work is also being moved from the office into the home. Perhaps the most persistent myth about the computer's effects on women's work lives is the idea that this computer "homeworking" will be a tremendous boon to women. Yet the history of "outwork"—factory piecework produced in the home on commission—shows how such work in the past has often entailed losses in workers' rights and wages, a result corroborated in the recent history of computer outwork.[14]

[11] Garson, 49.

[12] Judith Gregory, "The Next Move: Organizing Women in the Office," in Zimmerman, ed., 263–64; and Wendy Chavkin, ed., *Double Exposure: Women's Health on the Job and at Home* (New York: Monthly Review Press, 1984).

[13] "Study Links VDTs to Miscarriages," originally published in *American Journal of Industrial Medicine* (June 1988) and quoted by Leslie Fraser in "Study Links VDTs to Miscarriages," *Science for the People* 20, no. 4 (September–October 1988): 4. For more up-to-date information, send for the bimonthly *VDT News*, P.O. Box 1799, Grand Central Station, New York, N.Y. 10163.

[14] See Bettina Berch, "Home Sweet Sweatshop: The Resurrection of Outwork" (New York, 1985, typescript). Barbara Garson includes an interesting discussion

Because homeworkers are paid by the piece, not by the hour, they receive no benefits. They also often earn lower wages than their office counterparts. Home data processors at Blue Cross/Blue Shield, for example, working up to fifty-five hours a week, make $5,000 less per year than their office counterparts who work forty hours a week. In Sweden, too, wages are lower both for homework and for "remote work" (data processing performed in centers that are geographically removed from the main office) than for on-site workers.[15]

Homeworkers and remote workers have little bargaining power with their employers. They tend to have few other employment options, and their isolation from one another makes collective action difficult. For women with small children it may seem like a solution to the day care crisis, but it also means a reprivatization of their lives. It is obviously easier for a company providing "opportunities" for homework to insist that child care be each woman's individual responsibility. Unions not always sympathetic to women's particular concerns nevertheless recognize that homeworkers' low wages and lack of benefits depress all workers' wages. Some, such as the AFL-CIO and 9-to-5, have called for a federal ban on teleworking for clerical workers.[16]

The possibility of remote work centers has given a new reality to the metaphor of the global factory. In 1985, the *Wall Street Journal* described the process as follows: "West Publishing Company, St. Paul, Minnesota, sends some material to South Korea, where non-English-speaking workers keypunch complex legal documents into the firm's Westlaw data bank. Barbados workers earn $2.50 an hour keypunching data into American Airline computers. The work was previously done in Tulsa, Oklahoma by 200 workers who made $6.50 an hour."[17] While the use of Third World women's labor for data processing may be new, the labor pattern is familiar to the electronics industry. Indeed, the low U.S. dollar cost of the electronics revolution is to a large extent a reflection of the ability of multinational companies to exploit Third World labor. The desire

---

about how higher-level professionals also lose their job security and benefits through automation in her chapter "Piecework Professionals," 225–36.

[15] Gitte Vedel, "Telematics and Remote Office Work," summary statement of methods and main conclusions of Information Systems Research Group, August 1985, Institute for Industrial Research and Social Development, Copenhagen School of Economics and Social Science.

[16] Michael Miller, "Productivity Spies: Computers Keep Eye on Workers and See If They Perform Well," *Wall Street Journal* (June 3, 1985).

[17] "Clerical Jobs Are Moving to Countries with Cheaper Labor Costs," *Wall Street Journal* (February 26, 1985), quoted in Berch, "Home Sweet Sweatshop," 17.

for low assembly costs and high profits in a rapidly changing electronics industry has resulted in the need for a willing and vulnerable labor market—a need most often met by hiring young (and in most countries, single) Third World women in low-skilled, low-paying assembly and testing positions. In Hong Kong, the first off-shore assembly site for the U.S. semi-conductor industry and now a regional core of semi-conductor chip production, multinational companies like Motorola employ only women workers to load chips into test equipment.[18] In the Philippines, 84 percent of the assemblers at Philips Components Philippines, Inc. (PCPI) are women.[19]

The working conditions of this female labor force are particularly exploitative. Oftentimes wages are not high enough to cover workers' living expenses. At PCPI in 1987, monthly take-home pay averaged 1,341 pesos while monthly expenses averaged 2,135 pesos; maternity benefits covered a woman's first four "legitimate" children. In South Korea over 60 percent of fully employed women urban workers earn less than the minimum cost of living—a wage that makes it easier for companies to encourage or require overtime work. For Korean workers, the average work week is 54.4 hours.[20] In December 1988 electronic workers at Motorola's South Korean plant staged a sit-in in the company canteen to gain company recognition of their union. Motorola locked the protestors in the canteen and sent in *kusadae*—a militant save-the-company corps consisting of managerial staff and other male employees. Many workers were seriously injured.[21] In some cases the violence of the *kusadae* has been specifically directed at women workers, such as when the women union organizers at the Masan plant of TC Electronics, the South Korean subsidiary of Tandy Electronics, suffered "a series of violent attacks, including torture and sexual brutality."[22]

[18] Lenny Siegel, "Hong Kong: A Regional Case of Chip Production," *Global Electronics* 89 (December 1988): 2; published by Pacific Studies Center, 2220 View St., Mountain View, Calif. 94041. For a discussion of the global assembly line in the electronics industry, see also Barbara Ehrenreich, *Women in the Global Factory* (Boston: South End Press, 1983); Diane Elson and Ruth Pearson, "Nimble Fingers Make Cheap Workers: An Analysis of Women's Employment in Third World Manufacturing," *Feminist Review* 7 (1981): 87–107; Rachael Grossman, "Woman's Place in the Integrated Circuit," *Southeast Asia Chronicle* 66 (January/February 1979): 2–18; Steve Volk and Amy Wishner, "Electronics: The Global Industry," *NACLA Report on the Americas* 11 (April 1977): 1–25.

[19] Lenny Siegel, "PCPI Conditions," *Global Electronics* 76 (August 1987): 1.

[20] Ibid., and Lenny Siegel, "Korea," *Global Electronics* 79 (November 1987): 1.

[21] Lenny Siegel, "Korean Workers Organize," *Global Electronics* 89 (December 1988): 4.

[22] North American Coalition for Human Rights, quoted in *Global Electronics* 85 (August 1988): 2.

These are not the only issues that computers present to women. Still, these few examples suggest some ways in which computers are implicated in the stories of women in the contemporary workplace and how computers can reinforce particular social and economic structures. They support the power of capital by moving information and skills from workers to managers; they reinforce the power of patriarchy by pushing women, particularly women of color, into low-skilled, low-paying, and highly controlled jobs. These effects are certainly not inherent in the technology: to program a user-monitoring dimension into word-processing software is a sociopolitical choice, not a technological necessity. Professional women may value their computers' help in processing experimental information, writing and editing, or in expediting administrative tasks—but secretaries who do not control their own time and only use computers to process other people's words feel differently about the flexibility, potential, and power of these machines.

An examination of recent developments in employment patterns in the rapidly reorganizing insurance industry shows us what changes we can expect in the next stage of computer automation if it is driven by existing sociopolitical forces. The first stage of automation in this industry looked much like that in other industries: increased job fragmentation and a narrowing of function, more centralized administration of workers, greater occupational sex segregation, and isolation of data entry from other clerical tasks.[23] Yet there is much to be learned from analyzing the employment practices of the second stage of automation, still in the process of working itself out, a process hardly neutral with regard to race and gender. The hallmark of this second stage is the combining of professional and clerical functions, a reorganization accompanied by progressive "feminization" of the industry. Women may move into higher levels of management during this stage, but what was previously designated as "professional work" has been in many ways degraded, human decision making preempted by routinized, computer-based practices. At the same time, combined clerical activities such as data entry, insurance rating, and policy preparation are being transferred to newly intermediate multifunction workers.

Thus, although women appear to be moving up in the occupational hierarchy, what is in fact happening is that the work is being

[23] Barbara Baran, "Office Automation and Women's Work: The Technological Transformation of the Insurance Industry," in *High Technology, Space and Society,* ed. Manuel Castells, Urban Affairs Annual Reviews, vol. 28 (Beverly Hills: Sage, 1985), 143–71.

restructured. Professional women's wage rates are not so high as were the rates for male professionals in the previous stage, and their contribution is devalued. Meanwhile, whole all-woman occupational rungs at the bottom of the hierarchy such as keyboarding and filing—often the jobs of women of color—are being entirely eliminated from the ladder. The cost of women's labor is lower, and there are fewer jobs in all categories. Employers in the insurance industry are now targeting an educated, middle-class, largely white population of married women with small children to work part-time at home with computers in this new form of postindustrial, bureaucratic housework.[24]

In this example, it is not the logic of computer technology that causes these changes, but the prevailing social and economic system that educates its middle class to bureaucratic drudgery and encourages—with short-term profits—business practices that mechanize work and de-skill workers. We must learn to see computers in their cultural context—to parse the interacting political, economic, social, and technological forces that combine to create and define appropriate use of computers—as part of the process of imagining the kinds of technologies or adaptations of technologies that best reflect the social and political relations that we, as feminists, would like to see.

The history of women and computers

The story of women's place in the development of the computer is instructive—both for what it suggests about the relation of women to developing technologies in general and for the details of a historically specific construction of a field—computer science—in a context that includes but is not defined by the dimension of gender. Although the use of machines to assist in computation has a long history, the digital electronic computer is the child of our own times, and in particular of the first and second world wars. The development of the computer is inextricably linked with wartime needs. The British Colossus, completed in December of 1943, was a single-purpose decoding machine designed to unscramble German radio transmissions. It was not able to run stored programs, but in all other respects it was similar to modern computers, and it launched the British computer industry.[25] In the United States, the

[24] Ibid., 152–66.
[25] A history of Colossus and other early British machines can be found in Simon Lavington, *Early British Computers* (Bedford, Mass.: Digital, 1980), esp. 8–12.

Ballistic Research Laboratory and professors from the Moore School of Engineering collaborated on the design of the Electronic Numerical Integrator and Computer (ENIAC), a machine created to assist with the computation of ballistic tables.[26] These were firing and bombing tables considered necessary during World War II to assist gunners in targeting high speed aircraft. According to Goldstine, the computation of one firing table required approximately 3 million multiplications.

Prior to the ENIAC, women "computers" using hand calculators performed the mathematics to compile these ballistic tables. They worked too slowly for wartime needs, however. In the eyes of military leaders, the development of an electronic calculating machine was necessary to meet the war's demands. The close cooperation of universities and the military in developing computer technology and sharing material resources and personnel that began during a wartime regime continues to this day. Although it would seem to be accidental that it was women's labor that this new technology was designed to replace, this example corroborates the thesis of at least one historian of technology that the interpretation of technological development needs to be charted in relation to women's work insofar as many technologies have evolved to replace the labor of women.[27]

Because of the plasticity of the computer, it is difficult to imagine which developments might never have occurred during so-called peacetime civilian management, but some examples are suggestive. In the early 1950s, the Army Signal Corps's need for transistors capable of withstanding high temperatures and amplifying high-frequency signals led Bell Laboratories to develop devices appropriate to military needs but less useful for the commercial telephone system.[28] More recently, the military has encouraged the development of gallium arsenide (GaAs) semi-conductor devices. In contrast to the more traditional and less expensive silicon transistors, which currently satisfy most civilian transistor needs, GaAs devices are "radiation-hard." This means they might withstand the electromagnetic pulse effects of a nuclear war, or, in

[26] Herman Goldstine, one of the participants in the design of these machines, details their history in *The Computer from Pascal to von Neumann* (Princeton, N.J.: Princeton University Press, 1972), pt. 2, 121–236. This work makes the military-university cooperation particularly clear.

[27] This is the thesis of a forthcoming book by David Noble: *A World without Women: The Evolution of the Masculine Culture of Science* (New York: Knopf, 1991), in press.

[28] See Thomas J. Misa's essay "Military Needs, Commercial Realities and the Development of the Transistor, 1948–1958," in *Military Enterprise and Technological Change*, ed. Merritt Roe Smith (Cambridge, Mass.: MIT Press, 1986), 253–87.

a more realistic scenario, withstand current levels of cosmic irradiation while in orbit as part of the Strategic Defense Initiative (former President Reagan's Star Wars). Proponents argue that GaAs devices would be three to six times as fast as traditional ones and thus eventually preferable for civilian uses other than the current limited demand for them in satellites and microwave communications. However, in very small devices, switching speed may be limited by the ability of the material to dissipate heat.[29] Silicon can do this about six times as fast as GaAs; hence the primary reason for encouraging the latter can only be its suitability for the military. Examples of technological developments tied to military uses are legion; indeed the imperatives of defense research may be the most consistent form of determinism operating in the evolution of technology.

The military represents our culture's definition of masculinity in perhaps its clearest form. The ideology of Western manhood has historically linked male privilege with aggression, violence, and domination. The identification of military interests with masculine gender definition has affected the development of computers, in both their production and their use, as Paul Edwards's article in this issue states. Women now constitute noticeable percentages of both military personnel and computer scientists, reflecting gains made in the past fifteen years. Edwards is interested in the political and cultural implications of women's presence in these highly masculine fields. In considering the modes of thought that dominate computer science and the culture of engineering, as well as the deeply entangled institutions of military service and of masculinity, Edwards suggests that women's presence in these bastions of masculinity might threaten masculinity as a political institution. He sees the increasing militarization of computers and the corresponding computerization of the military—each sector reinforcing the other—as attempts to buttress the prevailing social order. Indeed, as we have seen, the increased use of computers in the workplace tends to intensify stratification of workers along gender and racial lines. Edwards concludes that this effect can be prevented only by concerted political action; simply increasing the numbers of women in each sector may not be sufficient.

Research on the history of the computer and its relationship to women still needs to be done because much of the early history is missing. The currently available history underwrites the standard story of the computer's masculine roots. The unwritten history may tell a slightly different tale. It seems possible that, while most of the

---

[29] See James P. Meindl, "Chips for Advanced Computing," *Scientific American* 257, no. 4 (October 1987): 78–88.

early hardware development was done by men, women created much of the necessary software.

Women have been involved with computers as programmers since the days of Ada Lovelace.[30] Grace Hopper's work with the early compilers and the development of COBOL (Common Business Oriented Language) has been often noted.[31] Women's as yet undocumented contributions to software development may have been enormous. For example, Adele Goldstine seems to have provided key leadership in designing software for the ENIAC, a job performed primarily by women until, as Edwards notes, men discovered its complexity and challenge—and its cash value.

This pattern of women's participation in the early stages of a technical discipline and subsequent exclusion from it as it gains status is duplicated in other scientific fields. For example, before the 1940s and 1950s revolution in molecular biology, work in biology was mainly taxonomic. Not enough was known about cellular processes and reproduction to develop rigorous explanations or mathematical models of the kind so successful in physics. In the late nineteenth and early twentieth centuries biology consisted largely of classification and description of new species—tasks seen as appropriate for women. Botany in fact was so identified with women that *Science* found it necessary to print an article in 1887 arguing that it was still a suitable field for men.[32] With the discovery of DNA, a workable, rigorous model for the mechanism of heredity, men reappropriated the field for themselves.[33]

[30] Ada Lovelace's most significant contribution to computer science was to introduce a binary system in computer mathematics in place of Charles Babbage's decimal system. For biographical information see D. W. Kear, "The Computer and the Countess," *Datamation* 19, no. 5 (1973): 60–63; and Doris Langley-Levy Moore, *Ada, Countess of Lovelace: Byron's Legitimate Daughter* (London: J. Murray, 1977). For references to Lovelace by her contemporary, see S. E. De Morgan, *Memoir of Augustus De Morgan, with Selections from His Letters* (London: Longmans & Green, 1882). The Department of Defense has named its newest computer language ADA in Lovelace's honor.

[31] See, e.g., Richard L. Wexelblat, ed., *History of Programming Languages* (New York: Academic Press, 1981), a collection of papers printed from a conference at which Grace Hopper gave the keynote address and in which she is cited throughout. See also Joel Shurkin, *Engines of the Mind: From Abacus to Apple—the Men and Women Who Created the Computer* (New York: Washington Square Press, 1985).

[32] Margaret Rossiter, *Women Scientists in America: Struggles and Strategies to 1940* (Baltimore: Johns Hopkins University Press, 1982), 61. See chap. 3, "Women's Work in Science," for a more detailed look at the ghettoization of women in particular scientific fields, 51–72.

[33] Compare, e.g., two narratives of the discovery of DNA and the way in which ideologies of gender shape the story. Anne Sayre, *Rosalind Franklin and DNA* (New York: Norton, 1975); and James D. Watson, *The Double Helix: A Personal Account of the Discovery of the Structure of DNA* (London: Weidenfeld & Nicolson, 1981).

One way of describing this phenomenon is that women's brain power often provides the intellectual venture capital for new fields but that the memory of this contribution drops away when the field becomes professionalized. The history of women herbalists, healers, and midwives in the early modern period is an example of this pattern.[34] Women often participate in the early stages of a new technical field, but once a field has stabilized and demonstrated its intellectual (and financial) potential, women are excluded. They no longer can be found in decision-making positions within the field, however invaluable their prior contributions.

The history of the computer seems to bear out this contention. Women's early presence in software development—which was considerable—is not reflected in their current levels of participation. Although the opportunities for women in programming are substantially better than in most technical fields, they are still limited.[35] In particular, although the pay differential between men and women is not large, women's employment is concentrated in areas considered less skilled and hence less financially rewarding (maintenance, coding), while men are more likely to be found in management positions. Women's increasing representation among computer personnel thus parallels their experience in most fields: ghettoization in low status, low pay, "de-skilled" job categories.

What, then, should be a feminist's relation to computer technology? Should we condemn the enterprise? Should we reject it as a still more sophisticated tool for the oppression of women? How can we as women gain control over the future of the computer? What do we want that future to look like? How can we positively direct the course of technological change, not merely redress some of its harms? These larger questions must influence our choice of tactics.

[34] See Alice Clark, *Working Life of Women in the 17th Century* (1919; reprint, New York: Kelley, 1968), 253–65; and Barbara Brandon Schnorrenberg, "Is Childbirth Any Place for a Woman? The Decline of Midwifery in Eighteenth-Century England," *Studies in Eighteenth-Century Culture* 10 (1981): 393–408. For a more polemical treatment of this history, see Barbara Ehrenreich and Dierdre English, *Witches, Midwives, and Nurses* (Old Westbury, N.Y.: Feminist Press, 1973).

[35] In 1986, 28 percent of the computer specialists in the United States were women—as compared to 13 percent of the practitioners in the physical sciences, 22 percent in the life sciences, and 3 percent of the practicing engineers. Four percent of all the women employed in computer science were Black; 5.4 percent were Asian. Salaries for women were lower than those for men across all fields of science and engineering, although the differential was less in computer science than in other fields. In the sciences, salaries for women averaged 76 percent of the salaries for men across the board; among engineers, women's salaries were 84 percent those of men; among computer specialists, "the fastest growing field for both men and women during the eighties," women's salaries averaged 86 percent of those for men. *Women and Minorities in Science and Engineering* (Washington, D.C.: National Science Foundation, January 1988).

The case of the frame-breaking Luddites in the early nineteenth century offers an interesting historical analogy to these problems, especially insofar as the epithet "Luddite" is frequently used to dismiss even moderate critics of technology. Their struggles with the first industrial revolution can help us analyze our own strategies for the second.

The Luddites were loosely connected groups of English stock-ingers who participated in the destruction of shearing frames, steam looms, and lace machines during the period 1810–17. They destroyed thousands of dollars worth of equipment. Although commonly viewed as protests against technological displacement and unemployment, it appears that their aims, at least in the midlands of England, were more complex.[36] They confined their attacks almost exclusively to machines engaged by owners in the production of cheap, inferior goods (thus undercutting costs) and to machines owned by hosiers paying low wages or barter goods instead of cash. They also attacked stockingers who trained more apprentices than were allowed (thus increasing the labor pool and lowering wages) or who manufactured inferior goods, thus destroying customer confidence and depressing the industry. The Luddites' motives were deep-seated economic ones, classic labor confrontations brought to a head but not caused by technological innovation.

The success of the Luddite movement, if judged by its ability to resist industrial developments, was almost nil. Under the immediate threat of the frame breakers the use of the larger machines was stopped, but as soon as the riots were quelled they were back in production. Nonetheless, the Luddites did have a lasting effect on British labor policy. The movement was at least partly responsible for drawing the attention of the British Parliament away from foreign policy to focus instead on its own industrial crises, which led to the legalization of trade unions and the passage of the Factory Acts, measures designed to alleviate to some degree the pain of rapid industrialization.[37] Frame breaking served as an effective attention getter and led to increased accountability of owners and politicians toward the working classes. Still, since the protests were couched in limited economic terms without long-term political aims, they did not lead to social control of the workplace or technology.

The introduction of wide frames in the stocking trade is an example of a new technology growing out of and reinforcing

[36] Frank O. Darvall, *Popular Disturbances and Public Order in Regency England* (New York: Augustus M. Kelley, 1969), 166–75.
[37] Ibid., chap. 8.

existing social and economic hierarchies. The response of the Luddites, while implicitly an economic and political one, concentrated on the machines, the physical manifestations of the current order. This emphasis led to the alleviation of some of the workers' most grievous needs but not to a redistribution of power.

This instructive example ought to inform our feminist understanding of our relationship to the computer. Hostility toward the computer in isolation from its social context will do nothing to change underlying economic and social inequalities. A more effective strategy would be to imagine and construct alternative visions of this technology: to choose our own future. Furthermore, we stand to learn less about issues concerning the intersections of computers and society from those who are hostile or indifferent to computer technology than we do from those who understand both the technology and how it is embedded in a social and economic context.

The story of a two-part conference on women and computers organized by the Massachusetts Institute of Technology (MIT) Women's Studies Program in the fall of 1984 and the spring of 1985 demonstrates this truism. The planners of the conference originally assumed that the participating women who were computer professionals would find useful the analyses of feminist theorists from other disciplines to help them formulate the ways in which computer science reflected the dominant patriarchal ideology. They theorized that an articulation of gender difference derived from philosophy, literature, and psychology might lead to speculation about the ways in which computer hardware, software, and theories of artificial intelligence reflected masculine assumptions— assumptions about thought, meaning, intellectual priorities, and function.

Although these issues were ultimately addressed, it became clear at the outset that the feminist agenda in computer science has its own sequence, independent of the feminist scholarship in the humanities and the social sciences. To ignore this agenda is to fail to recognize the diversity among feminists or to respect each others' differences. Just as the theory and practice of white, middle-class feminists has been challenged by the inclusion of women of color and women of other classes, so feminists in the humanities and social sciences have much to learn from the perceptions and experiences of women in scientific and technological fields. Computer professionals have their own stories to tell about how a new field of inquiry can be appropriated by men or by masculine values, and how developments in a seemingly neutral arena are driven by the familiar forces of the market and entrenched privilege. The women who work with this technology are in the best position to understand its potential effects on all our lives—its dangers and its possible benefits, how it is and will be affecting women's lives. Some are beginning to think about what it might mean to redirect the course of the technology, to take social control of it.

Virtually all of the computer professionals who participated in this conference considered themselves feminists, yet they felt to varying degrees that the women's movement tacitly excluded them, as if by working in such a traditionally masculine field they had forfeited their right to be considered as women and as sisters. In open discussion they kept returning to certain themes: the increasing marginalization of women in computer science, both in industry and the academy; the erasure of women's emotional labor; the absence of analyses of social relations in the most prestigious arena of computer science—artificial intelligence; the disturbing degree of complicity with the Department of Defense that most advanced work in computer science seems to entail. Indeed, all the women participating in the conference expressed concern about this particular moral dilemma.

They traded discouraging examples of computer courses rigidly sequenced, with hostile vocabulary (abort; slave), designed, it seemed, to weed out women and people of color and to prevent the recognition of the computer as a flexible medium adaptable to human needs.[38] They discussed the extent to which computer games and other software produced for popular consumption are designed by and for men and boys and not by and for women and girls.

Although many of the participants knew of one another, they had never been gathered together in such a large group (thirty) before. It was the first time any of them had discussed issues of gender and computer science with so many other knowledgeable women. All found this aspect of the conference exhilarating. It was universally lamented that there were so few other women working in computer science with whom to connect and make common cause. Moreover, many reported with dismay an ever-polarizing distribution of men at the top and women at the bottom in the computer industry.

The three essays printed here represent three attempts to analyze this current state of affairs with regard to women and

---

[38] The terminology of software documentation betrays attitudes that would not be comfortable for many women. In "X Toolkit Intrinsics—C Language Interface—X Window System X version 11, Release 3," by Joel McCormack, Paul Asente, and Ralph R. Swick (copyright 1988 MIT and Digital Equipment Corp.), e.g., subsidiary functions are called "children," and instructions are given for the "overall management of children from creation to destruction." We are indebted to Evelynn Hammonds for bringing this example to our attention.

computers. Each begins from the assumption that computer work,
like any work, is never culturally neutral but has a variety of social
meanings constructed by educators, practitioners, and advertisers.
Each essay explores different ways in which the sociologically
constructed practice of negotiating the world as male or female
might intersect with existing stereotypes about computers. Thus
Paul Edwards's article, "The Army and the Microworld: Computers
and the Politics of Gender Identity," explores the paradox of a
stubborn definition of computer work and of military institutions as
"masculine" despite increasing numbers of women working in
those arenas. He argues that they are the sites of powerfully
interlocking loci of personal, political, and cultural identity despite
the irony that computer technology makes physical strength irrelevant to the control of immense destructive power. The association
of masculine identity with clear hierarchies, unambiguous rules,
citizenship and patriotism, an appetite for games and for psychological separation—these are some of the elements he examines in
his sensitive analysis of the connections among the cultural codings
of gender, militarism, and computers. Edwards argues that feminist
pacifism in the form of the "Moral Mother" is an inadequate
position of resistance. One need not support his contention that the
most effective strategy is the one that places women in combat
alongside men to understand the immediate and pressing need to
confront the risks and responsibilities of living in a society where
computer and military power are joining forces. A radical feminist
pacifism based on a morally informed refusal to join the military, for
instance, could provide an alternative with greater agency than
Edwards's image of the "Moral Mother."

Sheila Lehman and Pamela Kramer also examine ways in which
computer use is determined by its social and economic contexts in
their article "Mismeasuring Women: A Critique of Research on
Computer Ability and Avoidance." They report on research that
compared a group of older minority women returning to college for
undergraduate engineering and management degrees with older
nonminority women reentering graduate-level education in similar
fields. Both groups needed a remedial mathematics course (in
algebra and trigonometry). An experimental review course designed especially for such students succeeded admirably; both
groups passed their college level precalculus and calculus courses.
However, while grades in this experimental math review course
were predictive of success in college math courses, they were not
predictive of success in college computer courses. Warning against
creating negative stereotypes of women's relation to technology,
Lehman and Kramer point out that computer literacy has often been

constructed differently for boys and girls: boys are exposed to programming while girls are expected to use the computer for word processing or other clerical skills. A similar point has been made by Shirley Malcom with regard to Afro-American students whose alienating experiences with computers used for rote drill make it hard for them to imagine the technology as flexible, hospitable, or creative.[39] In trying to explain why women and girls opt out of using computers, Lehman and Kramer's article also considers the effects on girls of teaching about computers in math and science courses that draw fewer girls in the first place. In addition, computers are seen by many girls as a tool for asocial and unpopular kids. Because girls have been taught to think more contextually and socially than boys, the isolation of the computer from other aspects of school life they value may lead them to consciously opt out of computer classes. Lehman and Kramer suggest a contextualized approach to further study of women and computers which takes into account the genesis of women's attitudes toward computers—the story of the processes by which women are introduced to computers as well as the content of women's complex relations to computers.

Sherry Turkle and Seymour Papert tell a number of such stories in their article "Epistemological Pluralism: Styles and Voices within the Computer Culture." Although the computer is ideally an expressive medium that different people can make use of in their own way, they report that frequently (women) students are forced to use particular programming strategies with computers, such as black-boxing (which allows one to plan something large without knowing in advance how the details will be managed) or other prepackaged programs that feel intellectually uncomfortable to the new and now resisting computer user. Distinguishing a "bricoleur" programming strategy (what Sherry Turkle once called "soft mastery") from the more standard top-down style of programming, they note that computer culture increasingly discriminates against this ad hoc style. That is, programmers and educators privilege an intellectual method that moves abstractly and hierarchically from

[39] Shirley Malcom, "Color Coded Systems: Computing and Women of Color" (MIT, Spring 1984, typescript). There is also evidence that Black students might prefer computer-aided instruction because it is color-blind, according to Sharon Traweek in a private communication (April 1989) about the Stanford-Brentwood CAI (Computer Assisted Instruction) project—sometimes referred to as the Suppes Project—in math education, 1966–68. According to Traweek, first, second, and third graders from an overcrowded, racially mixed but primarily Black school were given access to computers. Many of them preferred the machine-aided instruction to their grade school teachers, she said, because the machines remembered their names and where they left off in the last session, whereas their teachers did not always remember who they were or what they were learning.

axiom to theorem to corollary, whereas bricoleurs construct theories by arranging and rearranging, by negotiating and renegotiating with a set of well-known materials. Although this latter programming style seems to characterize women more than men, and girls more than boys, for all the usual reasons of sociological training and experience, Turkle and Papert are not arguing for a statistical correlation between gender and certain programming styles but investigating what lies behind the difference in styles and behind the resistance of computer culture to recognize and facilitate them both. They identify a variety of cognitive preferences within what they call the "bricoleur strategy"—preferences for treating symbols on the screen as physical objects rather than as abstractions, for anthropomorphizing the program, or for seeing things in terms of relationships rather than in terms of properties—preferences which are discouraged in the usual course of computer training. They argue that to recognize differences in programming styles would be one step toward epistemological pluralism in science, the need for which has been one of the hallmarks of the feminist critique of science.

All three essays explore different ways in which computer technologies key into existing cultural structures. Their analyses make clear how naive it is to assume the neutrality of any medium or technique with the power of the computer in a world of political, social, and economic interest. All three emphasize the need to understand simultaneously the ways in which computer culture is being shaped by these forces and the ways in which a particular set of gender constructions is implicated in the process. The uses to which computers have been most readily put, the ways in which their capabilities have been conceived, the language that has grown up to describe their functions, the social practices that mark computer rooms, classes, and businesses—all of these constitute a gender-coded system that is less hospitable to women than could be predicted from the characteristics of the technology itself. To accept these patterns as inevitable when they are the effects of existing social forces would be foolish—as foolish as accepting any other disempowering definition of women, of creativity, or of intellectual process. Understanding the socially constructed nature of computer use reveals the origin of technophobic reactions to be in social systems and not in machines.

Computers redefining gender

If the social patterns of computer use are not inevitable, might it be possible to appropriate the computer for our own uses as an aid to reimagining the social arrangements of our own American culture? For example, what changes in the definitions of masculinity and femininity might arise from the reconceptualization of human beings in terms of the computer? Gender roles, in contrast to biological sex, are quite plastic, and the particular traits considered to define the sexes vary considerably across cultures and over time. The common wisdom which associates computers with masculinity in Western culture arises partly from modeling computers as logical, linear, and objective—traits positively correlated with masculinity. In addition, the pedagogical conflation of computers with science/math/technology, all masculine domains, contributes to this impression. As computers permeate our culture and we define ourselves as a species as both like and unlike these "information processors," we may drastically redefine our conceptions of masculinity and femininity.[40] The possibilities for questioning the ideological associations between computers and masculinity, or for redefining what is meant by masculinity, could conceivably arise from philosophical discussions about the differences between human beings and computers, or from new research in artificial intelligence, or from socially conscious restructuring of the increasingly automated workplace.

The strongest challenges to the historical association between masculinity and computers are those arising from pressures within computer science itself and, in particular, from the new theories of artificial intelligence. Until recently, the model of mental processes traditionally used by researchers in the field of artificial intelligence was a linear one. Computation was described as a process that operates on a set of deficient objects to transform them into a set of desired objects, in a purposeful and systematic way. Recently, however, some computer scientists have redefined "intelligent" behavior to mean flexibility, the ability to respond to unexpected situations in meaningful ways, and the ability to make intuitive deductive leaps with insufficient information. These new models are less quintessentially masculine—less rigid, less linear, less task oriented.[41]

There is also a growing tendency to emphasize the quality of user interaction with the computer, to try to make the interface between the user and the computer more physically intuitive, something particularly attractive for those who practice a bricoleur style of programming. In the words of one (male) researcher, the

---

[40] Margaret Boden suggested this possibility ten years ago in her classic *Artificial Intelligence and Natural Man* (New York: Basic, 1977), 463.

[41] Ursula Huws, "The Effects of AI on Women's Lives," in *Artificial Intelligence for Society*, ed. K. S. Gill (West Sussex: Wiley, 1986), 169–79.

intent is to make the "interaction between the user and the computer more like cooperation than confrontation."[42] Turkle and Papert, for example, discuss the use of icons instead of textual instructions—screen symbols that look like familiar objects such as trashcans or pointing fingers—to represent abstract processes. Other current efforts include the invention of touch-sensitive screens and voice recognition, in which the computer responds to spoken commands.[43]

The next step for some is the creation of what is termed "virtual realities." With the aid of head-mounted monitors and a specially wired "DataGlove," users can interact with the computer by pointing, gesturing, or "handling" objects on the screen. The glove translates the user's physical motions into electrical signals; these signals allow the computer to move an image of the user's hand on the screen in imitation of the gesture of the real one. James Foley suggests that the DataGlove might, among other things, help students and researchers gain a kinesthetically based, intuitive feel for certain models of physical processes. A chemist, for example, might manipulate models of an enzyme and a substrate, and physically feel their attraction.[44] This extension of kinesthetic learning might make it easier for students uncomfortable with the traditional analytic framework to understand atomic phenomena.

While none of these technological developments are necessarily beneficial—most have clear and immediate military applications— they do represent, as Turkle and Papert note, a greater acceptance of object-oriented programming, which in turn could be interpreted as a reevaluation of acceptable intellectual styles and possibly a reconsideration of traditional conceptions of masculinity and femininity.

Pressures to reconsider definitions of gender are also likely to come from outside the computer industry, possibly from some of the computer-driven changes we have noted in the workplace. In many contemporary cultures, the separation of public and private spheres is the separation of male and female domains. The computer blurs these distinctions as employers utilize this new technology for outwork and for surveillance of formerly private aspects of workers' lives. The technology also allows the continued deskilling of workers at best and potentially massive unemployment at worst—moves that might eventually undermine the myth of the male provider, a reality for only a small and diminishing segment of

[42] James D. Foley, "Interfaces for Advanced Computing," *Scientific American* 257, no. 4 (October 1987): 126–35.
[43] Ibid.
[44] Ibid., 130–32.

the population in any case. For good and ill, these economic changes might begin to redefine male and female labor.

Philosophical questions about what it means to be a human being rather than a computer may also motivate a reinterpretation of contemporary gender roles. As computers permeate our workplaces, our homes, and language, more and more people come to define human beings as simply more complex information-processing systems. Social relations, artistic creativity, whimsical invention, imagination, faith, humor—all these drop away. This perception of ourselves as information processors (and inferior ones at that) may be the historical culmination of a hundred years of thinking of ourselves as machines—as things without purpose. As such, it is a counsel of despair. As Margaret Boden points out, when the self "is no longer seen as a truly purposive system, then relatively inhuman 'pathological' behavior can be expected in consequence."[45]

The alternative to despair is to define our humanity in a more complex fashion.[46] Perhaps the essence of our humanity is, as Aristotle suggested, our impulse to laughter. Even though we do process information—that is, learn, evaluate, and act on what we know—we may come to define our quintessential humanness not in those terms but as the ability to care, to feel, and to connect with other human beings. These are all characteristics considered feminine in our society and, as has been often argued, reproduced in women as part of the sexual division of labor in our culture. Because the cultural ties between femininity and empathy or connectedness are so strong, the reassignment of these characteristics to a definition of what is essentially human could have profound effects on our rigid gender norms. It might result in a restructuring of the sexual division of labor—who does the "caring" work and whether such work is considered masculine and valued or feminine and devalued—even if economic and political power were not redistributed.

Reclaiming computers for women

Where do we go from here? How do we, as women, gain control over the future of the computer? What do we want that future to look like? How can we positively direct the course of technological

[45] Boden, 455.
[46] See ibid., chaps. 13–15, 393–473, as well as Joseph Weizenbaum in *Computer Power and Human Reason: From Judgment to Calculation* (San Francisco: W. H. Freeman, 1976), passim.

change, not merely redress some of its harms? These questions are not unique to either women or computers but are part of a general concern that technological change meets the needs of the many, not the greed of the few. If we want to insure true democracy in a technological era, we need to demand broader participation in the allocation of resources and the design of technologies that affect people's lives. We need to select tools that are both environmentally sustainable and whose uses in social settings give more people a say about those uses. Using these criteria, for example, small-scale renewable energy sources are preferable to nuclear power because they are environmentally more benign and because they involve less centralized bureaucratic structures. The dangers inherent in a plutonium economy, in contrast, make it easier for governments to justify curtailing civil liberties in the interests of national security.[47]

There are obviously no simple "feminist" answers to these questions,[48] but the history and explorations offered here suggest a number of possible strategies that will help us counteract our learned helplessness about technological change. We need to educate women to use computers; we need to be vigilant about computer use in the workplace; and we need to explore the feminist possibilities of this new technology. We must continually remind each other—through education, organizing, and action— that we have the right, the responsibility, and the ability to control the future of the computer.

The first step in computer education will be to reach girls, who are at present heavily underrepresented in computer classes, after-school computer clubs, computer summer camps, and enrichment programs.[49] It appears that access to facilities alone is not sufficient.

[47] Our design criteria here are adapted from Richard Sclove's more comprehensive discussion. In his Ph.D. thesis (Massachusetts Institute of Technology, 1986) entitled "Technology and Freedom: A Prescriptive Theory of Technological Design," he evolved a set of "rationally contestable" criteria for evaluating the democratic implications of technology. See also Michael Goldhaber, *Reinventing Technology: Politics for Democratic Values* (New York: Routledge & Kegan Paul, 1986).

[48] Jannet Gronfeldt and Susanne Kandrup offer further feminist considerations of these questions in "Women, Work and Computerization; or Still Dancing after All These Years," in Olerup et al., eds. (n. 7 above), 205–21.

[49] See Nancy Kreinberg and Elizabeth Stage, "EQUALS in Computer Technology," in Zimmerman, ed. (n. 5 above), 251–60. See also S. J. Russell, J. R. Mokros, and J. C. Foster, "Ten Years and Counting: Who Will Use Computers?" (Cambridge, Mass.: Technical Education Research Center, 1984). Marlaine Lockheed in "Evaluation of Computer Literacy at the High School Level" (Princeton, N.J.: Evaluation of Computer Service, 1982) points out that only 5 percent of girls, as opposed to 60 percent of boys, enrolled in computer classes will use the computer outside of class time. The problem of girls' lower rate of participation in computer education is

We must instead address the reasons that girls are opting out of the computer field at early ages. Part of the problem is gender-inappropriate software: sex-role stereotyped games, games focused on violent examples, and a lack of female protagonists. There have been some recent efforts to develop nonsexist software.[50] Yet, as the papers in this issue demonstrate, the problem may require more far-reaching solutions, like rethinking the context in which computer classes are taught and allowing a greater variety of intellectual styles to flourish in relation to the computer.

We also need to educate girls and women to a familiarity not only with the existing computer technology but to their own needs in relation to this technology so that they can make decisions about the place of computers in their own lives and in the society in which they live. Just because we can learn to do something does not mean that it is desirable. In thinking about computer education we must remember that a feminist approach is not one that tries to "beat the boys at their own game" but instead is one that turns the game on its side and changes the rules. To effect this radical revision, we may need to structure our educational objectives around much broader demands than simple equity.

There have been several attempts to create alternative curricula for women that encourage the kinds of thinking about computers we envision here. Two of these, the British Women's Computer Course and the *Women's Computer Literacy Handbook,* teach women computing in environments that stress the social context of technology, discussing the history of computers along with programming. Introductory classes in this vein also cover some facts about hardware as well as software. These discussions have alleviated some of the women's fears about the machine—particularly their fears about breaking it! The author of the *Women's Computer Literacy Handbook* disputes the familiar saying that "you do not need to know how a car works in order to drive it," observing that what we do know about cars enables us to use them with greater

---

addressed by Jo Sanders and Antonia Stone in *The Neuter Computer: Computers for Girls and Boys* (New York: Neal-Schuman, 1986). They suggest some strategies for reducing this gender imbalance.

[50] Elaine Anderson and Margaret Wilsman, under the auspices of Microcomputer and Instructional Technology Supervisor, Wisconsin Department of Public Instruction (1125 S. Webster St., P.O. Box 7841, Madison, Wis. 53707) are studying the effects of sex-equitable software on girls' interest in computers. A pilot program in the Wisconsin public school system, begun in 1984, is implemented in *Solutions Unlimited,* a set of instructional materials released by the Indiana Agency for Instructional Television and billed as sex equitable.

confidence. When the turn signals on a car are not working, for example, one does know that the car is not about to explode. Descriptions of hardware can give women enough basic understanding of computer mechanisms to give them confidence to take risks with the machine.[51]

Education can provide the skills and confidence for organized resistance and creative change within the new sociopolitical arrangements created by computers. Such resistance is already occurring—from workers engaged in manufacturing electronic components in off-shore factories to those facing office automation. In spite of enormous obstacles, women electronics workers in Malaysia were able to obtain withheld overtime payments in 1987; in the same year (predominantly women) workers at South Korea's Anam Industrial, the world's largest assembly subcontractor, won a 27 percent raise.[52] There have been similar successes in office automation. For example, Swedish welfare workers have insisted that they will not use computers unless the time saved from paperwork can be used for direct social work.[53]

Most challenging to thinkers concerned with the intersections of gender and computers is to try to figure out how to use the computer to implement feminist values. Some examples might suggest future possibilities. One tactic is to use microcomputers to help small nonprofit organizations and individuals gain access to information that they need in order to work for social change. For example, the Virginia-based Micro Associates produces a database on disks—rather than on-line—for power structure research.[54] Their system, covering some 26,000 powerful groups and individuals, indexes investigative books and periodicals in such areas as the intelligence community, the right wing, Latin America, the East Coast foreign policy establishment, domestic surveillance, assassinations, and big business.

Another tactic is to exploit the power of the modem. PeaceNet and EcoNet currently allow concerned peace and environmental activists, respectively, to communicate with each other and share information, resources, and strategies. Such technology in the future might not simply link activist organizations but also help to

---

[51] The British "Women's Computer Course" is a teaching pack put out by Mary Jennings and Robin Smits in August 1985 (available from 157 Maryland Road, Woodgreen, London N22 5AS). *The Women's Computer Literary Handbook*, by Deborah L. Brecher, was published in 1985 by New American Library.

[52] Lenny Siegel, "Malaysian Women Resist," *Global Electronics* 76 (August 1987): 1.

[53] Garson (n. 8 above), 113.

[54] For more information, contact Micro Associates, Box 5369, Arlington, Va. 22205.

create them. It might be possible for computer-communication channels to be used by workers to communicate with each other, possibly on an international level, and thus serve liberatory ends.

All of these are potential models for projects explicitly addressed to women. The California-based National Women's Mailing List, founded by Deborah Brecher in 1982, links feminist individuals and organizations through a national database.[55] The creators of this mailing list have tried to incorporate features into it to protect the privacy of individuals while at the same time making it easier for groups and individuals to organize with it. An even more ambitious organization is the British "Microsyster," created by a group of women computer professionals in 1982 to develop ways to use microcomputers for women.[56] Microsyster was part of a broader British movement of the early 1980s whose goal was to make social needs rather than economic criteria the primary determinant for technological innovation. Local government councils in London, Sheffield, and the West Midlands viewed this transformation of the process of technological innovation as integral to their strategies to increase employment while involving more people in the planning process—in ways that both met broad social needs and were environmentally sound. In London, the Greater London Enterprise Board (GLEB) established a number of technology networks to "facilitate [the] organization of the innovation process by promoting the expertise in polytechnics and trade union and community groups developing alternate plans for employment."[57] The mission statement of Microsyster articulates the intention to provide computing services to women and to women's groups, to support feminists working in computing, to provide a feminist perspective on new technology and to introduce the skills and knowledge necessary for women to benefit from and critically assess new technologies. Among other things, they help women's groups decide whether or not a computer would be useful to them and, if so, what kind of hardware and software would be best. They develop packages for specific feminist applications and provide speakers and information to the feminist community. Each of these projects represents a step toward creating a technology—and a society—that reflects our feminist values.

[55] The National Women's Mailing List, P.O. Box 68, Jenner, Calif. 95450.

[56] Microsyster, Wesley House, Wild Court, London WC 2.

[57] Veronica Mole and David Elliot, *Enterprising Innovation: An Alternative Approach* (London: Frank Pinter, 1987), 65.

Technology and change

Whether or not we can predict future changes in computer technology accurately, we can predict that it will change. The meaning of those changes must be interpreted in human terms, for their political and social implications. When the gender distribution of jobs in the computer industry begins to replicate the stratification found in other fields after an early history of more equitable participation by women and men; when computer outwork extends the global assembly line for Third World women and locks them into meaningless, routine drudgery; when a programmer designs software that places more emphasis on efficiency in a narrowly defined sense than on a broader understanding of the workers' needs, styles, and experience—when all of these are documented and taken for granted, the insistence that technology is neutral can be understood only as naive or as disingenuous. We must attend to the political meanings of these facts.

As feminists, we must struggle to keep human concerns foremost in our critique of changing technology. We must develop new techniques for educating girls and women about current computer developments and new strategies for organizing women workers, to ensure equitable workforce participation. We must identify the ways in which the computer reinforces the current distribution of power internationally. We must see that hardware and software developments are designed to meet the needs of individuals and communities. We must remember that technology is never produced in a vacuum but in a particular social and economic context, one which can be changed by social and political action. The answer to our technological concerns lies not in our tools but in ourselves.

Literature Faculty
Massachusetts Institute of Technology (Perry)
Science for the People
Cambridge, Massachusetts (Greber)

Sex and Death in the Rational World of Defense Intellectuals

Carol Cohn

"I can't believe *that*," said Alice.

"Can't you?" the Queen said in a pitying tone. "Try again: draw a long breath, and shut your eyes."

Alice laughed. "There's no use trying," she said. "One *can't* believe impossible things."

"I daresay you haven't had much practice," said the Queen. "When I was your age, I always did it for half-an-hour a day. Why, sometimes I've believed as many as six impossible things before breakfast." [LEWIS CARROLL, *Through the Looking Glass*]

My close encounter with nuclear strategic analysis started in the summer of 1984. I was one of forty-eight college teachers (one of ten women) attending a summer workshop on nuclear weapons, nuclear strategic doctrine, and arms control, taught by distinguished "defense intellectuals." Defense intellectuals are men (and indeed, they are virtually all men) "who use the concept of deterrence to explain why it is safe to have weapons of a kind and number it is not safe to use."[1] They are civilians who move in and out of

[1] Thomas Powers, "How Nuclear War Could Start," *New York Review of Books* (January 17, 1985), 33.

[*Signs: Journal of Women in Culture and Society* 1987, vol. 12, no. 4]

government, working sometimes as administrative officials or consultants, sometimes at universities and think tanks. They formulate what they call "rational" systems for dealing with the problems created by nuclear weapons: how to manage the arms race; how to deter the use of nuclear weapons; how to fight a nuclear war if deterrence fails. It is their calculations that are used to explain the necessity of having nuclear destructive capability at what George Kennan has called "levels of such grotesque dimensions as to defy rational understanding."[2] At the same time, it is their reasoning that is used to explain why it is not safe to live without nuclear weapons.[3] In short, they create the theory that informs and legitimates American nuclear strategic practice.

For two weeks, I listened to men engage in dispassionate discussion of nuclear war. I found myself aghast, but morbidly fascinated—not by nuclear weaponry, or by images of nuclear destruction, but by the extraordinary abstraction and removal from what I knew as reality that characterized the professional discourse. I became obsessed by the question, How can they think this way? At the end of the summer program, when I was offered the opportunity to stay on at the university's center on defense technology and arms control (hereafter known as "the Center"), I jumped at the chance to find out how they could think "this" way.

I spent the next year of my life immersed in the world of defense intellectuals. As a participant observer, I attended lectures, listened to arguments, conversed with defense analysts, and interviewed graduate students at the beginning, middle, and end of their training. I learned their specialized language, and I tried to understand what they thought and how they thought. I sifted through their logic for its internal inconsistencies and its unspoken assumptions. But as I learned their language, as I became more and more engaged with their information and their arguments, I found that my own thinking was changing. Soon, I could no longer cling to the comfort of studying an external and objectified "them." I had to confront a new question: How can *I* think this way? How can any of us?

Throughout my time in the world of strategic analysis, it was hard not to notice the ubiquitous weight of gender, both in social relations and in the language itself; it is an almost entirely male world (with the exception of the secretaries), and the language contains many rather arresting metaphors.

[2] George Kennan, "A Modest Proposal," *New York Review of Books* (July 16, 1981), 14.

[3] It is unusual for defense intellectuals to write for the public, rather than for their colleagues, but a recent, interesting exception has been made by a group of defense analysts from Harvard. Their two books provide a clear expression of the stance that living with nuclear weapons is not so much a problem to be solved but a condition to be managed rationally. Albert Carnesale and the Harvard Nuclear Study Group, *Living with Nuclear Weapons* (Cambridge, Mass.: Harvard University Press, 1984); and Graham T. Allison, Albert Carnesale, and Joseph Nye, Jr., eds., *Hawks, Doves, and Owls: An Agenda for Avoiding Nuclear War* (New York: W. W. Norton & Co., 1985).

There is, of course, an important and growing body of feminist theory about gender and language.[4] In addition, there is a rich and increasingly vast body of theoretical work exploring the gendered aspects of war and militarism, which examines such issues as men's and women's different relations to militarism and pacifism, and the ways in which gender ideology is used in the service of militarization. Some of the feminist work on gender and war is also part of an emerging, powerful feminist critique of ideas of rationality as they have developed in Western culture.[5] While I am indebted to all of these bodies of work, my own project is most closely linked to the development of feminist critiques of dominant Western concepts of reason. My goal is to discuss the nature of nuclear stragetic thinking; in

---

[4] For useful introductions to feminist work on gender and language, see Barrie Thorne, Cheris Kramarae, and Nancy Henley, eds., *Language, Gender and Society* (Rowley, Mass.: Newbury Publishing House, 1983); and Elizabeth Abel, ed., *Writing and Sexual Difference* (Chicago: University of Chicago Press, 1982).

[5] For feminist critiques of dominant Western conceptions of rationality, see Nancy Hartsock, *Money, Sex, and Power* (New York: Longman, 1983); Sandra Harding and Merrill Hintikka, eds., *Discovering Reality: Feminist Perspectives on Epistemology, Metaphysics, Methodology and the Philosophy of Science* (Dordrecht: D. Reidel Publishing Co., 1983); Evelyn Fox Keller, *Reflections on Gender and Science* (New Haven, Conn.: Yale University Press, 1985); Jean Bethke Elshtain, *Public Man, Private Woman: Woman in Social and Political Thought* (Princeton, N.J.: Princeton University Press, 1981); Genevieve Lloyd, *The Man of Reason: "Male" and "Female" in Western Philosophy* (Minneapolis: University of Minnesota Press, 1984), which contains a particularly useful bibliographic essay; Sara Ruddick, "Remarks on the Sexual Politics of Reason," in *Women and Moral Theory*, ed. Eva Kittay and Diana Meyers (Totowa, N.J.: Rowman & Allanheld, in press). Some of the growing feminist work on gender and war is explicitly connected to critiques of rationality. See Virginia Woolf, *Three Guineas* (New York: Harcourt, Brace, Jovanovich, 1966); Nancy C. M. Hartsock, "The Feminist Standpoint: Developing the Grounds for a Specifically Feminist Historical Materialism," in Harding and Hintikka, eds., 283–310, and "The Barracks Community in Western Political Thought: Prologomena to a Feminist Critique of War and Politics," in *Women and Men's Wars*, ed. Judith Hicks Stiehm (Oxford: Pergamon Press, 1983); Jean Bethke Elshtain, "Reflections on War and Political Discourse: Realism, Just War and Feminism in a Nuclear Age," *Political Theory* 13, no. 1 (February 1985): 39–57; Sara Ruddick, "Preservative Love and Military Destruction: Some Reflections on Mothering and Peace," in *Mothering: Essays in Feminist Theory*, ed. Joyce Trebilcot (Totowa, N.J.: Rowman & Allanheld, 1984), 231–62; Genevieve Lloyd, "Selfhood, War, and Masculinity," in *Feminist Challenges*, ed. E. Gross and C. Pateman (Boston: Northeastern University Press, 1986). There is a vast and valuable literature on gender and war that indirectly informs my work. See, e.g., Cynthia Enloe, *Does Khaki Become You? The Militarization of Women's Lives* (Boston: South End Press, 1984); Stiehm, ed.; Jean Bethke Elshtain, "On Beautiful Souls, Just Warriors, and Feminist Consciousness," in Stiehm, ed., 341–48; Sara Ruddick, "Pacifying the Forces: Drafting Women in the Interests of Peace," *Signs: Journal of Women in Culture and Society* 8, no. 3 (Spring 1983): 471–89, and "Drafting Women: Pieces of a Puzzle," in *Conscripts and Volunteers: Military Requirements, Social Values, and the All-Volunteer Force*, ed. Robert K. Fullinwider (Totowa, N.J.: Rowman & Allanheld, 1983); Amy Swerdlow, "Women's Strike for Peace versus HUAC," *Feminist Studies* 8, no. 3 (Fall 1982): 493–520; Mary C. Segers, "The Catholic Bishops' Pastoral Letter on War and Peace: A Feminist Perspective," *Feminist Studies* 11, no. 3 (Fall 1985): 619–47.

particular, my emphasis is on the role of its specialized language, a language that I call "technostrategic."[6] I have come to believe that this language both reflects and shapes the nature of the American nuclear strategic project, that it plays a central role in allowing defense intellectuals to think and act as they do, and that feminists who are concerned about nuclear weaponry and nuclear war must give careful attention to the language we choose to use—whom it allows us to communicate with and what it allows us to think as well as say.

State I: Listening

Clean bombs and clean language

Entering the world of defense intellectuals was a bizarre experience—bizarre because it is a world where men spend their days calmly and matter-of-factly discussing nuclear weapons, nuclear strategy, and nuclear war. The discussions are carefully and intricately reasoned, occurring seemingly without any sense of horror, urgency, or moral outrage—in fact, there seems to be no graphic reality behind the words, as they speak of "first strikes," "counterforce exchanges," and "limited nuclear war," or as they debate the comparative values of a "minimum deterrent posture" versus a "nuclear war–fighting capability."

Yet what is striking about the men themselves is not, as the content of their conversations might suggest, their cold-bloodedness. Rather, it is that they are a group of men unusually endowed with charm, humor, intelligence, concern, and decency. Reader, I liked them. At least, I liked many of them. The attempt to understand how such men could contribute to an endeavor that I see as so fundamentally destructive became a continuing obsession for me, a lens through which I came to examine all of my experiences in their world.

In this early stage, I was gripped by the extraordinary language used to discuss nuclear war. What hit me first was the elaborate use of abstraction and euphemism, of words so bland that they never forced the speaker or enabled the listener to touch the realities of nuclear holocaust that lay behind the words.

---

[6] I have coined the term "technostrategic" to represent the intertwined, inextricable nature of technological and nuclear strategic thinking. The first reason is that strategic thinking seems to change in direct response to technological changes, rather than political thinking, or some independent paradigms that might be isolated as "strategic." (On this point, see Lord Solly Zuckerman, *Nuclear Illusions and Reality* [New York: Viking Press, 1982]). Even more important, strategic theory not only depends on and changes in response to technological objects, it is also based on a kind of thinking, a way of looking at problems—formal, mathematical modeling, systems analysis, game theory, linear programming—that are part of technology itself. So I use the term "technostrategic" to indicate the degree to which nuclear strategic language and thinking are imbued with, indeed constructed out of, modes of thinking that are associated with technology.

Anyone who has seen pictures of Hiroshima burn victims or tried to imagine the pain of hundreds of glass shards blasted into flesh may find it perverse beyond imagination to hear a class of nuclear devices matter-of-factly referred to as "clean bombs." "Clean bombs" are nuclear devices that are largely fusion rather than fission and that therefore release a higher quantity of energy, not as radiation, but as blast, as destructive explosive power.[7]

"Clean bombs" may provide the perfect metaphor for the language of defense analysts and arms controllers. This language has enormous destructive power, but without emotional fallout, without the emotional fallout that would result if it were clear one was talking about plans for mass murder, mangled bodies, and unspeakable human suffering. Defense analysts talk about "countervalue attacks" rather than about incinerating cities. Human death, in nuclear parlance, is most often referred to as "collateral damage"; for, as one defense analyst said wryly, "The Air Force doesn't target people, it targets shoe factories."[8]

Some phrases carry this cleaning-up to the point of inverting meaning. The MX missile will carry ten warheads, each with the explosure power of 300–475 kilotons of TNT: *one* missile the bearer of destruction approximately 250–400 times that of the Hiroshima bombing.[9] Ronald Reagan has

---

[7] Fusion weapons' proportionally smaller yield of radioactive fallout led Atomic Energy Commission Chairman Lewis Strauss to announce in 1956 that hydrogen bomb tests were important "not only from a military point of view but from a humanitarian aspect." Although the bombs being tested were 1,000 times more powerful than those that devastated Hiroshima and Nagasaki, the proportional reduction of fallout apparently qualified them as not only clean but also humanitarian. Lewis Strauss is quoted in Ralph Lapp, "The 'Humanitarian' H-Bomb," *Bulletin of Atomic Scientists* 12, no. 7 (September 1956): 263.

[8] I must point out that we cannot know whether to take this particular example literally: America's list of nuclear targets is, of course, classified. The defense analyst quoted, however, is a man who has had access to that list for at least two decades. He is also a man whose thinking and speaking is careful and precise, so I think it is reasonable to assume that his statement is not a distortion, that "shoe factories," even if not themselves literally targeted, accurately represent a category of target. Shoe factories would be one among many "military targets" other than weapons systems themselves; they would be military targets because an army needs boots. The likelihood of a nuclear war lasting long enough for foot soldiers to wear out their boots might seem to stretch the limits of credibility, but that is an insufficient reason to assume that they are not nuclear targets. Nuclear targeting and nuclear strategic planning in general frequently suffer from "conventionalization"—the tendency of planners to think in the old, familiar terms of "conventional" warfare rather than fully assimilating the ways in which nuclear weaponry has changed warfare. In avoiding talking about murder, the defense community has long been ahead of the State Department. It was not until 1984 that the State Department announced it will no longer use the word "killing," much less "murder," in official reports on the status of human rights in allied countries. The new term is "unlawful or arbitrary deprivation of life" (*New York Times*, February 15, 1984, as cited in *Quarterly Review of Doublespeak* 11, no. 1 [October 1984]: 3).

[9] "Kiloton" (or kt) is a measure of explosive power, measured by the number of thousands of tons of TNT required to release an equivalent amount of energy. The atomic bomb dropped on Hiroshima is estimated to have been approximately 12 kt. An MX missile is designed to

dubbed the MX missile "the Peacekeeper." While this renaming was the object of considerable scorn in the community of defense analysts, these very same analysts refer to the MX as a "damage limitation weapon."[10]

These phrases, only a few of the hundreds that could be discussed, exemplify the astounding chasm between image and reality that characterizes technostrategic language. They also hint at the terrifying way in which the existence of nuclear devices has distorted our perceptions and redefined the world. "Clean bombs" tells us that radiation is the only "dirty" part of killing people.

To take this one step further, such phrases can even seem healthful/curative/corrective. So that we not only have "clean bombs" but also "surgically clean strikes" ("counterforce" attacks that can purportedly "take out"—i.e., accurately destroy—an opponent's weapons or command centers without causing significant injury to anything else). The image of excision of the offending weapon is unspeakably ludicrous when the surgical tool is not a delicately controlled scalpel but a nuclear warhead. And somehow it seems to be forgotten that even scalpels spill blood.[11]

White men in ties discussing missile size

Feminists have often suggested that an important aspect of the arms race is phallic worship, that "missile envy" is a significant motivating force in the nuclear build-up.[12] I have always found this an uncomfortably reductionist explanation and hoped that my research at the Center would yield a more complex analysis. But still, I was curious about the extent to which I might find a sexual subtext in the defense professionals' discourse. I was not prepared for what I found.

---

carry up to ten Mk 21 reentry vehicles, each with a W-87 warhead. The yield of W-87 warheads is 300 kt, but they are "upgradable" to 475 kt.

[10] Since the MX would theoretically be able to "take out" Soviet land-based ICBMs in a "disarming first strike," the Soviets would have few ICBMs left for a retaliatory attack, and thus damage to the United States theoretically would be limited. However, to consider the damage that could be inflicted on the United States by the remaining ICBMs, not to mention Soviet bombers and submarine-based missiles as "limited" is to act as though words have no meaning.

[11] Conservative government assessments of the number of deaths resulting from a "surgically clean" counterforce attack vary widely. The Office of Technology Assessment projects 2 million to 20 million immediate deaths. (See James Fallows, *National Defense* [New York: Random House, 1981], 159.) A 1975 Defense Department study estimated 18.3 million fatalities, while the U.S. Arms Control and Disarmament Agency, using different assumptions, arrived at a figure of 50 million (cited by Desmond Ball, "Can Nuclear War Be Controlled?" Adelphi Paper no. 169 [London: International Institute for Strategic Studies, 1981]).

[12] The phrase is Helen Caldicott's in *Missile Envy: The Arms Race and Nuclear War* (Toronto: Bantam Books, 1986).

I think I had naively imagined myself as a feminist spy in the house of death—that I would need to sneak around and eavesdrop on what men said in unguarded moments, using all my subtlety and cunning to unearth whatever sexual imagery might be underneath how they thought and spoke. I had naively believed that these men, at least in public, would appear to be aware of feminist critiques. If they had not changed their language, I thought that at least at some point in a long talk about "penetration aids," someone would suddenly look up, slightly embarrassed to be caught in such blatant confirmation of feminist analyses of What's Going On Here.[13]

Of course, I was wrong. There was no evidence that any feminist critiques had ever reached the ears, much less the minds, of these men. American military dependence on nuclear weapons was explained as "irresistible, because you get more bang for the buck." Another lecturer solemnly and scientifically announced "to disarm is to get rid of all your stuff." (This may, in turn, explain why they see serious talk of nuclear disarmament as perfectly resistable, not to mention foolish. If disarmament is emasculation, how could any real man even consider it?) A professor's explanation of why the MX missile is to be placed in the silos of the newest Minuteman missiles, instead of replacing the older, less accurate ones, was "because they're in the nicest hole—you're not going to take the nicest missile you have and put it in a crummy hole." Other lectures were filled with discussion of vertical erector launchers, thrust-to-weight ratios, soft lay downs, deep penetration, and the comparative advantages of protracted versus spasm attacks—or what one military adviser to the National Security Council has called "releasing 70 to 80 percent of our megatonnage in one orgasmic whump."[14] There was serious concern about the need to harden our missiles and the need to "face it, the Russians are a little harder than we are." Disbelieving glances would occasionally pass between me and my one ally in the summer program, another woman, but no one else seemed to notice.

If the imagery is transparent, its significance may be less so. The temptation is to draw some conclusions about the defense intellectuals themselves—about what they are *really* talking about, or their motivations; but the temptation is worth resisting. Individual motivations cannot necessarily be read directly from imagery; the imagery itself does not originate in these particular individuals but in a broader cultural context.

Sexual imagery has, of course, been a part of the world of warfare since

---

[13] For the uninitiated, "penetration aids" refers to devices that help bombers or missiles get past the "enemy's" defensive systems; e.g., stealth technology, chaff, or decoys. Within the defense intellectual community, they are also familiarly known as "penaids."

[14] General William Odom, "C³I and Telecommunications at the Policy Level," Incidental Paper, Seminar on C³I: Command, Control, Communications and Intelligence (Cambridge, Mass.: Harvard University, Center for Information Policy Research, Spring 1980), 5.

long before nuclear weapons were even a gleam in a physicist's eye. The history of the atomic bomb project itself is rife with overt images of competitive male sexuality, as is the discourse of the early nuclear physicists, strategists, and SAC commanders.[15] Both the military itself and the arms manufacturers are constantly exploiting the phallic imagery and promise of sexual domination that their weapons so conveniently suggest. A quick glance at the publications that constitute some of the research sources for defense intellectuals makes the depth and pervasiveness of the imagery evident.

Air Force Magazine's advertisements for new weapons, for example, rival *Playboy* as a catalog of men's sexual anxieties and fantasies. Consider the following, from the June 1985 issue: emblazoned in bold letters across the top of a two-page advertisement for the AV-8B Harrier II—"Speak Softly and Carry a Big Stick." The copy below boasts "an exceptional thrust to weight ratio" and "vectored thrust capability that makes the . . . unique rapid response possible." Then, just in case we've failed to get the message, the last line reminds us, "Just the sort of 'Big Stick' Teddy Roosevelt had in mind way back in 1901."[16]

An ad for the BKEP (BLU-106/B) reads:

The Only Way to Solve Some Problems is to Dig Deep.
THE BOMB, KINETIC ENERGY
PENETRATOR
"Will provide the tactical air commander with efficient power to deny or significantly delay enemy airfield operations."
"Designed to maximize runway cratering by optimizing penetration dynamics and utilizing the most efficient warhead yet designed."[17]

(In case the symbolism of "cratering" seems far-fetched, I must point out that I am not the first to see it. The French use the Mururoa Atoll in the South Pacific for their nuclear tests and assign a woman's name to each of the craters they gouge out of the earth.)

Another, truly extraordinary, source of phallic imagery is to be found in descriptions of nuclear blasts themselves. Here, for example, is one by journalist William Laurence, who was brought to Nagasaki by the Air Force to witness the bombing. "Then, just when it appeared as though the thing had settled down in to a state of permanence, there came shooting out of the top a giant mushroom that increased the size of the pillar to a total of 45,000 feet. The mushroom top was even more alive than the pillar, seething and boiling in a white fury of creamy foam, sizzling upward and

---

[15] This point has been amply documented by Brian Easlea, *Fathering the Unthinkable: Masculinity, Scientists and the Nuclear Arms Race* (London: Pluto Press, 1983).

[16] *Air Force Magazine* 68, no. 6 (June 1985): 77–78.

[17] Ibid.

then descending earthward, a thousand geysers rolled into one. It kept struggling in an elemental fury, like a creature in the act of breaking the bonds that held it down."[18]

Given the degree to which it suffuses their world, that defense intellectuals themselves use a lot of sexual imagery does not seem especially surprising. Nor does it, by itself, constitute grounds for imputing motivation. For me, the interesting issue is not so much the imagery's psychodynamic origins, as how it functions. How does it serve to make it possible for strategic planners and other defense intellectuals to do their macabre work? How does it function in their construction of a work world that feels tenable? Several stories illustrate the complexity.

During the summer program, a group of us visited the New London Navy base where nuclear submarines are homeported and the General Dynamics Electric Boat boatyards where a new Trident submarine was being constructed. At one point during the trip we took a tour of a nuclear powered submarine. When we reached the part of the sub where the missiles are housed, the officer accompanying us turned with a grin and asked if we wanted to stick our hands through a hole to "pat the missile." *Pat the missile?*

The image reappeared the next week, when a lecturer scornfully declared that the only real reason for deploying cruise and Pershing II missiles in Western Europe was "so that our allies can pat them." Some months later, another group of us went to be briefed at NORAD (the North American Aerospace Defense Command). On the way back, our plane went to refuel at Offut Air Force Base, the Strategic Air Command headquarters near Omaha, Nebraska. When word leaked out that our landing would be delayed because the new B-1 bomber was in the area, the plane became charged with a tangible excitement that built as we flew in our holding pattern, people craning their necks to try to catch a glimpse of the B-1 in the skies, and climaxed as we touched down on the runway and hurtled past it. Later, when I returned to the Center I encountered a man who, unable to go on the trip, said to me enviously, "I hear you got to pat a B-1."

What is all this "patting"? What are men doing when they "pat" these high-tech phalluses? Patting is an assertion of intimacy, sexual possession, affectionate domination. The thrill and pleasure of "patting the missile" is the proximity of all that phallic power, the possibility of vicariously appropriating it as one's own.

But if the predilection for patting phallic objects indicates something of the homoerotic excitement suggested by the language, it also has another side. For patting is not only an act of sexual intimacy. It is also what one does to babies, small children, the pet dog. One pats that which is small,

[18] William L. Laurence, *Dawn over Zero: The Study of the Atomic Bomb* (London: Museum Press, 1974), 198–99.

cute, and harmless—not terrifyingly destructive. Pat it, and its lethality disappears.

Much of the sexual imagery I heard was rife with the sort of ambiguity suggested by "patting the missiles." The imagery can be construed as a deadly serious display of the connections between masculine sexuality and the arms race. At the same time, it can also be heard as a way of minimizing the seriousness of militarist endeavors, of denying their deadly consequences. A former Pentagon target analyst, in telling me why he thought plans for "limited nuclear war" were ridiculous, said, "Look, you gotta understand that it's a pissing contest—you gotta expect them to use everything they've got." What does this image say? Most obviously, that this is all about competition for manhood, and thus there is tremendous danger. But at the same time, the image diminishes the contest and its outcomes, by representing it as an act of boyish mischief.

Fathers, sons, and virgins

"Virginity" also made frequent, arresting, appearances in nuclear discourse. In the summer program, one professor spoke of India's explosion of a nuclear bomb as "losing her virginity"; the question of how the United States should react was posed as whether or not we should "throw her away." It is a complicated use of metaphor. Initiation into the nuclear world involves being deflowered, losing one's innocence, knowing sin, all wrapped up into one. Although the manly United States is no virgin, and proud of it, the double standard raises its head in the question of whether or not a woman is still worth anything to a man once she has lost her virginity.

New Zealand's refusal to allow nuclear-armed or nuclear-powered warships into its ports prompted similar reflections on virginity. A good example is provided by Retired U.S. Air Force General Ross Milton's angry column in *Air Force Magazine*, entitled, "Nuclear Virginity." His tone is that of a man whose advances have been spurned. He is contemptuous of the woman's protestation that she wants to remain pure, innocent of nuclear weapons; her moral reluctance is a quaint and ridiculous throwback. But beyond contempt, he also feels outraged—after all, this is a woman we have *paid* for, who *still* will not come across. He suggests that we withdraw our goods and services—and then we will see just how long she tries to hold onto her virtue.[19] The patriarchal bargain could not be laid out more clearly.

Another striking metaphor of patriarchal power came early in the summer program, when one of the faculty was giving a lecture on deter-

---

[19] U.S.A.F. Retired General T. R. Milton, "Nuclear Virginity," *Air Force Magazine* 68, no. 5 (May 1985): 44.

rence. To give us a concrete example from outside the world of military strategy, he described having a seventeen-year-old son of whose TV-watching habits he disapproves. He deals with the situation by threatening to break his son's arm if he turns on the TV again. "That's deterrence!" he said triumphantly.

What is so striking about this analogy is that at first it seems so inappropriate. After all, we have been taught to believe that nuclear deterrence is a relation between two countries of more or less equal strength, in which one is only able to deter the other from doing it great harm by threatening to do the same in return. But in this case, the partners are unequal, and the stronger one is using his superior force not to protect himself or others from grave injury but to coerce.

But if the analogy seems to be a flawed expression of deterrence as we have been taught to view it, it is nonetheless extremely revealing about U.S. nuclear deterrence as an operational, rather than rhetorical or declaratory policy. What it suggests is the speciousness of the defensive rhetoric that surrounds deterrence—of the idea that we face an implacable enemy and that we stockpile nuclear weapons only in an attempt to defend ourselves. Instead, what we see is the drive to superior power as a means to exercise one's will and a readiness to threaten the disproportionate use of force in order to achieve one's own ends. There is no question here of recognizing competing but legitimate needs, no desire to negotiate, discuss, or compromise, and most important, no necessity for that recognition or desire, since the father carries the bigger stick.[20]

The United States frequently appeared in discussions about international politics as "father," sometimes coercive, sometimes benevolent, but always knowing best. The single time that any mention was made of countries other than the United States, our NATO allies, or the USSR was in a lecture on nuclear proliferation. The point was made that younger countries simply could not be trusted to know what was good for them, nor were they yet fully responsible, so nuclear weapons in their hands would be much more dangerous than in ours. The metaphor used was that of parents needing to set limits for their children.

Domestic bliss

Sanitized abstraction and sexual and patriarchal imagery, even if disturbing, seemed to fit easily into the masculinist world of nuclear war planning. What did not fit, what surprised and puzzled me most when I first heard it, was the set of metaphors that evoked images that can only be called domestic.

---

[20] I am grateful to Margaret Cerullo, a participant in the first summer program, for reporting the use of this analogy to me and sharing her thoughts about this and other events in the program. The interpretation I give here draws strongly on hers.

Nuclear missiles are based in "silos." On a Trident submarine, which carries twenty-four multiple warhead nuclear missiles, crew members call the part of the submarine where the missiles are lined up in their silos ready for launching "the Christmas tree farm." What could be more bucolic—farms, silos, Christmas trees?

In the ever-friendly, even romantic world of nuclear weaponry, enemies "exchange" warheads; one missile "takes out" another; weapons systems can "marry up"; "coupling" is sometimes used to refer to the wiring between mechanisms of warning and response, or to the psycho-political links between strategic (intercontinental) and theater (European-based) weapons. The patterns in which a MIRVed missile's nuclear warheads land is known as a "footprint."[21] These nuclear explosives are not dropped; a "bus" "delivers" them. In addition, nuclear bombs are not referred to as bombs or even warheads; they are referred to as "reentry vehicles," a term far more bland and benign, which is then shortened to "RVs," a term not only totally abstract and removed from the reality of a bomb but also resonant with the image of the recreational vehicles of the ideal family vacation.

These domestic images must be more than simply one more form of distancing, one more way to remove oneself from the grisly reality behind the words; ordinary abstraction is adequate to that task. Something else, something very peculiar, is going on here. Calling the pattern in which bombs fall a "footprint" almost seems a willful distorting process, a playful, perverse refusal of accountability—because to be accountable to reality is to be unable to do this work.

These words may also serve to domesticate, to *tame* the wild and uncontrollable forces of nuclear destruction. The metaphors minimize; they are a way to make phenomena that are beyond what the mind can encompass smaller and safer, and thus they are a way of gaining mastery over the unmasterable. The fire-breathing dragon under the bed, the one who threatens to incinerate your family, your town, your planet, becomes a pet you can pat.

Using language evocative of everyday experiences also may simply serve to make the nuclear strategic community more comfortable with what they are doing. "PAL" (permissive action links) is the carefully constructed, friendly acronym for the electronic system designed to prevent the unauthorized firing of nuclear warheads. "BAMBI" was the acronym developed for an early version of an antiballistic missile system (for Ballistic Missile Boost Intercept). The president's Annual Nuclear Weapons Stockpile Memorandum, which outlines both short- and long-range plans for production of new nuclear weapons, is benignly referred to

---

[21] MIRV stands for "multiple independently targetable re-entry vehicles." A MIRVed missile not only carries more than one warhead; its warheads can be aimed at different targets.

as "the shopping list." The National Command Authorities choose from a "menu of options" when deciding among different targeting plans. The "cookie cutter" is a phrase used to describe a particular model of nuclear attack. Apparently it is also used at the Department of Defense to refer to the neutron bomb.[22]

The imagery that domesticates, that humanizes insentient weapons, may also serve, paradoxically, to make it all right to ignore sentient human bodies, human lives.[23] Perhaps it is possible to spend one's time thinking about scenarios for the use of destructive technology and to have human bodies remain invisible in that technological world precisely because that world itself now *includes* the domestic, the human, the warm, and play-ful—the Christmas trees, the RVs, the affectionate pats. It is a world that is in some sense complete unto itself; it even includes death and loss. But it is weapons, not humans, that get "killed." "Fratricide" occurs when one of your warheads "kills" another of your own warheads. There is much discussion of "vulnerability" and "survivability," but it is about the vulner-ability and survival of weapons systems, not people.

Male birth and creation

There is one set of domestic images that demands separate attention—images that suggest men's desire to appropriate from women the power of giving life and that conflate creation and destruction. The bomb project is rife with images of male birth.[24] In December 1942, Ernest Lawrence's

[22] Henry T. Nash, "The Bureaucratization of Homicide," *Bulletin of Atomic Scientists* (April 1980), reprinted in E. P. Thompson and Dan Smith, eds., *Protest and Survive* (New York: Monthly Review Press, 1981), 159. The neutron bomb is notable for the active political contention that has occurred over its use and naming. It is a small warhead that produces six times the prompt radiation but slightly less blast and heat than typical fission warheads of the same yield. Pentagon planners see neutron bombs as useful in killing Soviet tank crews while theoretically leaving the buildings near the tanks intact. Of course, the civilians in the nearby buildings, however, would be killed by the same "enhanced radiation" as the tank crews. It is this design for protecting property while killing civilians along with soldiers that has led people in the antinuclear movement to call the neutron bomb "the ultimate capitalist weapon." However, in official parlance the neutron bomb is not called a weapon at all; it is an "enhanced radiation device." It is worth noting, however, that the designer of the neutron bomb did not conceive of it as an anti-tank personnel weapon to be used against the Russians. Instead, he thought it would be useful in an area where the enemy *did not have* nuclear weapons to use. (Samuel T. Cohen, in an interview on National Public Radio, as reported in Fred Kaplan, "The Neutron Bomb: What It Is, the Way It Works," *Bulletin of Atomic Scientists* [October 1981], 6.)

[23] For a discussion of the functions of imagery that reverses sentient and insentient matter, that "exchange[s] . . . idioms between weapons and bodies," see Elaine Scarry, *The Body in Pain: The Making and Unmaking of the World* (New York: Oxford University Press, 1985), 60–157, esp. 67.

[24] For further discussion of men's desire to appropriate from women the power of giving life and death, and its implications for men's war-making activities, see Dorothy Dinnerstein,

telegram to the physicists at Chicago read, "Congratulations to the new parents. Can hardly wait to see the new arrival."[25] At Los Alamos, the atom bomb was referred to as "Oppenheimer's baby." One of the physicists working at Los Alamos, Richard Feynman, writes that when he was temporarily on leave after his wife's death, he received a telegram saying, "The baby is expected on such and such a day."[26] At Lawrence Livermore, the hydrogen bomb was referred to as "Teller's baby," although those who wanted to disparage Edward Teller's contribution claimed he was not the bomb's father but its mother. They claimed that Stanislaw Ulam was the real father; he had the all important idea and inseminated Teller with it. Teller only "carried it" after that.[27]

Forty years later, this idea of male birth and its accompanying belittling of maternity—the denial of women's role in the process of creation and the reduction of "motherhood" to the provision of nurturance (apparently Teller did not need to provide an egg, only a womb)—seems thoroughly incorporated into the nuclear mentality, as I learned on a subsequent visit to U.S. Space Command in Colorado Springs. One of the briefings I attended included discussion of a new satellite system, the not yet "on line" MILSTAR system.[28] The officer doing the briefing gave an excited recitation of its technical capabilities and then an explanation of the new Unified Space Command's role in the system. Self-effacingly he said, "We'll do the motherhood role—telemetry, tracking, and control—the maintenance."

The Mermaid and the Minotaur (New York: Harper & Row, 1977). For further analysis of male birth imagery in the atomic bomb project, see Evelyn Fox Keller, "From Secrets of Life to Secrets of Death" (paper delivered at the Kansas Seminar, Yale University, New Haven, Conn., November 1986); and Easlea (n. 15 above), 81–116.

[25] Lawrence is quoted by Herbert Childs in *An American Genius: The Life of Ernest Orlando Lawrence* (New York: E. P. Dutton, 1968), 340.

[26] Feynman writes about the telegram in Richard P. Feynman, "Los Alamos from Below," in *Reminiscences of Los Alamos, 1943–1945*, ed. Lawrence Badash, Joseph O. Hirshfelder, and Herbert P. Broida (Dordrecht: D. Reidel Publishing Co., 1980), 130.

[27] Hans Bethe is quoted as saying that "Ulam was the father of the hydrogen bomb and Edward was the mother, because he carried the baby for quite a while" (J. Bernstein, *Hans Bethe: Prophet of Energy* [New York: Basic Books, 1980], 95).

[28] The MILSTAR system is a communications satellite system that is jam resistant, as well as having an "EMP-hardened capability." (This means that the electromagnetic pulse set off by a nuclear explosion would theoretically not destroy the satellites' electronic systems.) There are, of course, many things to say about the sanity and morality of the idea of the MILSTAR system and of spending the millions of dollars necessary to EMP-harden it. The most obvious point is that this is a system designed to enable the United States to fight a "protracted" nuclear war—the EMP-hardening is to allow it to act as a conduit for command and control of successive nuclear shots, long after the initial exchange. The practicality of the idea would also appear to merit some discussion—who and what is going to be communicating to and from after the initial exchange? And why bother to harden it against EMP when all an opponent has to do to prevent the system from functioning is to blow it up, a feat certain to become technologically feasible in a short time? But, needless to say, exploration of these questions was not part of the briefing.

In light of the imagery of male birth, the extraordinary names given to the bombs that reduced Hiroshima and Nagasaki to ash and rubble—"Little Boy" and "Fat Man"—at last become intelligible. These ultimate destroyers were the progeny of the atomic scientists—and emphatically not just any progeny but male progeny. In early tests, before they were certain that the bombs would work, the scientists expressed their concern by saying that they hoped the baby was a boy, not a girl—that is, not a dud.[29] General Grove's triumphant cable to Secretary of War Henry Stimson at the Potsdam conference, informing him that the first atomic bomb test was successful read, after decoding: "Doctor has just returned most enthusiastic and confident that the little boy is as husky as his big brother. The light in his eyes discernible from here to Highhold and I could have heard his screams from here to my farm."[30] Stimson, in turn, informed Churchill by writing him a note that read, "Babies satisfactorily born."[31] In 1952, Teller's exultant telegram to Los Alamos announcing the successful test of the hydrogen bomb, "Mike," at Eniwetok Atoll in the Marshall Islands, read, "It's a boy."[32] The nuclear scientists gave birth to male progeny with the ultimate power of violent domination over female Nature. The defense intellectuals' project is the creation of abstract formulations to control the forces the scientists created—and to participate thereby in their world-creating/destroying power.

The entire history of the bomb project, in fact, seems permeated with imagery that confounds man's overwhelming technological power to destroy nature with the power to create—imagery that inverts men's destruction and asserts in its place the power to create new life and a new world. It converts men's destruction into their rebirth.

William L. Laurence witnessed the Trinity test of the first atomic bomb and wrote: "The big boom came about a hundred seconds after the great flash—the first cry of a new-born world. . . . They clapped their hands as they leaped from the ground—earthbound man symbolising the birth of a new force."[33] Watching "Fat Man" being assembled the day before it was dropped on Nagasaki, he described seeing the bomb as "being fashioned into a living thing."[34] Decades later, General Bruce K. Holloway, the commander in chief of the Strategic Air Command from 1968 to 1972,

---

[29] The concern about having a boy, not a girl, is written about by Robert Jungk, *Brighter Than a Thousand Suns*, trans. James Cleugh (New York: Harcourt, Brace & Co., 1956), 197.

[30] Richard E. Hewlett and Oscar E. Anderson, *The New World, 1939/46: A History of the United States Atomic Energy Commission*, 2 vols. (University Park: Pennsylvania State University Press, 1962), 1:386.

[31] Winston Churchill, *The Second World War*, vol. 6., *Triumph and Tragedy* (London: Cassell, 1954), 551.

[32] Quoted by Easlea, 130.

[33] Laurence (n. 18 above), 10.

[34] Ibid., 188.

described a nuclear war as involving "a big bang, like the start of the universe."[35]

God and the nuclear priesthood

The possibility that the language reveals an attempt to appropriate ultimate creative power is evident in another striking aspect of the language of nuclear weaponry and doctrine—the religious imagery. In a subculture of hard-nosed realism and hyper-rationality, in a world that claims as a sign of its superiority its vigilant purging of all nonrational elements, and in which people carefully excise from their discourse every possible trace of soft sentimentality, as though purging dangerous nonsterile elements from a lab, the last thing one might expect to find is religious imagery—imagery of the forces that science has been defined in *opposition to*. For surely, given that science's identity was forged by its separation from, by its struggle for freedom from, the constraints of religion, the only thing as unscientific as the female, the subjective, the emotional, would be the religious. And yet, religious imagery permeates the nuclear past and present. The first atomic bomb test was called Trinity—the unity of the Father, the Son, and the Holy Spirit, the male forces of Creation. The imagery is echoed in the language of the physicists who worked on the bomb and witnessed the test: "It was as though we stood at the first day of creation." Robert Oppenheimer thought of Krishna's words to Arjuna in the *Bhagavad Gita:* "I am become Death, the Shatterer of Worlds."[36]

Perhaps most astonishing of all is the fact that the creators of strategic doctrine actually refer to members of their community as "the nuclear priesthood." It is hard to decide what is most extraordinary about this: the easy arrogance of their claim to the virtues and supernatural power of the priesthood; the tacit admission (*never* spoken directly) that rather than being unflinching, hard-nosed, objective, empirically minded scientific describers of reality, they are really the creators of dogma; or the extraordinary implicit statement about who, or rather what, has become god. If this new priesthood attains its status through an inspired knowledge of nuclear weapons, it gives a whole new meaning to the phrase "a mighty fortress is our God."

[35] From a 1985 interview in which Holloway was explaining the logic of a "decapitating" strike against the Soviet leadership and command and control systems—and thus how nuclear war would be different from World War II, which was a "war of attrition," in which transportation, supply depots, and other targets were hit, rather than being a "big bang" (Daniel Ford, "The Button," *New Yorker Magazine* 61, no. 7 [April 8, 1985], 49).

[36] Jungk, 201.

Stage 2: Learning to speak the language

Although I was startled by the combination of dry abstraction and counter-intuitive imagery that characterizes the language of defense intellectuals, my attention and energy were quickly focused on decoding and learning to speak it. The first task was training the tongue in the articulation of acronyms.

Several years of reading the literature of nuclear weaponry and strategy had not prepared me for the degree to which acronyms littered all conversations, nor for the way in which they are used. Formerly, I had thought of them mainly as utilitarian. They allow you to write or speak faster. They act as a form of abstraction, removing you from the reality behind the words. They restrict communication to the initiated, leaving all others both uncomprehending and voiceless in the debate.

But, being at the Center, hearing the defense analysts use the acronyms, and then watching as I and others in the group started to fling acronyms around in our conversation revealed some additional, unexpected dimensions.

First, in speaking and hearing, a lot of these terms can be very sexy. A small supersonic rocket "designed to penetrate any Soviet air defense" is called a SRAM (for short-range attack missile). Submarine-launched cruise missiles are not referred to as SLCMs, but "slick'ems." Ground-launched cruise missiles are "glick'ems." Air-launched cruise missiles are not sexy but magical—"alchems" (ALCMs) replete with the illusion of turning base metals into gold.

TACAMO, the acronym used to refer to the planes designed to provide communications links to submarines, stands for "take charge and move out." The image seems closely related to the nicknames given to the new guidance systems for "smart weapons"—"shoot and scoot" or "fire and forget."

Other acronyms work in other ways. The plane in which the president supposedly will be flying around above a nuclear holocaust, receiving intelligence and issuing commands for the next bombing, is referred to as "kneecap" (for NEACP—National Emergency Airborne Command Post). The edge of derision suggested in referring to it as "kneecap" mirrors the edge of derision implied when it is talked about at all, since few believe that the president really would have the time to get into it, or that the communications systems would be working if he were in it, and some might go so far as to question the usefulness of his being able to direct an extended nuclear war from his kneecap even if it were feasible. (I never heard the morality of this idea addressed.) But it seems to me that speaking about it with that edge of derision is *exactly* what allows it to be spoken about and seriously discussed at all. It is the very ability to make fun of a concept that makes it possible to work with it rather than reject it outright.

In other words, what I learned at the program is that talking about nuclear weapons is fun. I am serious. The words are fun to say; they are racy, sexy, snappy. You can throw them around in rapid-fire succession. They are quick, clean, light; they trip off the tongue. You can reel off dozens of them in seconds, forgetting about how one might just interfere with the next, not to mention with the lives beneath them.

I am not describing a phenomenon experienced only by the perverse, although the phenomenon itself may be perverse indeed. Nearly everyone I observed clearly took pleasure in using the words. It mattered little whether we were lecturers or students, hawks or doves, men or women— we all learned it, and we all spoke it. Some of us may have spoken with a self-consciously ironic edge, but the pleasure was there nonetheless.

Part of the appeal was the thrill of being able to manipulate an arcane language, the power of entering the secret kingdom, being someone in the know. It is a glow that is a significant part of learning about nuclear weaponry. Few know, and those who do are powerful. You can rub elbows with them, perhaps even be one yourself.

That feeling, of course, does not come solely from the language. The whole set-up of the summer program itself, for example, communicated the allures of power and the benefits of white male privileges. We were provided with luxurious accommodations, complete with young black women who came in to clean up after us each day; generous funding paid not only our transportation and food but also a large honorarium for attending; we met in lavishly appointed classrooms and lounges. Access to excellent athletic facilities was guaranteed by a "Temporary Privilege Card," which seemed to me to sum up the essence of the experience. Perhaps most important of all were the endless allusions by our lecturers to "what I told John [Kennedy]" and "and then Henry [Kissinger] said," or the lunches where we could sit next to a prominent political figure and listen to Washington gossip.

A more subtle, but perhaps more important, element of learning the language is that, when you speak it, you feel in control. The experience of mastering the words infuses your relation to the material. You can get so good at manipulating the words that it almost feels as though the whole thing is under control. Learning the language gives a sense of what I would call cognitive mastery; the feeling of mastery of technology that is finally *not* controllable but is instead powerful beyond human comprehension, powerful in a way that stretches and even thrills the imagination.

The more conversations I participated in using this language, the less frightened I was of nuclear war. How can learning to speak a language have such a powerful effect? One answer, I believe, is that the *process* of learning the language is itself a part of what removes you from the reality of nuclear war.

I entered a world where people spoke what amounted to a foreign language, a language I had to learn if we were to communicate with one another. So I became engaged in the challenge of it—of decoding the acronyms and figuring out which were the proper verbs to use. My focus was on the task of solving the puzzles, developing language competency— not on the weapons and wars behind the words. Although my interest was in thinking about nuclear war and its prevention, my energy was elsewhere.

By the time I was through, I had learned far more than a set of abstract words that refers to grisly subjects, for even when the subjects of a standard English and nukespeak description seem to be the same, they are, in fact, about utterly different phenomena. Consider the following descriptions, in each of which the subject is the aftermath of a nuclear attack:

> Everything was black, had vanished into the black dust, was destroyed. Only the flames that were beginning to lick their way up had any color. From the dust that was like a fog, figures began to loom up, black, hairless, faceless. They screamed with voices that were no longer human. Their screams drowned out the groans rising everywhere from the rubble, groans that seemed to rise from the very earth itself.[37]

> [You have to have ways to maintain communications in a] nuclear environment, a situation bound to include EMP blackout, brute force damage to systems, a heavy jamming environment, and so on.[38]

There are no ways to describe the phenomena represented in the first with the language of the second. Learning to speak the language of defense analysts is not a conscious, cold-blooded decision to ignore the effects of nuclear weapons on real live human beings, to ignore the sensory, the emotional experience, the human impact. It is simply learning a new language, but by the time you are through, the content of what you can talk about is monumentally different, as is the perspective from which you speak.

In the example above, the differences in the two descriptions of a "nuclear environment" stem partly from a difference in the vividness of the words themselves—the words of the first intensely immediate and evoca-

---

[37] Hisako Matsubara, *Cranes at Dusk* (Garden City, N.Y.: Dial Press, 1985). The author was a child in Kyoto at the time the atomic bomb was dropped. Her description is based on the memories of survivors.

[38] General Robert Rosenberg (formerly on the National Security Council staff during the Carter Administration), "The Influence of Policymaking on C³I," Incidental Paper, Seminar on C³I (Cambridge, Mass.: Harvard University, Center for Information Policy Research, Spring 1980), 59.

tive, the words of the second abstract and distancing. The passages also differ in their content; the first describes the effects of a nuclear blast on human beings, the second describes the impact of a nuclear blast on technical systems designed to assure the "command and control" of nuclear weapons. Both of these differences may stem from the difference of perspective: the speaker in the first is a victim of nuclear weapons, the speaker in the second is a user. The speaker in the first is using words to try to name and contain the horror of human suffering all around her; the speaker in the second is using words to ensure the possibility of launching the next nuclear attack. Technostrategic language can be used only to articulate the perspective of the users of nuclear weapons, not that of the victims.[39]

Thus, speaking the expert language not only offers distance, a feeling of control, and an alternative focus for one's energies; it also offers escape—escape from thinking of oneself as a victim of nuclear war. I do not mean this on the level of individual consciousness; it is not that defense analysts somehow convince themselves that they would not be among the victims of nuclear war, should it occur. But I do mean it in terms of the structural position the speakers of the language occupy and the perspective they get from that position. *Structurally,* speaking technostrategic language removes them from the position of victim and puts them in the position of the planner, the user, the actor. From that position, there is neither need nor way to see oneself as a victim; no matter what one deeply knows or believes about the likelihood of nuclear war, and no matter what sort of terror or despair the knowledge of nuclear war's reality might inspire, the speakers of technostrategic language are positionally allowed, even forced, to escape that awareness, to escape viewing nuclear war from the position of the victim, by virtue of their linguistic stance as users, rather than victims, of nuclear weaponry.

Finally, then, I suspect that much of the reduced anxiety about nuclear

---

[39] Two other writers who have remarked on this division of languages between the "victims" and the professionals (variously named) are Freeman Dyson and Glenn D. Hook. Dyson, in *Weapons and Hope* (New York: Harper & Row, 1984), notes that there are two languages in the current discussion of nuclear weapons, which he calls the language of "the victims"and the language of "the warriors." He sees the resulting problem as being the difficulty the two groups have in communicating with each other and, thus, in appreciating each other's valid concerns. His project, then, is the search for a common language, and a good portion of the rest of the book is directed toward that end. Hook, in "Making Nuclear Weapons Easier to Live With: The Political Role of Language in Nuclearization," *Journal of Peace Research* 22, no. 1 (1985): 67–77, follows Camus in naming the two groups "the victims" and "the executioners." He is more explicit than Dyson about naming these as perspectives, as coming from positions of greater or lesser power, and points out that those with the most power are able to dominate and define the terms in which we speak about nuclear issues, so that no matter who we are, we find ourselves speaking as though we were the users, rather than the victims of nuclear weapons. Although my analysis of perspectives and the ways in which language inscribes relations of power is similar to his, I differ from Hook in finding in this fact one of the sources of the experts' relative lack of fear of nuclear war.

war commonly experienced by both new speakers of the language and long-time experts comes from characteristics of the language itself: the distance afforded by its abstraction; the sense of control afforded by mastering it; and the fact that its content and concerns are that of the users rather than the victims of nuclear weapons. In learning the language, one goes from being the passive, powerless victim to the competent, wily, powerful purveyor of nuclear threats and nuclear explosive power. The enormous destructive effects of nuclear weapons systems become extensions of the self, rather than threats to it.

Stage 3: Dialogue

It did not take very long to learn the language of nuclear war and much of the specialized information it contained. My focus quickly changed from mastering technical information and doctrinal arcana to attempting to understand more about how the dogma was rationalized. Instead of trying, for example, to find out why submarines are so hard to detect or why, prior to the Trident II, submarine-based ballistic missiles were not considered counterforce weapons, I now wanted to know why we really "need" a strategic triad, given submarines' "invulnerability."[40] I also wanted to know why it is considered reasonable to base U.S. military planning on the Soviet Union's military capabilities rather than seriously attempting to gauge what their intentions might be. This standard practice is one I found particularly troubling. Military analysts say that since we cannot know for certain what Soviet intentions are, we must plan our military forces and strategies as if we knew that the Soviets planned to use all of their weapons. While this might appear to have the benefit of prudence, it leads to a major problem. When we ask only what the Soviets *can* do, we quickly come to assume that that is what they *intend* to do. We base our planning on "worst-case scenarios" and then come to believe that we live in a world where vast resources must be committed to "prevent" them from happening.

   Since underlying rationales are rarely discussed in the everyday business of defense planning, I had to start asking more questions. At first,

[40] The "strategic triad" refers to the three different modes of basing nuclear warheads: at land, on intercontinental ballistic missiles; at sea, on missiles in submarines; and "in the air," on the Strategic Air Command's bombers. Given that nuclear weapons based on submarines are "invulnerable" (i.e., not subject to attack), since there is not now nor likely to be in the future any reliable way to find and target submarines, many commentators (mostly from outside the community of defense intellectuals) have suggested that the Navy's leg of the triad is all we need to ensure a capacity to retaliate against a nuclear attack. This suggestion that submarine-based missiles are an adequate deterrent becomes especially appealing when it is remembered that the other basing modes—ICBMs and bombers—act as targets that would draw thousands of nuclear attacks to the American mainland in time of war.

although I was tempted to use my newly acquired proficiency in techno-strategic jargon, I vowed to speak English. I had long believed that one of the most important functions of an expert language is exclusion—the denial of a voice to those outside the professional community.[41] I wanted to see whether a well-informed person could speak English and still carry on a knowledgeable conversation.

What I found was that no matter how well-informed or complex my questions were, if I spoke English rather than expert jargon, the men responded to me as though I were ignorant, simpleminded, or both. It did not appear to occur to anyone that I might actually be choosing not to speak their language.

A strong distaste for being patronized and dismissed made my experiment in English short-lived. I adapted my everyday speech to the vocabulary of strategic analysis. I spoke of "escalation dominance," "preemptive strikes," and, one of my favorites, "subholocaust engagements." Using the right phrases opened my way into long, elaborate discussions that taught me a lot about technostrategic reasoning and how to manipulate it.

I found, however, that the better I got at engaging in this discourse, the more impossible it became for me to express my own ideas, my own values. I could adopt the language and gain a wealth of new concepts and reasoning strategies—but at the same time as the language gave me access to things I had been unable to speak about before, it radically excluded others. I could not use the language to express my concerns because it was physically impossible. This language does not allow certain questions to be asked or certain values to be expressed.

To pick a bald example: the word "peace" is not a part of this discourse. As close as one can come is "strategic stability," a term that refers to a balance of numbers and types of weapons systems—not the political, social, economic, and psychological conditions implied by the word "peace." Not only is there no word signifying peace in this discourse, but the word "peace" itself cannot be used. To speak it is immediately to brand oneself as a soft-headed activist instead of an expert, a professional to be taken seriously.

If I was unable to speak my concerns in this language, more disturbing still was that I found it hard even to keep them in my own head. I had begun my research expecting abstract and sanitized discussions of nuclear war and had readied myself to replace my words for theirs, to be ever vigilant against slipping into the never-never land of abstraction. But no matter how prepared I was, no matter how firm my commitment to staying aware of the reality behind the words, over and over I found that I could not stay

[41] For an interesting recent discussion of the role of language in the creation of professional power, see JoAnne Brown, "Professional Language: Words That Succeed," *Radical History Review*, no. 34 (1986), 33–51.

connected, could not keep human lives as my reference point. I found I could go for days speaking about nuclear weapons without once thinking about the people who would be incinerated by them.

It is tempting to attribute this problem to qualities of the language, the words themselves—the abstractness, the euphemisms, the sanitized, friendly, sexy acronyms. Then all we would need to do is change the words, make them more vivid; get the military planners to say "mass murder" instead of "collateral damage" and their thinking would change.

The problem, however, is not only that defense intellectuals use abstract terminology that removes them from the realities of which they speak. There *is* no reality of which they speak. Or, rather, the "reality" of which they speak is itself a world of abstractions. Deterrence theory, and much of strategic doctrine altogether, was invented largely by mathematicians, economists, and a few political scientists. It was invented to hold together abstractly, its validity judged by its internal logic. Questions of the correspondence to observable reality were not the issue. These abstract systems were developed as a way to make it possible to "think about the unthinkable"—not as a way to describe or codify relations on the ground.[42]

So the greatest problem with the idea of "limited nuclear war," for example, is not that it is grotesque to refer to the death and suffering caused by *any* use of nuclear weapons as "limited" or that "limited nuclear war" is an abstraction that is disconnected from human reality but, rather, that "limited nuclear war" is itself an abstract conceptual system, designed, embodied, achieved by computer modeling. It is an abstract world in which hypothetical, calm, rational actors have sufficient information to know exactly what size nuclear weapon the opponent has used against which targets, and in which they have adequate command and control to make sure that their response is precisely equilibrated to the attack. In this scenario, no field commander would use the tactical "mini-nukes" at his disposal in the height of a losing battle; no EMP-generated electronic failures, or direct attacks on command and control centers, or human errors would destroy communications networks. Our rational actors would be free of emotional response to being attacked, free of political pressures from the populace, free from madness or despair or any of the myriad other factors that regularly affect human actions and decision making. They would act solely on the basis of a perfectly informed mathematical calculus of megatonnage.

So to refer to "limited nuclear war" is already to enter into a system that is de facto abstract and removed from reality. To use more descriptive

---

[42] For fascinating, detailed accounts of the development of strategic doctrine, see Fred Kaplan, *The Wizards of Armageddon* (New York: Simon & Schuster, 1983); and Gregg F. Herken, *The Counsels of War* (New York: Alfred A. Knopf, 1985).

language would not, by itself, change that. In fact, I am tempted to say that the abstractness of the entire conceptual system makes descriptive language nearly beside the point. In a discussion of "limited nuclear war," for example, it might make some difference if in place of saying "In a counterforce attack against hard targets collateral damage could be limited," a strategic analyst had to use words that were less abstract—if he had to say, for instance, "If we launch the missiles we have aimed at their missile silos, the explosions would cause the immediate mass murder of 10 million women, men, and children, as well as the extended illness, suffering, and eventual death of many millions more." It is true that the second sentence does not roll off the tongue or slide across one's consciousness quite as easily. But it is also true, I believe, that the ability to speak about "limited nuclear war" stems as much, if not more, from the fact that the term "limited nuclear war" refers to an abstract conceptual system rather than to events that might take place in the real world. As such, there is no need to think about the concrete human realities behind the model; what counts is the internal logic of the system.[43]

This realization that the abstraction was not just in the words but also characterized the entire conceptual system itself helped me make sense of my difficulty in staying connected to human lives. But there was still a piece missing. How is it possible, for example, to make sense of the following paragraph? It is taken from a discussion of a scenario ("regime A") in which the United States and the USSR have revised their offensive weaponry, banned MIRVs, and gone to a regime of single warhead (Midgetman) missiles, with no "defensive shield" (or what is familiarly known as "Star Wars" or SDI):

> The strategic stability of regime A is based on the fact that both sides are deprived of any incentive ever to strike first. Since it takes roughly two warheads to destroy one enemy silo, an attacker must expend two of his missiles to destroy one of the enemy's. A first strike disarms the attacker. The aggressor ends up worse off than the aggressed.[44]

"The aggressor ends up worse off than the aggressed"? The homeland of "the aggressed" has just been devastated by the explosions of, say, a thousand nuclear bombs, each likely to be ten to one hundred times more

---

[43] Steven Kull's interviews with nuclear strategists can be read to show that on some level, some of the time, some of these men are aware that there is a serious disjunction between their models and the real world. Their justification for continuing to use these models is that "other people" (unnamed, and on asking, unnameable) believe in them and that they therefore have an important reality ("Nuclear Nonsense," *Foreign Policy*, no. 58 [Spring 1985], 28–52).

[44] Charles Krauthammer, "Will Star Wars Kill Arms Control?" *New Republic*, no. 3,653 (January 21, 1985), 12–16.

powerful than the bomb dropped on Hiroshima, and the aggressor, whose homeland is still untouched, "ends up worse off"? How is it possible to think this? Even abstract language and abstract thinking do not seem to be a sufficient explanation.

I was only able to "make sense of it" when I finally asked myself the question that feminists have been asking about theories in every discipline: What is the reference point? Who (or what) is the *subject* here?

In other disciplines, we have frequently found that the reference point for theories about "universal human phenomena" has actually been white men. In technostrategic discourse, the reference point is not white men, it is not human beings at all; it is the weapons themselves. The aggressor thus ends up worse off than the aggressed because he has fewer weapons left; human factors are irrelevant to the calculus of gain and loss.

In "regime A" and throughout strategic discourse, the concept of "incentive" is similarly distorted by the fact that weapons are the subjects of strategic paradigms. Incentive to strike first is present or absent according to a mathematical calculus of numbers of "surviving" weapons. That is, incentive to start a nuclear war is discussed not in terms of what possible military or political ends it might serve but, instead, in terms of numbers of weapons, with the goal being to make sure that you are the guy who still has the most left at the end. Hence, it is frequently stated that MIRVed missiles create strategic instability because they "give you the incentive to strike first." Calculating that two warheads must be targeted on each enemy missile, one MIRVed missile with ten warheads would, in theory, be able to destroy five enemy missiles in their silos; you destroy more of theirs than you have expended of your own. You win the numbers game. In addition, if you do not strike first, it would theoretically take relatively few of their MIRVed missiles to destroy a larger number of your own—so you must, as they say in the business, "use 'em or lose 'em." Many strategic analysts fear that in a period of escalating political tensions, when it begins to look as though war may be inevitable, this combination makes "the incentive to strike first" well nigh irresistible.

Incentive to launch a nuclear war arises from a particular configuration of weapons and their hypothetical mathematical interaction. Incentive can only be so narrowly defined because the referents of technostrategic paradigms are weapons—not human lives, not even states and state power.

The fact that the subjects of strategic paradigms are weapons has several important implications. First, and perhaps most critically, there simply is no way to talk about human death or human societies when you are using a language designed to talk about weapons. Human death simply *is* "collateral damage"—collateral to the real subject, which is the weapons themselves.

Second, if human lives are not the reference point, then it is not only impossible to talk about humans in this language, it also becomes in some sense illegitimate to ask the paradigm to reflect human concerns. Hence, questions that break through the numbing language of strategic analysis and raise issues in human terms can be dismissed easily. No one will claim that the questions are unimportant, but they are inexpert, unprofessional, irrelevant to the business at hand to ask. The discourse among the experts remains hermetically sealed.

The problem, then, is not only that the language is narrow but also that it is seen by its speakers as complete or whole unto itself—as representing a body of truths that exist independently of any other truth or knowledge. The isolation of this technical knowledge from social or psychological or moral thought, or feelings, is all seen as legitimate and necessary. The outcome is that defense intellectuals can talk about the weapons that are supposed to protect particular political entities, particular peoples and their way of life, without actually asking if weapons *can* do it, or if they are the best *way* to do it, or whether they may even damage the entities you are supposedly protecting. It is not that the men I spoke with would say that these are invalid questions. They would, however, simply say that they are separate questions, questions that are outside what they do, outside their realm of expertise. So their deliberations go on quite independently, as though with a life of their own, disconnected from the functions and values they are supposedly to serve.

Finally, the third problem is that this discourse has become virtually the only legitimate form of response to the question of how to achieve security. If the language of weaponry was one competing voice in the discussion, or one that was integrated with others, the fact that the referents of strategic paradigms are only weapons would be of little note. But when we realize that the only language and expertise offered to those interested in pursuing peace refers to nothing but weapons, its limits become staggering, and its entrapping qualities—the way in which, once you adopt it, it becomes so hard to stay connected to human concerns—become more comprehensible.

Stage 4: The terror

As a newcomer to the world of defense analysts, I was continually startled by likeable and admirable men, by their gallows humor, by the bloodcurdling casualness with which they regularly blew up the world while standing and chatting over the coffee pot. I also *heard* the language they spoke—heard the acronyms and euphemisms, and abstractions, heard the imagery, heard the pleasure with which they used it.

Within a few weeks, what had once been remarkable became unnoticeable. As I learned to speak, my perspective changed. I no longer stood outside the impermeable wall of technostrategic language and, once inside, I could no longer see it. Speaking the language, I could no longer really hear it. And once inside its protective walls, I began to find it difficult to get out. The impermeability worked both ways.

I had not only learned to speak a language: I had started to think in it. Its questions became my questions, its concepts shaped my responses to new ideas. Its definitions of the parameters of reality became mine. Like the White Queen, I began to believe six impossible things before breakfast. Not because I consciously believed, for instance, that a "surgically clean counterforce strike" was really possible, but instead because some elaborate piece of doctrinal reasoning I used was already predicated on the possibility of those strikes, as well as on a host of other impossible things.[45]

My grasp on what *I* knew as reality seemed to slip. I might get very excited, for example, about a new strategic justification for a "no first use" policy and spend time discussing the ways in which its implications for our force structure in Western Europe were superior to the older version.[46] And after a day or two I would suddenly step back, aghast that I was so involved with the military justifications for not using nuclear weapons—as though the moral ones were not enough. What I was actually talking about—the mass incineration caused by a nuclear attack—was no longer in my head.

Or I might hear some proposals that seemed to me infinitely superior to the usual arms control fare. First I would work out how and why these proposals were better and then work out all the ways to counter the arguments against them. But then, it might dawn on me that even though these two proposals sounded so different, they still shared a host of assumptions that I was not willing to make (e.g., about the inevitable, eternal conflict of interests between the United States and the USSR, or the desirability of having some form of nuclear deterrent, or the goal of "managing," rather than ending, the nuclear arms race). After struggling to this point of seeing what united both positions, I would first feel as though I had really accomplished something. And then all of a sudden, I would realize that these new insights were things I actually knew *before I ever entered* this community. Apparently, I had since forgotten them, at least functionally, if not absolutely.

I began to feel that I had fallen down the rabbit hole—and it was a struggle to climb back out.

---

[45] For an excellent discussion of the myriad uncertainties that make it ludicrous to assume the targeting accuracies posited in the notion of "surgically clean counterforce strikes," see Fallows (n. 11 above), chap. 6.

[46] "No first use" refers to the commitment not to be the first side to introduce nuclear weapons into a "conventional" war. The Soviet Union has a "no first use" policy, but the United States does not. In fact, it is NATO doctrine to use nuclear weapons in a conventional war in Western Europe, as a way of overcoming the Warsaw Pact's supposed superiority in conventional weaponry and troop strength.

Conclusions

Suffice it to say that the issues about language do not disappear after you have mastered technostrategic discourse. The seductions remain great. You can find all sorts of ways to seemingly beat the boys at their own game; you can show how even within their own definitions of rationality, most of what is happening in the development and deployment of nuclear forces is wildly irrational. You can also impress your friends and colleagues with sickly humorous stories about the way things really happen on the inside. There is tremendous pleasure in it, especially for those of us who have been closed out, who have been told that it is really all beyond us and we should just leave it to the benevolently paternal men in charge.

But as the pleasures deepen, so do the dangers. The activity of trying to out-reason defense intellectuals in their own games gets you thinking inside their rules, tacitly accepting all the unspoken assumptions of their paradigms. You become subject to the tyranny of concepts. The language shapes your categories of thought (e.g., here it becomes "good nukes" or "bad nukes," not, nukes or no nukes) and defines the boundaries of imagination (as you try to imagine a "minimally destabilizing basing mode" rather than a way to prevent the weapon from being deployed at all).

Yet, the issues of language have now become somewhat less vivid and central to me. Some of the questions raised by the experiences described here remain important, but others have faded and been superseded by new questions. These, while still not precisely the questions of an "insider," are questions I could not have had without being inside, without having access to the knowledge and perspective the inside position affords. Many of my questions now are more practical—which individuals and institutions are actually responsible for the endless "modernization" and proliferation of nuclear weaponry? What role does technostrategic rationality actually play in their thinking? What would a reasonable, genuinely defensive "defense" policy look like? Others are more philosophical. What is the nature of the rationality and "realism" claimed by defense intellectuals for their mode of thinking? What are the many different grounds on which their claims to rationality can be shown to be spurious?

My own move away from a focus on the language is quite typical. Other recent entrants into this world have commented to me that, while it is the cold-blooded, abstract discussions that are most striking at first, within a short time "you get past it—you stop hearing it, it stops bothering you, it becomes normal—and you come to see that the language, itself, is not the problem."

However, I think it would be a mistake to dismiss these early impressions. They can help us learn something about the militarization of the mind, and they have, I believe, important implications for feminist scholars and activists who seek to create a more just and peaceful world.

Mechanisms of the mind's militarization are revealed through both listening to the language and learning to speak it. *Listening*, it becomes clear that participation in the world of nuclear strategic analysis does not necessarily require confrontation with the central fact about military activity—that the purpose of all weaponry and all strategy is to injure human bodies.[47] In fact, as Elaine Scarry points out, participation in military thinking does not require confrontation with, and actually demands the elision of, this reality.[48]

Listening to the discourse of nuclear experts reveals a series of culturally grounded and culturally acceptable mechanisms that serve this purpose and that make it possible to "think about the unthinkable," to work in institutions that foster the proliferation of nuclear weapons, to plan mass incinerations of millions of human beings for a living. Language that is abstract, sanitized, full of euphemisms; language that is sexy and fun to use; paradigms whose referent is weapons; imagery that domesticates and deflates the forces of mass destruction; imagery that reverses sentient and nonsentient matter, that conflates birth and death, destruction and creation—all of these are part of what makes it possible to be radically removed from the reality of what one is talking about and from the realities one is creating through the discourse.[49]

Learning to speak the language reveals something about how thinking can become more abstract, more focused on parts disembedded from their context, more attentive to the survival of weapons than the survival of human beings. That is, it reveals something about the process of militarization—and the way in which that process may be undergone by man or woman, hawk or dove.

Most often, the act of learning technostrategic language is conceived of as an additive process: you add a new set of vocabulary words; you add the reflex ability to decode and use endless numbers of acronyms; you add some new information that the specialized language contains; you add the conceptual tools that will allow you to "think strategically." This additive view appears to be held by defense intellectuals themselves; as one said to

[47] For an eloquent and graphic exploration of this point, see Scarry (n. 23 above), 73.

[48] Scarry catalogs a variety of mechanisms that serve this purpose (ibid., 60–157). The point is further developed by Sara Ruddick, "The Rationality of Care," in *Thinking about Women, War, and the Military*, ed. Jean Bethke Elshtain and Sheila Tobias (Totowa, N.J.: Rowman & Allanheld, in press).

[49] My discussion of the specific ways in which this discourse creates new realities is in the next part of this project, entitled, "The Emperor's New Armor." I, like many other social scientists, have been influenced by poststructuralist literary theory's discussion of deconstructing texts, point of view, and narrative authority within texts, and I take the language and social practice of the defense intellectuals as a text to be read in this way. For a classic introduction to this literature, see Josue Harari, ed., *Textual Strategies: Perspectives in Post-structuralist Criticism* (Ithaca, N.Y.: Cornell University Press, 1979); and Jacques Derrida, *Of Grammatology* (Baltimore: Johns Hopkins University Press, 1976).

me, "Much of the debate is in technical terms—learn it, and decide whether it's relevant later." This view also appears to be held by many who think of themselves as antinuclear, be they scholars and professionals attempting to change the field from within, or public interest lobbyists and educational organizations, or some feminist antimilitarists.[50] Some believe that our nuclear policies are so riddled with irrationality that there is a lot of room for well-reasoned, well-informed arguments to make a difference; others, even if they do not believe that the technical information is very important, see it as necessary to master the language simply because it is too difficult to attain public legitimacy without it. In either case, the idea is that you add the expert language and information and proceed from there.

However, I have been arguing throughout this paper that learning the language is a transformative, rather than an additive, process. When you choose to learn it you enter a new mode of thinking—a mode of thinking not only about nuclear weapons but also, de facto, about military and political power and about the relationship between human ends and technological means.

Thus, those of us who find U.S. nuclear policy desperately misguided appear to face a serious quandary. If we refuse to learn the language, we are virtually guaranteed that our voices will remain outside the "politically relevant" spectrum of opinion. Yet, if we do learn and speak it, we not only severely limit what we can say but we also invite the transformation, the militarization, of our own thinking.

I have no solutions to this dilemma, but I would like to offer a few thoughts in an effort to reformulate its terms. First, it is important to recognize an assumption implicit in adopting the strategy of learning the language. When we assume that learning and speaking the language will give us a voice recognized as legitimate and will give us greater political influence, *we are assuming that the language itself actually articulates the criteria and reasoning strategies upon which nuclear weapons development and deployment decisions are made.* I believe that this is largely an illusion. Instead, I want to suggest that technostrategic discourse functions more as a gloss, as an ideological curtain behind which the actual reasons for these decisions hide. That rather than informing and shaping decisions, it far more often functions as a legitimation for political outcomes that have occurred for utterly different reasons. If this is true, it raises some serious questions about the extent of the political returns we might get from using technostrategic discourse, and whether they can ever balance out the potential problems and inherent costs.

[50] Perhaps the most prominent proponent of this strategy is Sheila Tobias. See, e.g., "Demystifying Defense: Closing the Knowledge Gap," *Social Policy* 13, no. 3 (1983): 29–32; and Sheila Tobias, Peter Goudinoff, Stefan Leader, and Shelah Leader, *What Kinds of Guns Are They Buying for Your Butter?* (New York: William Morrow & Co., 1982).

I do not, however, want to suggest that none of us should learn the language. I do not believe that this language is well suited to achieving the goals desired by antimilitarists, yet at the same time, I, for one, have found the experience of learning the language useful and worthwhile (even if at times traumatic). The question for those of us who do choose to learn it, I think, is what use are we going to make of that knowledge?

One of the most intriguing options opened by learning the language is that it suggests a basis upon which to challenge the legitimacy of the defense intellectuals' dominance of the discourse on nuclear issues. When defense intellectuals are criticized for the cold-blooded inhumanity of the scenarios they plan, their response is to claim the high ground of rationality; they are the only ones whose response to the existence of nuclear weapons is objective and realistic. They portray those who are radically opposed to the nuclear status quo as irrational, unrealistic, too emotional. "Idealistic activists" is the pejorative they set against their own hard-nosed professionalism.

Much of their claim to legitimacy, then, is a claim to objectivity born of technical expertise and to the disciplined purging of the emotional valences that might threaten their objectivity. But if the surface of their discourse— its abstraction and technical jargon—appears at first to support these claims, a look just below the surface does not. There we find currents of homoerotic excitement, heterosexual domination, the drive toward competency and mastery, the pleasures of membership in an elite and privileged group, the ultimate importance and meaning of membership in the priesthood, and the thrilling power of becoming Death, shatterer of worlds. How is it possible to hold this up as a paragon of cool-headed objectivity?

I do not wish here to discuss or judge the holding of "objectivity" as an epistemological goal. I would simply point out that, as defense intellectuals rest their claims to legitimacy on the untainted rationality of their discourse, their project fails according to its own criteria. Deconstructing strategic discourse's claims to rationality is, then, in and of itself, an important way to challenge its hegemony as the sole legitimate language for public debate about nuclear policy.

I believe that feminists, and others who seek a more just and peaceful world, have a dual task before us—a deconstructive project and a reconstructive project that are intimately linked.[51] Our deconstructive task requires close attention to, and the dismantling of, technostrategic discourse. The dominant voice of militarized masculinity and decontextualized rationality speaks so loudly in our culture, it will remain difficult for any other voices to be heard until that voice loses some of its power to

---

[51] Harding and Hintikka, eds. (n. 5 above), ix–xix, esp. x.

define what we hear and how we name the world—until that voice is delegitimated.

Our reconstructive task is a task of creating compelling alternative visions of possible futures, a task of recognizing and developing alternative conceptions of rationality, a task of creating rich and imaginative alternative voices—diverse voices whose conversations with each other will invent those futures.

Center for Psychological Studies in the Nuclear Age
Harvard University Medical School

SCIENCE AND THE CONSTRUCTION OF GENDERED SUBJECTIVITIES

The Trials of Alice Mitchell: Sensationalism, Sexology, and the Lesbian Subject in Turn-of-the-Century America

Lisa Duggan

T HE YEARS 1880 to 1920 were a crucible of change in gender and sexual relations in the United States. This long transition was neither even nor easy; it was deeply marked by conflict and tragedy as well as by erotic excitements. As Victorian certainties faded and the possibilities of the modern slowly materialized, new sexualities took shape and the modern desiring subject emerged.

Historians writing about this transition now generally agree that the modern lesbian was one such new desiring subject appearing at the turn of the century in Europe and Anglo-America.[1] They argue not that sexual relations or love between women were new then, but that the subjectivity this lesbian embodied was a radical innovation. She came to see herself as an erotic subject—as a woman whose desire for women was felt as a fundamental component of her sense of self, marking her as erotically different from most other women. As the period progressed, this new subjective sense of self interacted in a complex way with the emergence of public lesbian identities and communities.

I would like to thank Nan D. Hunter, Jonathan Ned Katz, Cindy Patton, Carolyn Dean, Carroll Smith-Rosenberg, John D'Emilio, Paula Treichler, Sonya Michel, Martin Bauml Duberman, Esther Newton, Jenny Terry, Judith R. Walkowitz, Judith Butler, Liz Kennedy, and the *Signs* editors for comments and suggestions on successive versions of this article, and Jonathan Ned Katz, Allan Bérubé, and Eric Garber for supplying me with obscure but crucial citations. My progress in completing this research was partially supported by a generous grant from the Virginia Foundation for the Humanities.

[1] For overviews of this historical argument, see Weeks 1981, esp. "The Construction of Homosexuality," 96–121, and Foucault 1978. For a discussion of the emergence of the "lesbian" and "homosexual" in the American context, see Katz 1983, esp. "The Invention of the Homosexual, 1880–1950," 137–74, and D'Emilio and Freedman 1988, esp. "Toward a New Sexual Order, 1880–1930," 171–235.

[*Signs: Journal of Women in Culture and Society* 1993, vol. 18, no. 4]

The new lesbian relationships that formed in the midst of these changes significantly modified earlier forms of women's partnerships, which have been described by historians as falling within two broadly defined class-bound types—the romantic friendship in which bourgeois girls and women made passionate commitments to each other within a gender-segregated female world, and the "marriage" between a "female husband" who passed and worked as a man among workingmen and her "wife."[2] The historical picture of the transition from these earlier forms of relationship to modern lesbianism—the emergence of lesbian subjectivity into public visibility at the end of the nineteenth century—exists only in broad outline and mostly with respect to white women, both working class and bourgeois. The long historical process through which a new identity was constructed remains relatively obscure. At the heart of this obscurity lies the problematic relationship between the cultural representations (or texts) that historians use as sources and the living historical subjects who produced, consumed, and reproduced them.

The difficulty for historians is illustrated in the debate over the meaning of the figure of the "mannish lesbian"—a figure ubiquitous in published sources of many kinds by the early twentieth century (Newton 1989; Smith-Rosenberg 1989). Was this figure a distorted representation produced by antifeminist sexologists, intent on discrediting and stigmatizing the relationships of newly independent New Women? Or was the mannish lesbian in part a strategically deployed self-representation, used by some sexually active New Women to carve out a new identity? Underlying this debate are questions about the nature of the relationship between the representations of mannish lesbians in various texts and the subjectivities and identities of living women: Did hostile sexologists construct the mannish lesbian, or did she, in any meaningful way, construct herself?

Early in the nineteenth century, for instance, aristocratic British diarist Anne Lister represented herself as erotically interested in women exclusively and associated this interest with her appropriations of various aspects of masculinity (Lister [1791–1840] 1988). But women such as Lister were relatively isolated and did not form socially visible networks or forge connections linking their sexual subjectivity to public representations of lesbianism, as began to happen later in the century. Nonetheless, the manner in which they linked masculine traits, economic independence, and the erotic love of women drew on and reproduced tropes of sexual difference in combinations that presaged modern lesbian identities. The interrelations of their early representations with those of the

---

[2] For studies of romantic friendship, see Smith-Rosenberg 1975 and Faderman 1981. For discussions of "passing women," see Katz 1976 and San Francisco Lesbian and Gay History Project 1989.

first sexologists present historians with a polyvocal cultural dialogue not reducible to any single site of historical invention.

In these pages, I want to examine this complex dialogue in a new way. I want to look at the project of constructing identities as a historical process of contested narration, a process in which contrasting "stories" of the self and others—stories of difference—are told, appropriated, and retold as stories of location in the social world of structured inequalities. Looked at in this way, individual and collective subjectivities are inter-actively linked to representations (including self-representations) through historically and materially specific stories of identity. In illustration, I will show here how mass circulation newspapers fashioned stories out of living women's relationships, how sexologists then reappropriated those stories as "cases," and women themselves reworked them as "identities" in an extended battle over the meaning of women's erotic partnerships at the turn of the century. Out of this battle, the first publicly visible forms of modern lesbianism were born; as we shall see, it was a terrifyingly difficult birth.

*   *   *

Identity is defined in these pages as a narrative of a subject's location within social structure. As stories rather than mere labels, identities traverse the space between the social world and subjective experience, constituting a central organizing principle connecting self and world. Individual identities, usually multiple and often contradictory, structure and give meaning to personal experience. Collective identities—of gen-der, race, class, or nation—forge connections among individuals and provide links between past and present, becoming the basis for cultural representation and political action.

In an extended discussion of the problems facing feminists addressing such theoretical problems, Teresa de Lauretis modifies the poststructur-alist rejection of the notion of unmediated experience by redefining ex-perience "in the general sense of a process by which, for all social beings, subjectivity is constructed. Through that process one places oneself or is placed in social reality, and so perceives and comprehends as subjective (referring to, even originating in oneself) those relations—material, eco-nomic, and interpersonal—which are in fact social, and, in a larger per-spective, historical" (1984, 159). I use the term *experience* in de Laure-tis's sense. Identity, I argue, is the story or narrative structure that gives meaning to experience.

Stories of identity are never static, monolithic, or politically innocent. By situating people within shifting structures of social power and in-equality, they become contested sources of authority and legitimation. This is especially true during moments of radical social transformation.

Old stories assume new narrative meanings; new stories emerge, patched together from cultural fragments appropriated for new purposes.[3] Never created out of whole cloth, never uniquely individual, each narrative is a retelling, an act of social interaction, a positioned intervention in the shared, contested narratives of a given culture.[4]

"Lesbian" was just such a bitterly contested identity at the turn of the century, as new stories of lesbian life and experience developed at the changing nexus of gender identity and sexuality. The content of the identities "man" and "woman" shifted from their Victorian to their modern configurations, and the heterosexual/homosexual polarity emerged as a newly central preoccupation of gendered stories of identity.[5] Lesbianism in particular emerged as an issue in debates about female sexuality, aggression, economic independence, education, reform efforts, and feminism. Contests over the meanings of stories of lesbian identity expressed profound social anxiety over the boundary masculine/feminine itself. By tracing new stories of lesbian identity as they developed out of the earlier stories of romantic friends and female husbands and by examining how they were reworked and retold by different agents to different audiences for different and often conflicting social ends, we can observe the process of contested narration in motion.

*   *   *

One of the most sensational early accounts of a relationship perceived as of a new type was contained in the news reports of the 1892 murder of seventeen-year-old Freda Ward by nineteen-year-old Alice Mitchell in Memphis, Tennessee. Headlines nationwide announced that this was "A Very Unnatural Crime" in which the murderess claimed to have loved her victim so much that she killed her rather than live estranged from her. Though the murders of spouses and sweethearts—commonly called *love-murders*—were the frequent fare of sensational news, this one was treated as nearly incomprehensible and as unique on American soil. The *New York World*, for instance, reported that because of Alice Mitchell's act,

---

[3] These contests do not take place solely within various types of texts but are produced within and circulate through the material social world, both shaping and reflecting structured social antagonisms. For a particularly lucid discussion of this process, see Walkowitz 1989. Walkowitz stakes out a materialist grounding for her appropriation of poststructuralist theories of meaning production. See also Poovey 1988, where Poovey makes a specifically historical argument for the interdependence of material conditions and representations.

[4] This notion somewhat parallels Judith Butler's metaphor of *performance,* or the set of repetitive practices through which identity is constituted (Butler 1990). My version of this argument was also influenced by Barbara Herrnstein Smith's interesting analysis of narrative construction as a purposeful act (Smith 1981).

[5] For a provocative and influential argument placing the heterosexual/homosexual dyad at the center of cultural life in the modern West, see Sedgwick 1990.

a sober American community and an unimaginative American court must deal in matter-of-fact fashion with matters which have been discussed hitherto by French writers of fiction only. Gen. Luke E. Wright and Col. George Gantt, of Tennessee, find themselves compelled to do in open court the work that Balzac did in tracing to physical sources mental perversion. In the Criminal Court of Memphis, Shelby County, Adolphe Belot's *Mlle. [Giraud] Ma Femme* will be the only text-book at hand. Judge DuBose, of Tennessee, will have cited to him, as bearing on the case of an American girl, the creations of French writers whom he and all his associates have looked upon as perverted creatures, dealing with matters outside of real life, or at least outside of American life.

In all the long history of crime and insanity there is no such case recorded. [1892]

Other such cases were in fact recorded. By 1892, there was a developing medical literature on same sex love and its relation to crime and insanity produced by American doctors who adapted the theories of Krafft-Ebing and other Europeans. These doctors were captivated by Alice Mitchell's love-murder, which seemed a perfect illustration of their theories. Innumerable articles were published applying the new theories to this case, which was added in turn to later editions of Krafft-Ebing's *Psychopathia Sexualis* (1899, 550). By 1901 the first American edition of Havelock Ellis's *Sexual Inversion* stated that Alice Mitchell was "a typical invert of a very pronounced kind" and that "there have been numerous cases in America more recently" (1901, 121).

The story of Alice Mitchell's murder of Freda Ward persisted as a topic of newspaper sensationalism and of scientific sexology well into the twentieth century. The case also served as the partial basis for at least three works of fiction, a folk ballad that survived in oral tradition into the 1960s, and a proposed play for Sarah Bernhardt to be written by famed librettist Victorien Sardou (Bernhardt visited Mitchell in jail and kept a scrapbook on the case).[6]

Alice was not tried in criminal court for the murder. Instead, she appeared at a lunacy inquisition. The plan of the attorneys hired by her father was to have her declared "presently insane" and incompetent to stand trial, then confined to the state lunatic asylum as dangerous to the community. They brought physicians into the courtroom to testify as experts that Alice was insane. The prosecution countered that she was rational but vicious, degraded, and "fast."

[6] Sensationalism: Coppock 1930. Sexology: Cauldwell 1950. Fiction: Hatch 1895; Freeman [1895] 1927; Carhart 1895. Ballad: Howard 1961. Bernhardt: *Memphis Appeal Avalanche* 1892.

To make their case, the defense attorneys constructed Alice's life as a case history and presented it to expert witnesses as the basis for their opinions. The case history read, in part, as follows:

HYPOTHETICAL CASE[7]

Alice was a nervous, excitable child, somewhat undersize. As she grew she did not manifest interest in those childish amusements and toys that girls are fond of.

When only 4 or 5 years old she spent much time at a swing in the yard of the family, in performing such feats upon it as skinning the cat and hanging by an arm or leg. She was fond of climbing, and expert at it.

She delighted in marbles and tops, in base ball and foot ball. . . . She spent much time with her brother Frank. . . . She preferred him and his sports to her sisters. He practiced with her at target shooting with a small rifle, to her great delight. She excelled this brother . . . at feats of activity. She was fond of horses. . . . To the family she seemed a regular tomboy.

. . . She disliked sewing and needle work. . . . To most persons, even her relatives, she seemed distant and indifferent. She was wholly without that fondness for boys that girls usually manifest.

She had no intimates or child sweethearts among the boys, and when approaching womanhood . . . she had no beaux and took no pleasure in the society of young men. She was regarded as mentally wrong by young men toward whom she had thus acted. . . .

For Fred Ward, a girl about her own age, she had an extraordinary fondness. . . . The attachment seemed to be mutual, but was far stronger in Alice Mitchell than in Fred.

They were very different in disposition. Fred was girl-like and took no pleasure in the boyish sports that Alice delighted in. Her instincts and amusements were feminine. She was tender and affectionate. Time strengthened the intimacy between them. They became lovers in the sense of that relation between persons of different sexes. . . .

In Feb. 1891, Alice proposed marriage. She repeated the offer in three separate letters. To each Fred replied, agreeing to become her wife. Alice wrote her upon the third promise that she would hold her to the engagement, and that she would kill her if she broke the promise. . . .

---

[7] The defense team's "hypothetical case" was reprinted in an article in the *Memphis Commercial* 1892d and in Sim 1892. Freda Ward was referred to throughout by her nickname, Fred.

It was agreed that Alice should be known as Alvin J. Ward, so that Fred could still call her by pet name Allie, and Fred was to be known as Mrs. A. J. Ward. The particulars of formal marriage and elopement were agreed upon. Alice was to put on man's apparel, and have her hair trimmed by a barber like a man; was to get the license to marry, and Fred was to procure the Rev. . . . [or] a justice of the peace to marry them. The ceremony performed, they intended to leave for St. Louis. Alice was to continue to wear man's apparel, and meant to try and have a mustache, if it would please Fred. She was going out to work for Fred in men's clothes.

In the latter part of June, 1891, Ashley Roselle . . . began to pay court to Fred, who gave him one of her photographs. The watchful vigilance of Alice got track of this affair, and she remonstrated warmly with Fred, and charged her with deception and infidelity. Fred acknowledged she had done wrong, vowed unshaken fidelity to Alice, and promised never more to offend.

The scheme of marrying and eloping seemed almost ready for execution in the latter part of July. . . . By chance, Mrs. Volkmar, the married sister . . . with whom Fred was living, saw part of the correspondence of the girls, which disclosed the relations between them, and the plans to elope and marry. . . . An exciting scene ensued. Mrs. Volkmar wrote to Mrs. Mitchell, the mother of Alice, and at the same time wrote to Alice, returning the engagement ring, and other love tokens, and declaring that all intercourse between the girls must at once cease. . . .

The effect on Alice of the return of the engagement ring and the inhibition of all communication with Fred was almost crushing. She wept, passed sleepless nights, lost her appetite, frequently declined even to come to the table. . . .

. . . In her language she more than loved Fred. She took her life because she had told her she would, and because it was her duty to do it. The best thing would have been the marriage, the next best thing was to kill Fred. That would make sure that no one else could get her.

This account was, of course, a strategic construction, a case history designed to procure a particular medical opinion and a desired legal outcome. But unlike the medical case histories published in journals and texts, this one was corroborated by the testimony of witnesses and contested in court through cross-examination and the testimony of opposing witnesses. Family members and neighbors, as well as Alice herself, recounted their version of events, and Alice and Freda's letters were read aloud and printed in the papers. The newspaper reports of this hypothetical case, the testimony, and the trial summarized the many tellings and retellings of the story of love and murder from multiple points of view.

The relations of Alice and Freda emerged in these stories as a hybrid form developed from different class contexts. At first, their love was perceived as an ordinary, if excessive, schoolgirls' romantic friendship—in Memphis, such relations were called "chumming."[8] But their plans for cross-dressing and marriage pushed them beyond the bounds of that category. They had adopted a classic "passing" strategy—a strategy so rare among bourgeois white women that their plan was perceived as so radically inappropriate as to be insane. Though the local papers regularly noted cases of workingmen and farm laborers who turned out to be "passing" women, their lives and partnerships with other women were reported as simply eccentric or remarkable—not sexual, deviant, or insane. But at the trial, Alice's belief that she could marry Freda while disguised as "Alvin" was portrayed by her attorneys and their medical experts, and reported in the press, as a "morbid" or "imperative delusion" and a sign of sexual "perversion."

The descriptions of witnesses and experts at trial also reveal an emerging belief that Alice's plan to pass as Alvin was not merely a disguise but an expression of some deep and partially hidden truth—that Alice was masculine and that her masculinity and her desire for Freda were linked. For medical writers, this link was the basis for the construction of female sexual "inversion" (Chauncey 1982–83). But the link was also made by Alice before the interventions following the murder; it shaped her relations with Freda.

The "story" of Alice and Freda up to the time of the murder, as it was presented and reworked in the mass circulation press during 1892, was composed of three essential structural elements. First, the contrast drawn between Alice's "masculine" characteristics and Freda's "feminine" manner was universally agreed on—repeated not only by doctors but also by Alice's best friend Lillie, by the girls' school principal, and by neighbors. It also ran clearly through Alice's and Freda's published letters.

Second, conflict between Alice and Freda over the nature of their relationship was presented as the first and possibly the most important foundation for the later violence. Alice wanted Freda to commit herself totally to their love; Freda vacillated, making and breaking engagements with at least two young men. Alice was certain that she wanted to marry Freda and that she herself had no interest in men; Freda was full of doubt and treated Alice as one among several suitors. This conflict led Alice to

[8] For an account of this common phenomenon, also called "smashing" in a northern college setting, see Sahli 1979.

threats of violence and a suicide attempt. The plan to elope was a sign of and a means to ensure Alice's ultimate success in securing the relationship and in ensuring that Freda would not betray Alice by marrying a man.

The third structural element of the story is conflict between the "engaged" couple and their female relatives. Although Freda's older sister and Alice's mother did not object to the intensity of their attachment or the continual displays of physical affection, nor even to their exchange of engagement rings, the plan to elope with Alice posing as Alvin led the older women to end all contact between the lovers. Male relatives and the world of male authority were not brought into the affair until after the murder; only then did Alice come into direct conflict with the male-dominated institutions of law and medicine.

Running through all three elements of the story are themes of cross-gender identification and cross-dressing. Though there was no evidence reported of any sexual contact between Alice and Freda (and both those who claimed they were "pure" and those who claimed they indulged in "unnatural practices" had ulterior motives), there were indications in the news accounts that they recognized, played with, and eroticized a mas-culine/feminine difference between them. In her most affectionate letters, Freda referred to Alice as "Alvin" and included lines such as "If you chew tobacco, love, I won't let you kiss me" (*Memphis Commercial* 1892e). In their conflict over the nature of their relationship, Alice used the plan to cross-dress and marry as a strategy to define their love as a serious commitment equivalent to any of Freda's potential connections to a man. In their conflict with female relatives, the gender-crossing and elopement plans were a red flag signaling that these young women had gone too far and that their relationship had to be viewed as dangerous and possibly sexual rather than as foolishly but harmlessly romantic.

Overall, the cumulative newspaper story of Alice and Freda consti-tuted one version of a new narrative-in-formation—a cultural marker of the emergence of a partially cross-gender-identified lesbian and her sep-aration from and conflict with the family-based female world of the nineteenth century and, in this version of the story, from the bourgeois values of sexual purity and motherhood. In this story, I interpret Alice's "masculinity" as a paradoxical strategy, moving her both away from and closer to a life with other women. Her cross-gender identification worked as an expression of difference from other women, as a rejection of the pastimes and the conventional family-based relations of the female world, and as a mark of her commitment to the lasting erotic love of women. As part of her conflict with Alice, Freda expressed another kind of ambivalence toward the world of women represented by her sisters; she was ultimately reintegrated into its conventions through obedience to female authority. Her attachment to Alice might have been an interlude in an otherwise traditionally feminine life. But Alice's wish to leave the female world and to escape its conventions was so profound and unshakable that its frustration led her to destroy Freda and eventually herself as well. Alice, committed to the Tennessee State Insane Asylum at Bolivar in 1892, died in 1898; her death was reported as due to tuberculosis, but in a later interview one of the attorneys involved in the case claimed that she had killed herself by jumping into the water tower (Coppock 1930).

This narrative-in-formation appeared in various permutations in newspapers throughout the period 1880–1920. But such narratives were not merely the lurid, sensational productions of prosperous white male editors and reporters. Though the newspaper stories did stress the element of violence for shock value, they were nonetheless based on the stories women told about their own relationships. The newspaper retellings, altered to fit the worldview and assumptions of reporters and editors and the expectations, fears, and fantasies of readers, were not free of the shaping influence of women like Alice Mitchell and of the story she told her family, lawyers, trial experts, and court. They were, that is, not simply impositions but appropriations.

The press coverage of the Mitchell-Ward murder in 1892 stimulated especially intense attention to many similar cases. Some were cast as memories of cases past (see, e.g., *Memphis Public Ledger* 1892a). Others were accounts of rumors, denied by the principals (such as *Memphis Commercial* 1892b). The story of Alice and Freda as it appeared in the mainstream daily press also had precursors in the disreputable crime and police papers of earlier decades (see, e.g., the *National Police Gazette* 1879). Some of these were picked up and circulated in the mainstream press and in the medical literature after the Mitchell-Ward murder. The newspaper stories that resulted varied somewhat, especially with regard to the class and racial contexts within which they were situated, but all shared one or more of the three structural elements of the Mitchell-Ward tale.

On February 11, 1892, for instance, the *Memphis Public Ledger* (1892b) appended to an article on the Mitchell-Ward case a short report headlined "The Case of Male Impersonator Marie Hindle, Who Beaued the Girls at Broome's Variety Theater. Almost a Parallel Case." It read:

> Discussion of the Mitchell-Ward murder has brought to light a number of similar cases of abnormal affection existing between persons of the same sex, differing only in that they did not end in the death of one "lover" at the hands of the other. But there was a case of the kind located in Memphis, which narrowly missed being a prototype of that which is now engaging so much attention all over the country. It dates back nearly 23 years, but is still fresh in

the memory of citizens who were familiar with the local life after dark of that period.

In 1869–70 the bright particular star of Broome's Variety Theater, on Jefferson Street, was Marie Hindle, a very attractive woman, who played male parts. Nature had especially fitted her for that line of the business. Her features and voice were masculine, and her tastes in accord with her physical peculiarities. Though by no means chary of accepting the admiration of the other sex, she cared nothing for men as such. Her inclination was altogether toward women, and she inspired in them a like feeling toward herself. It was remarked by the stage hands and those among the habitues who were admitted to the inner circle of the performers that Marie was a reigning beau among the petticoat brigade, from the well-paid high kicker to the humblest "chair warmer."

Two of the former class were special favorites of hers. The girls were named Ione and Lizette, both pretty and clever and both madly in love with Marie. She distributed her favor with so much tact that each considered herself the queen bee in the Hindle hive, and neither had any eyes for the male creatures in their train when she was present. They were jealous of each other in a way, but Marie always managed to prevent active hostilities occurring between them. But the fires of rivalry were kindled and only needed occasion to break forth in flame.

The time came toward the close of the season when Marie had made ready to go on to New York to fill an engagement at the Bowery Theater. Ione and Lizette were wild with grief at the thought of parting from her, and would scarcely let her out of their sight. Naturally, each grudged the other a moment of their common idol's time, and jealousy gave place to hatred. When the day of separation came they were wrought up to a pitch that made them reckless of consequences. Both had laid on their war paint and got ready for action.

The night of Marie's departure found them in a state bordering on frenzy. Each had resolved to act as Marie's special escort from the Overton Hotel, where she was stopping, to the train that was to bear her away; and neither was aware of the other's intention. They chanced to meet at the ladies' entrance to the hotel. It was a match to the magazine. Instantly there came an explosion which attracted the attention of several men standing near, one of whom was Dick English, the river editor of the Appeal. He knew of the enmity existing between the two girls, and fearing lest they should do something desperate he ran toward them. By the time he reached the spot they had clinched and were struggling around in the alley.

He kept on after them and reached them just as they pulled out knives and began carving each other. He seized them, and with the assistance of another man, who had followed him, succeeded in separating them and wresting their weapons from their hands, but not until both had received ugly slashes on the face and bosom. But for his timely arrival and prompt action there would have been murder done.

Marie Hindle repeated in New York the professional conquests of her Memphis career. Again she became a successful rival of the gilded youth in the affections of the girls of the company and not a few among her audience. One of the latter she singled out for a favorite and they lived together up to the time of her death, which occurred not long ago. After this it was reported, and published in the papers, that she had actually married the girl.

"Mrs. Hindle" was interviewed by a New York paper soon after her partner passed away. She seemed overcome with grief at her loss and said that Marie had been "a dear, good husband."

This little story, both comic and contemptuous (and, of course, featuring male heroism), drew on and reframed various stock nineteenth-century narrative conventions. It was anything but "factual," and was full of gross errors as well as predictable distortions. Marie was actually Annie Hindle, the first male impersonator to make a name for herself on the American stage. (For a discussion of Annie Hindle's career, see Senelick [1982].) She did in fact marry a woman, Annie Ryan, with female impersonator Gilbert Saroney at her side. But it was Ryan who died in 1891. The story, both the apocryphal and the real, had little in common with the Mitchell-Ward case except for one important element—the masculine/feminine contrast between Hindle and her admirers, with only the manly Hindle believed to be inclined exclusively toward women in her affections. This difference was clearly eroticized, and the Variety Theater, on the very margins of respectability, provided a rare setting for its expression. Another 1892 article in a Lincoln, Nebraska entertainment paper, *Vanity Fair,* also linked the Mitchell-Ward case with the story of Hindle, getting more of the facts right and commenting that "it is a fact that this dashing singer was the recipient of as many 'mash' notes as ever went to a stage favorite of this country. Once she compared notes with H. J. Montague, that carelessly handsome actor at whose shrine so many silly women had worshipped; but Hindle's admirers outnumbered his, and they were all women, strange as it may seem" (1892).

The tragic conflicts that led to the Memphis murder never appeared in tales of Hindle's life and career (though she did have a brief and miserable marriage to the man who founded the Elks Lodge). Such good fortune was no doubt due to the theater's serving as an institution where collectivities of those with unconventional gender identifications and sexual lives could congregate relatively free from censure. For this reason Hindle's story also did not include isolation within the white bourgeois family, as did Alice Mitchell's. (Interestingly, both Alice and Freda were themselves "stage struck" and had fantasies of running off to join the theater.)

Another story published in the *Memphis Weekly Commercial* (1892) told a story of Addie Phillips, whose mother worried that her love for Minnie Hubbard would develop into a "Mitchell-Ward affair" and who was thrown into despair when Addie, after swearing never to marry a man, ran away from home and was found in a brothel. Male impersonation was associated in this era with the demimonde and geographically if not literally, with prostitution.[9] This story focused on young women from the barely respectable working class, at some social distance from Alice Mitchell's wealthy family. But the newspaper story drew many comparisons between them, finding some marked similarities across class lines and stressing the third element of the Mitchell-Ward "story"—the conflict between mother and daughter. The first element, the masculine/feminine contrast, was absent in this version, while the second element of conflict between the young women was only suggested: Addie was reported to have wished to marry Minnie, but when they ran away together, Minnie changed her mind and returned, to Addie's chagrin.

The mass circulation daily newspapers deliberately crossed class lines in their reporting as part and parcel of their marketing strategy—but the papers were controlled by local elites, and the stories of working-class life were (re)told from the elite perspective. The newspapers were explicitly racist, however. Comparisons across racial lines were much rarer and were laced with overt hostility or condescension. The *Memphis Commercial* (1892c) ran a series of stories under the heading "Similar Cases Recalled" on February 24, 1892, one of which follows:

Mobile, Ala.—Eleanora Richardson is now lying at her home in this city, between the borders of life and death from seven stab wounds, the most severe being through the lower rib. She will die. She is a handsome and well-formed mulatto, 17 years of age. Emma Williams, a black but comely woman of 23, is in jail, awaiting the results of the wounds she inflicted upon her friend. . . . The motive was a paroxysm of jealousy resulting from an unnatural passion

[9] The proximity of theatrical and prostitution districts in England is discussed in Tracy Davis's fascinating study (1991). The theatre's role as a haven for the unconventional is also examined in McArthur 1984.

similar to that case in Memphis, which has caused the world to wonder. The two women have been living in the same house for nearly a year. Eleanor says the past six months Emma Williams has been taking the most unusual interest in her. She has been showering caresses upon her daily and hourly, and though both were seen, the Williams girl went to work, and her wages supported and clothed her and the girl. If the Richardson girl spoke to a male acquaintance, the woman would upbraid her, and beg her not to allow any man to ever separate them. If any males called at the house the Williams woman would see them alone, invent excuses and resort to all artifices to prevent any interview with her companion. Last week Eleanora Richardson left the house where the Williams woman was and took up her residence with a married sister in another part of town. Her companion, wretched almost to the point of madness, yesterday afternoon was told by someone who knew of her unnatural infatuation, that Eleanora had left her because she was going to be married. This the Williams woman answered, "Never mind; I'll get her." She went immediately to the girl's house and . . . asked when . . . [she] was coming home. Her companion replied she would be back when her sister tired of her. Bursting into a fury of rage, the Williams woman said: "You are lying and trying to deceive me; you shall never marry that —— ," and rushing upon her she drew the murderous knife from her stocking and attacked her, plunging the knife into her body repeatedly, saying with each stab "Oh, you darling." The girl's screams finally brought her sister's husband on the scene, and the furious woman was seized and disarmed, but not until she had inflicted wounds which the physicians declare dangerous and possibly fatal.

This tale deploys the second element of the Mitchell-Ward narrative, the conflict between the two women over the nature of the relationship. Few of the many stories in the newspapers during the 1892 had all of the structural elements of the Alice and Freda case. All such elements were most likely to appear in stories about bourgeois white women and girls. Given that these narratives appeared in daily newspapers produced primarily by and for privileged white people, it is not surprising that most of them were "about" the gender and sexual disputes of this limited population. The stories of developing lesbian identity among working women and prostitutes or among African-American, Chicana, or Asian women were not entirely absent from the newspapers, but they were not developed at length there. Research into other sources of these narratives may show them to have been structured differently.

A typical account of love and conflict between young white bourgeois women appeared in a long article published in the *New York Sun* and reprinted in the *Memphis Commercial* (1892a)—a cautionary tale written by a girls' boarding school principal.

LIKE MISS MITCHELL

. . . When Blanche's parents brought her to our school and confided her to my care she had just passed her sixteenth birthday. She was of a vivacious disposition and of a will rather inclined to be imperious . . . Blanche was a very high-minded girl. Her ideals were all lofty. Though strangely ignorant of the real significance of love, courtship and marriage, she was very free with her criticisms of the attitude of men toward women. Her ideas on this subject were plainly derived from the literature of chivalry. . . .

Blanche lost no time in cultivating the friendship of Mary, the sweetest and most angelic of our flock. In disposition Mary was to Blanche as the soft spring rain is to the electricity which explodes and precipitates it to earth. She was of about the same age as Blanche, and equally innocent and ignorant. She seemed to yield with passive happiness to the new friendship held out to her. In a few weeks the individuality of Blanche seemed to have absorbed her individuality completely. They were constantly together, and both were supremely happy.

. . . Mary, like the ideal lady love, was softly and yieldingly affectionate. She leaned upon Blanche, looked up to her and trusted her as one whose strength and courage were wholly to be relied upon. Blanche on the other hand, exhibited the spirit, dash, and valor with the deferential devotion of the knight, the record of whose glorious career rested beneath her pillow. . . .

And when in a gayer mood I have seen her seize Mary unawares in the darkened hall or behind a door to steal a kiss, as is the fashion of more modern lovers. Neither made any attempt to conceal her infatuation from other pupils of the school, and as there were other cases of a similar kind, their behavior occasioned no particular comment. . . .

[Mary goes home to tend her sick mother and returns after several weeks, a changed girl.]

Mary had been playing a medley of gay dance music while Blanche stood regarding her gloomily from a corner of the room. Presently she approached the piano, and seizing Mary's hand to hers, exclaimed passionately: "Mary, Mary, don't you love me anymore?"

"Yes, my dicky bird—passionately," answered Mary gayily.

"But not as you used to," broke in the poor girl.

"Well, if you were a nice young man now, for instance," said Mary, smilingly, "the case would be—"

"Ah, you are false," broke in Blanche, wringing her hands. "You who promised to be true till death! What is it you have in that locket?" she demanded angrily. And while the rest of us looked on too astonished to move, Blanche snatched the gold ornament hanging at Mary's throat, opened it, and with a cry of rage dashed it on the floor. . . . A miniature photograph and a lock of dark hair were broken loose from their frame and lay on the carpet. Blanche stamped upon them and fled, weeping, to her room.

The photograph was that of a handsome, manly-looking young fellow, such as almost any girl might be pardoned for falling in love with. He was Mary's cousin, and it was their growing attachment for each other that had so long delayed Mary's return to school, after her mother had been pronounced convalescent.

Mary's compassion soon overcame her anger. She went to her friend's room and on the following day I noticed that their reconciliation seemed complete. But I was not at all pleased to see that Mary was again apparently under the influence of her irresistible girl friend. Day after day Blanche's attitude toward her grew more and more loverlike. They were constantly together. It was plain that the handsome dark-haired cousin was forgotten. . . . I noticed the sparkle of a little diamond on the third finger of Blanche's left hand.

"Why, what does this mean?" I asked.

"It means that we are engaged," said Blanche innocently. "I am so happy."

"Engaged!" To whom?" I demanded.

"Why, to my darling Mary, of course. To whom else?"

I glanced at Mary's left hand. The third finger bore the duplicate of Blanche's diamond. At first I was very much alarmed but gradually, as nothing further happened out of the ordinary, I concluded that my anxiety was groundless. . . .

In later years, when experience had burdened my knowledge of such matters, I would have acted on the warning which was now given in the actions of Blanche. She could not bear to have Mary out of her sight. . . .

[Blanche and Mary then make two attempted escapes from the school. On the first they are quickly caught, on the second they make it off the school grounds, leaving a note for the principal: "DEAR MISS LAGRANGE: It is useless for you to follow us. We have gone away, Mary and I, to be married, for we love each other, and have sworn never to be separated. Farewell, BLANCHE." But the girls are caught in the town and brought back.]

As Dr. Greene [from the town] came quite close, I saw beside him in his carriage the muffled-up figures of Blanche and Mary, while at their feet was the bundle which the eloping couple had taken with them. Mary was pale and frightened. Blanche was perfectly calm. Neither said a word.

When Dr. Greene drove back to the village he carried two telegrams. They were addressed to the parents of Blanche and Mary respectively, and urged their immediate presence at the school. Mary's parents arrived the next day, much alarmed. They agreed that it was best that Mary be taken home at once.

"Have you any objection to her cousin," I asked, "The manly-looking fellow with the dark hair?" They had not the slightest objection to him.

"Then," I said, "invite him to your house and Mary will be herself again in less than a week."

It was arranged that Mary's departure should be unknown to Blanche—at least, I supposed I had so arranged it. But the carriage had hardly passed the great gate when the sound of a pistol shot in the north dormitory created a panic in the house.

It was true. Poor Blanche had proven faithful to her ideal of lover, even to the extent of providing herself with the means of self-destruction. I had forgotten that her window commanded a view of the highway. She lay at full length on the floor. In one hand was the smoking pistol, and in the other a photograph of Mary.

The wound was not serious—the shock was even beneficial, for when Blanche was restored to consciousness after the lapse of several hours, she wept copiously, begged forgiveness for her rash act, and willingly accompanied her parents to her home. I learned afterward that a year of travel abroad not only restored her to a proper condition of mind, but supplied in the place of Mary a young gentleman who was in every way worthy of her, and to whom two years later she was happily married.

If the foregoing shall point a moral that will remain fixed in the memories of parents who read it, I am persuaded that they need never bewail such a misfortune as has plunged two Tennessee families into despair.

The narrative arrangement of this story suggests a clear motive—the principal is concerned to argue that schoolgirl friendships, even extremely intense ones, are not morbid or pathological as medical writers were beginning to argue, but simply based on ignorance and excessively romantic notions. Regulation of them could safely be left to vigilant female authority. She is therefore at considerable pains to portray the students as innocent of sexuality and to provide a suitably happy ending. It thus contrasts sharply with the more hostile, sensational newspaper stories, though it has all the elements of the masculine/feminine contrast, the conflict between the young women, and the conflict with female authority. This contrast shows how the narrative fragments could be recombined for a variety of purposes, as they continued to be over the next several decades.

During the 1890s, however, nearly all the newspaper stories had tragic endings. They were stories of struggle and failure; they ended with violence or loss. Only a very few, about women in exceptional circumstances like those of Annie Hindle, had happier endings. When successful partnerships between women were mentioned in the news columns, they almost always appeared in desexualized forms only. The suggestion of sexuality, however subtle or implicit, was generally paired with bloodletting.

This focus on violence was partly an artifact of the moralizing sensationalism of the press. The late-nineteenth century newspaper narratives of lesbian love featured violence as a boundary marker; murders or suicides served to abort the forward progress of the tale, signaling that such erotic love between women was not only tragic but ultimately hopeless. The selective nature of the reports made the exceptional cases of violent conflict among women seem characteristic of female sexual passion. The stories were thus structured to emphasize, ultimately, that no real love story was possible.

But the emphasis on conflict and violence in the newspaper stories must also have reflected the stories of overwhelming opposition and social isolation told by women whose erotic partnerships transgressed the boundaries of gender-appropriate, spiritual romantic friendship. Young women like Alice, Emma, and Blanche faced hostility and opposition not only from pathologizing sexologists and patriarchal social institutions but also from their closest female relatives and friends. In addition, they all struggled to establish a reciprocal love relationship with another woman who did not fully share their commitment to a life outside the traditional heterosexual family.

Such structural analysis of the newspaper narratives suggests that modern lesbian identity may have been constructed from an amalgam of elements drawn from the stories of romantic friendship and passing women. In 1892, Alice Mitchell did not present herself nor was she perceived as a "lesbian"—no such clear category yet existed. Rather, she combined her unremarkable story of schoolgirl "chumming" with a plan to cross-dress and marry Freda, and it was this combination and not either element by itself that signaled something new and incited opposition. It was Alice Mitchell's attempt to forge a new way of life—new in both material and social terms, a life outside the white bourgeois family and its hierarchical gender arrangements—that marked her as different and dangerous. Her love for other women was neither temporary nor complementary to heterosexual marriage; her appropriation of "masculinity" and her determination to marry Freda were not for the purpose of a temporary or superficial disguise but were the seeds of a new identity.

The relative powerlessness of lesbians (as of other marginalized groups) has been enforced historically by limiting their means of direct public self-representation, leaving lesbian historians few of women's own representations of their developing lesbian identities to use as sources. Instead, historians must make the most of mediated sources contaminated by hostility, like the turn-of-the-century newspaper narratives, by reading them "against the grain."[10] Not until the 1920s do we begin to have a body of self-representations, such as African-American blues songs outlining the exploits of masculine "bulldaggers" or *The Well of Loneliness,* Radclyffe Hall's widely circulated British novel featuring the "masculine" heroine Stephen Gordon.[11]

Both the hostile representations and the self-representations of lesbians at the turn of the century, however, suggest that for newly visible lesbians gender-crossing or cross-dressing became a term of address in several simultaneous dialogues. Through masculine identification they separated themselves from the family-based female world, defined their desire for other women as erotic, and declared their unyielding commitment to a new way of life. The feminine partners in developing lesbian relationships, from Freda Ward to *The Well's* Mary, along with the feminine pairs joined in romantic friendships, were not perceived as lesbian until the mid-twentieth century and later.[12]

Analysis of the newspaper narratives discussed here also shows that turn-of-the-century sexologists, far from creating or producing new lesbian identities, drew their "cases" from women's own stories and newspaper retellings of them as well as from French fiction and pornography as "empirical" bases for their theories.[13] They did not initiate or control

[10] For an exploration of the possibilities for reading "against the grain" for the history of lesbians, see Terry 1991, which draws from the work of Gayatri Spivak and Michel Foucault to construct such a method.

[11] On representations of "bulldaggers" in blues songs, see Carby 1990 and Garber 1989.

[12] Research by Elizabeth Kennedy and Madeline Davis suggests that, even after World War II, this issue of whether "fems" were really "lesbians" was still open to dispute (Kennedy and Davis 1989).

[13] I discuss at length this process of constructing a supposedly "empirical" basis for the typical lesbian case history of turn-of-the-century sexology in Duggan 1992, esp. in chap. 6, "Sapphic Slashers, or, the Scientific Construction of Lesbian Desire."

the social conversation from which lesbian identity developed but, rather, entered into it. Basing their descriptions on relationships like that of Alice and Freda, the sexologists took as their task the definition of *deviance,* the drawing of a line between acceptable romantic friends or simply eccentric passing women and intolerable lesbian lovers. In this they were not unique but, rather, like women such as Freda's sister who had drawn such a line in forbidding Freda any further contact with Alice. Sexologists' point of departure from all these other narratives of lesbian identity was their determination to interpret behaviors rooted in changing and contested social relations as biologically based and properly subject to medical regulation.

Sexologists decidedly did influence the conversations they entered. Many commentators have noted, for instance, the appropriation of medical language and biological assumptions in many lesbian self-representations, particularly in *The Well of Loneliness* (see Newton 1989; Smith-Rosenberg 1989). But in tracing the roots of Hall's narrative, it is equally important to note that *The Well* also shares the structure of the Mitchell-Ward newspaper stories—the masculine/feminine contrast, the conflict between the female partners, and the conflict with female authority (it is Stephen Gordon's mother who is most hostile to her, not her father). In Hall's version there is no violence, however—the conflict is experienced internally by Stephen Gordon, who releases the "normal" Mary rather than murdering her or killing herself. This narrative structure, imbricated with the difficult, conflict-laden history of the emergence of lesbian identities in the twentieth century, may help explain the book's widespread, enduring popularity despite its medicalized portrait of "inversion."

Thus, we can look back now at the figure of the turn-of-the-century mannish lesbian and see her as at least a double-edged construction—a representation used by sexologists and others to attack the independence and achievements of New Women, yet at the same time a self-represented historical subject who was attacked (sometimes even by feminists) for what she embodied: her rejection of the feminine body and the maternal body for herself. Her self-presentation took her outside the boundaries of the female world; for her, feminine dress and gestures were unnatural. She therefore existed largely beyond the categories of thought that, wedded to a fixed dualistic view of gender, can comprehend her only as a dupe of pathologizing sexologists who accepted the overvaluation of the masculine or as simply male identified.[14] Yet her history also defies any

[14] Such oversimple thought is represented in the work of Sheila Jeffreys, whose *The Spinster and Her Enemies: Feminism and Sexuality, 1880–1930* (1985) is structured as a stark melodrama with male villains and female victims and heroines appearing almost as cartoon characters. Jeffreys cannot conceive of the male-authored medical literature as

attempt to represent her as simply a hero of lesbian resistance, as Alice Mitchell's story, with its horrific act of murder, clearly shows.

The emerging new narratives of lesbian identity shaped new ways of living for some women, as new material possibilities and social positions outside the kin-based family also came into being at the turn of the century. These narratives both reproduced aspects of conventional gender hierarchy and were subversive of them. They suggest that it is useful to relinquish the fixed opposition of oppression versus resistance and to modify our own often too simple historical tales of lesbian innocence, romance, or heroism. Lesbians do not come from outside culture, outside history, or outside class, race, and gender to raise the flag for a self-evident version of freedom, justice, and equality. Rather, lesbian resistance consists instead of our determination to dissent—to retell our culture's dominant stories with an eye to reorganizing its distribution of cultural and material resources. With these new stories we re-present and re-make the world from the interaction of our own points of view and those of others in an ongoing process of re-vision.

Department of American Civilization
Brown University

References

Butler, Judith. 1990. *Gender Trouble: Feminism and the Subversion of Identity.* New York: Routledge.

Carby, Hazel. 1990. "It Jus' Be's Dat Way Sometime: The Sexual Politics of Women's Blues." In *Unequal Sisters: A Multicultural Reader in U.S. Women's History,* ed. Ellen DuBois and Vicki Ruiz, 238–49. New York: Routledge.

Carhart, J. W., M.D. 1895. *Norma Trist: A Story of the Inversion of the Sexes.* Austin, Tex.: Eugene von Boeckman.

Cauldwell, D. O., M.D. 1950. "Lesbian Love Murder." *Sexology* 16(12): 773–79.

Chauncey, George, Jr. 1982–83. "From Inversion to Homosexuality: Medicine and the Changing Conceptualization of Female Deviance." *Salmagundi* 58–59:114–46.

Coppock, Paul. 1930. "Memphis' Strangest Love Murder Had All Girl Cast." *Memphis Commercial Appeal,* September 7, sec. 4, p. 5.

Davis, Tracy. 1991. *Actresses as Working Women: Their Social Identity in Victorian Culture.* London: Routledge.

de Lauretis, Teresa. 1984. *Alice Doesn't: Feminism, Semiotics, Cinema.* Bloomington: Indiana University Press.

---

any kind of resource for subversive appropriation but only as pure evil opposed to the pure good of woman's true nature. Paradoxically, such paradigms only end up reproducing the very gendered categories they are meant to attack.

D'Emilio, John, and Estelle Freedman. 1988. *Intimate Matters: A Social History of Sexuality in America.* New York: Harper & Row.

Duggan, Lisa. 1992. "The Trials of Alice Mitchell: Sexual Science and Sexual Identity in Turn of the Century America." Ph.D. dissertation, University of Pennsylvania.

Ellis, Havelock. 1901. *Sexual Inversion.* Philadelphia: F. A. Davis.

Faderman, Lillian. 1981. *Surpassing the Love of Men: Romantic Friendship and Love between Women from the Renaissance to the Present.* New York: Morrow.

Foucault, Michel. 1978. *The History of Sexuality, vol. 1: An Introduction,* trans. Robert Hurley. New York: Pantheon.

Freeman, Mary Wilkins. [1895] 1927. "The Long Arm." In *American Detective Stories,* ed. Carolyn Wells, 134–78. New York: Oxford University Press.

Garber, Eric. 1989. "A Spectacle in Color: The Lesbian and Gay Subculture of Jazz Age Harlem." In *Hidden from History: Reclaiming the Lesbian and Gay Past,* ed. Martin Duberman, Martha Vicinus, and George Chauncey, Jr., 318–31. New York: New American Library.

Hatch, Mary P. 1895. *The Strange Disappearance of Eugene Comstock.* New York: G. W. Dillingham.

Howard, Edwin. 1961. "Resurrected Ballad Recalls a Strange Memphis Killing." *Memphis Press Scimitar,* November 13.

Jeffreys, Sheila. 1985. *The Spinster and Her Enemies: Feminism and Sexuality, 1880–1930.* London: Pandora.

Katz, Jonathan Ned. 1976. *Gay American History: Lesbians and Gay Men in the U.S.A.* New York: Crowell.

———. 1983. *Gay/Lesbian Almanac: A New Documentary.* New York: Harper & Row.

Kennedy, Elizabeth, and Madeline Davis. 1989. "The Reproduction of Butch-Fem Roles: A Social Constructionist Approach." In *Passion and Power: Sexuality in History,* ed. Kathy Peiss and Christina Simmons, 241–56. Philadelphia: Temple University Press.

Krafft-Ebing, Richard von. 1899. *Psychopathia Sexualis, with Special Reference to Antipathic Sexual Instinct: A Medico-Forensic Study.* London: Rebman.

Lister, Anne. [1791–1840] 1988. *I Know My Own Heart: The Diaries of Anne Lister,* ed. Helena Whitbread. London: Virago.

McArthur, Benjamin. 1984. *Actors and American Culture, 1880–1920.* Philadelphia: Temple University Press.

Memphis Appeal Avalanche. 1892. "Bernhardt At The Jail: The Great Actress Wanted to See Miss Alice Mitchell." *Memphis Appeal Avalanche,* February 17, 4.

Memphis Commercial. 1892a. "Like Miss Mitchell . . . An Infatuation Which Existed Between Two School Girls." *Memphis Commercial,* February 14, 13.

———. 1892b. "Like the Memphis Case: Another Story Which Furnishes Rich Food for the Gossips." *Memphis Commercial,* February 19, 5.

———. 1892c. "Unfolded, Revelation of Facts Surrounding Freda Ward's Death. . . . Similar Cases Recalled." *Memphis Commercial,* February 24, 1–3.

———. 1892d. "Sane or Insane? Is She Cruel Murderess or Irresponsible Lunatic?" *Memphis Commercial,* July 19, 1.

———. 1892e. "Still in Doubt, Alice Mitchell's Sanity Not Yet Determined." *Memphis Commercial,* July 20, 1.

Memphis Public Ledger. 1892a. "United in Death: A Tragedy Almost Identical with that of Monday: A Girl's Love for a Girl: How It Caused a Murder and a Suicide Twenty Years Ago." *Memphis Public Ledger,* January 27, 1.

———. 1892b. "The Plea for Bail." *Memphis Public Ledger,* February 11, 2.

Memphis Weekly Commercial. 1892. "A Strange Affection, Addie Phillips Shows Traces of Alice Mitchell-Fondness, Another Case Partially Paralleling the Famous One." *Memphis Weekly Commercial,* March 23, 12.

National Police Gazette. 1879. "A Female Romeo: Her Terrible Love for a Chosen Friend of Her Own Sex Assumes a Passionate Character that Blazes into Jealousy of so Fierce a Quality that it Fires Her to the Sacrifice of the Object of Her Unnatural Passion: A Queer Psychological Study." *National Police Gazette,* June 7, 6.

Newton, Esther. 1989. "The Mythic Mannish Lesbian: Radclyffe Hall and the New Woman." In *Hidden from History: Reclaiming the Lesbian and Gay Past,* ed. Martin Duberman, Martha Vicinus, and George Chauncey, Jr., 281–93. New York: New American Library.

New York World. 1892. "Alice Mitchell's Crime." *New York World,* January 31, 6.

Poovey, Mary. 1988. *Uneven Developments: The Ideological Work of Gender in Mid-Victorian England.* Chicago: University of Chicago Press.

Sahli, Nancy. 1979. "Smashing: Women's Relationships before the Fall." *Chrysalis* 8:17–27.

San Francisco Lesbian and Gay History Project. 1989. " 'She Even Chewed Tobacco': A Pictorial Narrative of Passing Women in America." In *Hidden from History: Reclaiming the Lesbian and Gay Past,* ed. Martin Duberman, Martha Vicinus, and George Chauncey, Jr., 183–94. New York: New American Library.

Sedgwick, Eve Kosofsky. 1990. *Epistemology of the Closet.* Berkeley and Los Angeles: University of California Press.

Senelick, Laurence. 1982. "The Evolution of the Male Impersonator on the Nineteenth Century Stage." *Essays in Theatre* 1(1):31–46.

Sim, F. L., M.D. 1892. "Forensic Psychiatry: Alice Mitchell Adjudged Insane." *Memphis Medical Monthly* 12(8):377–428.

Smith, Barbara Herrnstein. 1981. "Narrative Versions, Narrative Theories." In *On Narrative,* ed. W. J. T. Mitchell, 209–32. Chicago: University of Chicago Press.

Smith-Rosenberg, Carroll. 1975. "The Female World of Love and Ritual: Relations between Women in Nineteenth-Century America." *Signs: Journal of Women in Culture and Society* 1(1):1–29.

———. 1989. "Discourses of Sexuality and Subjectivity: The New Woman, 1870–1936." In *Hidden from History: Reclaiming the Lesbian and Gay Past,* ed. Martin Duberman, Martha Vicinus, and George Chauncey, Jr., 264–80. New York: New American Library.

Terry, Jennifer. 1991. "Theorizing Deviant Historiography." *differences* 3(2): 55–74.

Vanity Fair. 1892. "Marrying a Maiden! Can a Woman Legally Marry a Woman?" *Vanity Fair,* February 13, 1.

Walkowitz, Judith R. 1989. "Patrolling the Borders: Feminist Historiography and the New Historicism." *Radical History Review* 4:25–31.

Weeks, Jeffrey. 1981. *Sex, Politics and Society: The Regulation of Sexuality since 1800.* London: Longman.

Looking and Listening: The Construction of Clinical Knowledge in Charcot and Freud

Daphne de Marneffe

Introduction

I N T H E 1 8 7 0s, the French neuropathologist Jean-Martin Charcot and his staff at the Salpêtrière produced a series titled *Iconographie photographique de la Salpêtrière* (1876–77, 1878, 1879–80). The three volumes presented case histories of women diagnosed as hysterical or hystero-epileptic, amply illustrated by photographs and diagrams.[1] Long verbatim transcriptions of patients' utterances during hysterical attacks offer highly detailed and often gruesome allusions to past traumas. Yet these allusions, framed by concrete medical measurements (temperatures taken, drugs administered, attacks arrested), receive no direct analysis or attention. Why did the writers of the *Iconographie* introduce these transcriptions, only to ignore them? And why, in contrast, was such great attention paid to *photographing* these patients, when photography seemed so comparatively ill-equipped to capture the subjective information conveyed by their words?

Less than twenty years later, in 1895, Freud and Breuer published their *Studies on Hysteria*. Like the *Iconographie,* the *Studies* presented carefully crafted representations of cases. Unlike the earlier work, however, Freud's and Breuer's investigations relied on verbal information from the (women) patients themselves, rather than on visual representation of their bodies. The *Studies* were motivated by many of the same concerns as the Salpêtrière volumes, but were dependent on radically different modes of inquiry and presentation.

I would like to thank Carol Gilligan, Nancy Chodorow, Peter de Marneffe, and Gabrielle Weinberg Bodow for their helpful comments on an earlier draft of this paper. I am also grateful to Eric Sandweiss for his inspired editing.

[1] D. M. Bourneville and P. Regnard, *Iconographie photographique de la Salpêtrière,* 3 vols. (Paris: Aux Bureau du Progrès Médical, V. A. Delahaye & Cie, 1876–80). Hereafter cited as *IPS.*

[*Signs: Journal of Women in Culture and Society* 1991, vol. 17, no. 1]

What is the intrinsic difference between the two approaches? And what difference does this difference make in what they were able to reveal or obscure? A reading of the *Iconographie* and the *Studies* demonstrates that both Charcot and Freud had access to similar information—namely, the sexual trauma of their women patients—but that they approached this information in very different ways. It struck me as I studied the two approaches that a comparison between them offered insights into some of the most basic questions of concern to feminist and other contemporary scholars: How can we know others? How does the position and approach of the knower affect the portrayal of the known? When women cannot speak, or speak and are not heard, how is their subjectivity distorted or obscured? What are subjectivity and objectivity, and in what ways do we connect our understanding of these terms with notions of gender and gender difference?

A comparison of Charcot's and Freud's approaches to their hysterical women patients touches on a number of specific issues in recent feminist scholarship as well. First, there is an ongoing debate over the feminist or misogynist import of Freud's work on women. His work is clearly both, at different moments, and psychoanalytic feminists have each found their own ways of working with the ambiguities and challenges presented by Freud's equivocal corpus. In my discussion here, I attempt to illuminate overlooked aspects of his contribution to the psychology of women by placing that contribution in historical context.

Second, hysteria is of continuing interest to feminists, because of both its historical association with women and its enigmatic status as an actual or socially constructed illness. The term "hysteria" itself derives from the Greek word *hystera,* meaning uterus, and early Greek and Egyptian medicine attributed the hysterical woman's emotional instability to the "wandering" of her womb. This idea has had surprising resilience throughout medical history.[2] A number of feminist scholars have explored the interplay of sociological, historical, medical, and psychological factors in the longstanding association of hysteria and women.[3] In this essay, I attempt to show how the methods Charcot and Freud used to study hysteria interacted with the emotions and utterances of the women studied to produce very different accounts of the nature of the disorder and the process of cure.

[2] For discussions of the history of hysteria, see I. Veith, *Hysteria: The History of a Disease* (Chicago: University of Chicago Press, 1965); and A. Krohn, *Hysteria: The Elusive Neurosis*, Psychological Issues, monograph 45/46 (Madison, Conn.: International Universities Press, 1978).

[3] See, e.g., C. Smith-Rosenberg, *Disorderly Conduct: Visions of Gender in Victorian America* (New York: Oxford University Press, 1985); E. Showalter, *The Female Malady* (New York: Pantheon, 1985); and C. Bernheimer and C. Kahane, eds., *In Dora's Case: Freud-Hysteria-Feminism* (New York: Columbia University Press, 1985).

Finally, beyond these more particular theoretical and historical questions, I am centrally concerned with approaches to knowing—specifically, the methods of looking and listening used by Charcot and Freud. A great deal of recent writing has explored the relations of gender and epistemology, and these writings inform the perspective I take here.[4] In what follows, I describe the methods that Charcot and Freud each used in studying hysteria and hysterical patients, paying special attention to the kind of information each sought to obtain from the patient, and the role and status given that information. An inquiry into the differences between the two approaches illuminates, I believe, the ways in which Freud's innovations in clinical method offered a radical solution to the problem of how to study subjective information scientifically.

Charcot

Background

In the early 1850s, Jean-Martin Charcot served his medical internship at the Salpêtrière. A virtual warehouse for roughly five thousand deranged and sick women, the hospital held little interest for most other interns his age. Charcot, however, was attracted by the Salpêtrière's large and diverse patient population, which provided an ideal opportunity for the comparative study of disorders. He had little respect for theoretical or experimental medicine carried out separately from patient populations, and the Salpêtrière's great number of patients provided a basis for statistical inferences about the incidence and prevalence of diseases in the general population.[5] Charcot immediately set himself to the task of systematically categorizing the patients at the great hospital, which he would later enthusiastically refer to as "a museum of living pathology."[6]

Charcot's appointment in 1862 as chief physician of a large unit at the Salpêtrière ushered in the first major phase of his career in neurology. Between the years of 1862 and 1870, Charcot made important contributions to the medical description of sclerosis, tabes, aphasia, and cerebral and spinal localizations. His prolific output during this period established neurology as a science and solidified his own reputation as the

---

[4] Relevant works include S. Harding and M. B. Hintikka, eds., *Discovering Reality: Feminist Perspectives on Epistemology, Metaphysics, Methodology, and Philosophy of Science* (Dordrecht: Reidel, 1983; U.S. distributor, Boston: Kluwer, 1983); E. F. Keller, *Reflections on Gender and Science* (New Haven, Conn.: Yale University Press, 1985); and S. Harding and J. O'Barr, eds., *Sex and Scientific Inquiry* (Chicago: University of Chicago Press, 1987).

[5] A. R. G. Owen, *Hysteria, Hypnosis, and Healing: The Work of J.-M. Charcot* (New York: Garrett, 1971), 38; T. Gelfand, "Charcot and Freud Revisited" (lecture, University of California, Berkeley, March 10, 1989).

[6] G. Guillain, *J.-M. Charcot, 1825–1893: His Life and Work* (New York: Hoeber, 1959), 9–10; G. Guillain and P. Mathieu, *La Salpêtrière* (Paris: Masson & Cie, 1925).

foremost neurologist of the day. In 1870, the restructuring of the Salpêt-rière's wards led to the placement of women with the diagnosis of epi-lepsy and hysteria within the same ward. (This restructuring, as we shall see, had important implications for the clinical picture of hysteria that Charcot developed.) Charcot took charge of the ward and subsequently became interested in distinguishing epilepsy from hysteria. Charcot thus began working with hysterics in 1870 and pursued their study until his death in 1893. He became professor of pathological anatomy in 1872, and from 1872 to 1882 he delivered a series of influential lectures on his previous and current discoveries.

Between 1882 and 1893, Charcot devoted more than one-third of his lectures to hysteria. His service at the Salpêtrière continued to expand as more research space was commanded, more sophisticated technology was employed, and photography studios were equipped for the docu-mentation and study of hysteria and other disorders. The means by which Charcot examined his patients and carried out his research was the cel-ebrated clinicoanatomic method, developed in France during the late eighteenth and early nineteenth centuries. Through his use of this method, Charcot analyzed and categorized clinical phenomena into "ar-chetypes," fully developed examples of the disease, and analyzed these further to detect their anatomical bases.[7] The differentiation of an ar-chetype from its "variants" emerged from the careful observation of numerous cases. Freud, later describing what Charcot proudly called his "practicing nosography," wrote that the archetypes "could be brought into prominence with the help of a certain sort of schematic planning, and with these archetypes as a point of departure, the eye could travel over the long series of ill-defined cases—the *'formes frustes'*—which, branching off from one or other characteristic feature of the type, melt away into indistinctness."[8]

Since the central tenet of the clinicoanatomic method was that disease arose from an anatomical lesion, it was suited to the study of diseases with obvious biological bases but was less well adapted to disorders whose main manifestations were psychological. Before the method's de-velopment, clinically observed symptomatology had been a far more important basis for the categorization and treatment of disease, and "neurosis" had been an adequate term for nervous conditions of various kinds. With a shift in emphasis toward anatomical lesions and the im-portance of their localization, the concept of neurosis became problem-

[7] C. Goetz, annotator and trans., *Charcot, the Clinician: The Tuesday Lessons* (New York: Raven, 1987), 24–25, 110.

[8] S. Freud, "Charcot" (1893), in *The Standard Edition of the Complete Psychologi-cal Works of Sigmund Freud,* ed. J. Strachey (London: Hogarth, 1962), 3:12. Hereafter cited as *SE.*

atic, because few actual anatomical lesions could be found to account for them. By the time Charcot turned his attention to hysteria, he had been using the clinicoanatomic method on other disorders for many years and with great success. Diseases such as tabes yielded up the most precise information to Charcot's method. Yet hysteria proved more perplexing, because as a *grande névrose*, it gave no evidence of pathological lesions.

In his inaugural lecture in 1882 for the new university chair of diseases of the nervous system, Charcot discussed how conditions such as hysteria appeared to the physician:

> Epilepsy, chorea, hysteria . . . come to us like so many Sphinxes. . . . These symptomatic combinations deprived of anatomical substratum, do not present themselves to the mind of the physician with that appearance of solidity, of objectivity, which belong to affections connected with an appreciable organic lesion.
>
> There are some even who see in several of these affections only an assemblage of odd incoherent phenomena inaccessible to analysis, and which had better, perhaps, be banished to the category of the unknown. It is hysteria which especially comes under this sort of proscription.[9]

To account for the origins of hysteria, Charcot devised the concept of "dynamic lesions," or psychologically traumatic events. These he assigned, however, the limited role of *agents provocateurs,* capable of catalyzing a hereditary propensity for nervous disease. His view of exactly *what* was inherited remained relatively ill-defined and untested by comparison to the precise picture of symptoms yielded by his observational strategy. In his development of elaborate family trees to trace various forms of neurological "degeneracy," he did not consider those familial and sociological experiences that affected people at early ages psychologically rather than through bloodlines—a position to which Freud ultimately strongly objected.[10] In his clinical demonstrations with patients, Charcot regularly overruled his patients' pronouncements about actual predisposing experiences in favor of his own hereditary explanations.[11] The importance Charcot and his colleagues gave heredity constituted, in their view, a justification for detailed case histories; these histories were taken with the purpose of providing crucial information about family history relevant to the study of hereditary transmission of neurological disease.

[9] J.-M. Charcot, *Clinical Lectures on the Diseases of the Nervous System,* vol. 3, trans. T. Savill (London: New Sydenham Society, 1889), 12.

[10] Gelfand.

[11] See, e.g., the case presented in chap. 1 of Goetz, annotator and trans.

Charcot, like his predecessor Briquet, insisted that "hysteria is governed, in the same way as other morbid conditions, by rules and laws, which attentive and sufficiently numerous observations always permit us to establish."[12] By repeated scrutiny he developed a clinical picture of hysteria that conformed to rules and laws in much the same way as the other diseases he studied. In hysteria, the typical convulsive attack was preceded by the "aura"—a group of premonitory symptoms including palpitations, nervous cough, yawning, and the *globus hystericus,* a sensation of obstruction in the throat. Sharp pains in the ovaries were often present in this stage as well. The epileptoid stage marked the beginning of the attack proper and tended to last for a few minutes, although its duration and tempo varied. In the first epileptoid subphase, the "tonic phase," the patient's arms and legs stretched and oscillated violently. In the "stertorous phase," the patient fell backward and lost consciousness, breathing weakened, the neck swelled, and the mouth foamed. The muscles then relaxed and normal respiration resumed.

The second stage was named the "period of clownism" and was characterized by rapid movements of two possible sorts: the *arc de cercle* (as was seen in tetanus) and rhythmic chorea. The third stage in Charcot's series was the *attitudes passionnelles.* Though this stage differed critically from the preceding two stages in that it introduced the "psychical element," Charcot's description of it, like his account of the other stages, centered on visible physiognomic signs. The duration of this period varied, and the patient's outbursts, remonstrances, and conversations with hallucinated interlocutors were often repeated several times before the entire attack subsided. In some patients a fourth stage was recorded, a "posthysterical derangement" that lasted for several hours or days. The patient suffered a delirium during which the thoughts and ideas of the *attitude passionnelles* were repeatedly expressed.

As is clear from his clinical description of hysteria, Charcot's characterization of the disorder relied upon visually observable signs, through which its fundamental structure was deemed detectable. Charcot announced in 1882 that "an attack of hysteria major . . . is reduced at the present time to a very simple formula. Four periods succeed each other in the complete attack with mechanical regularity. . . . In the attack, . . . nothing is left to chance, everything follows definite rules—always the same whether the case is met within private or hospital practice, in all countries, all times, all races, in short universally."[13] Yet this "universal" sequence of stages that Charcot constructed was later discredited as being due to the witting or unwitting mimicry by hysterics of the seizures they

---

[12] Charcot, *Clinical Lectures on the Diseases of the Nervous System,* 3:13.
[13] Ibid.

had observed by epileptic patients with whom they shared the ward.[14] Thus, although the structural and social conditions of the ward played a role in producing the behaviors associated with hysteria, this role was overlooked by Charcot in his use of close, minute observation to develop his clinical description of the disease.

Visual method, photography, and art in the clinical enterprise

For anyone trying to understand Charcot's model of hysteria, it is important to examine the primary method used by the Salpêtrière doctors: visual observation. "To gaze, to look, to keep looking, always: thus only one comes to *see*. Charcot's penetrating observation [and his] precise look, often resulted in precious discoveries, revelations of illness unknown until then"—this was how Henri Meige described Charcot's method and its results.[15] Charcot relied on a natural and cultivated gift for seeing. Since early childhood he had decorated the carriages his father built, and he spent much of his reclusive and studious adolescence drawing. When he was eighteen, his father offered to sponsor his education as either a painter or a doctor; Charcot chose medicine.

The attention Charcot paid to visual information derived not only from his natural gifts, but from his concept of the scientist and of scientific objectivity. Two of his students wrote: "Meticulous clinical scrutiny, particularly of a visual type, was at the root of all Charcot's discoveries. The artist in him, who went hand in hand with the physician, played an interesting part in these discoveries."[16] Seeing provided the appropriate image for discovering: Freud remembered Charcot as saying that "the greatest satisfaction a man could have was to see something new—that is, to recognize it as new; and he remarked again and again on the difficulty and value of this kind of 'seeing.'"[17] According to Freud, Charcot answered a theoretical objection to his observational findings with the comment, "La théorie, c'est bon, mais ca n'empêche pas d'éxister" (Theory is good, but it doesn't keep something from existing).[18]

---

[14] In his lecture "The Mental State of Hystericals" in 1925, P. Janet retrospectively surmised that Charcot's description of the *grande attaque* was not stable but in fact highly variable in terms of both the number of stages represented in the actual attacks and their order of occurrence (see Owen, 66). Charcot, Janet said, "described a type of hysteria which disappeared with him" (*The Major Symptoms of Hysteria: Fifteen Lectures Given in the Medical School of Harvard University* [New York: Macmillan, 1925], 21).

[15] H. Meige, *Charcot—Artiste* (Paris: Masson, 1925), 13–15.

[16] Quoted in Guillain (n. 6 above), 51.

[17] *SE*, 3:12.

[18] Ibid., 1:139; ibid., 3:13. Charcot's emphasis on visual observation was related to his pride in the approach of French clinical medicine, superior in his view to the abstract theorizing and contrived laboratory study of the Germans. Gelfand (n. 5 above).

The visual observation that characterized Charcot's method of diagnosing his patients often came at the expense of direct interaction. His laudatory biographer Guillain, a pupil of several of Charcot's own students, describes how Charcot discontinued examining patients at bedside soon after his appointment at the Salpêtrière in 1862. Instead, Guillain writes, Charcot "spent the entire morning in his office, and had the patients brought to him one by one. In 1881, when he was appointed clinical professor of diseases of the nervous system, he rarely visited the wards of the hospital and did not leave his own office except on rare occasions to go to the autopsy room, to his laboratory of pathologic anatomy, or to his ophthalmologic office."[19]

Guillain quotes further from a description by two of Charcot's students, A. Souques and H. Meige:

He would seat himself near a table and immediately call for the patient who was to be studied. The patient then was completely undressed. The intern would read a clinical summary of the case, while the master listened attentively. Then there was a long silence, during which Charcot looked, kept looking at the patient while tapping his hand on the table. His assistants, standing close together, waited anxiously for a word of enlightenment. Charcot continued to remain silent. After a while he would request the patient to make a movement; he would induce him to speak; he would ask that his reflexes be examined and that his sensory responses be tested. And then again silence, the mysterious silence of Charcot. Finally he would call for a second patient, examine him like the first one, call for a third patient, and always without a word, silently making comparisons between them.[20]

For the clinicians at the Salpêtrière, photography provided the ideal method for accurately recording symptoms and their sequence. In their application of photographic method to medical study, these doctors belonged to a recently established tradition. Almost as soon as photography was invented, it had been applied to medical subject matter. The first photographer of madness, Hugh W. Diamond, had exclaimed in 1856 that "the Photographer secures with unerring accuracy the external phenomena of each passion, as the really certain indication of internal derangement."[21] Albert Londe, the director of the photographic service of

---

[19] Guillain, 51.

[20] Ibid., 52. As the pronouns attest, some of Charcot's patients, including some hysterical patients, were men.

[21] H. W. Diamond, "On the Application of Photography to the Physiognomic and Mental Phenomena of Insanity" (paper presented to the Royal Society of Medicine, Lon-

the Salpêtrière in the 1880s and 1890s, wrote that "the photographic plate is the true retina of the scientist."[22] In 1888, countering a view that hysterical phenomena might be produced by his own suggestion, Charcot exclaimed, "But in truth I am nothing but a photographer; I register what I see."[23] Photography was thus established as a more perfect extension of the clinician's eye, a means of recording objective truth and knowledge.

Charcot found in photography the appropriate tool for representing the distillation of general symptom characteristics from the observation of many cases. By capturing various hysterical poses on film and then superimposing negatives from different cases, a general picture of the syndrome was created that expunged individual difference.[24] Hysteria, the Sphinx of disorders, presented a challenge to the creation of a uniform clinical picture. But by carefully cataloging symptoms in sequence, Charcot was able to use documentary photographic evidence to ensure the veracity of his universal sequence of stages.

By far the most carefully rendered and complete series of photographs in the *Iconographie* is that of "Augustine," a patient who arrived at the Salpêtrière in October 1875, when she was fifteen and one-half years old.[25] We can see in her series how the photographic plates are generally sequenced to conform to Charcot's theory of the course of a hysterical attack. The series has seventeen plates in all, beginning with a picture of Augustine fully clothed in the "Etat normal" (normal state), staring out at the viewer with an arresting gaze. These are followed by "Debut de l'attaque" (beginning of the attack) and two manifestations of "Tétanisme" (tetanism). The next ten plates represent the "Attitudes passionnelles": "Menace" (threat) (two), "Appel" (call), "Supplication amoureuse" (amorous supplication), "Erotisme" (erotism), "Extase" (ecstasy) (two) (fig. 1), "Hallucination de l'ouie" (auditory hallucination), "Crucifiement" (crucifixion), and "Moquerie" (teasing). (The eleventh plate, not in sequence, depicts another aspect of the "Debut d'une attaque" [fig. 2], the extension of the tongue.) The final two images show the contractures of limbs (figs. 3 and 4).

The entire arrangement of photographs provides, in effect, a rendering of a "perfect attack," as seen from an omniscient view. We can witness the careful fashioning of this representation of the attack in a variety of

---

don, May 22, 1856), reprinted in S. Gilman, *The Face of Madness: Hugh W. Diamond and the Origins of Psychiatric Photography* (New York: Brunner/Mazel, 1976), 20.

[22] Quoted in G. Didi-Huberman, *Invention de l'hystérie: Charcot et l'iconographie de la Salpêtrière* (Paris: Macula, 1982), 35. Translations from the French are mine unless otherwise indicated.

[23] J.-M. Charcot, *Leçons du Mardi à la Salpêtrière* (Paris: Aux Bureaux du Progrès Médical, 1887–90), 178.

[24] For a more extensive description of this process, see Didi-Huberman, 51.

[25] *IPS* (n. 1 above), 2:123–86.

FIG I   *Attitudes passionnelles—extase (1878)*. (Plate 23, *Iconographie photographique de la Salpêtrière*, vol. 2.)

ways. First, in the text of Augustine's case itself, the display of the full sequence of hysterical symptoms is quite rare. Augustine is plagued by "incomplete" or "abortive" attacks; on March 9, her report documents thirty-five attacks, on March 17, forty-three attacks, and on March 18, sixty attacks.[26] Such a superabundance of hysterical symptoms suggests a more frenzied and chaotic expression than is depicted by the orderly sequence of photographs. In light of the variability in manifestations of symptoms, and the recorded difficulty with which an attack could be accurately observed, the arranged presentation of the stages of attacks in the photographs appears as a contrivance intended to support the medical veracity of their fixed sequence.

The photographs also validate Charcot's model of hysteria by giving fixed physiognomic, psychological, and medical content to the variable emotional states of the *attitudes passionnelles*. These states are actually

[26] Ibid., 139.

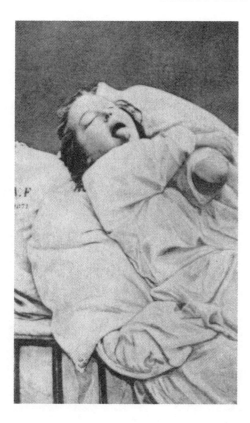

FIG 2   *Debut d'une attaque—cri.* (Plate 28, *Iconographie photographique de la Salpêtrière,* vol. 2.)

marked by variable duration and involve subjective utterances. Yet these fluctuating moods and expressions are presented as symptoms that share the stability of such neurological symptoms as *"tétanisme"* and *"contractures."* The very naming of the *attitudes passionnelles* ("passional attitudes" or "poses") renders primarily visual a subjectively meaningful state. The meaning of these variable states was further fixed through the use of captions, which ostensibly identified, but in fact constructed, the specific meaning of each gesture. Finally, the poses present as stereotyped depictions of emotion what were probably witnessed as chaotic gestures. In fact, the style of the photographs has much less in common with other early photographs of mental patients than with the theatrical portraiture of the day.[27]

[27] To observe their kinship to theatrical portraiture, see E. A. McCauley, *A. A. E. Disderi and the Carte de Visite Portrait Photograph* (New Haven, Conn.: Yale University Press, 1985).

FIG 3   *Hystéro-epilepsie—contracture.* (Plate 29, *Iconographie photographique de la Salpêtrière,* vol. 2.)

Charcot explicitly believed that his photographs satisfied both an artistic tradition and a scientific demand. Commenting on the series of photographs by Albert Londe in his lecture "On Six Cases of Hysteria in the Male Subject," Charcot said: "All this part of the seizure is very fine, if I may so express myself, and every one of these details deserves to be fixed by the process of instantaneous photography. . . . You see that from the point of view of art they leave nothing to be desired, and moreover they are very instructive."[28]

The *Iconographie photographique de la Salpêtrière* was by no means the only visual documentation of clinical material produced by Charcot and his colleagues. In the late 1880s, with others, Charcot's collaborator

[28] J.-M. Charcot, *Clinical Lectures on Certain Diseases of the Nervous System,* trans. E. P. Hurd (Detroit: George S. Davis, 1888), 129. A. Rouillé and B. Marbot provide the following quote from Albert Londe: "Medical photography had great importance from the didactic point of view, especially benefitting the doctors, but the sick person who was used as subject of observation did not benefit from it at all" (*Le corps et son image: Photographies du dix-neuvième siècle* [Paris: Contrejour, 1986], 60).

FIG 4 *Hystéro-epilepsie—contracture.* (Plate 30, *Iconographie photographique de la Salpêtrière*, vol. 2.)

Richer produced the *Nouvelle iconographie de la Salpêtrière*, "clinical picture books" that were half case histories and half discussions and reproductions from the Great Masters.[29] In *Les demoniaques dans l'art* (1887), Charcot and Richer argue that the portrayal of hysterics by photography offers a contemporary equivalent of the Great Masters' portrayal of "maniacs." They also state their view of the relation of artistic and scientific observation:

> Every resource is lacking to the painter, sculptor, actor, outside the exact observation of nature. For it does not suffice simply to deform

[29] P. Richer, G. de la Tourette, and A. Londe, *Nouvelle iconographie de la Salpêtrière*, 2 vols. (Paris: Lecrosnier & Babé, 1888–89). The phrase "clinical picture books" is drawn from Debora L. Silverman's highly informative history *Art Nouveau in Fin de Siècle France: Politics, Psychology, and Style* (Berkeley and Los Angeles: University of California Press, 1989), 94. I am also indebted to Silverman for biographical information on Charcot's youth.

things as pleases you and to make things strange as you see fit; beneath this apparent incoherence there is a hidden reason that arises from a morbid process, and, in the nature of the deformations of the parts or in the contortions of the whole, as well as in the order and grouping of all these phenomena, one finds, just as is demonstrated by our studies of the works of ancient and modern masters, the indisputable signs of a pre-established order, all the constancy and inflexibility of a scientific law.[30]

Since Charcot viewed artists and scientists alike as faithful renderers of a "pre-established order," the use of painterly techniques to retouch his photographs probably seemed a necessary enhancement rather than a selective distortion. The alignment of Augustine's photographs with representational traditions in art is effected through both the application of paint and the use of pose. A striking feature of the series taken as a whole is the liberal use of white paint or gouache on the surfaces of the drapery, and in some cases on Augustine's hair. Paint may have been applied in some cases to compensate for variable depth of field or badly focused shots; however, its application constitutes an aesthetic choice.[31] The application of paint to the drapery creates a sculptural effect, particularly in plates 16, 21, 28 (fig. 2), and 30 (fig. 4). These images, ostensibly taken at the precise moment of a hysterical attack, look timeless. They are made weighty and solid, and Augustine, surrounded by her heavy drapery, is imbued with static permanence. The addition of paint creates a contrast in dimensions and surfaces that renders Augustine's skin comparatively soft and luminous. Her vitality becomes tender and seductive in juxtaposition with the painted fabric. The photographs belie the prevalent notion of hysteria as an illness almost defined by the changeability of its manifestations.

The photographs of Augustine's *attitudes passionnelles* evoke traditional religious and erotic depictions of women. Plates 29 and 30 (figs. 3 and 4) offer a particularly interesting convergence of medical and aesthetic concerns. In these two images, Augustine gazes out at us; in plate 29 (fig. 3), her frank stare complements the frontal exposure of her body parts. Her body is posed to be viewed straight on, presumably so that the contracture may be fully inspected in an image offering the best opportunity for clinical observation. The perspective of the body is at odds with that of the chair and floor. The chair seems dwarfed by her, and her appearance of abnormality is heightened since the distortion of

---

[30] J.-M. Charcot and P. Richer, *Les demoniaques dans l'art* (Paris: V. A. Delahaye & E. Lecrosnier, 1887), 109.

[31] Walter Benjamin writes of the ways photographs were made to appear more artistic through the "arts of retouching." See "Walter Benjamin's Short History of Photography," trans. P. Patton, *Artforum* (February 1977), 46–51. I am grateful to Martha Sandweiss, director of the Mead Art Museum at Amherst College, for information on the history of photography.

the contracture is rendered more extreme by the inconsistency of planes. At the same time, her exposed flesh heightens her apparent vulnerability and seductiveness. Her bareness, the exposure of as many body surfaces as possible, and the angles at which these body parts meet each other, fulfill the demands of medical viewing and, at the same time, combine with Augustine's gaze to create an erotic allure. In plate 30 (fig. 4), medical and artistic concerns are in tension. The scientific rationale for Augustine's position is problematic, for the contracture would be better displayed if the disfigurement of the shoulder joint were not incorporated into a familiar posture of feminine seduction. The composition of plate 30 demonstrates for us, however, the subordination of medical to aesthetic concerns through its use of a stock female display pose.

The sexual content of the *attitudes passionnelles,* and the suggestiveness of their portrayal, are particularly interesting in light of Charcot's repeated statements that hysteria was not a disorder of sexuality at all. In an 1892 article, he and P. Marie wrote: "As to the sexual life, we protest against the opinion universally adopted by the public that all hysterical women have a tendency to lubricity, almost bearing on nymphomania. Far from this, our opinion founded on the observation of numerous hysterical females in the Salpêtrière is that hysterical women are less sexual than sane and normal individuals; we may even add that hysterical patients with total anesthesia show absolute indifference to intercourse."[32]

In *Studies on Hysteria,* Freud would excuse his own initial inattention to the sexual dimension of hysteria by saying, "I had come fresh from the school of Charcot, and I regarded the linking of hysteria with the topic of sexuality as a sort of insult—just as the women patients themselves do."[33] The contradiction between the photographic representations and Charcot's stated observations might have been resolved through attention to the actual effects of sexual trauma; it might have been possible, for instance, to discover in the experience of sexual trauma the reasons why hysterics both sought attention and showed "absolute indifference to intercourse." Yet the Salpêtrière doctors could only have gained such an understanding through listening to their patients' words.

The treatment of verbal information

In his renowned "Tuesday Lessons," Charcot demonstrated the extemporaneous application of his clinical technique.[34] Examining a

---

[32] J.-M. Charcot and P. Marie, "Hysteria," in *Dictionary of Psychological Medicine,* ed. D. H. Tuke (London: Churchill, 1892).

[33] *SE* (n. 8 above), 2:260.

[34] Charcot's case presentations were not, in fact, always extemporaneous. Although the Tuesday Lessons were promoted as Charcot's exposure to cases he had never seen before, in fact they were often cases he had seen at one point or another. For more information on the structure of Charcot's clinical presentations, see Goetz's preface and introduction to *Charcot, the Clinician* (n. 7 above).

woman in order to arrive at a differential diagnosis of epilepsy or hysteria, he says:

> Let us press again on the hysterogenic point. Here we go again. Occasionally subjects even bite their tongue, but this would be rare. Look at the arched back, which is so well described in the textbooks.
> *Patient:* Mother, I am frightened.
> *Charcot:* Note the emotional outburst. If we let things go unabated, we will soon return to the epileptoid behavior. Now we have a bit of tranquility, of resolution, followed by a type of static contracted posture. I consider this latter deformity as an accessory phenomenon to the basic attack. (*The patient cries again: "Oh! Mother."*)
> *Charcot:* Again, note these screams. You could say it is a lot of noise over nothing. True epilepsy is much more serious and also much more quiet."[35]

In its implicit linking of epilepsy's seriousness to an absence of subjective outbursts, this vignette suggests Charcot's view of the status, significance, and usefulness of patients' talk.

The case history of Augustine offers a vivid array of subjective information, remarkable for how uneasily it is fitted into the overarching biological-hereditary framework its authors attempt to provide. The case history opens with an exposition of the topic of primary medical interest (menstruation) and a summary specifying the topics to be covered. Bourneville offers this description of Augustine's appearance upon her arrival at the hospital: "L . . . [her name is given several different ways within the case] is blonde, tall, and strong for her age, and gives every appearance of a pubescent girl. She is active, intelligent, affectionate, impressionable, but capricious, loving to attract attention. She is coquettish, takes a great deal of care with her toilette, and with fixing her hair, which is abundant, arranging it sometimes in one way, sometimes in another, with ribbons, bright ones, making her especially happy."[36]

The case goes on to record the results of neurological examination and Augustine's symptoms (her aura, her digestive functions, and breathing). A year and a half of her stay in the Salpêtrière is recorded over thirty-six pages, detailing her periods, attacks, and treatment, and illustrated by the photographs. Fragments of her *périodes de délire* are given in the context of the course of her attacks. In the *périodes de délire,* Augustine engages

---

[35] Ibid., 105–6.
[36] *IPS* (n. 1 above), 2:127–28.

in what Bourneville calls her "bavardage" (chattering or gossip).[37] "More expansive" than the other patients, her "veritable delirium of words" occupies more than seven pages of fine print. In her hallucinations, she converses with what the doctors at the Salpêtrière call her "Invisibles," a term that refers to her hallucinated characters while inadvertently suggesting the workings of her mind, hidden from the observational techniques of the Salpêtrière doctors.

Augustine's history, entitled "Antécédents," supplies the lurid details of her young life. While she is a student at a religious school away from home, the husband of a woman she knows tries to rape her. She returns to her family in Paris on her vacation, where she meets Mr. C., her mother's employer. Her mother compels her to kiss this man and call him her father. She is then placed in his home, under the pretext of teaching his children to sew and sing. Lodged in a small isolated back room, Augustine is visited at night by Mr. C., "who was not on good terms with his wife," and who attempts to rape her twice without success. The third time, "[Mr.] C . . . after having made all sorts of promises shine before her eyes, having offered her pretty dresses, etc., seeing that she did not want to give in, threatened her with a razor; taking advantage of her fright, he made her drink a liqueur, undressed her, threw her on the bed, and had complete relations."[38]

Afterward, Augustine lost blood, "had pain in her genitals and was unable to walk." Her doctor thought she had begun her period. At this time Augustine was thirteen and a half. Soon thereafter she had her first hysterical attack.

Following these events, Augustine runs into Mr. C. on other occasions; he threatens her and thereby provokes renewed attacks. She is placed with an old woman as a chambermaid, at which time her brother introduces her to two of his friends, with whom she has sexual relations. She also realizes that Mr. C. was her mother's lover and that her mother procured her for him.

As her story unfolds, Augustine's delirious account is riddled with references to her mother who betrayed her, her father who did not protect her, her employer who raped her, and her brother who procured her for his friends. She dwells repeatedly, incessantly, on her own blamelessness, articulating her efforts to fend off unwelcome advances and to protect herself from pregnancy. In reference to Mr. C. and the rape itself, she says:

Then, I had Mr. C. . . . ; after that I would do well to tell Madame . . . to tell papa . . . but Mr. C. told me that he would kill me. What

[37] Ibid., 158, 172.
[38] Ibid., 126.

he showed me, I didn't know what it meant. He spread my legs . . .
I didn't know that it was an animal that was going to bite me . . .
I'm going to go out every night because he wants to go to bed with
me. He told me that he would kill me. He hurts me. . . . He says that
later on it will make me feel good. . . . But it's a sin. . . . I will be
forced to tell papa. . . . That's how people make children. What! a
baby! If Mr. C. . . were to make me a baby. . . . And mother claimed
that she was putting me in a safe house![39]

Battling with her brother Antonio about the sexual goings-on between
herself and his friend, she says: "Antonio, you are going to repeat what
he told you . . . that he had touched me. . . . But I didn't want it. . . .
Antonio, you lie! . . . It's true, he had a snake in his trousers, he wanted
to put it in my stomach, but he didn't even find me. . . . Me, I'm a lunatic?
. . . Antonio, you're joking. I'm going to smack you! (*Look of contempt
and disgust*)."[40]

The centrality of sexual trauma in hysteria is vividly suggested by these
utterances; in the medical accounts, however, it finds expression only in
the elaborate attention paid to symptoms involving female reproductive
biology. The doctors assiduously note, for instance, the onset, heaviness,
and length of menstrual periods and observe a relation between periods
and hysterical attacks. Although these facts and correlations are carefully
recorded and an enormous amount of evidence about sexuality is laid
out, the doctors do not cast these as correspondences whose meaning is
mediated by subjective experience.

This simultaneous fascination with, and neglect of, the relation between sexual functions and convulsive attacks is shown more clearly still
in the case of "Geneviève." "We insisted above," the authors write, "on
the relation that existed between *menstrual periods* and the *attacks*. We
must add again, that *sexual relations*, at least at first, diminished the
convulsive crises, of which the two *pregnancies* had augmented the number, whereas *breastfeeding* appeared to lead to a certain amelioration."[41]

The report reads as if biological signs had self-evident and unequivocal
meaning, and it does not address meanings for which Geneviève's verbal
utterances provide a wealth of suggestions. Her biographical information
reveals that she is an adopted child whose wet nurse died in her first
months of life. Her betrothed dies when she is fifteen; at sixteen she is
sexually approached by her employer. Soon after, her attacks begin and
she is put in a *hôtel-Dieu* where the nuns think she looks pregnant and
punish her. She is transferred to a mental hospital, where she cuts off her

[39] Ibid., 161.
[40] Ibid., 149.
[41] Ibid., 1:94. The emphasis is in the original.

right nipple. Geneviève goes from asylum to asylum, ending up at the Salpêtrière. She then escapes to Montbard, where Prussian soldiers hold her: "During eight days she had relations with one (?) Prussian officer, relations that resulted in a second pregnancy."[42] When she is returned to the Salpêtrière, Bourneville remarks that Geneviève's "attacks were very numerous and very strong during pregnancy," although she "insists that during the six weeks of breastfeeding she did not have one attack."[43] When her child dies at six weeks, the attacks resume.

At the Salpêtrière, "her talk rolls on without cease about the most striking events of her existence, which are the object of her preoccupation in her normal state."[44] In her hallucinations she complains that serpents and vipers are penetrating her stomach and making her suffer; she says that "if she refuses to eat, it's because she doesn't want to feed all those beasts."[45] Her imagery resonates with Augustine's reference to the erect penis of her brother's friend as "a snake in his trousers" that he wants to put in her stomach. The similarity of Augustine's and Geneviève's fears might have suggested to the Salpêtrière clinicians a common pool of misinformation, sexual theories, or fantasies whose meaning could be explored. However, hereditary-biological explanations provided a rationale for not interrogating these connections further.

Most critically, perhaps, the doctors did not take into account the emotions and motives of their women patients, or the interaction of their patients' emotional agendas and their own investigative procedures. Describing the social structure of the hospital wards, Bourneville writes: "G. is jealous of another sick person A. . . , with whom we are engaged for the purposes of research on magnetism, hypnotism, etc. Mr. Charcot addressed a sharp reprimand to her. She was profoundly mortified by it. Under the influence of this strong emotion the spinal pain completely disappeared and the attacks could no longer be provoked."[46]

This passage hints at the fraught emotional milieu in which the research was being conducted. It suggests triangular jealousies between patients and doctors, competition for attention, and direct links between symptomatology and emotional experiences. Yet G.'s response is not discussed in this light; instead, the spheres in which the hysterical patient's motives and feelings are most readily invoked include simulation, fraudulence, and the "natural" coquetry of the hysteric.

The question of fraudulence was a pressing one at the Salpêtrière, related as it was to the establishment of hysteria's legitimacy. Charcot

---

[42] Ibid., 2:67. The (?) is in the original.
[43] Ibid., 1:56.
[44] Ibid., 69.
[45] Ibid., 64.
[46] Ibid., 2:205.

betrays in his *Lectures on Diseases of the Nervous System* a mistrust of the patients' behavior altogether different from his unquestioning faith in visual evidence: "Simulation . . . is met with at every step in the history of hysteria. One finds oneself acknowledging the amazing craft, sagacity, and perseverance which women . . . especially under the influence of this great neurosis . . . will put into play . . . especially when a physician is to be the victim."[47] This pronouncement reveals an inconsistency in Charcot's opinion of the relationship of women and hysteria; for although he generally insisted that hysteria was not specific to women—contrary to a view that had prevailed since antiquity—here he implies that hysteria amounts to an exacerbation of female nature.

The hysteric's purported coquetry is illustrated in various descriptions of patients. One is described in this way: "Her face was quite sweet. Her air is somewhat nonchalant. Like all hysterics, she likes attention."[48] Of Augustine, Bourneville writes: "Everything about her, moreover, announces the hysteric. . . . It goes without saying that the sight of men pleases her, that she likes to show herself and wants them to pay her attention."[49]

The emphasis on coquetry by the doctors at the Salpêtrière had an ironic twist: the hysterical woman patient's display of exaggerated symptoms and sexual charms itself represented a threat to the truth derived from the visible realm of objective observation and the photographic lens. Yet it was precisely these exhibitionistic qualities that fitted her for participation in the enterprise of photographic representation. Her "hysterical tendencies" toward self-display and adornment were not simply recorded but, rather, encouraged when she was placed in front of the camera's eye for the purposes of medical documentation. In this meeting of the patient's desires and the doctor's intent, the question of "objective" knowledge through visual representation in photographs was thrown into confusion. The doctor's interpretation was that her desire for attention and self-display were typical hysterical signs; yet for the patient who had suffered severe trauma in the spheres of love and loyalty, the treatment of her illness and the "doctoring" of her photographs may both have been expressions of the attention and care she had been deprived of in the past.[50]

---

[47] Charcot, *Clinical Lectures on Certain Diseases of the Nervous System* (n. 28 above), 230.

[48] *IPS* (n. 1 above), 2:190.

[49] Ibid., 168.

[50] This hidden dynamic by which the needs of both doctor and patient are filled provides, Michel Foucault writes, an instance where "the sign no longer speaks the natural language of disease; it assumes shape and value only within the question posed by medical investigation. There is nothing, therefore, to prevent it being solicited and almost fabricated by medical investigation. It is no longer that which is spontaneously stated by the disease itself; it is the meeting point of the gestures of research and the sick organ-

Freud

Background

Richard Wollheim has written that "Freud's life work ... was a research into the deafness of the mind."[51] Ultimately for Freud, the deafness of the mind revealed itself in a special way in the symptomatology of hysteria: memories of events the conscious mind could not tolerate were expressed in physical symptoms. It was this commemoration of events by symptoms that Freud and Breuer sought to describe in their well-known aphorism, "Hysterics suffer mainly from reminiscences."[52] Freud's conceptualization of hysteria diverged from Charcot's, and it depended on a very different method—that of listening—for its construction.

Though Freud was a neuropathologist by training, his interest in medicine was by no means narrow or even particularly focused. His family noted in him a "lack of genuine medical temperament,"[53] and he took seven years to finish his medical studies, having plunged himself instead into the study of zoology, biology, and philosophy at university. A critical figure in Freud's philosophical training was Franz Brentano, with whom Freud studied for five semesters.[54] For Brentano the science of psychology stood on ground as firm as the natural sciences; in terms of method, Brentano advocated "a scientific working back and forth between the evidence of the inner 'subjective' world and the outer 'objective' world"—which, as McGrath points out, marked the mature method of Freud as well.[55]

Freud's wide-ranging interests, and his ambition to use medicine as a path to "realizing his intense curiosity in nature and human relations," were consonant with an interest in establishing the relationship of biological and psychological phenomena. With specific regard to hysteria, Freud's goal was to establish "a *combined psychophysiological basis* for both hypnotic and hysterical phenomena."[56] This is why Freud sought to study with Charcot, the reigning expert on the neurological aspects of hysteria.

---

ism" (*The Birth of the Clinic: An Archaeology of Medical Perception* [New York: Vintage, 1975], 162). Also see Michel Foucault, *The History of Sexuality* (New York: Vintage, 1980), 1:55–56 and 111–12, for specific discussion of the Salpêtrière.

[51] R. Wollheim, *Sigmund Freud* (New York: Viking, 1971), 272.

[52] *SE* (n. 8 above), 2:7.

[53] S. Bernfeld, "Sigmund Freud, 1882–85," *International Journal of Psychoanalysis* 32 (1951): 204–17, esp. 204.

[54] The influence of Brentano's philosophy of psychology on Freud has been explored in great detail by W. J. McGrath in *Freud's Discovery of Psychoanalysis: The Politics of Hysteria* (Ithaca, N.Y.: Cornell University Press, 1986).

[55] Ibid., 100.

[56] F. Sulloway, *Freud: Biologist of the Mind* (New York: Basic, 1979), 50. Original emphasis.

Throughout his published references to Charcot, Freud lavished praise upon his mentor for his method of diagnosis and classification, as well as for his use of hypnosis, which had begun to suggest the importance of the "psychical element" in hysteria. In terms of method, Freud was deeply influenced by Charcot's combined use of anatomical knowledge and clinical experience.[57] In his obituary of Charcot in 1893, he lauded Charcot's special gifts: "He was not a reflective man, not a thinker: he had the nature of an artist—he was, as he himself said, a *visuel,* a man who sees."[58] Freud was also impressed by the fruitful transfer of Charcot's method from the study of organic diseases to the study of neuroses; he credited Charcot with having made clear the lawful nature of these phenomena.[59] Through Charcot's use of the archetype as a way of understanding clinical disorders, hysteria was, by Freud's account, "lifted out of the chaos of the neuroses, was differentiated from other conditions with similar appearance, and was provided with a symptomatology, which though sufficiently multifarious, nevertheless makes it impossible any longer to doubt the rule of law and order."[60] Further, Freud was influenced by Charcot's use of hypnosis, both for its therapeutic effects and for the legitimacy it conferred upon what was still regarded in some Viennese medical circles as quackery.

Between 1886, when Freud returned from Paris, and 1895, when *Studies on Hysteria* was published, Freud's views diverged from Charcot's in three important areas: the etiology of hysteria, the use of hypnosis, and clinical method.[61]

In looking to sexuality as the critical link between the psychological and physical aspects of hysteria, Freud rejected the explanations he had received from Charcot. Charcot had eschewed the importance of sexuality in hysteria and had revealed himself to be relatively uninterested in exploring possible points of contact between the physiological and psychological origins of hysteria. Charcot's lack of interest in the role of sexuality later appeared to Freud in a strange light. Freud recounts an

[57] See, e.g., *SE,* 1:10 and 3:11–23.

[58] Freud, "Charcot" (n. 8 above), 3:9–23.

[59] Sulloway, 49.

[60] *SE,* 1:12.

[61] S. Freud, "Preface to the Translation of Charcot's Lectures on the Diseases of the Nervous System" (1886) in ibid., 19–22, "Preface to the Translation of Bernheim's Suggestion" (1888), in ibid., 73–88, "Hysteria" (1888), in ibid., 39–59, "Hypnosis" (1891), in ibid., 103–14, "Preface and Footnotes to Charcot's Tuesday Lectures" (1892–94), in ibid., 131–46, "Some Points for a Comparative Study of Organic and Hysterical Motor Paralyses" (1893), in ibid., 160–72, and "On the Psychical Mechanisms of Hysterical Phenomena" (1893), in ibid., 3:25–39; J. M. Masson, ed., *The Complete Letters of Sigmund Freud to Wilhelm Fliess, 1887–1904* (Cambridge, Mass.: Harvard University Press, 1985).

anecdote in his 1914 article, "On the History of the Psychoanalytic Movement":

> At one of Charcot's evening receptions, I happened to be standing near the great teacher at a moment when he appeared to be telling Brouardel some very interesting story from his day's work. I hardly heard the beginning, but gradually my attention was seized by what he was saying. A young married couple from the far East: the woman a confirmed invalid: the man either impotent or exceedingly awkward. *"Tachez donc,"* I hear Charcot repeating, *"je vous assure, vous y arriverez"* [Keep trying, I assure you, you'll get there]. Brouardel, who spoke less loudly, must have expressed his astonishment that symptoms such as the wife's could have been produced in such circumstances. For Charcot suddenly broke in with great animation, *"Mais, dans des cas pareils c'est toujours la chose génitale, toujours . . . toujours, toujours"* [In these kinds of cases, it's always a genital thing, always . . . always, always]; and he crossed himself with his arms over his stomach, hugging himself and jumping up and down on his toes several times in his own characteristic lively way. I know that for one second I was almost paralyzed with amazement and said to myself, "Well, but if he knows that, why does he never say so?" But the impression was soon forgotten; brain anatomy and the experimental induction of hysterical paralyses absorbed all available interest.[62]

Within his own developing psychological framework, Freud began to reinterpret some of the symptoms Charcot had observed. Reconceptualizing Charcot's *attitudes passionnelles,* Freud wrote: "The core of a hysterical attack, in whatever form it may appear, is a memory, the hallucinatory reliving of a scene which is significant for the onset of the illness. It is this event which manifests itself in a perceptible manner in the phase of '*attitudes passionnelles*'; but it is also present when the attack appears to consist only of motor phenomena."[63] In a letter to Fliess in late 1896, Freud devised a novel account of Charcot's *périodes de clownisme:* "The explanation of the phase of 'clownism' in Charcot's schema of [hysterical] attacks, lies in the perversion of the seducers who, by virtue of the compulsion to repeat what they did in their youth, obviously seek their satisfaction by performing the wildest capers, somersaults, and gri-

[62] *SE* (n. 8 above), 14:13–14.
[63] Ibid., 1:137.

maces."[64] Behaviors of hysterics were, to Freud, meaningful mimicry of traumatic past events.

Freud's overall dissatisfaction with, and shift away from, Charcot's method is evident in his 1893 view of Charcot's use of hypnotism: "The exclusively nosographical approach adopted at the School of the Salpêtrière was not suitable for a purely psychological subject. The restriction of the study of hypnosis to hysterical patients, the differentiation between major and minor hypnotism, the hypothesis of three stages of 'major hypnosis,' and their characterization by somatic phenomena—all this sank in the estimation of Charcot's contemporaries when Liébeault's pupil, Bernheim, set about constructing the theory of hypnotism on a more comprehensive psychological foundation and making suggestion the central point of hypnosis."[65]

Thus, Freud saw the approach of visual observation as simply inadequate to a "purely psychological subject" such as hysteria. This shift, combined with a change in his orientation to hypnosis, ushered in Freud's third critical divergence from Charcot, his use of a novel clinical-investigative method.

Listening, speaking, and the use of words in "Studies on Hysteria"

Freud visited Bernheim in Nancy in 1889 in order to perfect his hypnotic technique, but he soon became dissatisfied with the efficacy of suggestion and began experimenting with a method which, along the lines of Breuer's, used hypnotism to uncover memory of past events. Much earlier, in November 1882, Breuer had told Freud of his treatment of Anna O., which had been conducted between 1880 and 1882. Freud was extremely interested both by Breuer's use of hypnotism as a method of catharsis and by the young woman patient's response to it.

With Anna O., Breuer had found that hypnotism operated to reproduce the "hypnoid state" in which the symptoms first appeared. When Breuer returned her to her hypnoid state, she could recite the events that had originally brought on the symptom. In his treatment of Frau Emmy von N., which began in May of 1888 or 1889 and lasted a year, Freud used the cathartic method "to a large extent" for the first time.[66] His 1924 footnote to that case affirmed that he also used a great deal of direct therapeutic suggestion. His "first full-length analysis of hysteria,"[67] that of Fräulein Elisabeth von R., began in the fall of 1892, and the analysis of Miss Lucy R. began later that year. The fourth case study, that of Katha-

[64] Masson, ed., 218.
[65] *SE*, 3:22–23.
[66] Ibid., 2:105.
[67] Ibid., 139.

rina, is undated but occurred within the same time span. An exploration of the two most detailed cases, those of Emmy von N. and Elisabeth von R., offers a picture of the method Freud developed to investigate what he understood to be the *psychological* disorder of hysteria. Moreover, they emblematize Freud's approach to understanding and representing hysteria in the same way as Charcot's photographs emblematize his.[68]

Emmy von N. was a woman of about forty whose symptoms and personality interested Freud so greatly that, as he wrote, "I devoted a large part of my time to her and determined to do all I could for her recovery."[69] She was an exceptionally intelligent woman of "finely-cut features and noble character," who was able to conduct herself with great competence except during her bouts of hysteria. Freud visited her daily, usually twice, during the first three weeks of treatment at the nursing home where he had recommended she stay. Sometime in the course of Freud's first meeting with her, Emmy's coherent self-presentation and poised bearing gave way to "an expression of horror and disgust," and she exclaimed, "Keep still—Don't say anything—Don't touch me!" Freud conjectured that the words provided a "protective formula," an attempt to control her frightening thoughts.[70]

On the morning of May 10, as he massages Frau von N. (part of the acceptable practice of the day), Freud alleviates her doubt about an incident with Dr. Breuer, and her agitated tongue-clacking and grimaces stop. He remarks:

> So each time, even while I am massaging her, my influence has already begun to affect her; she grows quieter and clearer in the head, and even without questioning under hypnosis can discover the cause of her ill-humor on that day. Nor is her conversation during the massage so aimless as would appear. On the contrary, it contains a fairly complete reproduction of the memories and new impressions which have affected her since our last talk, and it often leads on, in a quite unexpected way, to pathogenic reminiscences of which she unburdens herself without being asked to. It is as though she had adopted my procedure and was making use of our conversation, apparently unconstrained and guided by chance, as a supplement to her hypnosis.[71]

[68] *Studies on Hysteria* is a joint work of Freud and Breuer, but here I am exploring two of Freud's cases. For a detailed summary of the two doctors' respective roles in producing the work, see J. Strachey, "Editor's Introduction," *SE*, 2:ix–xxviii.

[69] *SE*, 2:48.

[70] Ibid., 49.

[71] Ibid., 56. Strachey notes, "This is perhaps the earliest appearance of what later became the method of free association" (ibid.).

In some respects the passage contains in microcosm the development of Freud's technique. First, his "influence" begins to take hold without the necessity of actual hypnotism. His massage, his presence, and his attentiveness elicit her conversation, which, unlike the "babbling" of Charcot's patients, is not "so aimless as would appear." Frau von N. begins to recount her recent memories and impressions since their last talk and works her way back to pathogenic reminiscences. She herself makes use of the conversation for her own purposes, "without being asked to"; she thus participates in constructing the method in a context provided by Freud, a context that is, at least, not inimical to fluid self-expression.

When Freud does not provide Frau von N. with what she needs, she tells him. Asked about the meaning of each piece of her "protective formula," "she explained that when she had frightening thoughts she was afraid of their being interrupted in their course, because then everything would get confused and things would get even worse."[72] Two days later, Freud asks the hypnotized Emmy to remember by the next day why she had gastric pains; "She then said in a definitely grumbling tone that I was not to keep on asking her where this and that came from, but to let her tell me what she had to say. ... (I saw now that the cause of her ill-humour was that she had been suffering from the residues of this story which had been kept back)."[73]

Freud realizes from this exchange that by directing the conversation, he has been creating an impediment to his patient's "free association." He takes her statements as evidence that his procedure has not been "carried out exhaustively enough."[74] By noting Frau von N.'s moods following their sessions and relating these to the exhaustiveness with which he carried out the catharsis, Freud draws a theoretical conclusion that symptoms are attached "not solely to the initial traumas but to a long chain of memories associated with them," which must likewise be dealt with through catharsis.[75] When Freud uses visual cues, it is to read in the patient's face whether she has truthfully divulged her entire story. Even though Freud might at first prefer to cut his patient's words short, he realizes the importance of thoroughly listening to all the patient needs to say if a cure is to be reached and his theory is to be proven.

Freud, like Charcot, did not see himself as a therapist. In a letter to Fliess dated April 2, 1896, Freud conveyed his own reluctant involvement in psychotherapy: "As a young man I knew no longing other than for philosophical knowledge, and now I am about to fulfill it as I move from

[72] Ibid.
[73] Ibid., 63.
[74] Ibid., 74, n. 1.
[75] Ibid., 75, n. 2.

medicine to psychology. I became a therapist against my will."[76] Freud
may have had, at least initially, a distaste for therapeutics, but he recognized in therapy a process necessary to the study of the illness.

When Emmy von N. becomes fearful of how she will fare when her
treatment ends, Freud reassures her, telling her that she has become health-
ier and suggesting "that she would get in the habit of telling her thoughts
to someone she was on close terms with."[77] His injunction reveals the
importance he attributes to the act of verbal unburdening for the hysteric.
Freud also specifies a relational context for the unburdening—"someone
she was on close terms with." He thereby suggests a fundamental similarity
between the doctor's relationship to the patient and the patient's relationship to a friend or confidante in daily life.

In his treatment of Emmy von N., Freud further develops his opposition to Charcot's hereditary view of hysteria. He specifically objects to
Charcot's insufficient distinction between hereditary predisposition to
neurosis and the acquisition of nervous disease either through early childhood events or through the combination of trauma and inherited vulner-
ability.[78] Charcot's theory of the *famille névropathique*—"which, inci-
dentally, embraces almost everything we know in the form of nervous
diseases, organic and functional, systematic and accidental"[79]—was far
too general and dismissive in Freud's view. Statements in the *Studies* of
his opposition to the hereditary hypothesis show that Freud believed the
issues Charcot deemed biological belonged instead in the realm of relationships. The issue of degeneracy, important to Charcot, is only relevant
in cases where it impairs the ability of the patient to participate in the
process of psychotherapy: "The procedure is not applicable at all below
a certain level of intelligence, and it is made very much more difficult by
any trace of feebleness of mind. . . . It is almost inevitable that their
personal relation to him [the doctor] will force itself, for a time at least,
unduly into the foreground. It seems, indeed, as though an influence of
this kind on the part of the doctor is a *sine qua non* to a solution of the
problem."[80] Here "influence" refers to hypnotic suggestion, and it hints
at the concept of transference. Later in the chapter, Freud more fully
addresses the centrality of the doctor-patient relationship: "I have already indicated [*SE*, 2: 266] the important part played by the figure of the
physician in creating motives to defeat the psychical force of resistance.
In not a few cases, especially with women and here it is a question of
elucidating erotic trains of thought, the patient's cooperation becomes a

---

[76] Masson, ed. (n. 61 above), 180.
[77] *SE* (n. 8 above), 2:75.
[78] See, e.g., ibid., 294, and 1:139.
[79] Ibid., 1:142–43.
[80] Ibid., 2:265.

personal sacrifice, which must be compensated by some substitute for love. The trouble taken by the physician and his friendliness have to suffice for such a substitute. If, now, this relation of the patient to the physician is disturbed, her cooperativeness fails, too."[81]

To counter the hereditary hypothesis, however, Freud did not simply offer a psychological one. He invoked the exemplary qualities of the hysterical patients themselves in order to break the equation of hysteria with degeneracy. In closing the case of Emmy von N., Freud writes: "The woman we came to know was an admirable one. The moral seriousness with which she views her duties, her intelligence and energy, which were no less than a man's, and her high degree of education and love of truth impressed both of us greatly; while her benevolent care for the welfare of all her dependents, humility of mind and the refinement of her manners revealed her qualities as a true lady as well. To describe such a woman as a 'degenerate' would be to distort the meaning of that word out of all recognition."[82]

Freud's legitimation of his psychological theory, then, was intertwined with the question of the status or worthiness of the patient. Freud lays great stress on the refinement and high social standing of Frau von N.; though she has a "more lively and uninhibited way of expressing her emotions than [is] usual with women of her education and race,"[83] she is a highly educated woman nonetheless. And, interestingly, the measure of her superiority is described in terms of her equality with a man. If man is the measure, then the extent to which she is not "degenerated" is the extent to which she equals a man precisely in those qualities where man is superior. Freud's repeated emphasis on Emmy's character, breeding, and general superiority not only serves to correct some prejudices (incrimination by association) against the victims of the disorder and against the disease, but also buttresses the utility of his particular method of cure.

Describing the difficulties and disadvantages of his psychotherapy later on in the *Studies*, Freud writes: "The procedure is laborious and time-consuming for the physician. It presupposes great interest in psychological happenings, but personal concern for the patients as well. I cannot imagine bringing myself to delve into the psychical mechanism of a hysteria in anyone who struck me as low-minded or repellent, and who, on closer examination, would not be capable of arousing human sympathy."[84] Freud brings out with admirable candor the link of compassion and interest (both qualities of a personal relationship) to a sense of

[81] Ibid., 301.
[82] Ibid., 104.
[83] Ibid., 91.
[84] Ibid., 265.

respect for the patient. Aside from the virtue of his forthright tone, however, his suggestion that probing the mind of someone "low-minded" would not be worthwhile is consistent with, and in some sense justifies, Charcot's failure to question his destitute women patients at the Salpêtrière. High-mindedness and, by implication, membership in "an educated and literate social class"[85] made Freud perceive his patients as less distant and their subjective worlds as less strange and repellent.

The case of Elisabeth von R. is the most consummately crafted tale of the *Studies* and provides the best early account of the relation between therapist and patient. Freud introduces the case with his first interview and shares with us the suspense of his initial ignorance about this young woman and her disease. He leads us through his difficulties in settling on a technique and his slow realization of "the connection between the events in her illness and her actual symptom."[86] Freud then unfolds a very long and involved family drama, following which he writes: "If we put greater misfortunes on one side and enter into a girl's feeling, we cannot refrain from deep human sympathy with Fraülein Elisabeth. But what shall we say of the purely medical interest of this tale of suffering and of its relations to her painful locomotor weakness, and of the chances of an explanation and cure afforded by our knowledge of these psychical traumas?"[87] In answer to his own question, Freud says that "the patient's confession was at first sight a great disappointment."[88] Her life seems too mundane to bring on hysterical symptomatology; the reasons for her symptom choice are far from clear. Like most physicians, Freud does not regard her experiences as sufficiently important to precipitate hysteria. Yet, instead of contenting himself with the common medical view that she is a constitutional hysteric, he inquires into the meaning of her symptoms: What kind of excitations led to them? What would her motives have been, and when had an association between "her painful mental impressions and the bodily pains" taken place? These are questions that can only be answered by information elicited from Elisabeth herself—information that is not always available to her, but which must be made so.

In striking contrast to Charcot's technique, Freud uses cues about what holds Elisabeth's interest as indications of what course to pursue. Thus, after investigating the different pains she has in her legs, he admits, "I did not pursue further the delimitation of zones of pain corresponding to different psychical determinants, since I found that the patient's attention was directed away from this subject."[89]

---

[85] Ibid., xxix.
[86] Ibid., 138.
[87] Ibid., 144.
[88] Ibid.
[89] Ibid., 150.

Central both to the actual case and to its representation as a case history is Freud's explicit participation as one of the characters in the story. He attempts to achieve objectivity not through the eradication of his own presence but, rather, by carefully describing his own role and tracing the steps of his own logic. We are never allowed to forget his participation, since he often refers to his own questions and doubts about his technique, and continually inserts his own perspective on the conundrums raised by the case.

A major feature of Charcot's view of hysterics was an emphasis on hysterical dissimulation and the hysteric's goal of making the doctor a fool. Interestingly, Freud raises these same issues, but in the context of the relationship between doctor and patient. Proceeding first with his pressure technique, Freud finds that Elisabeth has made no confessions that have led to a cure. He remarks that "during this first period of her treatment she never failed to repeat that she was still feeling ill and that her pains were as bad as ever; and, when she looked at me as she said this with a sly look of satisfaction at my discomfiture, I could not help being reminded of old Herr von R.'s judgement about his favourite daughter — that she was often 'cheeky' and 'ill-behaved.' But I was obliged to admit that she was in the right."[90] Freud's self-disclosure makes clear the doctor's shared fallibility in the therapeutic enterprise. In this case as in others, Freud is ironic about his own ineptitude at pulling off a successful hypnosis. He gives dimension to the hysteric's obstinacy and wish to deceive by including his own role in the drama.

One of Freud's most quoted statements appears in the case of Elisabeth von R. and captures the essence of his innovative shift in method. He writes at the beginning of his "Discussion":

> I have not always been a psychotherapist. Like other neuropathologists, I was trained to employ local diagnoses and electro-prognosis, and it still strikes myself as strange that the case histories I write should read like short stories and that, as one might say, they lack the serious stamp of science. I must console myself with the reflection that the nature of the subject is evidently responsible for this, rather than any preference of my own. The fact is that local diagnoses and electrical reactions lead nowhere in the study of hysteria, whereas a detailed description of mental processes such as we are accustomed to find in the works of imaginative writers enables me, with the use of a few psychological formulas, to obtain at least some kind of insight into the course of that affection.[91]

[90] Ibid., 144–45.
[91] Ibid., 160–61.

In a familiar Freudian voice, he refers to his own training and orientation as a way to inform (and convince) the reader that he did not proceed from any natural desire to delve into the minds and lives of his women patients. Rather, he was reluctantly drawn there in response to the objective facts of the case. Similarly, he self-consciously refers to the product that has emerged from these investigations, case histories that "read like short stories" and "lack the serious stamp of science." He has listened to his patients, and their utterances have "dictated" to him an approach.

Although he almost apologizes for the narrative art of his account, its unorthodox form, it is precisely his worry about his role in constructing that account that is to his credit as a scientist. His innovative contribution operates in two related ways. The first is his inclusion of the subjective accounts of his patients in constructing his understanding of the disease. These early cases are marked by a relationship between doctor and patient in which both contribute to the building of the method, and both collaborate in the process of unearthing forgotten or repressed mnemic origins of the illness. Freud recognizes, even at this formative stage, the mutual interest of the two participants as central, and the relation of patient and doctor as a fundamental precondition of, or obstruction to, therapeutic progress. We can see in the development of Freud's technique a profoundly altered relationship to the patient.

The second and parallel innovation is Freud's acknowledgment of his own subjective contribution, his own hand in constructing the account of hysteria he has presented. His surprise at digressing from "serious science" is conveyed in a rhetorical strategy used repeatedly throughout the *Studies*. By referring to the position adopted by his colleagues, and by then indicating what observations required him to diverge from their view, Freud conveys the necessity and inevitability of his new approach. For example, in a discussion of an eighteen-year-old patient, Freud writes:

> To begin with I myself was unwilling to attach much importance to these details, and there can be no doubt that earlier students of hysteria would have been inclined to regard these phenomena as evidence of the stimulation of the cortical centres during a hysterical attack. It is true that we are ignorant of the locality of the centres for paraesthesias of this kind, but it is well known that such paraesthesias usher in partial epilepsy and constitute Charcot's sensory epilepsy. . . . But the explanation turned out to be a different one. When I had come to know the girl better I put a straight question to her as to what kind of thoughts came to her during these attacks. I told her not to be embarrassed and said that she

must be able to give an explanation of the two phenomena [facial pricking sensations and convulsive foot stretching].[92]

In this passage Freud moves from his initial emphasis (one shared by Charcot and others) on lesions and cortical stimulation to an explanation based on the causal role of the emotions and the therapeutic approach that must accompany this knowledge. He moves from a highly technical account of physiological symptoms to a question in plain language about the girl's own experience; thus he contrasts a specific biological diagnosis with a disarmingly simple remedy: "When I had come to know the girl better I put a straight question to her."

Just as Freud's treatment depended critically on talking and listening, the role of words was central both to the description of the disorder and to the disorder itself. In terms of his description of the disorder, Freud uses a number of similes in order to "throw light from different directions on a highly complicated topic which has never yet been represented."[93] In terms of his theory of the causes of the disorder, Freud sees words as critical to the process of symbolization, which he views as midway between conversion and autosuggestion. Examples of symbolization are drawn from the cases of Rosalia H., who hysterically lost her voice at having to suppress anger, and from Cäcilie M., whose facial neuralgia appeared as an embodiment of a slight she had received ("a slap in the face").[94] Freud shows that as the centrally charged themes in the patient's affective life are tapped, the implicated organ, in his words, "joins in the conversation," adding credence to the view that the organ is in fact involved in a psychologically meaningful way.[95] In Freud's view meanings traverse the mind and body more easily than we think, and words—their expression, use, and arrangement—develop out of bodily experience more readily than we credit.[96] The fluid interchange between words and bodily symptoms defies previously constructed barriers in much the same way as Freud's use of relationship in therapy.

The centrality Freud accorded verbal communication in uncovering hysteria's origins, on the one hand, and his rhetorical craft in presenting the cases, on the other, are intertwined but are not identical; after the *Studies*, each underwent further development. By the time of Freud's analysis of Dora in the autumn of 1900, he had developed his theory of

[92] Ibid., 93–94n.
[93] Ibid., 291.
[94] Ibid., 178. See also ibid., 275–76, 280.
[95] Ibid., 296.
[96] Freud comments wryly: "If anyone feels astonished at this associative connection between physical pain and psychical affect, on the ground of its being of such a multiple and artificial character, I should reply that this feeling is as little justified as astonishment at the fact that it is the rich people who own the most money" (ibid., 175).

dreams, had carried out an in-depth self-analysis, and was eager to prove the general importance of the Oedipal conflict he had discovered in himself. Freud's directive and in many ways clumsy application of these ideas to the situation of Dora, indeed his inability to listen and understand what she was telling him, has received extensive commentary from both psychoanalysts and literary critics.[97] Some writers have gone further to insist that Freud not only stopped listening but deliberately falsified what his women patients told him, by reinterpreting their accounts of sexual trauma as fantasies.[98] Proponents of this view ignore repeated statements by Freud throughout his career as to the central importance of sexual trauma in some (though not all) cases of psychopathology.[99] It is inarguable, however, that beginning with his conduct of the Dora case, Freud retrenched from his earlier reliance on his women patients for credible accounts and a share in the building of his method.

On the level of case presentation, Freud's impressive rhetorical mastery has also received a great deal of recent critical scrutiny, especially with reference to the Dora case.[100] Spence has written about the "Sherlock Holmes" tradition in psychoanalytic writing, which he dates from the case of Dora. The most problematic feature of this detective genre is the assumption that every case (detective or psychotherapeutic) has one possible solution or interpretation. Spence views this tradition as Freud's unfortunate legacy to psychoanalysts, whose clinical reports tend to present case material geared to confirming or disconfirming existing theory, rather than revealing the actual interchanges and inferences that take place in therapeutic sessions.[101]

It is in light of these later developments that the *Studies* emerge as an important, and hitherto relatively neglected, early document. The *Studies*

---

[97] The case of Dora is presented in Freud's "Fragment of an Analysis of a Case of Hysteria" (1905 [1901]), ibid., 7:3–122. For commentary on the case by psychoanalysts, see M. Kanzer and J. Glenn, eds., *Freud and His Patients* (New York: Jason Aronson, 1980), esp. the articles by M. A. Scharfman, R. J. Langs, and I. Bernstein. Literary critical perspectives (and two psychoanalytic articles) are provided in Bernheimer and Kahane, eds. (n. 3 above).

[98] See, e.g., J. M. Masson, *The Assault on Truth: Freud's Suppression of the Seduction Theory* (New York: Farrar, Straus, & Giroux, 1984); and J. L. Herman, with L. Hirschmann, *Father-Daughter Incest* (Cambridge, Mass.: Harvard University Press, 1981).

[99] For examples of such statements, see C. Hanly, "Review of *The Assault on Truth: Freud's Suppression of the Seduction Theory* by Jeffrey M. Masson," *International Journal of Psychoanalysis* 67, pt. 4 (1986): 517–19. For a more general discussion of the issue from a psychoanalyst's perspective, see L. Shengold, *Soul Murder: The Effects of Childhood Abuse and Deprivation* (New Haven, Conn.: Yale University Press, 1989), 32–40.

[100] See S. Marcus, "Freud and Dora: Story, History, Case History"; and N. Hertz, "Dora's Secrets, Freud's Techniques," both in Bernheimer and Kahane, eds.

[101] D. P. Spence, *The Freudian Metaphor: Toward Paradigm Change in Psychoanalysis* (New York: Norton, 1987), 113–59.

capture a moment when Freud's therapeutic techniques were explicitly pro-
visional and his rhetorical emphasis explicitly oriented to the process of the
clinical encounter. Freud's illuminating discoveries concerning the curative
process are made in the context of his consideration of alternative approaches, his attention to details, and his careful recounting of these details.
He attempts both to discern clinical realities and to lay bare the processes by
which he arrives at them. Freud was, like Charcot, an ambitious man of
science; but in the *Studies,* his desire to discover scientific truths compelled
him to humble himself before what he heard and to identify his patients'
utterances as a primary source of clinical knowledge.

Conclusion

I have charted the different methods used by Charcot and Freud to
investigate hysteria, and I have characterized these as depending primarily on processes of looking or listening. The questions that prompted my
investigation concerned the Salpêtrière's interest in photography and neglect of subjective patient accounts. These concerns can be captured in a
more general question: Why was the subjective information of patients
substantially ignored by Charcot, while for Freud it was central in building his theory of hysteria?

In providing an answer, I have tried to demonstrate that underlying Charcot's use of visual observation was a conception of empirical neurological
science and a tradition of the clinicoanatomic method. Gifted as a visual
artist, Charcot brought his natural abilities to the task of observing and
understanding neurological disease. When photography became available, it
was regarded by Charcot and others as providing, quite literally, a truly
objective record of reality. It was the retina of the scientist, with the supreme
advantage of being able not only to see but also to record visual information.

One might infer from the enthusiasm with which Charcot greeted photography that its value resided, at least in part, in the improvement it represented over drawing and painting. However, it is clear that Charcot did
not distinguish between painting and photography insofar as their ability to
create truthful records of the disorder was concerned. Rather, he treated
painters, photographers, and scientists as similarly accurate observers of
nature. It was perhaps not much of a leap, then, for Charcot to incorporate
his own documentation of hysteria into artistic tradition through pose,
paint, and picture books that linked depictions of hysteria across the ages.
Because art, photography, and clinical viewing all were seen by Charcot and
his colleagues as objective, the craft—and distortion—necessary to align his
representations of hysterics with artistic tradition went unnoticed.

The underside of Charcot's fascination with the visual was his inattention
to the subjective information conveyed by patients' words. What amazes me
about the *Iconographie* is the wealth of verbal information it presents and

the poverty of interpretation. This poverty can be understood on many levels. On the level of etiological explanation, the Salpêtrière doctors were limited by the global and relatively ill-defined model of heredity by which they understood hysteria and on which Charcot insisted throughout his career. Charcot's view of heredity operated through a deterministic logic by which anything that happened in the family, or that involved the reproductive functions, by virtue of its association with the course of hereditary transmission, was seen to be caused by it. In this light we can understand better how it was that any and all experiences involving menstruation, breastfeeding, pregnancy, childbirth, or sexual intercourse were collapsed together as the product of heredity and were regarded as unmediated by the meaning they might have for those who experienced them. Ironically, in their zeal to create a truly objective picture of hysteria, the Salpêtrière doctors were unable to see the ways in which the women patients' own subjective desires affected the picture they were constructing.

On the sociological level, one obstacle to Charcot's listening to his patients was that they seemed so different: they were women, they were poor, and they were sick. In a period when class, gender, and mental illness were considered more rigid categories than they are today, the disparities between the scientist and his subject gaped very large. To listen to (poor, sick) women's accounts, to see them as something other than "babbling," and to use these as scientific evidence was to throw into confusion accepted notions of knowledge and power. Had Charcot consciously and explicitly admitted these women's words as evidence (instead of recording and then ignoring them), he would also have had to admit that they could be tellers of truth and possessors of knowledge. He would have had to shift his notion of himself as a scientist from someone who talks only about, to someone who talks to, his subjects. With this shift Charcot's claim to the position of neutral observer would have been put into question. The fact that Freud did listen to his patients' accounts may rest in part on the fact that he saw a different group of patients, patients who were not warehoused en masse in an asylum but were able to visit his consulting room and to pay his fees.

On a psychological level, just as the psychoanalyst looks to areas of confusion or contradiction to locate intrapsychic conflict in his patient, one might detect in Charcot's own confused encounter with hysteria the evidence of some kind of internal conflict as well. The core question is why Charcot, who at least to some extent acknowledged the psychological component of hysteria, did not investigate it in his patients despite glaring evidence, carefully collected by the Salpêtrière chroniclers themselves. Successful as it was with strictly neurological diseases, his method rendered consideration of subjective evidence impossible and the subjective patient accounts themselves unintelligible. Parallel to Charcot's inability to take account of the subjectivity of the Salpêtrière patients was his inability to take account of the role his own subjectivity played. Charcot's and his colleagues' firm belief in their own objectivity itself constituted a threat to that very objectivity: first, by making them unable to question their own role in constructing the picture of the disease; and second, through their inability to see their own participation in recreating the pathogenic conditions of their patients' lives—neglect, lack of empathy, and exploitation. They were likewise unable to see how the attention that they gave to the patients who served as photographic subjects contributed to the patients' display of florid symptoms. What Charcot's practice does not address explicitly is the ever-present mutual effect of the doctors on the patients and the patients on the doctors.

By drawing attention to Charcot's problematic use of visual observation, I am not making a claim for the epistemological superiority of listening, nor do I claim with some feminist writers that looking is more closely aligned with masculine understanding, and listening with feminine, however these might be defined.[102] In my view, Charcot's inability to account for his own subjective contribution did not arise from his visual method per se but, rather, resulted from his opinion that visual observation yielded an unproblematic apprehension of truth. In tracing the uses of the metaphor of vision in our conceptions of knowledge, E. F. Keller and C. R. Grontkowski have pointed out that visual observation can be used both to communicate and to objectify.[103] In Western philosophical tradition, they argue, the objectifying function of vision gained ascendance at the expense of its communicative function. The Salpêtrière photographers privileged vision's objectifying function, with the effects noted by Keller and Grontkowski: the radical division of subject and object and the submersion of the communicative, connective functions of vision in the service of objectification. The Salpêtrière's use of photography can be seen as part of its overall tendency to disavow the observer's perspective in the process of fashioning reality.

The stance adopted by the Salpêtrière doctors was founded on—and foundered upon—an inability to see their position as interpretive. In a psychoanalytic sense, the ultimate effect of disavowing personal perspectives and aims inherent in one's enterprise is to create the conditions for their

[102] The notion that seeing and sight are linked to masculinity, while listening and voice are particularly female-identified activities, has been articulated by French feminists such as Hélène Cixous and Luce Irigaray (see E. Marks and I. de Courtivron, eds., *New French Feminisms* [New York: Schocken, 1980]), and developed in other forms by American psychologists and critics (e.g., M. Belenky, B. Clinchy, N. Goldberger, and J. Tarule, *Women's Ways of Knowing* [New York: Basic, 1986]). For an interesting slant on the issue, see C. Gilligan, L. M. Brown, and A. Rogers, "Psyche Embedded," in *Studying Persons and Lives*, ed. A. L. Rabin et al. (New York: Springer, 1990). Camille Paglia reverses the valorization of "feminine" words over "masculine" vision in her provocative *Sexual Personae: Art and Decadence from Nefertiti to Emily Dickinson* (New Haven, Conn.: Yale University Press, 1990).

[103] E. F. Keller and C. R. Grontkowski, "The Mind's Eye," in Harding and Hintikka, eds. (n. 4 above), 245–81.

reappearance in unconscious forms. At the Salpêtrière, sexuality was said to be unrelated to hysteria, yet it was used in hysteria's pictorial representation. Photographs were said to provide a completely objective picture of reality, yet their subject was contrived and surfaces "touched up." Charcot's scientific inquiry into hysteria was intended to incorporate the highest forms of art, yet the result was a hybrid representation that conveyed fully neither an artist's vision nor a scientist's precision.

Freud's approach to hysteria, characterized primarily by verbal communication, had both an interpretive and a relational dimension. His awareness of his own role was inseparable from his acknowledgment of his patients' perspective. The science that Freud constructed involved the study of an individual's subjective world, with the relationship of analyst and patient as the central activity of exploration. As an objective study of the subjective self, it did not insist that knowledge is acquired only at the price of impersonality, distance, or rigid division of self and object; it held instead that reliable and authentic knowledge could be gained from the involvement of two people in a relationship.

Charcot's and Freud's models of inquiry can be fruitfully conceptualized as differing along the lines of the concepts of "static" and "dynamic" objectivity developed in recent years by Evelyn Fox Keller in her work on the philosophy of science. Keller defines the "static objectivity" that characterizes traditional scientific method as "the pursuit of knowledge that begins with the severance of subject from object." "Dynamic objectivity," by contrast, is "a pursuit of knowledge that makes use of subjective experience," in which "the struggle to disentangle self from other is itself a source of insight."[104] That subjectivity and science are connected is undeniable, according to Keller, but we operate within an ideology that obscures that connection. Ideological pressures can be revealed, Keller suggests, by examining the irrational or inconsistent elements that pervade any given scientific enterprise.

Keller has illustrated, through historical example and psychological analysis, how extrascientific forces influence the development of scientific method and knowledge. She points out that "our 'laws of nature' are more than simple expressions of the results of objective inquiry or of political and social pressures: they must also be read for their personal— and by tradition, masculine—content. [Recent sociology of science] uncovers . . . the personal investment scientists make in impersonality; the anonymity of the picture they produce is revealed as itself a kind of signature."[105] Psychoanalysis is, in Keller's terms, "a form of knowledge

[104] Keller (n. 4 above), 117.
[105] Ibid., 10. The investment in impersonality derives, in Keller's view, from the culturally and historically pervasive link between objectivity and masculinity, and the origin of this link in problems of psychological gender development.

of other persons that draws explicitly on the commonality of feelings and experience in order to enrich one's understanding of another in his or her own right."[106] Ultimately, the concept of transference, present only in rudimentary form in the *Studies*, takes the doctor-patient relationship itself as the central process to be investigated. The centrality of transference in psychoanalysis is an instance of the dynamically objective "disentangling" of which Keller speaks.

In the early case studies, Freud's understanding of his women patients, his understanding of hysteria, and his dynamically objective approach powerfully converge. If feminism, as Keller writes, "seeks to enlarge our understanding of the history, philosophy, and sociology of science through the inclusion not only of women and their actual experiences but also of those domains of human experience that have been relegated to women: namely the personal, the emotional, and the sexual,"[107] then Freud's early work develops something of a "feminist" science. Freud's first gropings toward the theory of psychoanalysis incorporated both women's actual experiences and traditionally feminine domains. Further, Freud studied "women and their actual experiences" and integrated the domains relegated to them—"namely the personal, the emotional, and the sexual"—into his psychological theory.

I want to emphasize how short-lived this early phase of Freud's work was. By 1905 he had rejected his own theory of hysteria's necessary origins in sexual trauma and accorded fantasy a central role in its psychogenesis. He had also developed his conception of the Oedipus complex through his own self-analysis, under whose long shadow the analysis of Dora was carried out. Much recent feminist criticism has drawn attention to the ways Freud imposed his theory upon the subjective reality of Dora and other patients and has drawn a picture of Freud more akin to Charcot than the one I have drawn here.[108] Yet while feminist critiques of Freud have offered a necessary corrective, an exclusive focus on the dominating aspects of Freud's treatment results in too rigid a reading of his early cases. Moreover, it misses the opportunity to see in them a way of approaching the study of subjectivity. These critiques are more fruitfully applied, I think, to Freud's "Fragment of an Analysis of a Case of Hysteria" (1905) and to his later writings on femininity.

My purpose has been to examine an earlier period in Freud's work and to describe its contrast to Charcot's work before him. It would be useful now to begin to explore the developmental history of Freud's ideas about the psychology of women. A number of questions suggest

[106] Ibid., 117.
[107] Ibid., 9.
[108] For example, Bernheimer and Kahane, eds. (n. 3 above).

themselves. Specifically, how did changes in Freud's theoretical agenda make his relationship to Dora so different from his relationship to Elisabeth von R.? More generally, what circumstances fostered his ability to listen to women and what inhibited it? How did the language Freud used to describe women change over time? A number of psychoanalysts and writers have attempted to chart the unfolding of Freud's understanding of female psychology; such efforts bode well both for the study of psychoanalytic history and for feminist rereadings of Freud's work.[109]

The same contrasts I have described between Freud's and Charcot's work, and between Freud's early and later work, on a larger scale characterize the fields of both psychoanalysis and academic psychology. Within psychoanalysis, the question of whether the discipline is an objective science or a system of interpretation—and the question of what these terms themselves mean—reemerges from time to time with great intensity. These issues have proven central to debates on object relations versus drive theory, metapsychology versus clinical theory, and hermeneutic versus empiricist perspectives and approaches.[110] Until recently, practitioners of psychoanalysis have tended to insist upon the discipline's scientific stature, while remaining relatively ambiguous in their terminology and imprecise in describing their own role in the clinical process; they have tended, in other words, to insist

---

[109] Carol Gilligan has advanced the view that Freud began to misunderstand women beginning with the case of Dora, and that this had implications for the development of his concept of the Oedipus complex (see "The Conquistador of the Dark Continent: Reflections on the Psychology of Love," *Daedalus* 113, no. 3 [1984]: 75–97, and "Oedipus and Psyche: Two Stories about Love" [paper presented at the Conference on Complex Femininity: Changing Views of Women in Psychoanalytic Thought, Philadelphia Society for Psychoanalytic Psychology, February 1987]). The latter paper compares Freud's discussion of Elisabeth von R. and Dora. Nancy Chodorow has cataloged the multiplicity of accounts Freud gives of women, including women as patients, analysts, and figures in the male psyche, in her article "Freud on Women," in *Cambridge Companion to Freud*, ed. Jerome New (Cambridge: Cambridge University Press, 1991). A fascinating exploration of the relation of Freud's own psychology to the use of words and his approach to women is found in an interview with French analyst Monique Schneider in E. H. Baruch and L. J. Serrano, *Women Analyze Women: In France, England, and the United States* (New York: New York University Press, 1988). Elisabeth Young-Bruehl, in *Anna Freud: A Biography* (New York: Summit, 1988), points to the central role that Freud's analysis of his daughter Anna played in his later work on femininity.

[110] P. Buckley, ed., *Essential Papers on Object Relations* (New York: New York University Press, 1986); N. J. Chodorow, "Relational Individualism: The Mediation of Self through Psychoanalysis," in *Reconstructing Individualism: Autonomy, Individualism, and the Self in Western Thought*, ed. T. Heller, M. Sosna, and D. Wellbery (Stanford, Calif.: Stanford University Press, 1986); R. Schafer, *A New Language for Psychoanalysis* (New Haven, Conn.: Yale University Press, 1976); M. Gill, "The Point of View of Psychoanalysis: Energy Discharge or Person?" *Psychoanalysis and Contemporary Thought* 6, no. 4 (1983): 523–51; R. Wallerstein, "Psychoanalysis, Psychoanalytic Science, and Psychoanalytic Research—1986," *Journal of the American Psychoanalytic Association* 36, no. 1 (1988): 3–30.

on the discipline's "statically objective" legitimacy at the expense of its "dynamically objective" promise.[111]

In academic psychology there has been a historical tendency to minimize or refrain from investigating the effects of researchers on the researched. Research psychologists traditionally have viewed themselves as investigators of brute facts and have conceptualized methodological rigor as inhering in the removal of their own effects, as if such a thing were possible. More recently, it has become clearer that all research on fellow humans involves both interpretation and relationship, however implicit. Thus, a more accurate view would accept the researcher's influence as inevitable and demand honesty about its effects. Such honesty involves more than simply giving a short paragraph about the limitations of a study; it demands a richer inquiry into and description of one's effects. A persuasive demonstration of how one came to a given view must not obscure one's own emotional impetus; rather it should explore both the insights and distortions that that impetus has fueled. The possibility of grappling with questions of interpretation has been constricted by the empiricist values of the field, and psychology has lagged behind other social sciences in developing self-consciousness about its own enterprise.[112] Psychologists have seldom reflected critically on the philosophical and historical origins of their own practices. Too often, their conventional methods of inquiry have actually militated against historical reflection, because it seems to threaten the timelessness and universality of their findings.

Fortunately, these issues are slowly moving to the forefront of debate within psychology and psychoanalysis,[113] and both fields have begun to explore more fully what it means to be a science and what it means to be objective. Objectivity, as Keller defines it, is "the pursuit of a maximally authentic, and hence, maximally reliable, understanding of the world around oneself."[114] Charcot and Freud grappled with the problem of

[111] Spence (n. 101 above) offers a fuller description of this problem in *The Freudian Metaphor*, esp. 71–159.

[112] For a refreshing counterexample, see J. Haaken, "Field Dependence Research: A Historical Analysis of a Psychological Construct," *Signs: Journal of Women in Culture and Society* 13, no. 2 (Winter 1988): 311–30.

[113] Examples in the psychological literature include M. J. Packer, "Hermeneutic Inquiry in the Study of Human Conduct," *American Psychologist* 40, no. 10 (October 1985): 1081–93, esp. 1087; E. E. Jones and A. Thorne, "The Rediscovery of the Subject: Intercultural Approaches to Clinical Assessment," *Journal of Consulting and Clinical Psychology* 55, no. 4 (August 1987): 488–95; L. Brown, M. Tappan, C. Gilligan, B. Miller, and D. Argyris, "Reading for Self and Moral Voice: A Method of Interpreting Narratives of Real-Life Moral Conflict and Choice," in *Entering the Circle: Hermeneutic Investigations in Psychology*, ed. M. J. Packer and R. Addison (Albany: SUNY Press, 1989). The articles cited in n. 110 above provide examples of a similar trend in psychoanalytic writings.

[114] Keller (n. 4 above), 116.

understanding hysteria objectively, and came up with different solutions. To the extent that we can be flexible in our development of methods appropriate to what we study, and aware of the unwitting extrascientific considerations that color our theories and approaches, we will have done what we can to learn from their examples.

Department of Psychology
University of California, Berkeley

Field Dependence Research: A Historical Analysis of a Psychological Construct

Janice Haaken

Analyses of cultural and political bias in social science inquiry can tell us not only about the limits of our work but also about competing visions of human capabilities and society that underlie theory and research. In psychology, such analyses are often constrained by conceptions of what constitutes ideal social scientific science. The term "bias" carries a pejorative meaning—as a failure to maintain an objective, scientific stance—and its presence is viewed primarily as a methodological problem. The aim in mainstream psychology is to adopt methodological procedures that enable researchers to overcome sources of bias and to achieve impartial, value-neutral representations of reality. Challenges to this ideal that come from the study of the sociology of knowledge, for example, that knowledge is tied to specific social interests and ideologies and to historically problematic questions, have had relatively little impact on psychological inquiry. However, in recent years, a still small group of psychologists is cultivating an interest in the social and historical basis of psychological knowledge.[1]

I would like to thank Johanna Brenner, Norman Diamond, Nona Glazer, Cathleen Smith, and the readers for *Signs* for their helpful comments on earlier drafts of this manuscript.

[1] A. R. Buss, "The Emerging Field of the Sociology of Knowledge," in *Psychology in Social Context*, by A. R. Buss (New York: Irvington Publishers, 1979), 1–24.

[*Signs: Journal of Women in Culture and Society* 1988, vol. 13, no. 2]

I focus here on Herman Witkin. Key historical and social influences shaped Witkin's research on sex differences in field dependence-independence and shaped the extent to which it has been absorbed into psychology's corpus. Witkin was the first researcher to extend the study of psychological sex differences into the area of human perception. His findings, beginning in the late 1940s, that women were more field dependent than men—that is, they were more dependent on the external stimulus field in interpreting visual stimuli—are considered by many contemporary psychologists to be among the most stable findings concerning psychological sex differences in adulthood.[2] Witkin's field dependence-independence work is an attempt to use experimental methods to legitimize, on scientific grounds, the prevailing psychoanalytic theory of his time. By subjecting that theory to experimental verification, Witkin's research seemed to offer more definitive evidence of psychoanalytic ideas concerning gender development than the existing impression-based clinical accounts could offer.

My analysis, then, focuses on experimental psychology and how social and historical developments have influenced the construction of experimental problems, here, in particular, the study of gender and perceptual abilities. I offer Witkin's work—which began in the 1940s and extended over a period of over thirty years—as a case study in the social formation of a construct and its acceptance among professionals in psychology. Witkin's study of the role of context in perceptual abilities illustrates not only the limitations of experimental research in the behavioral sciences but also the ways in which research method becomes reified by its own findings. For instance, "decontextualization," to field-dependence theorists, means the perceptual ability to focus on a discrete stimulus while overcoming or ignoring the background context. I use the term to describe this tendency in positivist research at large, and I discuss the field-dependence literature as an example of the positivist rendering of a construct. To me, decontextualization means breaking down social reality into small units and focusing on a limited set of discrete interactions while ignoring the social context. It is what Parlee calls "context stripping."[3] That is, positivist research often omits a broad-based view of how everyday social experience influences the phenomenon under investigation. Such research typically lacks an analysis of how collective experiences (e.g., historical, ideological, and economic) shape individual experience—including the formation of research questions and constructs by scientists.

Ruth Bleier points out that the affinity for positivism in the social sciences has been particularly pronounced in psychology, where feminist

---

[2] E. Maccoby and L. Jacklin, *The Psychology of Sex Differences* (Stanford, Calif.: Stanford University Press, 1974), 351; C. Tavris and C. Offir, *The Longest War: Sex Differences in Perspective* (New York: Harcourt Brace Jovanovich, 1984).

[3] Mary Brown Parlee, "Psychology and Women," *Signs: Journal of Women in Culture and Society* 5, no. 1 (1979): 121–33, esp. 131.

scholarship and sociology of knowledge debates have had minimal impact.[4] In part, this emphasis on decontextualization is due to psychology's long-standing epistemological commitment to the experimental method, "directed toward finding and elucidating universal *laws* of human behavior by lifting behaviors out of the context within which they occur and subjecting them to scrutiny under 'controlled' laboratory conditions."[5]

I make a distinction here between the objectification of human experience that is present in all social science constructs and reification. Constructs involve more than simply naming phenomena; they point to a set of connections or underlying relationships. The construct of field dependence, for example, suggests a pattern that characterizes the organization of perceptual experiences and that connects the inner world and outer reality. The most useful constructs are those guided by a theoretical framework that explains how and why particular phenomena are related. What is interesting about Witkin's field-dependence construct is that it is more than a simple typology; it is guided by a body of theory that is also anchored in concrete empirical observations.

Reification is closely related to the problem of ideological and social domination in science. By approaching scientific constructs as metaphor, some have attempted to "de-reify" science by emphasizing the forms of social domination that underlie claims of scientific neutrality.[6] Constructs that are dissociated from the social reality that informs them can become reified in ongoing theoretical usage. In Witkin's case, key historical and ideological factors influenced his interest and interpretations of perceptual phenomena, which came to be understood as gender based.

The historical context

The term "field dependence-independence," introduced into psychology by Witkin in 1954, achieved wide currency in subsequent years. Based on a series of experiments in visual perception reported first by Witkin and Solomon Asch,[7] the construct referred to a subject's ability to separate a stimulus from its embedding context. Operationally, one of the main procedures involved placing subjects in a darkened room and asking them to place a luminous rod, suspended within a tilted frame, into a vertical

---

[4] Ruth Bleier, *Science and Gender* (New York: Pergamon Press, 1984), 68–69.

[5] Ibid., 69.

[6] See ibid.; Lynda Birke, *Women, Feminism and Biology* (New York: Methuen, 1986); Elizabeth Fee, "Women's Nature and Scientific Objectivity," in *Woman's Nature: Rationalizations of Inequality,* ed. M. Lowe and R. Hubbard (New York: Pergamon Press, 1983).

[7] H. A. Witkin and S. E. Asch, "Studies in Space Orientation, Part III: Perception of the Upright in the Absence of a Visual Field," *Journal of Experimental Psychology* 38 (December 1948): 603–14.

position. Subjects who did not or were unable to place the rod in a vertical position, relying more on the frame than on their own bodily and postural cues in positioning the rod, were labeled "field dependent." Witkin concluded that field dependence indicated a global, less differentiated mode of perception, whereas field independence was a more analytical approach that overcame misleading background cues in the stimulus field. Most significant was the apparent difference between men and women, with women tending to be significantly more field dependent than men.[8]

Considerable controversy surrounds Witkin's claim that field dependence is related to a larger constellation of personality attributes and analytical abilities.[9] Personality traits such as passivity, dependence, and conformity have been linked to field dependence as a perceptual style.[10] The empirical basis of these links has been recently reexamined by researchers in the psychology of women.[11] Most of the controversy focuses on the social significance of small but statistically significant sex differences and on Witkin's claims of a relationship between spatial abilities and other personality attributes and analytical abilities. The critiques of his work are limited, for the most part, to methodological problems, for example, construct validity and generalization from specific findings. Although Helen Block Lewis, a coinvestigator of Witkin's, has offered a feminist interpretation of sex differences in perception, that is, social explanations for women's greater field dependence,[12] she does not challenge the premises of Witkin's research nor his specific findings.[13]

[8] H. A. Witkin, "Sex Differences in Perception," *Transactions of New York Academy of Science* 12, no. 1 (November 1949): 25; H. A. Witkin, H. B. Lewis, M. Hertzman, K. Machover, P. B. Meissner, and S. Wagner, *Personality through Perception* (New York: John Wiley & Sons, 1954), 154.

[9] Maccoby and Jacklin, 104; J. Sherman, *Sex-related Cognitive Differences* (Springfield, Ill.: C. C. Thomas, 1978).

[10] H. Young, "A Test of Witkin's Field-Dependence Hypothesis," *Journal of Abnormal Social Psychology* 59 (September 1959): 188–92; Witkin et al., *Psychological Differentiation* (New York: John Wiley and Sons, 1962); C. Pitblado, "Orientation Bias in the Rod-and-Frame Test," *Perceptual and Motor Skills* 44 (June 1977): 891–900.

[11] Maccoby and Jacklin, 129; J. Levy, "Yes, Virginia, There Is a Difference: Sex Differences in Human Brain Assymetry and in Psychology," *L.S.B. Leakey Foundation News* 20 (Fall 1981): 3, 12–13.

[12] Helen B. Lewis, *Psychic War in Men and Women* (New York: New York University Press, 1976).

[13] Ibid. Lewis places the problem of sex roles and sex differences in psychological differentiation in the context of changing modes of production. She argues that capitalism promotes the division between an affective, private world of family life where dependency needs are permissably gratified and an objectified, exploitive world of work. The former world, with which women are primarily identified, propels women toward field dependence; the latter world, into which men are more consistently drawn, promotes field independence. Lewis also presents a persuasive analysis of the interdependence of internal processes, i.e., perceptual, cognitive, and emotional functioning, on the one hand, and internal and external reality, on the other. But she overstates the congruities within and between these various

Gender emerged as a specific theme of Witkin's research during the late 1940s and 1950s, but his early perceptual research did not explicitly focus on sex differences. His early studies, undertaken in 1942 and supported by a grant from the Civil Aeronautics Administration, were designed to identify problems of spatial orientation and visual perception in the training of airplane pilots. Thus, there was a practical aim relevant to the war effort that guided these early studies. Witkin and coinvestigator Asch shared a philosophical interest, however, in the dependency of the "ego" or "self" on the perceptual field. They were interested in challenging the notion that the self was an autonomous agent, inherently in opposition to the social world. In summarizing, retrospectively, the philosophical intent behind the early perceptual research, Asch states: "The usual way of explaining the limited operation of self-centeredness is to refer to the restrictions imposed by social demands or to the curbing of the ego-centrism of each by the ego-centrism of all. We have attempted to show that *the ego is not fundamentally ego-centered.* The ego is not dedicated solely to its own enhancement. It needs and wants to be concerned with its surroundings, to bind itself to others, and to work with them."[14]

While the term "field dependence" was not introduced into the literature until 1954, Asch's description of this perceptual phenomenon suggests that, in the early research, a positive value was placed on "field dependence" or, in Asch's terms, field "relatedness." However, during the postwar years, Witkin moved away from Asch in his theoretical interests, and his interpretations of perceptual phenomena took on a more conservative cast than those of Asch. Witkin turned away from the issue of the field's problematic nature and from the Gestalt emphasis on general human tendencies to *depend* on the field to focus instead on personality factors and individual differences in the ability to overcome the field and to perceive the "upright position."

In this new postwar emphasis on personality factors in perception, gender emerged as a central theme in Witkin's research. In the 1947–53 studies, reported in detail in *Personality through Perception*, Witkin pursued the relationship between personality differences and perceptual abilities. Among other research questions, he asked: "In what ways do men and women differ in perception, and are those differences related to differences in personality? Are the perceptual characteristics of women and men related to personality characteristics more commonly found within each

---

dimensions of experience. It is important to recognize differentiating tendencies in male and female personality development which correspond to the structure of the social world without overstating or reifying these tendencies. Women are not wholly dependent, along all dimensions of experience, nor are men wholly independent.

[14] S. E. Asch, *Social Psychology* (New York: Prentice-Hall, Inc., 1952), 320.

sex? Are there sex differences in perception at all ages or are these differences first manifested at a particular stage of development?"[15]

Witkin's new focus on sex differences during the late 1940s and 1950s took place during an important watershed in American history, one which shaped the content and growing influence of his work. During World War II, prior to Witkin's research on sex differences, large numbers of married women entered the American labor force. In 1943, the War Manpower Commission campaigned to draw women into traditionally male occupations such as welding, riveting, inspecting, and other industrial work.[16] Researchers and policymakers agreed that, when services such as child care were provided, women were as effective in these jobs as men.[17] But even though the war effort redefined and expanded job opportunities for women, propaganda all throughout World War II emphasized that women were working only temporarily, until the war was won, after which a more natural division of labor between the sexes would be restored.[18]

This belief in natural sex differences became increasingly important in the United States in the postwar period as public support for women in the work force shifted to support for the "domestic mystique."[19] As men returned from the war to resume their jobs and women workers were displaced, a renewed emphasis on enduring and essential differences between the sexes appeared in popular literature.[20] The contradiction between the belief in biological sex difference and the presence of women in traditionally men's jobs during the war could be reconciled with the caveat that, though one might learn to overcome natural differences, those differences were deeply fixed and enduring. This conflict—between the recognition of variability in women's roles and the assertion of polarized natural differences between men and women—also appears in Witkin's work.

Witkin was the first investigator to study sex differences in perception, emphasizing "the importance of knowing about sex differences in this area."[21] Though his initial research on sex differences in perception in 1949 was limited to technical aspects of perception, his results nonetheless provided a scientific rationale for the exclusion of women from industrial

[15] Witkin et al., 12.
[16] R. Baxandall, L. Gordon, and S. Riverby, *America's Working Women* (New York: Vintage Books, 1976), 284.
[17] Ibid., 291.
[18] K. Anderson, *Wartime Women: Sex Roles, Family Relations and the Status of Women during World War II* (Westport, Conn.: Greenwood Press, 1981), 59, 161; S. M. Hartmann, *The Home Front and Beyond: American Women in the 1940s* (Boston: Twayne Press, 1982), 23.
[19] B. Friedan, *The Feminine Mystique* (New York: W. W. Norton & Co., 1963), 44.
[20] B. Ehrenreich and D. English, *For Her Own Good* (New York: Doubleday & Co., 1978), 220–21; Hartmann, 169.
[21] Witkin (n. 8 above), 25.

jobs after the war because perceptual abilities are closely related to technical job skills.

Witkin did not necessarily condone this social application of field-dependence research, however. Coinvestigator Lewis maintains that Witkin did not believe initially that males and females would differ significantly in their performance.[22] She says that she and other members of the research team were concerned about the possible political uses of their findings, fearful of reporting sex differences that could be used politically against women in the postwar period. Witkin's emphasis on learned behavior and adaptation in his initial reporting of sex differences in 1949 may have been a concession to their concerns: "With continued testing under this condition, however, women became adapted to the unstable field and, in time, were able to do considerably better. Thus, when confronted with unstable surroundings, women are initially made much more unsteady than men, although they are eventually able to come to terms with this instability."[23]

In reporting findings of the studies undertaken from 1947 to 1953, Witkin noted women's capacity for adaptation, but the central theoretical focus was on passive submission and active coping as bipolar traits (i.e., the more the presence of one tendency, the less the capacity for the opposing tendency) associated with sex differences. Active coping, the central personality characteristic associated with males, meant the ability to function with "relatively little support from the environment."[24] Witkin concluded that "women, more often than men, passively accept a new visual framework 'as is,' without any effort or active analysis of it"[25] and, at the same time, women tend to give more variable performances than do men under different conditions.[26]

More recently, researchers have countered that Witkin's method resulted in overstating the frequency of field dependence by labeling as field dependent both those persons who respond consistently to the frame as a cue and those who respond inconsistently.[27] Some critics of trait theories have argued that individuals who are highly variable in their responses may have a "highly refined discriminative facility" in the ability to respond to subtle differences in situations.[28] These findings suggest that women's variable responses could have been interpreted differently by Witkin,

[22] H. B. Lewis, personal communication, May 1984.

[23] Witkin, 25.

[24] Witkin et al. (n. 8 above), 467.

[25] Ibid., 482.

[26] Ibid., 465.

[27] H. Nyborg and B. Isaksen, "A Method for Analyzing Performance in the Rod-and-Frame Test," *Scandinavian Journal of Psychology* 15, no. 2 (1974): 124–26.

[28] D. Bem and A. Allen, "On Predicting Some of the People Some of the Time: The Search for Cross-situational Consistencies in Behavior," *Psychological Review* 81 (November 1974): 517.

who concluded that "as a general rule" women are more field dependent than men.

I would suggest that Witkin overinterpreted his findings in a direction that was consistent with prevailing stereotypes of women during a postwar shift in ideas about essential differences between the sexes. Congruent with this shift, Witkin began to emphasize "enduring sets" (personality traits) in the structuring of perceptual tasks in contrast to the work of previous Gestalt theorists who stressed situational or transitory factors. Men, according to Witkin, consistently and enduringly exert control over the perceptual field, whereas women respond in a more variable and task-dependent way and so must have greater field dependence than men.[29] While Witkin concluded that "awareness of the body as a separate entity, independent of the surroundings, has progressed further in men than women," he noted that "when the situation makes it easy or necessary to utilize bodily experiences in performing the required task, they (women) are able to do so about as effectively as men."[30] In other words, men more readily drew on internal bodily cues to orient themselves in a destabilizing perceptual situation, but women could also draw on bodily cues when the task *required* them to do so. Historical disjunctures in what was "required" of women by social organizations, then, were reconciled with presumed substrative differences between the sexes.

The social assumptions that were embedded in Witkin's research are also evident in the naming of the phenomenon. In a society that valued independence and individual autonomy, field dependence had negative connotations. The phrase "inability to separate a stimulus from its embedding context" could have been interpreted positively to mean that women have greater sensitivity to the embedding context as they make judgments about a stimulus. During the postwar years, as women's productive capabilities were devalued and as exaggerated sex roles gained importance, field independence emerged as a masculine virtue, a decisively more desirable trait than field dependence. Then, in the 1970s, when the values attached to gender differences were called into question by feminists, Witkin began to stress the positive capabilities associated with field dependence, that is, that field-dependent individuals have a greater capacity for interpreting social cues than do field-independent individuals.[31]

The ideological context of Witkin's research extended, too, to Witkin's Gestalt predecessors, who fled Germany to escape political persecution and derived their research questions from their attempts to understand the rise of authoritarianism. In contrast, American psychologists pursued re-

---

[29] Witkin et al., 465.

[30] Ibid., 169, 171.

[31] H. A. Witkin, D. R. Goodenough, and P. K. Oltman, "Psychological Differentiation: Current Status," *Journal of Personality and Social Psychology* 37 (July 1979): 1127–45.

search problems related to U.S. military activity during and after World War II.[32] Perceptual research throughout the war was tied to military needs, for example, to problems of detecting camouflage or evaluating a terrain upon which a landing must be made.[33] During the postwar years, Witkin continued his research with funding from the Office of Naval Research. Like so many psychologists whose research activities were sponsored by military-related programs,[34] Witkin was influenced by program policies that encouraged quantitative, clinically based research and refinement of assessment tools. The military funded research, for instance, to develop scales for selecting recruits for specific kinds of military training.[35] The emphasis on testing and measurement gave psychology greater scientific and social legitimacy as a part of the effort to prepare the armed forces for the defense of American interests abroad and for maintaining peace at home.

While psychologists may not have endorsed these applications of testing, there was a heady confidence after the war in the predictive power and social utility of psychological tests. As Zigler noted in his 1963 review of Witkin's research, the promise was great: "If valid, such a typology (field dependence/independence) would be of great value. It would be marvelously efficient to administer a few simple perceptual tests and then be able to predict with a respectable degree of confidence, problem-solving behavior, impulse control, major psychological defenses and cognitive controls, activity level, attitudes towards and interactions with other persons, as well as the types of pathology to which [an individual] is susceptible."[36]

Governmental funding of training programs and research did not dictate specific research findings, but it did restrict the kinds of questions that could be pursued and the scope of the inquiry, that is, how much social reality could be called into question. Even though Witkin expanded the focus of his early research on visual perception to include a broader range of psychological factors, he was predominantly concerned with the organization of the internal psychological world. While recognizing the importance of the content of human experience as a source of variance within his typological groups—what people "wanted, were in conflict about, became angry over, believed in, as well as the life themes that ran through their histories"[37]—he never focused on this as important to his research in-

[32] D. Bernstein and M. Nietzel, *Introduction to Clinical Psychology* (New York: McGraw-Hill Book Co., 1980), 50–51.

[33] G. Murphy, "Introduction," in Witkin et al., *Personality through Perception* (n. 8 above), xvii.

[34] Birke (n. 6 above), 91–92.

[35] Bernstein and Nietzel, 50–51.

[36] Edward Zigler, "A Measure in Search of a Theory?" *Contemporary Psychology* 8 (1963): 133.

[37] Witkin et al., *Personality through Perception*, 8.

terests. This dissociation of personality structure from the content of lived experience contributed to the reification of both the field dependence-independence construct and psychological sex differences because the dissociation precludes recognition of the active, motivated subject and the dynamic tension between an inner world and an outer reality.

In a general way, Witkin's studies were concerned with problems of orientation and control in a disorienting world. In the experimental setting, the extent to which people could overcome the disorientation created by the tilted field—remaining faithful to internal cues that determined the upright position—was of central importance. The experiment itself, then, is a metaphor for the disorientation of the postwar period—a disorientation or confusion experienced with particular acuity by the socialists and left-wing intellectuals with whom Witkin associated.

A number of historians have described the public's preoccupation with stability following the destabilizing decades of the Depression and World War II.[38] But the combined impact of the Holocaust and Hiroshima created a particular despair and confusion for radicals as the political involvement of the Left declined.[39] Dorothy Dinnerstein, who worked closely with members of Witkin's research group, described it as a state of moral shock and "anesthesia" that radicals of her generation experienced after the war and into the 1950s. Many withdrew from large-scale social concerns and turned to more narrowly defined, psychological realities. According to Dinnerstein, "in these people, whose adolescence and youth had spanned the mid-thirties to mid-forties, capacities for connectedness—which in the preceding period had embraced historic considerations and a temporally and spatially extended human scene—were now focused on a world recreated in miniature."[40]

Witkin's research emphasized that it was possible to assert individual control over a confusing world. The field-independent person accomplished this by not "yielding" to distracting and regressive external cues. Witkin's interest in the individual's resources, and the implicit devaluing of relatedness, represented a very different stance from Asch's more pessimistic view of the possibilities for individual control over a disorienting world. Asch believed that the "contradictory and threatening world" in which people find themselves "takes a toll on the individual's very ability to establish and maintain contact with reality."[41]

[38] See discussion of this theme in Linda Gordon, *Woman's Body, Woman's Right* (New York: Penguin Books, 1977), 356–62; Stuart Ewen, *Captains of Consciousness* (New York: McGraw-Hill Book Co., 1976), 206; Stanley Aronowitz, *False Promises* (New York: McGraw-Hill Book Co., 1973), chap. 7.

[39] Christopher Lasch, *The Minimal Self* (New York: W. W. Norton & Co., 1984), chap. 7.

[40] Dorothy Dinnerstein, *The Mermaid and the Minotaur* (New York: Harper & Row, 1976), 258–62, esp. 261.

[41] Asch (n. 14 above), 604.

In contrast to Witkin, Asch saw the experiments as a metaphor for the individual's struggles in the social world.

Gestalt influences

Asch maintained his intellectual and political commitment to those issues that had informed and motivated the research base from which Witkin's work diverged. While Witkin's Gestalt predecessors did not focus on sex differences, their work suggests an interpretation of field dependence that emphasizes the social relational basis of perception.

Max Wertheimer, the intellectual leader of the German Gestalt movement, whose work guided Witkin's initial thinking, also conducted military-sponsored research early in his career. During World War I, his research in Germany focused on listening devices for submarines and harbor fortifications.[42] Unlike Witkin, whose research ties to the military continued harmoniously beyond the war years, Wertheimer had to carry on his research in a country suffering from postwar economic and political instability. Indeed, Wertheimer and Wolfgang Köhler, two of the major Gestalt theorists, came into growing conflict with the Nazi government and fled to the United States during the 1930s.[43]

Wertheimer's early experimental interest in "apparent motion" or illusions of movement—beginning in 1912—was congruent with his critique of industrial society. He was deeply concerned about prevailing notions of the nature and possibilities of human freedom and, in particular, about liberal thinkers who equated rapid change with progress and confused "freedom of business enterprise" with "real mutual freedom."[44] In the classic mirror experiment on which Witkin's work was based, Wertheimer concluded that people tended initially to "perceive the scene as tilted, but with continued inspection came gradually to regard it as upright and to see everything within it as normal."[45] This early perceptual research, then, focused on problematic aspects of perception, specifically the tendency to adapt to or perceive as "normal" a skewed world.

As important figures in left-wing German academia, Wertheimer and Kohler were aware of the politically conservative implications of restricting psychological research to observable phenomena.[46] Their own research

---

[42] Duane Schultz, *A History of Modern Psychology* (New York: Academic Press, 1969), 245.

[43] Ibid.

[44] M. Wertheimer, "On the Concept of Democracy" (1937), in *Documents of Gestalt Psychology*, ed. M. Henle (Berkeley: University of California Press, 1961), 50.

[45] Witkin et al., *Personality through Perception* (n. 8 above), 4.

[46] M. Leichtman, "Gestalt Theory and the Revolt against Positivism," in Buss, ed. (n. 1 above), 59.

examined the human capabilities that were restricted or diminished under particular social conditions. The capacity of human beings to recover meaning and coherence in a fragmenting, destabilizing environment was central to their philosophical and experimental interests. Human beings, they claimed, are bound by the requirements of existing conditions yet are capable of envisioning new possibilities and new meanings within a given reality.[47]

While he was influenced directly by Wertheimer's work on organizing factors in perception, Witkin was part of the "New Look" movement in experimental psychology. This approach attempted to demonstrate the importance of personality factors and unconscious processes in structuring the perceptual field.[48] Witkin was critical of the Gestalt theorists' exclusive concern with field factors and their neglect of developmental and motivational processes in structuring perception. "The individual is not 'subservient' to the field to the extent conceived in Gestalt theory; he is not a passive mirror-like recorder upon whom the field impresses itself, but an active agent who contributes to the progress and outcome of the act of perceiving."[49]

Witkin's conception of the self as active agent was an important corrective to theoretical tendencies within psychology to view humans as entirely governed by situational factors. But he attempted to resolve the conflict between subjective and objective factors by turning to psychoanalytic theory and its emphasis on the individual and early childhood as the primary context for understanding subjective experience. Indeed, his conception of the perceptual field was a narrowly defined configuration of stimuli, dissociated from social meaning.

While Witkin moved toward psychoanalysis in the 1950s, focusing on the primacy of the internal world in structuring outer reality, his early coinvestigator, Solomon Asch, pursued the relationship between independence, conformity, and the social world. Asch argued that relations with others are the basis of ego development and independence, not an inherent constraint on these capacities. This was the premise behind his critiques of classical psychoanalysis—which posited a fundamental opposition between the individual and society—and of bourgeois individualism and capitalism as an economic system.[50]

---

[47] See M. Wertheimer, "Some Problems in the Theory of Ethics" (1935), in Henle, ed. (n. 44 above), 39; and "On the Concept of Democracy," 51; W. Köhler, *The Place of Value in a World of Facts* (New York: Liveright Publishing Corp., 1938), 40.

[48] D. Goodenough, "History of the Field Dependence Construct," in *Field Dependence in Psychological Theory, Research and Application*, ed. M. Bertini, L. Pizzamiglio, and S. Wagner (Hillsdale, N.J.: Lawrence Erlbaum Associates, 1986), 6.

[49] Witkin et al., *Personality through Perception*, 497.

[50] Asch (n. 14 above), 313–16.

In discussing the social basis of psychological phenomena, Asch used examples from perceptual research to explain how people respond defensively to social conflict. For example, he pointed out that some individuals respond to social movements that call for equality (e.g., the early civil rights movement) with "efforts to keep parts of the field out of awareness or out of focus." Other individuals withdraw altogether from social conflict, reasserting conservative views of the past in order to "maintain clear lines in the field," avoiding "the danger of disorientation by clinging to the frame of reference [they] happen to have and resisting any change."[51]

Asch stressed the possibilities for human resistance to the prevailing socially constructed field, asserting that psychology "has almost exclusively stressed the slavish submission of individuals to group forces, has neglected to inquire into their possibilities for independence and for productive relations with the human environment, and has virtually denied the capacity of men under certain conditions to rise above group passion and prejudice."[52] If individualism meant that self-realization was achieved in contradistinction and opposition to the group, then, alternately, to "submerge" oneself in the group was to regress. In challenging a view of independence and conformity based on fear of group forces, Asch focused on social relational processes, emphasizing the importance of allies in resisting group pressures. The solitary individual was more likely than the social one to yield to an "oppressive majority."[53] Asch's work suggests that the individual is most vulnerable to persuasion when her or his independence is based on social isolation. Because we are by nature social beings, true autonomy and independence can be sustained only in a social context that supports and nurtures those capacities.

Witkin's asocial conception of field independence is in sharp contrast to the concepts of the individual's relationship to social context that were held by his Gestalt predecessors and his early coinvestigator. For Witkin, field independence became a stable, cross-situational human trait, the result of a psychology that had itself dissociated from the real world of political struggle. Asch's critical analysis of social psychology could have provided a basis for interpretations of sex differences in field-dependence research that challenged, rather than reinforced, normative assumptions about gender and dependence. One implication of Asch's analysis, for instance, is that field independence is not so much a masculine trait as it is a masculine illusion. Contemporary feminist psychoanalytic theorists observe that men often experience dependency longings as frightening and overwhelming

[51] Ibid., 604–5.
[52] S. E. Asch, "Group Pressure and Modification of Judgements" (1951), in Henle, ed. (n. 44 above), 233.
[53] Ibid., 213.

and, consequently, develop defensively a kind of pseudo-independence based on maintaining emotional distance from others.[54]

Psychoanalytic theory and the research field

The studies undertaken by Witkin from 1947 to 1953 were ambitious. In his theoretical formulations, Witkin combined psychoanalytic assumptions about motivational processes and Gestalt ideas about perceptual organization. He attempted to demonstrate the consistency of human perception and that personality dynamics determined perceptions of physical properties of the world just as they determined social situations.[55] Hence, he turned to the concept of differentiation to formulate a metapsychological bridge from Gestalt theory to psychoanalytic theory.[56]

Psychoanalytic theory posited that human development is a process of differentiation. According to Freud, the human infant exists in an undifferentiated state in which no boundaries are experienced between the self and others, between inner and outer reality.[57] External stimuli are assimilated into the internal rhythms of the infant's world. This is the stage of primary narcissism during which the infant is one with the object of its dependency. As the infant develops the conceptual capacity to differentiate between "me" and "not me," she or he experiences the ontological anxiety associated with separateness. This experience of anxiety stimulates ego development, however, as the child progressively internalizes the regulatory functions of caretakers. The ego emerges as an integrative, self-regulating capacity within the self.

For Witkin, field-independence experiments provided operational criteria for assessing ego strength. To make this link, subjects' scores on spatial orientation tasks were correlated with various measures of personality organization. The latter included projective tests (Rorschach and Thematic Apperception Test) and ratings based on clinical interviews.

The reliance on internal bodily cues in overcoming a distorted perceptual field indicated highly differentiated body image and ego boundaries. Joined to this conception of ego boundaries was Witkin's emphasis on the capacity for regression, defined as the ability to defend against distracting external and internal stimuli.

[54] See Nancy Chodorow, *The Reproduction of Mothering* (Berkeley: University of California Press, 1978); and Dinnerstein.

[55] Witkin et al., *Personality through Perception*, 502.

[56] I have limited the scope of my treatment of psychoanalysis since the social history of psychoanalysis has been more extensively documented and discussed than that of Gestalt theory.

[57] S. Freud, "On Narcissism: An Introduction," in *Standard Edition* (1914; 1937), 14:67–102; and *New Introductory Lectures on Psychoanalysis* (New York: W. W. Norton & Co., 1933), 93.

Witkin's conception of field independence had specific political implications. Field independence was presented as the higher form of development, indicating higher levels of differentiation between self and environment. Independence represented a reliance on "internal frames of reference" and a concomitant freedom from environmental influence. Field-dependent people, in contrast, "tend to be submissive to authority, to require environmental support, to deny inner events—a mechanism of defense especially characteristic of children—to have difficulty in impulse control and to make childish drawings of the human figure. The presence of such characteristics seems to suggest an 'arrest' in progress toward emotional maturity."[58]

In a period of repressive anticommunism, Witkin could argue to a receptive audience that it was more mature to be self-reliant and emotionally distant from the group. Of course, defending independent thought was an important emphasis of academics and intellectuals during the McCarthy era, particularly for the Leftists with whom Witkin associated. But Witkin's emphasis on independence as an individual trait and his assumption that the individual and the collective were inherent opposites made it possible for his work to be easily assimilated into conventional thought.

It was in this context, then, that Witkin's clinical data were collected. Inconsistencies and overinterpreted materials are evident in his psychoanalytically derived clinical data, that is, responses to projective tests and interview questions. The assumptions embedded in the research procedures, as well as the complexity of the phenomena under investigation, are especially apparent in the clinical data. They are more effectively concealed in the scientific or experimental data and in Witkin's final conclusions. The clinical data, by their phenomenological nature, offer fuller descriptive accounts of human experience than do the scientific data and so offer more opportunity to identify biases in clinical interpretation.

One area of ambiguity in Witkin's clinical data concerns the defensive nature of field independence. The case histories reported in 1954 suggest that field-independent subjects exhibited no less conflict in relation to dependency issues than did field-dependent subjects.[59] The primary difference was in the capacity for repression, mastery, and control. Outer reality was treated by Witkin as a projective field, that is, as a vehicle for the expression of internal conflict rather than as a source of such conflict for both independent and dependent subjects. Witkin did not ask what about the nature of the social world contributed to the apparent pervasiveness of dependence-independence conflicts.

Witkin's interpretation of his clinical data was also influenced by what

[58] Witkin et al., *Personality through Perception* (n. 8 above), 470.
[59] Ibid., 312–24.

we now see as problematic views of gender. Accepting the psychoanalytic account of gender development current in the 1950s, Witkin interpreted male and female strivings differently. In the clinical examples Witkin published, the field-independent female subject's attempts at control were described less favorably than those of her male counterpart. While the field-independent male was able to "maintain integration and control while undergoing great struggles,"[60] the field-independent female was described as self-assured, narcissistic, with "sadistic tendencies—especially toward men."[61] She took "considerable pleasure in exerting her power" while being "not at all aware of how deeply frightened she is of the 'surrender' of power which accepting a man represented to her."[62] The female field-dependent subject exhibited conflicts similar to those shown by males, but she defended herself against them less effectively: "Her penis envy seems only to increase her sexual confusion and guilt." Responses to Thematic Apperception Test (TAT) cards revealed that "the sexual scene was conceived of in terms of rape and death." The response to another TAT card: "The wife feels immobilized and must accept punishment, which, in this scene, is a form of blackmail."[63]

Once again, the outer world is conceived of largely as a projective field. Witkin did acknowledge the influence of socially constructed "sexual roles" in the acquisition of field dependence, concluding that "the more protected existence that is socially acceptable for women obviously places fewer demands on their functioning."[64] A more plausible interpretation of the clinical accounts described above would be that the women felt victimized, not protected, by men.

While acknowledging that cultural factors did influence gender development, Witkin emphasized biological factors in sex differences and personality development. He treated "penis envy" as an inevitable developmental "disappointment" for females that resulted in a "permanent sense of inferiority" and a diminished capacity for active mastery over the environment.[65] A stance more consistent with Freud's general methodology (the pursuit of the conflictual experiences that underlie symbolic representations) would have been that the phallus symbolizes domination and male privilege in patriarchal societies. Women both envy and resent what the phallus socially signifies. This stance, articulated by a few leading psychoanalysts in the 1940s and 1950s such as Clara Thompson,[66] had very

[60] Ibid., 287.
[61] Ibid., 298.
[62] Ibid., 299.
[63] Ibid., 296.
[64] Ibid., 487.
[65] Ibid., 489.
[66] C. Thompson, "Cultural Pressures in the Psychology of Women," *Psychiatry* 5, no. 3 (August 1942): 331–39, and "Penis Envy in Women," *Psychiatry* 6, no. 2 (May 1943): 123–25.

little impact on psychoanalytic thought in the postwar period. The reworking of psychoanalysis to take into account the social construction of gender and gender-based inequality emerged with more force and cohesion as a response to the women's movement in the 1970s.

The experimental context

Field independence, as a concept, idealizes individuality and the possibilities for individual control—particularly male control—over the environment. Specifically, it privileges the ability to attend to and control discrete events while ignoring or overcoming the context. Relatedly, field independence also describes the experimenter's self-conception and epistemological approach to the world. His or her research world is divided into discrete independent and dependent variables that can be studied apart from the context in which they occur normally. In the classical model of experimental design, the background of individual experience is viewed as something to be overcome—as a source of error variance. The relationship between the observer-scientist and the subject is understood in terms of the ability of the former to control the conditions of the latter's responses. At the same time, there has been a strong tendency in experimental psychology to deny evidence that the experimenter does influence her or his subject beyond the specific variables under investigation.[67] While Robert Rosenthal's research in the 1960s, demonstrating the effects of the experimenter's unconscious bias on research outcomes, casts doubt on the notion of experimental objectivity,[68] experimental psychologists have generally viewed such effects as idiosyncratic and as simply requiring more careful attention to technical aspects of research design.

Obviously, Witkin could not, years earlier, have known about these findings, but he was aware of the role of ego defenses in field independence, though he did not extend this understanding to the experimental field, that is, the psychodynamic meaning of the experiment and the experimenter's relation to the subject. Witkin viewed field independence as a higher-level response, developmentally, than field dependence, but he also acknowledged that some extremely field-independent people distorted reality in the use of defensive operations.[69] Certain cues were recognized by field-independent subjects while others were denied—particularly social and emotional cues. In emphasizing the problematic

[67] H. Gadlin and G. Ingle, "Through the One-Way Mirror: The Limits of Experimental Self-Reflection," *American Psychologist* 10 (October 1975): 1003–9.

[68] R. Rosenthal, *Experimenter Bias in Behavioral Research* (New York: Appleton-Century-Crofts, 1966).

[69] Witkin et al., *Personality through Perception*, 470.

aspects of masculine personality tendencies, coinvestigator Lewis[70] has more recently stressed the commonalities between field independence and obsessive compulsive neurosis and paranoia. Defenses such as emotional isolation, obsessive attention to detail, and overvaluation of control dominate responses to the world in both field independence and these psychopathological conditions.

In the design and interpretations of the research setting, Witkin became a perpetuator of his own field-independent ideology by not attending to the social and emotional properties of the experimental field. Given his psychoanalytic perspective, one would expect the phenomenology of the field to include transference and countertransference dimensions (i.e., the emotional connections between experimenter and subject) of the experimental setting as well as of the symbolic meaning of the stimulus materials. For the rod-and-frame test, which Witkin concluded to be the most reliable measure of field dependence, the subject enters a totally darkened room with the experimenter and is asked to sit in a reclining or upright position. She or he is then asked to make judgments in a perceptual task, that is, to locate the vertical position of an illuminated rod placed in a tilted illuminated frame. All of this takes place in the dark with the subject in a somewhat vulnerable position with a stranger.

While Witkin "ran subjects" himself, along with his male and female colleagues,[71] the sex of the experimenters is perhaps less crucial, psychoanalytically, than their shared belief in the predictive value of these experiments and their failure to recognize the ramifications of subjects' unconscious associations with the configuration of stimuli as a whole. This particular experimental situation could have evocative social meaning for female subjects. The experimental setting might have elicited associations with potential danger (the completely darkened room) and loss of control, and responses to the rod-and-frame task would be mediated by such social meaning. The stimulus materials and experimental task could have suggested, on an unconscious level, a reenactment of women's position in a patriarchal society; they were asked to orient themselves in relation to the phallus, the illuminated rod.

It has been demonstrated that anxiety and stress do influence responses to the rod-and-frame task,[72] a finding anticipated by Karen Machover, one of Witkin's coinvestigators. Machover suggested during the 1947–53 studies that a "dark room effect" might mediate the sex differences in their

[70] Lewis (n. 12 above), 184.

[71] H. B. Lewis, personal communication, March 1986.

[72] F. Gross, "The Role of Set in Perception of the Upright," *Journal of Personality* 27 (March 1959): 95–103; P. Quinlan and S. Blatt, "Field Articulation and Performance under Stress: Differential Predictions in Surgical and Psychiatric Nursing Training," *Journal of Consulting and Clinical Psychology* 39 (December 1972): 517.

findings.[73] However, Lewis said that this hypothesis was not pursued because it did not account for the correlations of the rod-and-frame scores with scores from other perceptual tests.[74] Continued exploration of field factors, beyond technical properties of the immediate task, was clearly not part of the research plan.

The dissociation of the task from its representational correspondence to the external world is a direct result of this field-independent orientation. Some critics of the experimental method have raised questions about whether laboratory conditions really do correspond to the conditions of "real life."[75] Others have argued that experimental tasks sometimes elicit different responses in males and females because of the sex role dimensions of the task rather than the inferred psychological attribute.[76] For example, Sheridan Fenwick Naditch found that when female subjects were told that the experiment was a test of empathy and a human figure was substituted for the rod, they scored significantly higher on field independence than when they were asked to judge a rod.[77] This is consistent with Lewis's thesis that, in capitalist societies, men are encouraged to be more "thing-oriented" and to view people and objects interchangeably, while women are more "people-oriented."[78] Witkin's claim that the physical properties of the world are perceived essentially in the same manner as social situations is consistent with this male point of view.

There is some evidence that Witkin was sensitive to the tendency in experimental psychology to overobjectify and oversimplify human phenomena. In the final chapter of *Personality through Perception*, he issues a caveat concerning the conclusions to be drawn from the reported findings: "While simplification of conditions is necessary, great care must be exercised in applying to nature itself in generalizing from these findings. The omission of critical elements of lived experience may result in misrepresenting phenomena."[79]

Throughout the course of his extensive research career, Witkin was not so much overinvested in a methodological stance as he was overinvested in his construct. Witkin did move from the narrowly circumscribed problems of experimental comparative (animal) psychology in the 1930s, that is,

[73] H. B. Lewis, personal communication, March 1986.

[74] Lewis was referring here to the Tilting-Room-Tilting-Chair Test and the Embedded-Figure Test, both tests of visual perception that were included in the studies published in 1954.

[75] Gadlin and Ingle (n. 67 above), 1003.

[76] I. Frieze, J. Parsons, P. Johnson, D. Ruble, and G. Zellman, *Women and Sex Roles: A Social Psychological Perspective* (New York: W. W. Norton & Co., 1975), 19.

[77] S. Sheridan Fenwick Naditch, "Effect of Experimental Artifact on Sex Differences in Field Dependence," (Ph.D. diss., Cornell University, 1975).

[78] Lewis (n. 12 above), 105.

[79] Witkin et al., *Personality through Perception* (n. 8 above), 507.

maze learning in rats, to increasingly broader domains of human phenomena and applied research in the 1960s and 1970s, that is, cross-cultural and ecological factors in the acquisition of field dependence. But as he cast his net further and further in search of theoretical and empirical links to field dependence, this construct continued to be the lens through which he organized the phenomenal world and upon which he built his career in psychology. This preoccupation with validating experimentally the field-dependence construct diminished his capacity to understand the meaning of the research for the subjects.

Once Witkin adopted it as a trait, field dependence lost much of its original theoretical meaning and descriptive power. For the early Gestalt theorists, who were the primary influence on Witkin's work, the perceptual field represented both an experimental problem and a metaphorical vehicle for a critique of society. For these theorists, human subjectivity was bound by the "requirements" of the field but contained the potential for conceiving of new possibilities and new arrangements in the field of experience.

Witkin took the most conservative and asocial premise shared by Gestalt theory and psychoanalysis—the idea that human development is a process of progressive differentiation of the self—and elaborated a construct that stressed individual autonomy and the primacy of the internal world in structuring outer reality. In attempting to demonstrate the merits of Gestalt theory and psychoanalysis on this narrowly defined empirical ground, he lost the self-critical and self-conscious dimensions of both perspectives as well as the possibility for broad-based social theorizing in field-dependence research.

Department of Psychology
Portland State University

Meta-Analysis and the Psychology of Gender Differences

Janet Shibley Hyde

Psychological research on gender differences has had a long, and sometimes dishonorable, history spanning more than a century.[1] The research ranges from early efforts to measure the cranial capacities of males and females to the current sophisticated meta-analyses of psychological gender differences. Here I will briefly review the history of research on gender differences, focusing particularly on the issue of gender differences in cognitive abilities, and then move to a discussion of recent meta-analyses of psychological gender differences.

Early research on gender differences in abilities

Stephanie Shields has provided an excellent analysis of the zeitgeist that influenced early research and writing on female psychol-

This research was supported by grants BNS 8508666, BNS 8696128, and MDR 8709533 from the National Science Foundation. I express my thanks for the insightful suggestions of an anonymous *Signs* reviewer.

[1] I use the term gender differences rather than sex differences throughout this essay because the data I discuss do not address the issue of whether such differences have a biological or cultural origin. I do not want to imply that the differences are biologically caused; "gender differences" allows me to focus on the existence and significance of differences regardless of origin.

[*Signs: Journal of Women in Culture and Society* 1990, vol. 16, no. 1]

ogy beginning around 1879, the date usually cited as the beginning of formal psychology.[2] Darwinism and functionalism dominated intellectual thought in the sciences. Evolutionary theory, because it highlighted the importance of variability, made it legitimate to study variations in behavior, including gender differences. Nonetheless, the outcome of such study was generally to provide further data supporting the notion of the evolutionary supremacy of the white male.

The topic of female intelligence was first investigated by phrenologists and neuroanatomists. The early belief was that male and female brains must be as different in their gross appearance as were male and female bodies in other selected areas. Franz Joseph Gall claimed that "if there had been presented to him in water, the fresh brains of two adult animals of any species, one male and the other female, he could have distinguished the two sexes."[3] The most popular argument was that females had smaller heads and smaller brains than males, that brain size was a direct indicator of intelligence, and that women must therefore be less intelligent than men.[4] Indeed, George Romanes considered brain size and its corollary, intelligence, to be among the secondary sex characteristics.[5] This argument overlooks the fact that there is a correlation between brain size and body size. The slightly larger size of male brains, on the average, is accounted for almost entirely by males' larger average body size.

Later theorizing was based on the notion of localization of function, that is, that different functions of the brain were localized in different regions. For a time it was thought that the frontal lobes of the brain were the site of the highest mental abilities; quickly, researchers claimed that males possessed larger frontal lobes.[6] Next, the parietal lobes were favored as the location of intelligence, and the parietal lobes of females were found wanting.[7]

In 1910, Helen Thompson Woolley provided the first review of psychological research on gender differences.[8] She quickly dis-

[2] Stephanie A. Shields, "Functionalism, Darwinism, and the Psychology of Women: A Study in Social Myth," *American Psychologist* 30, no. 7 (July 1975): 739–54.

[3] A. Walker, *Woman Physiologically Considered* (New York: J. & H. G. Langley, 1850), 317.

[4] A. Bain, *Mental Science* (New York: Appleton, 1875).

[5] George J. Romanes, "Mental Differences between Men and Women," *Nineteenth Century* 21, no. 123 (May 1887): 654–72.

[6] For example, P. J. Mobius, "The Physiological Mental Weakness of Woman," trans. A. McCorn, *Alienist and Neurologist* 22 (1901): 624–42.

[7] Henry Havelock Ellis, *Man and Woman: A Study of Secondary and Tertiary Sexual Characteristics*, 8th rev. ed. (London: Heinemann, 1934).

[8] Helen Thompson Woolley, "A Review of the Recent Literature on the Psychology of Sex," *Psychological Bulletin* 7, no. 18 (October 1910): 335–42.

missed the arguments on brain size: "It is now a generally accepted belief that the smaller gross weight of the female brain has no significance other than that of the smaller average size of the female."[9] She found only a meager amount of research using psychological methods to assess gender differences. She reviewed studies that measured rate and endurance in tapping a telegraph key, handwriting (women's was judged colorless, conventional, neat, and small, whereas men's was bold, careless, experienced, and individual), and tests of association. In the last case, participants were required to write a series of associations to a given word. The investigator of tests of association interpreted his results as indicating that women showed abnormality of reaction, meager presentations, a less active flow of ideas, less variety in ideas, more concrete forms of response, a more subjective attitude, and more indecision. Woolley's methodological critique of the research was devastating.

None of these measures has survived to have importance in modern psychology. Woolley's own evaluation of the research on gender differences available at the time is telling. "There is perhaps no field aspiring to be scientific where flagrant personal bias, logic martyred in the cause of supporting a prejudice, unfounded assertions, and even sentimental rot and drivel have run riot to such an extent as here."[10]

The mental testing movement

Research on gender differences in abilities entered a new phase with the rise of the mental testing movement and the development of standardized ability tests. The first viable intelligence test was devised by the French psychologist Alfred Binet. Binet was originally commissioned by the French minister of public instruction to accomplish a practical task: to find a means of identifying in advance those children who would not be successful when taught in normal public school classrooms and who might therefore benefit from special education. Given the myriad criticisms of intelligence tests (IQ tests), it is interesting that their origins were benign and pragmatic.[11] Binet's original test, published in 1905, included many quick, practical tasks, such as counting coins, that

[9] Ibid., 335.

[10] Ibid., 340.

[11] See, e.g., Stephen Jay Gould, *The Mismeasure of Man* (New York: Norton, 1981).

were intended to measure basic reasoning processes.[12] Stanford psychologist Lewis Terman expanded the test and published the first American version in 1916, naming it the Stanford Binet.[13]

Remarkably, given the popular views of the time, both Binet and Terman believed that there were no gender differences in general intelligence and so attempted to construct their tests to produce equal average scores for boys and girls. Repeated large-scale testing using the Binet has yielded no gender difference in this measure of general intelligence.[14] Noting that girls scored as well as boys in IQ measures, Terman decried women's limited access to the professions as both unjust and a waste of talent.[15] There is an irony here, of course. Because of the way the tests were constructed, a finding of no gender differences does not "prove" that there are no gender differences in general intelligence; rather, it only provides evidence that the test constructors succeeded in their goal of producing a test that resulted in no gender differences, by balancing items that would give advantages to males and females.

The next chapter in the testing movement that is of relevance is L. L. Thurstone's development of the Primary Mental Abilities (PMA) test in the 1930s and 1940s.[16] Until this time intelligence tests, including the Binet, had been based on the notion of general intelligence and yielded a single score, the intelligence quotient, or IQ, for each individual. Thurstone, in contrast, believed that there were multiple intellectual abilities and that he could identify them using a statistical technique called factor analysis. The PMA assesses seven abilities: verbal comprehension, word fluency, number (numerical computation), space (spatial visualizing), memory, perceptual speed (speed and accuracy on clerical tasks), and reasoning. This conceptualization of intelligence as composed of multiple abilities laid the foundation for research on gender differences in verbal ability, mathematical ability, and spatial ability.

[12] Alfred Binet and Theophile Simon, *A Method of Measuring the Development of the Intelligence of Young Children* (Lincoln, Ill.: Courier, 1912).

[13] Lewis M. Terman, *The Measurement of Intelligence* (Boston: Houghton Mifflin, 1916).

[14] Janet Shibley Hyde, *Half the Human Experience: The Psychology of Women*, 3d ed. (Lexington, Mass.: D. C. Heath, 1985), 186.

[15] Terman, *The Measurement of Intelligence*, 72, and *The Intelligence of School Children* (Boston: Houghton Mifflin, 1919), 278, 288.

[16] L. L. Thurstone, *Primary Mental Abilities* (Chicago: University of Chicago Press, 1938); L. L. Thurstone and Thelma G. Thurstone, *Factorial Studies of Intelligence*, Psychometric Monographs, no. 2 (Chicago: University of Chicago Press, 1941).

Reviews of research on gender differences

By the 1930s, sufficient data had begun to accumulate to do substantial reviews of research on gender differences in abilities. Some of the most authoritative and influential of these reviews were found in textbooks on differential psychology. Differential psychology as a specialty examines individual differences among humans, including differences in personality and intelligence, and group differences, including gender differences, race differences, social class differences, and age differences. Two works that present views typical of psychologists through the 1960s are Anne Anastasi's *Differential Psychology* (first published in 1937) and Leona Tyler's *The Psychology of Human Differences* (first published in 1947).[17] Anastasi concluded that females are superior in verbal and linguistic functions from infancy through adulthood; that males are superior in tests of spatial relations, although the difference is not found so early as the difference in verbal ability; and that males are superior on numerical tests, although the difference does not appear until well into elementary school and tends to be found on tests of numerical reasoning rather than computation, where girls are equal to or exceed boys in performance. Tyler's conclusions were quite similar: females are superior in verbal ability, although the difference is found on tests of verbal fluency, not vocabulary; males are superior in mathematical ability when the measure involves mathematical reasoning but not when it involves only mathematical computation; and males are superior on spatial ability tests. In her 1966 review, Eleanor Maccoby reached similar conclusions.[18]

By the publication of Eleanor Maccoby and Carol Nagy Jacklin's *The Psychology of Sex Differences*, literally thousands of studies had been published reporting data on gender differences in psychological characteristics, including not only abilities but also personality, social behavior, and memory.[19] One of the achievements of Maccoby and Jacklin's work was the systematic compilation of evidence so that a number of widely held beliefs about gender differences could be assessed for their empirical support.

---

[17] Anne Anastasi, *Differential Psychology: Individual and Group Differences in Behavior*, 3d ed. (New York: Macmillan, 1958); Leona E. Tyler, *The Psychology of Human Differences*, 3d ed. (New York: Appleton-Century-Crofts, 1965).

[18] Eleanor E. Maccoby, "Sex Differences in Intellectual Functioning," in *The Development of Sex Differences*, ed. E. E. Maccoby (Stanford, Calif.: Stanford University Press, 1966).

[19] Eleanor E. Maccoby and Carol Nagy Jacklin, *The Psychology of Sex Differences* (Stanford, Calif.: Stanford University Press, 1974).

Specifically, they concluded that the beliefs that girls are more social than boys, that girls are more suggestible than boys, that girls have lower self-esteem, that girls are better at rote learning and simple tasks whereas boys are better at higher-level cognitive processing, and that girls lack achievement motivation are unfounded. In contrast, they concluded that gender differences are well established in four domains: girls have greater verbal ability than boys, boys have greater visual-spatial ability, boys excel in mathematical ability, and boys are more aggressive. Thus, their conclusions, based on far more extensive evidence than were previous reviews, reaffirmed the belief in the holy trinity of gender differences in abilities: female superiority in verbal ability and male superiority in mathematical and spatial ability. Their conclusions have had a major impact on the field of psychology: they are taught to undergraduates in basic courses, and most introductory psychology and child development texts cite and discuss Maccoby and Jacklin's findings.[20]

Maccoby and Jacklin used a methodology that permitted systematic vote counting, that is; a listing of the studies according to the construct of interest (e.g., verbal ability, mathematical ability, aggressiveness). Consequently, it is possible to tally the percentage of studies that found a significant difference favoring females, the percentage that found no significant gender difference, and the percentage that found a significant difference favoring males. For example, in their analysis of mathematics performance, they located ten studies of subjects eleven years of age or younger; of those, seven found no significant gender difference and three found a significant difference favoring females. Among the remaining seventeen studies they located of older subjects, twelve found significant differences favoring males, five found no significant difference, and none found a difference favoring females (except for a few isolated findings favoring females on specific tests or in a specific age group). They concluded that the gender difference in mathematics performance emerges at twelve to thirteen years of age.[21]

In her 1976 critique of Maccoby and Jacklin's work, Jeanne Block pointed out, among other things, that Maccoby and Jacklin

[20] For examples, see Rita L. Atkinson, R. C. Atkinson, and E. R. Hilgard, *Introduction to Psychology*, 8th ed. (New York: Harcourt Brace Jovanovich, 1983); Henry Gleitman, *Psychology* (New York: Norton, 1981); E. Mavis Hetherington and Ross D. Parke, *Child Psychology: A Contemporary Viewpoint*, 3d ed. (New York: McGraw-Hill, 1986); and Paul H. Mussen, John J. Conger, Jerome Kagan, and Aletha C. Huston, *Child Development and Personality*, 6th ed. (New York: Harper & Row, 1984).

[21] Maccoby and Jacklin, 88–89.

were inconsistent in the criteria they used to decide whether the percentage of studies indicating a particular difference was sufficiently large to conclude that there is a true gender difference. Criticisms of their method of vote counting have also been raised. Statisticians have pointed out that this method can lead to false conclusions, specifically, that there is no significant difference when there actually is one.[22]

Meta-analysis and the new research on gender differences in abilities

In the 1980s the development of a new statistical method called meta-analysis, which uses quantitative methods to combine evidence from different studies, has radically altered the analysis of gender differences in abilities.[23] Essentially a quantitative or statistical method for doing a literature review, a meta-analysis proceeds in several stages. First, the researchers collect as many studies as possible that report data on the question of interest. Computerized literature searches can be helpful in assuring that there is a good sampling of studies. In the area of psychological gender differences, researchers can often obtain a very large sample of studies. For example, I was able to locate 143 studies reporting data on gender differences in aggression for one meta-analysis and 165 studies of gender differences in verbal ability for another.[24]

Second, the researchers perform a statistical analysis of the statistics reported in each article. For each study, an effect size statistic, d, is computed. For analyses of gender differences, the formula is $d = (M_M - M_F)/s$, where M_M is the mean or average of

[22] A detailed coverage of the statistical argument behind this assertion is beyond the scope of this article. The rationale is given by John E. Hunter, Frank L. Schmidt, and Gregg B. Jackson, *Meta-Analysis: Cumulating Research Findings across Studies* (Beverly Hills, Calif.: Sage, 1982). A discussion of the problem of vote counting as applied to research on gender differences is provided by Janet Shibley Hyde, "Introduction: Meta-Analysis and the Psychology of Gender," in *The Psychology of Gender: Advances through Meta-Analysis*, ed. Janet S. Hyde and Marcia C. Linn (Baltimore: Johns Hopkins University Press, 1986), 1–13.

[23] Larry V. Hedges and Ingram Olkin, *Statistical Methods for Meta-Analysis* (New York: Academic Press, 1985), 13.

[24] Janet Shibley Hyde, "How Large Are Gender Differences in Aggression? A Developmental Meta-Analysis," *Developmental Psychology* 20, no. 4 (July 1984): 722–36; and Janet Shibley Hyde and Marcia C. Linn, "Gender Differences in Verbal Ability: A Meta-Analysis," *Psychological Bulletin* 104, no. 1 (July 1988): 53–69.

males' scores and M_F is the mean or average of females' scores; s is the within-groups standard deviation, which is a measure of the variability of scores, that is, the within-sex variability. Essentially, d indicates how far apart the means for males and females are in standard deviation units. Positive values of d mean that males scored higher than females and negative values mean that females scored higher.

From a feminist point of view, one of the virtues of the d statistic is that it takes into account not only gender differences (the difference between male and female means), but also female variability and male variability (s, the standard deviation). That is, it recognizes that each sex is not homogeneous. According to earlier methods of assessment when reviewers concluded, as Maccoby and Jacklin did, that there were indeed gender differences in verbal, mathematical, and spatial ability, readers often assumed that because the differences were well established they were large. The d statistic assesses exactly how large, or small, the difference is.

In the third stage of the meta-analysis, the researchers average the d values obtained from all studies, which allows them to draw conclusions based on the average of the results of all of the studies.[25] For example, based on 100 values of d obtained from 100 studies, the average magnitude of the gender difference in spatial ability is $d = .45$. Recent developments in meta-analysis make it possible to proceed one step further, to analyzing variations in values of d, that is, in the magnitude of the gender difference, according to various features of the studies.[26] This step is called homogeneity analysis because it analyzes the extent to which the values of d in the set are uniform or homogeneous. When there are large variations in the values of d across the studies in the set, the meta-analyst must account for the inconsistencies in the findings. By grouping the studies into subsets, the meta-analyst attempts to find a classification scheme that yields relatively homogeneous values of d within each subset of studies. For example, in an analysis of gender differences in verbal ability, one could compute a value of d for those studies that measured vocabulary, another value of d for those that measured reading comprehension, and yet a third value for those that measured higher-order reasoning on tests such as anal-

---

[25] For a highly readable account of these statistical methods, designed for the beginner, see Larry V. Hedges and Betsy Jane Becker, "Statistical Methods in the Meta-Analysis of Research on Gender Differences," in Hyde and Linn, eds.

[26] See, e.g., Hedges and Olkin.

ogies. Thus the investigators could determine whether the gender difference was large for some kinds of verbal ability and small or perhaps zero for other kinds.

The interpretation of the magnitude of *d* values remains a point of contention among researchers. Because values can be lower or higher than 1, there is no absolute standard against which to measure any particular value of *d*. Jacob Cohen has offered as a somewhat arbitrary guideline the suggestion that an absolute value of .20 is small, a value of .50 is medium, and a value of .80 is large.[27] Robert Rosenthal and Donald Rubin have introduced another scheme using the statistic *r*, which translates into $d = 2r$.[28] Their method of assessing the magnitude of effect sizes is to use the binomial effect size display (BESD), which displays the change in success rate (e.g., recovery from cancer due to a particular treatment, compared with an untreated control group) as a function of the effect size. Thus, for example, an $r = .30$ ($d = .60$) translates into an improvement in recovery from cancer from 35 percent to 65 percent of patients studied. In the study of gender differences, an effect size of $d = .40$ means that approximately 40 percent of one sex falls above the median for both sexes and 60 percent of the other sex falls above the same median.

Yet a third scheme for interpreting the magnitude of an effect size is to compare it with other effect sizes that have been obtained either for related studies in the same field or for quite different studies. Thus, for example, one might compare the value of *d* for gender differences in verbal ability with one for gender differences in spatial ability. Drawing a broader comparison, one might compare the magnitude of gender differences in mathematics performance with the magnitude of the effects of psychotherapy (comparison of adjustment levels following therapy with untreated controls), which has been reported to be $d = .68$.[29] Ultimately it will be valuable for feminist research to be able to compare the magnitude of gender difference effects with the magnitude of other effects on that same phenomenon. For example, in a study of

[27] Jacob Cohen, *Statistical Power Analysis for the Behavioral Sciences* (New York: Academic Press, 1969).

[28] Robert Rosenthal and Donald B. Rubin, "A Simple, General Purpose Display of the Magnitude of Experimental Effect," *Journal of Educational Psychology* 74, no. 2 (April 1982): 166–69. The formula $d = 2r$ is a good approximation so long as values of *r* are small or moderate. For larger values of *r*, the exact formula should be used, $d = 2r / (1 - r^2)$.

[29] Mary Lee Smith and Gene V Glass, "Meta-Analysis of Psychotherapy Outcome Studies," *American Psychologist* 32, no. 9 (September 1977): 752–60.

mathematics performance, the effect of gender difference could be compared to the effect of social class difference, or the effect of differences in attitudes toward mathematics.

Meta-analyses of gender differences in abilities

The first published meta-analysis of gender differences in abilities appeared in 1981.[30] For that research, I reanalyzed and computed values of d for the studies collected by Maccoby and Jacklin, with the result that on the average, d = -.24 for gender differences in verbal ability, .45 for spatial ability, and .43 for mathematical ability. These results indicate that gender differences in abilities are not as large as the prominence of such findings in reviews and textbooks would indicate. According to Cohen's scheme, the gender difference in verbal ability is small, and the gender differences in spatial and mathematical ability are at most moderate in size. Another statistical analysis reported in the 1981 article indicated that within-gender differences were far larger than between-gender differences.

Gender differences in abilities have sometimes been used as an explanation for lopsided gender ratios in some occupations. The above meta-analysis made it possible to determine whether such explanations are adequate. For example, fewer than 5 percent of engineers in the United States are women, and possessing a high level of spatial ability is generally considered important for success at engineering. Assuming that spatial ability at least at the 95th percentile is required to become an engineer, and that d = .40 for gender differences in spatial ability, about 7.35 percent of men and 3.22 percent of women would possess sufficiently high spatial ability to be engineers. That result would support a 2:1 ratio of males:females in the profession, or 67 percent men and 33 percent women.[31] Thus, if women constitute fewer than 5 percent of

[30] Janet Shibley Hyde, "How Large Are Cognitive Gender Differences? A Meta-Analysis Using ω^2 and d," *American Psychologist* 36, no. 8 (August 1981): 892–901. Maccoby and Jacklin had computed a few effect sizes for their 1974 book, but they did not do so systematically. They concluded that d = .25 for verbal ability, but they found the variations in values of d for gender differences in mathematical ability to be so great that they did not hazard a guess as to an average value.

[31] This analysis ignores the issue of whether spatial performance can be learned. Many studies indicate that training can be successful, which might in turn narrow the gap between males and females. See, e.g., Maryann Baenninger and Nora Newcombe, "The Role of Experience in Spatial Test Performance: A Meta-Analysis," *Sex Roles* 20, nos. 5/6 (March 1989): 327–44; M. F. Blade and W. S.

engineers, they are seriously underrepresented in comparison with their spatial ability test performance, and other factors must be considered to account for the lopsided gender ratio.

Subsequent to my research, Marcia Linn and Anne Petersen performed a more sophisticated meta-analysis of gender differences in spatial ability, using homogeneity analyses.[32] Using studies published since 1974, they computed 172 values of d and concluded that there are actually three distinct types of spatial ability, each measured by different types of tests and each showing a different pattern of gender differences. The first type of spatial ability, which they term spatial perception (what I would call a sense of horizontality/verticality), is measured by tests such as the rod-and-frame test and the water-level task (see fig. 1). For these tests, $d = .44$, indicating a moderate advantage for males. The second type of spatial ability, which they term mental rotation, is a measure of participants' ability to rotate mentally a three-dimensional object pictured in two dimensions, to see whether it matches one of a number of other illustrations (see fig. 2). For these tests, $d = .73$. The third type of spatial ability, according to their analysis, is spatial visualization, or what I would term spatial disembedding. This type measures the participant's ability to extract visually a simpler figure from a more complex figure. Here $d = .13$. Thus, there is essentially no gender difference for spatial disembedding, a moderate difference for horizontality/verticality, and a rather large difference for mental rotation. Global statements about gender differences in spatial ability are therefore simplistic.

Linn and Petersen also analyzed the data for age trends in the magnitude of gender differences in spatial ability—an analysis motivated by Maccoby and Jacklin's previous arguments that gender differences in spatial ability do not emerge until adolescence and are therefore a result of biological changes—perhaps hormonal, perhaps brain lateralization—that occur at puberty. Their meta-analysis indicated that such assumptions are false; where gender differences were present, they were present throughout the life span. For example, for measures of horizontality/verticality, $d = .37$ for studies of persons under thirteen and $d = .37$ for studies of participants between the ages of thirteen and eighteen. Not all biological explanations of gender differences in spatial ability (e.g.,

Watson, "Increase in Spatial Visualization Test Scores during Engineering Study," *Psychological Monographs*, vol. 69, no. 397 (1955).

[32] Marcia C. Linn and Anne C. Petersen, "Emergence and Characterization of Sex Differences in Spatial Ability: A Meta-Analysis," *Child Development* 56, no. 4 (December 1985): 1479–98.

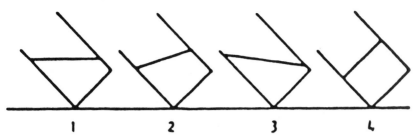

FIG. 1   A spatial perception item. Respondents are asked to indicate which tilted bottle has a horizontal water line.

sex-linked, genetic ones) predict a change in the pattern of gender differences at puberty, however, and the question of whether the differences in some aspects of spatial ability are rooted in biology or socialization remains an open one.

In our recently completed meta-analysis of gender differences in verbal ability, Marcia Linn and I used 165 studies that reported relevant data, and from those we were able to compute 120 values of d.[33] Over all studies, the mean $d = -.11$. This value is so small, even in comparison to Cohen's prescription, that we concluded that there is no gender difference in verbal ability. Meta-analysis is capable of yielding surprising conclusions that contradict widely held beliefs about gender differences. When we considered specific types of verbal tests, there was still no evidence of any substantial gender difference. For example, for vocabulary tests, $d = -.02$; for reading comprehension, $d = -.03$; and for essay writing, $d = -.09$.

As part of the analysis, we considered data from the SAT-Verbal, which includes a mixture of items measuring vocabulary, reading comprehension, and so on. For the 1985 administration of the SAT-Verbal, $d = +.11$, the positive value indicating superior male performance.[34] There are a number of possible explanations for why males outscore females on the test, including, for example, the test writers' selection of question topics and formats. Whatever the explanation, however, the difference is small (only about .1 standard deviation), which translates into a mean score of 437 for males and 425 for females.

One closely related project is the meta-analysis of gender differences in causal attributions done by Irene Frieze and her

[33] Hyde and Linn (n. 24 above).
[34] L. Ramist and S. Arbeiter, *Profiles, College-bound Seniors, 1985* (New York: College Entrance Examination Board, 1986).

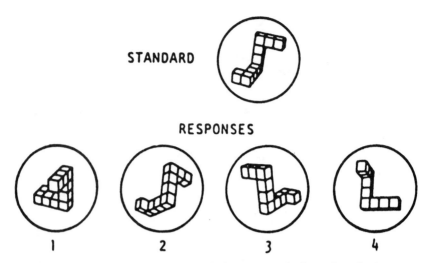

STANDARD

RESPONSES

1   2   3   4

FIG. 2 A mental rotation item. Respondents are asked to identify the two responses that show the standard in a different orientation.

colleagues.[35] Causal attributions are the mental explanations people generate for things that occur. For example, if a student gets an A on an exam, she might attribute that success to ability, to luck, to the exam's being easy, or to her own hard work. The four attributions studied most by social psychologists have been ability, luck, task ease, and effort. Ability and effort are regarded as internal attributions—that is, they involve factors in the individual—while luck and task ease are regarded as external attributions. Prior to Frieze and her colleagues' meta-analysis, the consensus in the field had been that females tend to make external attributions for their successes and internal attributions for their failures. These conclusions were used as an explanation for the lesser academic and occupational achievements of females. However, the meta-analysis indicated that gender differences were insignificant. For example, for attributions of success to ability, $d = .13$, suggesting that males are slightly more likely than females to make such attributions. For attributions of failure to (insufficient) ability, $d = .16$, indicating

[35] Irene H. Frieze, Bernard E. Whitley, Jr., Barbara H. Hanusa, and Maureen C. McHugh, "Assessing the Theoretical Models for Sex Differences in Causal Attributions for Success and Failure," *Sex Roles* 8, no. 4 (April 1982): 333–43; Bernard E. Whitley, Jr., Maureen C. McHugh, and Irene Hanson Frieze, "Assessing the Theoretical Models for Sex Differences in Causal Attributions of Success and Failure," in Hyde and Linn, eds. (n. 22 above), 102–35.

that males are also slightly more likely to make these attributions. Thus, widely held models of gender differences in attributions—which were female deficit models—were dismissed by the results of this meta-analysis, which led to a conclusion that there are no gender differences in patterns of attributions.[36]

Meta-analyses of gender differences in social behaviors

Although the present review concentrates on gender differences in cognitive abilities, a number of meta-analyses of gender differences in sociopsychological variables have been performed, and they yield interesting results.

Alice Eagly and Linda Carli performed a meta-analysis of studies of gender differences in influenceability.[37] Prior to their work, the consensus in the field of social psychology had been that women are more influenceable than men—that is, that they are more easily persuaded to change their opinion, that they are more suggestible, and that they are more conforming. Most of the relevant studies are of the laboratory experimental variety. For example, a standard measure of conformity is the Asch paradigm, in which a number of "subjects" give judgments of the length of a line, but in fact there is only one true experimental subject and the rest are confederates of the experimenter's who sometimes are unanimous in giving wrong answers: if the subject then also gives the same wrong answer, it is viewed as an indicator of conformity.[38] Eagly and Carli found that the magnitude of gender differentiation in the answers of males and females was small. For studies of influenceability, the average $d = -.16$; for studies in which there was group pressure to conform (as in Asch's paradigm), the average $d = -.32$; and for other conformity studies, in which group pressure was absent, the average $d = -.28$. Even in the set of studies

[36] Another effect-size analysis of gender differences in attributions was reported by David Sohn, "Sex Differences in Achievement Self-Attributions: An Effect-Size Analysis," *Sex Roles* 8, no. 4 (April 1982): 345–57. Although Sohn used a somewhat different statistical analysis, he reached essentially the same conclusion as Frieze and her colleagues: there was no evidence of a "consequential" relationship between sex and self-attributions.

[37] Alice H. Eagly and Linda L. Carli, "Sex of Researchers and Sex-typed Communications as Determinants of Sex Differences in Influenceability: A Meta-Analysis of Social Influence Studies," *Psychological Bulletin* 90, no. 1 (July 1981): 1–20.

[38] The original paradigm was presented in Solomon E. Asch, "Studies of Independence and Conformity: I. A Minority of One against a Unanimous Majority," *Psychological Monographs*, vol. 70, no. 416 (1956).

in which the gender difference was largest, where there was group pressure to conform, the studies may not necessarily be evidence of greater passivity on the part of females. An alternative interpretation is that these studies reflect the tendency of females to try to preserve harmony in a group.

Eagly and Carli's exploration of the relationship between the gender of the researchers and the results of their studies illustrates the way in which meta-analysis can be used to provide empirical answers to feminist questions about research methodology.[39] Male researchers found larger gender differences and greater persuasibility and conformity among women than did female researchers. In studies authored by women, no gender difference was found. There are many possible explanations for such an effect. For example, male researchers by their presence may encourage conformity in female participants. Male researchers may design experimental settings or stimulus materials that better measure males' responses or that contain more masculine content.[40]

Judith Hall reports a number of meta-analyses, including studies of gender differences in accuracy of judging facial expressions, gender differences in gazing, and gender differences in interpersonal distance, touch, body movement, and voice.[41] Her results indicate that females are better than males at understanding others' nonverbal cues ($d = -.42$), at recognizing faces ($d = -.34$), and at expressing emotions using nonverbal communication ($d = -.50$). Females have more expressive faces ($d = -.90$, but based on only five studies), are approached more closely by others ($d = -.86$), and emit fewer speech errors ($d = -.66$). These gender differences are generally larger than the differences in spatial and verbal abilities discussed earlier.

[39] It should be noted, however, that sex-of-author effects are not found consistently in all meta-analyses; relevant studies are discussed by Alice H. Eagly, *Sex Differences in Social Behavior: A Social-Role Interpretation* (Hillsdale, N.J.: Erlbaum, 1987), 144.

[40] For a meta-analysis addressed to some of these issues, see Betsy Jane Becker, "Influence Again: An Examination of Reviews and Studies of Gender Differences in Social Influence," in Hyde and Linn, eds., 178–209.

[41] Judith A. Hall, *Nonverbal Sex Differences: Communication Accuracy and Expressive Style* (Baltimore: Johns Hopkins University Press, 1984). In her reporting, Hall uses the statistic *r*, or the correlation between subject sex and behavioral measures, rather than the more conventional *d*. For the reader's convenience in comparing the results of different studies, I have converted all her *r* statistics to *d* statistics, using the formula $d = 2r$. Judith Hall should also be recognized for having reported, in 1978, what was probably the first meta-analysis of psychological gender differences; see her "Gender Effects in Decoding Nonverbal Cues," *Psychological Bulletin* 85, no. 4 (July 1978): 845–57.

Alice Eagly and Maureen Crowley have meta-analyzed studies on gender differences in helping behaviors.[42] Their article is particularly interesting because it is theory grounded, unlike many other meta-analyses with more applied orientations. Eagly and Crowley articulated a social-role theory of gender and helping behaviors, leading to the hypotheses that male gender roles foster helping that is heroic and chivalrous whereas female roles foster helping that is nurturant and caring. They noted that social psychologists have tended to study helping behaviors primarily in the context of short-term encounters with strangers. The consequence has been to neglect to study helping behaviors prescribed by the female role, which are most likely to occur in long-term, close relationships. In support of their theoretical formulations, the greatest differentials, in which males helped more than females, were in situations in which there was perceived danger in the testing situation and in which males feel most competent to help. For example, if the helping situation involves whether a motorist stops to help a person stopped by the roadside with a flat tire, most studies have found more helping by males because there is some danger involved to the helper and males feel more competent about automotive problems. In contrast, if the situation involves volunteering time to help a disturbed child, most studies have found more helping from females because there is little danger present for the helper and because females feel more competent in nurturing.

I and one other researcher have performed meta-analyses of studies of gender differences in aggression, with different focuses. The focus of my meta-analysis was developmental, concerning itself particularly with age trends in the patterns of gender differences in aggression.[43] Averaging over all ages and many different methods of measuring aggression, the magnitude of the gender difference was $d = .50$, indicating that males are indeed more aggressive but that the difference is moderate, not large. There was a negative correlation between participants' age and the magnitude of the gender difference; that is, gender differences were largest for studies of children and smallest for older participants. Specifically, for studies with participants six years of age or younger, $d = .58$, whereas for studies of college students, $d = .27$. One must view

[42] Alice H. Eagly and Maureen Crowley, "Gender and Helping Behavior: A Meta-analytic Review of the Social Psychological Literature," *Psychological Bulletin* 100, no. 3 (November 1986): 283–308.

[43] Janet S. Hyde, "How Large Are Gender Differences in Aggression?" (n. 24 above).

this difference with caution, however, since the measures of aggression in different age groups often differ. Many studies of preschoolers use direct observations of physical aggression (e.g., hitting, kicking) as the measure of aggression, whereas studies of college students more often use measures such as willingness to shock another person.

It is interesting that the magnitude of the gender difference in aggression indicated by such studies has declined over time. For studies published between 1966 and 1973, $d = .53$, whereas for studies published between 1978 and 1981, $d = .41$. Similar trends have been found in meta-analyses of cognitive abilities. For example, in my analysis of gender differences in verbal ability, studies published in 1973 or earlier showed $d = -.23$, whereas studies published after 1973 showed $d = -.10$.[44] This trend toward declining gender differences may represent an increasing tendency for psychologists to publish results when the gender difference is not significant. Alice Eagly has reviewed the evidence on trends over time in the magnitude of gender differences, finding the results to be inconsistent from one meta-analysis to another.[45] Alternatively, the trend toward diminished gender differences may be a real one. If that is the case, it provides remarkable evidence of the extent to which changes in gender roles in the past two decades have led to a diminishing of gender differences in behavior.

The other meta-analysis of gender differences in aggressive behavior was performed by Alice Eagly and Valerie Steffen.[46] Their focus was on social psychologists' research, the majority of it done with college students as subjects. They again used social-role theory to predict the pattern of results. Overall, men were more aggressive than women ($d = .29$). However, the pattern of results varied considerably depending on the way in which the aggressive

[44] Rosenthal and Rubin also investigated trends over time in the magnitude of gender differences, reanalyzing my 1981 meta-analysis of cognitive gender differences. They reported that their results indicated a "substantial gain in cognitive performance by females relative to males" (708) in more recent studies. However, the nature of their data cannot possibly support such a conclusion about improved levels of female performance on some absolute scale. Their data indicate only a trend toward diminished gender differences, which is consistent with the trends for aggression and verbal ability that are noted. See Robert Rosenthal and Donald B. Rubin, "Further Meta-analytic Procedures for Assessing Cognitive Gender Differences," *Journal of Educational Psychology* 74, no. 5 (October 1982): 708–12.

[45] Alice H. Eagly, *Sex Differences in Social Behavior: A Social-Role Interpretation* (n. 39 above).

[46] Alice H. Eagly and Valerie J. Steffen, "Gender and Aggressive Behavior: A Meta-analytic Review of the Social Psychological Literature," *Psychological Bulletin* 100, no. 3 (November 1986): 309–30.

behavior was assessed. The gender difference was larger when physical aggression was involved ($d = .40$) than when psychological aggression was involved ($d = .18$).[47] When women, more than men, believe the behavior to produce harm to the victim, guilt or anxiety to oneself, or danger to oneself, gender differences are larger. The results are therefore consistent with Eagly's social-role theory.

Summary and conclusions

We have come a long way from the belief, a century ago, that women's brains, and therefore their mental abilities, are smaller than men's. In the few decades before meta-analyses, reviewers consistently concluded that there are no gender differences in general intelligence, but that there are gender differences favoring females in verbal ability and males in mathematical and spatial ability. Meta-analysis, by quantitatively cumulating results from many studies, has permitted more sophisticated and convincing probing of these patterns of gender differences. A number of conclusions emerge from these meta-analyses. Gender differences in cognitive abilities are generally not large. The largest difference is for one type of spatial ability, mental rotations ($d = .73$), but the gender difference in mathematical performance is moderate ($d = .43$), and there is no gender difference in verbal ability.

In the realm of social behaviors such as aggression and helping behavior, whether gender differences are found in a particular study, and how large they are, depends greatly on the setting of the study and the ways in which the behaviors are measured; this variation in results is consistent with social-role theory. Gender differences in nonverbal behaviors are in some cases larger than other gender differences (e.g., females are approached more closely than males are), although here, too, most differences are small or moderate. Some (though not all) meta-analyses demonstrate a trend over approximately two decades toward a decline in the magnitude of gender differences.

---

[47] As most meta-analysts do, the authors calculated values of d so that they would be positive if the gender difference is in the hypothesized direction (in this case, greater male than female aggression) and negative if the gender difference is opposite to the hypothesis. Thus, although the gender difference is larger for physical than psychological aggression, the value of d is still positive for psychological aggression, meaning that males showed higher levels of psychological aggression than females did.

Meta-analysis is a useful statistical tool that allows one to perform a systematic and relatively unbiased assessment of existing research on any particular area of psychological gender differences.[48] It also allows detailed exploration of which types of tests or research settings are more likely to find gender differences and which are not. Although meta-analysis has been used in psychology and a few other disciplines such as education, it has yet to be used broadly in other social sciences, where it doubtless can contribute to feminist research. It has great promise because it cumulates large bodies of research findings and provides powerful quantitative answers to questions, thereby smashing many myths about gender differences.

Department of Psychology and Women's Studies Research Center
University of Wisconsin—Madison

[48] Meta-analysis has been used to address issues other than gender differences that are of interest to feminist psychologists. One example is Taylor and Hall's analysis of studies assessing the relation between androgyny and self-esteem. See Marylee C. Taylor and Judith A. Hall, "Psychological Androgyny: Theories, Methods, and Conclusions," *Psychological Bulletin* 92 (1982): 347–66.

SCIENCE AND THE
CONSTRUCTION OF
GENDERED BODIES

The Egg and the Sperm: How Science Has Constructed a Romance Based on Stereotypical Male-Female Roles

Emily Martin

> The theory of the human body is always a part of a world-picture. . . . The theory of the human body is always a part of a *fantasy.* [JAMES HILLMAN, *The Myth of Analysis*][1]

As an anthropologist, I am intrigued by the possibility that culture shapes how biological scientists describe what they discover about the natural world. If this were so, we would be learning about more than the natural world in high school biology class; we would be learning about cultural beliefs and practices as if they were part of nature. In the course of my research I realized that the picture of egg and sperm drawn in popular as well as scientific accounts of reproductive biology relies on stereotypes central to our cultural definitions of male and female. The stereotypes imply not only that

Portions of this article were presented as the 1987 Becker Lecture, Cornell University. I am grateful for the many suggestions and ideas I received on this occasion. For especially pertinent help with my arguments and data I thank Richard Cone, Kevin Whaley, Sharon Stephens, Barbara Duden, Susanne Kuechler, Lorna Rhodes, and Scott Gilbert. The article was strengthened and clarified by the comments of the anonymous *Signs* reviewers as well as the superb editorial skills of Amy Gage.

[1] James Hillman, *The Myth of Analysis* (Evanston, Ill.: Northwestern University Press, 1972), 220.

[*Signs: Journal of Women in Culture and Society* 1991, vol. 16, no. 3]

female biological processes are less worthy than their male counterparts but also that women are less worthy than men. Part of my goal in
writing this article is to shine a bright light on the gender stereotypes
hidden within the scientific language of biology. Exposed in such a
light, I hope they will lose much of their power to harm us.

Egg and sperm: A scientific fairy tale

At a fundamental level, all major scientific textbooks depict male
and female reproductive organs as systems for the production of
valuable substances, such as eggs and sperm.[2] In the case of
women, the monthly cycle is described as being designed to
produce eggs and prepare a suitable place for them to be fertilized
and grown—all to the end of making babies. But the enthusiasm
ends there. By extolling the female cycle as a productive enterprise,
menstruation must necessarily be viewed as a failure. Medical texts
describe menstruation as the "debris" of the uterine lining, the
result of necrosis, or death of tissue. The descriptions imply that a
system has gone awry, making products of no use, not to specifica-
tion, unsalable, wasted, scrap. An illustration in a widely used
medical text shows menstruation as a chaotic disintegration of form,
complementing the many texts that describe it as "ceasing," "dying," "losing," "denuding," "expelling."[3]
    Male reproductive physiology is evaluated quite differently. One
of the texts that sees menstruation as failed production employs a
sort of breathless prose when it describes the maturation of sperm:
"The mechanisms which guide the remarkable cellular transformation from spermatid to mature sperm remain uncertain. . . . Perhaps
the most amazing characteristic of spermatogenesis is its sheer magnitude: the normal human male may manufacture several hundred
million sperm per day."[4] In the classic text *Medical Physiology,*
edited by Vernon Mountcastle, the male/female, productive/des-
tructive comparison is more explicit: "Whereas the female *sheds*
only a single gamete each month, the seminiferous tubules *produce*
hundreds of millions of sperm each day" (emphasis mine).[5] The

[2] The textbooks I consulted are the main ones used in classes for undergraduate
premedical students or medical students (or those held on reserve in the library for
these classes) during the past few years at Johns Hopkins University. These texts are
widely used at other universities in the country as well.

[3] Arthur C. Guyton, *Physiology of the Human Body,* 6th ed. (Philadelphia:
Saunders College Publishing, 1984), 624.

[4] Arthur J. Vander, James H. Sherman, and Dorothy S. Luciano, *Human Physiology:
The Mechanisms of Body Function,* 3d ed. (New York: McGraw Hill, 1980), 483–84.

[5] Vernon B. Mountcastle, *Medical Physiology,* 14th ed. (London: Mosby, 1980),
2:1624.

female author of another text marvels at the length of the microscopic seminiferous tubules, which, if uncoiled and placed end to end, "would span almost one-third of a mile!" She writes, "In an adult male these structures produce millions of sperm cells each day." Later she asks, "How is this feat accomplished?"[6] None of these texts expresses such intense enthusiasm for any female processes. It is surely no accident that the "remarkable" process of making sperm involves precisely what, in the medical view, menstruation does not: production of something deemed valuable.[7]

One could argue that menstruation and spermatogenesis are not analogous processes and, therefore, should not be expected to elicit the same kind of response. The proper female analogy to spermatogenesis, biologically, is ovulation. Yet ovulation does not merit enthusiasm in these texts either. Textbook descriptions stress that all of the ovarian follicles containing ova are already present at birth. Far from being *produced,* as sperm are, they merely sit on the shelf, slowly degenerating and aging like overstocked inventory: "At birth, normal human ovaries contain an estimated one million follicles [each], and no new ones appear after birth. Thus, in marked contrast to the male, the newborn female already has all the germ cells she will ever have. Only a few, perhaps 400, are destined to reach full maturity during her active productive life. All the others degenerate at some point in their development so that few, if any, remain by the time she reaches menopause at approximately 50 years of age."[8] Note the "marked contrast" that this description sets up between male and female: the male, who continuously produces fresh germ cells, and the female, who has stockpiled germ cells by birth and is faced with their degeneration.

Nor are the female organs spared such vivid descriptions. One scientist writes in a newspaper article that a woman's ovaries become old and worn out from ripening eggs every month, even though the woman herself is still relatively young: "When you look through a laparoscope . . . at an ovary that has been through hundreds of cycles, even in a superbly healthy American female, you see a scarred, battered organ."[9]

To avoid the negative connotations that some people associate with the female reproductive system, scientists could begin to describe male and female processes as homologous. They might

[6] Eldra Pearl Solomon, *Human Anatomy and Physiology* (New York: CBS College Publishing, 1983), 678.

[7] For elaboration, see Emily Martin, *The Woman in the Body: A Cultural Analysis of Reproduction* (Boston: Beacon, 1987), 27–53.

[8] Vander, Sherman, and Luciano, 568.

[9] Melvin Konner, "Childbearing and Age," *New York Times Magazine* (December 27, 1987), 22–23, esp. 22.

credit females with "producing" mature ova one at a time, as they're needed each month, and describe males as having to face problems of degenerating germ cells. This degeneration would occur throughout life among spermatogonia, the undifferentiated germ cells in the testes that are the long-lived, dormant precursors of sperm.

But the texts have an almost dogged insistence on casting female processes in a negative light. The texts celebrate sperm production because it is continuous from puberty to senescence, while they portray egg production as inferior because it is finished at birth. This makes the female seem unproductive, but some texts will also insist that it is she who is wasteful.[10] In a section heading for *Molecular Biology of the Cell,* a best-selling text, we are told that "Oogenesis is wasteful." The text goes on to emphasize that of the seven million oogonia, or egg germ cells, in the female embryo, most degenerate in the ovary. Of those that do go on to become oocytes, or eggs, many also degenerate, so that at birth only two million eggs remain in the ovaries. Degeneration continues throughout a woman's life: by puberty 300,000 eggs remain, and only a few are present by menopause. "During the 40 or so years of a woman's reproductive life, only 400 to 500 eggs will have been released," the authors write. "All the rest will have degenerated. It is still a mystery why so many eggs are formed only to die in the ovaries."[11]

The real mystery is why the male's vast production of sperm is not seen as wasteful.[12] Assuming that a man "produces" 100 million (10^8) sperm per day (a conservative estimate) during an average reproductive life of sixty years, he would produce well over two

[10] I have found but one exception to the opinion that the female is wasteful: "Smallpox being the nasty disease it is, one might expect nature to have designed antibody molecules with combining sites that specifically recognize the epitopes on smallpox virus. Nature differs from technology, however: it thinks nothing of wastefulness. (For example, rather than improving the chance that a spermatozoon will meet an egg cell, nature finds it easier to produce millions of spermatozoa.)" (Niels Kaj Jerne, "The Immune System," *Scientific American* 229, no. 1 [July 1973]: 53). Thanks to a *Signs* reviewer for bringing this reference to my attention.

[11] Bruce Alberts et al., *Molecular Biology of the Cell* (New York: Garland, 1983), 795.

[12] In her essay "Have Only Men Evolved?" (in *Discovering Reality: Feminist Perspectives on Epistemology, Metaphysics, Methodology, and Philosophy of Science,* ed. Sandra Harding and Merrill B. Hintikka [Dordrecht: Reidel, 1983], 45–69, esp. 60–61), Ruth Hubbard points out that sociobiologists have said the female invests more energy than the male in the production of her large gametes, claiming that this explains why the female provides parental care. Hubbard questions whether it "really takes more 'energy' to generate the one or relatively few eggs than the large excess of sperms required to achieve fertilization." For further critique of how the greater size of eggs is interpreted in sociobiology, see Donna Haraway, "Investment Strategies for the Evolving Portfolio of Primate Females," in *Body/Politics,* ed. Mary Jacobus, Evelyn Fox Keller, and Sally Shuttleworth (New York: Routledge, 1990), 155–56.

trillion sperm in his lifetime. Assuming that a woman "ripens" one egg per lunar month, or thirteen per year, over the course of her forty-year reproductive life, she would total five hundred eggs in her lifetime. But the word "waste" implies an excess, too much produced. Assuming two or three offspring, for every baby a woman produces, she wastes only around two hundred eggs. For every baby a man produces, he wastes more than one trillion (10^{12}) sperm.

How is it that positive images are denied to the bodies of women? A look at language—in this case, scientific language—provides the first clue. Take the egg and the sperm.[13] It is remarkable how "femininely" the egg behaves and how "masculinely" the sperm.[14] The egg is seen as large and passive.[15] It does not *move* or *journey,* but passively "is transported," "is swept,"[16] or even "drifts"[17] along the fallopian tube. In utter contrast, sperm are small, "streamlined," [18] and invariably active. They "deliver" their genes to the egg, "activate the developmental program of the egg,"[19] and have a "velocity" that is often remarked upon.[20] Their tails are "strong" and efficiently powered.[21] Together with the forces of ejaculation, they can "propel the semen into the deepest recesses of the vagina."[22] For this they need "energy," "fuel,"[23] so that with a "whiplashlike motion and strong lurches"[24] they can "burrow through the egg coat"[25] and "penetrate" it.[26]

[13] The sources I used for this article provide compelling information on interactions among sperm. Lack of space prevents me from taking up this theme here, but the elements include competition, hierarchy, and sacrifice. For a newspaper report, see Malcolm W. Browne, "Some Thoughts on Self Sacrifice," *New York Times* (July 5, 1988), C6. For a literary rendition, see John Barth, "Night-Sea Journey," in his *Lost in the Funhouse* (Garden City, N.Y.: Doubleday, 1968), 3–13.

[14] See Carol Delaney, "The Meaning of Paternity and the Virgin Birth Debate," *Man* 21, no. 3 (September 1986): 494–513. She discusses the difference between this scientific view that women contribute genetic material to the fetus and the claim of long-standing Western folk theories that the origin and identity of the fetus comes from the male, as in the metaphor of planting a seed in soil.

[15] For a suggested direct link between human behavior and purportedly passive eggs and active sperm, see Erik H. Erikson, "Inner and Outer Space: Reflections on Womanhood," *Daedalus* 93, no. 2 (Spring 1964): 582–606, esp. 591.

[16] Guyton (n. 3 above), 619; and Mountcastle (n. 5 above), 1609.

[17] Jonathan Miller and David Pelham, *The Facts of Life* (New York: Viking Penguin, 1984), 5.

[18] Alberts et al., 796.

[19] Ibid., 796.

[20] See, e.g., William F. Ganong, *Review of Medical Physiology,* 7th ed. (Los Altos, Calif.: Lange Medical Publications, 1975), 322.

[21] Alberts et al. (n. 11 above), 796.

[22] Guyton, 615.

[23] Solomon (n. 6 above), 683.

[24] Vander, Sherman, and Luciano (n. 4 above), 4th ed. (1985), 580.

[25] Alberts et al., 796.

[26] All biology texts quoted above use the word "penetrate."

At its extreme, the age-old relationship of the egg and the sperm takes on a royal or religious patina. The egg coat, its protective barrier, is sometimes called its "vestments," a term usually reserved for sacred, religious dress. The egg is said to have a "corona,"[27] a crown, and to be accompanied by "attendant cells."[28] It is holy, set apart and above, the queen to the sperm's king. The egg is also passive, which means it must depend on sperm for rescue. Gerald Schatten and Helen Schatten liken the egg's role to that of Sleeping Beauty: "a dormant bride awaiting her mate's magic kiss, which instills the spirit that brings her to life."[29] Sperm, by contrast, have a "mission,"[30] which is to "move through the female genital tract in quest of the ovum."[31] One popular account has it that the sperm carry out a "perilous journey" into the "warm darkness," where some fall away "exhausted." "Survivors" "assault" the egg, the successful candidates "surrounding the prize."[32] Part of the urgency of this journey, in more scientific terms, is that "once released from the supportive environment of the ovary, an egg will die within hours unless rescued by a sperm."[33] The wording stresses the fragility and dependency of the egg, even though the same text acknowledges elsewhere that sperm also live for only a few hours.[34]

In 1948, in a book remarkable for its early insights into these matters, Ruth Herschberger argued that female reproductive organs are seen as biologically interdependent, while male organs are viewed as autonomous, operating independently and in isolation:

> At present the functional is stressed only in connection with women: it is in them that ovaries, tubes, uterus, and vagina have endless interdependence. In the male, reproduction would seem to involve "organs" only.
>
> Yet the sperm, just as much as the egg, is dependent on a great many related processes. There are secretions which mitigate the urine in the urethra before ejaculation, to protect the sperm. There is the reflex shutting off of the bladder connection, the provision of prostatic secretions, and various types of muscular propulsion. The sperm is no more inde-

[27] Solomon, 700.

[28] A. Beldecos et al., "The Importance of Feminist Critique for Contemporary Cell Biology," *Hypatia* 3, no. 1 (Spring 1988): 61–76.

[29] Gerald Schatten and Helen Schatten, "The Energetic Egg," *Medical World News* 23 (January 23, 1984): 51–53, esp. 51.

[30] Alberts et al., 796.

[31] Guyton (n. 3 above), 613.

[32] Miller and Pelham (n. 17 above), 7.

[33] Alberts et al. (n. 11 above), 804.

[34] Ibid., 801.

pendent of its milieu than the egg, and yet from a wish that it were, biologists have lent their support to the notion that the human female, beginning with the egg, is congenitally more dependent than the male.[35]

Bringing out another aspect of the sperm's autonomy, an article in the journal *Cell* has the sperm making an "existential decision" to penetrate the egg: "Sperm are cells with a limited behavioral repertoire, one that is directed toward fertilizing eggs. To execute the decision to abandon the haploid state, sperm swim to an egg and there acquire the ability to effect membrane fusion."[36] Is this a corporate manager's version of the sperm's activities—"executing decisions" while fraught with dismay over difficult options that bring with them very high risk?

There is another way that sperm, despite their small size, can be made to loom in importance over the egg. In a collection of scientific papers, an electron micrograph of an enormous egg and tiny sperm is titled "A Portrait of the Sperm."[37] This is a little like showing a photo of a dog and calling it a picture of the fleas. Granted, microscopic sperm are harder to photograph than eggs, which are just large enough to see with the naked eye. But surely the use of the term "portrait," a word associated with the powerful and wealthy, is significant. Eggs have only micrographs or pictures, not portraits.

One depiction of sperm as weak and timid, instead of strong and powerful—the only such representation in western civilization, so far as I know—occurs in Woody Allen's movie *Everything You Always Wanted To Know About Sex* *But Were Afraid to Ask*. Allen, playing the part of an apprehensive sperm inside a man's testicles, is scared of the man's approaching orgasm. He is reluctant to launch himself into the darkness, afraid of contraceptive devices, afraid of winding up on the ceiling if the man masturbates.

The more common picture—egg as damsel in distress, shielded only by her sacred garments; sperm as heroic warrior to the rescue—cannot be proved to be dictated by the biology of these events. While the "facts" of biology may not *always* be constructed in cultural terms, I would argue that in this case they are. The

---

[35] Ruth Herschberger, *Adam's Rib* (New York: Pelligrini & Cudaby, 1948), esp. 84. I am indebted to Ruth Hubbard for telling me about Herschberger's work, although at a point when this paper was already in draft form.

[36] Bennett M. Shapiro. "The Existential Decision of a Sperm," *Cell* 49, no. 3 (May 1987): 293–94, esp. 293.

[37] Lennart Nilsson, "A Portrait of the Sperm," in *The Functional Anatomy of the Spermatozoan*, ed. Bjorn A. Afzelius (New York: Pergamon, 1975), 79–82.

degree of metaphorical content in these descriptions, the extent to which differences between egg and sperm are emphasized, and the parallels between cultural stereotypes of male and female behavior and the character of egg and sperm all point to this conclusion.

New research, old imagery

As new understandings of egg and sperm emerge, textbook gender imagery is being revised. But the new research, far from escaping the stereotypical representations of egg and sperm, simply replicates elements of textbook gender imagery in a different form. The persistence of this imagery calls to mind what Ludwik Fleck termed "the self-contained" nature of scientific thought. As he described it, "the interaction between what is already known, what remains to be learned, and those who are to apprehend it, go to ensure harmony within the system. But at the same time they also preserve the harmony of illusions, which is quite secure within the confines of a given thought style."[38] We need to understand the way in which the cultural content in scientific descriptions changes as biological discoveries unfold, and whether that cultural content is solidly entrenched or easily changed.

In all of the texts quoted above, sperm are described as penetrating the egg, and specific substances on a sperm's head are described as binding to the egg. Recently, this description of events was rewritten in a biophysics lab at Johns Hopkins University— transforming the egg from the passive to the active party.[39]

Prior to this research, it was thought that the zona, the inner vestments of the egg, formed an impenetrable barrier. Sperm overcame the barrier by mechanically burrowing through, thrashing their tails and slowly working their way along. Later research showed that the sperm released digestive enzymes that chemically broke down the zona; thus, scientists presumed that the sperm used mechanical *and* chemical means to get through to the egg.

In this recent investigation, the researchers began to ask questions about the mechanical force of the sperm's tail. (The lab's goal was to develop a contraceptive that worked topically on sperm.) They discovered, to their great surprise, that the forward thrust of sperm is extremely weak, which contradicts the assumption that

[38] Ludwik Fleck, *Genesis and Development of a Scientific Fact*, ed. Thaddeus J. Trenn and Robert K. Merton (Chicago: University of Chicago Press, 1979), 38.

[39] Jay M. Baltz carried out the research I describe when he was a graduate student in the Thomas C. Jenkins Department of Biophysics at Johns Hopkins University.

sperm are forceful penetrators.[40] Rather than thrusting forward, the sperm's head was now seen to move mostly back and forth. The sideways motion of the sperm's tail makes the head move sideways with a force that is ten times stronger than its forward movement. So even if the overall force of the sperm were strong enough to mechanically break the zona, most of its force would be directed sideways rather than forward. In fact, its strongest tendency, by tenfold, is to escape by attempting to pry itself off the egg. Sperm, then, must be exceptionally efficient at *escaping* from any cell surface they contact. And the surface of the egg must be designed to trap the sperm and prevent their escape. Otherwise, few if any sperm would reach the egg.

The researchers at Johns Hopkins concluded that the sperm and egg stick together because of adhesive molecules on the surfaces of each. The egg traps the sperm and adheres to it so tightly that the sperm's head is forced to lie flat against the surface of the zona, a little bit, they told me, "like Br'er Rabbit getting more and more stuck to tar baby the more he wriggles." The trapped sperm continues to wiggle ineffectually side to side. The mechanical force of its tail is so weak that a sperm cannot break even one chemical bond. This is where the digestive enzymes released by the sperm come in. If they start to soften the zona just at the tip of the sperm and the sides remain stuck, then the weak, flailing sperm can get oriented in the right direction and make it through the zona— provided that its bonds to the zona dissolve as it moves in.

Although this new version of the saga of the egg and the sperm broke through cultural expectations, the researchers who made the discovery continued to write papers and abstracts as if the sperm were the active party who attacks, binds, penetrates, and enters the egg. The only difference was that sperm were now seen as performing these actions weakly.[41] Not until August 1987, more than three years after the findings described above, did these researchers reconceptualize the process to give the egg a more active role. They began to describe the zona as an aggressive sperm catcher, covered

[40] Far less is known about the physiology of sperm than comparable female substances, which some feminists claim is no accident. Greater scientific scrutiny of female reproduction has long enabled the burden of birth control to be placed on women. In this case, the researchers' discovery did not depend on development of any new technology. The experiments made use of glass pipettes, a manometer, and a simple microscope, all of which have been available for more than one hundred years.

[41] Jay Baltz and Richard A. Cone, "What Force Is Needed to Tether a Sperm?" (abstract for Society for the Study of Reproduction, 1985), and "Flagellar Torque on the Head Determines the Force Needed to Tether a Sperm" (abstract for Biophysical Society, 1986).

with adhesive molecules that can capture a sperm with a single bond and clasp it to the zona's surface.[42] In the words of their published account: "The innermost vestment, the *zona pellucida,* is a glyco-protein shell, which captures and tethers the sperm before they penetrate it. . . . The sperm is captured at the initial contact between the sperm tip and the *zona.* . . . Since the thrust [of the sperm] is much smaller than the force needed to break a single affinity bond, the first bond made upon the tip-first meeting of the sperm and *zona* can result in the capture of the sperm."[43]

Experiments in another lab reveal similar patterns of data interpretation. Gerald Schatten and Helen Schatten set out to show that, contrary to conventional wisdom, the "egg is not merely a large, yolk-filled sphere into which the sperm burrows to endow new life. Rather, recent research suggests the almost heretical view that sperm and egg are mutually active partners."[44] This sounds like a departure from the stereotypical textbook view, but further reading reveals Schatten and Schatten's conformity to the aggressive-sperm metaphor. They describe how "the sperm and egg first touch when, from the tip of the sperm's triangular head, a long, thin filament shoots out and harpoons the egg." Then we learn that "remarkably, the harpoon is not so much fired as assembled at great speed, molecule by molecule, from a pool of protein stored in a specialized region called the acrosome. The filament may grow as much as twenty times longer than the sperm head itself before its tip reaches the egg and sticks."[45] Why not call this "making a bridge" or "throwing out a line" rather than firing a harpoon? Harpoons pierce prey and injure or kill them, while this filament only sticks. And why not focus, as the Hopkins lab did, on the stickiness of the egg, rather than the stickiness of the sperm?[46] Later

[42] Jay M. Baltz, David F. Katz, and Richard A. Cone, "The Mechanics of the Sperm-Egg Interaction at the Zona Pellucida," *Biophysical Journal* 54, no. 4 (October 1988): 643–54. Lab members were somewhat familiar with work on metaphors in the biology of female reproduction. Richard Cone, who runs the lab, is my husband, and he talked with them about my earlier research on the subject from time to time. Even though my current research focuses on biological imagery and I heard about the lab's work from my husband every day, I myself did not recognize the role of imagery in the sperm research until many weeks after the period of research and writing I describe. Therefore, I assume that any awareness the lab members may have had about how underlying metaphor might be guiding this particular research was fairly inchoate.

[43] Ibid., 643, 650.

[44] Schatten and Schatten (n. 29 above), 51.

[45] Ibid., 52.

[46] Surprisingly, in an article intended for a general audience, the authors do not point out that these are sea urchin sperm and note that human sperm do not shoot out filaments at all.

in the article, the Schattens replicate the common view of the sperm's perilous journey into the warm darkness of the vagina, this time for the purpose of explaining its journey into the egg itself: "[The sperm] still has an arduous journey ahead. It must penetrate farther into the egg's huge sphere of cytoplasm and somehow locate the nucleus, so that the two cells' chromosomes can fuse. The sperm dives down into the cytoplasm, its tail beating. But it is soon interrupted by the sudden and swift migration of the egg nucleus, which rushes toward the sperm with a velocity triple that of the movement of chromosomes during cell division, crossing the entire egg in about a minute."[47]

Like Schatten and Schatten and the biophysicists at Johns Hopkins, another researcher has recently made discoveries that seem to point to a more interactive view of the relationship of egg and sperm. This work, which Paul Wassarman conducted on the sperm and eggs of mice, focuses on identifying the specific molecules in the egg coat (the zona pellucida) that are involved in egg-sperm interaction. At first glance, his descriptions seem to fit the model of an egalitarian relationship. Male and female gametes "recognize one another," and "interactions . . . take place between sperm and egg."[48] But the article in *Scientific American* in which those descriptions appear begins with a vignette that presages the dominant motif of their presentation: "It has been more than a century since Hermann Fol, a Swiss zoologist, peered into his microscope and became the first person to see a sperm penetrate an egg, fertilize it and form the first cell of a new embryo."[49] This portrayal of the sperm as the active party—the one that *penetrates* and *fertilizes* the egg and *produces* the embryo—is not cited as an example of an earlier, now outmoded view. In fact, the author reiterates the point later in the article: "Many sperm can bind to and penetrate the zona pellucida, or outer coat, of an unfertilized mouse egg, but only one sperm will eventually fuse with the thin plasma membrane surrounding the egg proper (*inner sphere*), fertilizing the egg and giving rise to a new embryo."[50]

The imagery of sperm as aggressor is particularly startling in this case: the main discovery being reported is isolation of a particular molecule *on the egg coat* that plays an important role in fertilization! Wassarman's choice of language sustains the picture. He calls the molecule that has been isolated, ZP3, a "sperm receptor." By

[47] Schatten and Schatten, 53.
[48] Paul M. Wassarman, "Fertilization in Mammals," *Scientific American* 259, no. 6 (December 1988): 78–84, esp. 78, 84.
[49] Ibid., 78.
[50] Ibid., 79.

allocating the passive, waiting role to the egg, Wassarman can continue to describe the sperm as the actor, the one that makes it all happen: "The basic process begins when many sperm first attach loosely and then bind tenaciously to receptors on the surface of the egg's thick outer coat, the zona pellucida. Each sperm, which has a large number of egg-binding proteins on its surface, binds to many sperm receptors on the egg. More specifically, a site on each of the egg-binding proteins fits a complementary site on a sperm receptor, much as a key fits a lock."[51] With the sperm designated as the "key" and the egg the "lock," it is obvious which one acts and which one is acted upon. Could this imagery not be reversed, letting the sperm (the lock) wait until the egg produces the key? Or could we speak of two halves of a locket matching, and regard the matching itself as the action that initiates the fertilization?

It is as if Wassarman were determined to make the egg the receiving partner. Usually in biological research, the *protein* member of the pair of binding molecules is called the receptor, and physically it has a pocket in it rather like a lock. As the diagrams that illustrate Wassarman's article show, the molecules on the sperm are proteins and have "pockets." The small, mobile molecules that fit into these pockets are called ligands. As shown in the diagrams, ZP3 on the egg is a polymer of "keys"; many small knobs stick out. Typically, molecules on the sperm would be called receptors and molecules on the egg would be called ligands. But Wassarman chose to name ZP3 on the egg the receptor and to create a new term, "the egg-binding protein," for the molecule on the sperm that otherwise would have been called the receptor.[52]

Wassarman does credit the egg coat with having more functions than those of a sperm receptor. While he notes that "the zona pellucida has at times been viewed by investigators as a nuisance, a barrier to sperm and hence an impediment to fertilization," his new research reveals that the egg coat "serves as a sophisticated biological security system that screens incoming sperm, selects only those compatible with fertilization and development, prepares sperm for fusion with the egg and later protects the resulting embryo from polyspermy [a lethal condition caused by fusion of more than one sperm with a single egg]."[53] Although this description gives the egg an active role, that role is drawn in stereotypically

---

[51] Ibid., 78.

[52] Since receptor molecules are relatively *immotile* and the ligands that bind to them relatively *motile*, one might imagine the egg being called the receptor and the sperm the ligand. But the molecules in question on egg and sperm are immotile molecules. It is the sperm as a *cell* that has motility, and the egg as a cell that has relative immotility.

[53] Wassarman, 78–79.

feminine terms. The egg *selects* an appropriate mate, *prepares* him for fusion, and then *protects* the resulting offspring from harm. This is courtship and mating behavior as seen through the eyes of a sociobiologist: woman as the hard-to-get prize, who, following union with the chosen one, becomes woman as servant and mother.

And Wassarman does not quit there. In a review article for *Science*, he outlines the "chronology of fertilization."[54] Near the end of the article are two subject headings. One is "Sperm Penetration," in which Wassarman describes how the chemical dissolving of the zona pellucida combines with the "substantial propulsive force generated by sperm." The next heading is "Sperm-Egg Fusion." This section details what happens inside the zona after a sperm "penetrates" it. Sperm "can make contact with, adhere to, and fuse with (that is, fertilize) an egg."[55] Wassarman's word choice, again, is astonishingly skewed in favor of the sperm's activity, for in the next breath he says that sperm *lose* all motility upon fusion with the egg's surface. In mouse and sea urchin eggs, the sperm enters at the *egg's* volition, according to Wassarman's description: "Once fused with egg plasma membrane [the surface of the egg], how does a sperm enter the egg? The surface of both mouse and sea urchin eggs is covered with thousands of plasma membrane-bound projections, called microvilli [tiny "hairs"]. Evidence in sea urchins suggests that, after membrane fusion, a group of elongated microvilli cluster tightly around and interdigitate over the sperm head. As these microvilli are resorbed, the sperm is drawn into the egg. Therefore, sperm motility, which ceases at the time of fusion in both sea urchins and mice, is not required for sperm entry."[56] The section called "Sperm Penetration" more logically would be followed by a section called "The Egg Envelops," rather than "Sperm-Egg Fusion." This would give a parallel—and more accurate—sense that both the egg and the sperm initiate action.

Another way that Wassarman makes less of the egg's activity is by describing components of the egg but referring to the sperm as a whole entity. Deborah Gordon has described such an approach as "atomism" ("the part is independent of and primordial to the whole") and identified it as one of the "tenacious assumptions" of Western science and medicine.[57] Wassarman employs atomism to

[54] Paul M. Wassarman, "The Biology and Chemistry of Fertilization," *Science* 235, no. 4788 (January 30, 1987): 553–60, esp. 554.

[55] Ibid., 557.

[56] Ibid., 557–58. This finding throws into question Schatten and Schatten's description (n. 29 above) of the sperm, its tail beating, diving down into the egg.

[57] Deborah R. Gordon, "Tenacious Assumptions in Western Medicine," in *Biomedicine Examined*, ed. Margaret Lock and Deborah Gordon (Dordrecht: Kluwer, 1988), 19–56, esp. 26.

his advantage. When he refers to processes going on within sperm, he consistently returns to descriptions that remind us from whence these activities came: they are part of sperm that penetrate an egg or generate propulsive force. When he refers to processes going on within eggs, he stops there. As a result, any active role he grants them appears to be assigned to the parts of the egg, and not to the egg itself. In the quote above, it is the microvilli that actively cluster around the sperm. In another example, "the driving force for engulfment of a fused sperm comes from a region of cytoplasm just beneath an egg's plasma membrane."[58]

Social implications: Thinking beyond

All three of these revisionist accounts of egg and sperm cannot seem to escape the hierarchical imagery of older accounts. Even though each new account gives the egg a larger and more active role, taken together they bring into play another cultural stereotype: woman as a dangerous and aggressive threat. In the Johns Hopkins lab's revised model, the egg ends up as the female aggressor who "captures and tethers" the sperm with her sticky zona, rather like a spider lying in wait in her web.[59] The Schatten lab has the egg's nucleus "interrupt" the sperm's dive with a "sudden and swift" rush by which she "clasps the sperm and guides its nucleus to the center."[60] Wassarman's description of the surface of the egg "covered with thousands of plasma membrane-bound projections, called microvilli" that reach out and clasp the sperm adds to the spiderlike imagery.[61]

These images grant the egg an active role but at the cost of appearing disturbingly aggressive. Images of woman as dangerous and aggressive, the femme fatale who victimizes men, are widespread in Western literature and culture.[62] More specific is the connection of spider imagery with the idea of an engulfing, devouring mother.[63] New data did not lead scientists to eliminate gender stereotypes in their descriptions of egg and sperm. Instead, scien-

[58] Wassarman, "The Biology and Chemistry of Fertilization," 558.

[59] Baltz, Katz, and Cone (n. 42 above), 643, 650.

[60] Schatten and Schatten, 53.

[61] Wassarman, "The Biology and Chemistry of Fertilization," 557.

[62] Mary Ellman, *Thinking about Women* (New York: Harcourt Brace Jovanovich, 1968), 140; Nina Auerbach, *Woman and the Demon* (Cambridge, Mass.: Harvard University Press, 1982), esp. 186.

[63] Kenneth Alan Adams, "Arachnophobia: Love American Style," *Journal of Psychoanalytic Anthropology* 4, no. 2 (1981): 157–97.

tists simply began to describe egg and sperm in different, but no less damaging, terms.

Can we envision a less stereotypical view? Biology itself provides another model that could be applied to the egg and the sperm. The cybernetic model—with its feedback loops, flexible adaptation to change, coordination of the parts within a whole, evolution over time, and changing response to the environment—is common in genetics, endocrinology, and ecology and has a growing influence in medicine in general.[64] This model has the potential to shift our imagery from the negative, in which the female reproductive system is castigated both for not producing eggs after birth and for producing (and thus wasting) too many eggs overall, to something more positive. The female reproductive system could be seen as responding to the environment (pregnancy or menopause), adjusting to monthly changes (menstruation), and flexibly changing from reproductivity after puberty to nonreproductivity later in life. The sperm and egg's interaction could also be described in cybernetic terms. J. F. Hartman's research in reproductive biology demonstrated fifteen years ago that if an egg is killed by being pricked with a needle, live sperm cannot get through the zona.[65] Clearly, this evidence shows that the egg and sperm *do* interact on more mutual terms, making biology's refusal to portray them that way all the more disturbing.

We would do well to be aware, however, that cybernetic imagery is hardly neutral. In the past, cybernetic models have played an important part in the imposition of social control. These models inherently provide a way of thinking about a "field" of interacting components. Once the field can be seen, it can become the object of new forms of knowledge, which in turn can allow new forms of social control to be exerted over the components of the field. During the 1950s, for example, medicine began to recognize the psychosocial *environment* of the patient: the patient's family and its psychodynamics. Professions such as social work began to focus on this new environment, and the resulting knowledge became one way to further control the patient. Patients began to be seen not as isolated, individual bodies, but as psychosocial entities located in an "ecological" system: management of "the patient's psychology was a new entrée to patient control."[66]

[64] William Ray Arney and Bernard Bergen, *Medicine and the Management of Living* (Chicago: University of Chicago Press, 1984).

[65] J. F. Hartman, R. B. Gwatkin, and C. F. Hutchison, "Early Contact Interactions between Mammalian Gametes *In Vitro,*" *Proceedings of the National Academy of Sciences (U.S.)* 69, no. 10 (1972): 2767–69.

[66] Arney and Bergen, 68.

The models that biologists use to describe their data can have important social effects. During the nineteenth century, the social and natural sciences strongly influenced each other: the social ideas of Malthus about how to avoid the natural increase of the poor inspired Darwin's *Origin of Species*.[67] Once the *Origin* stood as a description of the natural world, complete with competition and market struggles, it could be reimported into social science as social Darwinism, in order to justify the social order of the time. What we are seeing now is similar: the importation of cultural ideas about passive females and heroic males into the "personalities" of gametes. This amounts to the "implanting of social imagery on representations of nature so as to lay a firm basis for reimporting exactly that same imagery as natural explanations of social phenomena."[68]

Further research would show us exactly what social effects are being wrought from the biological imagery of egg and sperm. At the very least, the imagery keeps alive some of the hoariest old stereotypes about weak damsels in distress and their strong male rescuers. That these stereotypes are now being written in at the level of the *cell* constitutes a powerful move to make them seem so natural as to be beyond alteration.

The stereotypical imagery might also encourage people to imagine that what results from the interaction of egg and sperm—a fertilized egg—is the result of deliberate "human" action at the cellular level. Whatever the intentions of the human couple, in this microscopic "culture" a cellular "bride" (or femme fatale) and a cellular "groom" (her victim) make a cellular baby. Rosalind Petchesky points out that through visual representations such as sonograms, we are given "*images* of younger and younger, and tinier and tinier, fetuses being 'saved.' " This leads to "the point of visibility being 'pushed back' *indefinitely*."[69] Endowing egg and sperm with intentional action, a key aspect of personhood in our culture, lays the foundation for the point of viability being pushed back to the moment of fertilization. This will likely lead to greater acceptance of technological developments and new forms of scrutiny and manipulation, for the benefit of these inner "persons": court-ordered restrictions on a pregnant woman's activities in order to protect her fetus, fetal surgery, amniocentesis, and rescinding of abortion rights, to name but a few examples.[70]

[67] Ruth Hubbard, "Have Only Men Evolved?" (n. 12 above), 51–52.

[68] David Harvey, personal communication, November 1989.

[69] Rosalind Petchesky, "Fetal Images: The Power of Visual Culture in the Politics of Reproduction," *Feminist Studies* 13, no. 2 (Summer 1987): 263–92, esp. 272.

[70] Rita Arditti, Renate Klein, and Shelley Minden, *Test-Tube Women* (London: Pandora, 1984); Ellen Goodman, "Whose Right to Life?" *Baltimore Sun* (November

Even if we succeed in substituting more egalitarian, interactive metaphors to describe the activities of egg and sperm, and manage to avoid the pitfalls of cybernetic models, we would still be guilty of endowing cellular entities with personhood. More crucial, then, than what *kinds* of personalities we bestow on cells is the very fact that we are doing it at all. This process could ultimately have the most disturbing social consequences.

One clear feminist challenge is to wake up sleeping metaphors in science, particularly those involved in descriptions of the egg and the sperm. Although the literary convention is to call such metaphors "dead," they are not so much dead as sleeping, hidden within the scientific content of texts—and all the more powerful for it.[71] Waking up such metaphors, by becoming aware of when we are projecting cultural imagery onto what we study, will improve our ability to investigate and understand nature. Waking up such metaphors, by becoming aware of their implications, will rob them of their power to naturalize our social conventions about gender.

Department of Anthropology
Johns Hopkins University

17, 1987); Tamar Lewin, "Courts Acting to Force Care of the Unborn," *New York Times* (November 23, 1987), A1 and B10; Susan Irwin and Brigitte Jordan, "Knowledge, Practice, and Power: Court Ordered Cesarean Sections," *Medical Anthropology Quarterly* 1, no. 3 (September 1987): 319–34.

[71] Thanks to Elizabeth Fee and David Spain, who in February 1989 and April 1989, respectively, made points related to this.

The Medical Construction of Gender: Case Management of Intersexed Infants

Suzanne J. Kessler

The birth of intersexed infants, babies born with genitals that are neither clearly male nor clearly female, has been documented throughout recorded time.[1] In the late twentieth century, medical technology has advanced to allow scientists to determine chromosomal and hormonal gender, which is typically taken to be the real, natural, biological gender, usually referred to as "sex."[2] Nevertheless, physicians who handle the cases of intersexed infants consider several factors beside biological ones in determining, assigning, and announcing the gender of a particular infant. Indeed, biological factors are often preempted in their deliberations by such cultural factors as the "correct" length of the penis and capacity of the vagina.

I want to thank my student Jane Weider for skillfully conducting and transcribing the interviews for this article.

[1] For historical reviews of the intersexed person in ancient Greek and Roman periods, see Leslie Fiedler, *Freaks: Myths and Images of the Second Self* (New York: Simon & Schuster, 1978); Vern Bullough, *Sexual Variance in Society and History* (New York: Wiley, 1976). For the Middle Ages and Renaissance, see Michel Foucault, *History of Sexuality* (New York: Pantheon, 1980). For the eighteenth and nineteenth centuries, see Michel Foucault, *Herculine Barbin* (New York: Pantheon, 1978); and for the early twentieth century, see Havelock Ellis, *Studies in the Psychology of Sex* (New York: Random House, 1942).

[2] Suzanne J. Kessler and Wendy McKenna, *Gender: An Ethnomethodological Approach* (1978; reprint, Chicago: University of Chicago Press, 1985).

[*Signs: Journal of Women in Culture and Society* 1990, vol. 16, no. 1]

In the literature of intersexuality, issues such as announcing a baby's gender at the time of delivery, postdelivery discussions with the parents, and consultations with patients in adolescence are considered only peripherally to the central medical issues—etiology, diagnosis, and surgical procedures.[3] Yet members of medical teams have standard practices for managing intersexuality that rely ultimately on cultural understandings of gender. The process and guidelines by which decisions about gender (re)construction are made reveal the model for the social construction of gender generally. Moreover, in the face of apparently incontrovertible evidence—infants born with some combination of "female" and "male" reproductive and sexual features—physicians hold an incorrigible belief in and insistence upon female and male as the only "natural" options. This paradox highlights and calls into question the idea that female and male are biological givens compelling a culture of two genders.

Ideally, to undertake an extensive study of intersexed infant case management, I would like to have had direct access to particular events, for example, the deliveries of intersexed infants and the initial discussions among physicians, between physicians and parents, between parents, and among parents and family and friends of intersexed infants. The rarity with which intersexuality occurs, however, made this unfeasible.[4] Alternatively, physicians who have had considerable experience in dealing with this condition were interviewed. I do not assume that their "talk" about how they manage such cases mirrors their "talk" in the situation, but their words do reveal that they have certain assumptions about gender and that they impose those assumptions via their medical decisions on the patients they treat.

Interviews were conducted with six medical experts (three women and three men) in the field of pediatric intersexuality: one

[3] See, e.g., M. Bolkenius, R. Daum, and E. Heinrich, "Pediatric Surgical Principles in the Management of Children with Intersex," *Progressive Pediatric Surgery* 17 (1984): 33–38; Kenneth I. Glassberg, "Gender Assignment in Newborn Male Pseudohermaphrodites," *Urologic Clinics of North America* 7 (June 1980): 409–21; and Peter A. Lee et al., "Micropenis. I. Criteria, Etiologies and Classification," *Johns Hopkins Medical Journal* 146 (1980): 156–63.

[4] It is impossible to get accurate statistics on the frequency of intersexuality. Chromosomal abnormalities (like XOXX or XXXY) are registered, but those conditions do not always imply ambiguous genitals, and most cases of ambiguous genitals do not involve chromosomal abnormalities. None of the physicians interviewed for this study would venture a guess on frequency rates, but all agreed that intersexuality is rare. One physician suggested that the average obstetrician may see only two cases in twenty years. Another estimated that a specialist may see only one a year, or possibly as many as five a year.

clinical geneticist, three endocrinologists (two of them pediatric specialists), one psychoendocrinologist, and one urologist. All of them have had extensive clinical experience with various inter-sexed syndromes, and some are internationally known researchers in the field of intersexuality. They were selected on the basis of their prominence in the field and their representation of four different medical centers in New York City. Although they know one another, they do not collaborate on research and are not part of the same management team. All were interviewed in the spring of 1985, in their offices, and interviews lasted between forty-five minutes and one hour. Unless further referenced, all quotations in this article are from these interviews.

The theory of intersexuality management

The sophistication of today's medical technology has led to an extensive compilation of various intersex categories based on the various causes of malformed genitals. The "true intersexed" con-dition, where both ovarian and testicular tissue are present in either the same gonad or in opposite gonads, accounts for fewer than 5 percent of all cases of ambiguous genitals.[5] More commonly, the infant has either ovaries or testes, but the genitals are ambiguous. If the infant has two ovaries, the condition is referred to as female pseudohermaphroditism. If the infant has two testes, the condition is referred to as male pseudohermaphroditism. There are numerous causes of both forms of pseudohermaphroditism, and although there are life-threatening aspects to some of these conditions, having ambiguous genitals per se is not harmful to the infant's health.[6] Although most cases of ambiguous genitals do not repre-sent true intersex, in keeping with the contemporary literature, I will refer to all such cases as intersexed.

Current attitudes toward the intersex condition are primarily influenced by three factors. First are the extraordinary advance-

---

[5] Mariano Castro-Magana, Moris Angulo, and Platon J. Collipp, "Management of the Child with Ambiguous Genitalia," *Medical Aspects of Human Sexuality* 18 (April 1984): 172–88.

[6] For example, infants whose intersexuality is caused by congenital adrenal hyperplasia can develop severe electrolyte disturbances unless the condition is controlled by cortisone treatments. Intersexed infants whose condition is caused by androgen insensitivity are in danger of malignant degeneration of the testes unless they are removed. For a complete catalog of clinical syndromes related to the intersexed condition, see Arye Lev-Ran, "Sex Reversal as Related to Clinical Syndromes in Human Beings," in *Handbook of Sexology II: Genetics, Hormones and Behavior*, ed. John Money and H. Musaph (New York: Elsevier, 1978), 157–73.

ments in surgical techniques and endocrinology in the last decade. For example, female genitals can now be constructed to be indistinguishable in appearance from normal natural ones. Some abnormally small penises can be enlarged with the exogenous application of hormones, although surgical skills are not sufficiently advanced to construct a normal-looking and functioning penis out of other tissue.[7] Second, in the contemporary United States the influence of the feminist movement has called into question the valuation of women according to strictly reproductive functions, and the presence or absence of functional gonads is no longer the only or the definitive criterion for gender assignment. Third, contemporary psychological theorists have begun to focus on "gender identity" (one's sense of oneself as belonging to the female or male category) as distinct from "gender role" (cultural expectations of one's behavior as "appropriate" for a female or male).[8] The relevance of this new gender identity theory for rethinking cases of ambiguous genitals is that gender must be assigned as early as possible in order for gender identity to develop successfully. As a result of these three factors, intersexuality is now considered a treatable condition of the genitals, one that needs to be resolved expeditiously.

According to all of the specialists interviewed, management of intersexed cases is based upon the theory of gender proposed first by John Money, J. G. Hampson, and J. L. Hampson in 1955 and developed in 1972 by Money and Anke A. Ehrhardt, which argues that gender identity is changeable until approximately eighteen

---

[7] Much of the surgical experimentation in this area has been accomplished by urologists who are trying to create penises for female-to-male transsexuals. Although there have been some advancements in recent years in the ability to create a "reasonable-looking" penis from tissue taken elsewhere on the body, the complicated requirements of the organ (both urinary and sexual functioning) have posed surgical problems. It may be, however, that the concerns of the urologists are not identical to the concerns of the patients. While data are not yet available from the intersexed, we know that female-to-male transsexuals place greater emphasis on the "public" requirements of the penis (e.g., being able to look normal while standing at the urinal or wearing a bathing suit) than on its functional requirements (e.g., being able to carry urine or achieve an erection) (Kessler and McKenna, 128–32). As surgical techniques improve, female-to-male transsexuals (and intersexed males) might increase their demands for organs that look and function better.

[8] Historically, psychology has tended to blur the distinction between the two by equating a person's acceptance of her or his genitals with gender role and ignoring gender identity. For example, Freudian theory posited that if one had a penis and accepted its reality, then masculine gender role behavior would naturally follow (Sigmund Freud, "Some Psychical Consequences of the Anatomical Distinctions between the Sexes" [1925], vol. 18 of The Complete Psychological Works, ed. and trans. J. Strachey [New York: Norton, 1976]).

months of age.[9] "To use the Pygmalion allegory, one may begin with the same clay and fashion a god or a goddess."[10] The theory rests on satisfying several conditions: the experts must insure that the parents have no doubt about whether their child is male or female; the genitals must be made to match the assigned gender as soon as possible; gender-appropriate hormones must be administered at puberty; and intersexed children must be kept informed about their situation with age-appropriate explanations. If these conditions are met, the theory proposes, the intersexed child will develop a gender identity in accordance with the gender assignment (regardless of the chromosomal gender) and will not question her or his assignment and request reassignment at a later age.

Supportive evidence for Money and Ehrhardt's theory is based on only a handful of repeatedly cited cases, but it has been accepted because of the prestige of the theoreticians and its resonance with contemporary ideas about gender, children, psychology, and medi-

---

[9] Almost all of the published literature on intersexed infant case management has been written or cowritten by one researcher, John Money, professor of medical psychology and professor of pediatrics, emeritus, at the Johns Hopkins University and Hospital, where he is director of the Psychohormonal Research Unit. Even the publications that are produced independently of Money reference him and reiterate his management philosophy. Although only one of the physicians interviewed publishes with Money, all of them essentially concur with his views and give the impression of a consensus that is rarely encountered in science. The one physician who raised some questions about Money's philosophy and the gender theory on which it is based has extensive experience with intersexuality in a nonindustrialized culture where the infant is managed differently with no apparent harm to gender development. Even though psychologists fiercely argue issues of gender identity and gender role development, doctors who treat intersexed infants seem untouched by these debates. There are no renegade voices either from within the medical establishment or, thus far, from outside. Why Money has been so single-handedly influential in promoting his ideas about gender is a question worthy of a separate substantial analysis. His management philosophy is conveyed in the following sources: John Money, J. G. Hampson, and J. L. Hampson, "Hermaphroditism: Recommendations concerning Assignment of Sex, Change of Sex, and Psychologic Management," *Bulletin of the Johns Hopkins Hospital* 97 (1955): 284–300; John Money, Reynolds Potter, and Clarice S. Stoll, "Sex Reannouncement in Hereditary Sex Deformity: Psychology and Sociology of Habilitation," *Social Science and Medicine* 3 (1969): 207–16; John Money and Anke A. Ehrhardt, *Man and Woman, Boy and Girl* (Baltimore: Johns Hopkins University Press, 1972); John Money, "Psychologic Consideration of Sex Assignment in Intersexuality," *Clinics in Plastic Surgery* 1 (April 1974): 215–22, "Psychological Counseling: Hermaphroditism," in *Endocrine and Genetic Diseases of Childhood and Adolescence*, ed. L. I. Gardner (Philadelphia: Saunders, 1975): 609–18, and "Birth Defect of the Sex Organs: Telling the Parents and the Patient," *British Journal of Sexual Medicine* 10 (March 1983): 14; John Money et al., "Micropenis, Family Mental Health, and Neonatal Management: A Report on Fourteen Patients Reared as Girls," *Journal of Preventive Psychiatry* 1, no. 1 (1981): 17–27.

[10] Money and Ehrhardt, 152.

cine. Gender and children are malleable; psychology and medicine are the tools used to transform them. This theory is so strongly endorsed that it has taken on the character of gospel. "I think we [physicians] have been raised in the Money theory," one endocrinologist said. Another claimed, "We always approach the problem in a similar way and it's been dictated, to a large extent, by the work of John Money and Anke Ehrhardt because they are the only people who have published, at least in medical literature, any data, any guidelines." It is provocative that this physician immediately followed this assertion with: "And I don't know how effective it really is." Contradictory data are rarely cited in reviews of the literature, were not mentioned by any of the physicians interviewed, and have not diminished these physicians' belief in the theory's validity.[11]

The doctors interviewed concur with the argument that gender be assigned immediately, decisively, and irreversibly, and that professional opinions be presented in a clear and unambiguous way. The psychoendocrinologist said that when doctors make a statement about the infant, they should "stick to it." The urologist said, "If you make a statement that later has to be disclaimed or discredited, you've weakened your credibility." A gender assignment made decisively, unambiguously, and irrevocably contributes, I believe, to the general impression that the infant's true, natural "sex" has been discovered, and that something that was there all along has been found. It also serves to maintain the credibility of the medical profession, reassure the parents, and reflexively substantiate Money and Ehrhardt's theory.

Also according to the theory, if operative correction is necessary, it should take place as soon as possible. If the infant is assigned the male gender, the initial stage of penis repair is usually undertaken in the first year, and further surgery is completed before the child enters school. If the infant is assigned the female gender, vulva repair (including clitoral reduction) is usually begun by three months of age. Money suggests that if reduction of phallic tissue were delayed beyond the neonatal period, the infant would have traumatic memories of having been castrated.[12] Vaginoplasty, in those females having an adequate internal structure (e.g., the vaginal canal is near its expected location), is done between the ages of one and four years. Girls who require more complicated surgical procedures might not be surgically corrected until

---

[11] Contradictory data are presented in Milton Diamond, "Sexual Identity, Monozygotic Twins Reared in Discordant Sex Roles and a BBC Follow-up," *Archives of Sexual Behavior* 11, no. 2 (1982): 181–86.

[12] Money, "Psychologic Consideration of Sex Assignment in Intersexuality."

preadolescence.[13] The complete vaginal canal is typically constructed only when the body is fully grown, following pubertal
feminization with estrogen, although more recently some specialists have claimed surgical success with vaginal construction in the
early childhood years.[14] Although physicians speculate about the
possible trauma of an early childhood "castration" memory, there is
no corresponding concern that vaginal reconstructive surgery delayed beyond the neonatal period is traumatic.

Even though gender identity theory places the critical age limit
for gender reassignment between eighteen months and two years,
the physicians acknowledge that diagnosis, gender assignment, and
genital reconstruction cannot be delayed for as long as two years,
since a clear gender assignment and correctly formed genitals will
determine the kind of interactions parents will have with the
child.[15] The geneticist argued that when parents "change a diaper
and see genitalia that don't mean much in terms of gender assignment, I think it prolongs the negative response to the baby. . . . If
you have clitoral enlargement that is so extraordinary that the
parents can't distinguish between male and female, it is sometimes
helpful to reduce that somewhat so that the parent views the child
as female." Another physician concurred: parents "need to go home
and do their job as child rearers with it very clear whether it's a boy
or a girl."

Diagnosis

A premature gender announcement by an obstetrician, prior to a
close examination of an infant's genitals, can be problematic.
Money and his colleagues claim that the primary complications in
case management of intersexed infants can be traced to mishan-
dling by medical personnel untrained in sexology.[16] According to
one of the pediatric endocrinologists interviewed, obstetricians
improperly educated about intersexed conditions "don't examine
the babies closely enough at birth and say things just by looking,
before separating legs and looking at everything, and jump to

[13] Castro-Magana, Angulo, and Collipp (n. 5 above).

[14] Victor Braren et al., "True Hermaphroditism: A Rational Approach to Diagnosis and Treatment," *Urology* 15 (June 1980): 569–74.

[15] Studies of normal newborns have shown that from the moment of birth the
parent responds to the infant based on the infant's gender. Jeffrey Rubin, F. J.
Provenzano, and Z. Luria, "The Eye of the Beholder: Parents' Views on Sex of
Newborns," *American Journal of Orthopsychiatry* 44, no. 4 (1974): 512–19.

[16] Money et al. (n. 9 above).

conclusions, because 99 percent of the time it's correct. . . . People get upset, physicians I mean. And they say things that are inappropriate." For example, he said that an inexperienced obstetrician might blurt out, "I think you have a boy, or no, maybe you have a girl." Other inappropriate remarks a doctor might make in postdelivery consultation with the parents include, "You have a little boy, but he'll never function as a little boy, so you better raise him as a little girl." As a result, said the pediatric endocrinologist, "the family comes away with the idea that they have a little boy, and that's what they wanted, and that's what they're going to get." In such cases parents sometimes insist that the child be raised male despite the physician's instructions to the contrary. "People have in mind certain things they've heard, that this is a boy, and they're not likely to forget that, or they're not likely to let it go easily." The urologist agreed that the first gender attribution is critical: "Once it's been announced, you've got a big problem on your hands." "One of the worst things is to allow [the parents] to go ahead and give a name and tell everyone, and it turns out the child has to be raised in the opposite sex."[17]

Physicians feel that the mismanagement of such cases requires careful remedying. The psychoendocrinologist asserted, "When I'm involved, I spend hours with the parents to explain to them what has happened and how a mistake like that could be made, *or not really a mistake but a different decision*" (my emphasis). One pediatric endocrinologist said, "[I] try to dissuade them from previous misconceptions, and say, 'Well, I know what they meant, but the way they said it confused you. This is, I think, a better way to think about it.' " These statements reveal physicians' efforts not only to protect parents from concluding that their child is neither male nor female but also to protect other physicians' decision-making processes. Case management involves perpetuating the notion that good medical decisions are based on interpretations of the infant's real "sex" rather than on cultural understandings of gender.

"Mismanagements" are less likely to occur in communities with major medical centers, where specialists are prepared to deal with intersexuality and a medical team (perhaps drawing physicians from more than one teaching hospital) is quickly assembled. The team typically consists of the original referring doctor (obstetrician

[17] There is evidence from other kinds of sources that once a gender attribution is made, all further information buttresses that attribution, and only the most contradictory new information will cause the original gender attribution to be questioned. See, e.g., Kessler and McKenna (n. 2 above).

or pediatrician), a pediatric endocrinologist, a pediatric surgeon (urologist or gynecologist), and a geneticist. In addition, a psychologist, psychiatrist, or psychoendocrinologist might play a role. If an infant is born with ambiguous genitals in a small community hospital, without the relevant specialists on staff, she or he is likely to be transferred to a hospital where diagnosis and treatment are available. Intersexed infants born in poor rural areas where there is less medical intervention might never be referred for genital reconstruction. Many of these children, like those born in earlier historical periods, will grow up and live through adulthood with the condition of genital ambiguity—somehow managing.

The diagnosis of intersexed conditions includes assessing the chromosomal sex and the syndrome that produced the genital ambiguity, and may include medical procedures such as cytologic screening; chromosomal analysis; assessing serum electrolytes; hormone, gonadotropin, and steroids evaluation; digital examination; and radiographic genitography.[18] In any intersexed condition, if the infant is determined to be a genetic female (having an XX chromosome makeup), then the treatment—genital surgery to reduce the phallus size—can proceed relatively quickly, satisfying what the doctors believe are psychological and cultural demands. For example, 21-hydroxylase deficiency, a form of female pseudohermaphroditism and one of the most common conditions, can be determined by a blood test within the first few days.

If, on the other hand, the infant is determined to have at least one Y chromosome, then surgery may be considerably delayed. A decision must be made whether to test the ability of the phallic tissue to respond to (HCG) androgen treatment, which is intended to enlarge the microphallus enough to be a penis. The endocrinologist explained, "You do HCG testing and you find out if the male can make testosterone. . . . You can get those results back probably within three weeks. . . . You're sure the male is making testosterone— but can he respond to it? It can take three months of waiting to see whether the phallus responds." If the Y-chromosome infant cannot make testosterone or cannot respond to the testosterone it makes, the phallus will not develop, and the Y-chromosome infant is not considered to be a male after all.

Should the infant's phallus respond to the local application of testosterone or a brief course of intramuscular injections of low-potency androgen, the gender assignment problem is resolved, but possibly at some later cost, since the penis will not grow again at

[18] Castro-Magana, Angulo, and Collipp (n. 5 above).

puberty when the rest of the body develops.[19] Money's case management philosophy assumes that while it may be difficult for an adult male to have a much smaller than average penis, it is very detrimental to the morale of the young boy to have a micropenis.[20] In the former case the male's manliness might be at stake, but in the latter case his essential maleness might be. Although the psychological consequences of these experiences have not been empirically documented, Money and his colleagues suggest that it is wise to avoid the problems of both the micropenis in childhood and the still undersized penis postpuberty by reassigning many of these infants to the female gender.[21] This approach suggests that for Money and his colleagues, chromosomes are less relevant in determining gender than penis size, and that, by implication, "male" is defined not by the genetic condition of having one Y and one X chromosome or by the production of sperm but by the aesthetic condition of having an appropriately sized penis.

The tests and procedures required for diagnosis (and, consequently, for gender assignment) can take several months.[22] Although physicians are anxious not to make a premature gender assignment, their language suggests that it is difficult for them to take a completely neutral position and think and speak only of phallic tissue that belongs to an infant whose gender has not yet been determined or decided. Comments such as "seeing whether the male can respond to testosterone" imply at least a tentative male gender assignment of an XY infant. The psychoendocrinologist's explanation to parents of their infant's treatment program also illustrates this implicit male gender assignment. "Clearly this baby has an underdeveloped phallus. But if the phallus responds to this treatment, we are fairly confident that surgical techniques and hormonal techniques will help this child to look like a boy. But we want to make absolutely sure and use some hormone treatments and see whether the tissue reacts." The mere fact that this doctor refers to the genitals as an "underdeveloped" phallus rather than an overdeveloped clitoris suggests that the infant has been judged to

[19] Money, "Psychological Consideration of Sex Assignment in Intersexuality" (n. 9 above).

[20] Technically, the term "micropenis" should be reserved for an exceptionally small but well-formed structure. A small, malformed "penis" should be referred to as a "microphallus" (Lee et al. [n. 3 above]).

[21] Money et al., 26. A different view is argued by another leading gender identity theorist: "When a little boy (with an imperfect penis) knows he is a male, he creates a penis that functions symbolically the same as those of boys with normal penises" (Robert J. Stoller, Sex and Gender [New York: Aronson, 1968], 1:49).

[22] W. Ch. Hecker, "Operative Correction of Intersexual Genitals in Children," Pediatric Surgery 17 (1984): 21–31.

be, at least provisionally, a male. In the case of the undersized phallus, what is ambiguous is not whether this is a penis but whether it is "good enough" to remain one. If at the end of the treatment period the phallic tissue has not responded, what had been a potential penis (referred to in the medical literature as a "clitoropenis") is now considered an enlarged clitoris (or "penoclitoris"), and reconstructive surgery is planned as for the genetic female.

The time-consuming nature of intersex diagnosis and the assumption, based on gender identity theory, that gender should be assigned as soon as possible thus present physicians with difficult dilemmas. Medical personnel are committed to discovering the etiology of the condition in order to determine the best course of treatment, which takes time. Yet they feel an urgent need to provide an immediate assignment and genitals that look and function appropriately. An immediate assignment that will need to be retracted is more problematic than a delayed assignment, since reassignment carries with it an additional set of social complications. The endocrinologist interviewed commented: "We've come very far in that we can diagnose eventually, many of the conditions. But we haven't come far enough. . . . We can't do it early enough. . . . Very frequently a decision is made before all this information is available, simply because it takes so long to make the correct diagnosis. And you cannot let a child go indefinitely, not in this society you can't. . . . There's pressure on parents [for a decision] and the parents transmit that pressure onto physicians." A pediatric endocrinologist agreed: "At times you may need to operate before a diagnosis can be made. . . . In one case parents were told to wait on the announcement while the infant was treated to see if the phallus would grow when treated with androgens. After the first month passed and there was some growth, the parents said they gave it a boy's name. They could only wait a month."

Deliberating out loud on the judiciousness of making parents wait for assignment decisions, the endocrinologist asked rhetorically, "Why do we do all these tests if in the end we're going to make the decision simply on the basis of the appearance of the genitalia?" This question suggests that the principles underlying physicians' decisions are cultural rather than biological, based on parental reaction and the medical team's perception of the infant's societal adjustment prospects given the way her/his genitals look or could be made to look. Moreover, as long as the decision rests largely on the criterion of genital appearance, and male is defined as having a "good-sized" penis, more infants will be assigned to the female gender than to the male.

The waiting period: Dealing with ambiguity

During the period of ambiguity between birth and assignment, physicians not only must evaluate the infant's prospects to be a good male but also must manage parents' uncertainty about a genderless child. Physicians advise that parents postpone announcing the gender of the infant until a gender has been explicitly assigned. They believe that parents should not feel compelled to tell other people. The clinical geneticist interviewed said that physicians "basically encourage [parents] to treat [the infant] as neuter." One of the pediatric endocrinologists reported that in France parents confronted with this dilemma sometimes give the infant a neuter name, such as Claude or Jean. The psychoendocrinologist concurred: "If you have a truly borderline situation, and you want to make it dependent on the hormone treatment . . . then the parents are . . . told, 'Try not to make a decision. Refer to the baby as "baby." Don't think in terms of boy or girl.' " Yet, when asked whether this is a reasonable request to make of parents in our society, the physician answered: "I don't think so. I think parents can't do it."

New York State requires that a birth certificate be filled out within forty-eight hours of delivery, but the certificate need not be filed with the state for thirty days. The geneticist tells parents to insert "child of" instead of a name. In one case, parents filled out two birth registration forms, one for each gender, and they refused to sign either until a final gender assignment had been made.[23] One of the pediatric endocrinologists claimed, "I heard a story; I don't know if it's true or not. There were parents of a hermaphroditic infant who told everyone they had twins, one of each gender. When the gender was determined, they said the other had died."

The geneticist explained that when directly asked by parents what to tell others about the gender of the infant, she says, "Why don't you just tell them that the baby is having problems and as soon as the problems are resolved we'll get back to you." A pediatric endocrinologist echoes this suggestion in advising parents to say, "Until the problem is solved [we] would really prefer not to discuss any of the details." According to the urologist, "If [the gender] isn't announced people may mutter about it and may grumble about it, but they haven't got anything to get their teeth into and make trouble over for the child, or the parents, or whatever." In short, parents are asked to sidestep the infant's

[23] Elizabeth Bing and Esselyn Rudikoff, "Divergent Ways of Parental Coping with Hermaphrodite Children," *Medical Aspects of Human Sexuality* (December 1970), 73–88.

gender rather than admit that the gender is unknown, thereby collaborating in a web of white lies, ellipses, and mystifications.[24]

Even while physicians teach the parents how to deal with others who will not find the infant's condition comprehensible or acceptable, physicians must also make the condition comprehensible and acceptable to the parents, normalizing the intersexed condition for them. In doing so they help the parents consider the infant's condition in the most positive way. There are four key aspects to this "normalizing" process.

First, physicians teach parents normal fetal development and explain that all fetuses have the potential to be male or female. One of the endocrinologists explains, "In the absence of maleness you have femaleness. . . . It's really the basic design. The other [intersex] is really a variation on a theme." This explanation presents the intersex condition as a natural phase of every fetal development. Another endocrinologist "like[s] to show picture[s] to them and explain that at a certain point in development males and females look alike and then diverge for such and such reason." The professional literature suggests that doctors use diagrams that illustrate "nature's principle of using the same anlagen to produce the external genital parts of the male and female."[25]

Second, physicians stress the normalcy of the infant in other aspects. For example, the geneticist tells parents, "The baby is healthy, but there was a problem in the way the baby was developing." The endocrinologist says the infant has "a mild defect, just like anything could be considered a birth defect, a mole or a hemangioma." This language not only eases the blow to the parents but also redirects their attention. Terms like "hermaphrodite" or "abnormal" are not used. The urologist said that he advised parents

---

[24] These evasions must have many ramifications in everyday social interactions between parents and family and friends. How people "fill in" the uncertainty so that interactions remain relatively normal is an interesting issue that warrants further study. Indeed, the whole issue of parental reaction is worthy of analysis. One of the pediatric endocrinologists interviewed acknowledged that the published literature discusses intersex management only from the physicians' point of view. He asks. "How [do parents] experience what they're told; and what [do] they remember . . . and carry with them?" One published exception to this neglect of the parents' perspective is a case study comparing two couples' different coping strategies. The first couple, although initially distressed, handled the traumatic event by regarding the abnormality as an act of God. The second couple, more educated and less religious, put their faith in medical science and expressed a need to fully understand the biochemistry of the defect (ibid.).

[25] Tom Mazur, "Ambiguous Genitalia: Detection and Counseling," *Pediatric Nursing* 9 (November/December 1983): 417–31; Money, "Psychologic Consideration of Sex Assignment in Intersexuality" (n. 9 above), 218.

"about the generalization of sticking to the good things and not confusing people with something that is unnecessary."

Third, physicians (at least initially) imply that it is not the gender of the child that is ambiguous but the genitals. They talk about "undeveloped," "maldeveloped," or "unfinished" organs. From a number of the physicians interviewed came the following explanations: "At a point in time the development proceeded in a different way, and sometimes the development isn't complete and we may have some trouble . . . in determining what the *actual* sex is. And so we have to do a blood test to help us" (my emphasis); "The baby may be a female, which you would know after the buccal smear, but you can't prove it yet. If so, then it's a normal female with a different appearance. This can be surgically corrected"; "The gender of your child isn't apparent to us at the moment"; "While this looks like a small penis, it's actually a large clitoris. And what we're going to do is put it back in its proper position and reduce the size of the tip of it enough so it doesn't look funny, so it looks right." Money and his colleagues report a case in which parents were advised to tell their friends that the reason their infant's gender was reannounced from male to female is that "the baby was . . . 'closed up down there' . . . when the closed skin was divided, the female organs were revealed, and the baby discovered to be, *in fact*, a girl" (emphasis mine). It was mistakenly assumed to be a male at first because "there was an excess of skin on the clitoris."[26]

The message in these examples is that the trouble lies in the doctor's ability to determine the gender, not in the baby's gender per se. The real gender will presumably be determined/proven by testing, and the "bad" genitals (which are confusing the situation for everyone) will be "repaired." The emphasis is not on the doctors creating gender but in their completing the genitals. Physicians say that they "reconstruct" the genitals rather than "construct" them. The surgeons reconstitute from remaining parts what should have been there all along. The fact that gender in an infant is "reannounced" rather than "reassigned" suggests that the first announcement was a mistake because the announcer was confused by the genitals. The gender always was what it is now seen to be.[27]

Finally, physicians tell parents that social factors are more important in gender development than biological ones, even

[26] Money, Potter, and Stoll (n. 9 above), 211.

[27] The term "reassignment" is more commonly used to describe the gender changes of those who are cognizant of their earlier gender, e.g., transsexuals—people whose gender itself was a mistake.

though they are searching for biological causes. In essence, the physicians teach the parents Money and Ehrhardt's theory of gender development.[28] In doing so, they shift the emphasis from the discovery of biological factors that are a sign of the "real" gender to providing the appropriate social conditions to produce the "real" gender. What remains unsaid is the apparent contradiction in the notion that a "real" or "natural" gender can be, or needs to be, produced artificially. The physician/parent discussions make it clear to family members that gender is not a biological given (even though, of course, their own procedures for diagnosis assume that it is), and that gender is fluid. The psychoendocrinologist paraphrased an explanation to parents thus: "It will depend, ultimately, on how everybody treats your child and how your child is looking as a person. . . . I can with confidence tell them that generally gender [identity] clearly agrees with the assignment." Similarly, a pediatric endocrinologist explained: "[I] try to impress upon them that there's an enormous amount of clinical data to support the fact that if you sex-reverse an infant . . . the majority of the time the alternative gender identity is commensurate with the socialization, the way that they're raised, and how people view them, and that seems to be the most critical."

The implication of these comments is that gender identity (of all children, not just those born with ambiguous genitals) is determined primarily by social factors, that the parents and community always construct the child's gender. In the case of intersexed infants, the physicians merely provide the right genitals to go along with the socialization. Of course, at normal births, when the infant's genitals are unambiguous, the parents are not told that the child's gender is ultimately up to socialization. In those cases, doctors do treat gender as a biological given.

[28] Although Money and Ehrhardt's socialization theory is uncontested by the physicians who treat intersexuality and is presented to parents as a matter of fact, there is actually much debate among psychologists about the effect of prenatal hormones on brain structure and ultimately on gender role behavior and even on gender identity. The physicians interviewed agreed that the animal evidence for prenatal brain organization is compelling but that there is no evidence in humans that prenatal hormones have an inviolate or unilateral effect. If there is any effect of prenatal exposure to androgen, they believe it can easily be overcome and modified by psychosocial factors. It is this latter position that is communicated to the parents, not the controversy in the field. For an argument favoring prenatally organized gender differences in the brain, see Milton Diamond, "Human Sexual Development: Biological Foundations for Social Development," in *Human Sexuality in Four Perspectives*, ed. Frank A. Beach (Baltimore: Johns Hopkins University Press, 1976), 22–61; for a critique of that position, see Ruth Bleier, *Science and Gender: A Critique of Biology and Its Theories on Women* (New York: Pergamon, 1984).

Social factors in decision making

Most of the physicians interviewed claimed that personal convictions of doctors ought to play no role in the decision-making process. The psychoendocrinologist explained: "I think the most critical factors [are] what is the possibility that this child will grow up with genitals which look like that of the assigned gender and which will ultimately function according to gender . . . That's why it's so important that it's a well-established team, because [personal convictions] can't really enter into it. It has to be what is surgically and endocrinologically possible for that baby to be able to make it . . . It's really much more within medical criteria. I don't think many social factors enter into it." While this doctor eschews the importance of social factors in gender assignment, she argues forcefully that social factors are extremely important in the development of gender identity. Indeed, she implies that social factors primarily enter the picture once the infant leaves the hospital.

In fact, doctors make decisions about gender on the basis of shared cultural values that are unstated, perhaps even unconscious, and therefore considered objective rather than subjective. Money states the fundamental rule for gender assignment: "Never assign a baby to be reared, and to surgical and hormonal therapy, as a boy, unless the phallic structure, hypospadiac or otherwise, is neonatally of at least the same caliber as that of same-aged males with small-average penises."[29] Elsewhere, he and his colleagues provide specific measurements for what qualifies as a micropenis: "A penis is, by convention, designated as a micropenis when at birth its dimensions are three or more standard deviations below the mean. . . . When it is correspondingly reduced in diameter with corpora that are vestigial . . . it unquestionably qualifies as a micropenis."[30] A pediatric endocrinologist claimed that although "the [size of the] phallus is not the deciding factor . . . if the phallus is less than 2 centimeters long at birth and won't respond to androgen treatments, then it's made into a female."

These guidelines are clear, but they focus on only one physical feature, one that is distinctly imbued with cultural meaning. This becomes especially apparent in the case of an XX infant with normal female reproductive gonads and a perfect penis. Would the size and shape of the penis, in this case, be the deciding factor in assigning the infant "male," or would the perfect penis be surgically destroyed and female genitals created? Money notes that this

[29] Money, "Psychological Counseling: Hermaphroditism" (n. 9 above), 610.
[30] Money et al. (n. 9 above), 18.

dilemma would be complicated by the anticipated reaction of the parents to seeing "their apparent son lose his penis."[31] Other researchers concur that parents are likely to want to raise a child with a normal-shaped penis (regardless of size) as "male," particularly if the scrotal area looks normal and if the parents have had no experience with intersexuality.[32] Elsewhere Money argues in favor of not neonatally amputating the penis of XX infants, since fetal masculinization of brain structures would predispose them "almost invariably [to] develop behaviorally as tomboys, even when reared as girls."[33] This reasoning implies, first, that tomboyish behavior in girls is bad and should be avoided; and, second, that it is preferable to remove the internal female organs, implant prosthetic testes, and regulate the "boy's" hormones for his entire life than to overlook or disregard the perfection of the penis.[34]

The ultimate proof to these physicians that they intervened appropriately and gave the intersexed infant the correct gender assignment is that the reconstructed genitals look normal and function normally once the patient reaches adulthood. The vulva, labia, and clitoris should appear ordinary to the woman and her partner(s), and the vagina should be able to receive a normal-sized penis. Similarly, the man and his partner(s) should feel that his penis (even if somewhat smaller than the norm) looks and functions in an unremarkable way. Although there is no reported data on how much emphasis the intersexed person, him- or herself, places upon genital appearance and functioning, the physicians are absolutely clear about what they believe is important. The clinical geneticist said, "If you have . . . a seventeen-year-old young lady who has gotten hormone therapy and has breast development and pubic hair and no vaginal opening, I can't even entertain the notion that this

[31] John Money, "Hermaphroditism and Pseudohermaphroditism," in *Gynecologic Endocrinology*, ed. Jay J. Gold (New York: Hoeber, 1968), 449–64, esp. 460.

[32] Mojtaba Besheshti et al., "Gender Assignment in Male Pseudohermaphrodite Children," *Urology* (December 1983): 604–7. Of course, if the penis looked normal and the empty scrotum were overlooked, it might not be discovered until puberty that the male child was XX, with a female internal structure.

[33] John Money, "Psychologic Consideration of Sex Assignment in Intersexuality" (n. 9 above), 216.

[34] Weighing the probability of achieving a perfect penis against the probable trauma such procedures might involve is another social factor in decision making. According to an endocrinologist interviewed, if it seemed that an XY infant with an inadequate penis would require as many as ten genital operations over a six-year period in order to have an adequate penis, the infant would be assigned the female gender. In this case, the endocrinologist's practical and compassionate concern would override purely genital criteria.

young lady wouldn't want to have corrective surgery." The urologist summarized his criteria: "Happiness is the biggest factor. Anatomy is part of happiness." Money states, "The primary deficit [of not having a sufficient penis]—and destroyer of morale—lies in being unable to satisfy the partner."[35] Another team of clinicians reveals their phallocentrism, arguing that the most serious mistake in gender assignment is to create "an individual unable to engage in genital [heterosexual] sex."[36]

The equation of gender with genitals could only have emerged in an age when medical science can create credible-appearing and functioning genitals, and an emphasis on the good phallus above all else could only have emerged in a culture that has rigid aesthetic and performance criteria for what constitutes maleness. The formulation "good penis equals male; absence of good penis equals female" is treated in the literature and by the physicians interviewed as an objective criterion, operative in all cases. There is a striking lack of attention to the size and shape requirements of the female genitals, other than that the vagina be able to receive a penis.[37]

In the late nineteenth century when women's reproductive function was culturally designated as their essential characteristic, the presence or absence of ovaries (whether or not they were fertile) was held to be the ultimate criterion of gender assignment for hermaphrodites. The urologist interviewed recalled a case as late as the 1950s of a male child reassigned to "female" at the age of four or five because ovaries had been discovered. Nevertheless, doctors today, schooled in the etiology and treatment of the various intersex syndromes, view decisions based primarily on gonads as wrong, although, they complain, the conviction that the gonads are the ultimate criterion "still dictates the decisions of the uneducated and uninformed."[38] Presumably, the educated and informed now know that decisions based primarily on phallic size, shape, and sexual capacity are right.

---

[35] Money, "Psychologic Consideration of Sex Assignment in Intersexuality," 217.

[36] Castro-Magana, Angulo, and Collipp (n. 5 above), 180.

[37] It is unclear how much of this bias is the result of a general, cultural devaluation of the female and how much the result of physicians' greater facility in constructing aesthetically correct and sexually functional female genitals.

[38] Money, "Psychologic Consideration of Sex Assignment in Intersexuality," 215. Remnants of this anachronistic view can still be found, however, when doctors justify the removal of contradictory gonads on the grounds that they are typically sterile or at risk for malignancy (J. Dewhurst and D. B. Grant, "Intersex Problems," *Archives of Disease in Childhood* 59 [July–December 1984]: 1191–94). Presumably, if the gonads were functional and healthy their removal would provide an ethical dilemma for at least some medical professionals.

While the prospect of constructing good genitals is the primary consideration in physicians' gender assignments, another extra-medical factor was repeatedly cited by the six physicians interviewed—the specialty of the attending physician. Although generally intersexed infants are treated by teams of specialists, only the person who coordinates the team is actually responsible for the case. This person, acknowledged by the other physicians as having chief responsibility, acts as spokesperson to the parents. Although all of the physicians claimed that these medical teams work smoothly with few discrepancies of opinion, several of them mentioned decision-making orientations that are grounded in particular medical specializations. One endocrinologist stated, "The easiest route to take, where there is ever any question . . . is to raise the child as female. . . . In this country that is usual if the infant falls into the hands of a pediatric endocrinologist. . . . If the decision is made by the urologists, who are mostly males, . . . they're always opting, because they do the surgery, they're always feeling they can correct anything." Another endocrinologist concurred: "[Most urologists] don't think in terms of dynamic processes. They're interested in fixing pipes and lengthening pipes, and not dealing with hormonal, and certainly not psychological issues. . . . 'What can I do with what I've got.' " Urologists were defended by the clinical geneticist: "Surgeons here, now I can't speak for elsewhere, they don't get into a situation where the child is a year old and they can't make anything." Whether or not urologists "like to make boys," as one endocrinologist claimed, the following example from a urologist who was interviewed explicitly links a cultural interpretation of masculinity to the medical treatment plan. The case involved an adolescent who had been assigned the female gender at birth but was developing some male pubertal signs and wanted to be a boy. "He was ill-equipped," said the urologist, "yet we made a very respectable male out of him. He now owns a huge construction business—those big cranes that put stuff up on the building."

Postinfancy case management

After the infant's gender has been assigned, parents generally latch onto the assignment as the solution to the problem—and it is. The physician as detective has collected the evidence, as lawyer has presented the case, and as judge has rendered a verdict. Although most of the interviewees claimed that the parents are equal participants in the whole process, they gave no instances of parental participation prior to the gender assignment.[39] After the physicians assign the infant's gender, the parents are encouraged to establish the credibility of that gender publicly by, for example, giving a detailed medical explanation to a leader in their community, such as a physician or pastor, who will explain the situation to curious casual acquaintances. Money argues that "medical terminology has a special layman's magic in such a context; it is final and authoritative and closes the issue." He also recommends that eventually the mother "settle [the] argument once and for all among her women friends by allowing some of them to see the baby's reconstructed genitalia."[40] Apparently, the powerful influence of normal-looking genitals helps overcome a history of ambiguous gender.

Some of the same issues that arise in assigning gender recur some years later when, at adolescence, the child may be referred to a physician for counseling.[41] The physician then tells the adolescent many of the same things his or her parents had been told years before, with the same language. Terms like "abnormal," "disorder," "disease," and "hermaphroditism" are avoided; the condition is normalized, and the child's gender is treated as unproblematic. One clinician explains to his patients that sex organs are different in appearance for each person, not just those who are intersexed. Furthermore, he tells the girls "that while most women menstruate, not all do . . . that conception is only one of a number of ways to become a parent; [and] that today some individuals are choosing not to become parents."[42] The clinical geneticist tells a typical female patient: "You are female. Female is not determined by your genes. Lots of other things determine being a woman. And you are a woman but you won't be able to have babies."

A case reported by one of the pediatric endocrinologists involving an adolescent female with androgen insensitivity provides an

[39] Although one set of authors argued that the views of the parents on the most appropriate gender for their child must be taken into account (Dewhurst and Grant, 1192), the physicians interviewed denied direct knowledge of this kind of participation. They claimed that they personally had encountered few, if any, cases of parents who insisted on their child's being assigned a particular gender. Yet each had heard about cases where a family's ethnicity or religious background biased them toward males. None of the physicians recalled whether this preference for male offspring meant the parents wanted a male regardless of the "inadequacy" of the penis, or whether it meant that the parents would have greater difficulty adjusting to a less-than-perfect male than with a "normal" female.

[40] Money, "Psychological Counseling: Hermaphroditism" (n. 9 above), 613.

[41] As with the literature on infancy, most of the published material on adolescents is on surgical and hormonal management rather than on social management. See, e.g., Joel J. Roslyn, Eric W. Fonkalsrud, and Barbara Lippe, "Intersex Disorders in Adolescents and Adults," American Journal of Surgery 146 (July 1983): 138–44.

[42] Mazur (n. 25 above), 421.

intriguing insight into the postinfancy gender-management process. She was told at the age of fourteen "that her ovaries weren't normal and had been removed. That's why she needed pills to look normal. . . . I wanted to convince her of her femininity. Then I told her she could marry and have normal sexual relations . . . [her] uterus won't develop but [she] could adopt children." The urologist interviewed was asked to comment on this handling of the counseling. "It sounds like a very good solution to it. He's stating the truth, and if you don't state the truth . . . then you're in trouble later." This is a strange version of "the truth," however, since the adolescent was chromosomally XY and was born with normal testes that produced normal quantities of androgen. There were no existing ovaries or uterus to be abnormal. Another pediatric endocrinologist, in commenting on the management of this case, hedged the issue by saying that he would have used a generic term like "the gonads." A third endocrinologist said she would say that the uterus had never formed.

Technically these physicians are lying when, for example, they explain to an adolescent XY female with an intersexed history that her "ovaries . . . had to be removed because they were unhealthy or were producing 'the wrong balance of hormones.' "[43] We can presume that these lies are told in the service of what the physicians consider a greater good—keeping individual/concrete genders as clear and uncontaminated as the notions of female and male are in the abstract. The clinician suggests that with some female patients it eventually may be possible to talk to them "about their gonads having some structures and features that are testicular-like."[44] This call for honesty might be based at least partly on the possibility of the child's discovering his or her chromosomal sex inadvertently from a buccal smear taken in a high school biology class. Today's litigious climate is possibly another encouragement.

In sum, the adolescent is typically told that certain internal organs did not form because of an endocrinological defect, not because those organs could never have developed in someone with her or his sex chromosomes. The topic of chromosomes is skirted. There are no published studies on how these adolescents experience their condition and their treatment by doctors. An endocrinologist interviewed mentioned that her adolescent patients rarely ask specifically what is wrong with them, suggesting that they are accomplices in this evasion. In spite of the "truth" having been evaded, the clinician's impression is that "their gender identities and general senses of well-being and self-esteem appear not to have suffered."[45]

[43] Dewhurst and Grant, 1193.
[44] Mazur, 422.
[45] Ibid.

Conclusion

Physicians conduct careful examinations of intersexed infants' genitals and perform intricate laboratory procedures. They are interpreters of the body, trained and committed to uncovering the "actual" gender obscured by ambiguous genitals. Yet they also have considerable leeway in assigning gender, and their decisions are influenced by cultural as well as medical factors. What is the relationship between the physician as discoverer and the physician as determiner of gender? Where is the relative emphasis placed in discussions with parents and adolescents and in the consciousness of physicians? It is misleading to characterize the doctors whose words are provided here as presenting themselves publicly to the parents as discoverers of the infant's real gender but privately acknowledging that the infant has no real gender other than the one being determined or constructed by the medical professionals. They are not hypocritical. It is also misleading to claim that physicians' focus shifts from discovery to determination over the course of treatment: first the doctors regard the infant's gender as an unknown but discoverable reality; then the doctors relinquish their attempts to find the real gender and treat the infant's gender as something they must construct. They are not medically incompetent or deficient. Instead, I am arguing that the peculiar balance of discovery and determination throughout treatment permits physicians to handle very problematic cases of gender in the most unproblematic of ways.

This balance relies fundamentally on a particular conception of the "natural."[46] Although the deformity of intersexed genitals would be immutable were it not for medical interference, physicians do not consider it natural. Instead they think of, and speak of, the surgical/hormonal alteration of such deformities as natural because such intervention returns the body to what it "ought to have been" if events had taken their typical course. The nonnormative is converted into the normative, and the normative state is considered natural.[47] The genital ambiguity is remedied to conform to a "natural," that is, culturally indisputable, gender dichotomy. Sherry Ortner's claim that the culture/nature distinction is itself a

[46] For an extended discussion of different ways of conceptualizing "natural," see Richard W. Smith, "What Kind of Sex Is Natural?" in *The Frontiers of Sex Research*, ed. Vern Bullough (Buffalo: Prometheus, 1979), 103–11.

[47] This supports sociologist Harold Garfinkel's argument that we treat routine events as our due as social members and that we treat gender, like all normal forms, as a moral imperative. It is no wonder, then, that physicians conceptualize what they are doing as natural and unquestionably "right" (Harold Garfinkel, *Studies in Ethnomethodology* [Englewood Cliffs, N.J.: Prentice Hall, 1967]).

construction—a product of culture—is relevant here. Language and imagery help create and maintain a specific view of what is natural about the two genders and, I would argue, about the very idea of gender—that it consists of two exclusive types: female and male.[48] The belief that gender consists of two exclusive types is maintained and perpetuated by the medical community in the face of incontrovertible physical evidence that this is not mandated by biology.

The lay conception of human anatomy and physiology assumes a concordance among clearly dimorphic gender markers—chromosomes, genitals, gonads, hormones—but physicians understand that concordance and dimorphism do not always exist. Their understanding of biology's complexity, however, does not inform their understanding of gender's complexity. In order for intersexuality to be managed differently than it currently is, physicians would have to take seriously Money's assertion that it is a misrepresentation of epistemology to consider any cell in the body authentically male or female.[49] If authenticity for gender resides not in a discoverable nature but in someone's proclamation, then the power to proclaim something else is available. If physicians recognized that implicit in their management of gender is the notion that finally, and always, people construct gender as well as the social systems that are grounded in gender-based concepts, the possibilities for real societal transformations would be unlimited. Unfortunately, neither in their representations to the families of the intersexed nor among themselves do the physicians interviewed for this study draw such far-reaching implications from their work. Their "understanding" that particular genders are medically (re)constructed in these cases does not lead them to see that gender is always constructed. Accepting genital ambiguity as a natural option would require that physicians also acknowledge that genital ambiguity is "corrected" not because it is threatening to the infant's life but because it is threatening to the infant's culture.

Rather than admit to their role in perpetuating gender, physicians "psychologize" the issue by talking about the parents' anxiety and humiliation in being confronted with an anomalous infant. The physicians talk as though they have no choice but to respond to the parents' pressure for a resolution of psychological discomfort, and as though they have no choice but to use medical technology in the service of a two-gender culture. Neither the psychology nor the technology is doubted, since both shield physicians from respon-

[48] Sherry B. Ortner, "Is Female to Male as Nature Is to Culture?" in *Woman, Culture, and Society*, ed. Michelle Zimbalist Rosaldo and Louise Lamphere (Stanford, Calif.: Stanford University Press, 1974), 67–87.

[49] Money, "Psychological Counseling: Hermaphroditism" (n. 9 above), 618.

sibility. Indeed, for the most part, neither physicians nor parents emerge from the experience of intersex case management with a greater understanding of the social construction of gender. Society's accountability, like their own, is masked by the assumption that gender is a given. Thus, cases of intersexuality, instead of illustrating nature's failure to ordain gender in these isolated "unfortunate" instances, illustrate physicians' and Western society's failure of imagination—the failure to imagine that each of these management decisions is a moment when a specific instance of biological "sex" is transformed into a culturally constructed gender.

Division of Natural Sciences
State University of New York College at Purchase

Baboons with Briefcases: Feminism, Functionalism, and Sociobiology in the Evolution of Primate Gender

Susan Sperling

S TUDIES OF MONKEYS and apes have never been just about monkeys and apes. Historically, humans have wondered about the status of nonhuman primates, about the ways in which they are like and unlike us. With the rise of evolutionary thought in nineteenth-century Europe, our views of the nonhuman primates became firmly tied to our understanding of our own development over evolutionary time. In the Western imagination, primates are now central to the iconography of the human past, including the meanings of sexual divisions in human societies.

Modern Western primate studies arose largely through "natural" field studies in decolonized Africa and other Third World sites in the period following World War II.[1] Soon thereafter, anthropological primatologists and their advocates in other disciplines began to fit data about monkeys and apes into models of human evolution. The template for this enterprise had been set earlier in the century by Robert M. Yerkes and Clarence Ray Carpenter, both of whom worked with nonhuman primates to

Some of the ideas in this article are the result of a long, ongoing dialogue with Micaela di Leonardo about anthropology, feminism, and the relationship between social theory and evolutionary science. I gratefully acknowledge her help in the articulation of these topics as presented here. Donna Haraway's perspectives on modern primate studies have played an important role in my approach to various functionalist agendas in primatology.

[1] This article focuses on Western primatology, but it is important to note that Japan has also been a major center for primatological research. Africa was the initial location of the early postwar field studies, following which primatologists worked in Asia, South America, and the Caribbean. For a full account of these developments, see Donna Haraway, *Primate Visions: Gender, Race, and Nature in the World of Modern Science* (New York: Routledge, Chapman & Hall, 1989).

[*Signs: Journal of Women in Culture and Society* 1991, vol. 17, no. 1]

examine human evolutionary issues,[2] but it is in the period since World War II that the primatological enterprise has flourished. Field and laboratory observations of primates have produced a large body of data on the behavior of diverse species. The integration of these facts into models for human evolution has consumed over two decades of scholarship. Gender differences in hominids (humans and protohumans) have been a major focus of these models, which often have proposed that changing reproductive behavior is the central factor in the hominid transition.[3]

From media stars such as Jane Goodall and Dian Fossey to well-known academics such as Jeanne Altmann, Alison Richard, and Thelma Rowell, women always have been a visible presence in the demographics of modern primate research. This alone has sometimes produced a vague sense that feminist "correctives" to male models of primate behavior exist. However, such an impression can be deceptive. The history of accounts of gendered behaviors among primates is not encompassed by a simple evolutionary story of the triumph of good feminist research over bad sexist research. To assess the growth of the feminist tree in primatology, we must view it as part of an entire forest of modern intellectual developments.

Two theories of ultimate causality have dominated primatological models for the origins of monkey, ape, and human gendered behavior: structural-functionalism and sociobiology. The structural-functionalist model, British social anthropology's key contribution to twentieth-century social science, explains the structural pattern of social institutions in terms of how they function as integrated systems to fulfill individual and societal human needs. Anthropologists in the period following World War II translated this theory to their observations of nonhuman primates; they viewed savanna baboon behaviors as adaptations that "functioned" both to promote individual survival and to maintain stable troop life. As we shall see, this perspective structured much theory about the evolution of human gendered behaviors as extrapolated from studies of baboons and other monkeys and apes. Male dominance was viewed as functioning to organize and control the troop in much the same way as political leadership functions in human cultures. There are many problems with this simple analogy.

---

[2] Donna Haraway, "Animal Sociology and a Natural Economy of the Body Politic, Part I: A Political Physiology of Dominance," and "Animal Sociology and a Natural Economy of the Body Politic, Part II: The Past Is the Contested Zone: Human Nature and Theories of Production and Reproduction in Primate Behavior Studies," *Signs: Journal of Women in Culture and Society* 4, no. 1 (Autumn 1978): 21–36, 37–60.

[3] For opposing views on this issue, see Adrienne Zihlman, "Women and Evolution, Part II: Subsistence and Social Organization among Early Hominids," *Signs* 4, no. 1 (Autumn 1978): 4–20; and Owen Lovejoy, "The Origin of Man," *Science* 211, no. 4480 (1981): 341–50.

In the mid-1970s, sociobiology replaced structural-functionalism as the preeminent explanatory model. According to the sociobiologists, behaviors always evolve to maximize the reproductive fitness of individuals (the relative percentage of genes passed on to future generations). Although differing in some significant ways, both models explain the existence of gender-dimorphic behaviors as functioning to increase evolutionary fitness and as controlled in unspecified ways by genes. Both kinds of functionalist arguments for the origin of sexually dimorphic behaviors among humans explain these behaviors as adaptations to past selective pressures in primate or hominid phylogeny. In the past, many of these reconstructions have been overtly sexist; some more recent functionalist hypotheses have attempted to redress former androcentric biases. For instance, some sociobiologists have recently asserted that female primates harass each other in an effort to increase their own genetic advantages. According to this interpretation, attacks on pregnant monkeys and apes by other females are efforts by the attackers to gain a genetic advantage by reducing the number of competitors' offspring. Superficially, such models may seem at times to tell a "good" feminist primate story, by positing, for example, that female primates are aggressive strategists in pursuit of their own reproductive advantages rather than passive objects over which males compete. But these new narratives, although more palatable for some feminists, rest on poor empirical foundations. We do not fully understand the biological, social, and ecological roots of non-human primate aggression.

Donna Haraway has applauded "feminist sociobiology" as telling a better story for feminists than did earlier functionalist models, but she also notes its failure to posit a fully alternative theory about gender differences and human origins:

> Feminist contests for authoritative accounts of evolution and behavioral biology are not simply alternatives, but equally as biased as the masculinist stories so prominent in the early decades of the field. To count as better stories, they have to better account for what it means to be *human* and *animal*. They have to offer a fuller, more coherent vision, one that allows the monkeys and apes to be seen more accurately.

But what will count as more accurate, fuller, more coherent? Rarely will feminist contests for scientific meaning work by replacing one paradigm with another, by proposing and successfully establishing fully alternative accounts and theories. Rather, as a form of narrative practice or story-telling, feminist practice in primatology has worked more by altering a "field" of stories or possible explanatory accounts, by raising the cost of defending some accounts, by destabilizing the plausibility of some strategies or explanations.[4]

"Fully alternative accounts" of the development of gendered behaviors in primates can, and must, be developed. Feminist sociobiology does not represent progress for feminist evolutionary science because it suggests a biological essentialism at the heart of human behavior. In following its path, we abandon those research strategies that might lead us to insights about gendered aspects of human aggression, among other things.

Feminist sociobiologists have retold the story of evolution, giving females an active role, but in using the old narrative structures they tell us little about the development of complex behaviors and their context-dependent expressions. The new female primate is dressed for success and lives in a troop that resembles the modern corporation: now everyone gets to eat power lunches on the savanna. But is it advantageous merely to change one narrative element, as feminist sociobiology has done, so that the category "female," like "male," is constructed as active, dominant, and looking out for genetic advantages? I think not, and I want to argue instead for a deconstruction of all functionalist models, including sociobiological ones, of sex-linked primate behaviors. I think we can hope for more accurate, fuller, more coherent approaches to the study of primate gender differences (some of which may help us to understand aspects of human behavior) than those proposed by functionalists of the last two decades. New theoretical and methodological approaches must attend to the context-dependent nature of behavioral development in primates and the behavioral diversity among different species and in so doing abandon reductionist-functionalist models. But in order to understand feminist sociobiology and its deficiencies, we need a better sense of the unfolding story of primate studies and structural-functionalist and sociobiological models.

For two decades, functionalist reductionism in primatology has seemed almost immune to sophisticated arguments about evolutionary epistemology in other disciplines; primatologists who have addressed this problem have sometimes found themselves tarred with the brush of "anti-Darwinism" and "antievolutionism." Stephen Jay Gould has written of the frustrations involved in critiquing adaptationism: "A former student of mine recently completed a study proving that color patterns of certain clam shells did not have the adaptive significance usually claimed. A leading journal rejected her paper with the comment: 'Why would you want to publish such

---

[4] Haraway's assertion that feminist sociobiology tells a better feminist story is meant ironically (personal communication). See Donna Haraway, "Primatology Is Politics by Other Means: Women's Place Is in the Jungle," in *Feminist Approaches to Science,* ed. Ruth Blier (New York: Pergamon, 1986), 77–118.

nonresults?' "[5] As Gould points out, the study of gender differences suffers from the same bias, a problem in what is privileged as publishable. Measured gender differences are reported and attract attention from the press. What we do not know is how often such differences are not found and the results not published.[6]

Other things shape behavior besides genes and shape it in important ways for the organisms in question. In rodents, for instance, there are a number of maternal behavioral responses resulting from developmental sensitivity to normally invariant environmental conditions. In many species, only females show parental care behaviors, whereas males are always aggressive or indifferent toward infants. But this difference is not determined solely by genetics or hormones; parental caretaking is a developmental behavioral response in females, who are always present at the time of birth. Males develop some of the same caretaking patterns, such as posturing for nursing, when exposed to newborn young. From an evolutionary point of view, such new behaviors may develop and persist in a population either because of changes in the average genotype by natural selection or by enduring changes in the environment in which the average genotype develops.

As biologist Susan Oyama points out, an ant larva may become a worker or a queen, depending on nutrition, temperature, and other variables, just as a male rodent may exhibit nurturant behaviors when exposed to certain stimuli.[7] Control does not flow only from the gene outward. To understand the vastly more complex developmental sequences involved in the acquisition of gendered primate behavior, we must study it developmentally rather than attempting to reduce discourse to arguments about ultimate genetic fitness. There is much more to understanding the development of behavior than retrospectively hypothesizing its adaptive function.[8] Considering the presently confounding array of data on gender-role dimorphism in different primate species, it seems that three things are likely to provide both better questions and answers about behavioral dimorphism: emphasis on both context and development of behavior, a rejection of essentialism and gender dualism,

---

[5] Stephen J. Gould, "Cardboard Darwinism," *New York Review of Books* 33 (September 1986): 47–54.

[6] An excellent investigation of these null hypotheses may be found in Anne Fausto-Sterling, *Myths of Gender: Biological Theories about Women and Men* (New York: Basic, 1985).

[7] Susan Oyama, *The Ontogeny of Information: Developmental Systems and Evolution* (Cambridge: Cambridge University Press, 1985).

[8] Within the functionalist framework, development is usually viewed backward from the adult form, taking as the starting point sex differences in adult behavior. Linda Birke has made this point in her critique of the hormone and behavior literature of the 1950s and 1960s, in which hormones are reified as causal factors; see Linda Birke, *Women, Feminism, and Biology: The Feminist Challenge* (New York: Methuen, 1986).

and a focus on the interaction between organisms and their environments of development. This mandates not the complete abandonment of functionalist models but their integration with other levels of causality.

For over two decades, an obsession with gender-role dimorphism (sexually differing behaviors) as an adaptative mechanism has impeded our understanding of the origins and maintenance of such sexually distinct behaviors in primates—behaviors that, after all, vary greatly both within and across species. Functionalist interpretations of primate behavior view sexually dimorphic traits as end points of natural selection and attempt to explain the selective pressures that might have brought these traits into being, while failing to explain their mechanisms of development and great variety of expressions. These approaches propose a kind of Panglossian philosophy that all behavior is adaptive, although there is much accumulating evidence that this is by no means the case.

The uses of nonhuman primate behavior for understanding human evolution raise important epistemological questions about how we know things in evolutionary science; feminist scholars and others in the evolutionary sciences are beginning to address these questions. As Gould and others have argued, many aspects of morphology and behavior cannot be explained only as direct results of natural selection.[9] Researchers must begin to examine the multiply contingent pathways along which biological systems develop and the complex ways in which extraorganismic factors interact with organisms at every stage of development. Emphasis on contingency in the development of biological and behavioral systems leads inevitably away from the biological essentialism (the belief that gendered behaviors are genetically determined) so pervasive in functionalist evolutionary models in primatology.

But such epistemological critiques of functionalism are rarely raised outside the scholarly enclaves in which evolutionary biologists meet. Such discourse almost never reaches social scientists, among whom the debate has been disastrously constructed as one between reductionists in the biological and evolutionary sciences who contend that genetic mechanisms selected over phylogenetic history control important human behaviors and feminists and other cultural constructionists who deny that biology has any important role in human experience. In both scholarly and popular discussions, writers disseminate the currently privileged functionalist model in journals, at conferences, and in the popular press.[10] Although

[9] See Stephen J. Gould and E. Vrba, "Exaptation—a Missing Term in the Science of Form," *Paleobiology* 8 (1982): 4–15.

[10] For instance, the epistemological failures of sociobiology have been critiqued since the early 1980s by the Cambridge-based Sociobiology Study Group of Science for the People (Sociobiology Study Group of Science for the People, "Sociobiology—Another Biological Determinism," *Bioscience* 26, no. 3 [March 1976]: 182–86), and by other

a number of primatologists have argued for years against the obsession with ultimate causality that has come to dominate the field, their ideas have not been widely conveyed outside the discipline.[11]

Structural-functionalist models of primate gendered behavior

When I began my tenure as a graduate student in physical anthropology at the University of California, Berkeley, in the 1970s, modern primate studies had emerged from a period in which a relatively small number of researchers collected natural histories of a variety of primate species in the field and had entered an era of widespread structural-functionalist model building.[12] The first period, the natural history stage of primate studies, occurred roughly between 1950 and 1965. In the second stage (from the mid-1960s to the late 1970s), data from a variety of field studies, particularly those of savanna baboons and the chimpanzees of the Gombe Reserve in Tanzania, were incorporated into structural-functionalist models for human evolution centering on the sexual division of labor, the origins of the family, and the origins of human gendered behavior. The third phase came in the late 1970s with the hegemony of sociobiology as the functionalist model par excellence for understanding behavioral evolution.[13]

---

groups who find it scientifically flawed. The latter have had little voice in the popular diffusion of ideas about evolution and animal behavior. Gould's antisociobiological volleys in his "Cardboard Darwinism" are a rare exception. For a strong and exhaustive critique of sociobiology, see Phillip Kitcher, *Vaulting Ambition: Sociobiology and the Quest for Human Nature* (Cambridge, Mass.: MIT Press, 1985).

[11] A recent expression of this minority opinion is primatologist Bernstein's statement on functionalism in primatology: "Proof by assertion, plausible argument and consensual validation are no substitute for evidence. The scientific method consists of developing hypotheses from available observation or theory and then testing to see if the null hypothesis, that there is no relationship between the phenomenon under study and the hypothesized independent variable, can be rejected at some predetermined level of confidence. Many sociobiologists seem satisfied only to have proposed an hypothesis, and expect others to do the work of providing the evidence. . . . Ideas are cheap. Evidence from rigorous scientific tests is hard to produce" (Irwin S. Bernstein, "Primate Status Hierarchies," *American Zoologist* 8, no. 741 [1968]: 111).

[12] Primatologists work in a variety of disciplines such as zoology and comparative psychology. Although a concern with human evolution has never been universal among primatologists, it is ubiquitous among anthropologists who study prosimians, monkeys, and apes.

[13] Primate studies began early in the century with the work of Robert M. Yerkes and Clarence Carpenter, and the use of nonhuman primates as models for the evolution of human gendered behaviors predates the postwar period. Yerkes was concerned with questions of gender and dominance in his laboratory research with apes in the 1920s and 1930s, but his theory and methodology—while not unrelated to the modern studies reviewed in this article—are different in important ways from the works under review. For discussion of the origins of twentieth-century primate studies and the social agendas informing the early work, see Haraway, "Animal Sociology and a Natural Economy of the Body Politic, Part I" (n. 2 above).

The first wave of postwar anthropological primatology included a number of long-term studies that laid the foundations of the discipline.[14] Jeanne and Stuart Altmann studied baboon ecology and behavior at Amboseli National Park, Kenya; Stuart Altmann initiated research on rhesus monkeys on the Caribbean island of Cayo Santiago, followed by Donald Sade and his student Elizabeth Missakian and others; and several researchers worked on the Smithsonian project with howler monkeys at Barro Colorado.[15] Research accelerated in the 1960s: Goodall began her observations at the Gombe Stream Reserve in Tanzania (Japanese workers had studied chimpanzees in Tanzania since 1965); Thomas Struhsaker and others studied several species of monkeys in the Kibale Forest of Uganda; Sherwood Washburn and Irven DeVore studied savanna baboons in the Serengeti National Park, Kenya; Fossey initiated observations of mountain gorillas in 1967 in Rwanda's Parc de Volcans; and Phyllis Dolhinow researched Indian langur monkeys at several sites in India.[16] Most of these studies (and this is only a partial list) were descriptive natural histories with few explicit links made to human evolution.[17]

During the second stage of modern primatology, which began in the mid-1960s, structural-functionalist analysis became central to the problem-

[14] Haraway, *Primate Visions* (n. 1 above), 115–275.

[15] Stuart A. Altmann and Jeanne Altmann, *Baboon Ecology: African Field Research* (Basel, Munchen: S. Karger, 1970; distributed in the United States by Chicago: University of Chicago Press, 1970); Stuart A. Altmann, "A Field Study of the Sociobiology of Rhesus Monkeys, *Macaca mulatta*," *Annals of the New York Academy of Sciences* 102, no. 2 (1962): 338–435; Donald S. Sade, "Some Aspects of Parent-Offspring and Sibling Relations in a Group of Rhesus Monkeys, with a Discussion of Grooming," *American Journal of Physical Anthropology* 23, no. 1 (1965): 1–17, and "Determinants of Dominance in a Group of Free-ranging Rhesus Monkeys," in *Social Communication among Primates*, ed. Stuart A. Altmann (Chicago: University of Chicago Press, 1967); Nicholas E. Collias and Charles H. Southwick, "A Field Study of Population Density and Social Organization in Howling Monkeys," *Proceedings of the American Philosophical Society* 96 (1952): 143–56.

[16] Jane Goodall, "My Life among the Wild Chimpanzees," *National Geographic Magazine* 124, no. 2 (August 1963): 272–308; Toshisada Nishida, "Preliminary Information on the Pygmy Chimpanzee *(Pan paniscus)* of the Congo Basin," *Primates* 13 (1972): 415–25; Thomas Struhsaker, "Social Behavior of Mother and Infant Vervet Monkeys *(Cercopithecus aethiops),*" *Animal Behavior* 19 (1971): 233–50; Sherwood L. Washburn and Irven DeVore, "Social Behavior of Baboons and Early Man," in *The Social Life of Early Man*, ed. Sherwood Washburn (New York: Aldine, 1961), 91–105; Dian Fossey, "Making Friends with Mountain Gorillas," *National Geographic Magazine* 137, no. 1 (January 1970): 48–68; Phyllis Dolhinow, *Primate Patterns* (New York: Holt, Rinehart & Winston, 1972).

[17] A number of important organizational events served to consolidate modern primatology as a science. Important among these was the 1962–63 "Primate Year" organized by Washburn and Hamburg at the Stanford Institute for Advanced Study in the Behavioral Sciences, Stanford, Calif. Three major international conferences took place in 1962, producing edited volumes. See Haraway's *Primate Visions*, 123–24, for a list of these events.

oriented studies that replaced the earlier emphasis on natural history.[18]
Primatology was then, as it is today, a heterogeneous field that included
research on proximate causal factors affecting social behavior and on the
complex interaction between social structure, behavior, and ecology (socioecology).[19] But it is the structural-functionalist grand theory builders, those
who have focused exclusively on ultimate causality, who have been the
progenitors of the most influential and popular visions of primate behavior.
In the functionalist models of the 1960s and 1970s, all aspects of behavior
within a primate troop were explained as adaptive mechanisms. Thus, the
roles of females and males in different species were interpreted as selected
during the phylogenetic history of the species because they "functioned" to
promote survival.

Lynda Marie Fedigan has reviewed many of the evolutionary reconstructions by primatologists of this period.[20] She points out that the
"baboonization" of early human life in such models rested on a savanna
ecological analogy: since protohominids evolved on the African savanna,
presumably they would have shared certain selective pressures with modern baboon troops, particularly for predator protection by large males.
Washburn, DeVore, and other early baboon researchers had viewed male
dominance as functioning to organize troop members hierarchically and
to control overt aggression. Fedigan argues that the other primary model
for protohominid evolution, that of the chimpanzees studied by Goodall
at the Gombe Reserve in Tanzania, was far preferable. Here the analogy
rested on a phylogenetic relationship between chimp and human, which
is immensely closer. This model emphasized the mother-offspring bond,
sharing within the matrifocal family, the immigration of young females to
new groups, birth spacing, and temporary sex bonding. It is to this
chimpanzee behavioral model that the first wave of feminist authors, in
particular, the constructors of the "woman the gatherer" model, would
turn for primatological evidence of the social centrality of females in
early hominid evolution.[21]

The savanna baboon model was compatible with, and tended to bol-
ster, a Hobbesian view of human society, while the chimpanzee model

[18] See Lynda Marie Fedigan, *Primate Paradigms: Sex Roles and Social Bonds* (Montreal: Eden, 1982); and Haraway, *Primate Visions*, for discussions of the periodization of
primatology.
[19] A number of primatologists have seen primate studies as part of socioecology,
viewing primates within the context of mammalian social and ecological adaptations
rather than as human surrogates. For this approach, see Alison Richard, *Primates in Nature* (New York: Freeman, 1985).
[20] For a thorough review of this model and its many offshoots, see Fedigan, *Primate
Paradigms*.
[21] Nancy Tanner and Adrienne Zihlman, "Women in Evolution, Part 1: Innovation
and Selection in Human Origins," *Signs* 1, no. 3 (Spring 1976): 585–608.

originally tended to reflect a more benign view, stressing the mother-infant pair and a more flexible, less hierarchical social structure. But many of the assumptions underlying the early use of ape and baboon behavioral data in models for hominid evolution were equivalent: ape and monkey behaviors were microcosms of human social behavior and political life.

Fedigan points out that the "baboonization" of protohominids became so common that by the early to mid-1970s not a single introductory text in human evolution omitted reference to it. As Rowell and other critics of this model stressed, many of the generalizations and assumptions about the functions of male dominance made by early baboon researchers like Washburn and DeVore were unsubstantiated by data from other research sites.[22] Rowell's studies of troop movement among forest baboons, for instance, indicated that the direction of daily foraging routes was determined by a core of mature females rather than by the dominant males. As feminist scholars such as Sandra Harding and Donna Haraway note, women primatologists often have had a different vision of group structure and behavior because they attended to female actors in a way that male primatologists did not.[23] This focus on female behavior in baboons and in a variety of other species became fuel for the critical deconstructions of the baboon model during the 1970s. In addition, a number of studies questioned the assumption that male dominance conferred a reproductive advantage on particular males, thus contributing to selection for male aggression.[24]

An article by psychologists Carol McGuinness and Karl Pribram illustrates a pervasive phenomenon of the second wave of primatology, the insertion of primatological data into structural-functionalist models for the evolution of gendered human behavior: "In all primate societies the division of labor by gender creates a highly stable social system, the dominant males controlling territorial boundaries and maintaining order among lesser males by containing and preventing their aggression, the females tending the young and forming alliances with other females. Human primates follow this same pattern so remarkably that it is not difficult to argue for biological bases for the type of social order that channels aggression to guard the territory which in turn maintains an equable environment for the young."[25]

[22] Thelma Rowell, "The Concept of Dominance," *Behavioral Biology* 11 (1974): 131–54.

[23] Sandra Harding, *The Science Question in Feminism* (Ithaca, N.Y.: Cornell University Press, 1986); Haraway, *Primate Visions*.

[24] Lynda Marie Fedigan, "Dominance and Reproductive Success in Primates," *Yearbook of Physical Anthropology* 26 (1983): 91–129.

[25] Quoted in David Goldman, "Special Abilities of the Sexes: Do They Begin in the Brain?" *Psychology Today* 12, no. 6 (November 1978): 56.

McGuinness's and Pribram's interpretation appeared in *Psychology Today*, one of many popular journals publishing articles on human nature and its biological roots. Although the template here is the savanna baboon troop as described by Washburn and DeVore—and contested early in this period by Rowell and others who call into question all of the fundamental assumptions of the savanna model—"all primate species" collapsed the diversity and specificity of data on primates into a single category, "primate societies." Here, and in a plethora of popular books and articles published during this period, monkeys and apes were used explicitly as exemplars of earlier stages of human evolution. The ubiquitous primate ancestral group now occupied a position like that of "tribal societies" in the evolutionary schemas of nineteenth-century anthropologists. The diffusion of cultural relativism into all branches of modern social science had made it embarrassing and untenable to fit tribal groups into this early evolutionary slot. If "primitives" were to be considered our equals with complex and meaningful cultures, they could not also represent the protohuman past. In this new way of thinking, monkeys and apes became the early ancestral group from which human institutions could be seen to have evolved.

This replacement of human "primitives" by nonhuman primates also relates to global political events of the postwar period: "With the progressive disappearance of human 'primitives' as legitimate objects of knowledge and colonial rule, and with the discrediting of pre-war eugenics, Western anthropologists had to rethink the meaning and processes of the formation of 'man.' "[26] The substitution of primates for "primitives" thus neatly retained an important Western cosmological category for use in the era of decolonization and the construction of the Third World.

One consequence of this key insertion of the nonhuman primate in the Western symbolic niche for "primitive progenitor" was an implied obliteration of the border between human and nonhuman.[27] The passage by McGuinness and Pribram is a mass of terminological ambiguities. What is meant by terms such as "the division of labor" when referring to nonhuman primates? Does this term mean the same thing when applied to human groups? Monkeys and apes do not have a division of labor along gender lines as do human cultures; each animal performs subsistence tasks in approximately the same way as the others, consuming on the spot what is individually foraged. Human divisions of labor by sex are complex historical and socioeconomic phenomena embroidered with

[26] Haraway, *Primate Visions* (n. 1 above), 7.

[27] See Susan Sperling, *Animal Liberators: Research and Morality* (Berkeley and Los Angeles: University of California Press, 1988), for discussion of the relationship between primate ethnology and the current animal rights movement.

symbolic meanings unavailable to animals. But when DeVore and Hall wrote that "the baboon troop is organized around the dominance hierarchy of adult males," they meant it both literally and figuratively.[28] They perceived dominant males as "culturally" binding together a loose, potentially chaotic aggregate of females, subadult males, and young. In the same work, they offered a spatial schematization of primate societies, a series of concentric circles with the most dominant animals in the center. DeVore and Hall visualized male dominance as the cement of primate social organization.

Social anthropologist and popularizer Robin Fox is typical of the many writers who sought evolutionary legitimations of male dominance among humans in primate field studies. In *Biosocial Anthropology* (1975), Fox was quite explicit about his use of nonhuman primates as replacements for human "primitives":

> Older theorists speculated on the "earliest conditions of man," and as we know debates raged between proponents of "primitive promiscuity" and "primitive monogamy." The former were usually seen as a prelude to "matriarchy" (now popular again) and the latter to "patriarchy." This has all been dismissed as ridiculous for well-known reasons. But I think we can now go back to the question in a different way. We know a great deal about primates which can tell us what is behaviorally available to our order in general and, therefore, what must have been available by way of a behavioral repertoire to our ancestors . . . "early man" then, in this sense, was less like modern man gone wild than like a primate tamed. *And even if we cannot deduce accurately the kinship systems of early man [sic] from those of the most primitive humans, we can do something better, we can distill the essence of kinship systems on the basis of comparative knowledge and find the elements of such systems that are logically, and hence in all probability chronologically, the "elementary forms of kinship."*[29]

The differences between Fox's assumptions and those of the Victorian evolutionists are negligible. Fox traced the evolution of human kinship through the primates, borrowing, as he admits, "somewhat recklessly from the jargon of social anthropology, descent and alliance."[30] According to his analysis, these two elements are present in nonhuman primate

---

[28] Irven DeVore and K. R. L. Hall, "Baboon Social Behavior," in *Primate Behavior: Field Studies of Monkeys and Apes,* ed. Irven DeVore (New York: Holt, Rinehart & Winston, 1965), 54.

[29] Robin Fox, *Biosocial Anthropology* (New York: Wiley, 1975), 11; emphasis mine.

[30] Ibid., 11.

social systems but are combined only in human groups. He divides primate social systems into two types, single-male and multi-male groups, of which all have in common "a threefold division of the larger group into: a) adult males; b) females and young; c) peripheral males. We can look at any primate social system, including our own, in terms of the 'accommodations' made between these three blocks."[31] According to Fox, in single-male groups (gorillas and hamadryas baboons) the basic unit is the "polygenous family," while in the multi-male group (common baboons, chimpanzees), "if the sexual relationship is brief and unenduring, the consanguineal relationship is long lasting and of central importance."[32] The phylogenetic histories of different primates are thus collapsed into several categories with a certain internal consistency but little relationship to actual data. Once Fox raises the question of the relationship of complex human behaviors to nonhuman primate behavioral variation, his evidence becomes a confusing array of randomly chosen bits and pieces of behavior from species with varying phylogenetic relationships to one another and to humans. Although nodding briefly at the issue of variation, Fox goes on to the heart of his argument about nonhuman primates and human culture: "The real question is do the rules represent more than a 'labeling' procedure for behavior that would occur anyway? . . . If group A and B were called 'Eaglehawk' and 'Crow,' and the various lineages 'snake,' 'beaver,' 'bear,' and 'antelope,' etc., then a picture emerges of a proto-society on a clan moiety basis."[33] An important consequence of this approach is that it obscures many of the culturally unique aspects of human kinship, among them the widespread existence of putative kin among human cultures, that make it fundamentally different from social relations among nonhumans.

Examples of this missing link approach to the use of nonhuman primate behavior abound in the literature of this period, often focusing on gendered behavior and its presumed "functions." Many popularizations of this approach have had a wide audience.[34] In one such account, the sexologist and gerontologist Alex Comfort explained the presumed continual receptivity of human females: "At some point in primate evolution, the female became receptive all year round and even throughout pregnancy. This apparently trifling change in behavior was probably the trigger, or one of the triggers, which set off the evolution of man [*sic*].

---

[31] Ibid., 13.

[32] Ibid., 15.

[33] Ibid.

[34] Robert Ardry, *The Territorial Imperative: A Personal Inquiry into the Animal Origins of Property and Nations* (New York: Atheneum, 1966); Desmond Morris, *The Naked Ape* (New York: McGraw-Hill, 1967); Lionel Tiger and Robin Fox, *The Imperial Animal* (New York: Holt, Rinehart & Winston, 1971).

Between baboons and higher apes we find the effects of this change. Baboons behave very like other pack-living animals. Higher apes, with sexual activity continuing all the˙year round, and unrelated to heat, develop a heterosexual social life which is not confined to the coital encounter."[35] Comfort's order of ascent is baboon, ape, and human, and the characteristic "continual sexual receptivity" is traced along this ladder in much the same way that the Victorians associated "primitive promiscuity" with savages, group marriage with barbarians, and monogamy with civilized humans.

As we move up and down the phylogenetic scale, monkeys and apes are anthropomorphized, and behaviors of diverse species are used as simple analogues of human characteristics. Much of the second-wave scholarly and popular evolutionary writing that uses nonhuman primate models reproduces this logical failing. Selected examples of group structure, kinship, and dominance behavior in nonhuman primates are viewed as precursors of human social structure and behavior. The influence of these models on popular perceptions of the relationship of humans to animals and of the meanings of gender divisions has been profound.

Nonhuman primates became the missing link in the evolutionary models of the late 1960s and 1970s. But nonhuman primates are as unwieldy a link as were the "primitives" of the early evolutionists. All living species of organisms have undergone separate histories combining both evolutionary and chance events. There is immense variation in behavior among primate species, and cross-phylum generalizations are hard to make. For instance, sexual behavior among monkeys and apes exhibits a wide variety of patterns that defy neat phylogenetic analysis. Monkeys display a variety of mating patterns, but the most telling data in this regard are from the apes.[36] There are significant differences between the sexual behavior of chimpanzees, gorillas, and orangutans that in no way relate to their phylogenetic closeness to humans. For instance, hormonal and behavioral states appear closely correlated in gorilla reproductive behavior, somewhat less so in chimps, and least of all in orangutans. But chimpanzees are much more closely related to humans than are orangutans. This finding contradicts the linear evolutionist's view that the closer a species' phylogenetic relationship to humans, the less its sexual behavior is hormonally controlled and the greater the resemblance to human reproductive behavior.

[35] Alex Comfort, *The Nature of Human Nature* (New York: Harper & Row, 1966), 13.
[36] Thelma Rowell, *The Social Behaviour of Monkeys* (Middlesex: Penguin, 1972); Ronald Nadler, "Laboratory Research on the Sexual Behavior of the Great Apes," in *Reproductive Biology of the Great Apes,* ed. Charles E. Graham (New York: Academic Press, 1975).

Sociobiology and the evolution of gendered behavior in primates

The 1975 publication of *Sociobiology: The New Synthesis* by Harvard entomologist Edward O. Wilson was a signal event for students of animal behavior in numerous disciplines.[37] Wilson makes two major assertions in *Sociobiology*: that all important social behaviors are genetically controlled and that natural selection of the genome is caused by a set of specific adaptive mechanisms (kin selection) that produce behaviors maximizing an organism's ability to contribute the greatest number of genes to the next generation. The historical roots of sociobiology lie in nineteenth- and early twentieth-century arguments about the level at which natural selection operates, that of the group or of the individual. Evolutionists like Darwin, Haldane, and Wynne-Edwards contended that traits may be selected because they are advantageous for populations.[38] In the 1960s, William Hamilton and Robert Trivers proposed that traits can be selected only at the individual level and that all social behaviors are tightly genetically controlled.[39]

Hamilton's theory of kin selection is based on the concept that the "fitness" of an organism has two components: "fitness" gained through the replication of its own genetic material by reproduction and "inclusive fitness" gained from the replication of copies of its own genes carried in others as a result of its actions. According to this theory, when an organism behaves altruistically toward related individuals, fitness benefits to kin also benefit the organism, but the actor's benefits are devalued by the coefficient of relatedness between actor and relatives. Thus, genes are viewed as being selected because they contribute to their own perpetuation, regardless of the organism of which they are a part. Trivers defined reciprocal altruism as behavior that appears to be altruistic but which, given mutual dependence in a group, may be selected if it confers indirect benefits on the altruist.[40]

---

[37] Edward O. Wilson, *Sociobiology: The New Synthesis* (Cambridge, Mass.: Harvard University Press, 1975).

[38] Charles Darwin, *On the Origin of Species by Means of Natural Selection* (London: John Murray, 1859); J. B. S. Haldane, *The Causes of Evolution* (London: Longmanns, Green, 1932); V. C. Wynne-Edwards, *Animal Dispersion in Relation to Social Behaviour* (New York: Hafner, 1962).

[39] William D. Hamilton, "The Genetical Evolution of Social Behavior, Parts 1 and 2," *Journal of Theoretical Biology* 7 (1964): 1–52; Robert Trivers, "Parental Investment and Sexual Selection," in *Sexual Selection and the Descent of Man, 1871–1971*, ed. Bernard Campbell (Chicago: Aldine, 1972), 136–79.

[40] The roots of these arguments can be traced to the works of the evolutionists V. C. Wynne-Edwards, William D. Hamilton, and Robert Trivers. Altruism was defined as any behavior that benefits another organism, not closely related, while being apparently detrimental to the organism performing the behavior, benefit and detriment being defined in terms of their contributions to inclusive fitness. Examples of such altruistic behaviors might be sharing of food with nonrelatives and the aiding of nonrelatives in times of danger.

Wilson took the concept of kin selection and applied it to all animal and human behavior from the social insects to humans, suggesting that the social sciences and biological sciences be subsumed by sociobiology. It is not surprising that many scientists viewed the idea of their disciplines' cannibalistic incorporation into the body of sociobiology as an unsavory prospect. Some objected on political grounds to its explicit reductionism and potential for racist and sexist interpretations. The Boston-based collective Science for the People issued a critical attack on sociobiology, calling it another form of biological determinism like nineteenth-century eugenics and Social Darwinism.[41] At the same time, sociobiology began to establish a foothold in American and European departments of anthropology, zoology, and psychology. The American Anthropological Association sponsored a two-day symposium on sociobiology at its 1976 yearly meeting, and departments in the biological and social sciences began to offer seminars and classes on the topic. By the late 1980s, it had become the dominant paradigm among anthropological primatologists, replacing the structural-functionalist models of the second period of modern primatology.

I cannot here discuss the many reasons, from national political trends to individual departmental politics, for the ascendance of sociobiology over structural-functionalism in primate studies. Researchers studying proximate mechanisms, many of them socioecologists, continued to work at various sites with little interest or involvement in postulations of ultimate causality. Nevertheless, as structural-functionalism had earlier, sociobiology became the grand theory conveyed to social scientists interested in human evolution and widely popularized through newspaper and magazine articles and popular books.[42] By the mid-1980s, a number of important empirical critiques appeared, deconstructing the logic of sociobiological arguments. But these have yet to be widely circulated outside classes and seminars in evolutionary theory.

Early sociobiological views of the evolution of human gendered behaviors incorporated primatological data and viewed males and females as having differential reproductive strategies. Because of the presumably greater "investment" of female primates in infant rearing, female behaviors were viewed as selected because they advanced a female's chances of gaining male protection during vulnerable periods for herself and her offspring (offspring are seen as fleshy packets of shared genes). Females frequently were pictured as conservative, coy, and passive. By contrast, it behooved males to inseminate as many females as possible, thus forward-

---

[41] Sociobiology Study Group of Science for the People (n. 10 above).

[42] See Haraway, *Primate Visions* (n. 1 above), for a history of the actors involved in the demise of structural-functionalism and the ascendance of sociobiology.

ing their attempted genetic monopoly of the future. Wilson wrote: "It pays males to be aggressive, hasty, fickle and undiscriminating. In theory it is more profitable for females to be coy, to hold back until they can identify the male with the best genes. Human beings obey this biological principle faithfully."[43] DeVore and other sociobiologists have maintained that the sexual and romantic interest of middle-aged men in younger women and their presumed lack of interest in their female age cohort stem from selective pressures on male primates to inseminate as many fertile females as possible.[44]

Wilson applied sociobiological arguments to the meaning of the middle-class nuclear family in American culture:

> The building block of nearly all human societies is the nuclear family. The populace of an American industrial city, no less than a band of hunter-gatherers in the Australian desert, is organized around this unit. In both cases the family moves between regional communities, maintaining complex ties with primary kin by means of visits (or telephone calls and letters) and the exchange of gifts. During the day the women and children remain in the residential area while the men forage for game or its symbolic equivalent in the form of money. The males cooperate in bands or deal with neighboring groups.[45]

It is no coincidence that sociobiology and the second wave of Western feminism were simultaneous occurrences. Early sociobiologists clearly envisioned their new model as "disproving" feminism. The sociobiologist Pierre Van den Berghe wrote: "Neither the National Organization for Women nor the Equal Rights Amendment will change the biological bedrock of asymmetrical parental investment."[46] Phillip Kitcher (1985) has commented on the sexism of many sociobiological arguments:

> Sometimes the expression is tinged with regretful sympathy for ideals of social justice (Wilson), at other times with a zeal to *epater les feministes* (Van den Berghe). [I]t is far from clear that sociobiologists appreciate the political implications of the views they pro-

[43] Edward O. Wilson, *On Human Nature* (Cambridge, Mass.: Harvard University Press, 1978).

[44] DeVore is an actor in the primatological drama who has made a smooth transition from the functionalist agendas of the 1960s to those of the 1980s. He was an important proponent of the use of the baboon troop as a functionalist's microcosm of human society and later became a strong advocate of sociobiology.

[45] Wilson, *Sociobiology*, 553.

[46] Pierre Van den Berghe, *Human Family Systems* (New York: Simon & Schuster, 1979), 2, quoted in Kitcher (n. 10 above), 5.

mulgate. These implications become clear when a *New York Times* series on equal rights for women concludes with a serious discussion of the limits that biology might set to women's aspirations, and when the new right in Britain and France announces its enthusiasm for the project of human sociobiology.[47]

More recently, a feminist discourse in sociobiology has shifted attention to the presumed gender-specific reproductive strategies of female primates. By stressing female variance, feminist sociobiologists assert that selection acts on females as well as males to encode genetic programs for enhanced fitness. The primatologist Sarah Hrdy, an important contributor to this literature, has lauded the emphasis in sociobiology on variance in reproductive success for contributing a bracing dose of feminism to primatology.[48] Thus, these researchers see female mate choice and female elicitation of male support and protection in rearing young as integral to the competitive strategies of females vis-à-vis other females.[49] They describe "prolonged female receptivity" in some nonhuman primates and human females as an evolved mechanism to manipulate male behavior. Variation in mothering styles and skills, and the degree of selfishness of caretakers, are said to reflect variance in reproductive interests that are sometimes at odds with those of offspring. They also describe (as kin-selection strategies) competition between females whenever fertility and the rearing of young are limited by access to resources and the competition of dominant females on behalf of their offspring by eliminating competitors or forestalling reproduction in the mothers of potential competitors: "Female primates have evolved to be fierce competitors and they are obsessed with signs of status differences or disrespect only when it pays off in terms of access to energy resources. . . . Female primates may compete sexually . . . they may harass other females, especially low-status ones, to such an extent that they are unable to conceive effectively, maintain gestation or adequately lactate. There are also scattered reports that females may kill and cannibalize the infants of low-status females, or seize them and 'aunt' them to death."[50]

This new view of females among academic sociobiologists is mirrored in popular journalism about primate infanticide and infant abuse and

---

[47] Kitcher, 6.

[48] Sarah B. Hrdy and George C. Williams, "Behavioral Biology and the Double Standard," in *Social Behavior of Female Vertebrates*, ed. Samuel K. Wasser (New York: Academic Press, 1983), 3–17.

[49] Sarah B. Hrdy, *The Woman That Never Evolved* (Cambridge, Mass.: Harvard University Press, 1981); Jane B. Lancaster, introduction to *Female Primates: Studies by Women Primatologists*, ed. Meredith Small (New York: Liss, 1984), 1–12.

[50] Jane B. Lancaster, quoted in Small, ed., 1.

interfemale aggression and competition. Here, human females are portrayed as bearers of behavioral homologues from their nonhuman primate ancestors and early hominid past, predisposing them toward certain modes of interindividual competition, rather than as the passive and nurturant weaklings of some former functionalist models. In these newer accounts, female competition has taken center stage. It is tempting to blame journalists and science writers for these lurid images and their extension to human females, but that would be a mistake: the academic sociobiological model is clearly meant to apply across the primate order to humans. DeVore, for example, interprets soap operas to reflect his vision of female reproductive strategies:

> Soap operas have a huge following among college students, and the female-female competition is blatant. The women on these shows use every single feminine wile. On the internationally popular soap *Dynasty*, for example, a divorcee sees her ex-husband's new wife riding a horse nearby. She knows the woman to be newly pregnant, so she shoots off a gun, which spooks the horse, which throws the young wife, and makes her miscarry. The divorcee's own children are living with their father and this woman; the divorcee doesn't want this new young thing to bring rival heirs into the world to compete with her children.
>
> Whole industries turning out everything from lipstick to perfume to designer jeans are based on the existence of female competition. The business of courting and mating is after all, a negotiation process, in which each member of the pair is negotiating with those of the opposite sex to get the best deal possible, and to beat out the competition from one's own sex. . . . I get women in my class saying I'm stereotyping women, and I say sure, I'm stereotyping the ones who make lipstick a multibillion dollar industry. It's quite a few women. Basically, I appeal to students to look inside themselves: what are life's little dilemmas? When your roommate brings home a guy to whom you're extremely attracted, does it set up any sort of conflict in your mind?[51]

Many sociobiologists disclaim the reductionism of their popular interpreters; Wilson and Hrdy have both published statements about the importance of human cultural transmission and the possibility of change in human social relations caused by cultural factors.[52] This is disingen-

---

[51] Duncan M. Anderson, "The Delicate Sex: How Females Threaten, Starve, and Abuse One Another," *Science 7*, no. 3 (April 1986): 43–48.

[52] Wilson, *On Human Nature;* Hrdy.

uous; it has now become fashionable for both biological and environmental reductionists to claim interactionism as the only reasonable view and then to revert immediately to the reductionist theories that belie their assertions. In fact, academic sociobiologists draw the same conclusions as their journalistic interpreters.[53]

What we know about gendered primate behavior

Scientists now criticize many former assertions about reliably differentiating behavioral dimorphisms across primate phyla as based on incomplete data.[54] The more we know about nonhuman primate behavior, the more examples of intraspecific and interspecific variety emerge. Several common functionalist assertions about gender differences now appear to be unsubstantiated. For instance, male monkeys and apes of a variety of different species have been described as more aggressive than conspecific females. Barbara B. Smuts, however, finds no consistent gender difference in frequencies of aggression in numerous primate species.[55] She focuses on the contextual factors influencing agonistic behaviors in both males and females, including how males and females influence each other, rather than positing inherent, genetically controlled behavioral dimorphisms.

Another recently challenged functionalist theory about nonhuman primates is that social dominance is highly correlated with reproductive success and that dominance behaviors have been selected over the phylogenetic histories of species. Irwin S. Bernstein, in reviewing data from numerous primate studies, suggests that there is little association between dominance rank and reproductive success.[56] Fedigan summarizes the whole era of reports on male copulations, mating success, consortship, and male dominance and concludes that none of the measures provides

[53] Oyama's *The Ontogeny of Information* (n. 7 above) discusses the many ways that biological reductionists hedge their bets by making sociobiological assertions about the different reproductive interests of the sexes but adding that cultural factors are "important for humans." As she points out, this is an additive model of human culture pinned onto the "primate biogram" (83).

[54] Irwin S. Bernstein, "The Evolution of Nonhuman Primate Social Behavior," *Genetica* 73 (1987): 99–116; Fedigan, "Dominance and Reproductive Success in Primates" (n. 24 above); Barbara B. Smuts, "Gender, Aggression, and Influence," in *Primate Societies*, ed. Barbara B. Smuts et al. (Chicago: University of Chicago Press, 1986), 400–412.

[55] Smuts's "Gender, Aggression, and Influence" is a very useful review of gender dimorphism in aggression. Her interpretations of baboon data in *Sex and Friendship in Baboons*, ed. Barbara B. Smuts (New York: Aldine, 1985), are generally consistent with the feminist sociobiology critiqued in this article.

[56] Bernstein, "The Evolution of Nonhuman Primate Behavior."

a convincing picture of dominant males monopolizing estrous females.[57] High levels of male aggression and wounding during the breeding season may have more to do with male mobility, "xenophobia," and rank instability among males during the breeding season than with fighting over females.[58]

Aggression, reproduction access, and dominance are emerging as more complex, variable, and context dependent and as less subject to generalizations easily applied cross-phyla. And not all primate species show a pattern of male protection from predators for females and young (their own or those of other males); indeed, many do not. Robert S. O. Harding and Dana K. Olson report that the vivid displays of male patas (a type of African monkey), long assumed to distract predators from females and young, who remained frozen in the grass, now appear to be associated with intermale competition during the breeding season.[59] To complicate the picture further, these large African cercopithecines were thought to live in exclusively single-male groups. In fact, it is now clear that patas females mate with a variety of males.

How can we generalize with any certainty about gendered behavior in nonhuman primates? We know that female primates conceive, gestate, and lactate, and that in most species it is the female primarily who nurtures the young (although nonhuman primate "nurturance" should not be confused with the cultural traditions with which this word is associated in human groups). Males inseminate females. There is little or no sexual division in subsistence labor among nonhuman primates, one fact among many others that makes them strikingly different from human beings. All nonhuman primates forage for themselves and there is little sharing of food, with a few exceptions, such as the occasional opportunistic hunting by some male chimps and baboons. In many, but not all, species of monkeys and apes, males are larger than females, more muscular, and have larger canines. Size dimorphism seems to be important in a number of species in giving priority of access to environmental incentives (such as desired grooming partners or preferred foods), but larger males by no means always dominate smaller females. Aggressive and affiliative behaviors of male and female primates vary depending on the species, social context, and individual. In fact, we are confronted with an enormous range of variations in intraspecific and interspecific behavior that defies neat classificatory schemas. Yet, rather than study the ontogeny of behaviors across the life span of individual animals, a daunt-

---

[57] Fedigan, "Dominance and Reproductive Success in Primates."

[58] Bernstein, "The Evolution of Nonhuman Primate Behavior."

[59] Robert S. O. Harding and Dana K. Olson, "Patterns of Mating among Male Patas Monkeys *(Erythrocebus patas)* in Kenya," *American Journal of Primatology* 11 (1986): 343–58.

ing task but one likely to yield some important clues about the development and maintenance of behaviors, many primatologists have generally continued to posit tidy ex post facto explanations about function.

Toward an epigenetic perspective on gendered primate behavior

A recent and more refined discourse in evolutionary studies has suggested that important influences on the development of organisms cannot be explained by reductionist-adaptationist models.[60] Bernstein has noted the concentration on function rather than mechanism in the literature and points out that while functional consequences may influence genetic change in a population's future, they do not always reflect evolutionary history. The concept that evolution always produces ideal solutions ignores many other factors that may have had varying degrees of importance in a species' history: random processes, phylogenetic inertia, environmental change, and the random nature of mutation. The zoologist Hans Kummer noted: "Discussions of adaptiveness sometimes leave us with the impression that every trait observed in a species must by definition be ideally adaptive, whereas all we can say with certainty is that it must be tolerable, since it did not lead to extinction."[61]

Whether they propose masculinist or feminist arguments, both structural-functionalism and sociobiology commit the fallacy of affirming the consequent. In 1951 the ethologist Niko Tinbergen posed a set of questions for understanding the reason for the existence of a biological structure: (1) What were the immediate preceding events leading to changes producing the structure or behavior? (2) What are the consequences of the structure (its functions)? (3) What processes from conception to the present have influenced the attributes of the structure? and (4) What were the evolutionary selective pressures that influenced the genetic contributions to the structure? It is important to note that the second and fourth questions are separate: function is a future consequence; it is not the same as evolutionary history, because environments are not constant.[62] The first and third questions deal with proximal and developmental factors that bring about behaviors, levels of analysis often completely ignored by functionalists but likely to yield the most interesting developmental data on gendered behavior. Tinbergen's classic construction throws into relief the error of trying to answer all questions at

---

[60] Patrick Bateson, "Ontogeny of Behaviour," *British Medical Bulletin* 37, no. 2 (1981): 159–64; Fausto-Sterling (n. 6 above); Gould and Vrba (n. 9 above); Kitcher; Oyama.

[61] Quoted in Bernstein, "The Evolution of Nonhuman Primate Behavior," 101.

[62] Ibid.

the level of function alone, as so many of the grand theory builders in modern primatology have done, without explicating proximal cause and mechanism.[63]

Although linear functionalist agendas have prevailed in reconstructions of the evolution of human gendered behavior, views of what female and male monkeys and apes are doing, and why they are doing it, have changed considerably.[64] The new assertions of "feminist sociobiology" can be analyzed in the light of recent epistemological discourse in feminist theory. Haraway and others have contextualized primatology both historically and culturally; some compelling feminist deconstructions have viewed primatology as a mythic science of "good stories" and "bad stories." Primates are icons for us. They seem to live at the boundary of nature and culture, and, as Haraway has brilliantly elucidated, the ways they appear in current Western symbolism reflect the political and socioeconomic discourses of the historical periods during which primate studies have developed as a discipline.[65] But postmodern feminist deconstructions of primatology have tended to avoid the issue of good science versus bad science in relationship to feminist goals.[66]

Sandra Harding's recent treatment of the "science question in feminism" provides a useful way to frame the epistemological issues raised when primatologists study the evolution of gendered behavior.[67] Harding discusses three feminist epistemologies, which she calls "feminist empiricism," "the feminist standpoint," and "feminist postmodernism." Feminist empiricism assumes that more women in science will create a less patriarchal agenda and that the selection of appropriate problems for inquiry will change as women become practitioners. Critics of the early androcentric foci of male primatological researchers have pointed out that their models were mascu-

---

[63] I am following Irwin S. Bernstein's use of Niko Tinbergen's construction of causality in behavior, as outlined in ibid.

[64] The ascendance of functionalist models in primate studies mirrors the debate over hierarchical vs. nonhierarchical models in interactionist theories in biology throughout the twentieth century. In many cases, the proponents of hierarchy have won out. For a discussion of this point, see Evelyn Fox Keller, *A Feeling for the Organism: The Life and Work of Barbara McClintock* (New York: Freeman, 1983).

[65] Haraway, *Primate Visions* (n. 1 above).

[66] Evelyn Fox Keller has made this point: "The intellectual danger resides in viewing science as pure social product; science then dissolves into ideology and objectivity loses all intrinsic meaning. In the resulting cultural relativism, any emancipatory function of modern science is negated, and the arbitration of truth recedes into the political domain. Against this background, the temptation arises for feminists to abandon their claim for representation in scientific culture and, in its place, to invite a return to a purely 'female' subjectivity, leaving rationality and objectivity in the male domain, dismissed as products of a purely male consciousness" (Evelyn Fox Keller, *Reflections on Gender and Science* [New Haven, Conn.: Yale University Press, 1985], 113).

[67] Harding, *The Science Question in Feminism* (n. 23 above).

linist and have suggested correcting this by removing their biases and thus "fixing" the bad science involved in their construction.

As we have seen, many primatologists in the early 1970s showed the centrality of female agency. Early feminist critics exposed the androcentric bias of much former research, which focused on male agonistic behavior to the exclusion of other axes of social life in the baboon troop. A number of women primatologists sought to redress the masculinist models of the past by describing female roles and behaviors within the baboon troop and by privileging female behaviors as integral to troop structure.[68] The work of women primatologists on a multitude of species has given us a more balanced description of behavior by focusing on female animals and their interactions, showing that female primates are active and important to troop life.

As important as these feminist correctives are, an emphasis on female primates and female personnel does not challenge the functionalism that underlies much primatology of this period. Once these new data on female behavior were linked to functionalist models, they often suffered from the same empirical inadequacies as did the male-centered models, using adaptationist hypotheses in a way that seems to tell a better story for feminists but nevertheless ultimately defeats scientific goals.

In Sandra Harding's second epistemology, "the feminist standpoint," men's dominating role in science is seen as resulting in "partial and perverse" understandings (the subjugated position of women allowing for the possibility of a more complete vision). Women are disproportionately represented in the ranks of primatologists as compared to other areas of evolutionary studies. But the social experiences of women vary enormously according to class, race, and culture; and the social and economic privilege enjoyed by bourgeois women primatologists may itself produce perverse understandings. This is not a minor issue: professional male and female primatologists in the United States have come, almost without exception, from the white upper-middle or upper classes. Feminist primatologists from the economically privileged classes of the West have focused much energy on identifying and describing status roles of female primates. We do not know what primatological issues might emerge from scholars whose social experiences are radically different. For example, primatologists of a different class background might place less emphasis upon social dominance and more on the mutually supportive interactions of non-"alpha" monkeys and apes.[69]

[68] For examples of this emphasis, see Small, ed. (n. 49 above).

[69] I do not mean to imply that a simple relationship exists between social position and ideology. But in aggregate the ideas of working-class and minority members have

Some primatologists have been slow to realize that the primates they studied were part of a changing Third World ecology and that opportunities must be created for human communities if nonhuman primates are to survive in the context of rapidly changing political economies. For example, the role of the poacher as entrepreneur and the need for viable alternatives for those who depend economically on poaching are rarely considered in primatological accounts. The naive conservationism of some primatologists and their supporters is evident in the *National Geographic* vision of the African apes: innocent hairy primates defended against Africans by the lone white women who study them.[70]

Sandra Harding's third epistemology, "feminist postmodernism," challenges many of the assumptions on which the first two are based. Like structuralism, semiotics, deconstruction, and psychoanalysis, feminist postmodernism "requires seeking a solidarity in our oppositions to the dangerous fiction of the naturalized, essentialized, uniquely 'human' (read 'manly') and to the distortion and exploitation perpetrated on behalf of this fiction."[71] Some of the most interesting critiques of evolutionary models have come from postmodernist deconstructionists who read primatology as text in order to reveal its cultural meanings.

Like practitioners of the recent "ethnography as text" deconstruction of cultural anthropology, a growing number of historians and sociologists of science have viewed the evolutionary models of primatologists as a series of myths, one replacing another, and contextualized them in relation to wider social and political issues. Haraway is the most important exemplar of this school. She writes in "Primatology Is Politics by Other Means": "But *values* seems an anemic word to convey the multiple strands of meaning woven into the bodies of monkeys and apes. So I prefer to say that the life and social sciences in general, and primatology in particular, are story-laden; these sciences are composed through complex, historically specific storytelling practices. Facts are theory-laden; theories are value-laden; values are story-laden. Therefore, facts are meaningful within stories."[72] Postmodernists have tended to see less sexist and more female-centered origin myths as good for feminism. Such perspectives have led firmly away from considerations of the role of biology in human behavior in favor of analysis of the textual content of evolutionary stories. But there are problems with this approach, for it is one thing to say that science is socially constructed but another to deny,

---

been little represented in primatology, whose practitioners tend to come from an elite homogeneous class background and to be white.

[70] Haraway, *Primate Visions.*

[71] Harding, *The Science Question in Feminism,* 28.

[72] Haraway, *Primate Visions.*

as postmodernists have often done, that biology has a role in human evolution and behavior. Postmodernism leaves untouched the question of the relative worth of epistemologies in evolutionary science, because postmodernists tend to view all epistemologies as equally mythic social constructions.

Sandra Harding discusses the tensions inherent in each of these approaches and endorses a radical enterprise that considers not the "woman question" in science but, rather, the "science question" in feminism: she sees the elimination of masculine bias in science as requiring a "fundamental transformation of concepts, methods and interpretations; an examination of the very logic of scientific inquiry."[73] The movement away from linear functionalist models in primatology toward a more robust epigenetic vision of evolutionary biology fits squarely within this last enterprise. The resistance to this change is strong: the linear reductionism of the past is clean and orderly, whereas for many, the ambiguity of the kind of approach I am suggesting is often unbearably messy. Such an approach is also time-consuming; primates are long-lived species, and the research strategies necessary for a full explication of gendered behavior require life history studies, a difficult prospect within the current structure of academic science (in which most primatological data are acquired for doctoral dissertations during one or two field seasons).

Can there can be a feminist evolutionary biology that does more than retell functionalist stories in a less sexist format? Although feminist functionalism has "told new stories" about male and female primates, the narrative logic of functionalist models of primate behavior is ultimately antithetical to feminist goals. It proposes a reductionist science of genetic essences of maleness and femaleness that does not explain the diversity observed in nature. An approach that looks at genetic and extragenetic factors in the origin, diversity, and persistence of gender dimorphic behavior is more useful, although more complicated and problematic, than reductionist-functionalist models.[74] Life history studies of primates, which view development from the perspective of both proximate and ultimate causality, are necessary to our future understanding of all aspects of behavior, including gendered behaviors.

---

[73] Harding, The Science Question in Feminism, 108.

[74] In A Feeling for the Organism (n. 64 above), Fox Keller uses geneticist McClintock's radical interactionism as an example of this approach: "In lieu of the linear hierarchy described by the central dogma of molecular biology, in which the DNA encodes and transmits all instructions for the unfolding of a living cell, her research yielded a view of the DNA in delicate interaction with the cellular environment—an organismic view. Far more important that the genome as such (i.e., the DNA) is the 'overall organism.' " As she sees it, the genome functions "only in respect to the environment in which it is found." In this work, the program encoded by the DNA is itself subject to change (121).

Feminists in the social sciences have often turned away from a consideration of evolutionary biology because of their awareness of the dangers of its frequently reductionist paradigms. But a more robust and sophisticated primate ethology may have something to offer by elucidating developmental mechanisms that apply across primate phyla and by defining the important differences between human and nonhuman primates. Human gendered behavior involves uniquely human cultural, cognitive, and linguistic characteristics that appear to be recent developments in hominid evolution and that are not shared by other primates. Biological anthropologists can contribute to an understanding of human gendered behavior only by attending first to its historical, economic, and cultural causes. Without a sophisticated grasp of human social behavior, they have little to offer the social sciences by way of theorizing about biological "roots" of complex human behaviors.

Feminist theory is dependent on the larger intellectual ecology. Recent discourse in the social and biological sciences points out problems with normative studies that assume that behaviors are fixed dimorphisms to be measured in adulthood. Recent critiques in evolutionary theory challenge reductionist-adaptationist models that collapse variation into theories of male and female reproductive strategies. Primatologists must attend to these arguments as well as acknowledge that the human world has never existed before and that its conditions are constantly changing.[75] This fact sets important limitations on what we can know about human evolution from studies of monkeys and apes.

Ultimately, langurs in lipstick are not an improvement over baboons with briefcases: we must return them all to their natural environments. This mandates changes in research style involving description and coherent explanation of what actually happens during life-cycle development. With more sophisticated methodologies and more robust theoretical models, primatology may yet have something valuable to offer those of us interested in gendered human behavior.

Social Science Division
Chabot College

[75] I am here paraphrasing Oyama (n. 7 above).

Engendering Reproductive Policy and Practice in Peasant China: For a Feminist Demography of Reproduction

Susan Greenhalgh and Jiali Li

INCE THE INTRODUCTION of China's forceful one-child-per-family policy in 1979, there have been reports of abandonment and infanticide of baby girls and, more recently, widespread abortion of female fetuses.[1] As a result of these and other gender-differentiated practices, the sex ratio at birth has been rising steadily. Between 1982 and 1989 the number of boys born per 100 girls born rose from 107 to 114, well above the biologically normal level of 105 to 106. For third and higher-order children the ratio of boys to girls exceeds 125 (Zeng et al. 1993, 284). The sex ratios are most distorted in the rural areas, where the bulk of the population lives: in 1989 the sex ratio was 110 in China's cities, 113 in the towns, and 114 in the largely rural counties (Hull and Wen 1992, 29). The numbers tell a frightening story: little girls are being eliminated from Chinese society—at close to 1.2 billion, the largest society on earth—on a massive scale.

The problem of China's missing girls has attracted sporadic international attention, largely from Western journalists and from demographers, both Western and Chinese, who discovered the gender gap in births in the course of analyzing their large-scale data sets. Despite the importance of this issue to feminism, remarkably few feminist scholars have written on it.[2] Whatever the reason(s)—distaste for quantitative research, distrust of demography, or simply lack of relevant expertise and

Preparation of this article was supported by a grant from the National Institute for Child Health and Human Development, RO1 HD 28689. The 1988 fieldwork was funded by a grant from the National Science Foundation, BNS-8618121. We are grateful to Terence Hull, Kay Johnson, Peter Schneider, G. William Skinner, and several anonymous reviewers for *Signs* for their detailed comments on an earlier version of this article. Kay Johnson and Bill Skinner deserve special thanks for their thorough and thoughtful critiques.

[1] See Yan 1983; *Beijing Review* 1989; Johnson 1993; and Kristof 1993.
[2] Some who have are Johnson 1993; and Croll, Davin, and Kane 1985.

[*Signs: Journal of Women in Culture and Society* 1995, vol. 20, no. 3]

research experience—the result has been that demographers have defined the terms in which the issue is now understood.

This silence about the skewed sex ratios in China is symptomatic of the relative detachment of feminism generally from demography.[3] While the other social sciences have been thoroughly interrogated and to varying extents transformed by feminist scholars, demography has taken only the first step of adding women to the equation (Riley 1993). The more fundamental tasks—of challenging basic assumptions and reformulating central concepts—remain largely undone.[4] Today, as books in feminist anthropology, sociology, and political science proliferate, the term *feminist demographer* remains an oxymoron.

Yet the feminist remaking of demography—the critique of demographic thought and praxis and the construction of a politically engaged demography motivated by feminist concerns and informed by feminist theory—is a critical project for feminist scholarship. Its importance rests on empirical, theoretical, and political grounds. The empirical importance of this critique stems from the value of demographic data to feminist scholarship. Male-female demographic differentials, because they deal with vital matters such as life and death and because they provide a bird's-eye view of the whole population under study, can provide stark clues to the changing relations between the genders in the society as a whole. Changes in the sex ratio at birth in China, for example, could shed light on transformations in the value of females in the reform era. Demographic data such as these, however, remain underexploited, as the many feminists in the mainstream social sciences rely increasingly on qualitative data and the few feminists in demography, working in isolation from the larger feminist community, labor away at their computers trying to convince their colleagues in demography that sex-based disparities merit more attention.

The theoretical need for a feminist demography lies in the narrowness and general weakness of demographic theories of reproduction, problems widely recognized by demographers themselves (Schofield and Coleman 1986; McNicoll 1994). A highly mathematical discipline known for being long on methods but short on ideas, demography remains wedded to positivist methods of data collection and analysis.[5] Theory construction is highly constrained by the fact that only elements of social life that can be quantified and treated as individual-level variables can easily be incorporated into causal models. While some social and economic factors

---

[3] An exception is the critique of demography's role in the design of family planning programs; see esp. Hartmann 1987; and Dixon-Mueller 1993.

[4] A recent contribution to this project is Riley 1993; see also Folbre 1983.

[5] Not all demographers rely exclusively on positivist methods. McNicoll's institutional demography (1994) draws on a very different methodological tradition.

are adequately measured in this way, hard-to-quantify forces such as power and politics, which many feminists place at the heart of reproductive dynamics, remain outside the scope of analysis. Moreover, in recent decades demography has not kept up with theoretical developments in social science at large.[6] Concepts such as culture and gender, when treated at all, tend to be regarded as residual variables and formulated in the sorts of apolitical and ahistorical ways that prevailed before social constructionist approaches became popular.

These theoretical limitations are apparent in the demographic treatment of the missing Chinese girls. As in demography generally, the bulk of the demographic literature on the missing girls is devoted to quantifying the trend and describing its spatial and temporal patterning.[7] Some of this work, however, deals with causal forces. Although the authors concentrate on proximate causes (such as the underreporting of girls and sex-selective abortion), implicit in their discussions is a simple causal model of the larger forces at work. According to this model, growing discrimination against infant girls is a product of traditional (so-called feudal) patriarchal culture, which valued sons more than daughters. Although the demographic manifestations of this traditional bias disappeared during the first few decades after the revolution of 1949—sex ratios at birth were normal from the early 1960s to the late 1970s (Li and Duan 1986; Coale 1993)—values that had lain dormant for decades resurfaced in the 1980s with the introduction of the one-child policy. That policy restricts peasant couples to one, or at most two, children, forcing them to discriminate against their daughters in order to get the culturally treasured son.

While demographers have made a valuable contribution in exposing the growing discrimination against baby girls, their theoretical framework is limited by their exclusive reliance on aggregate demographic data. Such data tell the end of the story but shed little light on the complex processes leading up to it. The demographic interpretation, for example, has little to say about such matters as politics, the role of the state, and historical transformations in gender values.[8] Yet these are fundamental features of reproductive reality in the People's Republic,

---

[6] Readers of this journal may be surprised to learn that demographic theories of fertility still draw heavily on modernization theory, whose popularity in other fields peaked in the 1950s and 1960s. A critique of demographic theories of fertility from the perspective of contemporary anthropological theory is developed in Greenhalgh 1995. Some of the reasons for the intellectual isolation of demography from the more humanistic social sciences are explored by Szreter 1993.

[7] Li and Duan 1986; Liu 1988; Hull 1990; Johansson and Nygren 1991; Xu and Guo 1991; Hull and Wen 1992; Tuan 1992; Coale 1993; Zeng et al. 1993.

[8] Some demographers have been sensitive to the role of state policy in fostering the increase in the sex ratio at birth. A notable example is Terence Hull (esp. 1990).

where the politics of policy formulation and implementation forms a central dynamic of reproductive change; where the party-state is an ever-present force in reproductive decision making; and where patriarchal culture—that is, gender ideologies—has been made and remade many times since the Communist regime took control in 1949. The aggregate data also do not allow for very sophisticated notions of culture. Thus, while giving culture its due (what else could account for the gender disparities?), the demographic work relies on an ahistorical view of culture, presenting culture as simply surviving from the past and neglecting contemporary forces that may impinge on its reproduction. To see these forces in operation, we need types of data that demographers characteristically do not collect, in particular local-level case studies of policy enforcement in political-economic and sociocultural contexts. Until such evidence is brought to bear on these questions, our understanding of the growing gender inequalities will be badly incomplete and traditional peasant culture will be blamed for an outcome to which other parties have heavily contributed.

Finally, the political urgency of the feminist critique stems from the fact that demography is a powerful field whose definitions of and solutions to "the population problem" sometimes serve as tools of domination (Hartmann 1987). The field's overriding emphasis on relieving what it considers a global population crisis through the implementation of fertility control projects in southern countries has kept feminist concerns—which are often in conflict with the high-tech, top-down strategies of fertility control generally employed—off the research and policy agenda (Jaquette and Staudt 1985). As a result, relations between feminism and demography have been strained for decades.[9] Individual demographers who may be sympathetic to feminist concerns are likely to find themselves constrained by the institutional configuration of their discipline. Heavily dependent on governments for their large-scale data sets, research funds, and in many cases also employment, demographers have a harder time than most criticizing official policies that produce adverse consequences for specific groups such as women or girls.

Such political problems are extreme in the Chinese case. Because of their dependence on the Chinese state for demographic data and access to China itself, specialists in Chinese demography must be circumspect in the extreme. While many of these demographers personally are appalled by the rising sex ratios at birth,[10] they must couch their criticisms in

---

[9] Relations have improved in the past year or so as both demographers and feminists have come to see that investments in women's education and earning ability can both improve women's lives and lower the fertility rate. These issues rose to the top of the international population policy agenda in anticipation of the UN International Conference on Population and Development, which was held in Cairo in September 1994.

[10] There are some, however, who feel that the end justifies the means.

oblique language that does not direct blame at the one-child policy, designated a "basic state policy" of the People's Republic, that is, off limits to criticism. Chinese demographers who overstep these bounds risk being labeled enemies of the state and losing their jobs in government bureaucracies or state-supported universities. Overly critical foreign demographers are likely to lose access to carefully cultivated contacts in key state bureaucracies and, with them, their ability to monitor developments in the future.

With these and other critical voices muffled, the political dynamics surrounding the issue of the missing girls tend to reflect the underlying sexist strands in Chinese cultural and political life (Honig and Hershatter 1988; Gilmartin et al. 1994). Public concern focuses not on the fate of the abandoned or aborted girls but on the plight of the men who will be unable to find brides twenty years hence. Since mid-1993, when the rise in the sex ratio was first officially acknowledged, virtually the only policy that has been adopted to counteract it is a ban on the use of ultrasound B equipment for prenatal sex determination, an ineffective step at best. Meanwhile, top officials continue to boast of the country's extraordinarily low fertility level—today in the area of 1.8 to 2.0 children per woman—not mentioning the fact that it has been achieved at the cost of violence against untold numbers of infants. Politics of this sort is unlikely to reverse the tide of missing girls any time soon.

Clearly, or so it seems to us, demographic-cum-political issues like these are too important for feminists to ignore. Moreover, relative to demographers, feminist scholars enjoy certain advantages in dealing with these questions. Less dependent on governmental support, they have more political space in which to criticize existing practices and propose alternatives more favorable to women's interests. Not tied to positivist approaches, feminists can draw from a wider range of conceptual, theoretical, and methodological resources. These include political theories of reproduction, social constructionist concepts of culture and other forces, and the field research methods of some of their home disciplines. Using analytic tools such as these, feminists can appropriate demographic data for feminist purposes, supplementing them with qualitative information to ensure their proper interpretation.

Focusing on the demography of gender among the youngest Chinese, we (an anthropologist and a sociologist/demographer) seek to make a small contribution to this larger project of feminist critique and reconstruction. We deal here with the theory and politics of the missing girls, leaving the critique of demographic methods and underlying epistemologies for the future. Our approach draws on a politics-of-reproduction approach advanced by other feminist scholars and extends that framework to embrace the demographic consequences of reproductive politics. Field data from three villages in northwestern China allow us to enrich the demographic account, showing how growing gender inequality emerged from a complex interweaving of cultural values with political processes involving peasants and representatives of the party-state. We see the gender dimensions of reproductive values not as contemporary manifestations of traditional culture but as something newly constructed out of the residues of the past and the exigencies of contemporary life. Thus, politics, the state, and history, which are missing from the demographic account, take center stage in ours. We first develop these arguments and then elaborate them with ethnographic and demographic data from the study villages.

Politics, state, history: Analytic issues

Over the last decade or so, feminist scholars in history, sociology, and anthropology have begun to probe the politics of reproduction—itself a deeply gendered process—and the consequences of these negotiations and contests for women's lives and for gender relations and ideologies in society as a whole. Through studies of a wide array of topics, from the new reproductive technologies (Stanworth 1987; Strathern 1992) to the politics of abortion (Petchesky [1984] 1990; Ginsburg 1989) and the medical metaphors of reproduction (Martin 1987, 1991), to name but a few, these scholars have contested the notion that reproduction is a "natural" process that unfolds in the private domain. To the contrary, this work shows, reproduction is a social and political process involving contests over the means, the ends, and the meanings of childbearing.[11] While women and their bodies are usually the object of these struggles, the political drama is much larger, involving individuals and groups at multiple levels of the social system, all with interests in the outcome.

The consequences of such contests for women and gender hierarchies are highly variable and often paradoxical. For example, the use of modern contraception may liberate women from the burden of unwanted pregnancies but at the same time subject them to increased social control by state and medical establishments. Women's efforts to conceal their reproductive secrets that are aimed at inverting gender hierarchies may end up reproducing them instead (Browner and Perdue 1988).

Although rarely applied to demographic outcomes, a politics-of-reproduction perspective provides a useful analytic framework for developing a feminist understanding of demographic issues. Such an approach has particular appeal in a place like China, where the state has subjected reproduction to extensive political controls. The feminist literature on China suggests that throughout the post-1949 period the party-state (or

---

[11] An excellent overview is Ginsburg and Rapp 1991.

simply state) has been complicit in perpetuating gender inequality in many realms of life.[12] It would come as no surprise if the state promoted gender disparities in the reproductive domain as well.

In China two main sets of actors have been involved in the struggle to shape reproductive outcomes, the party-state and peasant society.[13] Both have vital interests at stake. The Dengist regime that took over in the late 1970s promised economic progress to the Chinese people, staking its legitimacy on its ability to achieve prosperity by century's end. Having seen rampant population growth eat up economic gains in the past, China's leaders were convinced that their economic project would fail if it could not stanch the growth of the population, especially the rural component of it, which made up over three-quarters of the total.[14] The one-child policy provided a drastic solution to this problem: radically curtailing population growth by asking all couples to limit themselves to one child.[15] Peasant society, the main target of the policy, was profoundly threatened by it. The socioeconomics and culture of village life necessitated having more than one child and at least one son. A policy restricting couples to one child imperiled cherished values and undermined the family's ability to reproduce itself.

Reproductive politics and policy

What kinds of politics were involved? Working in the United States, where reproduction is heavily medicalized, anthropologists such as Emily Martin (1987, 1991) and Rayna Rapp (1990, 1991) have shown that women resist the medical model of pregnancy and birth, accepting images, technologies, and practices that serve their interests while rejecting those that do not. Individual and group protests serve not only to contest malpractices but also to alter them. The process is depicted as one of negotiation, in which women can challenge denigrating or harmful practices of more powerful actors and at times transform dominant ideas and practices to better advance their objectives (Ginsburg 1989; Ginsburg and Tsing 1990).

We argue that similar processes mark the implementation of state-run family planning programs, domains of reproductive life as yet little ex-

[12] See, e.g., Johnson 1983; Wolf 1985; Woo 1994.

[13] Of course, contests over reproductive issues also occurred between spouses, between neighbors, and between communities. In this article we focus on the biggest reproductive struggle in contemporary China, that between the party-state and peasant society. Following conventional practice in Chinese studies, *peasant* is used for the Chinese term *nongmin*, a member of the rural population engaged in agriculture.

[14] Although demographers in China and abroad widely believe that current population growth rates pose serious economic and environmental problems, some recent scholarship challenges this alarmist position. See Johnson 1994.

[15] This call was issued in an Open Letter from the Central Committee of the Communist Party in September 1980 (CPIC 1983,1).

plored by students of reproductive politics. Where the state is involved in the process, we must consider not only *politics* but also *policy,* for it is the state's population policy that guides the design and implementation of the family planning program. Moreover, we must distinguish between formal and informal policy. *Formal policy* is specified in the written laws and regulations. *Informal policy,* by contrast, is actually implemented on the ground.

In China's state-directed birth control program,[16] we argue, women have fiercely resisted the formal policies of the state, forcing local enforcers to negotiate new, informal policies to guide implementation in village society. To understand reproductive politics in China, we must consider not only what transpires at the local level, or point of implementation, but also what happens at higher levels of the bureaucracy, where formal policy is made. Despite a common perception that the policy process in China is an exclusively top-down affair, historically top-down initiatives have generally been followed by bottom-up processes, in which the results of local enforcement are used to "perfect" state policy and thereby improve implementation.[17] Thus, there is a third political process, that of state accommodation of locally negotiated reproductive norms by officials at higher levels of the political system.

Finally, in state-socialist societies like China, where the party-state possesses the power to exert great social control, there is a fourth kind of reproductive politics, one involving submission of local society, peasants and local officials alike, to the will of the political center. This sort of politics emerges when the state decides that achievement of its demographic goals is so urgent that the needs of local society must be temporarily overridden in the service of what the state defines as compelling economic and political priorities of the country as a whole.

Political transformations and their gender consequences

Because politics is constantly evolving, as the resolution of one conflict gives birth to the next, analyses of reproductive politics must be sensitive to historical variation. In China the politics surrounding the one-child policy unfolded in three relatively distinct phases. Although the processes overlapped somewhat, to show how one led into the other, it is useful for analytic purposes to discuss them as though they occurred at different points in time.

[16] Birth planning (*jihua shengyu*), China's solution to the population problem, differs from the Western liberal notion of family planning in that the role of the party-state is paramount: births are planned by the state to bring the production of human beings into line with the production of material goods.

[17] Known as the "mass line," this strategy was formulated by Mao Zedong in the early 1940s and has been central to party leadership since then. For a classic statement, see Lewis 1963, 70–100. A convenient overview of the policy-making process in China is Liu 1986, esp. 247–60.

The initial phase of the one-child policy (roughly 1979–83) was dominated by the *politics of resistance*. The original policy, with its strict demands for one child for all, was starkly out of touch with the realities of life in the countryside. When the economic reforms dismantled the collective structures of rural life, creating space for the politics of resistance, peasant women began to actively defy the policy, insisting on having more children (in many places two), at least one of which was a son.

The second phase (roughly 1984–87) was marked by the *politics of negotiation* at the local level and the *politics of accommodation* at higher levels, leading to the engenderment of informal and formal policy. Faced with determined resistance from the peasants and, after dismantling of the rural collectives, a massive loss of power and resources, local officials (cadres) had no choice but to negotiate new terms of policy enforcement. The two groups struck a deal, working out an informal policy that allowed women to have two children and a son in exchange for agreement not to press for more.[18] While the process of policy engenderment took root at the local level, the political center could not remain a passive actor for long. The original policy of 1979 was ungendered; that is, gender was not a factor guiding reproductive behavior. However, when policymakers at provincial and national levels discovered that increased gender inequality was the price they had to pay for enforcing a restrictive policy among the peasantry, they reluctantly supported it and even institutionalized it by rewriting the regulations so that two children were allowed if the first was a girl. Formal policy thus became engendered as well.

The third and most recent phase (roughly 1988–93) was dominated by the *politics of submission* to state authority. Unfortunately for all groups involved, the politics of negotiation led to a big surge in rural fertility. Fearing that crucial economic targets would not be met, in the late 1980s the political center took resolute steps to strengthen enforcement of formal policy. By introducing a set of tough new enforcement measures, higher officials overrode locally devised policies, smudging out the politics of resistance, leaving in its place the politics of submission to state demographic demands.

These fluctuating politics had crucial consequences for gender relations. While the existing literature on the gender consequences of reproductive politics focuses on the implications for adult women, in China the struggle over birth control touched the lives of the next generation of females as well. Mothers of baby girls were subject to verbal and physical assault from unhappy husbands and in-laws (Wasserstrom 1984; Croll,

[18] Of course, the specific norms negotiated varied from place to place. The two-child-one-son rule, which was implemented in the area we studied, may have been quite widespread, since the fertility desires it reflected—for two children and one son—were very common (Whyte and Gu 1987).

Davin, and Kane 1985), but their daughters suffered too. We will show that as reproductive policy was engendered, so too was reproductive practice, as peasant women discriminated against their baby daughters in order to ensure the birth and survival of a son. The result was growing gender inequality among the littlest Chinese, visible not only in sex ratios at birth but in other areas of demographic behavior such as breast-feeding and adoption. Male bias in demographic behavior evolved over time, changing in form and degree as the politics of resistance gave rise to the politics of negotiation, accommodation, and submission.

The literature on reproductive politics cited above underscores the potentially contradictory effects on gender hierarchies. In China, too, we will see that the effects were paradoxical. For even as couples were subjecting their daughters to gross discrimination, they were beginning to recognize a daughter's value to the family. Ironically, growing demographic discrimination against girls was accompanied by growing cultural appreciation of them.

Culture as historically situated construction

While culture—in this case, gender ideologies or the cultural images and values associated with the two genders—played a crucial role in these outcomes, our view of culture differs substantially from that of the demographers discussed above. The demographic position—that the gender ideologies of peasants today are residues of traditional culture—reflects an older, ahistorical conception of culture as something "out there" or external to its bearers. In social science at large this perspective has been replaced by one that sees cultural values as constructions of human agents acting in historical time.[19] Adopting the constructionist view allows us to question the assumption that today's values are mirror reflections of yesterday's and to look critically at possible differences between the two. In China, we argue, the gender ideologies of the 1980s and 1990s resemble those of the past in their valuation of sons over daughters. On close inspection, however, there are important differences. By placing these gender values in historical context, we will show that they are human constructions reflecting traditional biases that have been reworked in response to specific changes in the political economy of village life in the 1970s, 1980s, and 1990s.

The Shaanxi village research

We now elaborate these arguments with data from three villages in the northwestern province of Shaanxi. A relatively backward province both economically and demographically, Shaanxi has experienced smaller in-

---

[19] A succinct statement is Rosaldo 1989.

creases in the sex ratios at birth than the more developed provinces to the east. In 1989 Shaanxi's sex ratio was 111.6, 2 percent below the national average of 113.8 (although 6 percent above the biological norm) (Zeng et al. 1993, 294).

These three villages were the site of ethnographic-cum-demographic field research by one of us (Greenhalgh) and collaborators at Xi'an Jiaotong University. Most of the research was conducted in 1988; during a brief restudy in 1993 we updated some of the findings and the municipal Birth Planning Association implemented a special survey on fertility. Carried out during the first six months of 1988, the initial project involved the collection of reproductive histories from all women in the villages who had ever married (941 women), intensive interviews with 150 randomly selected families, in-depth interviews with present and former cadres, and documentary research in local newspapers, journals, and other sources. During the research period Greenhalgh lived in the largest village for one month, commuting from Xi'an during the rest of the time. Village residence as well as regular village visits afforded the opportunities to engage in casual conversations and make ethnographic observations throughout the research period. All interviews and discussions with ordinary peasants were conducted in the privacy of people's homes or family fields, with no cadre present. Our empirical analyses focus on the period 1979–87, for which our data are most complete. However, we also deal briefly with the most recent period (1988–93), when trends in gender inequality took a sharp turn for the worse.

Rural reform and the remaking of gender ideology in three Shaanxi villages

Located in the Wei River valley just west of the provincial capital of Xi'an, the three study villages belong to Weinan Township (a pseudonym, 1993 population 28,510), a subdivision of Xianyang City. Although the villages vary in size—their mid-1993 populations were 1,716, 1,126, and 797—because of shared political and economic histories, as well as social and cultural backgrounds, we can treat them as a single locality for the study of reproductive policy and politics.

Rural reform: Transforming the economics and politics of village life

Vegetable growers for the nearby urban populations, the villagers are fairly well-off by Shaanxi standards, although only lower-middling by China-wide criteria. In 1991 their per capita incomes stood at 800 yuan, 50 percent higher than the provincial average (for the rural population [Shaanxi Provincial Bureau of Statistics 1992]). Rising incomes have brought dramatic improvements in consumption standards. In 1987 two in five families owned a television, while washing machines, motorcycles, and other trappings of modern life adorned the homes and courtyards of the wealthier villagers.

These striking improvements in economic well-being were a product of the economic and political reforms of the late 1970s and early 1980s. In 1979 and 1980 private plots were turned over to peasant households, free markets were opened, and short-term wage work was sanctioned, allowing villagers to supplement their meager income from the collective with private earnings. The key package of reforms—division of the collective land, dismantling of the collective workpoint system, and introduction of household responsibility systems—was put in place in late 1982 and early 1983. Since that time peasant households in the three villages have had virtually total control over the use of their plots and marketing of their produce. Political reforms followed in 1984. By eliminating the production brigade and production team structures and transforming them into villages and neighborhoods run by small committees, the political reforms sharply reduced the number and power of the cadres controlling peasant life.[20]

The dismantling of collective institutions also had profound effects on reproductive life, transforming both the politics of reproduction and the socioeconomics and culture of childbearing. Here we discuss the impact on politics, leaving socioeconomics and culture for the following section. As the local cadres tell it, birth control and other policies were relatively easy to enforce in the 1970s, when the collective socioeconomic regime was still in place. Brigade and team cadres controlled access to all the essentials of peasant life—work assignments, income, rations of basic necessities, and medical care, to name a few. If a couple failed to comply with the reproductive rules, team cadres could simply deduct the stipulated fine from their income and/or withhold essential goods and services. The reforms destroyed that system of near-total control, turning the enforcement of birth control into a major headache for local officials.[21] By eliminating collective income accounting, allowing peasant incomes to rise rapidly, and reducing the power and prestige of local cadres, the reforms opened up space for the politics of peasant resistance to the one-child policy and the politics of peasant-cadre negotiation of a new, informal policy on reproduction.

Reproductive ideologies and their gender dimension

The reforms also had striking effects on the socioeconomics of family life and, in turn, parents' ideas about childbearing. While the economic

[20] For details, see Shue 1984. On the impact of these reforms on local cadres, see White 1987; White 1991.

[21] For a discussion of the devastating effects of the reforms on the enforcement of the one-child policy, see Greenhalgh 1993. For a description of the process in China generally, see White 1991, 1992.

advantages of having many children remained limited—plot sizes were small and industry and commerce remained undeveloped—the direct and indirect costs of raising the next generation soared.[22] In 1988 parents worried about the escalating costs of food, schooling, and weddings, all of which had to be paid for in cash. By 1993, these worries had grown more intense and focused on the exceptionally high cost of raising three children and two sons. Caring for three children, informants said, would engage a mother full-time (with only two children she could take them to the fields), while having two sons would require the construction of a second house.

Increases in the costs of child rearing were, of course, not the only factors affecting reproductive decisions. Since the early 1970s the birth planning program has been inundating the villagers with propaganda explaining the societal benefits of limiting population growth. These messages, especially when reiterated by local leaders and backed up with tough administrative and economic sanctions, must have had some unmeasurable effect on childbearing aspirations. We might also expect that cultural values such as the desire for a son to carry on the family name and perpetuate the descent line would carry weight in these decisions. Oddly, though, the villagers never mentioned these factors. It was economic considerations—especially the "heavy burdens" (*fudan zhong*) of raising children—that dominated discussions about family ideals.

Peasant reproductive ideologies bore the clear mark of these concerns. Both in 1988 and in 1993 the villagers expressed strong preferences for two children. This reproductive ideal was remarkably pervasive: in the reproductive histories gathered in 1988, 86 percent of the nearly one thousand women in the three villages named the two-child family as the best. (Three percent thought one child was best, while 11 percent believed three or more were just right.) The two-child norm was even stronger among young people: 92 percent of those married during the period 1979–87 considered two children ideal. The villagers settled on two children because neither three nor one was acceptable: raising three was too costly, while one child was simply not enough—if that child died, the couple would be without issue, a social, cultural, and economic tragedy in peasant China.[23]

---

[22] For details, see Greenhalgh 1994b. Many observers feared that economic reforms would have pronatalist effects by increasing the labor value of children. Perhaps because of the skill-intensive nature of vegetable production, such effects did not materialize in the area studied.

[23] The uniformity of these answers might lead some readers to suspect that they were tailored to the demands of the regnant policy. Several facts argue against this interpretation. First, the answers were given in a period of policy relaxation; even the deputy township head in charge of birth planning was fairly relaxed about policy implementation. Second, informants of all ages and both genders, including many who could not possibly be policy targets, gave the same reply. Third, the villagers had compelling social

As important as the number of children was their gender: at least one had to be a son. Despite (or because of) decades of Communist intervention in peasant family life, in the 1980s the families of Weinan remained patrilineal (property was passed through the male line) and patrilocal (newly married couples lived with the husbands' parents). These features of family organization made sons much more essential to the reproduction of the family than daughters, who would join their husbands' families at marriage. Most important, a son was needed to support his parents in old age. A son was also needed to carry on the family line, although, as we have seen, few villagers mentioned this factor. In a village culture that continued to view women and girls as lesser beings, girls were restricted from engaging in some crucial agricultural activities, making sons the prized members of the family labor force.

While the necessity of having a son was a persistent theme in discussions with the villagers, the image of the ideal family also included a daughter. Indeed, in the reproductive histories only 4 percent of the women in the three villages considered a family with no daughter ideal. The great majority—94 percent—said one daughter was the best number. Extended discussions on this subject left the impression that sons were expected to meet parents' economic needs, while daughters were to fulfill their emotional ones. The result was a strong and insistent demand for a son and a weaker but still present longing for a daughter.

The construction of gender ideology in the reform era

The demographic literature on China has portrayed such gender ideologies, in particular the preference for sons, as reflections of a traditional culture that has survived relatively unaltered from the past. While the past is almost always carried forward in some form into the present, field data allow us to develop a more complex view of the connections between past and present. These data reveal that the preference for sons has persisted but that beneath this global gender preference lie subtle changes in the valuation of sons and daughters. Moreover, the roots of today's views can be traced to specific changes in the political economy of village life in the 1970s, 1980s, and 1990s. In this section we trace out those roots, arguing that the gender ideologies of today are best viewed as contemporary constructions forged by the villagers as some of their most fundamental family traditions were undermined by the massive political, economic, and social changes of the late Maoist and early Dengist eras.

Traditionally, sons were thought to bring many benefits, while daughters carried few if any. Today these ideas are being discarded. While the

---

and economic reasons to support their beliefs. And finally, the answers were offered with such strong conviction in the interviews that I (Greenhalgh) came away with the feeling that they reflected deeply held personal beliefs.

old saying "Many sons [bring] much happiness" was something of an idealization, the fact that some older villagers still defended it in the late 1980s suggests that it contained more than a kernel of truth. Before the policies of the Communist state eliminated significant private property and altered the distribution of resources in favor of the young, the parents of two, three, or four sons could realistically hope to be relatively well-off and to enjoy a comfortable old age surrounded by at least one son, his wife, and some grandchildren. In the 1980s and early 1990s the connection between a houseful of sons and family prosperity was no longer apparent to the villagers. Asked to reflect on the wisdom embodied in the above saying, most villagers scoffed at it, adding that, far from being sources of wealth, sons were onerous economic burdens. One informant reminded us of the heavy fines imposed on couples having a second son, implying that the question was less than sensible.

Today, as we have seen, peasant couples want at most two sons. Increasingly, they want only one. These ideas were formed in response to the political-economic realities of contemporary life. Many villagers interviewed in 1988 believed that having three or four sons was a bad idea because they often fight over who will have to support the elderly parents, causing humiliation and even economic hardship for the parents. While such squabbles between brothers have always been part of Chinese family life, during the collective era they may have had increasingly negative consequences for the parents, as family division began to occur sooner after marriage (i.e., earlier in the parents' lives). As older villagers tell it, fraternal fights have become even noisier and more prevalent during the reform years, because young people, now free to pursue economic activities on their own, no longer want to be saddled with the burdens of listening to and caring for old people, whom they consider hopelessly old-fashioned and an obstacle to getting ahead. Increasingly, older parents are finding themselves left entirely alone, as even the last son demands his freedom and separates from his parents. Cases of older people abandoned by their sons and unable to fend for themselves in the rapidly changing, highly competitive reform environment[24] have convinced many people that sons just cannot be counted on any more even to honor their most fundamental obligation. As one older man put it, "These days sons are useful to parents only after the parents die; then they throw huge funerals to show how filial they have been."

Peasant attitudes toward daughters have also shifted. In the past daughters were considered "goods on which one loses": they required time and money to raise, then married out of the family, cutting off ties with their

---

[24] In families in which all the sons divide from the parents, one or more sons usually send small amounts of money to cover the older couple's living expenses. Destitution results when these sums are too small to cover basic living expenses, forcing the older folk to try to support themselves through agricultural production.

parents. While such disparaging views can occasionally be heard today, more young people now actively want a daughter, albeit not as keenly as they want a son. The reasons are many and complex,[25] but the explanation most frequently given in the interviews was to provide emotional support in old age. Some even imagined relying on their adult daughters for economic support—that is, they envisioned moving in with their married daughters if their sons failed to provide for them, something quite unheard of in the past.[26] Such notions could have arisen only in recent decades, when married women have gained more resources and personal freedom and marriages within the village have became common, making it feasible for married daughters to return home for a few hours and tend their aging parents. Intravillage marriages have also enabled parents to maintain contact with their married daughters, a prerequisite to joining them in later years.

It was not only the proximity of married daughters that underlay the strikingly new imagery of grown daughters tending their aging parents. Also important was the growing emotional distance between older parents and the culturally preferred caregivers, their sons and daughters-in-law. During the field research older people complained bitterly about the unfiliality of sons, who often refused to provide pocket money, and the coldness of daughters-in-law, who were known to undertake small acts of cruelty in order to precipitate family division. While stories of daughters-in-law breaking up the large family have long been part of the cultural repertoire, what has changed is the daughter-in-law's ability to force the division. Now important income earners, daughters-in-law are using their economic power to advance their personal agendas. One young newlywed, finding her husband siding with his parents in the great division debate, simply refused to go into the fields. Fearing that their crops would be ruined, the other family members gave in and agreed to split up the family. Such stories have become more common during the reform years, as young people, impatient for economic progress, try to hasten the arrival of the future by ridding themselves of the burdens of the past. Facing these distressing new realities, people are beginning to construct new, regendered images of family life. In these imaginings a daughter has not replaced a son but, unlike the past, she now has a place.

Today's ideas reflect themes in traditional culture, but these themes are being reworked to form part of a different cultural imaginary. The vision

---

[25] Because they have been encouraged to take part in agricultural labor, daughters now have much greater economic value to their parents than they did before 1949. For a discussion of these and related issues, see Parish and Whyte 1978, esp. 180–92. The preference for daughters appears to be much stronger in the cities. These issues are explored with subtlety by Wolf 1985.

[26] The social histories of 150 families that were gathered in 1988 include no cases of parents moving in with their married daughters. The histories cover the half-century 1937–87.

of a big family with many sons, one of whom lives with and supports the elderly parents, is fast disappearing, undermined by the changing political-economic realities of village life. In its stead is another image: the small-hearted son and selfish daughter-in-law refusing to honor their obligations to their elders and, in their place, the faithful daughter, appreciated at last, coming home to render personal services and comfort in her parents' final years.

The politics of engenderment: Resistance, negotiation, accommodation, and submission

When it introduced the one-child policy in 1979, the Chinese party-state did not intend to foster gender bias in reproductive policy and practice. Top leaders were aware that the policy might produce an excess of males over females, but they dismissed the problem as unlikely and in any case fixable through proper ideological work (CPIC 1983). The original policy was gender-neutral, asking all Han Chinese couples to have only one child. Yet by 1988 two-thirds of China's provinces had incorporated gender considerations into their reproductive regulations, and reproductive practice had become deeply differentiated by gender. Focusing on the three Shaanxi villages, in this section we illuminate the complex political processes out of which gender disparities among the young arose. We will see that, far from being passive bystanders, agents of the state were active parties to the negotiations.

Resisting the one-child rule

Soon after the one-child policy was introduced, peasants in the Weinan villages began seeking means to escape its harshest provisions. In the early years of economic reform, before decollectivization, the means of resistance available to them were relatively limited. The dismantling of the collectives in 1982–83 vastly widened the villagers' circle of freedom, opening up many ways to defy the birth control policy.

Resistance took many forms: economic means such as refusing to pay fines; social strategies such as adopting out second and third daughters; migrational tactics such as temporarily moving to another city to give birth; and bodily techniques such as illegally removing an intrauterine device (IUD), refusing to adopt the stipulated contraception, and concealing unauthorized pregnancies until it was presumably too late to have an abortion.[27]

Reflecting deep-seated desires for a son and much weaker although tenacious yearnings for a daughter, peasant resistance to the policy was

---

[27] For more on these bodily techniques, see Greenhalgh 1994a; economic strategies are documented in Greenhalgh 1993.

profoundly gendered. We look here at the imprint of these gender preferences, as well as the desire for two children, on the willingness of
women to undergo contraceptive surgery and on the size and gender
composition of the families they constructed. (Here and below family size
is used as shorthand for the number of children a woman has.) The
demographic data provide a particularly rich resource for studying resistance. Unlike individual case studies, the demographic data give an
overall picture of the number of women resisting the policy and the forms
that resistance took. We focus here on the resistances of the early one-
child policy period (1979–83). Although peasants continued to evade the
birth restrictions into the mid-1980s, the political actions of the earlier
years actually provided the impetus for the renegotiation of local policy.

Under the one-child policy all married couples of reproductive age
with one or more children were required to adopt effective contraception
(i.e., an IUD or sterilization). This demand was clearly spelled out in the
provincial birth planning regulations, which specified economic and administrative sanctions for failure to comply.[28] The obligation to contracept was also national policy, enshrined in the Marriage Law of 1980 and
the Constitution of 1982.[29] Thus, to choose not to contracept was a bold
action, one that defied laws on the books at the highest levels of the
political system.

Despite the severity of the offense, many couples refused to protect
themselves against conception. At the end of 1983, five years after the
one-child policy was introduced, the level of contraceptive use fell far
below the level required by law. Patterns of contraception by family size
and composition suggest why. While a substantial majority of couples
with two or three children complied with the demand to contracept (74
and 82 percent, respectively), only 22 percent of couples with one child
did so, bespeaking fierce resistance to the notion of limiting family size to
one.

The gender of the first child did not affect the desire for two children:
that is, regardless of whether the first child was a girl or boy, the low
contraceptive use rates (about 20 percent) suggest that couples wanted a
second child. However, gender preferences emerge clearly at larger family
sizes. While fully 85 percent of couples with one son and one daughter
were contracepting, only 12 percent of those with only two daughters
were doing so, indicating an exceptionally strong desire for a son. Al-

[28] The birth planning regulations of Xianyang City also guided the reproductive activities of the villagers. Since the municipal regulations differ little from the provincial
ones, we limit our discussion to the latter.
[29] Article 14 of the 1980 Marriage Law and Article 49 of the 1982 Constitution
state: "Husband and wife are in duty bound to practice [birth] planning" (*Population
and Development Review* 1981, 369–72; National People's Congress 1983).

though a great deal weaker, the desire for a daughter is also evident in the villages. Among couples with two sons but no daughter, the contraceptive level was 81 percent, 4 percent lower than that found among couples with one child of each sex. The desire for a daughter is weaker in couples with three children, but it is evident nevertheless.[30]

Beneath these aggregate figures, of course, were individual women struggling to produce the children they, their husbands, and in-laws badly wanted while not running afoul of the birth planning cadres. Biologically fortunate women, who got a son and a daughter on the first two tries, had a relatively easy reproductive career, evading only the widely violated rules that each couple have but one child and women with one child wear an IUD. The biologically unlucky ones, who had two sons or, worse yet, two daughters, had to resort to politically and physically riskier measures such as illegally removing their IUDs and hiding pregnancies as long as possible in hopes of avoiding the mandatory abortion that was supposed to end all unauthorized pregnancies.

The gendered character of resistance also emerges from the data on fertility. In the early years of the one-child policy, all couples, regardless of circumstances, were "encouraged" (i.e., pressured) by birth planning workers to limit themselves to one child. Second children were to be strictly limited to couples in exceptional circumstances (some of which are described below), while third and higher-order children were to be "resolutely prohibited." These injunctions were laid out in the provincial birth planning regulations and backed by strong economic and administrative sanctions.[31]

Tough penalties notwithstanding, in the Weinan villages many peasants refused to stop at one child. During the years 1979–83, fully 44 percent of women with one child went on to have a second. Defiance of the rules on second children depended partly on the gender of the first; while 39 percent of women with a son pressed for a second, 50 percent of those with a daughter did so. Resistance became even more gendered as birth order rose. Twenty-two percent of all couples with two children had a third during these years, but 54 percent of those with two daughters and no sons did so. And while only 4 percent of couples with three children defied intense pressures to have a fourth, 25 percent of couples with three daughters took this risky step in hopes of being blessed with a son.

What stands out most boldly from these patterns of childbearing is the intensity of son preference. However, we can also discern the desire for

[30] Couples with three sons but no daughter were slightly less likely to contracept than those with at least one daughter. The percentages were 76 and 83, respectively.

[31] Unlike contraception, family size has never been regulated by national law. Such a law has been drafted and discussed many times but never formally passed.

a daughter. The strongest evidence for daughter preference is that nearly 40 percent of couples with only a son went on to have a second child. (Of course, this behavior might reflect simply a desire for two children.) As the number of children increases, however, the desire for a daughter appears to weaken. While 12 percent of couples with one son and one daughter went on to have a third child, a slightly higher 18 percent of couples with two sons but no daughters did so. A minuscule 2 percent of couples with at least one child of each gender had a fourth child, but 7 percent of those with three sons and no daughters had another child.

The results of this gender-specific resistance can be seen in the gender composition of the families that village couples had constructed by the end of the fifth year of implementation (see fig. 1). At that time, 57 percent of couples with one child had a son, while only 43 percent had a daughter. Clearly, couples were playing with biology, for if biological factors alone were at work, we would expect rough parity in the proportion of couples with one son and one daughter. As families grew in size, the gender gap also grew. Of all couples with two children, 60 percent had the village ideal of one child of each sex. Twenty-seven percent had two sons, while only 12 percent had two daughters. If gender composition were not being manipulated, we would expect a ratio closer to 50-25-25. The gender gap widens even farther in three-child families. Eighty percent of families with three children had at least one child of each sex, 16 percent had all sons, and only 5 percent had all daughters.

Negotiating informal policy

Faced with resolute resistance to the strict one-child rule and, after decollectivization, a massive loss of power and resources, during the mid-1980s local birth planning cadres had little choice but to negotiate new, informal terms of implementation. The political and economic climate at middecade was unusually conducive to reproductive deal making at the village level. Most likely, village-level birth planning workers had long secretly sympathized with peasant desires for two children and a son. After all, unlike higher-level officials, village cadres were members of village society who shared its culture and daily life (Shue 1988). Under the economic reforms, however, the cadres' identification with the villagers—and thus sympathy for their reproductive plight—deepened. By eliminating many of the cadres' official duties and by giving them allocations of land under the household responsibility system, the reforms turned them into nearly full-time peasants whose interests were virtually identical to those of ordinary villagers.

A second factor encouraging local politicking over the reproductive rules was a softening of the demographic demands of the state. In general, local officials in China are duty bound to enforce all state policies,

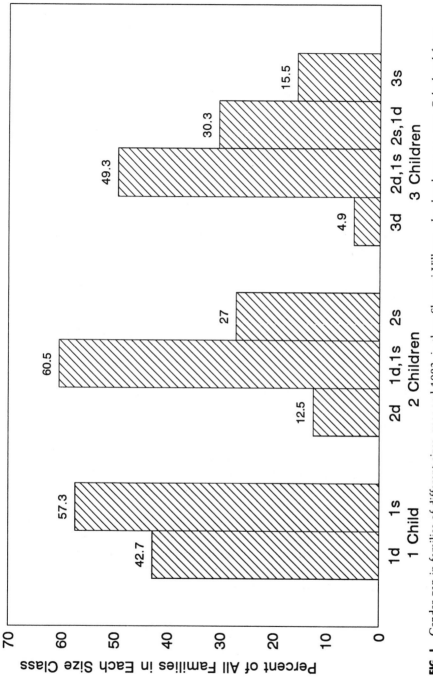

FIG. 1 Gender gap in families of different sizes, year-end 1983, in three Shaanxi Villages. *d* = daughters; *s* = son. Calculated from reproductive histories.

including unpopular ones such as the birth control policy. Research shows, however, that the extent to which these cadres actually do so varies according to the amount of pressure exerted on them from above (Unger 1989). In the early 1980s state pressure to achieve demographic targets was great, leaving village cadres few options but to press the villagers to comply. In the mid-1980s, however, the central government slightly relaxed its demands on the birth planning bureaucracy, creating room for bargaining and constructing more lenient, informal policies in localities throughout the country.

Although the reproductive rules of thumb worked out in the Weinan villages were not written down anywhere—to do so would have been politically risky, exposing the pervasive, ongoing violation of formal policy—everyone concerned with childbearing seemed to know what they were. We pieced them together from conversations with birth planning workers and peasants and from individual cases that represented limiting situations. Although there is space here only to introduce a few of these cases, ethnographic and demographic evidence presented elsewhere (Greenhalgh 1993, 1994a) confirms the existence of such rules and charts the implicit and explicit negotiations that led to their formulation.

The informal policy on reproduction can be distilled into three sets of rules or understandings: those regarding the number of children, the sex of children, and the treatment of couples who had reached the ideal of two children and one son. The application of these rules on childbearing can best be seen by examining the more detailed and again, informal, behavioral guidelines for contraception, which was the major means of controlling fertility. These three rules and the associated contraceptive guidelines are as follows:

First, virtually all couples, regardless of their circumstances, were allowed to have two children. Formal policy notwithstanding, women with one child were encouraged but not required to have an IUD inserted, and women with one child who became pregnant out of plan were not required to undergo an abortion.[32]

The case of Zhu Xiuhua illustrates this rule.[33] In December 1980 Zhu had a son. Following township regulations, in May 1981 she had an IUD inserted. However, five months later she had her IUD removed, hoping to have a second child. The local birth planning worker allowed her to carry the pregnancy to term, and in October 1982 Zhu gave birth to another boy.

[32] All births were supposed to be planned, i.e., to take place only after a couple requested and received an official birth quota. Local cadres allocated birth quotas according to a priority system in which certain categories of couples (those with no children, e.g.) were given preference. The total number of quotas given out in a specific year depended on the number of births assigned to the locality by higher levels of the administrative system. All pregnancies occurring outside the plan were supposed to be aborted.

[33] All names used in this article are pseudonyms.

Second, virtually all women were allowed to have a son. In contravention to the written regulations, which forbade third and higher-order childbearing, women with two daughters who became pregnant again were allowed to carry the pregnancy to term.

The case of the party secretary of one of the villages aptly illustrates this one-son-for-all rule. The secretary quietly allowed his daughter-in-law to have a third child because the first two were girls. This case bears special import, because party secretaries are the most powerful members of village society. It is what they do, not what the written regulations say, that sets the policy in the villages they head.

Third, these liberties were granted on the understanding that peasants who had reached the reproductive ideal would not seek to exceed it. Women with at least one son and one daughter were expected to undergo sterilization. They were strongly pressured to do so, however, only if they caused trouble for the cadres by attempting to have another child.

The application of this rule can be seen in the case of Cao Lihua. After bearing two daughters, Cao finally had a son in April 1983. However, wanting another child, she became pregnant again. Her pregnancy was discovered and aborted in August 1985, and in October of that year Cao was required to undergo sterilization.

In addition to these rules of thumb on number and sex of children and contraception, informal policymakers also waived the state's requirement that births be spaced four years apart and ignored children born but later adopted out when determining a couple's birth quota. These other guidelines will figure in the story told below.

Accommodating local values: Engendering formal policy

Although detailed micropolitical data are unavailable, evidence of other sorts suggests that patterns of peasant defiance and peasant-cadre negotiation such as those documented above were common throughout rural China.[34] Reading the political signals, in 1984 the central leadership conceded that the original, strict version of the one-child policy was unimplementable in the rural areas. Unwilling to abandon the policy, which was a crucial component of their larger economic development plan, leaders in Beijing sought ways to "perfect" the policy to make it work. In 1984 they issued a high-level directive authorizing the provinces—the administrative units with primary responsibility for fertility policy—to adapt the policy to local realities within their borders. Under the slogan "Open a small hole to close a big hole" (*Kai xiaokou du dakou*), provinces were permitted to increase the number of conditions

---

[34] Such a picture emerges from ethnographic information from villages in Fujian and Guangdong (Huang 1989; Potter and Potter 1990), demographic data on contraception and fertility in all the provinces and the country as a whole (Arnold and Liu 1986; Tuan 1992), and numerous accounts in the Chinese press (Wasserstrom 1984).

under which couples, especially rural couples, would be allowed to have second children. The aim was not to increase freedom of reproductive choice but to improve enforcement by bringing policy into line with practice.

In Shaanxi, provincial policymakers adapted formal policy to local conditions by incorporating informal policy of the sort adopted in Weinan into the written regulations. Since informal practice was male-biased, the process of "opening a small hole" resulted in the writing of gender inequality into provincial legislation. In a step that would prove fateful for the villagers in later years, provincial policymakers adapted formal policy to one of the peasants' desires—for a son—but not the other—for two children for all.[35]

The process of policy engenderment can be traced in the provincial birth planning regulations. Since the introduction of the one-child policy, Shaanxi Province has issued four major sets of regulations advocating one child for all couples, those of 1981, 1982, 1986, and 1991. (Another set of regulations issued in 1979 reflected the previous policy of recommending one but permitting two children.) Between successive sets of regulations, the number of conditions under which peasant couples were allowed to have a second child increased from five to seven to eleven, and then dropped to ten. In the Temporary Regulations of 1981 and 1982, conditions such as the disability of the first child, remarriage of the couple, or non-Han ethnicity enabled some couples to have second children; the gender of the first child was not a factor.

By 1986 gender had become a consideration for second childbearing, although policymakers apparently felt uncomfortable enough about it that they used a code word for the provision on gender in the written regulations. The final condition of the 1986 regulations stated that rural couples who find themselves "in real difficulties" (*shiji kunnan*) were allowed to have a second child in a planned fashion (i.e., after spacing four years and receiving an official birth quota). Although this last item was not further elaborated in the regulations themselves, its meaning was very clear to everyone involved in birth planning work. A document prepared for Greenhalgh and her Chinese colleagues by the Provincial Birth Planning Commission stated clearly that the 1986 provision for couples with "real difficulties" meant those with only a girl. By 1991 policymakers had shed their reticence about incorporating gender disparities into the regulations. According to the last condition of the 1991 regulations, "when both husband and wife have only one daughter and the family has real difficulties," they may have a second child in a planned fashion.

---

[35] A few provinces did modify their policies to allow all rural couples to have two children.

Shaanxi was not the only province that institutionalized—indeed, actually legalized—male bias in reproductive behavior. By 1989, eighteen provinces had formalized what came to be known as the "daughter-only" (*dunuhu*) policy (Zeng 1989; Feng and Hao 1992). That is, two-thirds of all provinces formally recognized the unequal value of daughters and sons and made the gender of the first child a legitimate basis for reproductive behavior. The legalization of gender inequality was in direct contravention to the Chinese Constitution, which holds men and women to be equal before the law.

Submitting to the political center

In the late 1980s and early 1990s, the climate for reproductive politicking at the local level turned hostile. When state policymakers relaxed the pressure in 1984 and allowed localities to increase the number of conditions for second childbearing, they did not imagine that villages throughout the country would go further and allow two children for all. Unfortunately for all parties involved, the enforcement of such informal policies led to sharp increases in rural fertility.[36] Believing that too-rapid population growth would jeopardize achievement of crucial economic goals, in the late 1980s the political center began to turn up the pressure on the birth planning establishment to meet demographic targets. A central-level document issued in May 1991 reflects this toughened stance on birth control. The document affirmed the more liberal daughter-only policy but called for greatly enhanced efforts to implement that policy in the rural areas (Xinhua 1991).

Shaanxi responded to these new demands with considerable alacrity (Greenhalgh, Zhu, and Li 1994). In 1991 policymakers issued a new set of provincial regulations to guide childbearing throughout the province. The aim was to unify policy provincewide, eliminating the hundreds, perhaps thousands, of local policies, both formal and informal, that had guided childbearing in the province during the mid-1980s.[37] Reiterating previous policy on childbearing, the regulations continued to encourage one child for all and prohibit third children. With regard to second children, as we have seen, they allowed two if the first was a girl but insisted that couples with a son stop at one.

In this new politicized climate, birth cadres in the Weinan villages had little choice but to abandon the informal policies of the mid-1980s.

---

[36] Western scholars, using sophisticated techniques, estimate that the total fertility rate rose from 2.27 in 1985 to 2.45 in 1987 (Feeney et al. 1989). Official Chinese data show a much sharper rise, from 2.20 to 2.59 countrywide and from 2.48 to 2.94 in the rural townships (*China Population Newsletter* 1989). It is these latter estimates, one can presume, that lay behind the program modifications of the late 1980s.

[37] Interview with officials at Shaanxi Provincial Birth Planning Commission, July 14, 1993.

Although they continued to sympathize with peasant desires for two children and a son, the villages' officials now faced intense pressure to promote the formal policy of the province instead. This pressure was no longer just political; economic pressures were also evident in new "cadre responsibility systems" that docked wages and blocked promotions of those failing to meet targets. In addition, the problems of enforcement they had faced in the mid-1980s had been solved by the creation of a battery of new, highly effective mechanisms specifically designed to work in the late-reform environment. Most of these enforcement instruments were designed by officials at higher levels of the political system and promoted for use throughout the province. Some of them, such as the new, party-controlled Birth Planning Association, were deliberately designed to bypass the local cadres, taking over some of the work they had been unable—or unwilling—to do. Other techniques of control involved linking compliance to access to crucial economic resources and new "service-oriented" administrative measures that were mandatory for all women of reproductive age. These measures, which are detailed elsewhere (Greenhalgh, Zhu, and Li 1994), were apparently every bit as powerful as the collective-based mechanisms that had supported enforcement in the late 1970s and early 1980s.

Finding their local bargains overridden and feeling strong pressure from above, village birth cadres had no choice but to submit to state authority. This meant going back on their earlier promises to the villagers. While couples whose first child was a girl were allowed to have a second, they were now required to wait the stipulated four years. (As noted above, spacing rules had always been on the books but were not enforced in the more lenient environment of the mid-1980s.) Couples with a son were expected to stop at one. Although the brevity of our 1993 field research limited the number of individual cases that we could collect, conversations with cadres and peasants alike made it clear that a tough policy was in force. One case must suffice to make the point. In mid-1993 Tian Fangfang, a shy mother of a three-year-old girl, was awaiting a quota to have a second child. Asked what she would do if her next child was another daughter, she said she would have no more children. Why? "Because the policy is so rigid" (*zhuade henjin*), she replied softly.

Thus, through a complex, historically situated political process involving resistance, negotiation, accommodation, and submission, son preference moved from being a peasant value[38] (deeply embedded, of course, in social institutions) to becoming a component of informal reproductive

---

[38] Of course, patriarchal values were not the exclusive property of the peasantry but were shared by most groups in Chinese society.

policy in the villages, to being incorporated into the formal population policy of the province. Neither intended nor desired by any of the parties involved, the extension and formalization of gender bias was the only compromise that proved feasible when peasant patriarchal values clashed head-on with state demands for population control.

Distorting the demography of gender: Consequences for the young

The reproductive compromises reached by diverse groups of adults, each with its own pressing agenda, had devastating consequences for the next generation, especially the female portion of it. During the one-child policy period the demography of gender among the young became very unbalanced, as peasant women struggled to meet their most basic reproductive needs in a fluctuating policy environment that confronted them with a succession of political constraints. Distortions in the demography of gender were not confined to the sex ratio at birth, the subject that has gotten most attention. As we will see, patterns of adoption and breast-feeding also bore the imprint of political forces impressing patriarchal values into demographic behavior.

In the following sections we examine changes in the demography of gender over four policy periods: before 1970, that is, before a forceful birth control policy was in force, and three phases of the one-child policy period, 1979–83, 1984–87, and 1988–93. To keep an already complicated story from becoming more so, we omit discussion of the 1970s (more specifically, 1970–78), when the "later-longer-fewer" (*wanxishao*) policy was in effect.[39] During these years gender differentials in the demographic measures explored here were intermediate between those of the 1960s and 1980s.

Sex ratios at birth

Of all the demographic effects of these struggles over reproduction, the most consequential was the change in the number of boys and girls born. Trends in the sex ratio at birth in the three villages are shown in table 1. For all children combined, the sex ratio of reported births fluctuated sharply over time, measuring 105 (close to the biological norm) before 1970, rising to 121 during the strict early one-child period, falling to 109 during the phase of policy liberalization, and rising steeply to 153 during the recent period of strong enforcement. The data thus suggest a

---

[39] During the 1970s China's population control efforts were guided by the "later-longer-fewer" (*wanxishao*) policy, so named because it stressed later marriage, longer spacing between children, and fewer births.

TABLE 1   SEX RATIOS OF REPORTED BIRTHS BY PERIOD AND PARITY IN THREE
SHAANXI VILLAGES

	Period Child Born			
Birth Order	Before 1970	1979–83	1984–87	1988–93*
All birth orders	105 (1,525)	121 (301)	109 (389)	153 (299)
Parity 1	122 (348)	126 (163)	91 (174)	133 (189)
Parity 2	102 (309)	96 (90)	106 (181)	172 (98)
Parity 3+	100 (868)	167 (48)	386 (34)	1,100 (12)
Parities 1 and 2	112 (656)	114 (253)	98 (355)	145 (287)

Sources: Data for periods up to 1987 from reproductive histories. Data for 1988–93
provided by Xianyang City Birth Planning Association.
Note: The sex ratio is the number of sons born per 100 daughters born. Numbers in
parentheses are sample sizes.
*Data cover first six months of 1993 only.

connection between intensity of policy enforcement and sex ratio at
birth: the stronger the enforcement, the greater the dearth of daughters.

What underlies the extraordinarily high sex ratios of the 1980s and
1990s? The subject of the missing girls was an extremely sensitive one in
Weinan, making it difficult for Greenhalgh and her field research collaborators to learn what was going on. Indeed, during the 1993 research,
the township cadres who provided information on the number of births
intentionally neglected to supply data on the sex of the children born.
The figures presented in table 1 came from village officials, who apparently did not know that their superiors had wanted to keep the information confidential. (At the time we asked the village cadres for the information, we did not know of the intent to keep it secret either.) Not
surprisingly, given the political risks of divulging such information, peasant informants in the villages were extremely reluctant to tell us what
they or their neighbors were doing to produce so many sons. Indeed, both
cadres and peasants successfully resisted our efforts to find out what was
going on.

Despite the extreme sensitivity of the issue, in 1993 we tried to get a
sense of what was happening to the missing girls. We probed for each of
the four possibilities offered by the literature on China as a whole: sex-
selective abortion of female fetuses, underreporting of girls, informal
forms of adoption, and infanticide and/or abandonment of infant girls.

Unlike some other parts of the country, where the use of ultrasound
for prenatal sex determination followed by abortion of females is apparently an open secret (Kristof 1993), in the Xi'an area the practice is
concealed deep within the sociopolitical fabric. Individual peasants,
asked if they knew of a way to tell the sex of an unborn child, reacted
with surprise, saying they knew of no such method and pointing out that

that sort of technique, if available, would attract a great deal of interest. Village cadres were more elusive, refusing, quite understandably, to answer our intrusive questions. The officials of one village said they did not know whether residents of their village were using ultrasound for sex determination, something we found difficult to believe. Given this dearth of information, the only conclusion we can draw about sex-selective abortion is that suggested by a municipal birth planning official: that it occurs, but to an unknown extent.

Probes about underreporting of female births met with strong denial from the cadres. The birth cadre of the largest village, a longstanding friend of the researchers, insisted vehemently that the data were absolutely correct and had not been tampered with. Asked why, if that was true, the sex ratio was so high, she replied with audible anguish, "I just don't know!" Given her response, as well as the high degree of social control and surveillance that makes secrets impossible to keep in Chinese villages, we believe that underenumeration of children born and raised in the village was minimal. In other words, we believe that underreporting of a sort the village cadres might find out about is likely to be small in scope.

Concealment of other sorts, however, may well be going on. For example, the villagers may have been using informal types of adoption in which infant girls were not reported to the officials and were "loaned" to relatives or friends elsewhere for a few years, then brought back to the village after the threat of severe sanctions receded. Cautious inquiries into the questions of infanticide and abandonment met with hostility and silence. With the exception of underreporting, therefore, we have no grounds for ruling out any of the possible explanations for the missing girls. We hope for the best but, knowing of the crowded orphanages and babies abandoned in the streets in some other parts of the country, fear the worst.

While we do not know what combination of practices was used to distort the sex ratios in the villages, by looking at the differentials in sex ratio by parity, or birth order, we can discover which children were discriminated against. Returning to table 1, we find that for children born before 1970, the sex ratio is high for the first child, then falls to normal for other children. The high sex ratio among first-borns probably reflects a combination of differential care of first children—that is, passive neglect of unhealthy first daughters—and selective memory about girls allowed to die so long ago.

Trends during the one-child policy period reflect the fluctuating politics surrounding the birth control program. (We assume that selective memory did not affect the data for these more recent years.) The sex ratio for first and second births together (presented in the bottom row) fell from 114 in the initial period of strong enforcement to 98 in the mid-1980s, when informal policy was liberalized to accommodate peasant desires for two children and a son, before rising to 145 in the late 1980s and early 1990s, when the state overrode local policy in order to drastically reduce the birth rate.

Trends in the sex ratio of third and higher births show clearly the growing pressure to eliminate such births. From 100 in the years before 1970, the sex ratio for higher-order births climbed to 167 in the early 1980s, 386 in the mid-1980s, and 1,100 in the late 1980s and early 1990s. This latter figure should be interpreted with great caution, for it is based on only twelve births. Nevertheless, the trend is unmistakable: over time third-born girls simply vanished from the demographic scene.

Taken together, the evidence suggests that little girls fared best during the mid-1980s, when the relatively lenient, informal two-child-one-son policy was in effect. They fared worst during the late 1980s and early 1990s; although a daughter-only policy was in effect at that time, intense pressures from above apparently led couples to fear that they would be allowed only one child, inducing them to take drastic steps to ensure that that one was a son.

Adoption

Village couples not only gave birth to fewer daughters but they also gave away more of the daughters they bore. Changes in adoption practices are shown in table 2. The data presented here include all formal adoptions reported by the village women during the 1988 field research. (Unfortunately, it was not possible to collect comparable information on adoption or breast-feeding, discussed below, in 1993.) Thus, these data exclude the more informal types of adoption described above.

Before the imposition of a forceful birth control policy in the early 1970s, a small but significant proportion of village children—5 percent of sons and 4 percent of daughters—were adopted in and out of their families.[40] In general, young children were adopted out when there were already too many of their gender in the family. Males were most often adopted in by couples who had no sons. Females were adopted for a number of reasons, including to serve as little daughters-in-law (*tongyangxi*) for their adoptive brothers (for more see Wolf and Huang 1980) and to act as talismans, protection against the early death of later children.

These practices changed after the introduction of the one-child policy. With strict limits on the number of children allowed, sons became too precious to give away, and the villagers stopped adopting them out altogether. Girls, by contrast, became more dispensable. Facing stringent restrictions on the total number of children allowed and strongly desiring

---

[40] The figures on the prevalence of adoption in the villages roughly parallel estimates for the country as a whole. See Johansson and Nygren 1991, 45.

TABLE 2   ADOPTION BY GENDER IN THREE SHAANXI VILLAGES

| | Period Child Born | | | | | |
| | Before 1970 | | 1979–83 | | 1984–87 | |
	Number	%	Number	%	Number	%
Children adopted out:						
Female	10	1.3	4	2.9	7	3.8
Male	27	3.5	0	.0	0	.0
Children adopted in:						
Female	18	2.4	2	1.5	2	1.1
Male	11	1.4	0	.0	0	.0
All children adopted out and in:						
Female	28	3.8	6	4.4	9	4.8
Male	38	4.9	0	.0	0	.0
Total number of children:						
Female	744	. . .	136	. . .	186	. . .
Male	782	. . .	165	. . .	203	. . .

Source: Reproductive histories.
Note: Includes only permanent adoptions. For discussion of other forms, see text.

a son, couples with two or three daughters adopted the younger one out in hopes of being allowed another try for a son. (This practice was explicitly forbidden by formal policy but permitted informally.) The proportion of daughters adopted out rose from 1.3 percent before 1970 to 2.9 percent in 1979–83 to 3.8 percent in 1984–87. Although couples were generally allowed to have a son in the mid-1980s, some couples apparently still felt it necessary to get rid of a daughter. These couples may have foreseen a crash birth control campaign and rushed to adopt out one of their girls before being forced to undergo sterilization. In this way a practice that historically involved children of both sexes came to be a girl-only strategy used by couples apparently desperate to have a son.[41]

The decision to adopt out a daughter was not lightly made. It was especially difficult because the child in question was one of only two or three the parents would ever have, making her, if not quite as precious as a son, precious nonetheless. The case of Li Hua illustrates the anguish many parents probably felt about giving away their daughters. In spring of 1993 Li and her husband had two children, both girls, aged 8 and 3. A few months earlier Li's brother-in-law and his wife had their second

[41] The feminization of adoption was a nationwide phenomenon. In China as a whole, during 1980 1.8 girls were given away in adoption for every 1.0 boys who were adopted out. By 1987 that figure had risen to 3.7; see Johansson and Nygren 1991, 44.

TABLE 3   DURATION OF BREAST-FEEDING BY GENDER (F and M) and PARITY OF CHILD IN THREE SHAANXI VILLAGES

| | Period Child Born | | | | | | | | |
| | Before 1970 | | | 1979–83 | | | 1984–87 | | |
	F	M	F-M	F	M	F-M	F	M	F-M
Parity 1	21.2	21.0	+.2	16.4	16.9	–.5	13.9	14.7	–.8
Parity 2	21.1	23.7	–2.6	24.5	24.2	+.3	17.6	21.3	–3.7
Parity 3+	25.0	25.0	.0	21.6	29.0	–7.4	18.0*	20.4	–2.4
All parities	23.3	23.5	–.2	19.2	21.0	–1.8	15.6	18.4	–2.8

Source: Reproductive histories.
Note: Duration expressed in months. For sample sizes, see table 1.
*Based on two valid cases.

child. Like the first, the child was a boy. The brother-in-law, badly wanting a daughter instead of a son, suggested that they swap their younger children. Li and her husband agonized over the decision for a long time. Despite the many problems they were certain to encounter throughout life—lack of labor, old-age support, and a culturally appropriate heir, among other things—in the end they decided they just could not give up their daughter. Their reason was simple: "She is ours."

Breast-feeding

Not only were fewer girls born and raised but girls who were brought up by their birth parents were given less of their mother's milk than their brothers (see table 3). In the years before births became subject to state planning, the total number of months that sons and daughters were breast-fed was about the same, roughly twenty-three (see bottom line of table). During the one-child policy period, however, a gender disparity emerged and grew in size. Reflecting the changing value of sons and daughters as the politics of resistance gave way to the politics of negotiation, the gender gap moved from 1.8 months to the boys' advantage in 1979–83 to 2.8 months in the boys' favor in 1983–87.

During the one-child policy period, a distinct differential by birth order emerged. For children born before 1970, birth order made no difference in the gender gap in breast-feeding. By the early 1980s birth order had begun to be a factor. While the difference between boys and girls was very small at the first and second parities, at the third parity boys enjoyed a 7.4-month advantage. This differential by birth order continued into the mid-1980s, when a differential appeared between first and second births as well: at first parity boys enjoyed 0.8 month more of breast-feeding; at second parity that advantage was 3.7 months. Unfortunately, the extremely small number of third-order girls born during these years makes it impossible to draw conclusions about the gender gap among higher-order children.

The significance of this gender gap in breast-feeding lies not in the health or mortality consequences for the daughters who got less; child survival is much more sensitive to the timing of breast milk supplementation than to the total duration of breast-feeding. The differential is significant, rather, because it is indicative of a larger pattern of discrimination against baby girls that continues into childhood and beyond. Other data gathered in the villages suggest that these early demographic inequalities laid the groundwork for a girlhood of disparities in cultural attention, social investment, and economic opportunity.

The creation of gender gaps in reproductive practice

What is striking about the village data when they are read together is that in all three areas of reproductive life, gender gaps appeared where they had not existed in previous decades. Of course, throughout Chinese history gender has been a major axis of social differentiation. The degree of inequality, however, has varied across time, place, and type of social behavior. In the Shaanxi villages, gender disparities in the behaviors explored here were very modest at midcentury. That changed with the advent of forceful birth control policies. For all children together, the sex ratio at birth, which fell at a biologically normal level of 105 in the decades before 1970, soared to 153 by 1988–93. Under the one-child policy, adoption was transformed from a two-gender practice to a girl-only practice, as boys came to be considered too precious to give away. Breast-feeding, which had favored neither sex, became increasingly advantageous to boys. Thus, during the 1980s and 1990s gender was created—or, from a longer historical perspective, perhaps re-created—as an active force in demographic life.[42]

Not all girls were equally disadvantaged. To the contrary, because of the parity-specific demands of the birth policy and the cultural demands for at least one son, later-born girls suffered the most. Adoption, for example, was confined to girls unfortunate enough to be born later in the reproductive period. During the most intense periods of policy enforcement, girls falling near the end of the sibling string were breast-fed a much shorter period of time than their brothers. Sex ratios at birth, while mildly disadvantageous to girls in the lower birth orders, were extremely disadvantageous for third and higher-order daughters. Indeed, the sex

[42] The process actually began to occur during the 1970s, when the first strong birth planning policy, the later-longer-fewer policy, was put into effect. We will explore the impact of that policy on gender differentials in early childhood in a future publication.

ratios suggest that, as time went by, third-born daughters virtually disappeared from village homes.

While it is clear that the engendering of reproductive policy had deleterious consequences for little girls, just how harmful these were depended on the strength of state pressure on the villages to drastically limit births. When pressure from above was reduced in the mid-1980s, creating space for both the negotiation and the enforcement of an informal two-child-one-son policy, the sex ratio at birth improved dramatically (although adoption and breast-feeding continued to become less favorable to girls). However, when state pressure became intense in the late 1980s and early 1990s and the formal policy permitting two children only for families with a girl was reimposed, the sex ratio deteriorated to its worst level ever.

Conclusion

The case of the missing Chinese girls makes plain the need for a feminist demography of reproduction. While conventional demography has performed a valuable service in documenting the growing discrimination against little girls, because of its reliance on aggregate demographic data and dependence on the Chinese government, its explanations of this trend have been limited and its politics circumscribed. Feminists can and should respond in a different way.

Drawing on a much richer, although smaller-scale, body of data, in this article we have sought to develop a feminist understanding of transformations in the demography of gender among the youngest Chinese. Our explanation is feminist because we are motivated by feminist concerns and recognize the fundamentally political and public rather than "natural" and private nature of reproductive processes. We have argued that this trend is part of a larger social phenomenon in China—the engendering of population policy and practice—that is rooted in a complex interweaving of traditional culture with contemporary politics. Drawing on local-level ethnographic and demographic data, we have shown how the engenderment of reproductive practice in the study villages arose out of a complex, historically situated politics involving peasant couples and state officials at multiple levels of the administrative hierarchy. Male bias in reproductive behavior evolved over time, changing character and intensity as resistance gave way to negotiation, negotiation to accommodation, and accommodation to submission.

While existing explanations underscore the importance of peasant culture, the role of the party-state was equally fundamental. Far from being a helpless observer as "feudal culture" worked its evil, the state was in fact a central actor in this drama. Faced with intense pressure from peasants resisting the policy, state officials at the point of implementation and, later, officials in charge of policy formulation were forced to accommodate peasant demands and rewrite the policy to allow most rural couples to have a son. As patriarchal values made their way from the bottom to the top of the system and then, most recently, from the top back down to the bottom, the party-state became complicit in supporting male bias in reproductive practice. Because it saw population growth as a critical drag on economic development and because it had declared the achievement of economic progress as the basis of its own right to rule, the party-state reluctantly supported patriarchy despite the ideological and practical contradictions that support entangled it in. Like the Maoist party-state before it—indeed, like socialist states in many other times and places—the Dengist regime set its promises to women aside and sacrificed the goal of gender equality for the achievement of what it deemed the higher goods of economic progress for the country and political legitimacy for the regime.[43]

A feminist demography of reproduction involves not only a remaking of demographic thought but also a critique of existing policy and practice. While we have tried hard to achieve a full and balanced understanding of the actions taken by the Chinese state in light of its goals for economic development and the constraints it faced, from a feminist perspective its policies on reproduction can only be judged harshly. From the vantage point of the mid-1990s, the original one-child policy, although formally gender-neutral, appears to have been callously sexist in its willful neglect of well-known prejudices against girls and their likely life-and-death consequences when the number of children allowed was drastically restricted.[44] In the late 1980s, when top policymakers turned up the heat again, they could have had no doubt whatsoever about the repercussions for China's littlest girls.

Although Chinese policymakers have expressed concern about these developments, their policy solutions—banning the use of ultrasound equipment for prenatal sex determination and promising policy relaxation in the future—are far from adequate. An immediate liberalization of the one-child policy, coupled with a vigorous condemnation of discrimination against baby girls, would seem to be necessary and urgent first steps in stopping the practices that lead to their disappearance. A relaxation of policy would not eliminate gender biases, but it can be expected to reduce them measurably. Such steps would, of course, require a reordering of political priorities in which the pace of fertility reduction

---

[43] On the relations of the Maoist party-state to women, see Johnson 1983; Stacey 1983; Wolf 1985. The fate of women in other socialist states is explored by Lapidus 1978; Wolchik 1989.

[44] We are grateful to Kay Johnson for discussion on these points.

is slowed to eliminate gross abuses directed at girls (and adult women). Given the extraordinarily low level of fertility China has already achieved and the party's long-standing ideological commitment to gender equality, one would think that this trade-off might be acceptable to the country's leaders. Further significant reduction of gender bias in demographic behavior is a long-term task that is likely to require remaking the institutions of social, economic, and political life to refigure females as more valuable members of society.

The China material shows how a feminist demography can deepen our understanding of reproduction by broadening the empirical scope of feminist research. Reflecting the suspicion with which many feminists regard quantitative data and methods, students of the consequences of reproductive politics have neglected demographic data, instead focusing on social and cultural evidence. Yet the data themselves are not inherently objectifying; when appropriated for feminist purposes, demographic data and measures can usefully inform feminist scholarship by revealing patterns of gender relations and practices not observable through qualitative research (cf. Jayaratne and Stewart 1991). Indeed, it may be that the more politicized the arena of reproduction, the more crucial demographic evidence becomes, for where reproduction is heavily contested, people work hard to hide their secrets, not only from other members of their society but from social scientists as well. In China the discrimination and violence directed against little girls were thickly cloaked until large-scale demographic evidence brought them to light.[45] The demography of gender can thus enrich the analysis of reproductive politics by uncovering some of the hidden life-affecting consequences of these politics and by providing a sense of how common such consequences are in the society as a whole.

While we have been concerned here with the gender effects of the politics surrounding the one-child policy, we cannot leave this subject without noting that the consequences extend far beyond gender relations to touch every area of life. Enforcement of this policy has been a wrenching experience for Chinese society. It has shrunk the basic unit of social life; allowed the state to penetrate one of the few private spaces left by Chinese collectivism; pitted husband against wife, neighbor against neighbor, city against countryside; and raised terribly painful ethical dilemmas that can be dimly perceived through the haze of silence and shame that surrounds the issue of the missing girls in China's villages.

---

[45] From the early 1980s local newspapers have occasionally published egregious cases of violence against women and girls as warnings that such behavior would be condemned. Such cases, however, were dismissed as local anomalies. Only when demographic evidence of the huge number of missing girls came to light did the scale of the gender violence become known.

Consequences such as these demand a place on the future agenda of a politics of reproduction.

Finally, we must ask about the future prospects of the girls born under the one-child reproductive regime. The literature on reproductive politics highlights the contradictory effects these politics have on gender hierarchies. For China's little girls, the effects are supremely ironic. For just as their numbers are declining and demographic discrimination against them is worsening, their cultural worth is rising in the eyes of parents who have been abandoned by unfilial sons. While this more accepting view of daughters is encouraging, one must remember that it failed to protect them from even greater discrimination when state pressure to limit births grew intense. To those who imagine that the lot of girls will improve as they become scarcer, we can only say that this outcome cannot be taken for granted, for the impact of demographic factors such as relative numbers is powerfully conditioned by the political, cultural, and economic context in which they operate. The case of India, where women's numbers are below par and falling, provides little reason for comfort (Basu 1993). In any case, the hope for an eventual, demographically induced evening of gender relations should not divert attention from the injuries of gender that are being inflicted today.

Department of Anthropology
University of California, Irvine (Greenhalgh)
Research Division
Population Council (Li)

References

Arnold, Fred, and Liu Zhaoxiang. 1986. "Sex Preference, Fertility, and Family Planning in China." *Population and Development Review* 12(2):221–46.

Basu, Alaka Malwade. 1993. "Fertility Decline and Increasing Gender Imbalance in India: Including the South Indian Turnaround." Paper presented at the workshop "Understanding Replacement Fertility: What Policy Options Do Asians Have?" Beijing.

Beijing Review. 1989. "Stop Sex Checks of Fetuses." *Beijing Review* 32, no. 28 (July 10–16): 8–9.

Browner, C. H., and Sondra T. Perdue. 1988. "Women's Secrets: Bases for Reproductive and Social Autonomy in a Mexican Community." *American Ethnologist* 15(1):84–97.

China Population Newsletter. 1989. "Surveys and Data." *China Population Newsletter* 6(2):7.

Coale, Ansley J. 1993. "Excess Ratios of Males to Females by Birth Cohort in the Censuses of China, '53 to '90, and in the Births Reported in the Fertility Surveys, '82 and '88." Revision of paper presented at International Seminar on China's 1990 Population Census, Beijing.

CPIC (China Population Information Centre). 1983. "Open Letter from the Central Committee of the Communist Party of China to All Members of the Party and the Communist Youth League Concerning the Problem of Controlling the Country's Population Growth." In *China: Population Policy and Family Planning Practice*, 1–4. Beijing: CPIC.

Croll, Elisabeth, Delia Davin, and Penny Kane, eds. 1985. *China's One-Child Family Policy*. New York: St. Martin's.

Dixon-Mueller, Ruth. 1993. *Population Policy and Women's Rights: Transforming Reproductive Choice*. Westport, Conn.: Praeger.

Feeney, Griffith, Wang Feng, Zhou Minkun, and Xiao Baoyu. 1989. "Recent Fertility Dynamics in China: Results from the 1987 One Percent Population Survey." *Population and Development Review* 15(2):297–32.

Feng Guoping, and Hao Linna. 1992. "Zhongguo 28 ge difang jihua shengyu tiaoli zongshu" (Summary of 28 regional birth planning regulations in China). *Renkou Yanjiu* (Population research), no. 4, 28–33.

Folbre, Nancy. 1983. "Of Patriarchy Born: The Political Economy of Fertility Decisions." *Feminist Studies* 9(2):261–84.

Gilmartin, Christina K., Gail Hershatter, Lisa Rofel, and Tyrene White, eds. 1994. *Engendering China: Women, Culture, and the State*. Cambridge, Mass.: Harvard University Press.

Ginsburg, Faye. 1989. *Contested Lives: The Abortion Debate in an American Community*. Berkeley and Los Angeles: University of California Press.

Ginsburg, Faye, and Rayna Rapp. 1991. "The Politics of Reproduction." *Annual Review of Anthropology* 20:311–43.

Ginsburg, Faye, and Anna Lowenhaupt Tsing, eds. 1990. *Uncertain Terms: Negotiating Gender in American Culture*. Boston: Beacon.

Greenhalgh, Susan. 1993. "The Peasantization of the One-Child Policy in Shaanxi." In *Chinese Families in the Post-Mao Era*, ed. Deborah Davis and Stevan Harrell, 219–50. Berkeley and Los Angeles: University of California Press.

———. 1994a. "Controlling Births and Bodies in Village China." *American Ethnologist* 21(1):1–30.

———. 1994b. "The Peasant Household in the Transition from Socialism." In *The Economic Anthropology of the State*, ed. Elizabeth Brumfiel, 43–64. Lanham, Md.: University Press of America.

———. 1995. "Anthropology Theorizes Reproduction: Integrating Practice, Political Economic, and Feminist Perspectives." In *Situating Fertility: Anthropology and Demographic Inquiry*, ed. Susan Greenhalgh. Cambridge: Cambridge University Press.

Greenhalgh, Susan, Zhu Chuzhu, and Li Nan. 1994. "Restraining Population Growth in Three Chinese Villages, 1988–1993." *Population and Development Review* 20(2):365–95.

Hartmann, Betsy. 1987. *Reproductive Rights and Wrongs: The Global Politics of Population Control and Contraceptive Choice*. New York: Harper & Row.

Honig, Emily, and Gail Hershatter. 1988. *Personal Voices: Chinese Women in the 1980s*. Stanford, Calif.: Stanford University Press.

Huang Shu-min. 1989. *The Spiral Road: Change in a Chinese Village through the Eyes of a Communist Party Leader*. Boulder, Colo.: Westview.

Hull, Terence H. 1990. "Recent Trends in Sex Ratios at Birth in China." *Population and Development Review* 16(1):63–83.

Hull, Terence H., and Wen Xingyan. 1992. "Rising Sex Ratios at Birth in China: Evidence from the 1990 Population Census." Paper presented at International Seminar on China's 1990 Population Census, Beijing.

Jaquette, Jane, and Kathleen A. Staudt. 1985. "Women as 'At Risk' Reproducers: Biology, Science, and Population in U.S. Foreign Policy." In *Women, Biology, and Public Policy,* ed. Virginia Sapiro, 235–68. Beverly Hills, Calif.: Sage.

Jayaratne, Toby Epstein, and Abigail J. Stewart. 1991. "Quantitative and Qualitative Methods in the Social Sciences: Current Feminist Issues and Practical Strategies." In *Beyond Methodology: Feminist Scholarship as Lived Research,* ed. Mary Margaret Fonow and Judith A. Cook, 85–106. Bloomington: Indiana University Press.

Johansson, Sten, and Ola Nygren. 1991. "The Missing Girls of China: A New Demographic Account." *Population and Development Review* 17(1):35–51.

Johnson, D. Gale. 1994. "Effects of Institutions and Policies on Rural Population Growth with Application to China." *Population and Development Review* 20(3):503–31.

Johnson, Kay Ann. 1983. *Women, the Family, and Peasant Revolution in China.* Chicago: University of Chicago Press.

———. 1993. "Chinese Orphanages: Saving China's Abandoned Girls." *Australian Journal of Chinese Affairs* 30:61–87.

Kristof, Nicholas D. 1993. "Peasants of China Discover New Way to Weed out Girls." *New York Times,* July 21, 1.

Lapidus, Gail Warshofsky. 1978. *Women in Soviet Society: Equality, Development, and Social Change.* Berkeley: University of California Press.

Lewis, John Wilson. 1963. *Leadership in Communist China.* Ithaca, N.Y.: Cornell University Press.

Li Bohua and Duan Jixian. 1986. "Dui Zhongguo chusheng yinger xingbiebi de guji" (An estimation of China's infant sex ratio at birth). *Renkou yu Jingji* (Population and economics), no. 4, 19–23.

Liu, Alan P. L. 1986. *How China Is Ruled.* Englewood Cliffs, N.J.: Prentice-Hall.

Liu Shuang. 1988. "Dui Zhongguo renkou chusheng xingbiebi de fenxi" (An analysis of the sex ratio at birth in China). *Renkou Yanjiu* (Population research), no. 3, 33–36.

Martin, Emily. 1987. *The Woman in the Body: A Cultural Analysis of Reproduction.* Boston: Beacon.

———. 1991. "The Egg and the Sperm: How Science Has Constructed a Romance Based on Stereotypical Male-Female Roles." *Signs: Journal of Women in Culture and Society* 16(3):485–501.

McNicoll, Geoffrey. 1994. "Institutional Determinants of Fertility Change." In *Population, Development, and the Environment,* ed. Kerstin Lindahl-Kiessling and Hans Landberg. New York and Oxford: Oxford University Press.

National People's Congress. 1983. *The Constitution of the People's Republic of China.* Beijing: National People's Congress.

Parish, William L., and Martin K. Whyte. 1978. *Village and Family in Contemporary China.* Chicago: University of Chicago Press.

Petchesky, Rosalind Pollack. (1984) 1990. *Abortion and Women's Choice: The State, Sexuality, and Reproductive Freedom.* Boston: Northeastern University Press.

Population and Development Review. 1981. "China's New Marriage Law." *Population and Development Review* 7(2):369–72.

Potter, Sulamith Heins, and Jack M. Potter. 1990. *China's Peasants: The Anthropology of a Revolution.* Cambridge: Cambridge University Press.

Rapp, Rayna. 1990. "Constructing Amniocentesis: Maternal and Medical Discourses." In Ginsburg and Tsing 1990, 28–42.

———. 1991. "Moral Pioneers: Women, Men, and Fetuses on a Frontier of Reproductive Technology." In *Gender at the Crossroads of Knowledge: Feminist Anthropology in the Postmodern Era,* ed. Micaela di Leonardo, 383–95. Berkeley and Los Angeles: University of California Press.

Riley, Nancy. 1993. "Challenging Demography: Contributions from Feminist Theory." Unpublished manuscript, Bowdoin College.

Rosaldo, Renato. 1989. *Culture and Truth: The Remaking of Social Analysis.* Boston: Beacon.

Schofield, Roger, and David Coleman. 1986. "Introduction: The State of Population Theory." In *The State of Population Theory: Forward from Malthus,* ed. David Coleman and Roger Schofield, 1–13. Oxford: Basil Blackwell.

Shaanxi Provincial Bureau of Statistics. 1992. *Shaanxi Tongji Nianjian, 1992* (Shaanxi statistical yearbook, 1992). Xi'an: Shaanxi Provincial Bureau of Statistics.

Shue, Vivienne. 1984. "The Fate of the Commune." *Modern China* 10(3):259–83.

———. 1988. *The Reach of the State: Sketches of the Chinese Body Politic.* Stanford, Calif.: Stanford University Press.

Stacey, Judith. 1983. *Patriarchy and Socialist Revolution in China.* Berkeley and Los Angeles: University of California Press.

Stanworth, Michelle, ed. 1987. *Reproductive Technologies: Gender, Motherhood and Medicine.* Minneapolis: University of Minnesota Press.

Strathern, Marilyn. 1992. *Reproducing the Future: Essays on Anthropology, Kinship, and the New Reproductive Technologies.* New York: Routledge.

Szreter, Simon. 1993. "The Idea of Demographic Transition and the Study of Fertility: A Critical Intellectual History." *Population and Development Review* 19(4):659–701.

Tuan Chi-hsien. 1992. "Gender Selection and Fertility Regulation in the Process of Family Building in China." *Chinese Journal of Population Science* 4(1):33–54.

Unger, Jonathan. 1989. "State and Peasant in Post-Revolution China." *Journal of Peasant Studies* 17(1):114–36.

Wasserstrom, Jeffrey. 1984. "Resistance to the One-Child Family." *Modern China* 10(3):345–74.

White, Gordon. 1987. "The Impact of Economic Reforms in the Chinese Countryside." *Modern China* 13(4):411–40.

White, Tyrene. 1991. "Birth Planning between Plan and Market: The Impact of Reform on China's One-Child Policy." In *China's Economic Dilemmas in the*

1990s: The Problems of Reforms, Modernization, and Interdependence, 1:252–69. Study Papers Submitted to the Joint Economic Committee, Congress of the United States. Washington, D.C.: Government Printing Office.

————. 1992. "The Population Factor: China's Family Planning Policy in the 1990s." In *China Briefing, 1991*, ed. William A. Joseph, 97–117. Boulder, Colo.: Westview.

Whyte, Martin K., and S. Z. Gu. 1987. "Popular Response to China's Fertility Transition." *Population and Development Review* 13(3):471–93.

Wolchik, Sharon. 1989. "Women and the State in Eastern Europe and the Soviet Union." In *Women, the State, and Development*, ed. Sue Ellen M. Charlton, Jana Everett, and Kathleen Staudt, 44–65. Albany: State University of New York Press.

Wolf, Arthur P., and Huang Chieh-shan. 1980. *Marriage and Adoption in China, 1845–1945*. Stanford, Calif.: Stanford University Press.

Wolf, Margery. 1985. *Revolution Postponed: Women in Contemporary China*. Stanford, Calif.: Stanford University Press.

Woo, Margaret Y. K. 1994. "Chinese Women Workers: The Delicate Balance between Protection and Equality." In Gilmartin et al. 1994, 279–95.

Xinhua. 1991. "Decision of CPC Central Committee, State Council on Stepping up Family Planning Work, Strictly Controlling Population Growth." June 12 broadcast. In *Daily Report—China*, Foreign Broadcast Information Service, FBIS-CHI-91-119, 33–36.

Xu Yi, and Guo Weiming. 1991. "Zhongguo chusheng xingbiebi de xianzhuang ji youguan wenti de tantao" (Exploration of the current situation and some related questions regarding the sex ratio at birth in China), *Renkou yu Jingji* (Population and economics), no. 5, 9–12, 54.

Yan Keqing. 1983. "Problems and Prospects in Population Planning." *China Reconstructs* (June), 11–13.

Zeng Yi. 1989. "Is the Chinese Family Planning Program 'Tightening Up'?" *Population and Development Review* 15(2):333–37.

Zeng Yi, Tu Ping, Gu Baochang, Xu Yi, Li Bohua, and Li Yongping. 1993. "Causes and Implications of the Recent Increase in the Reported Sex Ratio at Birth in China." *Population and Development Review* 19(2):283–302.

COLLEEN BALLERINO COHEN is associate professor of anthropology and women's studies and director of women's studies at Vassar College. She is coeditor of *Beauty Queens on the Global Stage: Gender, Contests, and Power* (New York: Routledge, 1995), and her articles have appeared in *Signs, Social Analysis, Journal of the History of Sexuality,* a special gender issue of the *Annals of Tourism Research,* and in edited collections. Since 1989 she has conducted ethnographic research on tourism, national culture, and identity in the British Virgin Islands, and she is completing a book based on this research.

CAROL COHN is assistant professor of women's studies and sociology at Bowdoin College. She is working on a book-length manuscript on the discourses and institutions of national security and gender.

PATRICIA HILL COLLINS is professor of African-American studies and women's studies at the University of Cincinnati. She is completing *Fighting Words,* a book on oppositional social theory (Minneapolis: University of Minnesota Press, in press).

DESLEY DEACON teaches American studies and sociology at the University of Texas at Austin, where she moved from the Australian National University ten years ago. "Political Arithmetic" was written in 1982 as the first chapter of her dissertation, which was published as *Managing Gender: The State, the New Middle Class and Women Workers, 1830–1930* (Oxford: Oxford University Press, 1989). She has completed a biography of the American feminist intellectual Elsie Clews Parsons, titled *Elsie Clews Parsons: Constructing Sex and Culture in Modernist America* (Chicago: University of Chicago Press, 1997, in press). She is working on a study of transnationalism in the United States and Mexico in the 1920s and 1930s, based on the life of anthropologist, political activist, and cultural critic Anita Brenner.

DAPHNE DE MARNEFFE is a clinical psychologist practicing psychotherapy in San Francisco. Her current research examines how young children begin to make sense of gender.

LISA DUGGAN teaches histories of gender and sexuality and lesbian/gay studies in the American studies program at New York University. She is the coauthor of *Sex Wars: Sexual Dissent and Political Culture*

(New York: Routledge, 1995) and the author of *Sapphic Slashers: Love, Murder and Lesbian Desire, 1880–1920* (Berkeley and Los Angeles: University of California Press, in press).

LISA GREBER confesses that in the years since this article was written she has fallen in love with the Internet. But that is another story. She is interested in understanding and helping facilitate the kinds of changes needed in ourselves, our technologies, and our communities in order to live in a more compassionate and ecologically sustainable world. She has worked on these questions through political action, computer modeling of sustainable futures, and, with her current job, direct implementation of energy conservation measures, but she would really rather make change through science fiction, at the place where science, politics, and poetry meet.

SUSAN GREENHALGH is associate professor in the anthropology department at the University of California at Irvine. She is writing a book on the gendered science and politics of reproductive control in China.

JANICE HAAKEN is professor of psychology at Portland State University and a clinical psychologist. She has published extensively in the areas of psychoanalysis and feminism, gender and psychopathology, and the psychology of social movements. Her current research focuses on sexual abuse narratives and the debate over recovered memory of childhood abuse.

EVELYNN M. HAMMONDS is assistant professor of the history of science in the Program in Science, Technology and Society at Massachusetts Institute of Technology. Her research involves the history of medicine and public health, and gender, race, and science. She is completing a manuscript on the history of the control of diphtheria in New York City at the turn of the century.

MARY E. HAWKESWORTH is professor of political science and women's studies at the University of Louisville. Her research interests include contemporary political philosophy, feminist theory, and social policy. She is the author of *Beyond Oppression: Feminist Theory and Political Strategy* (New York: Continuum Press, 1990) and *Theoretical Issues in Policy Analysis* (Albany: State University of New York Press, 1988); and the editor of *The Encyclopedia of Government and Politics* (London: Routledge, 1992) and a special issue of *Policy Sciences* (vol. 27, nos. 2–3 [1994]) on feminism and public policy.

JANET SHIBLEY HYDE is professor of psychology and women's studies at the University of Wisconsin—Madison. She continues to do research involving meta-analysis of psychological gender differences. Most recently, she published a meta-analysis of gender differences in sexuality (*Psychological Bulletin* [1993]) and is working on a meta-analysis of gender differences in self-esteem. She also is studying maternity leave and women's mental health.

SUZANNE J. KESSLER is professor of psychology at Purchase College, State University of New York. With Wendy McKenna, she is the co-author of *Gender: An Ethnomethodological Approach* (New York: Wiley-Interscience, 1978; reprint, Chicago: University of Chicago Press, 1985). Since the publication of the article reprinted in this volume, she has extended her analysis of intersex management to include the perspective of parents and adult intersexuals who are part of the transgender movement.

SALLY GREGORY KOHLSTEDT is professor of the history of science at the University of Minnesota and is affiliated with the Center for Advanced Feminist Studies. She served terms as associate/advisory editor for *Signs* under its first three editors. She publishes on the history of science in American culture, with recent emphasis on nature study, museums, and women's participation. Her recent articles include "Women in the History of Science: An Ambiguous Place," *Osiris* 10 (1995): 27–38.

BARBARA LASLETT is professor of sociology at the University of Minnesota. With Ruth-Ellen B. Joeres, she edited *Signs* from 1990 to 1995. Her research and writing have focused primarily on the historical sociology of gender relations, the family, social reproduction, and the history of American sociology. She edited *Contemporary Sociology* between 1983 and 1986 and is past president of the Social Science History Association.

JIALI LI is an associate research scientist at the National Center for Children in Poverty at Columbia University School of Public Health. Much of her current research focuses on the impact of poverty on child well-being.

HELEN LONGINO teaches women's studies, philosophy, and science studies at the University of Minnesota. She is the author of *Science as Social Knowledge* (Princeton, N.J.: Princeton University Press, 1990) and most recently of "Gender, Politics, and the Theoretical Virtues," *Synthese* 105, no. 3 (1995): 53–68.

EMILY MARTIN   is professor of anthropology at Princeton University. Beginning with *The Woman in the Body: A Cultural Analysis of Reproduction* (Boston: Beacon, 1987), she worked on the anthropology of science and reproduction in the United States, in particular on how gender stereotypes have shaped medical language and how they circulate among and are contested by women in different age groups and communities. In *Flexible Bodies: Tracking Immunity in America from the Days of Polio to the Age of AIDS* (Boston: Beacon, 1994), she analyzed the manner in which the concept of flexibility in immune discourse has been invoked in a transformation of contemporary notions of health and business practices. Her current work addresses theories of normalization and the evolving constitution of selfhood in contemporary society.

FRANCES E. MASCIA-LEES   teaches anthropology and cultural studies at Simon's Rock College of Bard. She and Pat Sharpe are at work on two books, a collection of their essays—which will include their most recent articles "The Anthropological Unconscious," *American Anthropologist* 96, no. 3 (1994): 649–60, and "Piano Lessons," *American Anthropologist* 97, no. 4 (1995): 763–73. The books are tentatively titled *Looking Back: Postmodern/Feminist Reflections on Writing Culture* and *Cultural Stories.*

RUTH PERRY   is professor of literature at Massachusetts Institute of Technology, where she has watched the gendering of science and technology at close quarters. She founded MIT's women's studies department in 1984. The author of four books and dozens of articles on eighteenth-century English letters and culture, she is working on a history of kinship and the family in relation to the novel in England from 1750 to 1810.

PATRICIA SHARPE   is dean of academic affairs at Simon's Rock College of Bard. She and Fran Mascia-Lees are at work on two books, a collection of their essays—which will include their most recent articles "The Anthropological Unconscious," *American Anthropologist* 96, no. 3 (1994): 649–60, and "Piano Lessons," *American Anthropologist* 97, no. 4 (1995): 763–73. The books are tentatively titled *Looking Back: Postmodern/Feminist Reflections on Writing Culture* and *Cultural Stories.*

SUSAN SPERLING   teaches in the medical anthropology program at the University of California, San Francisco, and the social science program at Chabot College. She is researching human attitudes toward animals in a number of contexts including ecotourism and food processing. This work is part of a larger project looking at changing political economic contexts of human-animal interaction.

NANCY M. THERIOT   is associate professor of history and chair of the women's studies program at the University of Louisville. She is author of *Mothers and Daughters in Nineteenth-Century America: The Biosocial Construction of Femininity* (rev. ed. [Lexington: University Press of Kentucky, 1996]), as well as articles and papers focusing on gender and medical discourse. She is working on a book manuscript tentatively titled "Deciphering Illness: Nineteenth-Century Women and Their Physicians."

Index